Lecture Notes in Computer Science 4904

Commenced Publication in 1973
Founding and Former Series Editors:
Gerhard Goos, Juris Hartmanis, and Jan van Leeuwen

T0189997

Shrisha Rao   Mainak Chatterjee
Prasad Jayanti   C. Siva Ram Murthy
Sanjoy Kumar Saha (Eds.)

Distributed Computing and Networking

9th International Conference, ICDCN 2008
Kolkata, India, January 5-8, 2008
Proceedings

 Springer

Volume Editors

Shrisha Rao
International Institute of Information Technology – Bangalore
26/C Keonics Electronics City, Hosur Road, Bangalore 560 100, India
E-mail: srao@iiitb.ac.in

Mainak Chatterjee
University of Central Florida, School of EECS
P.O. Box 162450, Orlando, FL 32816-2450, USA
E-mail: mainak@eecs.ucf.edu

Prasad Jayanti
Dartmouth College, Department of Computer Science
6211 Sudikoff Lab for Computer Science, Hanover, NH 03755, USA
E-mail: prasad@cs.dartmouth.edu

C. Siva Ram Murthy
Indian Institute of Technology Madras, Dept. of Computer Science and Engineering
Chennai 600 036, India
E-mail: murthy@iitm.ac.in

Sanjoy Kumar Saha
Jadavpur University, Department of Computer Science and Engineering
Kolkata 700 032, India
E-mail: sks_ju@yahoo.co.in

Library of Congress Control Number: 2007941816

CR Subject Classification (1998): C.2, D.1.3, D.2.12, D.4, F.2, F.1, H.4

LNCS Sublibrary: SL 1 – Theoretical Computer Science and General Issues

ISSN   0302-9743
ISBN-10   3-540-77443-2 Springer Berlin Heidelberg New York
ISBN-13   978-3-540-77443-3 Springer Berlin Heidelberg New York

Springer is a part of Springer Science+Business Media

springer.com

© Springer-Verlag Berlin Heidelberg 2008
Printed in Germany

Typesetting: Camera-ready by author, data conversion by Scientific Publishing Services, Chennai, India
Printed on acid-free paper   SPIN: 12209491   06/3180   5 4 3 2 1 0

Message from the General Chairs

The 2008 International Conference on Distributed Computing and Networking (ICDCN 2008) was the ninth event in this series. This event, formerly known as IWDC (International Workshop on Distributed Computing), became an international conference in 2007, and it was renamed International Conference on Distributed Computing and Networking to remark the growth in scope, quality and visibility and the increasing relevance of networking research. Over the years, ICDCN has become a leading forum for disseminating the latest research results in distributed computing and networks. This year's conference brought together worldwide researchers in Kolkata (India), during January 5–8, 2008, to present and discuss a wide variety of aspects such as networks, systems, algorithms and applications.

The program of the conference lasted four days and included, in addition to a high-quality technical program, four tutorials giving young researchers and students an excellent opportunity to learn about the hottest research areas in wireless networking, complex systems and high-performance computing.

A conference of this magnitude would not have been possible without the hard and excellent work of all the members of the Organizing Committee. Our special thanks are due to Prasad Jayanti and C. Siva Ram Murthy (Program Co-chairs) and to Mainak Chatterjee (Program Vice Chair), for coordinating and leading the effort of the Program Committee culminating in an excellent technical program. We are grateful to the Keynote Chair, Sajal K. Das, for arranging three high-quality keynote talks by eminent leaders in the field: Roger Watthenhofer (ETH Zurich), Jie Wu (NSF and Florida Atlantic University), and Sankar Kumar Pal (Indian Statistical Institute, Kolkata). We would also like to express our appreciation to the Tutorial Co-chairs, Sajal K. Das and Sarmistha Neogy, and to the Panel Chair, Kalyan Basu.

We are indebted to all the other members of the Organizing Committee for their excellent work. Atal Chaudhuri (Organizing Chair) and Subhadip Basu and Nibaran Das (Organizing Vice Chairs) coordinated the local arrangements. Shrisha Rao and Sanjoy K. Saha (Publication Co-chairs) managed the publication of the conference proceedings. We also take this opportunity to acknowledge the contribution to the conference's success of the Registration Chair, Mridul S. Barik, and of the Finance Chair Salil K. Sanyal.

Last but not least, we extend our heartfelt thanks to the authors, reviewers and participants of the conference, for their vital contribution to the success of this conference.

January 2008

Marco Conti
Pradip K. Das
Nicola Santoro

Message from the Technical Program Chairs

Welcome to the Proceedings of the Ninth International Conference on Distributed Computing and Networking (ICDCN) 2008! This annual event started off nine years ago as a small workshop for distributed computing researchers in India, and has gradually matured into a true international conference, while simultaneously widening its scope to cover most aspects of distributed computing and networking.

We received 185 submissions from all over the world, including Australia, Bangladesh, Brazil, Canada, China, France, Greece, Iran, Israel, Italy, Malaysia, Poland, Singapore, South Africa, South Korea, Spain, Switzerland, Tunisia, United Kingdom, and United States, besides India, the host country. The submissions were read and evaluated by the Program Committee, which consisted of 25 members for the Distributed Computing Track and 34 members for the Networking Track, with the additional help of external reviewers. The Program Committee selected 30 regular papers and 27 short papers for inclusion in the proceedings and presentation at the conference.

We were fortunate to have several distinguished scientists as keynote and invited speakers. Roger Wattenhofer (ETH, Zurich) and Jie Wu (Florida Atlantic University and NSF) delivered the keynote address, and Sudhir Dhawan (IBM India) and Sushil Prasad (Georgia State University) were the invited speakers. Sankar Pal from the Indian Statistical Institute, Kolkata, delivered the A.K. Choudhury Memorial talk. By inviting these speakers to contribute an article to the proceedings, we ensured that most of the content of these valuable talks appeared in print in this volume.

The main conference program was preceded by a day of tutorial presentations. We had four tutorials, presented by Sunghyun Choi (Seoul National University) on "High-Speed WLAN and Wireless Mesh," Vipin Chaudhary and John Paul Walters (University of Buffalo) on "Fault-Tolerant High Performance Computing," Romit Roy Choudhury (Duke University) on "Exploiting Smart Antennas," and Niloy Ganguly (Indian Institute of Technology, Kharagpur) on "Complex Network Theory."

We thank all authors for their interest in ICDCN 2008, and the Program Committee members and external reviewers for their careful reviews despite a tight schedule. We used the EasyChair system to handle the submissions, reviews, discussions, and notifications. The system was easy to use and very helpful.

We hope that you will find the ICDCN 2008 proceedings to be technically rewarding.

January 2008

Mainak Chatterjee
Prasad Jayanti
C. Siva Ram Murthy

Organization

ICDCN 2008 was organized by Jadavpur University, Kolkata, India.

General Chairs

Marco Conti, Institute for Informatics and Telematics, Italy
Pradip K. Das, Jadavpur University, Kolkata, India
Nicola Santoro, Carleton University, Canada

Program Chairs

Prasad Jayanti, Dartmouth College, USA (Distributed Computing Track)
C. Siva Ram Murthy, IIT Madras, India (Networking Track)
Mainak Chatterjee, University of Central Florida, USA (Vice Chair, Networking Track)

Keynote Chair

Sajal Das, University of Texas at Arlington, USA

Tutorial Chairs

Sajal Das, University of Texas at Arlington, USA
Sarmistha Neogy, Jadavpur University, India

Panel Chair

Kalyan Basu, University of Texas at Arlington, USA

Publicity Chairs

Arobinda Gupta, IIT Kharagpur, India
Ajay Kshemkalyani, University of Illinois at Chicago, USA
Goutam K. Paul, Jadavpur University, India

Organizing Chair

Atal Chaudhuri, Jadavpur University, India

Organizing Vice Chairs

Subhadip Basu, Jadavpur University, India
Nibaran Das, Jadavpur University, India

Publication Chairs

Shrisha Rao, IIIT Bangalore, India
Sanjoy K. Saha, Jadavpur University, India

Registration Chair

Mridul S. Barik, Jadavpur University, India

Finance Chair

Salil K. Sanyal, Jadavpur University, India

Steering Committee Chair

Sukumar Ghosh, University of Iowa, USA

Steering Committee Members

Gautam Barua, IIT Guwahati, India
Pradip K. Das, Jadavpur University, Kolkata, India
Sajal Das, University of Texas at Arlington, USA
Sukumar Ghosh, University of Iowa, Iowa City, USA
Anurag Kumar, Indian Institute of Science, Bangalore, India
David Peleg, Weizmann Institute of Science, Israel
Michel Raynal, IRISA, France
Indranil Sengupta, IIT Kharagpur, India
Bhabani Sinha, ISI, Kolkata, India

Organizing Committee

Shibaji Bandyopadhyay, Jadavpur University, India
Mridul S. Barik, Jadavpur University, India
Dipak K. Basu, Jadavpur University, India
Bijan B. Bhaumik, Jadavpur University, India
Samiran Chattopadhyay, Jadavpur University, India

Rana Dattagupta, Jadavpur University, India
Chandan Majumdar, Jadavpur University, India
Nandini Mukherjee, Jadavpur University, India
Mita Nasipuri, Jadavpur University, India

Program Committee

Debopam Acharya, Georgia Southern University, USA
Dharma P. Agrawal, University of Cincinnati, USA
Marcos Aguilera, HP Lab, USA
Arzad Alam, IIT Delhi, India
Lorenzo Alvisi, University of Texas at Austin, USA
Amiya Bhattacharya, New Mexico State University, USA
Saad Biaz, Auburn University, USA
Azzedine Boukerche, University of Ottawa, Canada
Soma Chaudhuri, Iowa State University, USA
Carla-Fabiana Chiasserini, Polytechnic of Turin, Italy
Nabanita Das, ISI, Kolkata, India
Samir R. Das, SUNY at Stony Brook, USA
Vijay K. Garg, University of Texas at Austin, USA
Ratan Ghosh, IIT Kanpur, India
Sukumar Ghosh, University of Iowa, USA
Kartik Gopalan, State University of New York at Binghamton, USA
Isabelle Guerin-Lassous, INRIA, France
Rachid Guerraoui, EPFL, Switzerland
Ashwin Gumaste, IIT Bombay, India
Arobinda Gupta, IIT Kharagpur, India
Danny Hendler, Ben-Gurion University, Israel
Maurice Herlihy, Brown University, USA
Sridhar Iyer, IIT Bombay, India
Prasad Jayanti, Dartmouth College, USA
Kamal Karlapalem, IIIT Hyderabad, India
Holger Karl, University of Paderborn, Germany
Taskin Kocak, University of Bristol, UK
Rastislav Kralovic, Comenius University, Bratislava, Slovakia
Rajeev Kumar, IIT Kharagpur, India
Kevin Kwiat, Air Force Research Lab, USA
Yonghe Liu, University of Texas at Arlington, USA
Victor Luchangco, Sun Labs, USA
D. Manjunath, IIT Bombay, India
B.S. Manoj, University of California, San Diego, USA
Mahesh Marina, The University of Edinburgh, UK
Keith Marzullo, University of California, San Diego, USA
Ravi R. Mazumdar, University of Waterloo, Canada
Prasant Mohapatra, University of California, Davis, USA

Yoram Moses, Technion, Israel
Sukumar Nandi, IIT Guwahati, India
Asis Nasipuri, University of North Carolina, USA
Lionel Ni, Hong Kong University of Science & Technology, Hong Kong
Alessandro Panconesi, La Sapienza University, Rome, Italy
Sriram Pemmaraju, University of Iowa, USA
Srdjan Petrovic, Google, USA
Marius Portmann, The University of Queensland, Australia
Sergio Rajsbaum, UNAM, Mexico
R. Ramanujam, Institute of Mathematical Sciences, Chennai, India
Ramachandran Ramjee, Microsoft Research, Bangalore, India
Shrisha Rao, IIIT Bangalore, India
Manivasakan R., IIT Madras, India
Romit Roy Choudhury, Duke University, USA
Rajarshi Roy, IIT Kharagpur, India
Pavan S. Nuggehalli, Indian Institute of Science, Bangalore, India
Vinod Sharma, Indian Institute of Science, Bangalore, India
C. Siva Ram Murthy, IIT Madras, India
Kannan Srinathan, IIIT Hyderabad, India
Vikram Srinivasan, National University of Singapore
Srikantha Tirthapura, Iowa State University, USA
Sam Toueg, University of Toronto, Canada
Pallapa Venkataram, Indian Institute of Science, Bangalore, India
Krishnamurthy Vidyasankar, Memorial University of New Foundland, Canada

Additional Referees

Anas Abutaleb	Umesh Deshpande	Long Le
Sankar Adida	Shruti Dubey	Jun Luo
Jayaraj Alavelli	Stefan Dziembowski	Michael Ma
Chrisil Arackaparambil	Hugues Fauconnier	Neeraj Mittal
Manoj Balakrishnan	Antony Franklin	Hrushikesha Mohanty
Bharath	Sameh Gabrail	Subhamoy Moitra
Balasubramanian	Soumya K. Ghosh	Raymond Hoi-lun Ngan
Torsha Banerjee	R.K. Ghosh	Vinit Ogale
Giacomo Bernardi	Bing He	Puviyarasan Pandian
Vibhor Bhatt	Stephanie Horn	Saurav Pandit
Subhasis Bhattacharjee	Chien-Chung Huang	Himadri Sekhar Paul
Quanbin Chen	Sujatha Kashyap	Sofia Pediaditaki
Yi Cheng	Ashok Khanal	Sasa Pekec
Rajib K. Das	R. Kiran	Srinath Perur
Samir Das	Michael Kistler	Imran Pirwani
Ashoke Deb	Purushottam Kulkarni	Marius Portmann
Carole Delporte-Gallet	Yunhuai Liu	Chen Qian
Hongmei Deng	Bibudh Lahiri	Kiran R.

Vijay Raisinghani
HariShankar
   Ramachandran
Manivasakan Rathinam
Nityananda Sarma
Sanand Sasidharan

Nicolas Schiper
Shamik Sengupta
Bhabani P. Sinha
Shamik Sural
S.P. Suresh
Venkatesh Tamarapalli

Alessandro Tiberi
Demin Wang
Yun Wang
Jungang Wang

Table of Contents

A.K. Choudhury Memorial Lecture

Rough-Fuzzy Knowledge Encoding and Uncertainty Analysis: Relevance
in Data Mining 1
   Sankar K. Pal

Keynote Talks

Utility-Based Data-Gathering in Wireless Sensor Networks with
Unstable Links 13
   Mingming Lu and Jie Wu

Sensor Networks Continue to Puzzle: Selected Open Problems 25
   Thomas Locher, Pascal von Rickenbach, and Roger Wattenhofer

Distributed Coordination of Workflows over Web Services and Their
Handheld-Based Execution 39
   *Janaka Balasooriya, Jaimini Joshi, Sushil K. Prasad, and
   Shamkant Navathe*

Distributed Computing Track Papers

Agreement Protocols

The Building Blocks of Consensus................................. 54
   *Yee Jiun Song, Robbert van Renesse, Fred B. Schneider, and
   Danny Dolev*

Continuous Consensus with Ambiguous Failures 73
   Tal Mizrahi and Yoram Moses

On Optimal Probabilistic Asynchronous Byzantine Agreement 86
   Amjed Shareef and C. Pandu Rangan

Narrowing Power vs. Efficiency in Synchronous Set Agreement 99
   Achour Mostefaoui, Michel Raynal, and Corentin Travers

Fault Tolerance and Synchronization

Highly-Concurrent Multi-word Synchronization (Extended Abstract) ... 112
   Hagit Attiya and Eshcar Hillel

Fault Tolerance in Finite State Machines Using Fusion 124
    Bharath Balasubramanian, Vinit Ogale, and Vijay K. Garg

Wait-Free Dining Under Eventual Weak Exclusion 135
    Scott M. Pike, Yantao Song, and Srikanth Sastry

On the Inherent Cost of Atomic Broadcast and Multicast in Wide Area
Networks 147
    Nicolas Schiper and Fernando Pedone

Detection of Disjunctive Normal Form Predicate in Distributed
Systems 158
    Hongtao Huang

Solving Classic Problems in Distributed Systems: The Smart-Message
Paradigm (Short) 170
    Sandip Dey

Design of Concurrent Utilities in Jackal: A Software DSM
Implementation (Short) 176
    Pradeep Kumar Nalla, Rajeev Wankar, and Arun Agarwal

Self-stabilization

Anonymous Daemon Conversion in Self-stabilizing Algorithms by
Randomization in Constant Space 182
    W. Goddard, S.T. Hedetniemi, D.P. Jacobs, and Pradip K. Srimani

Snap-Stabilizing Waves in Anonymous Networks 191
    Christian Boulinier, Mathieu Levert, and Franck Petit

Self-stabilizing Distributed Protocol Switching (Short) 203
    Sushanta Karmakar and Arobinda Gupta

A Self-stabilizing Algorithm for the Minimum Color Sum of a Graph
(Short) 209
    Huang Sun, Brice Effantin, and Hamamache Kheddouci

Scheduling, Clustering, and Data Mining

Global Fixed-Priority Scheduling of Arbitrary-Deadline Sporadic Task
Systems 215
    Sanjay Baruah and Nathan Fisher

Scalable and Distributed Mechanisms for Integrated Scheduling and
Replication in Data Grids 227
    Anirban Chakrabarti and Shubhashis Sengupta

DGDCT: A Distributed Grid-Density Based Algorithm for Intrinsic
Cluster Detection over Massive Spatial Data....................... 239
  Sauravjyoti Sarmah, Rosy Das, and Dhruba Kumar Bhattacharyya

An Abstraction Based Communication Efficient Distributed Association
Rule Mining (Short)... 251
  P. Santhi Thilagam and V.S. Ananthanarayana

List Heuristic Scheduling Algorithms for Distributed Memory Systems
with Improved Time Complexity (Short)............................ 257
  Maruf Ahmed, Sharif M.H. Chowdhury, and Masud Hasan

Parallel Architectures and Algorithms

CG-Cell: An NPB Benchmark Implementation on Cell Broadband
Engine 263
  Dong Li, Song Huang, and Kirk Cameron

Parallel Algorithm for Conflict Graph on OTIS-Triangular Array
(Short) 274
  Keny T. Lucas, Dheeresh K. Mallick, and Prasanta K. Jana

A Deadlock Free Shortest Path Routing Algorithm for WK-Recursive
Meshes (Short) 280
  Mostafa Rezazad, M. Hoseiny Farahabady, and Hamid Sarbazi-Azad

Mobile Agents and Cryptography

Proving Distributed Algorithms for Mobile Agents: Examples of
Spanning Tree Computation in Anonymous Networks (Short).......... 286
  *M.A. Haddar, A. Hadj Kacem, Y. Métivier, M. Mosbah, and
  M. Jmaiel*

Mobile Agent Rendezvous in a Ring Using Faulty Tokens (Short) 292
  Shantanu Das

A New Key-Predistribution Scheme for Highly Mobile Sensor
Networks (Short) 298
  Abhijit Das and Bimal Kumar Roy

Alternative Protocols for Generalized Oblivious Transfer (Short) 304
  Bhavani Shankar, Kannan Srinathan, and C. Pandu Rangan

Networking Track Papers

Sensor Networks I

The Crossroads Approach to Information Discovery in Wireless Sensor
Networks 310
  Robin Doss, Gang Li, Shui Yu, Vicky Mak, and Morshed Chowdhury

Tree-Based Anycast for Wireless Sensor/Actuator Networks 322
    Michal Koziuk and Jaroslaw Domaszewicz

A Distributed Algorithm for Load-Balanced Routing in Multihop
Wireless Sensor Networks (Short) 332
    Punyasha Chatterjee and Nabanita Das

Using Learned Data Patterns to Detect Malicious Nodes in Sensor
Networks (Short) 339
    Partha Mukherjee and Sandip Sen

An Efficient Key Establishment Scheme for Self-organizing Sensor
Networks (Short) 345
    Yong Ho Kim, Kyu Young Choi, Jongin Lim, and Dong Hoon Lee

Internet and Security

SuperTrust – A Secure and Efficient Framework for Handling Trust in
Super Peer Networks 350
    Tassos Dimitriou, Ghassan Karame, and Ioannis Christou

A Highly Flexible Data Structure for Multi-level Visibility of P2P
Communities 363
    Debmalya Biswas and Krishnamurthy Vidyasankar

Mathematical Performance Modelling of Stretched Hypercubes 375
    Sina Meraji and Hamid Sarbazi-Azad

A Family of Collusion Resistant Symmetric Key Protocols for
Authentication (Short) 387
    Bruhadeshwar Bezawada and Kishore Kothapalli

An Escalated Approach to Ant Colony Clustering Algorithm for
Intrusion Detection System (Short).................................... 393
    L. Prema Rajeswari, A. Kannan, and R. Baskaran

Sensor Networks II

Interplay of Processing and Routing in Aggregate Query Optimization
for Sensor Networks 401
    Niki Trigoni, Alexandre Guitton, and Antonios Skordylis

Exploiting Resource-Rich Actors for Bridging Network Partitions in
Wireless Sensor and Actor Networks................................... 416
    Ka. Selvaradjou, B. Goutham, and C. Siva Ram Murthy

A New Top-Down Hierarchical Multi-hop Routing Protocol for Wireless
Sensor Networks (Short) 428
    M.P. Singh and M.M. Gore

PROBESYNC: Platform Based Synchronization for Enhanced Life of
Large Scale Wireless Sensor Networks (Short) 434
  Virendra Mohan and R.C. Hansdah

Optical Networks

An Adaptive Split Reservation Protocol (SRP) for Dynamically
Reserving Wavelengths in WDM Optical Networks 440
  Malabika Sengupta, Swapan Kumar Mondal, and Debashis Saha

Routing and Wavelength Assignment in All Optical Networks Based on
Clique Partitioning 452
  Tanmay De, Ajit Pal, and Indranil Sengupta

Fault Detection and Localization Scheme for Multiple Failures in
Optical Network (Short) 464
  A. Pal, A. Paul, A. Mukherjee, M.K. Naskar, and M. Nasipuri

A Heuristic Search for Routing and Wavelength Assignment in
Distributed WDM Optical Networks with Limited Range Wavelength
Conversion (Short) 471
  Sahadeb Jana, Kajla Basu, and Subhabrata Chowdhury

QoS and Multimedia

An Efficient Storage Mechanism to Distribute Disk Load in a VoD
Server (Short) 478
  D.N. Sujatha, K. Girish, K.R. Venugopal, and L.M. Patnaik

Multi Level Pricing for Service Differentiation and Congestion Control
in Communication Networks (Short)............................. 484
  Vineet Kulkarni, Sanjay Srivastava, and R.B. Lenin

Revenue-Driven Bandwidth Management for End-to-End Connectivity
over IP Networks (Short) 490
  K. Ravindran, M. Rabby, and X. Liu

Modeling and Predicting Point-to-Point Communication Delay of
Circuit Switching in the Mesh-Connected Networks (Short) 496
  F. Safaei, A. Khonsari, M. Fathy, and M. Ould-Khaoua

Wireless Networks

Maximizing Aggregate Saturation Throughput in IEEE 802.11 Wireless
LAN with Service Differentiation................................ 503
  A.V. Babu and Lillykutty Jacob

Overloading Cellular DS-CDMA: A Bandwidth-Efficient Scheme for
Capacity Enhancement 515
    Preetam Kumar, M. Ramesh, and Saswat Chakrabarti

Enhancing DHCP for Address Autoconfiguration in Multi-hop
WLANs 528
    Raffaele Bruno, Marco Conti, and Antonio Pinizzotto

Channel Assignment in Multimedia Cellular Networks (Short) 540
    Goutam K. Audhya and Bhabani P. Sinha

Ad Hoc Networks

On Routing with Guaranteed Delivery in Three-Dimensional Ad Hoc
Wireless Networks 546
    Stephane Durocher, David Kirkpatrick, and Lata Narayanan

Energy-Efficient Dominating Tree Construction in Wireless Ad Hoc
and Sensor Networks 558
    Ruiyun Yu, Xingwei Wang, Yonghe Liu, and Sajal K. Das

A Location-Aided Content Searching Mechanism for Large Mobile
Ad Hoc Network Using Geographic Clusters 570
    Parama Bhaumik and Somprokash Bandyopadhyay

A Centralized Algorithm for Topology Management in Mobile Ad-Hoc
Networks through Multiple Coordinators (Short) 581
    Abhishek Bhattacharyya, Anand Seetharam, and M.K. Naskar

Author Index 587

Rough-Fuzzy Knowledge Encoding and Uncertainty Analysis: Relevance in Data Mining

Sankar K. Pal

Indian Statistical Institute, Kolkata
sankar@isical.ac.in

Abstract. Data mining and knowledge discovery is described from pattern recognition point of view along with the relevance of soft computing. The concept of computational theory of perceptions (CTP), its characteristics and the relation with fuzzy-granulation (f-granulation) are explained. Role of f-granulation in machine and human intelligence, and its modeling through rough-fuzzy integration are discussed. Three examples of synergistic integration, e.g., rough-fuzzy case generation, rough-fuzzy c-means and rough-fuzzy c-medoids are explained with their merits and role of fuzzy granular computation. Superiority, in terms of performance and computation time, is illustrated for the tasks of case generation (mining) in large scale case based reasoning systems, segmenting brain MR images, and analyzing protein sequences.

Keywords: soft computing, fuzzy granulation, rough-fuzzy computing, bioinformatics, MR image segmentation, case based reasoning.

1 Introduction

In recent years, the rapid advances being made in computer technology have ensured that large sections of the world population have been able to gain easy access to computers on account of falling costs worldwide, and their use is now commonplace in all walks of life. Government agencies, scientific, business and commercial organizations are routinely using computers not just for computational purposes but also for storage, in massive databases, of the immense volumes of data that they routinely generate, or require from other sources. Large-scale computer networking has ensured that such data has become accessible to more and more people. In other words, we are in the midst of an information explosion, and there is urgent need for methodologies that will help us bring some semblance of order into the phenomenal volumes of data that can readily be accessed by us with a few clicks of the keys of our computer keyboard. Traditional statistical data summarization and database management techniques are just not adequate for handling data on this scale, and for extracting intelligently, information or, rather, knowledge that may be useful for exploring the domain in question or the phenomena responsible for the data, and providing support to decision-making processes. This quest had thrown up some new phrases, for example, *data mining* [1, 2] and *knowledge discovery in databases (KDD).*

S. Rao et al. (Eds.): ICDCN 2008, LNCS 4904, pp. 1–12, 2008.
© Springer-Verlag Berlin Heidelberg 2008

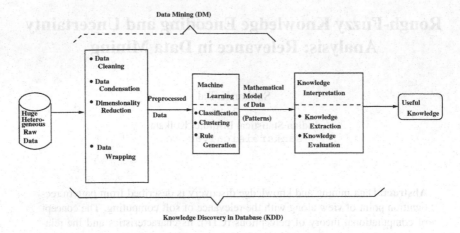

Fig. 1. Block diagram for knowledge discovery in databases [3]

Data mining is that part of knowledge discovery which deals with the process of identifying valid, novel, potentially useful, and ultimately understandable patterns in data, and excludes the knowledge interpretation part of KDD (Fig 1). From pattern recognition (PR) point of view, data mining can be viewed as applying PR and machine learning principles in the context of voluminous, possibly heterogeneous data sets. Furthermore, soft computing-based (involving fuzzy sets, neural networks, genetic algorithms and rough sets) PR methodologies and machine learning techniques hold great promise for data mining. The motivation for this is provided by their ability to handle imprecision, vagueness, uncertainty, approximate reasoning and partial truth and lead to tractability, robustness and low-cost solutions [4]. An excellent survey demonstrating the significance of soft computing tools in data mining problem is provided by Mitra et al. [5]. Some of the challenges arising out of those posed by massive data and high dimensionality, nonstandard and incomplete data, and over-fitting problems deal mostly with issues like user interaction, use of prior knowledge, assessment of statistical significance, learning from mixed media data, management of changing (dynamic) data and knowledge, integration of different classical and modern soft computing tools, and making knowledge discovery more understandable to humans by using linguistic rules, visualization, etc. Recently, a detailed review explaining the state of the art and the future directions for *web mining* research in soft computing framework is provided by Pal et al. [6]. One may note that web mining, although considered to be an application area of data mining on the WWW, demands a separate discipline of research. The reason is that web mining has its own characteristic problems (e.g., page ranking, personalization), because of the typical nature of the data, components involved and tasks to be performed, which can not be usually handled within the conventional framework of data mining and analysis. Moreover, being an interactive medium, human interface is a key component of most web applications.

Bioinformatics which can be viewed as a discipline of using *computational methods to make biological discoveries* [7] has recently been considered as another important candidate for data mining applications. It is an interdisciplinary field mainly involving biology, computer science, mathematics and statistics to analyze biological sequence data, genome content and arrangement, and to predict the function and structure of macromolecules. The ultimate goal is to enable the discovery of new biological insights as well as to create a global perspective from which unifying principles in biology can be derived. There are three major sub-disciplines dealing with the following three tasks in bioinformatics:

a) Development of new algorithms and models to assess different relationships among the members of a large biological data set;
b) Analysis and interpretation of various types of data including nucleotide and amino acid sequences, protein domains, and protein structures; and
c) Development and implementation of tools that enable efficient access and management of different types of information.

First one concerns with the mathematical and computational aspects, while the other two are related to the biological and data base aspects respectively. Data analysis tools used earlier in bioinformatics were mainly based on statistical techniques like regression and estimation. With the need of handling large heterogeneous data sets in biology in a robust and computationally efficient manner, soft computing, which provides machinery for handling uncertainty, learning and adaptation with massive parallelism, and powerful search and imprecise reasoning, has recently gained the attention of researchers for their efficient mining.

While talking about pattern recognition and data mining in the 21st century, it will remain incomplete without the mention of the *Computational Theory of Perceptions (CTP)*, explained by Zadeh [8, 9], which has a significant role in the said tasks. In the following section we discuss its basic concepts and features, and relation with soft computing.

The organization of the paper is as follows. Section 2 introduces the basic notions of computational theory of perceptions and f-granulation, while Section 3 presents rough-fuzzy approach to granular computation, in general. Section 4 explains the application of rough-fuzzy granulation in case based reasoning. Sections 5 and 6 demonstrate the concept of rough-fuzzy clustering and their key features with applications to segmenting brain MR images and analyzing protein sequence. Concluding remarks are given in Section 7.

2 Computational Theory of Perceptions and F-Granulation

Computational theory of perceptions (CTP) [8, 9] is inspired by the remarkable human capability to perform a wide variety of physical and mental tasks, including recognition tasks, without any measurements and any computations. Typical everyday examples of such tasks are parking a car, driving in city traffic, cooking meal, understanding speech, and recognizing similarities. This capability is due to the crucial ability of human brain to manipulate perceptions of time, distance, force, direction, shape, color, taste, number, intent, likelihood, and truth, among others.

Recognition and perception are closely related. In a fundamental way, a recognition process may be viewed as a sequence of decisions. Decisions are based on information. In most realistic settings, decision-relevant information is a mixture of measurements and perceptions; e.g., the car is six year old but looks almost new. An essential difference between measurement and perception is that in general, measurements are crisp, while perceptions are fuzzy. In existing theories, perceptions are converted into measurements, but such conversions in many cases, are infeasible, unrealistic or counterproductive. An alternative, suggested by the CTP, is to convert perceptions into propositions expressed in a natural language, e.g., it is a warm day, he is very honest, it is very unlikely that there will be a significant increase in the price of oil in the near future.

Perceptions are intrinsically imprecise. More specifically, perceptions are f-granular, that is, both fuzzy and granular, with a granule being a clump of elements of a class that are drawn together by indistinguishability, similarity, proximity or functionality. For example, a perception of height can be described as very tall, tall, middle, short, with very tall, tall, and so on constituting the granules of the variable 'height'. F-granularity of perceptions reflects the finite ability of sensory organs and, ultimately, the brain, to resolve detail and store information. In effect, f-granulation is a human way of achieving data compression. It may be mentioned here that although information granulation in which the granules are crisp, i.e., c-granular, plays key roles in both human and machine intelligence, it fails to reflect the fact that, in much, perhaps most, of human reasoning and concept formation the granules are fuzzy (f-granular) rather than crisp. In this respect, generality increases as the information ranges from singular (age: 22 yrs), c-granular (age: 20-30 yrs) to f-granular (age: "young"). It means CTP has, in principle, higher degree of generality than qualitative reasoning and qualitative process theory in AI [10, 11]. The types of problems that fall under the scope of CTP typically include: perception based function modeling, perception based system modeling, perception based time series analysis, solution of perception based equations, and computation with perception based probabilities where perceptions are described as a collection of different linguistic *if-then* rules.

F-granularity of perceptions puts them well beyond the meaning representation capabilities of predicate logic and other available meaning representation methods. In CTP, meaning representation is based on the use of so called constraint-centered semantics, and reasoning with perceptions is carried out by goal-directed propagation of generalized constraints. In this way, the CTP adds to existing theories the capability to operate on and reason with perception-based information.

This capability is already provided, to an extent, by fuzzy logic and, in particular, by the concept of a linguistic variable and the calculus of fuzzy if-then rules. The CTP extends this capability much further and in new directions. In application to pattern recognition and data mining, the CTP opens the door to a much wider and more systematic use of natural languages in the description of patterns, classes, perceptions and methods of recognition, organization, and knowledge discovery. Upgrading a search engine to a question- answering system is another prospective candidate in web mining for CTP application. However, one may note that dealing with perception-based information is more complex and more effort-intensive than dealing with measurement-based information, and this complexity is the price that has to be paid to achieve superiority.

3 Granular Computation and Rough-Fuzzy Approach

Rough set theory [12] provides an effective means for analysis of data by synthesizing or constructing approximations (upper and lower) of set concepts from the acquired data. The key notions here are those of "information granule" and "reducts". Information granule formalizes the concept of finite precision representation of objects in real life situation, and reducts represent the core of an information system (both in terms of objects and features) in a granular universe. *Granular computing* refers to that where computation and operations are performed on information granules (clump of similar objects or points). Therefore, it leads to have both data compression and gain in computation time, and finds wide applications. An important use of rough set theory and granular computing in data mining has been in generating logical rules for classification and association. These logical rules correspond to different important regions of the feature space, which represent data clusters.

For the past few years, rough set theory and granular computation has proven to be another soft computing tool which, in various synergistic combinations with fuzzy logic, artificial neural networks and genetic algorithms, provides a stronger framework to achieve tractability, robustness, low cost solution and close resembles with human like decision making. For example, rough-fuzzy integration can be considered as a way of emulating the basis of f-granulation in CTP, where perceptions have fuzzy boundaries and granular attribute values. Similarly, rough neural synergistic integration helps in extracting crude domain knowledge in the form of rules for describing different concepts/classes, and then encoding them as network parameters; thereby constituting the initial knowledge base network for efficient learning. Since in granular computing computations/operations are performed on granules (clump of similar objects or points), rather than on the individual data points, the computation time is greatly reduced. The results on these investigations, both theory and real life applications, are being available in different journals and conference proceedings. Some special issues and edited volumes have also come out [13-15].

4 Rough-Fuzzy Granulation and Case Based Reasoning

Case based reasoning (CBR) [16], which is a novel Artificial Intelligence (AI) problem-solving paradigm, involves adaptation of old solutions to meet new demands, explanation of new situations using old instances (called cases), and performance of reasoning from precedence to interpret new problems. It has a significant role to play in today's pattern recognition and data mining applications involving CTP, particularly when the evidence is sparse. The significance of soft computing to CBR problems has been adequately explained in a recent book by Pal, Dillon and Yeung [17] and Pal and Shiu [18]. In this section we demonstrate an example [19] of using the concept of f-granulation, through rough-fuzzy computing, for performing an important task, namely, *case generation*, in large scale CBR systems.

A case may be defined as a contextualized piece of knowledge representing an evidence that teaches a lesson fundamental to achieving goals of the system. While case selection deals with selecting informative prototypes from the data, case generation concerns with construction of 'cases' that need not necessarily include any of the given data points. For generating cases, linguistic representation of patterns is used to obtain a fuzzy granulation of the feature space. Rough set theory is used to generate dependency rules corresponding to informative regions in the granulated feature space. The fuzzy membership functions corresponding to the informative regions are stored as cases. Figure 2 shows an example of such case generation for a two dimensional data having two classes. The granulated feature space has $3^2 = 9$ granules. These granules of different sizes are characterized by three membership functions along each axis, and have ill-defined (overlapping) boundaries. Two dependency rules: $class_1 \leftarrow L_1 \wedge H_2$ and $class_2 \leftarrow H_1 \wedge L_2$ are obtained using rough set theory. The fuzzy membership functions, marked bold, corresponding to the attributes appearing in the rules for a class are stored as its case.

Unlike the conventional case selection methods, the cases here are cluster granules and not sample points. Also, since all the original features may not be required to express the dependency rules, each case involves a reduced number of relevant features. The methodology is therefore suitable for mining data sets, large both in dimension and size, due to its low time requirement in case generation as well as retrieval.

The aforesaid characteristics are demonstrated in Figures 3 and 4 [19] for two real life data sets with features 10 and 649 and number of samples 586012 and 2000 respectively. Their superiority over IB3, IB4 [16] and random case selection algorithms, in terms of classification accuracy (with one nearest neighbor rule), case generation (t_{gen}) and retrieval (t_{ret}) times, and average storage requirement (average feature) per case, are evident. The numbers of cases considered for comparison are 545 and 50 respectively.

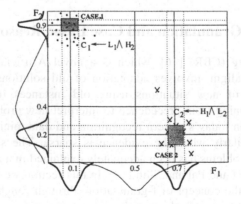

Fig. 2. Rough-fuzzy case generation for a two dimensional data [15]

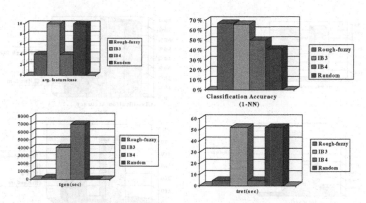

Fig. 3. Performance of different case generation schemes for the forest cover-type GIS data set with 7 classes, 10 features and 586012 samples

5 Rough-Fuzzy Clustering and Segmentation of Brain MR Images

Incorporating both fuzzy and rough sets, a new clustering algorithm is described, termed as rough-fuzzy c-means (RFCM). The proposed c-means adds the concept of fuzzy membership of fuzzy sets, and lower and upper approximations of rough sets into c-means algorithm. While the membership of fuzzy sets enables efficient handling of overlapping partitions, the rough sets deal with uncertainty, vagueness, and incompleteness in class definition [26].

In the proposed RFCM, each cluster is represented by a centroid, a crisp lower approximation, and a fuzzy boundary. The lower approximation influences the fuzziness of final partition. According to the definitions of lower approximations and boundary of rough sets, if an object belongs to lower approximations of a cluster, then the object does not belong to any other clusters. That is, the object is contained in that cluster definitely. Thus, the weights of the objects in lower approximation of a cluster should be independent of other centroids and clusters, and should not be coupled with their similarity with respect to other centroids. Also, the objects in lower approximation of a cluster should have similar influence on the corresponding centroids and cluster. Whereas, if the object belongs to the boundary of a cluster, then the object possibly belongs to that cluster and potentially belongs to another cluster. Hence, the objects in boundary regions should have different influence on the centroids and clusters. So, in RFCM, the membership values of objects in lower approximation are 1, while those in boundary region are the same as fuzzy c-means. In other word, RFCM first partitions the data into two classes - lower approximation and boundary. Only the objects in boundary are fuzzified. The new centroid is calculated based on the weighting average of the crisp lower approximation and fuzzy boundary. Computation of the centroid is modified to include the effects of both fuzzy memberships and lower and upper bounds. *In essence, Rough-Fuzzy clustering tends to compromise between restrictive (hard clustering) and descriptive (fuzzy clustering) partitions.*

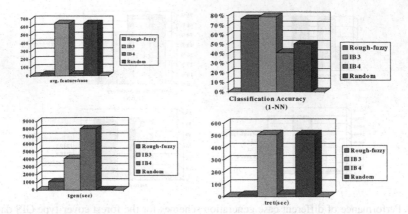

Fig. 4. Performance of different case generation schemes for the handwritten numeral recognition data set with 10 classes, 649 features and 2000 samples

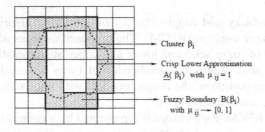

Fig. 5. Rough-fuzzy c-means: each cluster is represented by crisp lower approximations and fuzzy boundary [26]

The effectiveness of RFCM algorithm is shown, as an example, for classification of Iris data set and segmentation of brain MR images. The Iris data set is a four-dimensional data set containing 50 samples each of three types of Iris flowers. One of the three clusters (class 1) is well separated from the other two, while classes 2 and 3 have some overlap.

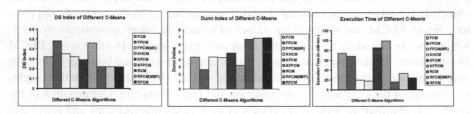

Fig. 6. Comparison of DB and Dunn Index [25], and execution time of HCM, FCM [21], RCM [22], RFCM^{MBP} [23], and RFCM

The performance of different c-means algorithms is shown with respect to DB and Dunn index [25] in Fig. 6. The results reported establish the fact that RFCM provides best result having lowest DB index and highest Dunn index with lower execution time.

For segmentation of brain MR images, 100 MR images with different sizes and 16 bit gray levels are tested. All the MR images are collected from Advanced Medicare and Research Institute (AMRI), Kolkata, India. The comparative performance of different c-means is shown in Fig. 7 with respect to β index [24].

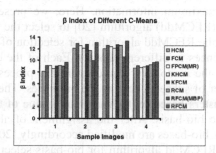

Fig. 7. Comparison of β index [24] of HCM, FCM [21], RCM [22], RFCM^{MBP} [23], and RFCM

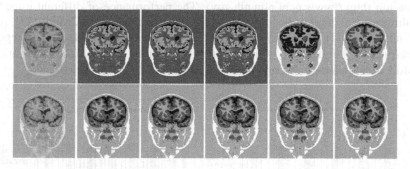

Fig. 8. Some original and segmented images of HCM, FCM [21], RCM [22], RFCM^{MBP} [23], and RFCM

Some of the original images along with their segmented versions with different c-means are shown in Fig. 8. The results confirm that the RFCM algorithm produces segmented images more promising than do the conventional methods, both visually and in terms of β index.

6 Rough Fuzzy C-Medoids and Amino Acid Sequence Analysis

In most pattern recognition algorithms, amino acids cannot be used directly as inputs since they are non-numerical variables. They, therefore, need encoding prior to input. In this regard, bio-basis function maps a non-numerical sequence space to a numerical feature space. It uses a kernel function to transform biological sequences to feature vectors directly. Bio-bases consist of sections of biological sequences that code for a feature of interest in the study and are responsible for the transformation of biological data to high-dimensional feature space. Transformation of input data to high-dimensional feature space is performed based on the similarity of an input sequence to a bio-basis with reference to a biological similarity matrix. Thus, the biological content in the sequences can be maximally utilized for accurate modeling. The use of similarity matrices to map features allows the bio-basis function to analyze biological sequences without the need for encoding.

One of the important issues for the bio-basis function is how to select the minimum set of bio-bases with maximum information. Here, we present the application of rough-fuzzy c-medoids (RFCMdd) algorithm [20] to select the most informative bio-bases. The objective of the RFCMdd algorithm for selection of bio-bases is to assign all amino acid subsequences to different clusters. Each of the clusters is represented by a bio-basis, which is the medoid for that cluster. The process begins by randomly choosing desired number of subsequences as the bio-bases. The subsequences are assigned to one of the clusters based on the maximum value of the similarity between the subsequence and the bio-basis. After the assignment of all the subsequences to various clusters, the new bio-bases are modified accordingly [20].

The performance of RFCMdd algorithm for bio-basis selection is presented using five whole human immunodeficiency virus (HIV) protein sequences and Cai-Chou HIV data set, which can be downloaded from the National Center for Biotechnology Information (http://www.ncbi.nlm.nih.gov). The performance of different c-medoids algorithms such as hard c-medoids (HCMdd), fuzzy c-medoids (FCMdd) [27], rough c-medoids (RCMdd) [20], and rough-fuzzy c-medoids (RFCMdd) [20] is reported with respect to β index and γ index [20]. The results establish the superiority of RFCMdd with lowest γ index and highest β index.

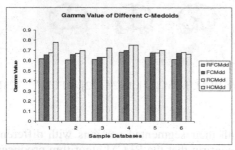
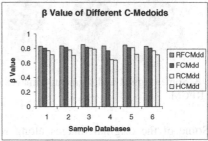

7 Conclusions

Data mining and knowledge discovery in databases, which has recently drawn the attention of researchers significantly, have been explained from the view-point of pattern recognition. The concept of rough-fuzzy computing is given more emphasis. Three examples of judicious integration, viz., rough-fuzzy case generation, rough-fuzzy c-means and rough-fuzzy c-medoids are explained along with their merits. Problems of rough-fuzzy clustering in protein sequence analysis and segmentation of brain MR images are considered. Fuzzy granulation through rough-fuzzy computing, and performing operations on fuzzy granules provide both information compression and gain in computation time; thereby making it suitable for data mining applications. As it appears, soft computing methodologies, coupled with computational theory of perception (CTP), have great promise for efficient mining of large, heterogeneous data, including web mining and bioinformatics [28], and providing solution of real-life recognition problems.

References

1. Shanahan, J.G.: Soft Computing for Knowledge Discovery: Introducing Cartesian Granule Feature. Kluwer Academic, Boston (2000)
2. Pal, S.K., Pal, A. (eds.): Pattern Recognition: From Classical to Modern Approaches. World Scientific, Singapore (2002)
3. Pal, A., Pal, S.K.: Pattern recognition: Evolution of methodologies and data mining. In: Pal, S.K., Pal, A. (eds.) Pattern Recognition: From Classical to Modern Approaches, pp. 1–23. World Scientific, Singapore (2002)
4. Zadeh, L.A.: Fuzzy logic, neural networks and soft computing. Communications of the ACM 37, 77–84 (1994)
5. Mitra, S., Pal, S.K., Mitra, P.: Data Mining in Soft Computing Framework: A Survey. IEEE Trans. Neural Networks 13(1), 3–14 (2002)
6. Pal, S.K., Talwar, V., Mitra, P.: Web Mining in Soft Computing Framework: Relevance, State of the Art and Future Directions. IEEE Trans. Neural Networks 13(5), 1163–1177 (2002)
7. Baldi, P., Brunak, S.: Bioinformatics: The Machine Learning Approach. MIT Press, Cambridge (1998)
8. Zadeh, L.A.: A new direction in AI: Toward a computational theory of perceptions. AI Magazine 22, 73–84 (2001)
9. Zadeh, L.A., Pal, S.K., Mitra, S.: Neuro-Fuzzy Pattern Recognition: Methods in Soft Computing. Wiley, New York (1999)
10. Kuipers, B.J.: Qualitative Reasoning. MIT Press, Cambridge (1984)
11. Sun, R.: Integrating Rules and Connectionism for Robust Commonsense Reasoning. Wiley, NewYork (1994)
12. Pawlak, Z.: Rough Sets: Theoretical Aspects of Reasoning about Data. Kluwer Academic, Dordrecht (1991)
13. Pal, S.K., Skowron, A. (eds.): Rough-Fuzzy Hybridization: A New Trend in Decision Making. Springer, Singapore (1999)
14. Pal, S.K., Polkowski, L., Skowron, A. (eds.): Rough-neuro Computing: A Way to Computing with Words. Springer, Berlin (2003)
15. Pal, S.K., Skowron, A. (eds.): Special issue on Rough Sets, Pattern Recognition and Data Mining, Pattern Recognition Letters, 24(6) (2003)
16. Kolodner, J.L.: Case-Based Reasoning. Morgan Kaufmann, San Mateo (1993)
17. Pal, S.K., Dillon, T.S., Yeung, D.S. (eds.): Soft Computing in Case Based Reasoning. Springer, London (2001)
18. Pal, S.K., Shiu, S.C.K.: Foundations of Soft Case Based Reasoning. John Wiley, NewYork (2003)
19. Pal, S.K., Mitra, P.: Case generation using rough sets with fuzzy discretization. IEEE Trans. Knowledge and Data Engineering 16(3), 292–300 (2004)

20. Maji, P., Pal, S.K.: Rough-Fuzzy C-Medoids Algorithm and Selection of Bio-Basis for Amino Acid Sequence Analysis. IEEE Trans. Knowledge and Data Engineering 19(6), 859–872 (2007)
21. Bezdek, J.C.: Pattern Recognition with Fuzzy Objective Function Algorithm. Plenum, New York (1981)
22. Lingras, P., West, C.: Interval Set Clustering of Web Users with Rough K-Means. Journal of Intelligent Information Systems 23(1), 5–16 (2004)
23. Mitra, S., Banka, H., Pedrycz, W.: Rough-Fuzzy Collaborative Clustering. IEEE Trans. on Systems, Man, and Cybernetics - Part B: Cybernetics 36, 795–805 (2006)
24. Pal, S.K., Ghosh, A., Sankar, B.U.: Segmentation of Remotely Sensed Images with Fuzzy Thresholding, and Quantitative Evaluation. International Journal of Remote Sensing 21(11), 2269–2300 (2000)
25. Bezdek, J.C., Pal, N.R.: Some New Indexes for Cluster Validity. IEEE Trans. on System, Man, and Cybernetics, Part B 28, 301–315 (1988)
26. Maji, P., Pal, S.K.: Rough Set Based Generalized Fuzzy C-Means Algorithm and Quantitative Indices. IEEE Trans. on System, Man and Cybernetics, Part B (to appear)
27. Krishnapuram, R., Joshi, A., Nasraoui, O., Yi, L.: Low Complexity Fuzzy Relational Clustering Algorithms for Web Mining. IEEE Trans. Fuzzy System 9, 595–607 (2001)
28. Bandyopadhyay, S., Pal, S.K.: Classification and Learning Using Genetic Algorithms: Applications in Bioinformatics and Web Intelligence. Springer, Berlin (2007)

Utility-Based Data-Gathering in Wireless Sensor Networks with Unstable Links

Mingming Lu and Jie Wu*

Department of Computer Science and Engineering
Florida Atlantic University
Boca Raton, FL 33431
{mlu2@, jie@cse.}fau.edu

Abstract. Traditional utility-based data-gathering models consider the maximization of the gathered information and the minimization of energy consumption in WSNs with reliable channels. In this paper, we extend the model to include retransmissions caused by link failure to improve network utility. The challenge lies in balancing two competing factors: energy loss (and hence utility) through retransmissions and increased reliability (and hence utility) through retransmissions. We adopt a utility-based metric proposed in our previous work [9] and show the NP-hardness of the problem, regardless of the number of source sensors. We design several approximation heuristics for either case and compare their performances through simulation. We also study the impact of retransmissions on the maximization of network utility. Extensive simulations through a customized simulator are conducted to verify our results.

Keywords: Data-gathering, heuristic solution, network utility, routing, stability, wireless sensor networks (WSNs).

1 Introduction

A typical data-gathering wireless sensor network (WSN) consists of one or more sinks which subscribe specific data by expressing interests. Many sensors act as data sources that detect environmental events and push the relevant data to the subscriber sinks. We consider a general many-to-one (one sink and many sensors) WSN with unstable wireless links, where the sink assigns different weights (*benefit*) to different types of events according to their importance. Sensors periodically sense the subscribed events and send data through a data-gathering tree to the sink in each round of communication.

Since the wireless channels are unstable, the reliability of data delivery from sensors to the sink cannot be guaranteed. This unreliability causes data loss and energy waste, and in turn decreases the amount of information collected by the sink and increases the total energy consumption by the sensors. To address the inefficiency caused by the unreliability, we integrate the energy consumption, the instability of wireless channels, and the benefit of sensed data (to the sink) into a single metric-*network utility*-which

* This work was supported in part by NSF grants ANI 0073736, EIA 0130806, CCR 0329741, CNS 0422762, CNS 0434533, CNS 0531410, and CNS 0626240.

S. Rao et al. (Eds.): ICDCN 2008, LNCS 4904, pp. 13–24, 2008.

is the same as social welfare [11], which studies the efficient allocation of limited resources in a society to optimize the resource utilization. It is well known that a system is efficient if and only if the system's social welfare is maximized. The social welfare of a system = the system benefit − the system cost. Because the systems we study are the data-gathering WSNs and the purpose of the data-gathering WSNs is to collect sensed data, the system benefit (called *network benefit*) is the total amount of weighted (non-redundant) information gathered by the sink in a round, and the system cost (called *network energy consumption*) is the the total energy consumed by all sensors in a round.

The challenges in maximizing network utility in data-gathering WSNs are as follows. First, the selection of the path from any sensor to the sink depends not only on the network topology (including the energy consumption and the instability of wireless channels), but also the benefit value for each operation (collection of a particular type of data). Second, data from different sensors can share the same path (to the sink) in order to save energy, but this also introduces additional problems as it is vulnerable to link failure since multiple data share the same path/link. Third, there is a question as to whether the number of sensors that have data to send affects the complexity of the problem. Lastly, retransmission can increase the delivery ratio for a path/link, but can also increase transmission delay and energy consumption.

To assess the complex trade-offs one at a time, we assume the availability of a sufficient bandwidth for each channel so that contention for the channel is not an issue. Moreover, we assume that sensors are static and the benefit values for different data are predetermined. Under these assumptions, we can focus on the determination of the optimal reverse broadcast/multicast trees (in terms of maximum network utility).

2   Preliminaries

We first consider the path selection problem, i.e., choosing a path for any sensor to the sink according to the network topology and the benefit value. A network is modeled as an undirected disk graph. Each link (i, j) has two properties: link cost $c_{i,j}$ and link stability $p_{i,j}$. Link cost $c_{i,j}$ is node i's minimal transmission cost to send a packet to node j in a single transmission attempt. Link stability $p_{i,j}$ is the ratio of received packets by node j to transmitted packets by node i in a single transmission attempt. The costs and stabilities of all links compose the topology information of the network.

To illustrate the basic idea of the expected utility, we first consider a single-link route (i, j), where j is the sink. We assume that i has data with benefit v to send. Since the data will be delivered to j with probability $p_{i,j}$, the expected benefit is $v \times p_{i,j}$. Because sensor i will consume energy cost $c_{i,j}$ regardless whether j receives the data or not, the expected utility of this data delivery is:

$$v \times p_{i,j} - c_{i,j}. \tag{1}$$

We observe that the above calculation of the expected utility can extend to the case of a multi-hop route. For example, consider a route $R = < 1, \cdots, i, i+1, \cdots, r >$, where node 1 is the source sensor (the sensor with data to send), and node r is the sink. We can pretend node $r - 1$ is also a source sensor; thus, according to Formula (1), the expected utility from node $r - 1$ to the sink r is $v \times p_{r-1,r} - c_{r-1,r}$. For simpler presentation, we denote it as the residual expected utility u_{r-1}. Similarly, the expected utility from node $r - 2$ to the sink r is $u_{r-2} = u_{r-1} \times p_{r-2,r-1} - c_{r-2,r-1}$. In general, we have

$$u_i = u_{i+1} \times p_{i,i+1} - c_{i,i+1}. \tag{2}$$

By applying Formula (2) recursively, we obtain the expected utility $U = u_1 = u_2 \times p_{1,2} - c_{1,2}$.

We observe that the value of $u_i - u_j$ can be regarded as the *distance* between node i and node j. Therefore, the distance between each two neighboring nodes can be regarded as the weight of the link connecting the two nodes, and hence, the weight information composes the topology information of WSNs with unstable links. Based on this topology information, it is straightforward to apply a Dijkstra-based algorithm to select the best path in terms of the shortest distance. However, the tricky part is that this topology information changes with the change of the benefit value, and therefore, different benefit values cause different topologies. Moreover, the weights of different links are interdependent, which complicates the construction of the data-gathering tree.

3 The Model

In this work, our main consideration is WSNs, where sensors periodically sense the environment and have data to send in each round (period) of communication. The problem lies in finding a routing scheme to deliver collected data from the designated sensors to the sink so that the expected network utility (in a round) is maximized. We assume that each sensor has only one unit of data to send in each round.

We consider path-sharing to save energy because each packet has a minimum fixed overhead provided by the sequence number, the radio header and CRC, etc. This cost is fixed and independent of the size of the packet payload. Path-sharing can improve transmission efficiency by having proportionally less overhead per useful bit transmitted in the payload. Without loss of generality, we assume that the size of the fixed overhead is 1 and the size of one unit of data is α. Hence, the packet size of transmitting k units of aggregated data is $1 + k\alpha$.

Formally, in our model, a WSN is modeled as an undirected disk graph $(\mathcal{N} \cup \{d\}, E)$, where $\mathcal{N} = \{1, 2, \cdots, N\}$ is the set of sensor nodes, d is the sink, and E is the set of links connecting the sensors. A subset $S \subseteq \mathcal{N}$ consists of all source sensors, each of which has 1 unit of data to send in each round. Let p_i be the delivery ratio from source sensor i to the sink d along the path in a spanning tree T, and c_i be the expected cost of node i in T. $\sum_{i \in S} v \times p_i$ and $\sum_{i \in T} c_i$ are the expected network benefit and the expected network consumption, respectively. Thus, our data-gathering problem can be defined as follows: find a spanning tree T rooted as the sink d that maximizes the expected network utility,

$$\sum_{i \in S} v \times p_i - \sum_{i \in T} c_i, \tag{3}$$

with the constraint that the cost of k units of data transmitted through link $c_{i,j}$ is $(1 + k\alpha)c_{i,j}$.

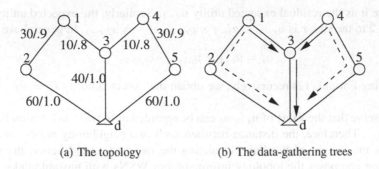

(a) The topology   (b) The data-gathering trees

Fig. 1. An example of utility-based data-gathering tree

Through a simple example shown in Fig. 1(a), we can see that the optimal data-gathering tree depends not only on the topology information but also on the benefit value and the value of α. There is one sink and two sources (nodes 1 and 4) in Fig. 1(a). In the gathering tree described by the flows in solid lines in Fig. 1(b), the expected utility is $0.8 \times 2v - 10 \times (1 + \alpha) \times 2 - 0.8 \times 40 \times (1 + 2\alpha) = 1.6v - 52 - 84\alpha$ because path $< 1, 3, d >$ and path $< 4, 3, d >$ share link $(3, d)$. In the gathering tree described by the flows in dashed lines in Fig. 1(b), the expected utility of path $< 1, 2, d >$ is $0.9v - 84(1 + \alpha)$. Because path $< 1, 2, d >$ and path $< 4, 5, d >$ are symmetrical and do not share a path, the expected utility is $[0.9v - 84(1 + \alpha)] \times 2 = 1.8v - 168(1 + \alpha)$. Comparing the expected utilities from the two data-gathering trees, their difference is $0.2v - 116 - 84\alpha$. Note that $\alpha \geq 0$. If $v = 100$, the optimal data-gathering scheme is path-sharing. If $\alpha = 0.1$ and $v = 630$, the optimal scheme is to not share a path.

Both the reverse broadcast tree problem and the reverse multicast tree problem are NP-hard. If all of the links' stabilities are 1, the reverse broadcast tree problem can be reduced to the correlated data gathering problem [5], which has been proven to be NP-hard. Similarly, if all links' stabilities are 1 and the data cost is excluded, i.e., $\alpha = 0$, the reverse multicast tree problem can be reduced to the geometric spanning tree problem, which is also NP-hard. Therefore, our reverse broadcast/multicast tree problem is NP-hard. If we restrict the overhead cost, the data cost α, the link stability, the benefit v, and the source sensor set S, the problem can be reduced to different well-known or solved subproblems. For example, if the overhead cost is not counted, the problem is reduced to the maximum expected utility path tree problem, whose special case that $|S| = 1$ (only one source sensor) has been studied in our prior work [9] and an optimal algorithm with complexity of $O((|E| + |\mathcal{N}|)log|\mathcal{N}|)$ was designed to solve the problem. Furthermore, if all links are reliable, the problem is reduced to the shortest-path tree problem. If link stability is not 1 but the benefit $v \rightarrow \infty$ and $|S| = 1$, it is equal to the most reliable path problem, i.e. find the path with the highest delivery ratio from s to d. On the other hand, if only the overhead cost is considered ($\alpha = 0$), all links' stabilities are 1, and the source set $S = \mathcal{N}$, the problem is the standard broadcast tree problem, which can be solved via the Prime algorithm to construct a minimum spanning tree.

4   The Construction of the Data-Gathering Tree

4.1   Build the Reverse Broadcast Tree

Maximum Expected Utility Path Tree. A nave method of constructing the reverse broadcast tree is to build the maximum expected utility path for each sensor, i.e. build the maximum expected utility (MEU) path tree. This heuristic is similar to the shortest-path tree. The difference is that in a MEU path tree, a sensor's distance to the sink depends not only on the link cost, but also on the link stability and the data's benefit to the sink. Different benefit values usually cause different MEU path trees.

Algorithm 1. MEUPT$(\mathcal{N}, d, v)$

1: Initialize;
2: **while** $\mathcal{N} \neq \emptyset$ **do**
3:     Find the maximum EU sensor i from $\mathcal{N}$;
4:     Remove i from $\mathcal{N}$ to T;
5:     For each i's neighbor j not in T, Relax(i, j);

Relax(i, j)
1: **if** i can increase j's utility **then**
2:     $u_j \leftarrow u_i \cdot p_{j,i} - \delta \cdot c_{j,i}$;

The formal description of this heuristic is given in Algorithm MEUPT. The input of this algorithm is the sensor set $\mathcal{N}$, the sink d, and the benefit v. The link cost $c_{i,j}$ and link stability $p_{i,j}$ for each link (i, j) are also given. Initially, the sink's expected utility is v, if a sensor j can directly communicate with the sink, its expected utility is $v \cdot p_{j,d} - \delta \cdot c_{j,d}$, and all the other sensor's expected utilities are $-\infty$. The reverse broadcast tree T first contains only the sink. In each iteration of the construction phase, the algorithm chooses a link that connects a frontier node (node in T) with a node not in T and has the maximum expected utility, and removes the node from the sensor set. Then, the sensor relaxes its neighbors that are still in the sensor set.

The relaxation consists of two steps. First, the chosen node calculates the expected utility of each neighbor according to the recursive definition of the expected utility (Formula (2)) with a small modification because of the consideration of the data cost and overhead cost. Second, the node compares each neighbor's calculated expected utility with its original expected utility and saves the larger value as the neighbor's new expected utility. This procedure repeats until all sensor nodes are included in T.

Note that in line 2 of the Relax(i, j) function, the coefficient of the cost δ can be either $1 + \alpha$ or α. If $\delta = \alpha$, it means the overhead cost is excluded from the energy cost, and hence, there is no need for path-sharing. If $\delta = 1 + \alpha$, it means that data flows do not share paths. Without path-sharing, the MEU path tree is the optimal data gathering tree. Thus, the expected network utilities of the MEU path tree with $\delta = \alpha$ and the MEU path tree with $\delta = 1 + \alpha$ can be used as an upper bound and a lower bound of the optimal data-gathering tree, respectively.

To illustrate the algorithm, we describe the execution of the algorithm on the simple example given in Fig. 1(a). Assume that the benefit is 200 and $\delta = \alpha = 1$. Among d's three neighbors 2, 3, and 5, node 3 has the maximum expected utility 160 while both node 2 and node 5's expected utilities are 140. Thus, link $(3, d)$ is first added into T, and then node 1 and 4's expected utilities are both relaxed through node 3 from $-\infty$ to $160 \times 0.8 - 10 = 118$. Since both node 2 and node 5's expected utilities are larger than node 1 and node 4's expected utilities, node 2 and node 5 are selected earlier than node 1 and 4. Node 2 (5) will try to relax node 1 (4) but fails to improve nodes 1 and 4's expected utilities. Finally, node 1 and 4 will be selected, and the MEU path tree consists of link $(1, 3)$, $(4, 3)$, $(3, d)$, $(2, d)$ and $(5, d)$. If the overhead is not counted, the expected network utility is $160 + 140 \times 2 + 118 \times 2 = 676$. The actual expected network utility of the MEU path tree is $676 - 180 = 496$, where 180 is the overhead of the entire MEU path tree.

Maximum Incremental ENU Link First. Although the nave method is simple, it does not take advantage of path-sharing. Therefore, we propose a greedy-based heuristic, MIENULF, to utilize path-sharing. In each iteration of the construction phase, the MIENULF heuristic selects a link that can increase the expected network utility the most. The only difference between the MIENULF heuristic and the MEUPT heuristic is the relaxation part.

Algorithm 2. MIENULF($\mathcal{N}, d, v$)

1: The main part is the same as Algorithm MEUPT;

Relax(i, j)
1: **if** i can increase j's utility **then**
2:      $p_j \leftarrow p_i \cdot p_{j,i}$;
3:      $c_j \leftarrow c_i \cdot p_{j,i} + c_{j,i}$;
4:      $u_j \leftarrow v \cdot p_j - \alpha \cdot c_i \cdot p_{j,i} - (1 + \alpha)c_{j,i}$;

Besides the expected utility from each sensor, algorithm MIENULF has to memorize the delivery ratio and the expected cost from each sensor to the sink. Therefore, the algorithm maintains two additional variables for each node: p_i and c_i - the current delivery ratio and the current expected cost from node i to the sink along the current path, respectively. Initially, $p_i = 0$ and $c_i = 0$ if $i \neq d$; otherwise, $p_d = 1$ and $c_d = 0$. The reason to maintain p_i and c_i for each node is that the expected cost consists of two parts: the first part is the cost of the new relaxed link, i.e., $(1 + \alpha)c_{j,i}$, which consists of the data cost and the overhead; the second part is the cost shared with other sensors, i.e., $\alpha \cdot c_i \cdot p_{j,i}$, in which the overhead has been included in other nodes's expected cost.

We illustrate algorithm MIENULF by running the example given in Fig. 1(a) and still set $v = 200$ and $\alpha = 1$. After d's relaxation, node 2, 3, and 5's expected utilities are 80, 120, and 80, respectively. Then link $(3, d)$ is selected and node 3 will relax node 1 and node 4, whose expected utilities will change to $200 \times 0.8 - 40 \times 0.8 - 2 \times 10 = 108$. Therefore, in MIENULF, nodes 1 and 4 are selected before nodes 2 and 5, whose orders are different from the execution of MEUPT, although the final trees are the same.

Spanning Tree-Based Heuristic. The spanning tree-based method builds the data-gathering tree by applying the Prime algorithm to construct the minimum spanning tree. The reason is that if we omit the data cost, and hence the utility, the weigh of each link (i, j) is just $-c_{i,j}$, i.e., the negative value of the overhead. Therefore, finding a data-gathering tree that maximizes the weight of the tree is equal to finding the minimal spanning tree. For the example in Fig. 1(a), the minimum spanning tree, which is different from the MEU path tree, consists of links $(3, d)$, $(1, 3)$, $(4, 3)$, $(1, 2)$, and $(4, 5)$. The cost of the overhead is 120, and the expected network utility is $160 + 118 \times 2 + 76.2 \times 2 - 120 = 428.4$.

SLT-Based Approximation Algorithm. The SLT-based heuristic utilizes the property that the expected utility of a tree rooted at the sink can be separated into two parts: the expected utility excluding the overhead energy cost and the overhead energy cost. Each part alone can be optimized by a polynomial algorithm. This heuristic is inspired by the shallow light tree (SLT) [5, 8]. The SLT is a spanning tree that has two properties: the cost of the SLT is no more than $1 + \frac{\sqrt{2}}{\gamma}$ times the cost of the minimal spanning tree, and the cost of the path from any node to the sink in the SLT is no more than $1 + \sqrt{2\gamma}$ times the cost of the shortest path, where γ can be any positive constant. But our SLT-based heuristic cannot have the approximation ratio because the metrics for the overhead cost and the modified expected utility are different, unlike those for the MST and the shortest path.

The construction of the SLT-based approximation algorithm is as follows. First, a minimum spanning tree is constructed. Starting from the sink, a depth-first-search of the tree is made. When a node is visited the first time, its expected utility is compared to its maximum expected utility (along the maximum expected utility path). If its expected utility is less than θ ($\theta < 1$) times its maximum expected utility, the link connecting its parent node will be removed, and the maximum expected utility path from the node to the sink is added.

For the example in Fig. 1(a), assume that $v = 200$, $\alpha = 1$, and $\theta = 0.75$. First, the MST is constructed. When searching the MST from the sink in the depth first order, since the expected utilities for nodes 3, 1, and 4 are equal to their maximum expected utilities, links $(3, d)$, $(1, 3)$, and $(3, 4)$ remain the same. However, when nodes 2 and 5 are visited, their expected utilities are $76.2 < 0.75 \times 140$, where 140 is the maximum expected utility. Thus, links $(1, 2)$ and $(4, 5)$ are removed, and links $(2, d)$ and $(5, d)$ are inserted. In this example, the data-gathering tree produced by the SLT-based algorithm is the same as the MEU path tree.

4.2 Build the Reverse Multicast Tree

All the algorithms used in building the reverse broadcast tree can be used to build the reverse multicast tree by pruning the redundant, useless branches in order to connect source sensors to the sink. Besides these algorithms, we propose an algorithm that builds the reverse multicast tree directly.

Maximum Incremental ENU Path First. The maximum incremental ENU path first (MIENUPF) approach is similar to the MIENULF heuristic. The difference is that instead of adding one link at each iterative step, the MIENUPF inserts a path that connects an unconnected source to the current T. After the selection of the new branch, each node in the new branch will relax the remaining source sensors. This procedure repeats until all required source sensors are included in T.

The MIENUPF heuristic uses a modified MIEUIF heuristic as a building block. In the modified MIEUIF heuristic, line 2 (the loop termination condition) changes from $\mathcal{N} \neq \emptyset$ to $S \cap \mathcal{N} \neq \emptyset$ because we intend to build a reverse multicast tree instead of the reverse broadcast tree. After the selection of the maximum expected utility node i, besides removing i from $\mathcal{N}$, node i should also removed from S if $i \in S$.

Initially, only the expected utility of the sink is set to v, and the expected utilities of all the other nodes are set to $-\infty$. At each iterative step, after the execution of the modified MIEUIF heuristic, the MIENUPF heuristic will select an unconnected source sensor with the maximum expected utility and add the branch that connects the source sensor to T. Although a lot of nodes' expected utilities were updated in the execution of the modified MIEUIF heuristic, only the expected utilities of the nodes on the new branch will be kept.

Algorithm 3. MIENUPF($\mathcal{N}, S, d, v$)

1: Initialize;
2: **while** $S \cap T \neq \emptyset$ **do**
3:     MIENULF($\mathcal{N}, S, d, v$);
4:     Find the maximum EU sensor i from S;
5:     Remove i from S;
6:     Insert into T the branch connecting i to T;
7:     Keep the u_j of each node j on the new branch;

For the example in Fig. 1(a), assume that $v = 200$, $\alpha = 1$. After the first round of the MIENULF, all five nodes have been relaxed, and path $< 1, 3, d >$ (or $< 4, 3, d >$, depending on the tie-breaking rule; here we adopt the smallest node ID) is inserted into T. The expected utilities of nodes 2, 4, and 5 change back to $-\infty$ at the end of this round. In the next round, T starts with the path $< 1, 3, d >$ and link $(3, 4)$ will be inserted in the end.

5 Simulation

All approaches are simulated on our customized simulator. We empirically study the performance of different heuristics for the reverse broadcast/multicast tree and the effect of various network parameters on the performance of the proposed heuristics. The network parameters include the network density n (i.e., node population), the size of a unit data (α), link stability, the value of the benefit v, the source sensor set S, the local quota, and the parameter θ in SLT-based heuristic. The simulation is set up in a $100m \times 100m$ area, where all sensors are homogeneous and can be deployed in this area arbitrarily. The energy cost between any two nodes is proportional to their distance. The

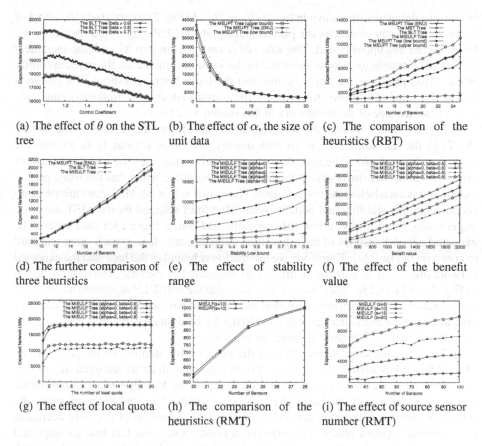

(a) The effect of θ on the STL tree

(b) The effect of α, the size of unit data

(c) The comparison of the heuristics (RBT)

(d) The further comparison of three heuristics

(e) The effect of stability range

(f) The effect of the benefit value

(g) The effect of local quota

(h) The comparison of the heuristics (RMT)

(i) The effect of source sensor number (RMT)

Fig. 2. Simulation results of the heuristics in building the reverse broadcast/multicast tree

stability of each link is randomly generated (uniform distribution) in the range $[\beta, \gamma]$, where $0 \le \beta \le \gamma \le 1$.

5.1 Simulation Results

First, we study the effect of θ on the performance of the STL-based algorithm. θ is the control coefficient in the SLT-based heuristic, in which the value of θ controls whether a node's maximum expected utility path should be inserted into the existing spanning tree or not. As shown in Fig. 2 (a), when $\theta \approx 1.1$, the SLT-based heuristic has the best performance. Because the link stability has direct impact on the SLT-based heuristic, we adopt three different stability low bounds $\beta = 0.7, 0.8$, and 0.9 as comparisons. The three settings show a similar curve, which means the selection of θ is independent of the link stability.

In section 4, we argue that the expected network utilities of the MEU path tree with $\delta = \alpha$ and the MEU path tree with $\delta = 1 + \alpha$ can be used as the upper bound and the low bound for the optimal data-gathering tree, respectively. Our claim can be verified by the simulation results shown in Fig. 2 (b) and (c). In Fig. 2 (b), we study the effect of α, the size of a unit of data on the performance of the MEUPT algorithm and verify the lower bound and upper bound. The value of α ranges from 0 to 30 with the increment being 2. The simulation results show that as the value of α increases, the expected utility of the MEU path tree, the upper bound, and the lower bound converge. The reason is that as the value of α grows, the effect of the overhead decreases. In the extreme case, as $\alpha \to \infty$, the size of the overhead can be omitted, i.e., $1 + \alpha \to \infty$.

In Fig. 2 (c), we compare the four algorithms in building the reverse broadcast tree (RBT) in the test dimension of network density, and range it from 10 to 25 with the increment being 1. As expected, the network density increases the expected network utility for all the heuristics except the MST-based heuristic, which has the worst performance and is even below the lower bound. The reason is that the MST does not take into account the link stability and benefit issues. The links selected by the MST are close in geometry but may have a low delivery ratio, and hence, cause a lot data losses. The expected network utilities of the other three heuristics are close to each other and hard to compare in Fig. 2 (c). Therefore, we use the lower bound as the base and the expected network utilities of all the three heuristics are subtracted by the base. The result is shown in Fig. 2 (d). From Fig. 2 (d), we can conclude that the MIEULF algorithm has the best performance and the MEUPT algorithm has the worst performance because it does not take into account path-sharing. Since the MIEULF heuristic has the best performance, we will use MIEULF in the following simulations.

In Fig. 2 (e), we simulate the effect of the range of link stability on the performance of the MIEULF heuristic. We increase β from 0 to 0.9 with an incremental step of 0.1. As β increases, the links become stable. We compare the MIEULF trees with different values of α, the size of unit data. The simulation results show that the more stable the links, the higher the expected network utility, and the increment of data size decreases the expected network utility. The simulation results reflect the fact that the expected network utility can be affected from two causes. On one hand, the expected network utility increases with the increment of the link stability. On the other hand, the expected network utility decreases with the increment of the transmission cost.

Fig. 2 (f) shows the results of the simulation on the effect of benefit value. We use the MIEULF heuristic to simulate and adopt four combinations of stability range and the value of α ($\alpha = 0, \beta = 0.5$, $\alpha = 0, \beta = 0.8$, $\alpha = 2, \beta = 0.5$, and $\alpha = 0, \beta = 0.8$). The benefit value varies from 500 to 2000 with an increment of 100. As expected, the increment of the benefit improves the expected network utility, the increment of the data size decreases the expected network utility, and the increment of the stability increases the expected network utility.

We also study the effect of the local quota on the performance. We use the same setting as the previous experiment. The local quota increases from 1 to 20 with an increment of 1. According to the simulation results shown in Fig. 2 (g), the increment of the local quota can increase the expected network utility, but as the number of the local quota reaches 6, the impact of the continuous increment of the local quota becomes less essential. The reason for this is that retransmissions increase the delivery ratio the most in the first several retry attempts.

Finally, we compare the proposed heuristics for constructing the reverse multicast tree and study the effect of the size of the source sensor set on the performance. The simulation results are plotted in Fig. 2 (h) and (i). Because the MIEULF heuristic has the best performance in building the reverse broadcast tree, we adopt the pruning heuristic based on the MIEULF heuristic as the representative pruning method. We set the benefit value to 1000, $\beta = 0.9$, and $\alpha = 2$. Because the expected network utilities of the MIEULF-based heuristic and the MIEUPF heuristic are close, we subtract 5000 from both utilities. Fig. 2 (h) shows that the MIEULF-based pruning heuristic has better performance. Since the MIEULF-based pruning heuristic has better performance, we use it as the method to study the effect of the size of the source sensor set. The other settings are the same. Fig. 2 (i) illustrates that the increment of the number of the source sensors can increase the expected utilities.

6 Related Work

Many existing data-gathering models [5, 10, 12] assume that wireless channels are reliable, or the channels are unstable but the reliability can be achieved through retransmissions. However, wireless communication is unreliable in practice, and 100% reliability is not achievable due to practical issues such as the constraint on the maximum number of retransmissions in link layer technologies. Therefore, we proposed a new-data gathering model that takes this unreliability into account.

Existing link reliability models [1, 3, 7] usually adopted the packet-delivery ratio to define the link reliability, and defined the expected link cost as the link cost divided by the link reliability. This definition is based on the assumption of unbounded retransmissions. Our previous work [9] proposed a more reasonable definition of the expected link costs, which does not allow unlimited retransmissions and involves the interdependence of the stabilities among different links.

Many energy-efficient data-gathering models adopt the reverse broadcast/multicast tree models [12], which utilizes in-network aggregation and fusion to reduce energy consumption. To reduce the complexity, the reverse broadcast tree model [12] assumed the energy consumption of the aggregated data flow is equal to that of a single data flow. A more reasonable model [4, 5, 6] assumed the existence of data correlation so that the energy consumption of an aggregated flow from two flows is less than two single flows and more than one single flow. Our model admits the existence of data correlation, and adopts a utility metric to balance the reliability and energy cost. Chen and Sha [2] also adopted the utility-based model in data-gathering WSNs. They assumed that different data have different levels of importance, and the sink would assign different weights to different types of data according to their importance.

7 Conclusion

In this paper, we study the data-gathering problem in wireless sensor networks from the maximization of the expected network utility point of view by considering resource scarcity and the unstable nature of wireless channels. We model the data-gathering problem as an optimization problem, prove its NP-hardness, propose several heuristics for both the reverse broadcast tree and the reverse multicast tree problems, and use simulation to study the effects of different parameters and to compare the performance of various heuristics. In the future, we will explore the effect of the data redundance on the evaluation of the network benefit and the effect compression technique on reducing the energy consumptions, as well as the effect of signal strength on stability.

References

[1] Banerjee, S., Misra, A.: Minimum energy paths for reliable communication in multi-hop wireless networks. In: MobiHoc 2002. Proceedings of the 3rd ACM international symposium on Mobile ad hoc networking & computing, pp. 146–156 (2002)

[2] Chen, W., Sha, L.: An energy-aware data-centric generic utility based approach in wireless sensor networks. In: IPSN 2004. Proceedings of the third international symposium on Information processing in sensor networks, pp. 215–224 (2004)

[3] Couto, D.S.J.D., Aguayo, D., Bicket, J., Morris, R.: A high-throughput path metric for multi-hop wireless routing. In: Proceedings of ACM MOBICOM 2003 (2003)

[4] Cristescu, R., Beferull-Lozano, B., Vetterli, M.: On network correlated data gathering. In: INFOCOM (2004)

[5] Cristescu, R., Beferull-Lozano, B., Vetterli, M., Wattenhofer, R.: Network correlated data gathering with explicit communication: Np-completeness and algorithms. IEEE/ACM Trans. Netw., 41–54 (2006)

[6] Cristescu, R., Vetterli, M.: Power efficient gathering of correlated data: Optimization, np-completeness and heuristics. SIGMOBILE Mob. Comput. Commun. Rev. 7(3), 31–32 (2003)

[7] Dong, Q., Banerjee, S., Adler, M., Misra, A.: Minimum energy reliable paths using unreliable wireless links. In: MobiHoc 2005. Proceedings of the 6th ACM international symposium on Mobile ad hoc networking and computing, pp. 449–459 (2005)

[8] Khuller, S., Raghavachari, B., Young, N.: Balancing minimum spanning and shortest path trees. In: SODA 1993. Proceedings of the fourth annual ACM-SIAM Symposium on Discrete algorithms, pp. 243–250 (1993)

[9] Lu, M., Wu, J.: Social welfare based routing in ad hoc networks. In: Proceedings of ICPP 2006 (accepted to appear)

[10] Luo, H., Luo, J., Liu, Y.: Energy efficient routing with adaptive data fusion in sensor networks. In: DIALM-POMC 2005. Proceedings of the 2005 joint workshop on Foundations of mobile computing, pp. 80–88. ACM Press, New York, NY, USA (2005)

[11] Mas-Collel, A., Whinston, W., Green, J.: Microeconomic Theory. Oxford University Press, Oxford (1995)

[12] Tan, H.O., Korpeoglu, I.: Power efficient data gathering and aggregation in wireless sensor networks. In: SIGMOD 2003 (2003)

Sensor Networks Continue to Puzzle:
Selected Open Problems

Thomas Locher, Pascal von Rickenbach, and Roger Wattenhofer

Computer Engineering and Networks Laboratory, ETH Zurich, Switzerland
{lochert, pascalv, wattenhofer}@tik.ee.ethz.ch

Abstract. While several important problems in the field of sensor networks have already been tackled, there is still a wide range of challenging, open problems that merit further attention. We present five theoretical problems that we believe to be essential to understanding sensor networks. The goal of this work is both to summarize the current state of research and, by calling attention to these fundamental problems, to spark interest in the networking community to attend to these and related problems in sensor networks.

1   Introduction

Algorithmic sensor network research has been around for almost a decade now,[1] and it has meanwhile reached a semi-mature state: Many essential questions have been studied; some exemplary ones such as, e.g., min-energy [1,2] and min-time [3,4,5] broadcasting or geo-routing [6,7,8] are understood to a pleasing degree, belying those who accuse the sensor networking community of not producing any rigid results.

However, sensor networks continue to puzzle as many fundamental aspects are not well understood; in this paper we present five brainteasers in the sensor network domain, covering various areas such as scheduling, topology control, clustering, positioning, and time synchronization. The five open problems have in common that they all pertain to data gathering, an important task in sensor networking. As it is often essential to know when and where data has been collected, the data needs to be enriched with time (Section 6) and position (Section 5) information. Additionally, the structure of the network has to be tuned in order to gather data in an energy-efficient manner. In Section 4 we save energy by turning off unneeded nodes, in Section 3 by reducing interference. Finally, in Section 2 we study the capacity of sensor networks, i.e., the achievable throughput of scheduling algorithms.

The five problems have in common that they all allow for a precise "zero parameters" definition. This is probably rare in a research area that still mostly revolves around the question which questions to ask. In that sense, these five

---

[1] Alas, there is no clear date of birth of this research area; however, some of the first workshops such as, e.g., DialM or MobiHoc were started about a decade ago.

S. Rao et al. (Eds.): ICDCN 2008, LNCS 4904, pp. 25–38, 2008.

problems are prototypical for an algorithmic approach to networking. However, primarily they have in common that the authors of this article are familiar with them. Our five open problems are by no means the most important problems that remain to be solved in the sensor network domain. We are sure that three other authors would come up with a completely different set of open problems, at least equally worthy of being studied. Nevertheless, we do believe that advancing the state of the art of any of the problems discussed in this paper will not only advance sensor networks but also networking and distributed computing in general.

2   Scheduling

Spatial reuse is fundamental in wireless networking. Due to channel interference, concurrent transmissions may hinder a successful reception at the intended destinations. Thus, it is vital to coordinate channel access in order to prevent collisions and to increase network throughput. The task of a scheduling algorithm is to order a given set of transmission requests such that the correct reception of messages is not prevented due to interference caused by concurrent transmissions. Apart from timing message transmissions, scheduling algorithms have another degree of freedom to optimize their schedule: They can adjust the transmission power for each message individually to fully benefit from spatial reuse in order to minimize the total time needed to successfully complete all requests. This is important since a successful message reception depends on the ratio between received signal strength on the one hand and interference and ambient noise on the other hand (also known as SINR).[2]

More formally, consider the network nodes $X = \{x_1, \ldots, x_n\}$. Furthermore, let P_r be the signal power received by a node x_r and let I_r denote the amount of interference generated by other nodes. Finally, let N be the ambient noise power level. Then, a node x_r receives a transmission if and only if $\frac{P_r}{N+I_r} \geq \beta$, where β denotes the minimum signal-to-noise-plus-interference ratio that is required for a message to be successfully received.

In wireless networks, the value of received signal power P_r is a decreasing function of the distance $d(x_s, x_r)$ between transmitter node x_s and receiver node x_r. More specifically, given the distance $d(x_s, x_r)$ between sender and receiver, the decay of the signal power is proportional to $d(x_s, x_r)^{-\alpha}$. The so-called path-loss exponent α is a constant between 2 and 6 and depends on external conditions of the medium, as well as the exact sender-receiver distance [9]. Let P_i be the power level assigned to node x_i. A message transmitted from a node $x_s \in X$ is successfully received by a node x_r if

$$\frac{\frac{P_s}{d(x_s, x_r)^{\alpha}}}{N + \sum_{x_i \in X \setminus \{x_s\}} \frac{P_i}{d(x_i, x_r)^{\alpha}}} \geq \beta.$$

---

[2] The communication model adopting this notion of signal-to-noise-plus-interference ratio is also known as the physical model [9].

In [10,11] the scheduling complexity of basic network structures, namely strongly connected networks, is studied. It is shown that adjusting the transmission power gives an exponential advantage over uniform or linear power assignment schemes. This gives an interesting complement to the more pessimistic bounds for the capacity in wireless networks [9]. The authors of [12] define a measure called disturbance that comprises the intrinsic difficulty of finding a short schedule for a problem instance. Furthermore, they propose an algorithm that achieves provably efficient performance in any network and request setting that exhibits a low disturbance. For the special case of many-to-one communication with data aggregation in relaying nodes, [13] derives a scaling law describing the achievable rate in arbitrarily deployed sensor networks. It is show that for a large number of aggregation functions a sustainable rate of $1/\log^2 n$ can be achieved.

In the context of routing, [14] studies the problem of constructing end-to-end schedules for a given set of routing requests such that the delay is minimized. That is, each node is assigned a distinct power level, the paths for all requests are determined, and all message transmissions are scheduled to guarantee successful reception in the SINR model. In this setting, [14] presents a polynomial-time algorithm with provable worst-case performance for the problem.

Despite all the work discussed in this section considering transmission scheduling problems with specific constraints, the basic problem is still not fully understood.

Problem 1. *A communication request consists of a source and a destination, which are arbitrary points in the Euclidean plane. Given n communication requests, assign a color (time slot) to each request. For all requests sharing the same color specify power levels such that each request can be handled correctly, i.e., the SINR condition is met at all destinations. The goal is to minimize the number of colors.*

While uniform power assignment is understood well [15], it is unknown how difficult the problem is if nodes can adapt their transmission power. This is indisputably a most fundamental problem in the field of sensor networks. A deeper understanding of scheduling will potentially shed new light also on other advanced open problems.

3 Topology Control

Energy is a scarce resource in wireless sensor networks. In a very general way, topology control can be considered as the task of, given a network communication graph, constructing a subgraph with certain desired properties while minimizing energy consumption. The subgraph needs to meet some requirements, the minimum requirement being to maintain connectivity. However, sometimes one has stronger demands, e.g., the subgraph should not only be connected but a spanner of the original graph. At the same time the subgraph should be sparse as low node degrees allow for simpler neighborhood management at the nodes; additionally, symmetric links are desired as they permit simpler higher-layer protocols, and, if the constructed graph is planar, geo-routing protocols can be used. The most important goal however is energy-efficiency. Energy is saved by several means, the simplest being to eliminate distant neighbors, and thereby energy-inefficient connections, since the energy consumption of a transmission is believed to grow at least quadratically with distance.[3] Almost as a side effect, this reduction also results in less interference. Confining interference additionally lowers the power consumption by reducing the number of collisions and consequently the number of packet retransmissions on the media access layer.

Early work focused on topology control algorithms emphasizing locality while exhibiting more and more desirable properties [16,17,18,19], sometimes presenting distributed algorithms that optimize various design goals concurrently. All these approaches have in common, however, that they address interference reduction only implicitly. The intuition was that a low (constant) node degree at all nodes would solve the interference issue automatically. This intuition was proved wrong in [20], starting a new thread that explicitly studies interference reduction in the context of topology control [21,22,23]. The interference model introduced in [24] in the context of data-gathering structures, which is generalized in [25], proposes a natural way to define interference in sensor networks. The general question is: How can one connect the nodes such that as few nodes as possible disturb each other? In the following, we discuss the network and interference model presented in [25].

The wireless network is modeled as a geometric graph. The graph consists of a set of nodes represented by points in the Euclidean plane; we want to connect these nodes by choosing a set of edges. In order to prevent already basic communication between neighboring nodes from becoming unacceptably cumbersome [26], it is required that a message sent over a link can be acknowledged by sending a corresponding message over the same link in the opposite direction. In other words, only undirected edges are considered. A node is able to adjust its transmission power to any value between zero and its maximum power level to reach other nodes. An edge exists if and only if the maximum transmission range of both incident nodes mutually include their counterpart. The minimum requirement of a topology control algorithm reducing transmission power levels is then to compute a subgraph of the given network graph that preserves connectivity. The interference of a node v is then defined as the number of other nodes that potentially affect message reception at node v.[4] The maximum interference of a graph is then defined as the maximum node interference.

So far, not many results have been published in the context of explicit interference minimization. For networks restricted to one dimension the authors in

---

[3] In sensor networks, one has to be careful about this model, as generally transmission distances are short, and the base transmission or even reception energy washes this quadratic behavior out.

[4] In practice, the shape of a node's interference region is not restricted to be circular. In particular, it depends on the antenna in use; the interference range is typically larger than the reception range.

[25] present a $\sqrt[4]{n}$-approximation of the optimal connectivity-preserving topology that minimizes the maximum interference. For the two dimensional case, the authors in [27] propose an algorithm that bounds the maximum interference to $O(\sqrt{n})$. If average interference of a graph is considered, there is an asymptotically optimal algorithm achieving an approximation ratio of $O(\log n)$ [28]. This leads us to the open problem:

Problem 2. *Given n nodes in the plane. Connect the nodes by a spanning tree. For each node v we construct a disk centering at v with radius equal to the distance to v's furthest neighbor in the spanning tree. The interference of a node v is then defined as the number of disks that include node v. Find a spanning tree that minimizes the maximum interference.*

This problem is still not understood well. We do not know the complexity of the problem (solvable optimally in polynomial time, or $\mathcal{NP}$-complete), and it is unknown whether efficient approximation algorithms exist. Once we understand interference, we can try to combine it with other optimization goals such as planarity or constant node degree. And once we understand these, we can start looking for distributed (or even local) algorithms for the problem. Furthermore, we can abandon the strict geometric representation of interference and think about more general interference models [28].

Clearly, there is a relation between Problem 2 and the scheduling problem studied in Section 2 [10], as in both problems the goal is to increase spatial reuse by understanding interference. However, we do not believe that solving one problem would help solving the other, as the scheduling problem allows for a more general power control approach. It was shown in [11] that there is an exponential difference between these two models. The next section is related to this one as well: The goal is also to reduce energy consumption, however with a different approach.

4   Dominating Set

An alternative method to ensure an efficient operation in dense graphs is to completely "shut down" a large fraction of all nodes and delegate their responsibilities to a few neighboring nodes. This is in stark contrast to the approach taken in topology control algorithms where all nodes continue to handle messages themselves. Naturally, it must be guaranteed that every node has a neighbor that is in the position to take over its tasks. Ideally, this set of nodes that remain awake and handle all tasks is as small as possible in order to minimize energy consumption. New sets of nodes that must stay awake can be constructed periodically in order to even out the burden of communication among all nodes in the network.

More formally, we again model the network as a graph where edges between nodes indicate that these nodes can communicate directly. A set of nodes S for which it holds that every node that is not in S has a direct neighbor in S has to be found. Such a set is commonly referred to as a *dominating set*. The goal of the *minimum dominating set* (MDS) problem is to find the dominating set of minimum size. For certain applications, it is mandatory or at least beneficial if the nodes in the dominating set are connected. Thus, a variation of the MDS problem is the problem of finding a minimum *connected dominating set*.

Computing a minimum dominating set is a hard problem. It has been shown that the MDS problem is $\mathcal{NP}$-complete not only for arbitrary graphs [29], but also for special topologies such as *unit disk graphs* (UDGs) [30,31]. Moreover, dominating sets cannot be approximated in polynomial time to within a factor of $(1 - o(1)) \ln n$ [32] unless $\mathcal{NP}$ has quasi-polynomial time algorithms. However, this bound only holds for general graphs, and in various special cases, constant approximations can be computed efficiently. For example, there is a simple constant approximation algorithm for dominating sets in UDGs [33]. Note that a DS can trivially be extended to a connected dominating set by means of a spanning tree with only a constant overhead. This result has been generalized in [34], where it is shown that a constant-factor approximation is even possible if all nodes are *weighted*, and the goal is to find a (connected) dominating set that minimizes the sum of the weight of all nodes in the dominating set. In the unweighted case, there is a PTAS for the minimum dominating set problem in unit disk graphs [35].

Distributed algorithms for the MDS problem have also been studied extensively. The algorithms in the following papers belong to the class of *local algorithms* in which all nodes are allowed to communicate k times, for a particular value k, with their neighboring nodes. In this model, nodes can basically gather information about nodes in their k-neighborhood and can thus base their decisions on this information only. Similarly to the centralized case, it has also been shown that once a dominating set has been built, this set can be used to construct a connected dominating set in a distributed fashion [36].

In general graphs, a *maximum independent set* (MIS) can be constructed using a randomized algorithm in $O(\log n)$ time [37]. Naturally, a MIS is also a dominating set, but the constructed MIS does not guarantee any bounds on the approximation ratio. The algorithm presented in [38] computes an $O(\log \Delta)$-approximation in $O(\log n \log \Delta)$ rounds with high probability, where Δ denotes the maximum node degree. The first constant-time distributed algorithm achieving a non-trivial approximation ratio is presented in [39]: An $O(k\Delta^{2/k} \log \Delta)$-approximation is computed in $O(k^2)$ rounds for an arbitrary (constant) k. By setting $k = \Theta(\log \Delta)$, the algorithm achieves an approximation ratio of $O(\log^2 \Delta)$ in $O(\log^2 \Delta)$ rounds. This result was later improved to an $O(\log \Delta)$-approximation algorithm also requiring $O(\log^2 \Delta)$ rounds [40].

There has also been a lot of work on computing dominating or maximum independent sets in unit disk graphs. Note that in unit disk graphs a maximum independent set is a good approximation of the optimal dominating set, thus the two problems are basically equivalent. A PTAS for UDGs is also achievable by means of a local algorithm [41]. If the nodes know the distance to all other nodes, a MIS can be constructed in $O(\log^* n)$ time in unit disk graphs and also in a large class of bounded independence graphs [42], which matches a MIS lower bound of $\Omega(\log^* n)$ [43]. The fastest *deterministic* algorithm for the MIS problem in unit disk graphs—in fact, in any growth-bounded graph—requires $O(\log \Delta \log^* n)$ time [44] to construct a MIS. A MIS can be constructed faster using a randomized algorithm whose running time is only $O(\log \log n \log^* n)$ with high probability [45].

It is, however, still unclear if a dominating set that is only a constant factor larger than the smallest possible dominating set can be constructed very quickly in unit disk graphs.

Problem 3. *Let each node in a unit disk graph know its k-neighborhood for a constant k, i.e., each node knows all nodes up to distance k including their interconnections. Given this information, each node must decide locally without any further communication whether it joins the dominating set or not. Is it possible to construct a valid dominating set that is only a constant factor larger than the optimal dominating set?*

While there are lower bounds to find a MIS or a coloring, there is no lower bound for the MDS problem. It is unclear if a constant-time algorithm can compute a dominating set in UDGs, and conversely if a constant-factor approximation requires $\omega(1)$ time. There are many related open problems such as the problem of finding a MIS or a coloring with a small approximation ratio as quickly as possible.

5 Embedding

Many envisioned application scenarios in the field of wireless sensor networks rely on positioning information: sensing the environment is only useful if one knows where the data has actually been measured. Knowledge of location information can also improve the performance of routing algorithms because it allows the use of geo-routing techniques [6,7]. Equipping all sensor nodes with specific hardware such as GPS receivers would be one option to gain position information at the nodes. However, GPS reception might be obstructed by climatic conditions or in-door environments. Another solution is to provide only a few nodes (so-called anchor or landmark nodes) with GPS and have the rest of the nodes compute their position by using the known coordinates of the anchor nodes [46,47]. One characteristic inherent to all these approaches is that the solution quality is determined by the anchor density and their actual placement.

Obviously, in the absence of anchors, nodes are clueless about their real coordinates. However, recent work has pointed out that for many applications it is not necessary to have real coordinates but it suffices to have virtual coordinates—two nodes having similar coordinates implies that they are physically close together. Moreover, a deeper understanding of anchorless positioning would likely advance the state of the art of anchor-based positioning algorithms. A mapping of all the nodes to virtual coordinates, in this case coordinates in the Euclidean plane, is called an *embedding*.

Sensor networks are typically modelled as *unit disk graphs* in which there is an edge between two nodes if and only if the Euclidean distance between them is less or equal to 1. It has been shown that the problem of deciding whether a given graph is a unit disk graph is $\mathcal{NP}$-hard [48]. A more general model for sensor networks is given by *d-quasi unit disk graphs*. A graph is called a *d*-quasi unit disk graph (*d*-QUDG, $d \leq 1$) if there is an embedding that respects the following two rules: If two nodes are connected, the distance between their respective coordinates must be at most 1, and if there is not edge between two nodes, the distance between their coordinates must exceed d. Note that a 1-QUDG corresponds to a UDG graph and that the definition of a *d*-QUDG does not specify whether there is an edge between two nodes at a distance in the range $(d, 1]$ for $d < 1$. In that sense, a *d*-QUDG is a relaxed version of a UDG. A QUDG can generally be regarded as a more realistic model for sensor networks since nodes at a critical distance may or may not be able to communicate. The quality $q(e)$ of an embedding e in this model is defined as

$$q(e) = \frac{\max_{\{u,v\} \in E} dist(u, v)}{min_{\{u,v\} \notin E} dist(u, v)}.$$

A good embedding has a *small* value for its quality. It has been shown that it is also $\mathcal{NP}$-hard to find an embedding such that $q(e) < \sqrt{3/2}$ [49]. In the same work, it has further been proven that it is $\mathcal{NP}$-hard to decide whether a graph can be realized as a *d*-quasi unit disk graph with $d \geq 1/\sqrt{2}$. Surprisingly, the problem remains hard even if additional information is available. For example, each node might know the exact distance to each of its neighbors. Given this distance information, it is still $\mathcal{NP}$-hard to decide whether the graph is a UDG or not [50]. Instead of having distance information, the nodes might be aware of the angle between itself and any two of its neighbors. The problem remains $\mathcal{NP}$-hard also in this context [51].

In [52], the first approximation algorithm for this problem is presented, which heavily borrows techniques introduced by Vempala [53], claiming an $O(\log^{2.5} n \sqrt{\log \log n})$-quality embedding in polynomial running time.[5] The currently best known algorithm for this problem is due to Pemmaraju and Pirwani [54], which computes a $O(\log^{2.5} n)$-quality embedding of a given unit disk graph.

In practice, many heuristics are used to compute embeddings efficiently. Various approaches based on, e.g., distance measurements [55], using eigenvectors [56] or linear programming [51] etc. have been shown to produce acceptable results. Still, in theory the problem is not well understood.

Problem 4. *Given the adjacency matrix of a unit disk graph, find positions for all nodes in the Euclidean plane such that the ratio between the maximum distance between any two adjacent nodes and the minimum distance between any two non-adjacent nodes is as small as possible.*

---

[5] A subsequent paper [54] corrects the bound on the quality to $O(\log^{3.5} n \sqrt{\log \log n})$.

Apparently, there is a large gap between the best known lower bound, which is a constant, and the polylogarithmic upper bound. It is a challenging task to either come up with a better approximation algorithm or prove a stronger lower bound.

6   Time Synchronization

Many protocols require that the participants be closely *synchronized* in order to guarantee an efficient and successful execution. It is therefore mandatory to provide a distributed clock synchronization algorithm whose objective is to ensure that the nodes are able to acquire a common notion of time. As the state of the system is distributed, the participating nodes can synchronize their clocks by exchanging messages with their neighboring nodes and thereby learn about the current state of other nodes.

We consider distributed clock synchronization algorithms in the following setting. Given an arbitrary graph $G = (V, E)$ in which nodes can communicate directly with all other node to which they are directly connected in G. The nodes that are directly connected to a node v are referred to as the neighboring nodes of v. The communication between neighboring nodes is assumed to be reliable, but all messages can have variable delays in the range $[0, 1]$. The *distance* between nodes i and j is defined as the length of the shortest path between i and j, and the *diameter* D of G is the maximum distance between any two nodes.

We assume that each node is equipped with a *hardware clock* $H(\cdot)$ whose value at time t is $H(t) := \int_0^t h(\tau)\, d\tau$, where $h(\tau)$ is the *hardware clock rate* at time τ. Furthermore, we make the assumption that the hardware clocks have bounded drift, i.e., there is a constant $0 \leq \epsilon < 1$ such that $1 - \epsilon \leq h(t) \leq 1 + \epsilon$ at all times t.

In addition to the hardware clock, each node i is further equipped with a second, so-called *logical clock* $L(\cdot)$. The logical clock also increases steadily, just like the hardware clock, but potentially at a different rate. However, the deviation between the hardware and the logical clock rate is lower and upper bounded by specific constants, e.g., the logical clock rate has to be at least half and at most twice the hardware clock rate at any given time. This restriction ensures that the logical clock can neither be slowed down nor sped up arbitrarily, which would trivialize the problem and destroy the relation between the hardware and the logical clock.

Due to different clock rates the hardware clocks of different nodes might drift apart. As the hardware clocks cannot be manipulated, the goal is therefore to minimize the clock skew of the logical clocks. At any point in time, a node may inform its neighboring nodes about its current logical time. A node receiving such an update can decide to increase its own logical clock in order to counterbalance the skew between the clocks. However, the logical clock is not allowed to run backwards.

A desirable goal is to guarantee that the clock skew between any two nodes in the network is as small as possible. The bound achievable for this goal is denoted the *global property* of the clock synchronization algorithm. It can be shown that the skew between two nodes at distance d cannot be synchronized better than $\Omega(d)$ by using simple indistinguishability type arguments. Srikanth and Toueg [57] presented a clock synchronization algorithm, which is asymptotically optimal in the sense that it guarantees a clock skew of at most $O(D)$ between any two nodes in a network of diameter D. However, there are executions of this algorithm causing a clock skew of $\Theta(D)$ even between neighboring nodes.

For several distributed applications, such as, e.g., media access control or event detection, it is mandatory that the clocks between any node and particularly all nodes in its vicinity are closely synchronized. This is known as the *gradient property* of the algorithm that requires a minimal clock skew between all neighboring nodes. This property was introduced in [58] where a surprising lower bound on the worst-case clock skew of $\Omega(\frac{\log D}{\log \log D})$ between neighboring nodes is proven. If the logical clocks are allowed to remain constant for a certain period of time, the clock skew between neighboring nodes can in fact be kept constant [59]. In general, the best known clock synchronization algorithm with a non-trivial gradient property guarantees that the worst-case skew between any two neighbors at distance d is at most $O(d + \sqrt{D})$ [60]. Obviously, the gap between the lower and the upper bound is still fairly large and the goal is to close this gap.

Problem 5. *Nodes in an arbitrary graph are equipped with an unmodifiable hardware clock and a modifiable logical clock. The logical clock must make progress roughly at the rate of the hardware clock, i.e., the clock rates may differ by a small constant. Messages sent over the edges of the graph have delivery times in the range* $[0, 1]$. *Given a bounded, variable drift on the hardware clocks, design a message-passing algorithm that ensures that the logical clock skew of adjacent nodes is as small as possible at all times.*

The algorithm that guarantees a skew of $O(\sqrt{D})$ [60] between neighboring nodes requires that a large amount of messages are sent. Another natural question is whether a good gradient property can also be ensured if bounds on the message complexity are imposed. Further future work might include faulty or even byzantine nodes which deliberately try to hinder the correct nodes from synchronizing their clocks.

7   Conclusions

In this paper, we presented five open problems in the field of sensor networks, all with an algorithmic flavor. Craving for progress, we offer a bag of Swiss chocolate to anybody who solves one of our problems. As stated before, our selection is rather random, and other authors for sure would promote other problems at least equally worthy of being studied. Actually, we would also be quite keen to learn about these other problems and encourage you to tell us about them. An official repository of open problems could ignite a fresh way of organizing research in this area—a way that actually uses the Internet—and could help keeping track of progress.

References

1. Wan, P.J., Calinescu, G., Li, X.Y., Frieder, O.: Minimum-Energy Broadcast Routing in Static Ad Hoc Wireless Networks. In: INFOCOM. Proc. of the 20th Annual Joint Conf. of the IEEE Computer and Communications Societies (2001)
2. Ambühl, C.: An Optimal Bound for the MST Algorithm to Compute Energy Efficient Broadcast Trees in Wireless Networks. In: Caires, L., Italiano, G.F., Monteiro, L., Palamidessi, C., Yung, M. (eds.) ICALP 2005. LNCS, vol. 3580, Springer, Heidelberg (2005)
3. Alon, N., Bar-Noy, A., Linial, N., Peleg, D.: A Lower Bound for Radio Broadcast. J. Comput. Syst. Sci. 43, 290–298 (1991)
4. Czumaj, A., Rytter, W.: Broadcasting Algorithms in Radio Networks with Unknown Topology. J. Algorithms 60, 115–143 (2006)
5. Peleg, D.: Time Efficient Broadcasting in Radio Networks: A Review. In: Janowski, T., Mohanty, H. (eds.) ICDCIT 2007. LNCS, vol. 4882, Springer, Heidelberg (2007)
6. Bose, P., Morin, P., Stojmenovic, I., Urrutia, J.: Routing with Guaranteed Delivery in ad hoc Wireless Networks. In: DIAL-M. Proc. of the 3rd Int. Workshop on Discrete Algorithms and Methods for Mobile Computing and Communications (1999)
7. Kuhn, F., Wattenhofer, R., Zollinger, A.: Worst-Case Optimal and Average-Case Efficient Geometric Ad-Hoc Routing. In: MOBIHOC. Proc. of the 4th ACM Int. Symposium on Mobile Ad Hoc Networking and Computing (2003)
8. Durocher, S., Kirkpatrick, D., Narayanan, L.: On Routing with Guaranteed Delivery in Three-Dimensional Ad Hoc Wireless Networks. Personal communication (2007)
9. Gupta, P., Kumar, P.R.: The Capacity of Wireless Networks. IEEE Trans. Information Theory 46, 388–404 (2000)
10. Moscibroda, T., Wattenhofer, R.: The Complexity of Connectivity in Wireless Networks. In: INFOCOM. Proc. of the 25th Annual Joint Conf. of the IEEE Computer and Communications Societies (2006)
11. Moscibroda, T., Wattenhofer, R., Zollinger, A.: Topology Control Meets SINR· The Scheduling Complexity of Arbitrary Topologies. In: MOBIHOC. Proc. of the 7th ACM Int. Symposium on Mobile Ad Hoc Networking and Computing (2006)
12. Moscibroda, T., Oswald, Y.A., Wattenhofer, R.: How Optimal are Wireless Scheduling Protocols? In: INFOCOM. Proc. of the 26th Annual Joint Conf. of the IEEE Computer and Communications Societies (2007)
13. Moscibroda, T.: The Worst-Case Capacity of Wireless Sensor Networks. In: IPSN. Proc. of the 6th Int. Conf. on Information Processing in Sensor Networks (2007)
14. Chafekar, D., Kumar, V.S.A., Marathe, M., Pathasarathy, S., Srinivasan, A.: Cross-Layer Latency Minimization in Wireless Networks with SINR constraints. In: MOBIHOC. Proc. of the 8th ACM Int. Symposium on Mobile Ad Hoc Networking and Computing (2007)
15. Goussevskaia, O., Oswald, Y.A., Wattenhofer, R.: Complexity in Geometric SINR. In: MOBIHOC. Proc. of the 8th ACM Int. Symposium on Mobile Ad Hoc Networking and Computing (2007)
16. Wattenhofer, R., Li, L., Bahl, P., Wang, Y.M.: Distributed Topology Control for Power Efficient Operation in Multihop Wireless Ad Hoc Networks. In: INFOCOM. Proc. of the 20th Annual Joint Conf. of the IEEE Computer and Communications Societies (2001)

17. Santi, P.: Topology Control in Wireless Ad Hoc and Sensor Networks. Wiley, Chichester (2005)
18. Li, X.Y., Song, W.Z., Wan, W.: A Unified Energy Efficient Topology for Unicast and Broadcast. In: MOBICOM. Proc. of the 11th Int. Conf. on Mobile Computing and Networking (2005)
19. Damian, M., Pandit, S., Pemmaraju, S.: Local Approximation Schemes for Topology Control. In: PODC. Proc. of the 25th Annual ACM Symposium on Principles of Distributed Computing (2006)
20. Burkhart, M., von Rickenbach, P., Wattenhofer, R., Zollinger, A.: Does Topology Control Reduce Interference? In: MobiHoc. Proc. of the 5th ACM Int. Symposium on Mobile Ad-hoc Networking and Computing (2004)
21. Moaveni-Nejad, K., Li, X.Y.: Low-Interference Topology Control for Wireless Ad-hoc Networks. Ad Hoc & Sensor Wireless Networks: An International Journal 1 (2005)
22. Johansson, T., Carr-Motyčková, L.: Reducing Interference in Ad hoc Networks through Topology Control. In: DIALM-POMC. Proc. of the 3rd ACM Joint Workshop on Foundations of Mobile Computing (2005)
23. Benkert, M., Gudmundsson, J., Haverkort, H., Wolff, A.: Constructing Interference-Minimal Networks. Computational Geometry: Theory and Applications (2007)
24. Fussen, M., Wattenhofer, R., Zollinger, A.: Interference Arises at the Receiver. In: WIRELESSCOM. Proc. of the Int. Conf. on Wireless Networks, Communications, and Mobile Computing (2005)
25. von Rickenbach, P., Schmid, S., Wattenhofer, R., Zollinger, A.: A Robust Interference Model for Wireless Ad-Hoc Networks. In: WMAN. Proc. of the 5th Int. Workshop on Algorithms for Wireless, Mobile, Ad Hoc and Sensor Networks (2005)
26. Prakash, R.: Unidirectional Links Prove Costly in Wireless Ad-hoc Networks. In: DIALM. Proc. of the 3rd Int. Workshop on Discrete Algorithms and Methods for Mobile Computing and Communications (1999)
27. Halldórsson, M.M., Tokuyama, T.: Minimizing Interference of a Wireless Ad-Hoc Network in a Plane. In: ALGOSENSORS. Proc. of the 2nd Int. Workshop on Algorithmic Aspects of Wireless Sensor Networks (2006)
28. Moscibroda, T., Wattenhofer, R.: Minimizing Interference in Ad Hoc and Sensor Networks. In: DIALM-POMC. Proc. of the 3rd ACM Joint Workshop on Foundations of Mobile Computing (2005)
29. Karp, R.: Reducibility Among Combinatorial Problems. J. ACM 45, 634–652 (1998)
30. Masuyama, S., Ibaraki, T., Haseqawa, T.: The Computational Complexity of the M-Center Problems in the Plane. Trans. IECE Japan E64, 57–64 (1981)
31. Clark, B.N., Colbourn, C.J., Johnson, D.S.: Unit Disk Graphs. Discrete Math. 86, 165–177 (1990)
32. Feige, U.: A Threshold of ln n for Approximating Set Cover. J. ACM 45, 634–652 (1998)
33. Marathe, M., Breu, H., Ravi, H., Rosenkrantz, D.: Simple Heuristics for Unit Disk Graphs. Networks 25, 59–68 (1995)
34. Ambühl, C., Erlebach, T., Mihalak, M., Nunkesser, M.: Constant-Factor Approximation for Minimum-Weight (Connected) Dominating Sets in Unit Disk Graphs. In: APPROX. Proc. of the 9th Int. Workshop on Approximation Algorithms for Combinatorial Optimization Problems (2006)
35. Nieberg, T., Hurink, J.L.: A PTAS for the Minimum Dominating Set Problem in Unit Disk Graphs. Memorandum 1732, Universiteit Twente, Dep't of Applied Mathematics (2004)

36. Dubhashi, D., Mei, A., Panconesi, A., Radhakrishnan, J., Srinivasan, A.: Constant-Factor Approximation for Minimum-Weight (Connected) Dominating Sets in Unit Disk Graphs. In: APPROX. Proc. of the 9th Int. Workshop on Approximation Algorithms for Combinatorial Optimization Problems (2006)
37. Luby, M.: A Simple Parallel Algorithm for the Maximal Independent Set Problem. SIAM Journal on Computing 15, 1036–1053 (1986)
38. Jia, L., Rajaraman, R., Suel, R.: An Efficient Distributed Algorithm for Constructing Small Dominating Sets. In: PODC. Proc. of the 20th ACM Symposium on Principles of Distributed Computing (2001)
39. Kuhn, F., Wattenhofer, R.: Constant-Time Distributed Dominating Set Approximation. In: PODC. Proc. of the 22nd ACM Symposium on Principles of Distributed Computing (2003)
40. Kuhn, F., Moscibroda, T., Wattenhofer, R.: The Price of Being Near-Sighted. In: SODA. Proc. of the 17th ACM-SIAM Symposium on Discrete Algorithms (2006)
41. Kuhn, F., Moscibroda, T., Nieberg, T., Wattenhofer, R.: Local Approximation Schemes for Ad Hoc and Sensor Networks. In: DIALM-POMC. Proc. of the 3rd ACM Joint Workshop on Foundations of Mobile Computing (2005)
42. Kuhn, F., Moscibroda, T., Wattenhofer, R.: On the Locality of Bounded Growth. In: PODC. Proc. of the 24th ACM Symposium on Principles of Distributed Computing (2005)
43. Linial, N.: Locality in Distributed Graph Algorithms. SIAM Journal on Computing 21, 193–201 (1992)
44. Kuhn, F., Moscibroda, T., Nieberg, T., Wattenhofer, R.: Fast Deterministic Distributed Maximal Independent Set Computation on Growth-Bounded Graphs. In: Fraigniaud, P. (ed.) DISC 2005. LNCS, vol. 3724, Springer, Heidelberg (2005)
45. Gfeller, B., Vicari, E.: A Randomized Distributed Algorithm for the Maximal Independent Set Problem in Growth-Bounded Graphs. In: PODC. Proc. of the 26th ACM Symposium on Principles of Distributed Computing (2007)
46. Savvides, A., Han, C.C., Strivastava, M.B.: Dynamic Fine-Grained Localization in Ad-Hoc Networks of Sensors. In: MOBICOM. Proc. of the 7th Annual Int. Conf. on Mobile Computing and Networking (2001)
47. O'Dell, R., Wattenhofer, R.: Theoretical Aspects of Connectivity-based Multi-hop Positioning. Theoretical Computer Science 344, 47–68 (2005)
48. Breu, H., Kirkpatrick, D.: Unit Disk Graph Recognition is NP-hard. Computational Geometry: Theory and Applications 9, 3–24 (1998)
49. Kuhn, F., Moscibroda, T., Wattenhofer, R.: Unit Disk Graph Approximation. In: DIALM-POMC. Proc. of the 2nd ACM Joint Workshop on Foundations of Mobile Computing (2004)
50. Aspnes, J., Goldenberg, D., Yang, Y.R.: On the Computational Complexity of Sensor Network Localization. In: ALGOSENSORS. Proc. of the 1st Int. Workshop on Algorithmic Aspects of Wireless Sensor Networks (2004)
51. Bruck, J., Gao, J., Jiang, A.: Localization and Routing in Sensor Networks By Local Angle Information. In: MOBIHOC. Proc. of the 6th ACM Int. Symposium on Mobile Ad Hoc Networking and Computing (2005)
52. Moscibroda, T., O'Dell, R., Wattenhofer, M., Wattenhofer, R.: Virtual Coordinates for Ad hoc and Sensor Networks. In: DIALM-POMC. Proc. of the 2nd ACM Joint Workshop on Foundations of Mobile Computing (2004)
53. Vempala, S.: Random Projection: A New Approach to VLSI Layout. In: FOCS. Proc. of the 39th Annual Symposium on Foundations of Computer Science (1998)

54. Pemmaraju, S., Pirwani, I.A.: Good Quality Virtual Realization of Unit Ball Graphs. In: ESA. Proc. of the 15th Annual European Symposium on Algorithms (2007)
55. Priyantha, N.B., Balakrishnan, H., Demaine, E.D., Teller, S.: Anchor-free Distributed Localization in Sensor Networks. Technical Report TR-892, MIT, LCS (2003)
56. Gotsman, C., Koren, Y.: Distributed Graph Layout for Sensor Networks. In: Pach, J. (ed.) GD 2004. LNCS, vol. 3383, Springer, Heidelberg (2005)
57. Srikanth, T.K., Toueg, S.: Optimal Clock Synchronization. J. ACM 34, 626–645 (1987)
58. Fan, R., Lynch, N.: Gradient Clock Synchronization. In: PODC. Proc. of the 23rd Annual ACM Symposium on Principles of Distributed Computing (2004)
59. Fan, R., Chakraborty, I., Lynch, N.: Clock Synchronization for Wireless Networks. In: Higashino, T. (ed.) OPODIS 2004. LNCS, vol. 3544, Springer, Heidelberg (2005)
60. Locher, T., Wattenhofer, R.: Oblivious Gradient Clock Synchronization. In: DISC. Proc. of the 20th Int. Symposium on Distributed Computing (2006)

Distributed Coordination of Workflows over Web Services and Their Handheld-Based Execution

Janaka Balasooriya[1], Jaimini Joshi[2], Sushil K. Prasad[2], and Shamkant Navathe[3]

[1] Arizona State University
Tempe, AZ
janakab@asu.edu
[2] Georgia State University
Atlanta, GA, USA
sprasad@gsu.edu
[3] Georgia Institute of Technology
Atlanta, GA, USA
sham@cc.gatech.edu

Abstract. The current state of the art of workflow composition over web services employ a centralized composite process to coordinate the constituent web services. Therefore, the coordinator process is complex, less scalable, and bulky. This paper introduces an architecture and associated techniques for distributed coordination of these workflows, and a prototype system, namely BondFlow system, with capability to control workflow execution using a handheld device. We distribute the centralized coordination logic of traditional workflows by (i) extending the stateless web services into self-coordinating entities using coordinator proxy objects, and (ii) creating the workflow over these entities by interconnecting them into a distributed network of objects using web bond primitives. Previously, we have developed web bond primitives to enforce interdependencies among autonomous entities. The prototypedr BondFlow systeh provides a platform to configure such distributed workflows, producing coordination components with a footprint small enough to be executed on a handheld (footprint no larger than 150 KB).

1 Introduction

Web Services (WSs) based applications span domains as diverse as enterprise e-commerce applications [3], personal applications [1, 7, 10, 11], and scientific applications [4, 6]. Thus, the users and developers of these applications are usually non-computer scientists. Efficient technologies are required to rapidly develop and deploy robust collaborative applications leveraging off the existing web services [15]. Several of these collaborative applications involve workflows [8], which is the focus of this paper.

Fig. 1 illustrates a purchase order workflow presented in the WS-BPEL specification (Web Services Business Process Execution Language) [16]. In Fig. 1a, dark arrows depict the control flow dependencies while dashed arrows depict data flow

S. Rao et al. (Eds.): ICDCN 2008, LNCS 4904, pp. 39–53, 2008.

dependencies. Fig. 1b illustrates the software architecture of the WS-BPEL based implementation of the workflow. Here, each workflow activity has been modeled as a web service. WS-BPEL models the composite workflow process as a separate state-preserving web process encapsulating all the data flow and control flow requirements. This software architecture typically results in complex and centralized logic for workflow coordination. This model has two significant drawbacks:

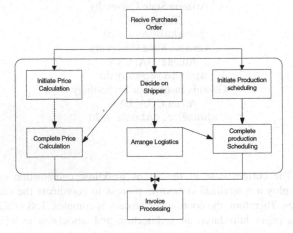

(a) A purchase order workflow

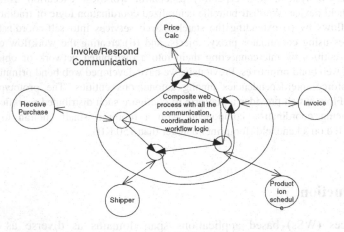

(b) Architecture of traditional WS-BPEL Implementation

Fig. 1. Web Service Workflow Development

i) Centralized Coordination: There are both pros and cons in centralized coordination: the positive point is to have total control over the behavior of the web process at the cost of complex and intricate programming. However, distributed coordination has two kinds of advantages over centralized coordination: (i) due to security, privacy, or licensing imperatives, some web-based objects will only allow direct pair-wise interactions without any coordinating third-party entity; and (ii) centralized workflows suffer from issues of scalability, performance, and fault tolerance [5]. In Section 6, we compare and contrast current efforts towards distributed workflow.

ii) Deployment Platforms: Executing and monitoring workflows over wireless devices has significant benefits [9, 10, 11, 12, 22]. Portions of long-running workflows can reside on handheld devices providing real-time monitoring and controlling capabilities. The current platforms consume significant amount of resources and are difficult to deploy on resource-constrained wireless devices. In Section 6, we also discuss handheld-based web service deployment and execution platforms.

1.1 Our Approach and Contributions

This paper discusses a two-layered software architecture for distributed coordination, and demonstrates a handheld-based execution capability of workflows using our prototype BondFlow system [13, 14].

i) Distributed Coordination: We propose a two-layered workflow software architecture, which greatly simplifies the workflow development task by distributing the complexity of the centralized workflow coordination logic over stateless web services of traditional systems such as BPEL. The stateless web services are empowered by "Coordinator Proxy Objects (CPOs)" into self-coordinating stateful entities. Next, the high-level web bond primitives are employed to interlink the coordinator proxy objects, capturing the workflow logic. Each CPO maintains and enforces its own dependencies during the execution of the workflow. The workflows we create are inherently distributed. Details of our two-layered architecture are presented in Section 3.

ii) Handheld-Based Execution: This was an exercise in engineering as well as in system design, given the limited capabilities of handhelds such as iPAQs. The footprint of the coordinator objects generated by Bondflow system is small (~10KB). The intermediate system-generated files are less than 100 KB for sufficiently large workflows. The footprint of the BondFlow runtime system is 24KB. Thus the byte size of our workflows are no more than 150KB. The additional third party software packages, such as those of SOAP client and XML parser, account for 115KB. The execution time workspace on a Java-enabled handheld used by the BondFlow system is 5.4 MB including JVM (Jeode 1.2 handheld Java version). Therefore, we have been able to execute our workflows on both wired and wireless infrastructures. For communication among the coordinator objects, we employed SOAP in wired devices and our SyD middleware in wireless devices. SyD is our recently prototyped middleware platform to develop and execute distributed applications over handheld devices [1]. Lightweight SyD Listener component enables handheld devices to host server objects.

The remainder of the paper is organized as follows. Section 2 describes the background work on web coordination bonds, the SyD middleware framework, and the BondFlow system design and implementation details. Section 3 presents a two-layered workflow software architecture and distributed workflow coordination methodology of the BondFlow system. Section 4 discusses the handheld-based execution of workflows. Section 5 presents details of our system evaluation. In Section 6, we discuss the related work. Finally, Section 7 presents our future plan of work and conclusions.

2 Background

Here, we briefly discuss web coordination bonds, SyD middleware platform, and the BondFlow system architecture.

Web Bonds [13]: We have proposed the ideas of web bonds as a set of primitives for web service coordination/choreography. There are two types of web bonds: subscription bonds and negotiation bonds. The subscription bonds allow automatic flow of information and control from a source entity to other entities that subscribe to it. This can be employed for synchronization as well as for more complex changes, needing data or event flows. The negotiation bonds enforce dependencies and constraints among entities and trigger changes based on constraints satisfaction. A negotiation bond from A to B has two interpretations: pre-execution and post-execution. In case of pre-execution, in order to start the activity A, B needs to complete its execution. In case of post-execution, in order to start the activity A, A needs to make sure that B can be completed afterwards. Both pre- and post-execution interpretations of negotiation bonds enforce atomicity. In this paper, unless specified, we have implicitly employed the pre-execution type of negotiation bonds.

It has been established that web bonds have the modeling power of extended Petri nets. They can express all the benchmark patterns for workflow and for inter-process communication; a feat that almost all previously proposed artifacts and languages are not capable of comprehensively [13]. Here we illustrate the use of negotiation and subscription bonds for modeling workflow dependencies by modeling producer-consumer scenario.

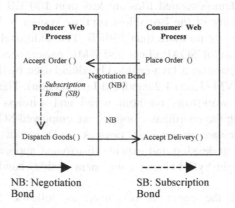

Fig. 2. Coordinating Producer-Consumer web Processes

Modeling Dependencies Using Web Bonds

Fig. 2 shows how a classic relationship of a producer and consumer web process can be modeled using two negotiation bonds. The *"Place_Order"* method at a consumer process needs to ensure that the producer has enough inventories such that the corresponding *"Accept_Order"* method will get executed successfully.   Before guaranteeing this, the *"Accept_Order"* probably will check the current and projected inventory. A negotiation bond is created from consumer web process to producer web process. This is the basic situation for deploying a negotiation bond. Once order has been placed by the consumer and accepted by the producer, a subscription bond serves notice to *"Dispatch_Goods"* method.   Note that the web bonds are useful within a web process as well. Again before *"Dispatch_Goods"* executes, it needs to ensure that consumer's *"Accept_Delivery"* method can be completed successfully (ensuring that enough space is available, for example).

SyD Middleware [1]: The System on Mobile Devices (SyD) middleware platform addresses the key problems of heterogeneity of device, data format and network, and of mobility. Each device is managed by a SyD deviceware that encapsulates it to present a uniform and persistent object view of the device. One of the main components of the SyD middleware is SyD Directory service. The SyD Directory provides user/group/service publishing, management, and lookup services to SyD users and device objects. SyD deviceware consists of SyDListener and SyD Engine components. SyD Listener provides a uniform object view of device services, and receives and responds to clients' synchronous or asynchronous XML-based remote invocations of those services.   It also allows SyD device objects to publish their services locally to the listener and globally through the directory service. SyD Engine allows users/clients to invoke individual or group services remotely via XML-based messaging and aggregates responses.

BondFlow System [14]: The BondFlow system has been developed as a platform to configure and execute workflows over web services (Fig. 3). Workflow configuration module consists of web service interface module, coordinator proxy object generator module, and workflow configuration module. Workflow execution module consists of web bond manager, communication layer, and JVM runtime.

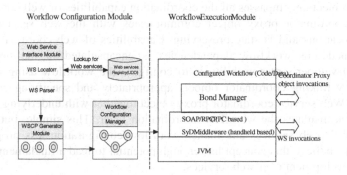

Fig. 3. BondFlow System

The WS Interface module is the system's interface to the web services. It deals with locating the web services of interest for the user and parsing those web service descriptions (WSDL) for desired data. Note that selecting a suitable web service itself is a significant research issue and in this paper we rely on available web services directories such as UDDI. We have used Apache-Axis implementation of the web services. The WSDL parser uses WSDL4J API for WSDL parsing. It parses the WSDL file for required components, and then the methods and parameter list is shown to the user for his/her reference. A parsed WSDL file is stored in the persistence storage if the user opts to save the web service. Data is stored in an XML format. Upon selection of a particular WS for the workflow, a coordinator proxy object is generated. The coordinator object code is generated based on the parsed WSDL file of the selected WS and the proxy generator template (Section 3.1). The responsibility of the configuration manager is twofold. First, it handles bond related operations such as creating, deleting, and updating web bonds, and generating the bond repository for each web service selected. Second, it allows expert users to add customized features to the workflow. This is one of the key modules in our system that guarantees high-level programmability for expert users. Collection of coordinator objects together with corresponding bond repository represents a configured workflow.

The BondFlow execution module consists of two modules: web bond manager and the runtime information handler. The web bond manager enforces workflow constraints at runtime whilst runtime information handler stores method invocation information and other workflow related dynamic information for long-lived workflows (Section 3.2).

3   A Two-Layered Workflow Software Architecture

As shown in Fig. 4a, the architecture of the traditional workflow code is "single layered" where developer needs to program the workflow from scratch (ensure communication, workflow coordination, and intermediate data processing - Fig. 4a). In contrast, in the BondFlow system, workflow coordination has been encapsulated as a separate layer using web coordination bonds. In addition, the system generates Java-based coordinator objects to represent participating web services in the workflow. The coordinator object encompasses all the coordination capabilities of web bond artifacts (Fig. 4b). Coordinator proxy object communicates with the web service through method invocations and is state preserving. Capabilities of web coordination bonds including modeling workflow dependencies is encapsulated in the upper layer (Fig. 4b). Developer's responsibility is to configure the workflow using high level constructs by linking coordinator objects appropriately and specifying constraints. The idea of Web service coordinator proxy object together with underlying web bond primitives encapsulates the workflow coordination layer. This simple, but powerful idea empowers web services and makes workflow configuration less programming intensive. We believe this concept has enough potential to lead a fundamental shift in workflow development over web services.

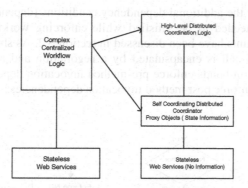

(a) Architecture of workflow using traditional systems

(b) Architecture of workflow using the BondFlow system

Fig. 4. Two-Layered Workflow Software Architecture

3.1 Web Service Coordinator Proxy Object (CPO)

Fig. 5 illustrates components of the coordinator proxy object. The coordinator object provides the same interface as the web service provides to the outer world. Web service method invocations of the workflow take place through the coordinator object and the web bond coordination layer ensures that pre and post method invocation dependencies are satisfied. Each coordinator object has a bond repository, a set of user-defined constraints (if nay), and runtime information associated with it. The bond repository consists of all the workflow dependences related to the coordinator object (participating web service).

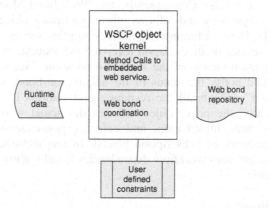

Fig. 5. Web Service Coordinator Proxy Object

This indirection allows us to bring transparency to the system and hide the necessary coordination and communication logic behind it. It also maintains the status of method invocations such as intermediate date and partial results. User defined constraints represent the additional dependency conditions (dependencies not defined using web bonds) needed to be satisfied while enforcing workflow dependencies. User defined constraints have been discussed in section 3.2. As shown in Fig. 6, each web service method call is encapsulated by a negotiation and a subscription bond check. The negotiation bonds enforce pre-method invocation dependencies while the subscription bonds enforce post method invocation dependencies.

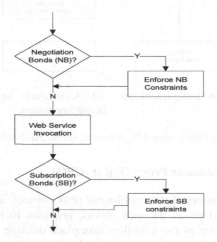

Fig. 6. Flow within a Proxy Object

This logic ensures that workflow dependencies are satisfied with associated WS method invocation. For example, upon receiving an invocation, CPO requests the "Execution Module" to enforce pre-execution dependencies (enforced using a network of negotiation bonds). Consequently, the "Web Bond Manager" checks the corresponding bond repository and informs other coordinator objects to enforce the dependency (Fig. 4). Here, enforcing dependency implies successful invocation of corresponding web service methods. Upon receiving the request, other objects check their runtime information (status of the method invocation - success or failure and intermediate data) and notify the status of the negotiation bond dependencies. The "Web Bond Manager" collects all the responses and informs the proxy about the outcome. Subsequently, the proxy object invokes the actual web service method, updates its runtime state information, and enforces post-execution dependencies (enforced using a network of subscription bonds). In this architecture, each proxy object maintains and enforces workflow dependencies locally, allowing decentralized workflow coordination.

3.1.1 Bond Repository
The workflow configuration process starts by creating bonds among methods of selected web services to reflect dependencies (negotiation and subscription bonds). Bond constraints are specified during the bond creation time and the bond configuration is stored in a persistent storage in XML format.

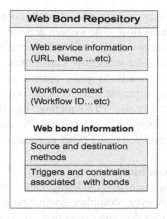

Fig. 7. Elements of a Typical "Bond" Repository

Fig. 7 shows the structure of a typical bond repository. The bond data store (repository) consists of four elements. The first element is to identify the web service (hence the coordinator objects) the repository belongs to. The second element identifies the workflow/application to which the repository belongs. Source and destination methods and associated constraints among bonds are in the next two elements.

3.2 Web Bond Layer

Here, we illustrate the workflow configuration using high-level web coordination bond constructs using purchase order case study workflow. Fig. 8 illustrates the modeling of

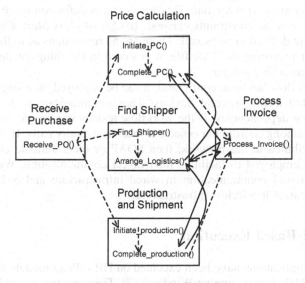

Fig. 8. Purchase Order Workflow

purchase order workflow using a network of web coordination bonds. Five web services are involved in the workflow. The system generates coordinator proxy objects for each web service. Then a network of web bonds is created among methods of these coordinator objects to enforce the workflow constraints. For example, the "receive purchase order" web service needs to pass control to "price calculation", "find shipper", and "production and shipment web services" once it is completed. In order to model this split-dependency, *Receive_PO()* method has three subscription bonds to each of *Initiate_PC()*, *Find_Shipper()*, and *Initiate_Production()* methods. Similarly, rest of the dependencies are modeled using other negotiation and subscription bonds.

3.2.1 High-Level Programmability
Simple workflow constraints such as AND-split can easily be enforced using web coordination bonds [13]. However, complex control patterns such as "Sync-merge" and "Milestone" need developer designed selection criteria [13]. Such customizations can be incorporated by developing user-defined libraries (Java classes) and integrating them to the system library (typically complex workflow need such customizations). Then the triggers/constraints portion of the bond repository refers to the user-defined library (Figure 6). The BondFlow system is capable of extending the default web bond constraints allowing a plug-in architecture that extends the scalability of the system. Furthermore, it empowers the system's ability not only to support the well known workflow patterns but also any arbitrary patterns to be created and deployed.

The extended bond constraints (user defined constraints) define one or more "Roles." Each role performs a set of coordinating activities in order to enforce the semantics of the role. Furthermore, these roles are to be assigned to specific web services (nodes) in the workflow, thus allowing distributed coordination among this web services. The BondFlow system provides a common interface where new web bond constraints can be plugged-in. The extended bond constraints define a JAR file. This package contains: (i) *roles.xml*: This file contains definition of all the roles and their binding to specific constraints classes: (ii) *Set of class files*: These class files relate to each role defined in roles.xml. There are no restrictions as to the name of the class files. After preparing the JAR file, it is stored in the /plug-ins directory of the workflow configuration manager.

Once the workflow has been configured, it can be deployed on a single device or it can be distributed among several devices. They communicate with each other to enforce workflow dependencies. If the workflow resides in a single device, then the communication among coordinator objects is local in-memory calls. If the coordinator objects are distributed in the network, then SOAP or other suitable communication protocol can be employed to facilitate inter-object communication. We have implemented SOAP based communication in wired infrastructure and SyD middleware based communication in wireless infrastructure.

4   Handheld-Based Execution

The workflow applications have been executed on HP's iPAQ models 3600 and 3700 with 32 and 64 MB storage running Windows CE. There are two possible deployment strategies. First, the entire workflow can reside in a single wireless device. In this case, communication among coordinator objects is via local in-memory calls. Actual web service call is made using SOAP (kSOAP). Second, the workflow can be distributed among several iPAQ's (Fig. 9). This scenario is important in cases where some portions of the workflow can be monitored and executed by a selected set of users on specific devices and/or with specific security settings.

In this case, coordinator objects need to communicate using a remote messaging system to enforce dependences. We have employed the SyD Listener of the SyD middleware. The SyD Listener enables handheld devices to communicate among applications deployed on other peer devices (Fig. 9). SyD Listener is a lightweight module in our SyD middleware framework for enabling mobile devices to host server objects. In order to communicate using SyD Listener, first coordinator objects need to be registered in the SyD Directory. SyD Directory maintains its own database to store information about all the SyD application objects together with associated devices and delivers location information of devices and services (methods) dynamically. SyD objects can lookup remote objects through SyD Directory. The SyD Engine facilitates the object to actually invoke a remote object. SyD Listener keeps listening for any connection requests and delegates the control to the SyD Engine module.

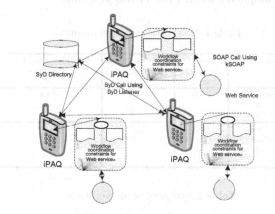

Fig. 9. Workflow Distributed among Several iPAQ's

Coordinator Object Registration as a SyD Application Object [1]: The proxy objects register all the method names along with the list of parameters (their data types) with the registry. Initially, all the entities are converted into required XML format using SyD Doc and then the registration process with SyD Directory begins. Once bound in the registry, these coordinator objects wait for invocation from other proxies. In this scenario, the registered proxies act as servers waiting for invocation from clients.

Coordinator Object Invocation through SyD Engine [1]: When a workflow containing SyD coordinator application object encounters the presence of web bonds with other applications, it looks up the desired web service proxy in the SyD Directory (Fig. 8). SyD Directory returns the list of parameters for the specified method. Depending upon the parameters, required values are passed to the SyD Engine as an XML document. The SyD Engine of the client (in this case the source web service) invokes its SyD Listener that in turn calls the server's SyD Listener by opening a socket connection. The result is returned to the client as an XML document. In this architecture, each device can act as both server and the client. They become capable of hosting server objects. As shown in Fig. 8, an actual web service call is made using SOAP (kSOAP).

5 System Evaluation

Hardware software setup: We ran our experiments on a high performance SunOS 5.8 server. We built wrappers using JDK 1.4.2. The WSDL parser has been built using WSDL4J API. WSLD4J API is an IBM reference implementation of the JSR-110 specification (JavaAPI's for WSDL). NanoXML 2.2.1 is used as the XMLparser for JAVA. Various publicly available web services including Xmethod's SOAP based web services (http://www.xmethods.net/) have been used for our experiments. For wireless device experiments we have used HP's iPAQ models 3600 and 3700 with 32 and 64 MB storage running Windows CE/Pocket PC OS interconnected through IEEE 802.11 adapter cards and a 11 MB/s Wireless LAN. Jeode EVM personal Java 1.2 compatible has been employed as the Java Virtual Machine.

Table 1. Workflow execution timings

Workflow	Total execution time (ms)	BondFlow related timings (ms)	BondFlow related (%) computation
Purchase order # of NB= 4, #of SB= 9	7820	1048	13.4
Online book purchase # of NB= 5 #of SB= 6	2483	102	4.1

Table 2. Footprint of the workflow

Workflow	Bond repository (KB)	Proxy objects (KB)	Total workflow (KB)
Purchase order	7.10	25.4	32.5
Online book purchase	5.82	19.8	25.62

System performance details: We have deployed and executed workflows from the above case studies including the purchase order workflow on both wired and wireless infrastructure. Table 1 shows that the workflow execution timings for the two case study workflows for both wired and wireless settings. Bond related time for both workflows are approximately ~10% of the time without the BondFlow system. The bond related time accounts for times taken to check workflow dependencies in bond repository and initiate appropriate method calls on remote web services (coordinator objects). Table 2 shows the footprints of two workflows. The coordinator objects and corresponding bond repositories accounts for ~25% and ~75% respectively. The footprint of the proxy object is small (~10KB) and typically increases by 0.3 KB per additional operation (method) of the web service. Intermediate system generated files are less than 100 KB for a sufficiently large workflow. Typically the footprint of the bond repository increases 0.3 KB per each additional bond. Thus, within a very small amount of additional storage for the proxy objects, we have been able to get substantial gains in the speed of the workflow.

6 Related Work and Discussion

Several approaches have been proposed toward distributed web service coordination and peer-to-peer interaction among web services. Among such systems, IBM symphony [5] decentralizes the coordination by partitioning centralized workflow specification into separate modules so that they can run in a distributed setting. However, there are limitations to such efforts. First, it is necessary to develop the centralized BPEL code and then partition and distribute it among participant entities. Second, usually, there are problems partitioning the code in complex application scenarios such as long-running transactional applications without proper infra-structure support. The Self-Serv project presented in [15] proposes a peer-to-peer orchestration model for web services. It introduces a "coordinator," which can act as a scheduler for participating web services. Several coordinators can control the execution of the workflow in peer-to-peer fashion. In [17] authors propose a distributed and decentralized process approach called OSIRIS that allows peer-to-peer communication among participating web services. However, their approach needs meta information to be stored in a central location. Also, in order to enforce fork/join dependencies they introduce a new join node exclusive from workflow nodes. In contrast to the Self-Serv and OSIRIS approaches, our coordinator proxy object is dynamically generated based on the description of participating web service and it encapsulates all the coordination capabilities. The proxy object enforces its own dependencies. This enhances each web service facilitating more fine-grained decentralization of the coordination. In [19] authors propose a system to distribute the execution of business applications using web services by adding business rules into the SOAP messages. Business rules encoded in the SOAP header specify the order of execution. Messages are decoded and processed by special processing units called SOAP intermediaries. In [18] authors propose a service-oriented distributed business rules system and its implementation based on WS-Coordination. Web Service Resource (WSRF) framework is another proposal towards stateful web services. It provides standardization representation to stateful resources and the web service interface provides functionalities to access (read, update and query) state information. This state information is used to process web service messages [21]. Comparative study of various implementations of WSRF is presented in [20]. In contrast to WSRF approach, the BondFlow system maintains state information of workflow execution and processes messages. State is attached to the coordinator proxy object. Web service interface need not be changed and web service is relieved from state handling functionalities.

In [2, 22], authors describe issues related to service composition in mobile environ-ments and evaluate criteria for judging protocols that enable such composition. The composition protocols are based on distributed brokerage mechanisms and utilize a distributed service discovery process over ad-hoc network connectivity. In [7] authors present an architecture for mobile device collaboration using web services. In [10] authors present a rapid application development environment for mobile web services. Authors of [11, 12] present web service based mobile application integration framework. However, a key limitation of most of these technologies is that they treat handheld devices only as clients. However, our SyD middleware gives the server capabilities to small hanheld device. The BondFlow system uses the SyD middleware to facilitate device to device communication and coordination among devices. Also, the small footprint (~150 KB) of our software system make it easily deployable on handheld devices.

7 Conclusions and Future Work

In this paper, we presented the decentralized workflow coordination architecture of the BondFlow system. The concept of the coordinator proxy object is central to our decentralized architecture. A preliminary study of implementation prototype shows that the bond related time is less than ~10% of the workflow execution time. Also, the small footprint of coordinator proxy object (~10KB) enables them to reside on Java-enabled handheld devices. In contrast to other systems such as Self-Serv, the idea of the coordinator proxy object enhances each web service facilitating more fine-grained decentralization of the coordination. Our goal is to use this infrastructure to model and implement actual workflows in typical biological and E-commerce applications to help biological researchers on one hand and international supply-chain technology users on the other.

References

[1] Prasad, S.K., Madisetti, V., Navathe, S., et al.: System on Mobile Devices (SyD): A Middleware Testbed for Collaborative Applications over Small Heterogeneous Devices and Data Stores. In: Proc. ACM/IFIP/USENIX 5th International Middleware Conference, Toronto, Ontario, Canada (October 18th - 22nd, 2004)

[2] Chakraborty, D., Joshi, A., Finin, T., Yesha, Y.: Service Composition for Mobile Environments. Journal on Mobile Networking and Applications, Special Issue on Mobile Services (February 2004)

[3] Ko, I.-Y., Neches, R.: Composing Web Services for Large-Scale Tasks. In: Internet Computing, vol. 7(5), pp. 52–59. IEEE, Los Alamitos (2003)

[4] Indrakanti, S., Varadharajan, V., Hitchens, M.: Authorization Service for Web Services and its Application in a Health Care Domain. International Journal of Web Services Research 2(4), 94–119 (2005)

[5] Chafle, G., Chandra, S., Mann, V., Nanda, M.G.: Decentralized Orchestration of Composite Web Services. In: WWW 2004. Proc. of the Alternate Track on Web Services at the 13th International World Wide Web Conference, New York, NY (May 2004)

[6] Sinderson, E., Magapu, V., Mak, R.: Portal of NASAs Mars Exploration Rovers Mission-Middleware and Web Services for the Collaborative Information. In: Proc. ACM/IFIP/USENIX 5th International Middleware Conference, Toronto, Ontario, Canada, October 18th - 22nd 2004, pp. 1–17 (invited paper)

[7] Ranganathan, A., McFaddin, S.: Using Workflows to Coordinate Web Services in Pervasive Computing Environments. In: ICWS 2004. Proc. of the IEEE International Conference on Web Services. Proc. of the IEEE International Conference on Web Services, San Diego, California, USA, June 6-9, 2004, pp. 288–295. IEEE Computer Society, Los Alamitos (2004)

[8] zur Muehlen, M., Stohr, E.A.: Internet-enabled Workflow Management. Editorial to the Special Issue of the Business Process Management Journal 11 (2005)

[9] Dustdar, S., Gall, H., Schmidt, R.: Web Services for Groupware in Distributed and Mobile Collaboration. In: PDP 2004, p. 241 (2004)

[10] Mnaouer, A.B., Shekhar, A., Yi-Liang, Z.: A Generic Framework for Rapid Application Development of Mobile Web Services with Dynamic Workflow Management. In: IEEE SCC 2004, pp. 165–171 (2004)

[11] Steele, R.A.: Web Services-based System for Ad-hoc Mobile Application Integration. In: Proc. of IEEE Intl. Conf. on Information Technology: Coding and Computing 2003 (2003)

[12] Hawryszkiewycz, I., Steele, R.: Extending Collaboration to Mobile Environments. In: Proc. of the International Conference on Web Technologies, Applications and Services, Calgary, Canada (July 4-6, 2005)

[13] Prasad, S.K., Balasoorya, J.: Fundamental Capabilities of Web Coordination Bonds: Modeling Petri Nets and Expressing Workflow and Communication Patterns over Web Services. In: Proc. Hawaii Intl. Conf. in Syst. Sc. (HICSS-38), Big Island (January 4-8, 2005)

[14] Balasooriya, J., Padye, M., Prasad, S., Navathe, S.B.: BondFlow: A System for Distributed Coordination of Workflows over Web Services. In: 14th HCW in conjunction with IPDPS 2005, Denver, Colorado, USA (April 2005)

[15] Benatallah, B., Dumas, M., Sheng, Q.Z.: Facilitating the Rapid Development and Scalable Orchestration of Composite Web Services. Distributed and Parallel Databases 17(1), 5–37 (2005)

[16] Barros, A., Dumas, M., Oaks, P.: Standards for Web Service Choreography and Orchestration: Status and Perspectives. In: Proc. of the Workshop on Web Services Choreography and Orchestration for Business Process Management, Nancy, France (September 2005)

[17] Schuler, C., Weber, R., Schuldt, H., Schek, H.-J.: Scalable Peer-to-Peer Process Management - The OSIRIS Approach. In: ICWS 2004, pp. 26–34 (2004)

[18] Rosenberg, F., Dustdar, S.: Towards a Distributed Service-Oriented Business Rules System. In: ECOWS. IEEE European Conference on Web Services, November 14-16, 2005, IEEE Computer Society Press, Los Alamitos (2005)

[19] Schmidt, R.: Web services based execution of business rules. In: Proc. of the Intl. Workshop on Rule Markup Languages for Business Rules on the Semantic Web (2002)

[20] Humphrey, M., Wasson, G., Jackson, K., et al.: State and Events for Web Services: A Comparison of Five WS-Resource Framework and WS-Notification Implementations. In: 14th IEEE Intl. Symposium on High Performance Distributed Computing (HPDC-14), Research Triangle Park, NC (July 24-27, 2005)

[21] Czajkowski, K., Ferguson, D., Foster, I., et al.: The WS-Resource Framework (2004), http://www-106.ibm.com/developerworks /library/ws-resource/ws-wsrf.pdf

[22] Jørstad, I., Dustdar, S., van Do, T.: Service-Oriented Architectures and Mobile Services. In: 3rd Intl. Workshop on Ubiquitous Mobile Information and collaboration Systems (UMICS), co-located with CAiSE 2005, June 13-14, 2005 Porto, Portugal (2005)

The Building Blocks of Consensus*

Yee Jiun Song[1], Robbert van Renesse[1], Fred B. Schneider[1], and Danny Dolev[2]

[1] Cornell University
[2] The Hebrew University of Jerusalem

Abstract. Consensus is an important building block for building replicated systems, and many consensus protocols have been proposed. In this paper, we investigate the building blocks of consensus protocols and use these building blocks to assemble a skeleton that can be configured to produce, among others, three well-known consensus protocols: Paxos, Chandra-Toueg, and Ben-Or. Although each of these protocols specifies only one quorum system explicitly, all also employ a second quorum system. We use the skeleton to implement a replicated service, allowing us to compare the performance of these consensus protocols under various workloads and failure scenarios.

1 Introduction

Computers will fail, and for many systems it is imperative that such failures be tolerated. Replication, a general approach for supporting fault tolerance, requires a protocol so replicas will agree on values and actions. The *agreement* or *consensus* problem was originally proposed in [1]. Many variants and corresponding solutions have followed (see [2] for a survey of just the first decade, containing well over 100 references).

This paper focuses on protocols for Internet-like systems — systems in which there are no real-time bounds on execution or message latency. Such systems are often termed *asynchronous*. The well-known FLP impossibility [3] result proved that consensus cannot be solved even if only one process can fail. Practical consensus algorithms sidestep this limitation using one of two approaches: i) *leader-based* algorithms use a failure detector that captures eventual timing assumptions, and ii) *randomized* algorithms solve a non-deterministic version of consensus and eventually decide with probability 1.

Guerraoui and Raynal [4] point out similarities between different consensus protocols. They provide a generic framework for consensus algorithms and show that differences between the various algorithms can be factored out into a function called Lambda. Each consensus algorithm employs rather different implementations of Lambda. Later, Guerraoui and Raynal [5] show that leader-based

* This work is supported by AFOSR grants FA8750-06-2-0060, FA9550-06-1-0019, FA9550-06-1-0244, the National Science Foundation under grants 0424422, 0430161 and CCF-0424422 (TRUST), a gift from Microsoft Corporation, and ISF, ISOC, and CCR. Any opinions expressed in this publication are those of the authors and do not necessarily reflect the views of the funding agencies.

S. Rao et al. (Eds.): ICDCN 2008, LNCS 4904, pp. 54–72, 2008.
© Springer-Verlag Berlin Heidelberg 2008

algorithms can be factored into an `Omega` module and an `Alpha` module, where all differences are captured by differences in `Omega`.

This paper is a next step in unifying consensus algorithms. By breaking down consensus algorithms into building blocks, we show that different consensus algorithms can be instantiated from a single *skeletal algorithm*:

- Going beyond the work reported in [5], we present the building blocks of consensus algorithms and how they can be used to build a skeletal consensus algorithm. The skeletal algorithm provides insight into how consensus protocols work, and we show that consensus requires not one but two separate quorum systems;
- We show that both leader-based and randomized algorithms can be instantiated from our skeletal algorithm by configuring the two quorums systems that are used and the way instances are started. This approach can be used to instantiate three well-known consensus protocols: Paxos [6], Chandra-Toueg [7], and Ben-Or [8];
- The skeleton provides a natural platform for implementation of multiple consensus protocols from a single code base;
- And we present a performance comparison of these protocols under varying workload and crash failures. The implementation reveals interesting trade-offs between various design choices in consensus algorithms.

The rest of this paper is organized as follows. Section 2 describes the consensus problem and proposes terminology. Next, we present the building blocks of consensus protocols in Section 3; these building blocks are used to build a skeletal consensus algorithm in Section 4. Section 5 illustrates the instantiation of particular consensus algorithms using the skeletal algorithm. Section 6 describes the implementation of the skeleton and compares the performance of three well-known consensus protocols. Section 7 concludes.

2   The Consensus Problem

Computers that run programs – nodes – are either *honest*, executing programs faithfully, or *Byzantine* [9], exhibiting arbitrary behavior. We will also use the terms *correct* and *faulty*, but not as alternatives to honest and Byzantine. A correct node is an honest node that always eventually makes progress. A faulty node is a Byzantine node or an honest node that has crashed or will eventually crash. Note that honest and Byzantine are mutually exclusive, as are correct and faulty. However, a node can be both honest and faulty.

We assume that each pair of nodes is connected by a *link*, which is a bi-directional reliable virtual circuit and therefore messages sent on this link are delivered, eventually, and in the order in which they were sent (*i.e.*, an honest sender keeps retransmitting a message until it receives an acknowledgment or crashes). A receiver can tell who sent a message (*e.g.*, using MACs), so a Byzantine node cannot forge a message so it is indistinguishable from a message sent by an honest node.

Because our model is asynchronous, we do not assume timing bounds on execution of programs or on latency of communication. We also do not assume that a node on one side of a link can determine whether the node on the other side of the link is correct or faulty. Timeouts cannot reliably detect faulty nodes in an asynchronous system, even if only crash failures are allowed.

In the consensus problem nodes run *actors* that are either *proposers*, each of which proposes a *proposal*, or *deciders*, each of which *decides* one of the proposals. Assuming there exists at least one correct proposer (*i.e.*, a proposer on a correct node), the goal of a consensus protocol is to ensure each correct decider decides the same proposal, even in the face of faulty proposers. A node may run both a proposer and a decider—in practice a proposer often would like to learn the outcome of the agreement.

Why is the consensus problem hard? Consider the following strawman protocol: each decider collects proposals from all proposers, determines the minimum proposal from among the proposals it receives (in case it received multiple proposals), and decides on that one. If no nodes were faulty, such a protocol would work, albeit limited in speed by the slowest node or link.

Unfortunately, even if only crash failures are possible, deciders do not know how long to wait for proposers. If deciders use time-outs, then each might time-out on different sets of proposers, so these deciders could decide different proposals. Thus, each decider has no choice but to wait until it has received a proposal from all proposers. But if one of the proposers is faulty, such a decider will wait forever and never decide.

In an asynchronous system with crash failures (Byzantine failures include crash failures), there exists no deterministic protocol in which correct deciders are guaranteed to decide eventually [3]. We might circumvent this limitation by allowing some correct deciders not to decide. Instead, we will embrace a slightly stronger requirement: that the consensus protocol never reach a state in which some correct decider can never decide. Since the strawman protocol of deciding the minimum proposal can reach a state in which deciders wait indefinitely for a faulty proposer, it is not a consensus protocol, even with respect to the relaxed requirement.

Formally, a protocol that solves the consensus problem must satisfy:

Definition 1. *Agreement. If two honest deciders decide, then they decide the same proposal.*

Definition 2. *Unanimity. If all honest proposers propose the same proposal v, then an honest decider that decides must decide v.*

Definition 3. *Validity. If a honest decider decides v, then v was proposed by some proposer.*

Definition 4. *Non-Blocking. For any run of the protocol that reaches a state in which a particular correct decider has not yet decided, there exists a continuation of the run in which that decider does decide on a proposal.*

Agreement is a safety property that captures what is informally meant by "consensus;" **Unanimity** and **Validity** are non-triviality properties; and **Non-Blocking** is a weaker version of the non-triviality requirement that all correct deciders eventually decide. **Non-Blocking** makes consensus solvable without trivializing the problem. Such a weakening of the problem is present in all algorithms that "solve" the consensus problem, since there cannot exist a solution to consensus with a strong liveness requirement [3].

3 Building Blocks

The strawman (viz., decide the minimum proposal) protocol presented in Section 2 is not a solution to the consensus problem because a faulty proposer can cause correct deciders to wait indefinitely, violating **Non-Blocking**. To remedy this, a consensus protocol might invoke multiple *instances*, where an instance is an execution of a sub-protocol that itself might not decide. Such instances have also been called *rounds*, *phases*, or *ballots*. Ensuring consistency among decisions made by multiple instances is central to the design of consensus protocols. In this section, we give building blocks in common to different consensus protocols; in the next section, we show how these building blocks can be combined to create full consensus protocols.

3.1 Instances

Instances may run in parallel with other instances. An instance decides a proposal if an honest decider in that instance decides a proposal. All honest deciders that decide in an instance must be guaranteed to decide the same proposal. An instance may not necessarily decide any proposals. If multiple instances decide, they must decide the same proposal.

Instances are identified by instance identifiers $r, \ldots$ from a totally ordered set $\tilde{\mathbb{N}}$ (which can be, but does not have to be, the set $\mathbb{N}$ on naturals). Instance identifiers induce an ordering on instances, and we say that one instance is *before* or *after* another instance, even though instances may execute concurrently.

We name proposals $v, w, \ldots$. Within an instance, proposals are paired with instance identifiers. A pair (r, v) is called a *suggestion*, if v is a proposal and r an instance identifier. A special suggestion $\bot$ is used to indicate the absence of a specific proposal.

3.2 Actors

We employ two new types of actors in addition to proposers and deciders: *archivers* and *selectors*.[1] A proposer sends its proposal to the selectors. Selectors and archivers exchange messages and occasionally archivers inform deciders about potential values for decision. Deciders apply a filter to reach a decision.

---

[1] A node may run multiple actors, although each node can run at most one archiver and at most one selector.

Selectors *select* proposals, and archivers *archive* suggestions. Each archiver remembers the last suggestion that it has archived. The initial archived suggestion of an archiver is $\perp$.

The objective of selectors is to reach a decision within an instance, while the objective of archivers is to maintain a collective memory that ensures decisions are remembered across instances and therefore conflicting decisions are avoided.

At any point in time, a selector or archiver executes within a single instance; it sends and receives messages that are part of the instance execution. Selectors can lose their state on a crash and subsequently join any instance upon recovery, even a prior one. Archivers can switch instances but must progress to later instances, and therefore keep their state on non-volatile storage.

3.3   Extended Quorum Systems

In order to ensure consistency in decisions, actors in a consensus protocol use *quorums*. An *extended quorum system* is a quadruple $(\mathcal{P}, \mathcal{M}, \mathcal{Q}, \mathcal{G})$. $\mathcal{P}$ is a set of nodes called the *participants*. $\mathcal{M}, \mathcal{Q}$, and $\mathcal{G}$ are each a collection of subsets of participants (that is, each is a subset of $2^{\mathcal{P}}$). $\mathcal{M}$ is the collection of *maximal-wait sets*, $\mathcal{Q}$ the collection of *quorum sets*, and $\mathcal{G}$ the collection of *guarded sets*. Each is defined below.

Crashed or Byzantine participants might never respond to requests. In an instance, an actor tries to collect as many responses to a broadcast request as possible; it stops awaiting responses when it is in danger of waiting indefinitely. $\mathcal{M}$ characterizes this — it is a set of subsets of $\mathcal{P}$, none contained in another, such that some $M \in \mathcal{M}$ contains all the correct nodes.[2] An actor stops waiting for responses after receiving replies from all participants in M.

A *quorum set* is a subset of $\mathcal{P}$ such that the intersection of any two quorum sets must contain at least one correct node. A subset of $\mathcal{P}$ is a *guarded set* if and only if it is guaranteed to contain at least one honest participant. Note, a guarded set may consist of a single participant that could be crashed but is not Byzantine.

An extended quorum system must satisfy the follow properties:

Definition 5. *Consistency. The intersection of any two quorum sets (including a quorum set with itself) is guaranteed to contain a correct participant.*

Definition 6. *Opaqueness. Each maximal-wait set contains a quorum consisting entirely of honest participants.*

The simplest example of extended quorum system are threshold quorum systems; Table 1 summarizes requirements for $\mathcal{P}, \mathcal{M}, \mathcal{Q}$, and $\mathcal{G}$ in (n, t)-threshold systems. Other quorum systems may be more appropriate for particular applications. See [11] and [10] for advantages and disadvantages of various quorum systems for crash and arbitrary failure models respectively.

---

[2] For those familiar with Byzantine Quorum Systems [10], $\mathcal{M}$ is the set of complements of the fail-prone system $\mathcal{B}$. For the purposes of this paper, it is often more convenient to talk about maximal-wait sets.

One degenerate extended quorum system, used in some well-known consensus protocols, is a *leader extended quorum system*: it involves one participant (the leader), and that participant by itself forms the only maximal-wait set in $\mathcal{M}$, quorum in $\mathcal{Q}$, and guarded set in $\mathcal{G}$. Because quorum sets have to satisfy consistency, the leader has to be honest.

Table 1. Size requirements for Threshold Quorum Systems that satisfy consistency and opaqueness

	Crash	Byzantine
guarded set (in $\mathcal{G}$)	> 0	$> t$
quorum set (in $\mathcal{Q}$)	$> n/2$	$> (n+t)/2$
maximal-wait set (in $\mathcal{M}$)	$= n - t$	$= n - t$
set of participants ($\mathcal{P}$)	$> 2t$	$> 5t$

3.4 Guarded Proposal

Selectors in some instance r must be careful about selecting proposals that can conflict with decisions of instances earlier than r. Before selecting a proposal in an instance, a selector obtains a set L of suggestions from each participant in a maximal-wait set of archivers. A proposal v is considered a *potential-proposal* if L contains suggestions containing v from a guarded set and, therefore, at least one honest archiver sent a suggestion containing v. The selector identifies a *guarded proposal* of L, if any, as follows:

1. Consider each potential-proposal v separately:
    (a) Consider all subsets of suggestions containing v from guarded sets of archivers. The minimum instance identifier in a subset is called a *guarded-instance-identifier*;
    (b) The maximum among the guarded-instance-identifiers for v is called the *associated-instance-identifier* of v. (Note, because v is a potential-proposal, at least one guarded-instance-identifier exists and thus the maximum is well-defined.) The *support-sets* for v are those subsets of suggestions for which the guarded-instance-identifier is the associated-instance-identifier;
2. Among the potential-proposals, select all proposals with the maximal associated-instance-identifier. If there is exactly one such potential-proposal v', and $v' \neq \bot$, then this is the guarded proposal. Otherwise there is no guarded proposal.

If a decider obtains suggestions (r, v) from a quorum of archivers (and consequently decides), then any honest selectors in instances at least r are guaranteed to compute a guarded proposal v' such that $v' = v$ (unless they crash). If a selector fails to compute a guarded proposal in a particular instance, then this is both evidence that no prior instance can have decided and a guarantee that no prior instance will ever decide. However, the reverse is not true. If a selector computes a guarded proposal v', it is not guaranteed that v' is or will be decided.

4   Assembling the Pieces

The building blocks described in the previous section can be used to populate a *skeletal algorithm*, which in turn can be instantiated to obtain particular consensus algorithms. The skeletal algorithm specifies the interaction between the actors. It does not, however, define the quorums that are used, the mechanisms for invoking new instances, or other protocol-specific details. A consensus protocol must specify these details, and some options are described in Section 5.

4.1   The Skeletal Algorithm

The skeletal algorithm defines actions by actors in each instance. Figure 1 shows the behavior of each actor.

Each selector, archiver, and decider participates in an extended quorum system and exchanges messages of the form

$$\langle message\text{-}type, instance, source, suggestion \rangle$$

An extended quorum system $\mathcal{E} = (\mathcal{P}, \mathcal{M}, \mathcal{Q}, \mathcal{G})$ has the following interface:

- $\mathcal{E}.broadcast(m)$: send message m to all participants in $\mathcal{P}$;
- $\mathcal{E}.wait(pattern)$: wait for messages matching the given pattern (specifies, for example, the message type and instance number). When the sources of the collected messages form an element or a superset of an element of $\mathcal{M}$, return the set of collected messages;
- $\mathcal{E}.uni\text{-}quorum(set\ of\ messages)$: if the set of messages contains the same suggestion from a quorum, then return that suggestion.[3] Otherwise, return $\perp$;
- $\mathcal{E}.guarded\text{-}proposal(set\ of\ messages)$: return the guarded proposal among these messages, or $\perp$ if there is none.

The skeletal algorithm uses two separate extended quorum systems. Archivers form an extended quorum system $\mathcal{A}$ that is the same for all instances; selectors use $\mathcal{A}$ to find the guarded proposal, preventing selection of proposals that conflict with decisions in earlier instances. Selectors form a second extended quorum system $\mathcal{S}^r$, which may be different for each instance r; archivers in instance r use quorums of $\mathcal{S}^r$ to prevent two archivers from archiving different suggestions in the same instance.

Deciders, although technically not part of an instance, try to obtain the same suggestion from a quorum of archivers in each instance. For simplicity of presentation, we associate deciders with instances and have them form a third extended quorum system, $\mathcal{D}$.

Returning to Figure 1, archivers start a new instance by sending their currently archived suggestion c_i to the selectors (A.1). Each selector awaits select messages from a maximal wait set (S.1) and determines if one of the suggestions it receives could have been decided in a previous instance (S.2). If so, it selects

---

[3] Quorum consistency ensures at most one such suggestion.

the corresponding proposal. If not, it selects one of the proposals issued by the proposers (S.3). The selector composes a suggestion from the selected proposal using the current instance identifier, and sends that suggestion to the archivers (S.4).

If an archiver receives the same suggestion from a quorum of selectors (A.3), it (i) archives that suggestion (A.4), and (ii) broadcasts the suggestion to the deciders (A.5). If a decider receives the same suggestion from a quorum of archivers (D.2), the decider decides the corresponding proposal in those suggestions (D.3).

Each selector i maintains a set P_i containing proposals it has received (across instances). A selector waits for at least one proposal before participating in the rest of the protocol, so P_i is never empty during execution of the protocol. (Typically, P_i first contains a proposal from the proposer on the same

At the **start of instance** r, each **archiver** i executes:

(A.1) send c_i to all participants (selectors) in $\mathcal{S}^r$:

$\qquad \mathcal{S}^r.broadcast(\langle \texttt{select}, r, i, c_i \rangle)$

Each **selector** j in $\mathcal{S}^r$ executes:

(S.1) wait for **select** messages from archivers:

$\qquad L_j^r := \mathcal{A}.wait(\langle \texttt{select}, r, *, * \rangle);$

(S.2) see if there is a guarded proposal:

$\qquad v_j^r := \mathcal{A}.guarded\text{-}proposal(L_j^r);$

(S.3) if not, select from received proposals instead:

$\qquad$ if $v_j^r = \bot$ then $v_j^r := P_j.pick(r)$ fi;

(S.4) send a suggestion to all archivers:

$\qquad \mathcal{A}.broadcast(\langle \texttt{archive}, r, j, (r, v_j^r) \rangle);$

Each **archiver** i (still in instance r) executes:

(A.2) wait for **archive** messages from selectors:

$\qquad M_i^r := \mathcal{S}^r.wait(\langle \texttt{archive}, r, *, * \rangle);$

(A.3) unanimous suggestion from a quorum?

$\qquad q_i^r := \mathcal{S}^r.uni\text{-}quorum(M_i^r);$

(A.4) *archive* the suggestion:

$\qquad c_i := $ if $q_i^r = \bot$ then $(r, \bot)$ else q_i^r fi;

(A.5) send the suggestion to all deciders:

$\qquad \mathcal{D}.broadcast(\langle \texttt{decide}, r, i, c_i \rangle)$

Each **decider** k executes:

(D.1) wait for **decide** messages from archivers:

$\qquad N_k^r := \mathcal{A}.wait(\langle \texttt{decide}, r, *, * \rangle);$

(D.2) unanimous suggestion from a quorum?

$\qquad d_k^r := \mathcal{A}.uni\text{-}quorum(N_k^r);$

(D.3) if there is, and not $\bot$, decide:

$\qquad$ if ($d_k^r = (r, v')$ **and** $v' \neq \bot$)

$\qquad$ **then** decide v' fi;

Fig. 1. The skeletal algorithm of consensus protocols

node as selector i.) For simplicity, we assume an honest proposer sends a single proposal. The details of how P_i is formed and used differ across consensus protocols, so this is discussed below when full protocols are presented. P_i has an operation $P_i.pick(r)$ that returns either a single proposal from the set or some value as a function of r. Different protocols use different approaches for selecting that value, and these too are discussed below. Note, selectors may lose their state, starting again with an empty P_i.

Archivers' states survive crashes and recoveries. So, an archiver j running on an honest node maintains: r_j, the current instance identifier and c_j, the last archived suggestion, which is initialized with the value $\perp$.

Note that steps (A.1), (S.1), and (S.2) can be skipped in the lowest numbered instance, because c_i is guaranteed to be $\perp$ for all archivers. This is an important optimization in practice and eliminates one of the three message rounds necessary for a proposal to be decided in the normal (failure-free) case.

4.2   Agreement

We now show that the skeletal algorithm satisfies **Agreement**, that is, if two honest deciders decide, then they decide the same proposal. We omit the proofs of lemmas that are relatively straightforward. For complete proofs please refer to [12].

Lemma 1. *In the skeletal algorithm of Figure 1:*

(a) *if any honest archiver i computes a suggestion $q_i^r \neq \perp$ in Step (A.3) of instance r, then any honest archiver that computes a non-$\perp$ suggestion in that step of that instance, computes the same suggestion.*

(b) *if any honest decider k computes a suggestion $d_k^r \neq \perp$ in Step (D.2) of instance r, then any honest decider that computes a non-$\perp$ suggestion in that step of that instance, computes the same suggestion.*

Note that Step (S.2) does *not* satisfy (a) and (b) of Lemma 1. because selectors do not try to obtain a unanimous suggestion from a quorum.

Corollary 1. *In the skeletal algorithm of Figure 1, if any honest archiver archives a suggestion (r, v) with $v \neq \perp$ in Step (A.4) of instance r, then any honest archiver that archives a suggestion with a non-$\perp$ proposal in that step of that instance archives the same suggestion.*

Lemma 2. *In the skeletal algorithm of Figure 1, if any honest archiver sends a suggestion $(\bar{r}, v)$ with $v \neq \perp$ in Step (A.1) of instance r then any honest archiver that sends a suggestion $(\bar{r}, v')$ with $v' \neq \perp$ in that step of that instance, sends the same proposal, i.e., $v = v'$.*

Lemma 3. *In the skeletal algorithm of Figure 1:*

(a) *if each honest selector that completes Step (S.4) of instance r sends the same suggestion, then any honest archiver that completes Step (A.3) of that instance computes the same suggestion;*

(b) *if each honest archiver that completes Step (A.4) of instance r sends the same suggestion, then any honest decider that completes Step (D.2) of that instance computes the same suggestion;*

(c) if each honest archiver that completes Step (A.1) of instance r sends the same suggestion, then any honest selector that completes Step (S.2) of that instance computes the same proposal.

The most important property we need to prove is:

Lemma 4. *In the skeletal algorithm of Figure 1, if r' is the earliest instance in which a proposal w is decided by some honest decider, then for any instance r, $r > r'$, if an honest archiver archives a suggestion in Step (A.4), then it is (r, w).*

Proof. Since instances are totally ordered, any subset of them are totally ordered. The proof will be by induction on all instances, past instance r', in which eventually some honest archiver archives a suggestion.

Let $w \neq \perp$ be the proposal decided by an honest decider in Step (D.4) of instance r'. Let $Q^{r'} \in \mathcal{A}$ be the quorum in instance r' whose suggestions caused the decider to decide w.

Let $r_1 > r'$ be the first instance past r' at which some honest archiver eventually completes Step (A.4). Since this archiver completes Step (A.4), it must have received **archive** messages from a maximal-wait set of selectors following Step (A.2) of instance r_1. Each honest selector that sent such a message received **select** messages from a maximal-wait set of archivers sent in their Step (A.1) of instance r_1. Each honest archiver that completes Step (A.1) did not archive any new suggestion in any instance r'' where $r' < r'' < r_1$ holds, because r_1 is the first such instance. Moreover, the archiver will not archive such a suggestion in the future, since all such instances r'' aborted before sending **select** messages in Step (A.1) of instance r_1.

In Step (A.1), an archiver sends the last suggestion it archived. Some archivers may send suggestions they archived prior to instance r' while other archivers send suggestions they archived in Step (A.5) of instance r'. Each honest selector j awaits a set of messages L_j from a maximal-wait set in Step (S.1). L_j contains suggestions from a quorum Q^{r_1} consisting entirely of honest archivers (by the opaqueness property of $\mathcal{A}$). By the consistency property of $\mathcal{A}$, the intersection of Q^{r_1} and $Q^{r'}$ contains a guarded set, and thus Q^{r_1} contains suggestions from a guarded set of honest archivers that archived (r', w). There cannot be such a set of suggestions for a later instance, prior to r_1. By Corollary 1 and Lemma 2, there cannot be any suggestions from a guarded set for a different proposal in instance r'. Thus, each honest selector will select a non-$\perp$ proposal and those proposals are identical. By Lemma 3, every honest archiver that completes Step (A.4) will archive the same suggestion. Thus the proof holds for r_1.

Now assume that the claim holds for all instances r'' where $r' < r'' < r$ holds; we will prove the claim for instance r. There is an honest archiver that completes Step (A.4) in instance r and archives (r, w). Following Step (A.2) of instance r, it must have received **archive** messages from a maximal-wait set of selectors. Each honest selector that sent such a message received **select** messages from a maximal-wait set of archivers in Step (S.1) of instance r.

Each honest archiver sends the last suggestion it archived. Some honest archivers might send suggestions they archived prior to instance r', while other honest archivers send suggestions archived in Step (A.4) of instance r'', where $r' \leq r'' < r$ holds. By the induction hypothesis, all honest archivers that send a suggestion archived by an instance ordered after instance r' use proposal w in their suggestions.

In instance r, each honest selector j awaits a set of messages L_j from a maximal-wait set in Step (S.1). L_j has to contain suggestions from a quorum Q^r consisting entirely of honest archivers (by the opaqueness property of $\mathcal{A}$). By the consistency property of $\mathcal{A}$, the intersection of Q^r and $Q^{r'}$ contains a guarded set, so Q^r has to contain suggestions from a guarded set of honest archivers that archived (r', w) in instance r' and that might have archived (r'', w) in some later instance. Therefore, selector j obtains w as a possible potential-proposal. Since all honest archivers that archive a suggestion past instance r' archive the same proposal, there is a support-set for w with associated-instance-identifier $\bar{r} \geq r'$.

There cannot be any other possible potential-proposal with an associated-instance-identifier ordered larger than r' since, by induction, no honest archiver archives a suggestion with a different proposal later than r'. Therefore, each honest selector selects proposal w. By Lemma 3, every honest archiver that completes Step (A.4) archives the same suggestion. Thus, the proof holds for r.

Theorem 1 (Agreement). *If two honest deciders decide, then they decide the same proposal.*

Proof. If the deciders decide in the same instance, the result follows from Lemma 1. Say one decider decides v' in instance r', and another decider decides v in instance r, with $r' < r$. By Lemma 4, all honest archivers that archive in instance r archive (r, v'). By the consistency property of $\mathcal{A}$, an honest decider can only decide (r, v') in instance r, so $v = v'$.

5   Full Protocols

The skeletal algorithm described above does not specify how instances are created, how broadcasts are done in steps (A.1), (S.4), and (A.5), what specific extended quorum systems to use for $\mathcal{A}$ and $\mathcal{S}^r$, how a selector j obtains proposals for P_j, or how j selects a proposal from P_j. We now show how Paxos [6], the algorithm by Chandra and Toueg [7], and the early protocol by Michael Ben-Or [8] resolve these questions.

5.1   Paxos

Paxos [6] was originally designed only for honest systems. In Paxos, any node can create an instance r at any time, and that node becomes the *leader* of the instance. The leader creates a unique instance-identifier r from its node identifier along with a sequence number per node that is incremented for each new instance created on that node. The leader runs both a proposer and a selector. $\mathcal{S}^r$ is a leader extended quorum system consisting only of that selector.

The leader starts the instance by broadcasting a `prepare` message containing the instance identifier to all archivers. Upon receipt, an archiver i checks that $r > r_i$, and, if so, sets r_i to r and proceeds with Step (A.1). Since there is only one participant in $\mathcal{S}_r$, the broadcast in (A.1) is actually a point-to-point message back to the leader, now acting as selector. In Step (S.3), if the leader has to pick a proposal from P_j, it selects the proposal by the local proposer. Thus, there is no need for proposers to send their proposals to all selectors.

Unanimity and **Validity** follow directly from the absence of Byzantine participants. To support **Non-Blocking**, Paxos has to assume that there is always at least one correct node that can become a leader and create a new instance. Consider a state in which some correct decider has not yet decided. Now consider the following continuation of the run: one of the correct nodes creates a new instance with an instance identifier higher than used before. Because there are always correct nodes and there is an infinite number of instance identifiers, this is always possible. The node sends a `prepare` message to all archivers. All honest archivers start in Step (A.1) of the instance on receipt, so the selector at the leader will receive enough `select` messages in Step (S.1) to continue. Due to Lemma 3 and there being only one selector in $\mathcal{S}^r$, all honest archivers archive the same suggestion in Step (A.4). The deciders will each receive a unanimous suggestion from a quorum of archivers in Step (D.1) and decide in Step (D.3).

5.2   Chandra-Toueg

The Chandra-Toueg algorithm [7] is another consensus protocol designed for honest systems. It requires a coordinator in each instance; the role of the coordinator is similar to the leader in Paxos. Unlike Paxos, Chandra-Toueg instances are consecutively numbered $0, 1, \dots$. The coordinator of each instance is determined by the instance number modulo the number of nodes in the system, so the role of the coordinator shifts from node to node at the end of each instance. Each node in the system is both a proposer and a archiver. For each instance r, selector quorum $\mathcal{S}^r$ is the extended quorum consisting only of the coordinator of that instance.

To start the protocol, a proposer sends a message containing a proposal to all nodes. Upon receiving the first proposal, an archiver starts in instance 0 and executes (A.1). The coordinator of each instance starts (S.1) upon receiving a `select` message for that instance. In (S.3), $P_i.pick(r)$ returns the first proposal received by the coordinator. Archivers that successfully complete (A.2-5) move to the next instance. Archivers must be prepared to time-out while awaiting an `archive` message from the selector of a particular instance, because the selector can fail. When this happens, archivers proceed to (A.1) in the next instance. When an archiver receives an `archive` message with a larger instance number than it has thus far received, it aborts the current instance and skips forward to the instance identified in the `archive` message.

In the original description of the Chandra-Toueg algorithm, the coordinator for an instance is the only decider for that instance. This necessitates an additional round of communication, where the coordinator broadcasts a decision so that all nodes become aware of the decision. The Chandra-Toueg algorithm can be changed so that all nodes are deciders in all instances without affecting the rest of the protocol. This eliminates one round of communication while increasing the number of messages sent in (A.5) of the skeletal algorithm. This is similar to the algorithm proposed in [13]. A comparison of the original Chandra-Toueg algorithm and this modified version is given in [14].

As in the case of Paxos, **Unanimity** and **Validity** follow directly from the absence of Byzantine participants. **Non-blocking** follows from that fact that a honest, correct selector can always receive sufficient `select` messages in (S.1) to continue. All honest archivers will always receive the same suggestion in (A.3), since there is only one selector in each instance. If the coordinator for an instance fails, then archivers for that instance will time-out and move to the next instance.

5.3 Ben-Or

In this early protocol [8], each node runs a proposer, a selector, an archiver, and a decider. Instances are numbered with consecutive integers. Proposals are either "0" or "1" (that is, this is a binary consensus protocol), and each $P_i = \{0, 1\}$. $P_i.pick(r)$ selects the local proposer's proposal for the first instance, or a random one in later instances.

Each of the selectors, archivers, and deciders starts in instance 1 and loops. The loop at selector j consists of steps (S.1) through (S.4), with r_j incremented right after Step (S.4). The loop at archiver i consists of steps (A.1-5), with r_i incremented after Step (A.4). The broadcasts in steps (A.1) and (A.5) are to the same destination nodes and happen in consecutive steps, so they can be merged into a single broadcast, resulting in just two broadcasts per instance. Finally, the loop at decider k consists of steps (D.1) through (D.3), with r_k incremented after Step (D.3).

S^r is the same extended quorum system as $\mathcal{A}$ for every instance r; both consist of all nodes and use a threshold quorum system. Ben-Or works equally well in honest and Byzantine environments as long as opaqueness is satisfied. It is easily shown that if a decider decides, then all other deciders decide either in the same or the next instance.

Unanimity follows from the rule that selectors select the locally proposed proposal in the first instance: if all selectors select the same proposal v, then by Lemma 3 the archivers archive v, and, by opaqueness of $\mathcal{A}$, the deciders decide v. **Validity** is ensured by the rule that selectors pick the local proposal in the first instance and random proposals in subsequent instances. Selectors have to pick random proposals in an instance iff there was not a unanimous suggestion computed in (A.3) of the previous instance. This can only happen if both of the binary proposals have been proposed by some proposer. **Non-Blocking** follows from the rule that honest selectors pick their proposals at random in all but the first instance, so it is always possible that they pick the same proposal, after which a decision in Step (D.3) is guaranteed because of opaqueness for $\mathcal{A}$.

6   Implementation and Evaluation

The descriptions of the Paxos, Chandra-Toueg, and Ben-Or protocols above show that these protocols share common building blocks. Having observed their similarities, we now investigate how their differences affect their performance. To do this, we implemented the skeletal algorithm, and built each of the three protocols using different configurations of the algorithm. In this section, we present the implementation and the performance of the three instantiations.

6.1   Implementation

We built a simple replicated logging service, consisting of a set of servers that use *epochs* of consensus to agree on the sequence of values to add to the log. Clients submit values to any server; that server then attempts to have that value decided in the current epoch by proposing that value. When a value is decided in an epoch, the client that submitted the value is informed of the epoch number in which the value was decided, and servers move to the next epoch. Each server maintains an internal queue of values it has received from clients but that are not yet decided, and attempts to get the values decided in FIFO order.

Paxos requires a leader election mechanism that was not described in the original protocol [6]. We explored two different leader election mechanisms. First, we built a version of Paxos where each node that wants to propose a value simply makes itself the leader. By having each node pick instance numbers for instances where it is the leader from a disjoint set of instance numbers, we ensure that each instance can only have one unique leader. We call this version of Paxos *GreedyPaxos*.

We also built a variant of Paxos that uses a token-passing mechanism to determine the leader. We call this version of Paxos *TokenPaxos*. The current leader holds a token that is passed to other nodes when the leader no longer has any local requests to commit. Token request and token passing messages are piggy-backed on **select** and **archive** messages. Further details of this protocol are outside the scope of this paper.

For the implementation of Chandra-Toueg, we modified the original algorithm to have all nodes be deciders in all instances. As described in Section 5.2, this avoids requiring deciders to broadcast a decision when a value is decided, thus improving the performance of our particular application where all servers need to learn about decisions.

All of our implementations use a simple threshold quorum system for the archiver and decider quorums, as well as for Ben-Or's selector quorums.

6.2   Experimental Setup

We evaluate the protocols using simulation. In our experiments, the logging service consists of a set of 10 servers. 10 clients generate the workload. Each client sends requests to the servers according to a Poisson distribution with a mean λ_c requests per minute. Each client chooses a server at random and sends

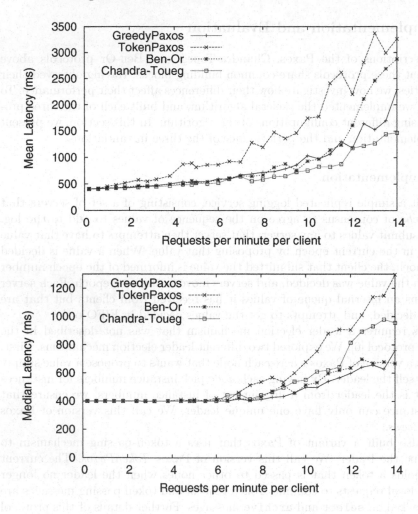

Fig. 2. Mean time (left) and median time (right) to decide under varying request rates

its requests to that server. All client to server and server to server messages have a latency that is given by a lognormal distribution with mean 100 ms and standard deviation 20 ms. For each set of experiments, we measure the elapsed time between when a server first receives a value from a client until the time that the server learns the value has been decided.

6.3   Results

In the first set of experiments, we run the service with varying loads until 100 values are decided by the logging service. We vary the request rate λ_c from each client from 0.5 requests per minute to 14 requests per minute. We report the mean and median values of 100 decisions averaged over 8 runs of each experiment.

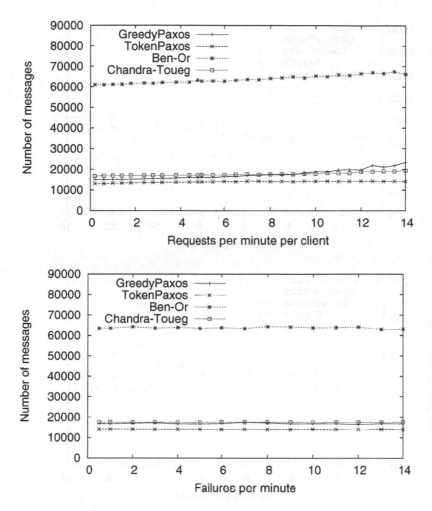

Fig. 3. Communication overhead under varying request rates (left) and failure rates (right)

Figure 2 shows the mean and the median latency for a single value to be decided. The graphs show that as load increases, the time it takes for a value to be decided increases gradually. At low loads, the performance of all four algorithms is quite close. This is because in the ideal case, all four algorithms take four rounds of communication for a value to be decided.

As load increases, performance degrades, because of contention between servers trying to commit different values. GreedyPaxos consistently outperforms TokenPaxos latency, particularly under heavy load. This is because selectors in GreedyPaxos do not need to wait for the token before creating a new instance. Under heavy load, each GreedyPaxos leader sends a `prepare` message in the beginning of each epoch without having to wait. The leader with the largest instance number wins and gets its value decided. TokenPaxos, on the other hand,

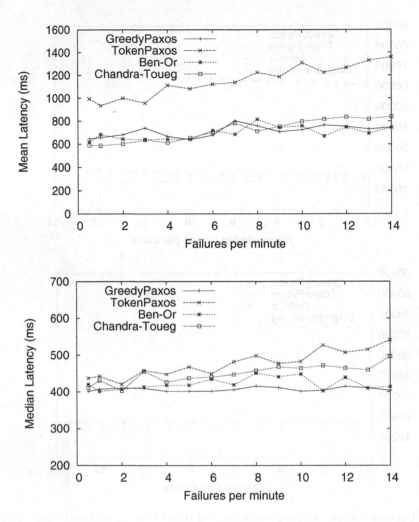

Fig. 4. Mean time (left) and median time (right) to decide under varying failure rates

will always decide values of the node with the token before passing the token to the next node with requests. This has two implications: i) if the leader keeps getting new requests, other nodes can starve, and ii) one round of communication overhead is incurred for passing the token.

The left graph in Figure 3 shows the number of messages that each protocol uses to commit 100 values under different request rates. Ben-Or incurs a larger overhead than the other protocols. This is because Ben-Or uses a selector quorum that consists of all nodes rather than just a leader/coordinator, so (A.1) and (S.4) of the skeletal algorithm send n^2 messages in each instance, rather than just n messages in Paxos and Chandra-Toueg.

Also observe that compared to TokenPaxos, GreedyPaxos sends more messages as load increases. Under heavy load, each GreedyPaxos node broadcasts a prepare message to all other nodes in the beginning of every round. This results in n^2 messages being sent rather than the n prepare messages that are sent in the case of TokenPaxos.

Next we investigate the performance of each protocol under crash failures. We model failure event occurrences as a Poisson distributed rate of λ_f failures per minute. When a failure event occurred, we failed a random server until the end of the epoch. To ensure that the system is able to make progress, we limit the number of failures in an epoch to be less than half the number of servers in the system in order to satisfy the threshold assumption of the quorum systems that we use. Keeping the request rate from clients steady at 7 requests per minute per client, we vary the failure rate from 0.5 failures per minute to 12 failures per minute.

Figure 4 shows the mean and median decision latency for the four protocols under varying failure rates. Note that GreedyPaxos and Ben-Or are not affected significantly by server failures. Chandra-Toueg and TokenPaxos, on the other hand, see significant performance degradation as the failure rate increases. This is because Chandra-Toueg and TokenPaxos both depend on time-out to recover from failures of particular nodes. In the case of Chandra-Toueg, failure of the coordinator requires that all archivers time-out and move to the next instance; in the case of TokenPaxos, if the node that is holding the token crashes, then a time-out is required to generate a new token.

A comparison study presented by Hayabashibara et al. [15] found that Paxos outperforms Chandra-Toueg under crash failures. We find that this result depends on the leader election protocol used by Paxos. In our experiments, Greedy-Paxos outperforms Chandra-Toueg, but TokenPaxos performs worse under certain failure scenarios.

The right graph in Figure 3 shows the message overhead of each protocol under varying failure rates, clearly showing that the number of messages sent is not significantly affected by failures.

7   Conclusion

We investigated several well-known consensus protocols and showed that they share the same basic building blocks. We used the building blocks to develop a skeletal algorithm that can be instantiated to obtain Paxos, Chandra-Toueg, and Ben-Or consensus protocols simply by configuring the quorum systems that are used, the way instances are started, and other protocol-specific details. We implemented the skeletal algorithm and used it to instantiate Ben-Or, Chandra-Toueg, and two variants of the Paxos algorithm. Simulation experiments using those implementations allowed the performance differences between these algorithms to be measured for different workloads and crash failures. This approach thus provides a basis for understanding consensus protocols and comparing their performance. The skeletal algorithm also provides a novel platform for exploring other possible consensus protocols.

References

1. Pease, M., Shostak, R., Lamport, L.: Reaching agreement in the presence of faults. J. ACM 27(2), 228–234 (1980)
2. Barborak, M., Malek, M.: The consensus problem in fault-tolerant computing. ACM Computing Surveys 25(2) (1993)
3. Fischer, M., Lynch, N., Patterson, M.: Impossibility of distributed consensus with one faulty process. J. ACM 32(2), 374–382 (1985)
4. Guerraoui, R., Raynal, M.: The information structure of indulgent consensus. In: Proc. of 23rd IEEE International Conference on Distributed Computing Systems (2003)
5. Guerraoui, R., Raynel, M.: The alpha of indulgent consensus. The Computer Journal (2006)
6. Lamport, L.: The part-time parliament. Trans. on Computer Systems 16(2), 133–169 (1998)
7. Chandra, T., Toueg, S.: Unreliable failure detectors for reliable distributed systems. J. ACM 43(2), 225–267 (1996)
8. Ben-Or, M.: Another advantage of free choice: Completely asynchronous agreement protocols. In: ACM SIGOPS-SIGACT. Proc. of the 2nd ACM Symp. on Principles of Distributed Computing, Montreal, Quebec, pp. 27–30 (August 1983)
9. Lamport, L., Shostak, R., Pease, M.: The Byzantine generals problem. Trans. on Programming Languages and Systems 4(3), 382–401 (1982)
10. Malkhi, D., Reiter, M.: Byzantine Quorum Systems. Distributed Computing 11, 203–213 (1998)
11. Naor, M., Wool, A.: The load, capacity, and availability of quorum systems. SIAM Journal on Computing 27(2), 423–447 (1998)
12. Song, Y.J., van Renesse, R., Schneider, F.B., Dolev, D.: Evolution vs. intelligent design in consensus protocols. Technical Report CUL.CIS/TR2007-2082, Cornell University (May 2007)
13. Mostéfaoui, A., Raynal, M.: Solving consensus using Chandra-Toueg's unreliable failure detectors: A general quorum-based approach. In: Proc. of the International Symposium on Distributed Computing, pp. 49–63 (1999)
14. Urbán, P., Schiper, A.: Comparing distributed consensus algorithms. In: Proc. of International Conference on Applied Simulation and Modelling, pp. 474–480 (2004)
15. Hayashibara, N., Urbán, P., Schiper, A., Katayama, T.: Performance comparison between the Paxos and Chandra-Toueg consensus algorithms. In: Proc. of International Arab Conference on Information Technology, Doha, Qatar, pp. 526–533 (December 2002)

Continuous Consensus with Ambiguous Failures

Tal Mizrahi and Yoram Moses

Department of Electrical Engineering, Technion, Haifa, 32000 Israel
deweastern@yahoo.com, moses@ee.technion.ac.il

Abstract. *Continuous consensus* (CC) is the problem of maintaining an identical and up-to-date core of information about the past at all correct processes in the system [1]. This is a primitive that supports simultaneous coordination among processes, and eliminates the need of issuing separate instances of consensus for different tasks. Recent work has presented new simple and efficient *optimum* protocols for continuous consensus in the crash and (sending) omissions failure models. For every pattern of failures, these protocols maintain at each and every time point a core that subsumes that maintained by any other continuous consensus protocol. This paper considers the continuous consensus problem in the face of harsher failures: general omissions and authenticated Byzantine failures. Computationally efficient optimum protocols for CC do not exist in these models if $P \neq NP$. A variety of CC protocols are presented. The first is a simple protocol that enters every interesting event into the core within $t + 1$ rounds (where t is the bound on the number of failures), provided there are a majority of correct processes. The second is a protocol that achieves similar performance so long as $n > t$ (i.e., there is always guaranteed to be at least one correct process). The final protocol in the general omissions model makes use of active failure monitoring and failure detection to include events in the core much faster in many runs of interest. Its performance is established based on a nontrivial property of minimal vertex covers in undirected graphs. The results are adapted to the authenticated Byzantine failure model, in which it is assumed that faulty processes are malicious, but correct processes have unforgeable signatures. Finally, the problem of *uniform* CC is considered. It is shown that a straightforward version of uniform CC is not solvable in the setting under study. A weaker form of uniform CC is defined, and protocols achieving it are presented.

Keywords: Distributed computing, fault tolerance, consensus, continuous consensus.

1 Introduction

Fault-tolerant systems often require a means by which independent processes or processors can arrive at an exact mutual agreement of some kind. As a result, reaching consensus is one of the most fundamental problems in fault-tolerant distributed computing, dating back to the seminal work of Pease, Shostak, and Lamport [2]. When the independent processes need to reach compatible decisions *at the same time*, they often need to reach *simultaneous consensus* about particular aspects of the execution. While early protocols in the synchronous model achieved consensus at the same round

S. Rao et al. (Eds.): ICDCN 2008, LNCS 4904, pp. 73–85, 2008.

(e.g. [2]), it was noticed by Dolev et al. [3] that non-simultaneous solutions are sometimes advantageous. Later work showed that simultaneous consensus required *common knowledge* and this is a nontrivial requirement [4]. Nevertheless, the need for simultaneous decisions to be compatible is very natural in many cases: E.g., when different processes need to access distinct physical resources 'at the same time, or when one distributed algorithm ends and another one begins, and the two use similar message texts for different purposes.

We consider a synchronous message-passing system in which processes receive external inputs from the outside world at various times. Suppose that we are interested in maintaining a simultaneously consistent view regarding a set of events $\mathcal{E}$ in the system. The particular events that would be of interest is application-dependent, but it will typically record events such as inputs that processes receive at various times, values that certain variables obtain at given times, and faulty behavior in the form of failed or inconsistent message deliveries. A continuous consensus (CC) protocol maintains at all times $k \geq 0$ a *core* $M_i[k]$ of events of $\mathcal{E}$ at every site i. In every run of this protocol the following properties are required to hold, for all nonfaulty processes i and j.

Accuracy: All events in $M_i[k]$ occurred in the run.
Consistency: $M_i[k] = M_j[k]$ at all times k.
Completeness: If the occurrence of an event $e \in \mathcal{E}$ is known to process j at any point, then $e \in M_i[k]$ must hold at some time k.

Decisions performed by different correct processes in the same round can be chosen in a consistent manner if they are based on the core of a CC protocol. Indeed, once an event recording a particular value or vote enters the core, the processes automatically have simultaneous consensus regarding it. Finally, a CC protocol can replace the need for initiating separate instances of a consensus protocol. By monitoring different events in $\mathcal{E}$, the protocol can automatically ensure consensus on a variety of issues.

The continuous consensus problem was introduced in [1], where it was studied in the crash and sending omissions failure models. This generalized and simplified the earlier related work in [5]. The main results of [1] are simple and efficient optimum CC protocols for both crash and sending omissions failures, in the synchronous message-passing model and assuming an upper bound of $t < n - 1$ on the total number of failures. The core provided by their protocol at time k given a particular behavior of the adversary is the union of *all* the cores provided by *all* correct CC protocols under the same adversarial conditions.

In this paper we extend the study of the continuous consensus problem to more problematic failure models: General omissions and Authenticated Byzantine failures. In the former, a faulty process may fail to send a subset of the messages prescribed by its protocol, *as well as* failing to receive a subset of the messages sent to it in a given round. In the authenticated Byzantine failure model, faulty processes are malicious, but correct processes have unforgeable signatures. This ability to sign messages implies that correct processes cannot be misquoted about messages that contain their signatures. As a result, the two failure models are actually quite similar. One property that they share is the fact that when a process i reports not having received a message that another process j was supposed to have sent it, this is proof that one of them is faulty. But this proof is ambiguous regarding which one of them is the culprit. This is in contrast to the situation in the crash and sending omissions models. In those models, an unreceived message provides unambiguous proof that the intended sender is faulty. This distinction turns out to have significant implications on the efficiency of solutions to the continuous consensus problem. While the optimum protocols in [1] for the simpler failure models can be implemented using linear-time computations and $O(n)$-bit messages, we adapt a result of [5] to show:

Lemma 1. *If $P \neq NP$ then there exists no polynomial-time protocol implementing an optimum solution to continuous consensus in the general omission (resp. in the authenticated Byzantine) failure model.*

This result is not detrimental, since optimum solutions are rare in general. For eventual consensus, for example, it has been shown in [5] that no optimum protocol exists at all, even in the crash failure model. Moreover, searching for continuous consensus protocols that are not optimum is still quite subtle in the presence of failures. Finding relatively efficient ones (and proving their correctness) turns out to be a nontrivial task.

The further contributions of this paper are:

- We present a simple CC protocol that enters every interesting event into the core within $t + 1$ rounds (where t is the bound on the number of failures), provided there are a majority of correct processes (i.e., $n > 2t$).
- We improve this protocol to one that achieves similar performance so long as $n > t$ (i.e., there is always guaranteed to be at least one correct process).
- Finally, we use fault monitoring and failure detection to obtain a protocol that in many runs will include events in the core within much fewer than $t + 1$ rounds of their discovery by a correct process. This protocol (called VC-CC) is based on the construction of a conflict graph [5,6,7] and an analysis of failures in such a graph. Intuitively, this is a graph whose nodes are process names, and where an edge appears if there is an inconsistency between the two nodes implying that at least one of them must be faulty. The faulty processes must at all times form a vertex cover of the (edges of the) conflict graph. The correctness of the VC-CC protocol depends on a nontrivial graph-theoretical result that shows the following: If the size of the minimal vertex cover of a graph is b, then the size of the union of all minimal vertex covers of G is at most $2b$ (see Appendix C).

    To this end, we present two types of protocols. One type consists of computationally efficient protocols that have good behavior in the best case, and more theoretical protocols that make use of an NP oracle and produce good performance much more often.
- We then turn to consider the problem of obtaining uniform solutions to CC. In the simpler crash and sending omission failure models [1], the basic optimum protocol is enhanced to yield an optimum solution for uniform CC. The resulting protocol guarantees that all processes—both faulty and nonfaulty—have the same core at all times. Moreover, the core contains exactly what it would under the optimal (non-uniform) protocol. In the general omission and the authenticated Byzantine models, solutions to CC in which all processes have the same core are shown to be impossible. Essentially, if a faulty process might be blocked from receiving any messages for arbitrarily long periods, then there is no way to ensure that it will

maintain a growing core with useful and up-to-date information. We define weaker notion of uniformity that requires the cores of the faulty processes to always be a subset of those of the nonfaulty ones, and show that this version is attainable.

2   Continuous Consensus in the Generalized Omission Model

Using Authentication

Our analysis of the CC problem in the generalized omission model uses an authentication scheme. Pease, Shostak and Lamport [2] presented an algorithm that reaches agreement in a fault-prone system using authentication. Since the generalized omissions model is in fact a simplified private case of the authenticated Byzantine model, this analysis is valid in the generalized omissions model as well. Thus, our algorithms in this section are presented for the authenticated Byzantine model.

We assume that all messages sent in the system are authenticated by unforgeable signatures that enable processes to verify the source of the information they send and receive. Since there are no "liars" in the generalized model, a process may sign a message by simply adding its name to the message. In the authenticated Byzantine model, it is assumed that the signatures are unforgeable despite the fact that some of the processes may be "liars", and thus the signatures are also used to verify the reliability of the information.[1]

Adding signatures to the data sent in the system enables each process to keep track of the knowledge of other processes. When a process receives a piece of information, it can deduce about which processes have received and signed this piece of information by observing the signatures added to this information by other processes.

Notation

We now present some terminology and definitions referring to the usage of authentication in our system. Similar to the notation in [1], our logical language consists of propositions referring to a set of monitored events in our system. For simplicity, we identify the set of monitored events $\mathcal{E}$ with a subset $\Phi_{\mathcal{E}} \subseteq \Phi$, and restrict monitored events to depend only on the external inputs in the current run.

Define $\text{SENT}_i(k)$ as the message that process i sends in round k to each of the other processes. We assume that each message is a sequence of atomic messages called *datagrams*. A datagram is either a proposition, $\varphi \in \Phi_{\mathcal{E}}$, or a *signed* proposition. A signed proposition consists of a proposition and a list of process signatures. Denote by Ψ as the set of all possible datagrams in the system. Clearly, $\Phi_{\mathcal{E}} \subset \Psi$. We also define the operation $sign_i : \Psi \to \Psi$ for a process i, so that if $\alpha \in \Psi$ then $sign_i(\alpha)$ is a datagram containing the information in α signed by process i. Notice that Ψ is defined inductively with primitive elements $\Phi_{\mathcal{E}}$, and is closed under the operations $sign_i(\cdot)$ for all $i \in \mathbb{P}$. In a given run, we denote by $\text{RCVD}_i(k)$ the set of datagrams received by i in round k.

---

[1] In practice, by having a public-key infrastructure in our system, one may produce cryptographic signatures which are unforgeable with a very high degree of probability.

Let α be a datagram such that $\alpha = sign_{p_d}(\ldots sign_{p_2}(sign_{p_1}(\varphi)))$ with $d \geq 1$. If $p_1, \ldots, p_d$ are pairwise distinct processes, then α is a d-*signed* datagram, and φ is d-*authenticated* by α. We further define a function $\mathcal{F} : \Psi \rightarrow \Phi_{\mathcal{E}}$. Intuitively, $\mathcal{F}(\alpha)$ is the proposition embedded in the datagram α. Formally, for every datagram α, we have $\mathcal{F}(\alpha) = \varphi$ if there exists a sequence of processes (not necessarily distinct), $\langle p_1, \ldots, p_s \rangle$, such that $\alpha = sign_{p_s}(\ldots sign_{p_2}(sign_{p_1}(\varphi)))$.

A CC Protocol with Authentication

In this subsection we present two protocols that solve the continuous consensus problem in the generalized omissions model using Authentication.

In Figure 1 we present the first protocol, ACC (which stands for *Authenticated Continuous Consensus*). Each process i runs the protocol individually, and computes a *core* $M_i[k]$ in every round k. The core is guaranteed to be shared among the nonfaulty processes. Process i places a proposition φ in its core when it receives a $(t+1)$-*signed* datagram, α, such that $\mathcal{F}(\alpha) = \varphi$. Every process sends and receives messages according to a protocol we call SFIP, which is a full-information protocol in which signatures are used to authenticate every piece of information delivered in the system. In SFIP every process broadcasts its information adding its signature to it. More formally, an SFIP is a protocol with the following properties:

– An SFIP is, in particular, a FIP, i.e., in every round, every process sends a message encoding all of its information to all other processes.
– Every primitive proposition $p \in \Phi_{\mathcal{E}}$, sent by process i is signed by i.
– In every round k, each process i relays all datagrams received in the previous round, adding its own signature to every datagram.

ACC(i)
    $M_i[k] \leftarrow \emptyset$ for all $k \geq -1$
    for $k \geq 0$ in round k
        do
1   send and receive messages according to SFIP
2   for $\alpha \in \text{RCVD}_i(k)$
3   if α is a $(t+1)$-*signed* datagram then
4            $M_i[k] \leftarrow M_i[k] \cup \mathcal{F}(\alpha)$
5   end for
6        $M_i[k] \leftarrow M_i[k-1] \cup M_i[k]$
    end for

Fig. 1. The ACC protocol for process i

Intuitively, once a process receives a sequence of $t+1$ signatures for φ, it is guaranteed that at least one nonfaulty process has received information about φ, and has forwarded it to all nonfaulty processes. These, in turn, are able to sign and forward the datagram. Thus, as stated in Lemma 2, all nonfaulty processes will add φ to their cores simultaneously.

Lemma 2. *Let R be a system with $n > 2t$. Then* ACC *solves the continuous consensus problem in R.*

In Figure 2 we present ACCD, which is a slight variant of ACC. In ACCD, for every datagram φ that i receives, it computes the round in which φ is expected to become a $(t+1)$-*authenticated* proposition. In a way, this is a bit similar to the concept of *horizon* presented in [1]: in each round of the CONCON protocol presented there every process i tries to compute a *horizon* based on the number of processes known to be faulty. The idea in ACCD also uses a "horizon," which is defined and computed differently. While in CONCON the core is uniquely determined by a *critical time* and a *critical set*, our approach in ACCD is different; The "horizon" is computed for *each* proposition individually, and thus the core cannot be represented by a particular critical time.

ACCD(i)

> $M_i[k] \leftarrow \emptyset$ for all $k \geq -1$
>   **for** $k \geq 0$ in round k
>>   **do**
>
> 1   send and receive messages according to SFIP
> 2   **for** $\alpha \in \text{RCVD}_i(k)$
> 3   **if** α is a d-*signed* datagram for some $1 \leq d \leq t+1$ **then**
> 4 $M_i[k+(t+1)-d] \leftarrow M_i[k+(t+1)-d] \cup \mathcal{F}(\alpha)$
> 5   **end for**
> 6 $M_i[k] \leftarrow M_i[k-1] \cup M_i[k]$
>   **end for**

Fig. 2. The ACCD protocol for process i

Lemma 3. *Let R be a system with $n > t$. Then* ACCD *solves the continuous consensus problem in R.*

Discussion of ACC and ACCD

Lower Bound on n. Notice that while ACC requires $n > 2t$, ACCD requires just $n > t$. The reason we require $n > 2t$ for ACC is that a proposition is included in the core once it is signed by $t+1$ signatures. Thus, as the proof of Lemma 2 shows, once a proposition reaches a nonfaulty process, it is forwarded sequentially to other non-faulty processes, and within at most $t+1$ rounds it is bound to become a $(t+1)$-*authenticated* proposition. Specifically, an event that occurs at a nonfaulty process i, must be forwarded through a sequence of t different nonfaulty processes in order for it to be included in the core. It must therefore by assumed that there are at least $t+1$ nonfaulty processes. ACCD, on the other hand, does not require $n > 2t$, since if a d-*signed* datagram α reaches a nonfaulty process at time m, it forwards the datagram to all nonfaulty processes in round $m+1$, enabling them to include $\mathcal{F}(\alpha)$ in the core at $m+(t+1)-d$.

More efficient implementations of SFIP. We previously defined a full-information protocol with signatures, SFIP, as a protocol similar to FIP except that it authenticates all messages using signatures. While it has been shown in [1] that a FIP in our context may be implemented quite efficiently, a first glance at SFIP shows that the overhead added by the authentication mechanism may by quite high. Since every datagram in SFIP is relayed by every process i, adding its own signature, it is easy to see that if a primitive proposition p is sent by some process i at time 0, then the number of datagrams regarding p in round k is $O(n^k)$. If every signature has length sl, and every datagram has $O(k)$ signatures, then a message regarding p requires a length of $O(sl \cdot k \cdot n^k)$. Since we have n such messages in round k, we obtain communication complexity of $O(sl \cdot k \cdot n \cdot n^k)$ of signatures regarding every proposition p in every round. It is possible, though, to derive a more efficient implementation of SFIP, by applying the following techniques:

(i) **Avoid multiple instances:** In order to avoid multiple datagrams for every proposition, we can have each process i, relay at most one datagram corresponding to every primitive proposition, p, in every round. In particular, for every such p, process i chooses a datagram corresponding to p with the maximal number of signatures. In addition, i completely ignores datagrams which already include i's signature, since they have already been sent by i. Avoiding multiple instances of the same proposition helps reduce the communication complexity of signatures regarding p to $O(n^2)$ in every round.

(ii) **Early stopping:** Since in ACC we are not interested in datagrams with more than $t+1$ signatures, once process i receives a $(t+1)$-*signed* datagram α, it stops sending any datagrams containing $\mathcal{F}(\alpha)$. This reduces the communication complexity of sending p to $O(n \cdot t)$ in every round. As for ACCD, once process i receives a message containing a datagram α, it relays the datagram just *once*. In all future rounds, process i ignores all datagrams β with $\mathcal{F}(\alpha) = \mathcal{F}(\beta)$, which reduces the communication complexity of signatures about p to $O(n)$.

(iii) **Nominating relay processes:** In ACC it is possible to nominate $2t+1$ processes to sign the data they send, while the rest of the processes follow the standard FIP. This allows for a communication complexity of $O(t^2)$, while still enabling the protocol to work correctly. Similarly, in ACCD we can nominate $t+1$ processes, reducing the comm. complexity to $O(t)$.

Uniformity. The uniform continuous consensus (UCC) problem was presented in [1]. UCC requires all processes, including the faulty ones, to have the same core at all times. It is an interesting observation that in the crash and omission models, the protocol ACC that we presented above solves UCC. Since in these models a faulty process is assumed to receive all messages sent to it, it is easy to verify that every faulty process receives a $(t+1)$-*signed* datagram α at the exact same time that the nonfaulty processes receive it, and can thus include α in its core. On the other hand, ACCD is not uniform, since its correctness depends on the process i running the protocol being nonfaulty; only a nonfaulty process may assume that a d-*signed* datagram is guaranteed to be relayed to all the nonfaulty processes, and become common knowledge in $t+1-d$ rounds.

In the generalized omissions model, however, we do not have uniformity for ACC, since a faulty process may fail to receive many or even all of the messages sent to it, keeping its core from growing as it should. Consequently, no protocol can guarantee both Completeness (which is defined for nonfaulty processes) and Uniform Consistency in the generalized omission model (see [1]). It is possible, however, to obtain a weaker variant of the Uniform Consistency property. Let j be a nonfaulty process, and let z be an arbitrary process, then:

Weak Uniform Consistency: $M_z[k] \subseteq M_j[k]$ at all times k.

We say that a protocol solves the *weak* UCC problem (WUCC for short), if it satisfies Accuracy, Consistency and Completeness, and in addition it also satisfies Accuracy for the cores of faulty processes and Weak Uniform Consistency, which is related to the cores of faulty and nonfaulty processes. It is easy to see that ACC solves the WUCC problem in the generalized omissions model.

3   CC in the Generalized Omission Model - Improved Protocols

In the previous section we presented ACCD and ACC. Both of these protocols solve the CC problem in the generalized model. However, in both of these protocols no event may be included in the core earlier than $t + 1$ rounds after it occurs. In this section we discuss different solutions to the CC problem, which provide a richer core, and enable some propositions to join the core earlier than they would in either of the two protocols above.

Similar to the protocols in the previous section, our protocol uses message authentication. The idea is that if in round k it is confirmed that a subset $S(k) \subset \mathbb{P}$ contains at least s faulty processes, then we know that $\overline{S}(k)$, the complement of $S(k)$, contains at most $t - s$ faulty processes, allowing us to add $(t - s + 1)$-*authenticated* propositions to the core.

The Conflict Graph

In [5] Moses and Tuttle prove that the problem of testing for common knowledge in the generalized omission model is NP-hard by showing a Turing reduction from the Vertex Cover problem to the problem of testing for common knowledge. It follows by their analysis that information about the number and identities of faulty processes can be obtained by a Vertex Cover computation, as we shall now describe.

Assume that at the end of every round k, process i constructs a graph, $G_i(k) = (V, E_i(k))$. V consists of n vertices, each labelled by a unique process name. $E_i(k)$ contains an edge $\{p_j, p_s\}$ i knows at the end of round k that at least one message between p_j and p_s has not been delivered successfully. $G_i(k)$ is called a *Conflict Graph*, since each of its edges stands for a conflict between its adjacent nodes: At most one of them is nonfaulty. It is thus easy to see that the nodes representing the processes which have displayed faulty behavior up to round k form a vertex cover of $G_i(k)$. It follows that if $G_i(k)$ has a *minimum* vertex cover of size s, then there must be at least s faulty processes in r. Our protocol, VC-CC is based on these properties of the conflict graph.

The analysis in this section uses the conflict graph to solve the CC problem. As we shall see, since the conflict graph represents information about potential failures in the

ACCI(i)

    $M_i[k] \leftarrow \emptyset, B_M[k] \leftarrow \emptyset$ for all $k \geq -1$

    for $k \geq 0$ in round k

        do

1   **repeat** iteratively until $B_M[k]$ stabilizes

2   send and receive messages according to SFIP

3   **for** $\alpha \in \mathrm{RCVD}_i(k)$

4   **if** α is $(t - |B_M[k]| + 1)$-*signed* by $\mathbb{P} \setminus B_M[k]$ **then**

5                  $M_i[k] \leftarrow M_i[k] \cup \mathcal{F}(\alpha)$

6   **end for**

7            $M_i[k] \leftarrow M_i[k-1] \cup M_i[k]$

8   **for** all $j \in \mathbb{P}$

9                $B_M[k] \leftarrow j$ if $M_i[k]$ implies that j is faulty

10   **end repeat**

    end for

Fig. 3. The ACCI protocol for process i in the generalized omission model

system, this information may be used to include some facts in the core earlier than they would in either ACC or ACCD.

A Simple Protocol Using the Conflict Graph

We first present a very simple protocol, which is an extension of ACC. The protocol is called ACCI (short for Improved ACC). The idea is that instead of defining the core as all $t + 1$-*signed* facts, we allow the information *in the core* to reduce this $t + 1$ round margin. For example, if the fact that process z is faulty is included in the core, then the fact that there are at most $t - 1$ faulty processes among $\mathbb{P} \setminus \{z\}$ is also in the core. Thus, receiving t signatures from processes in the set $\mathbb{P} \setminus \{z\}$ should be enough to include a fact in the core.

In ACCI, in every round, each process constructs a conflict graph according to the information in the core. We define $B_M[k]$ as the set of processes that are *confirmed* to be faulty according to information in $M_i[k]$. Specifically, once the conflict graph contains edges from a process z to at least $t + 1$ different processes, z is confirmed to be faulty, and thus $z \in B_M[k]$. More generally, if a process z has at least $t - B_M[k] + 1$ conflicts with processes from $\mathbb{P} \setminus B_M[k]$, then z must be faulty, and thus we can include z in $B_M[k]$. Notice that updating $B_M[k]$ may require iterative repetition of the steps above, until $B_M[k]$ stabilizes. It is important to note that ACCI has polynomial running time, since it requires counting the number of edges connected to each node, which requires polynomial computations.

VC-CC

We now present VC-CC. In each round, every process computes a *conflict graph*, $\mathcal{G}_i(k)$. It is essential that the conflict graphs constructed by all processes are the same in every round, since the computation of the core is based on the information in the conflict graph, $\mathcal{G}_i(k)$. Thus we require that $\mathcal{G}_i(k)$ is constructed by i according to $M_i[k-1]$,

VC-CC(i)

```
0   M_i[k] ← 0 for all k ≥ -1
    for k ≥ 1 in round k do
1       send and receive messages according to SFIP
2       M_i[k] ← M_i[k − 1]
3       ℓ ← 0
4       compute G_i^(ℓ)(k)
        repeat
5          for α ∈ RCVD_i(k)
6             if F(α) ∉ M_i[k] and AUTHENTICATEDVC(G_i^(ℓ)(k), α) then M_i[k] ← M_i[k] ∪ F(α)
7             ℓ ← ℓ + 1
8             compute G_i^(ℓ)(k)
9          until G_i^(ℓ)(k) = G_i^(ℓ−1)(k)
    end for
```

Fig. 4. The VC-CC protocol for process i in the generalized omission model

which guarantees a consistent conflict graph for all nonfaulty processes. The subroutine AUTHENTICATEDVC(G, α) (used on line 6 in the protocol) performs a test on α according to G, and returns TRUE if α is to be included in the core, and FALSE otherwise.

After updating the core $M_i[k]$ at time k (lines 5 and 6), a new conflict graph, $G_i(k)$ may now be constructed (line 8), based on recent information. Thus we iteratively update $M_i[k]$ according to $G_i^{(\ell)}(k)$, and construct $G_i^{(\ell)}(k)$ according to the recent computation of $M_i[k]$, until a fixed-point of $G_i^{(\ell)}(k)$ is reached (line 9).

The subroutine AUTHENTICATEDVC(G, α) performs a test on α according to G, the conflict graph. It returns TRUE if the conflict graph G and the signatures in α verify that $F(\alpha)$ should be included in the core.

Lemma 4. VC-CC *solves the Continuous Consensus problem for* $n > 3t$.

We will now briefly discuss the intuition behind the proof of Lemma 4. The challenging part of the proof is to show that VC-CC satisfies Consistency. There are three locations where the subroutine AUTHENTICATEDVC(G, α), returns TRUE, indicating that α should be included in the core. We consider each of these cases separately:

(i) α **is a** d-*signed* **datagram by a set of processes** D, **and it is guaranteed that at least one of the processes in** D **is nonfaulty** (lines 2 to 5 in the AUTHENTICATEDVC subroutine). For every α which is d-*signed* by a set of processes, D, we compute the min-VC of the set $\mathbb{P} \setminus D$. If the size of the min-VC is b, then the set D contains at most $t - b$ faulty processes, and thus any if $d > t - b$, then at least one nonfaulty process exists in D. In this case α is inserted into the core at $k+t+1-d$, i.e., to $M_i[k+t+1-d]$. Proving consistency for this case is the delicate part of the proof. It depends on the following graph-theoretical property:[2]

---

[2] As with all claims in this paper, the proof of Lemma 5 is deferred to the full paper.

Lemma 5. *If the size of the minimum vertex cover of an undirected graph is b, then the union of all its vertex covers has size 2b at most.*

(ii) α is $(t - c + 1)$-*signed* **by processes from** $\mathbb{P} \setminus C$ (lines 6 to 8 in the protocol). AUTHENTICATEDVC computes all vertex covers of G with at most t nodes. Let $v_1, \ldots, v_s$ be these VC's. Define $C \triangleq \bigcap_{j=1}^{m} v_j$, and $c \triangleq |C|$. The set C is the conjunction of all vertex covers of size t, and thus includes all nodes which are *guaranteed* to represent a faulty process. It follows that the set $\mathbb{P} \setminus C$ contains at most $t - c$ faulty processes, and thus $t - c + 1$ signatures are enough to authenticate a datagram and return TRUE.

(iii) α is $t + 1$-*signed* (lines 9 and 10).

We note that proving the consistency property in cases (ii) and (iii) above, is very similar to proving the consistency of ACC.

4 Byzantine Continuous Consensus

So far we discussed the generalized omission model. However, since we are using an authentication scheme, a natural extension to our analysis is to consider the authenticated Byzantine model. Our assumption in this model is that although faulty processes may be "liars," they can only lie about their own local states and inputs, and cannot alter any relayed information.

When analyzing the CC problem in the context of the authenticated Byzantine model, we find that satisfying the Accuracy property may prove a bit problematic: a faulty process, z, may falsely claim that an event e occurred, without any process ever realizing that z is faulty. In this case including e in the core would spoil its Accuracy. We solve this problem by modifying the sets of primitive propositions and monitored events, Φ and $\mathcal{E}(V)$, defined above. Let Φ^B be a set of primitive propositions of the form "process i claims that p" for $i \in \mathbb{P}$ and $p \in \Phi$. Similar to our definition in Section 2, we restrict our analysis to a set $\mathcal{E}^B$ of monitored events that is identified with $\Phi^B_{\mathcal{E}} \subseteq \Phi^B$, such that monitored events depend only on what processes *claim* about their inputs.

AUTHENTICATEDVC(G, α)

```
1   compute C and c according to G
2   if α is d-signed by a set of processes D such that d ≤ t then
3       G' ← G ↾ ℙ \ D
4       b ← size of min-VC of G'
5       if d ≥ t − b + 1 then return TRUE
6   h ← t − c
7   if α is signed by a sequence of processes, at least h + 1 of which are from P \ C then
8       return TRUE
9   if α is a t + 1-signed datagram then
10      return TRUE
11  return FALSE
```

Fig. 5. The AUTHENTICATEDVC procedure used in VC-CC

When using authentication, propositions from $\Phi_{\mathcal{E}}^B$ cannot be forged, since when a process receives a proposition $p \in \Phi_{\mathcal{E}}^B$, it may verify its signature. Thus, in this context the Accuracy property does not present a problem in the authenticated Byzantine model.

By restricting the core to the set $\mathcal{E}^B$ of monitored events, it is easy to verify that both the protocols shown in Section 2, as well as the ones shown in Section 3 provide a solution to the CC problem. The usage of authentication eliminates the possibility of forging *relayed* messages, while a message *produced* by a faulty process j regarding a proposition q is not considered a lie in our context, since it is indeed true that "j claims that q". Notice, however, that the core may still contain both "j claims that q" and "j claims that $\neg q$", provided that j is faulty. Such inconsistencies may be settled by protocols for Byzantine agreement that are beyond the scope of this work.

5 Conclusion

In this paper we discussed the continuous consensus problem in the generalized omission model. We presented two very simple protocols, ACC and ACCD, that solve the CC problem in this model by using an authentication. We showed that these protocols may be implemented quite efficiently. Whereas ACC requires $n > 2t$, we have shown that ACCD applies for $n > t$. In addition, we have shown that ACCD is early stopping, and that ACC, on the other hand, satisfies the *weak uniformity* property.

While ACC and ACCD both solve the CC problem in the crash and omission models, none of them is optimal. In both protocols it takes at least $t + 1$ rounds from the time that an event takes place until it is included in the core. As shown in [1], in the crash and in the sending omission models, some events may enter the core much sooner than this, by using a protocol called CONCON.

It was shown that by maintaining a *conflict graph* of the system, processes obtain information about failures in the run, which allows them to add facts to the core sooner than $t + 1$ rounds after their occurrence. We showed a very simple protocol called ACCI, which uses the conflict graph to identify a set of confirmed faulty processes, thus enabling processes to include in the core datagrams with less than $t + 1$ signatures.

Finally, we presented VC-CC, which, in addition to the techniques used by the previously described protocols, uses a subtle vertex-cover computation to obtain further information about failures in the system. While this solution produces a richer core, it is computationally problematic, since it requires computing the minimal vertex-cover, which is an NP-hard computation.

References

1. Mizrahi, T., Moses, Y.: Continuous consensus via common knowledge. Distributed Computing. In: The Proceedings of TARK X, pp. 236–252 (2005) (to appear, 2008)
2. Pease, M., Shostak, R., Lamport, L.: Reaching agreement in the presence of faults. Journal of the ACM 27(2), 228–234 (1980)
3. Dolev, D., Reischuk, R., Strong, H.R.: Eventual is earlier than immediate. In: Proc. 23rd IEEE Symp. on Foundations of Computer Science, pp. 196–203 (1982)

4. Dwork, C., Moses, Y.: Knowledge and common knowledge in a Byzantine environment: Crash failures. Information and Computation 88(2), 156–186 (1990)
5. Moses, Y., Tuttle, M.R.: Programming simultaneous actions using common knowledge. Algorithmica 3, 121–169 (1988)
6. Berman, P., Garay, J.A.: Cloture votes: $n/4$-resilient distributed consensus in $t + 1$ rounds. Mathematical Systems Theory 26(1), 3–19 (1993)
7. Garay, J.A., Moses, Y.: Fully polynomial byzantine agreement for $n > 3t$ processors in $t + 1$ rounds. SICOMP: SIAM Journal on Computing 27, 247–290 (1998)

On Optimal Probabilistic Asynchronous Byzantine Agreement

Amjed Shareef and C. Pandu Rangan

Department of Computer Science and Engineering,
Indian Institute of Technology Madras, Chennai - 600036, India
amjedshareef@gmail.com, rangan@cse.iitm.ernet.in

Abstract. An important problem in the fault tolerant distributed systems is reaching a consensus among a set of non faulty processes, even in the presence of some corrupted processes. The problem is couched in terms of generals attempting to decide on a common plan of attack. This is in fact the well known *Byzantine Generals Problem*. We present a consensus protocol of $O(ln)$ communication complexity in asynchronous networks (there is no common global clock and message delivery time is indefinite) with a small error probability where n is the number of players and l is the length of message, given l is sufficiently large, such that $l \geq n^3$. This improves the previous result with $O(ln^2)$ communication complexity[5]. Further more, we have proposed a reliable broadcast protocol in asynchronous networks with the assumption that messages delivery time is finite. Both of our protocols can tolerate up to $t < \frac{n}{3}$ corrupted players and is computationally secure.

Keywords: Distributed computing, byzantine agreement problem, fault tolerance, computationally bounded byzantine adversary.

1 Introduction

The Problem of Byzantine agreement was proposed by Lamport, Pease and Shostak[11] in 1980. It was formulated to solve the problem of Byzantine generals, in which, the generals, some of whom may be faulty, try to decide whether or not to carry out an attack. Some traitorous generals may lie about whether they will support a particular plan or what other generals told them. Formally, each player starts with an input value, from a finite set, V and decides on an output value from same set. The players have to attain the consensus, given the fact that some of the players may be faulty and may behave in a malicious manner. The conditions for consensus are specified as follows.

1. **Agreement:** No two non faulty players decide on different values.
2. **Validity:** If all non-faulty players start with the same initial value, $v \in V$, then v is the only possible decision value for non-faulty player.
3. **Termination:** The termination condition requires that all non-faulty players must eventually decide.

S. Rao et al. (Eds.): ICDCN 2008, LNCS 4904, pp. 86–98, 2008.
© Springer-Verlag Berlin Heidelberg 2008

Another variant of this problem is *the broadcast problem*, which aims at achieving broadcast in the distributed environment. The protocol for solving this problem is known as *the reliable broadcast*. A unique player, known as the sender begins the protocol by sending the message to other players. The reliable broadcast protocol aims at broadcasting this value to all the players, so that each player decides on an output value. For broadcast, the agreement and the termination conditions remain the same but validity condition differs. The conditions for broadcast are specified as follows.

1. **Agreement:** No two non faulty players decide on different values.
2. **Validity:** The players must decide on the sender's value, if the sender is honest.
3. **Termination:** The termination condition requires that all non-faulty players must eventually decide.

Byzantine fault is an arbitrary fault that occurs during the execution of a protocol in a distributed system. There are a variety of byzantine faults, like, the byzantine adversary may not follow the protocol. He may choose either not to send any values or to send different values to different players. The synchronous model of underlying network assumes the presence of global clock and has fixed bound on message delivery times. The asynchronous model assumes no such bounds. So, messages can be arbitrarily delayed. An adversary can be static (chooses its victims before the start of the protocol) or dynamic (can chose its victims during the course of execution of the protocol). Attaining security against a dynamic adversary is often much harder than against a static adversary.

Related Work

A fundamental result in this area is the impossibility of the byzantine agreement[9] in asynchronous networks which rules out the existence of deterministic protocol. So, to solve the consensus, the asynchronous distributed systems have to be enriched with additional power. Common coins[12], randomization[1] (probabilistic protocols) and unreliable failure detectors[7] are some examples of such additions that make it possible to solve the consensus, despite asynchrony and failures. Several protocols[2,3,5] in the literature are of $O(ln^2)$. Recently, Ramasamy[13] proposed atomic broadcast protocol of $O(ln)$, but the worst case complexity is $O(ln^2)$ and it works only for static adversary. The atomic broadcast protocol can be reduced to consensus[7].

Motivation and Contribution

We attempt to solve the open problem left by Fitzi and Hirt[10]. Their paper extends the synchronous short message broadcast protocol to the long message multivalued consensus protocol. We propose the long message multi-valued consensus protocols in the asynchronous networks (there is no common global clock and messages delivery time is indefinite) using the asynchronous short message broadcast protocol as a black box. The asynchronous reliable broadcast protocol with an assumption that messages delivery time is finite is proposed. The communication complexity of our protocol is $O(ln)$ with a negligibly small error probability, given l is sufficiently large, such that $l \geq n^3$. We used the reliable broadcast protocol proposed by Cachin[4] as a black box. Our reduction protocol works for byzantine failures, dynamic adversary and is computationally secure.

Model

We propose a solution for the agreement problem in the asynchronous networks. We assume that underlying network is completely connected and the communication channel between every pair of players is secure. The Adversary is dynamic, this means the adversary can choose corrupted players at any time of the protocol execution. The Adversary is computationally bounded and the byzantine faults are considered (messages can be delayed, wrongly sent or may not be sent at all). Adversary controls at most t number of players, in other words there are at most t malicious players among n players.

Paper Organization

The paper is organized as follows. Section 2 explains the components used by the protocol: black box, universal hash functions and threshold_broadcast() protocol. Section 3 presents an overview of the proposed protocol. Section 4 elaborates the consensus protocol and analyzes the security of each stage. Section 5 presents the reliable broadcast protocol. Sections 6 discusses the communication complexity of the protocol and finally, Section 7 concludes the paper.

2   Preliminaries

Black box

Any asynchronous reliable broadcast protocol[3,4] with order of $O(ln^2)$ can be used as black box. We use the protocol proposed by Cachin et.al.[4] for asynchronous networks as a black box. The communication complexity of this protocol is $O(ln^2)$. The Adversary is dynamic, computationally secure and the protocol works for byzantine faults. Optimal resilience ($n \geq 3t + 1$) is achieved.

Universal Hashing[6]

It is a randomized algorithm for selecting a hash function G with the following property: for any two distinct inputs x_1 and x_2, the probability that $G(x_1) = G(x_2)$ (i.e., there can be a hash collision between x_1 and x_2) is $\frac{1}{r}$, where G has function values in a range of size r.

2.1   Cryptographic Primitives

We use well known digital signature schemes and non-interactive dual threshold signatures[14]. The Dealer distributes the keys at the beginning of the protocol.

2.1.1   Non-interactive Dual-Threshold Signatures

The (n, κ, t)-dual threshold signature scheme[8,14] has n players and at most t malicious players. Every player holds the share of the secret key of the signature scheme, and generates the signature share on individual messages. κ is the threshold of the signature shares required to construct the signature, $t < \kappa \leq n - t$.

Generation of keys
Let $p_1, p_2, \cdots p_n$ be the set of players. The dealer sets up the system, generates a public key PK, a global verification key VK, the secret key shares $SK_1, \ldots, SK_n$ and the local verification keys $VK_1, \ldots, VK_n$. Initially, each player p_i has the secret key SK_i along with the public key PK. The *sender* sends the message to all the players at the beginning of the threshold_broadcast protocol. The sender additionally has the verification keys. A practical scheme that satisfies these definitions in the random-oracle model was proposed by Shoup[14]. In a non-interactive dual threshold signature scheme, generation and verification of signatures is non-interactive.

Algorithms involved in (n, κ, t)-dual threshold signature scheme

1. The *signing algorithm* (run by P_i)
   Input : A message m.
   Output : A signature share s'_i on the submitted message signed by secret key share SK_i.
2. The *share verification algorithm* (run by *sender*)
   Input : A message m, a signature share s'_i on the submitted message signed by SK_i and other keys PK, VK_i, VK.
   Output : TRUE if and only if the signature share s'_i is valid.
3. The *share combining algorithm SCA()* (run by *sender*)
   Input : A message m, κ valid signature shares on the message, PK, VK, $\{VK_i, 1 \leq i \leq n\}$.
   Output : A valid signature on the message m.
   Let *shares* = { set of all κ valid signatures s'_i }
   $m' = SCA(m, s'_1, s'_2, \cdots s'_n, VK_1, \cdots VK_n)$
4. The *signature verification algorithm* (run by P_i other than *sender*)
   Input : A message m, a signature m' (generated by the share-combining algorithm), PK.
   Output : TRUE iff the signature is valid. Verified by VK.

Security Requirements
1. *Robustness*: It is computationally infeasible for an adversary to produce κ valid signature shares such that the output of the share combining algorithm is not a valid signature.
2. $Non - forgeability$: It is computationally infeasible to output a valid signature on a message that was submitted as a signing request to less than $\kappa - t$ honest players.

2.1.2   The Threshold_broadcast() Protocol
We briefly explain the *Threshold_broadcast()* protocol in this section. To obtain a signature on a message m, the sender broadcasts the message through

the *Threshold_broadcast*() protocol to all the players and obtains the message m' with threshold signature. In the proposed protocol, whenever a player wants to broadcast his value, he obtains signature on the message through *Threshold_broadcast*(m) protocol. The protocol is similar to consistent broadcast protocol found in the literature[4]. The *Threshold_broadcast(m)* protocol returns the signed message m'. The steps involved in the protocol are as follows:

1. The sender broadcasts the message m to all the players.
2. Every player p_i upon receiving the message m from the sender, signs the message with his secret key share SK_i and obtains the signature share s'_i on the message m using *signing algorithm* and sends his share s'_i to the sender.
3. The Sender waits for the arrival of s'_i and checks the validity of message once received using *share verification algorithm*.
4. As soon as the sender receives $\lceil \frac{n+t+1}{2} \rceil$ valid shares, he generates valid signature on the message m using *share combining algorithm*.
   $m' = SCA(m, shares, VK_1, \ldots, VK_n)$.
5. *return*(m').

Lemma 1: *The sender definitely gets the message with threshold signature, m' if he is honest.*

Proof: As the sender is honest, he sends the correct message to all the players. All honest players generate a signature share on m as soon as they receive it from sender and send back to the sender. Since, at least $\lceil \frac{n+t+1}{2} \rceil$ honest players return their share to the sender, sender can correctly obtain the m'. Hence proved.   □

Lemma 2: *The sender can obtain at most one message with threshold signature irrespective of whether he is honest or dishonest.*

Proof: From lemma 1, if the sender is honest, he can obtain m'. We prove that even if the sender is dishonest he obtains at most message with threshold signature, m. We prove this by contradiction. Suppose the sender obtains two messages with threshold signature, say m'_1, m'_2. So, there should be at least $\lceil \frac{n+t+1}{2} \rceil$ signature shares for each of the messages, that is totally $(n + t + 1)$. Since there are $(n - t)$ honest players, at most $n - t$ signature shares can be obtained from distinct honest players. The adversary controls at most t players and therefore they can contribute at most $2t$ signature shares. Totally, at most $n - t + 2t = n + t$ signature shares can be obtained. As sender obtained both messages, at least one honest party might have signed both m'_1 and m'_2 signature shares, which is impossible according to protocol. Hence, $m'_1 = m'_2$.   □

Communication Complexity
Given the length of the signature is T and length of the message is l, the communication complexity is $(l + T)n$.

3 The Byzantine Agreement Protocol Overview

We briefly discuss the major parts of the protocol in this section.

Let P be the set of all players and P_{honest} be the set of all honest players. The protocol has 3 important stages: *First Stage*, *Set Creating Stage* and *Final Stage*.

First Stage

Initially, the sender sends the message m and the signature m' to all the players. This stage acts as a supporting stage to the *set creating stage*.

Set Creating Stage

The goal of the set creating stage is to identify a set $A \subseteq P$ of size at least $\lceil \frac{n+t+1}{2} \rceil$, such that all the players in A hold the same input message m.

- Each player sends the hash value of his message to other players and compares his message with other players and jointly determines the subset.
- If at least $\lceil \frac{n+t+1}{2} \rceil$ players do not have the same message, then all the players are set to the predefined default value.

Final Stage

In the Final Stage, every player $p_i \in A$ distributes his message to all the players in the set $(P-A)$. In order to keep the communication cost low, every honest player is distributing only part of the message rather than the full-length message. This stage will never be aborted. After the final stage all the honest players will have the same message and the protocol execution completes.

4 The Consensus Protocol

The *set creating stage* and *final stage* together will act as the consensus protocol. We name our protocol as Hash_consensus. Initially, every player p_i has his own value as input, that is m_i has some random value at the beginning of the protocol. The *set creating stage* and *final stage* protocols are described below in detail.

4.1 Set Creating Stage

The goal of the set creating stage is to identify a set $A \subseteq P$ of size at least $(n - t)$, such that all the players in A hold the same input message m. For the players to mutually agree on the fact that both the players have the same message, we use universal hash function. We are considering ϵ - almost two universal hash functions introduced by Carter[6]. This is a family $U = \{U_k, k = 0 \text{ to } 2^q - 1, q \geq 1\}$, where each hash function U_k maps arbitrary strings $(0, 1)^*$ to constant length q-bit strings. As we are using universal hash function[6], given two distinct messages, the probability that they have the same hash value is negligibly small. In other words, for two distinct messages m_1 and m_2, the probability that $U_k(m_1)$ is equal to $U_k(m_2)$ is $\frac{l}{2^{-q}}$, for given message length l and random key k, $q = |U_k(m_i)|$.

The Set Creating Stage Protocol

1. Every player $p_i \in P$ using the key k for a universal hash function U_k, computes hash value of the message, $h(m_i) = (k, U_k(m_i))$.
2. By using the reliable broadcast protocol (black box $B()$), player p_i broadcasts his hash value and other players agree on $< k, h(m_i) >$ value, if he is honest. Otherwise they agree on the default value.
3. All the players agree on the same set of hash values.
4. For every player, out of the received values, if there are at least $\lceil \frac{n+t+1}{2} \rceil$ players with same hash value, then those players belong to the set A and remaining players belong to the set B. Each player knows, to which set he belongs to and to which set every other player belongs to. Thus, the *set creating stage* succeeds.
5. If there are less than $\lceil \frac{n+t+1}{2} \rceil$ players with same hash value, then all the players agree on the default value. Hence, the protocol execution terminates.

In the next stage, every player belonging to A should send their value to every player belonging to B. A player belonging to the set B trusts a received value only if it is sent by at least $(t + 1)$ players. But if $|A| = t + 1$, there can be t dishonest players in the set A and they may not send correct values to the players of the set B. So, the size of the set A should be at least $(2t + 1)$. In the above case, the size of the set A is $\lceil \frac{n+t+1}{2} \rceil$ which is greater than $(2t + 1)$.

Lemma 3: *In the consensus protocol, at the end of the set creating stage, at least $\lceil \frac{n+t+1}{2} \rceil$ players agree on a common message, m or all the honest players agree on the default value.*

Proof: In the *set creating stage*, if at least $\lceil \frac{n+t+1}{2} \rceil$ players start with the same value, then their hash values will be equal (as $m_i = m_j$, $h(m_i) = h(m_j)$). Hence, a set A of players of size at least $\lceil \frac{n+t+1}{2} \rceil$ will be created, such that all players agree on a common value. If at least $\lceil \frac{n+t+1}{2} \rceil$ players do not start with the same value, then at the end of the *set creating stage*, all the players agree on the default value.   □

4.2   Final Stage

The players belonging to the set B know the hash value on which the players belonging to the set A agreed, but they do not know the corresponding message. In this stage, the players of the set A send the message to the players of the set B. Let m_A be the value agreed by all the players belonging to the set A. We use the same universal hash function mentioned in *set creating stage*.

Every player $p_i \in A$ sends a share of the message m_A to every player $p_j \in B$. This is done in the following manner. The message m_A is divided into d pieces (each of length $\lceil \frac{l+1}{d} \rceil$) and by using these d values as coefficients, every player forms a unique polynomial f_m of degree $(d - 1)$, calculates $f_m(i)$ and sends it to every player $p_j \in B$. As the value of i varies from 1 to $|A|$, x can take a maximum value of $|A|$. Let us denote $f_m(i)$ by y_i. The maximum length of y_i is

$\lceil \frac{l+1}{d} \rceil + d \log |A|$. A player $p_j \in B$ needs d points to compute the polynomial, so we set $d = |A| - t$ (as at most t players can be malicious). For eg., the message, $a_1 a_2 a_3 a_4 a_5 a_6$ can be divided into 3 pieces and by using them as coefficients, a polynomial like, $a_1 a_2 x^2 + a_3 a_4 x + a_5 a_6$ can be formed.

The Final Stage Protocol

Exponential Solution

1. Every player $p_i \in A$ computes $|y_i|$, d and f_m as described above, and sends the $|y_i|$ bit length piece y_i to every player p_j belonging to the set B.
2. Every player $p_j \in B$ waits for the arrival of at least d values of y_i from players p_i belonging to A.
3. As soon as every player $p_j \in B$ receives the d values, he forms the polynomial, retrieves the message m and computes the hash value of message.
4. If this hash value matches with the hash value received in the *set creating stage*, that is, $h(m_A)$, then received message is correct, otherwise there is at least one wrong value of y_i, so the player waits for arrival of one more y_i.
5. Every player $p_j \in B$, after receiving one more value, forms polynomials for all combinations of d values. From every combination he retrieves the message and calculates its hash value and checks whether this hash value equals to $h(m_A)$ value. If all values fails, he waits for the arrival of one more y_i value. For checking all possible combinations it takes exponential time. Players repeat step 5 until they retrieve the correct message.

Polynomial Solution

1. Every player $p_i \in A$ computes d and f_m as described above, and sends piece y_i to every player $p_j \in B$
2. Every player $p_i \in A$ selects random key k for a universal hash function U_k, computes the hash values $H_i = (k, U_k(y_1), \ldots, U_k(y_{|A|}))$, and sends them to every player $p_j \in B$.
3. Every player $p_j \in B$ waits for arrival of d number of y_i values, and $(t+1)$ number of H values as every H includes $U_k(y_i)$
4. If

>at least $(t+1)$ number of $U_k(y_i)$ hash values match with hash value of y_i then the received value is correct.

else

>If

>>at least $(t+1)$ number of $U_k(y_i)$ hash values do not match with hash value of y_i then the received value y_i is wrong, so wait for arrival of one more y_i value.

>else

>>wait for arrival of one more $U_k(y_i)$ hash value. In other words, wait for arrival of one more H_i value.

5. Step. 3 and Step. 4 are repeated till d number of correct y_i values are obtained and the message is retrieved. The hash value of this message is equal to the hash value received in *set creating stage*. It takes polynomial time as we are not checking all combinations.

Lemma 4: *At the end of final stage, all the honest players agree on a common value.*

Proof: The goal of this stage is to transfer the the message agreed by the players of the set A to the players of the set B. From lemma 3, at least $\lceil \frac{n+t+1}{2} \rceil$ players agree on the message m. As $\lceil \frac{n+t+1}{2} \rceil \geq (2t+1)$, it is possible for the players of set A to send their value to B.

Case 1: Exponential Solution
After this stage, all the players belonging to the set B checks whether the value obtained in final stage is equal to $h(m_A)$ or not, and they retrieve the correct value with high probability.

Case 2: Polynomial Solution
Every good piece y_i of an honest player, $p_i \in A$ will be confirmed by at least $(t+1)$ players (i.e. at least one honest player). Then, every player belonging to the set B receives d number of correct y_i values. All these points indeed lie on a polynomial and a unique polynomial of degree $(d-1)$ can be obtained by interpolation. Hence, the message m is retrieval.   □

Theorem 1: *The **Hash_consensus** protocol solves the consensus problem with a small arbitrary error, $\frac{l}{2^q}$ and can tolerate at most $\frac{n}{3}$ dishonest players, where l is the length of the message and q is the length of the hash message.*

Proof: As we are using universal hash function, we have a small arbitrary error probability of $\frac{l}{2^q}$. We prove that the protocol follows all conditions of the consensus.

Agreement: From lemma 3, at the end of the *set creating stage*, either all of the players agree on the default value or there will be a set A, of size at least $\lceil \frac{n+t+1}{2} \rceil$ such that all the honest players $\in A$ have the same value. From lemma 4, this value will be sent to the remaining players. Hence, all the honest players agree on the same value.

Validity: If all the honest players start with the same value, then there will be a set A, of size at least $(n-t)$ such that all the players $\in A$ have the same value (as $m_1 = m_2$, $h(m_1) = h(m_2)$). From lemma 3, at least $\lceil \frac{n+t+1}{2} \rceil$ players agree on the message m. From lemma 4, it is successfully transmitted to the remaining players. Hence, all the non faulty players agree on m.

Termination: The protocol terminates after either *set creating stage* or *final stage*.   □

5   The Reliable Broadcast Protocol

The reliable broadcast protocol consists of three consecutive stages, *first stage*, *set creating stage* and *final stage*. The *first stage* and *the set creating stage* together construct a set of players, A of size at least $\lceil \frac{n+t+1}{2} \rceil$ such that all the players of set A have the same value. In *final stage*, this message is sent to the remaining players. We name our protocol as **Byz-hash.** The description of each of the stages is given below.

5.1   First Stage

This stage uses the sub-protocol *Threshold_broadcast()*, mentioned in section 2.3.2, to obtain the threshold signature on the message m.

The First Stage Protocol

1. Initially every player p_i sets his value m_i to default value.
2. The sender obtains threshold signature m' on his message m.
   $m' = Threshold\_broadcast(m)$
3. The sender sends the messages $< m, m' >$ to all the players.
4. If a player p_i receives the value $< m, m' >$, he checks its validity. If it is valid then he sets his message m_i to m'.

The *set creating stage* is similar to section 4.1 except that at beginning of the *set creating protocol* players assign their message to the value obtained in *first stage*. The *final stage* is similar to section 4.2.

Lemma 5: *If the sender is honest, at the end of the first stage all the honest players learn the message m' and set their value to m' (m' is the message with the threshold signature).*

Proof: If the sender is honest, from lemma 1, he gets m' (message with the threshold signature) and sends the message m' to all the players. Because of finite time message delivery, all the players receives m' in fixed amount of time from sender (it is valid as sender is honest). In this way, all the honest players set their value to m'.   □

Lemma 6: *If the sender is honest, then after the set creating stage there will be a set A of size at least $(n - t)$ such that all the honest players $\in A$ have the same value.*

Proof: If the sender is honest, then from lemma 5, after the first stage at least $(n - t)$ players holds the message m'. In the set creating stage, their hash values will be equal (as $m_1 = m_2$, $h(m_1) = h(m_2)$). Hence, all the honest players agree on the value m'.   □

Lemma 7: *In the reliable broadcast protocol, at the end of set creating stage, either there will be set A of size at least $\lceil \frac{n+t+1}{2} \rceil$ such that all of them agree on same message or all honest players agree on default value.*

Proof: If the sender is honest from lemma 6, there will be a set A of size at least $(n-t)$. If the sender is dishonest, from lemma 2, at most he can obtain one message with threshold signature. Worst case, sender may not send the messages in threshold_broadcast() protocol or *first stage*, in that case all players agree on default value. The sender may sends m' to few players only, if at least $\lceil \frac{n+t+1}{2} \rceil$ players do not have the same value, then all the players agree on default value. □

Theorem 2: *The **Hash_broadcast** protocol solves the Asynchronous Multivalued Byzantine Agreement problem with a small arbitrary error $\frac{l}{2^{-k}}$ and tolerates at most $\frac{n}{3}$ dishonest players (l and k are lengths of message and hash message respectively).*

Proof: We prove that the protocol follows all conditions of reliable broadcast. *Agreement:*From lemma 7, after set creating stage either all honest players agree on default value or there will be set of players of size at least $\lceil \frac{n+t+1}{2} \rceil$ such that all the honest players have same value. From lemma 4, this value sent to all the remaining players. Hence all the honest players agree on same value.

Validity: From lemma 6, if the sender is honest, then after set creating stage there will be a set A of size at least $(n-t)$ such that all the honest players $\in A$ have the same value. From lemma 4, this value sent to all the remaining players. Hence all the honest players agree on same value.

Termination: The protocol terminates after either *set creating stage* or *final stage*. □

6   Communication Complexity of the Protocol

For the message length l, number of players n and q is hash value which is of constant length.

The communication complexity of first stage: $O(ln)$.

The communication complexity of set creating stage:
The protocol communicates $2nB(q)$ bits, where $B(b)$ denotes the communication complexity for broadcasting a b bit message with the short-message broadcast protocol. $B(q)$ is of $O(nq^2)$. The complexity is $O(2n^2q^2)$. As $l \geq n^3$ and q is of constant length, the communication complexity is of $O(ln)$.

The communication complexity of final stage:
The length of the point y_i is $\lceil \frac{l+1}{d} \rceil + d \log |A|$

Case 1: Exponential Solution
As every player $p_i \in A$ sends y_i to every player $p_i \in B$, overall communication complexity is $|A|(n-|A|)(\lceil \frac{l+1}{d} \rceil + d\log|A|)$. It is of order $O((l+1+d^2\log|A|)n)$. As $l \geq n^3$, the complexity is $O(ln)$.

Case 2: Polynomial Solution
Additionally to the exponential solution every player $p_i \in A$ sends hash values, $H_i = (k, U_k(y_1), \ldots, U_k(y_{|A|}))$. Its communication complexity is nq and q is of constant length. Hence, the overall communication complexity is

$$|A|(n - |A|)(\lceil \tfrac{l+1}{d} \rceil + d\log|A|) + |A|(n - |A|)nq.$$

As $l \geq n^3$, the complexity is $O(ln)$. As the communication complexity of each stage is $O(ln)$, the communication complexity of the entire protocol is $O(ln)$.

7   Conclusion

We have proposed an asynchronous (there is no common global clock and messages delivery time is indefinite) long message consensus protocol using the asynchronous short message reliable broadcast protocol as a black box. The asynchronous reliable broadcast protocol is proposed with an assumption that messages delivery time is finite. The communication complexity of both the protocols is $O(ln)$, with a small error probability, for $l \geq n^3$. The reduction can tolerate up to $\frac{n}{3}$ corrupted players and is computationally secure. In the Final stage, at least $\lceil \frac{n+t+1}{2} \rceil$ players who agree on a common message, send their message to all the other players with communication complexity of $O(ln)$.

References

1. Ben-Or, C.M.: Another Advantage of Free Choice: Completely Asynchronous Agreement Protocols. In: PODC 1983. Proc. Second ACM Symp. Principles of Distributed Computing, pp. 27–30 (1983)
2. Berman, P., Garay, J.A.: Randomized distributed agreement revisited. In: 23th International Symposium on Fault-Tolerant Computing (FTCS-23), pp. 412–413 (1993)
3. Bracha, G.: An asynchronous $[(n-1)/3]$-resilient consensus protocol. In: PODC. Proc. 3rd ACM Symposium on Principles of Distributed Computing, pp. 154–162 (1984)
4. Cachin, C., Kursawe, K., Petzold, F., Shoup, V.: Secure and efficient asynchronous broadcast protocols (extended abstract). In: Kilian, J. (ed.) CRYPTO 2001. LNCS, vol. 2139, pp. 524–541. Springer, Heidelberg (2001)
5. Cachin, C., Kursawe, K., Shoup, V.: Random oracles in Constantinople: Practical asynchronous Byzantine agreement using cryptography. Journal of Cryptology 18(3), 219–246 (2005)
6. Carter, L., Wegman, M.N.: Universal classes of hash functions. Journal of Computing and system sciences (JCSS) 18(4), 143–154 (1979) (Preliminary version appeared in STOC 1977)

7. Chandra, T.D., Toueg, S.: Unreliable Failure Detectors for Reliable Distributed Systems. J. ACM 43(2), 225–267 (1996)
8. Desmedt, Y., Kurosawa, K.: A Generalization and a Variant of Two Threshold Cryptosystems Based on Factoring. In: ISC 2007. Proceedings of 10th International Conference, vol. 4779, pp. 351–361. Springer, Heidelberg (2007)
9. Fischer, C.M.J., Lynch, N., Paterson, M.S.: Impossibility of Distributed Consensus with One Faulty Process. J. ACM 32(2), 374–382 (1985)
10. Fitzi, M., Hirt, M.: Optimally efficient multi-valued byzantine agreement. In: PODC 2006. Proceedings of the 25th annual ACM symposium on Principles of distributed computing, Denver, Colorado, USA (July 23 - 26, 2006)
11. Pease, M., Shostak, R., Lamport, L.: Reaching agreement in the presence of faults. Journal of the ACM 27(2), 228–234 (1980)
12. Rabin, C.M.: Randomized Byzantine Generals. In: FOCS 1983. Proc. 24th IEEE Symp. Foundations of Computer Science, pp. 403–409 (1983)
13. Ramasamy, C.H.V., Cachin, C.: Parsimonious asynchronous Byzantine-fault-tolerant atomic broadcast. In: Anderson, J.H., Prencipe, G., Wattenhofer, R. (eds.) OPODIS 2005. LNCS, vol. 3974, Springer, Heidelberg (2006)
14. Shoup, V.: Practical threshold signatures. In: Preneel, B. (ed.) EUROCRYPT 2000. LNCS, vol. 1807, pp. 207–220. Springer, Heidelberg (2000)

Narrowing Power vs. Efficiency
in Synchronous Set Agreement

Achour Mostefaoui, Michel Raynal, and Corentin Travers

IRISA, Campus de Beaulieu, 35042 Rennes Cedex, France
{achour,raynal,ctravers}@irisa.fr

Abstract. The k-set agreement problem is a generalization of the uniform consensus problem: each process proposes a value, and each non-faulty process has to decide a value such that a decided value is a proposed value, and at most k different values are decided. It has been shown that any algorithm that solves the k-set agreement problem in synchronous systems that can suffer up to t crash failures requires $\lfloor \frac{t}{k} \rfloor + 1$ rounds in the worst case. It has also been shown that it is possible to design early deciding algorithms where no process decides and halts after $\min \left(\lfloor \frac{f}{k} \rfloor + 2, \lfloor \frac{t}{k} \rfloor + 1 \right)$ rounds, where f is the number of actual crashes in a run ($0 \leq f \leq t$).

This paper explores a new direction to solve the k-set agreement problem in a synchronous system. It considers that the system is enriched with base objects (denoted $[m, \ell]$_SA objects) that allow solving the ℓ-set agreement problem in a set of m processes ($m < n$). The paper has several contributions. It first proposes a synchronous k-set agreement algorithm that benefits from such underlying base objects. This algorithm requires $O(\frac{t\ell}{mk})$ rounds, more precisely, $R_t = \lfloor \frac{t}{\Delta} \rfloor + 1$ rounds, where $\Delta = m\lfloor \frac{k}{\ell} \rfloor + (k \bmod \ell)$. The paper then shows that this bound, that involves all the parameters that characterize both the problem (k) and its environment (t, m and ℓ), is a lower bound. The proof of this lower bound sheds additional light on the deep connection between synchronous efficiency and asynchronous computability. Finally, the paper extends its investigation to the early deciding case. It presents a k-set agreement algorithm that directs the processes to decide and stop by round $R_f = \min \left(\lfloor \frac{f}{\Delta} \rfloor + 2, \lfloor \frac{t}{\Delta} \rfloor + 1 \right)$. These bounds generalize the bounds previously established for solving the k-set problem in pure synchronous systems.

1 Introduction

Context of the work. The k-set agreement problem generalizes the uniform consensus problem (that corresponds to the case $k = 1$). That problem has been introduced by S. Chaudhuri to investigate how the number of choices (k) allowed to the processes is related to the maximum number (t) of processes that can crash during a run [4]. The problem can be defined as follows. Each of the n processors (processes) defining the system starts with a value (called a "proposed" value). Each process that does not crash has to decide a value (termination), in such a way that a decided value

S. Rao et al. (Eds.): ICDCN 2008, LNCS 4904, pp. 99–111, 2008.

is a proposed value (validity), and no more than k different values are decided (agreement)[1].

When we consider asynchronous systems, the problem can trivially be solved when $k > t$. Differently, it has been shown that there is no solution in these systems as soon as $k \leq t$ [3,14,23]. (The asynchronous consensus impossibility, case $k = 1$, was demonstrated before using a different technique). Several approaches have been proposed to circumvent the impossibility to solve the k-set agreement problem in asynchronous systems (e.g., probabilistic protocols [20], unreliable failure detectors with limited scope accuracy [12,19], or conditions associated with input vectors [17]).

The situation is different in synchronous systems where the k-set agreement problem can always be solved, whatever the respective values of t and k. This has an inherent cost, namely, the smallest number of rounds (time complexity measured in communication steps) that have to be executed in the worst case scenario is lower bounded by $\lfloor \frac{t}{k} \rfloor + 1$ [5]. (That bound generalizes the $t+1$ lower bound associated with the consensus problem [1,7].)

Although failures do occur, they are rare in practice. For the uniform consensus problem ($k = 1$), this observation has motivated the design of early deciding synchronous protocols [6,15], i.e., protocols that can cope with up to t process crashes, but decide in less than $t + 1$ rounds in favorable circumstances (i.e., when there are few failures). More precisely, these protocols allow the processes to decide in $\min(f + 2, t + 1)$ rounds, where f is the number of processes that crash during a run, $0 \leq f \leq t$, which has been shown to be optimal (the worst scenario being when there is exactly one crash per round).

In a very interesting way, it has also been shown that the early deciding lower bound for the k-set agreement problem is $\min(\lfloor \frac{f}{k} \rfloor + 2, \lfloor \frac{t}{k} \rfloor + 1)$ [10]. This lower bound, not only generalizes the corresponding uniform consensus lower bound, but also shows an "inescapable tradeoff" among the number t of faults tolerated, the number f of actual faults, the degree k of coordination we want to achieve, and the best running time achievable. It is important to notice that, when compared to consensus, k-set agreement divides the running time by k (e.g., allowing two values to be decided halves the running time).

Related work. To our knowledge, two approaches have been proposed and investigated to circumvent the $\min(\lfloor \frac{f}{k} \rfloor + 2, \lfloor \frac{t}{k} \rfloor + 1)$ lower bound associated with the synchronous k-set agreement problem.

The first is the *fast failure detector* approach that has been proposed and developed in [2] to expedite decision in synchronous consensus. That approach assumes a special hardware that allows a process to detect the crash of any process at most d time units after the crash occurred, where $d < D$, D being the maximum message delay provided by the synchronous system. Both d and D are a priori known by the processes. A fast failure detector-based consensus algorithm that terminates in $D + fd$ is proposed in [2], where it is also shown that $D + fd$ is a lower bound for any algorithm based on a

---

[1] This paper considers the crash failure model. The reader interested by the k-set agreement problem in more severe send/receive/general omission failure models can consult the introductory survey [22].

fast failure detector[2]. To our knowledge, this approach has been considered only for the consensus problem.

A second approach that has been proposed to circumvent the $\min(f+2, t+1)$ lower bound is the use of conditions [18]. That approach considers that the values proposed by the processes define an input vector with one entry per process. Basically, a *condition* C_t^d (t and d are two parameters that allow defining instances of the condition) is a set of input vectors I such that $\forall I \in C_t^d$, there is a value that appears in I more than $t - d$ times. A deterministic way to define which value has to appear enough times in a vector I (e.g., the maximal value of the vector [16]) allows defining a hierarchy of conditions such that $C_t^0 \subset \cdots \subset C_t^x \subset \cdots \subset C_t^t$ (where C_t^t is the condition including all the input vectors).

[18] presents two main results. Let I be the input vector of the considered run, and C_t^d be a condition. The first result is a synchronous consensus algorithm that allows the processes to decide in (1) one round when $I \in C_t^d$ and $f = 0$, (2) two rounds when $I \in C_t^d$ and $f \le t - d$, (3) $\min(d+1, f+2, t+1)$ rounds when $I \in C_t^d$ and $f > t - d$, and (4) $\min(f+2, t+1)$ when $I \notin C_t^d$. The second result is a proof showing that $\min(d+1, f+2, t+1)$ rounds are necessary in the worst case when $I \in C_t^d$ (and $I \notin C_t^{d-1}$).

Problem addressed in the paper. The paper is on the efficiency (measured as the number of rounds required to decide) of synchronous set agreement algorithms. As it has just been shown, fast failure detectors and conditions are two ways to circumvent the synchronous lower bound. The paper investigates a third approach. That approach is based on base objects that allow narrowing the set of proposed values. Their aim is to play a part similar to fast failure detectors or conditions, i.e., allow expediting consensus.

Let us consider as a simple example a test&set object. This object has consensus number 2 [11], which means that it allows solving consensus in an asynchronous system made up of two processes (where one of them can crash), but not in a system made up of $n > 2$ processes (where up to $n-1$ can crash)[3]. Is it possible to use such base objects to speed up synchronous set agreement in a system made up of n processes where up to t may crash? More generally, let $[m, \ell]$_SA denote an object that allows solving ℓ-set agreement in a synchronous system of m processes. As fast failure detectors or conditions, these objects are assumed given for free. So, the previous question becomes:

- Is it possible to benefit from $[m, \ell]$_SA objects to build a t-resilient synchronous $[n, k]$_SA object (i.e., a k-set agreement object that has to cope with up to t process crashes)?
- If such a construction is possible, is its cost smaller than $\lfloor \frac{t}{k} \rfloor + 1$, or smaller than $\min(\lfloor \frac{f}{k} \rfloor + 2, \lfloor \frac{t}{k} \rfloor + 1)$ if we are interested in an early deciding $[n, k]$_SA object?

If m, ℓ, n and k are such that there is an integer a with $n \le am$ and $a\ell \le k$, it is possible to solve the k-set agreement problem without exchanging any value (i.e., in 0

---

[2] Without a fast failure detector, the cost would be $D \times \min(f+2, t+1)$.

[3] The consensus number of a concurrent object type is the maximum number of processes that can solve consensus (despite any number of process crashes) using only atomic registers and objects of that type. The consensus number of test&set objects, queues, and stacks is 2 [11].

round!) whatever the value of t. This is trivially obtained by partitioning the n processes into a subsets of at most m processes, and using in each subset a $[m, \ell]$_SA object in order that each process be provided with a decided value. So, the interesting cases are when the values m, ℓ, n and k do not allow a trivial partitioning such as the previous one.

Another way to present the previous question is the following: how much crashes can we tolerate when we want to build a synchronous $[10, 3]$_SA object from $[2, 1]$_SA objects, if one wants to decide in at most one round? In at most two rounds? In at most three rounds?

From a more practical point of view, we can see the system as made up of clusters of m processes, such that an operation involving only processes of a given cluster can be performed very efficiently, i.e., in a time that is smaller than the maximal message transfer delay involving processes belonging to different clusters. That is the sense in which the sentence "the $[m, \ell]$_SA objects are given for free" has to be understood.

Results. The paper presents the following results.

- It first presents a synchronous message-passing algorithm that builds a $[n, k]$_SA object from $[m, \ell]$_SA objects. This algorithm works for any values of n, k, m, and ℓ (assuming, of course, $n > k$ and $m > \ell$).
- The paper then shows that the number of rounds (R_t) of the previous algorithm varies as $O(\frac{t\ell}{mk})$. This means that R_t (1) decreases when the coordination degree k increases (i.e., when less synchronization is required), or when the number of processes m involved in each underlying object increases, and (2) increases when the underlying object is less and less powerful (i.e., when ℓ increases) or when the number of process crashes that the algorithm has to tolerate increases. More precisely, we have:

$$R_t = \left\lfloor \frac{t}{m\lfloor \frac{k}{\ell} \rfloor + (k \bmod \ell)} \right\rfloor + 1.$$

When we consider the previous example of building, in a synchronous system, a $[10, 3]$_SA object from $[2, 1]$_SA objects, we can conclude that $R_t = 1$ requires $t < 6$, while $R_t = 2$ allows $t = 9$. Moreover, as there are only $n = 10$ processes, there is no value of t that can entail an execution in which $R_t = 3$ are required (for it to occur, we should have $12 \leq t < 18$ and $n > t$).

To have a better view of R_t, it is interesting to look at special cases.

- Case 1. Build a consensus object in a synchronous system from $[1, 1]$_SA base objects or $[m, m]$_SA objects (i.e., from base objects that have no power). It is easy to see that $R_t = t+1$ (that is the well-known lower bound for synchronous t-resilient consensus).
- Case 2. Build a $[n, k]$_SA object in a synchronous system from $[1, 1]$_SA base objects or $[m, m]$_SA objects (base objects without power). It is easy to see that $R_t = \lfloor \frac{t}{k} \rfloor + 1$, (that is the lower bound for synchronous t-resilient k-set agreement).
- Case 3. Build a synchronous consensus from $[m, 1]$_SA base objects (i.e., consensus objects). In that case $R_t = \lfloor \frac{t}{m} \rfloor + 1$.

- Case 4. Build a synchronous $[n, \ell]$_SA object from $[m, \ell]$_SA base objects. In that case, $R_t = \lfloor \frac{t}{m} \rfloor + 1$.
- Case 5. Build a synchronous $[n, k]$_SA object from $[m, 1]$_SA base objects (i.e., consensus objects). We then have $R_t = \lfloor \frac{t}{mk} \rfloor + 1$.

These particular instances show clearly how the coordination degree and the size of the base objects (measured by the value m) affect the maximal number of rounds executed by the algorithm and consequently allow expediting the decision.

- The paper then shows that the value R_t is optimal when, one wants to build, in a synchronous system, an $[n, k]$_SA object from $[m, \ell]$_SA base objects. This optimality result generalizes previous lower bounds proved for special cases such as consensus [1,7,15], and set agreement [5].

  The optimality proof relies on two theorems, one from Gafni [9], the other from Herlihy and Rajsbaum [13]. Gafni's theorem establishes a deep connection between solvability in asynchronous system and lower bounds (efficiency) in synchronous systems. Herlihy and Rajsbaum's theorem is on the impossibility to solve some set agreement problems in asynchronous systems.
- Finally, the paper extends the algorithm to the early decision case. More specifically, the maximal number of rounds of the early deciding version of the algorithm is the following:

$$ R_f = \min\left(\lfloor \frac{f}{\Delta} \rfloor + 2, \lfloor \frac{t}{\Delta} \rfloor + 1\right) \quad \text{where} \quad \Delta = m\lfloor \frac{k}{\ell} \rfloor + (k \bmod \ell). $$

It is easy to see that this early decision bound generalizes the lower bounds that are known for the special consensus and set agreement cases.

This paper is an endeavor to capture the essence of the synchronous set agreement and provide the reader with a better understanding of it. To that end, it considers design simplicity as a first-class citizen when both designing algorithms and proving lower bound results[4].

As already noticed, the lower bound proof relies on previous theorems. We do think that Gafni's theorem [9] (that states that an asynchronous system with at most t' crashes can implement the first $\lfloor \frac{t}{t'} \rfloor$ rounds of a synchronous system with up to t failures) is a fundamental theorem of fault-tolerant distributed computing. The lower bound proof of this paper paper shows an application of this powerful theorem.

Roadmap. The paper is made up of 5 sections. Section 2 introduces the system model and definitions. Section 3 presents the algorithm that builds an $[n, k]$_SA object from $[m, \ell]$_SA objects in R_t synchronous rounds. Section 4 proves that R_t is a lower bound on the number of rounds for any synchronous algorithm that builds an $[n, k]$_SA object from $[m, \ell]$_SA objects. Section 5 considers the early decision case.

2   Computation Model and the Set Agreement Problem

The k-set agreement problem. The problem has been informally stated in the Introduction: every process p_i *proposes* a value v_i and each correct process has to *decide* on

---

[4] The paper strives to modestly follow Einstein's advice "Make it as simple as possible, but no more".

a value in relation to the set of proposed values. More precisely, the *k-set agreement* problem [4] is defined by the following three properties (as we can see 1-set agreement is the uniform consensus problem):

- **Termination**: Every correct process eventually decides.
- **Validity**: If a process decides v, then v was proposed by some process.
- **Agreement**: No more than k different values are decided.

Process model. The system model consists of a finite set of n processes, namely, $\Pi = \{p_1, \ldots, p_n\}$. A process is a sequence of steps (execution of a base atomic operation). A process is *faulty* during an execution if it stops executing steps (after it has crashed a process executes no step). As already indicated, t is an upper bound on the number of faulty processes, while f denotes the number of processes that crash during a particular run, $0 \leq f \leq t < n$. (Without loss of generality we consider that the execution of a step by a process takes no time.)

In the following, we implicitly assume $k \leq t$. This is because k-set agreement can trivially be solved in synchronous or asynchronous systems when $t < k$ [4].

Communication/coordination model. The processes communicate by sending and receiving messages through channels. Every pair of processes p_i and p_j is connected by a channel. The sending of a message and the reception of a message are atomic operations. The underlying communication system is assumed to be failure-free: there is no creation, alteration, loss or duplication of message.

In addition to messages, the processes can coordinate by accessing $[m, \ell]\_SA$ objects. Such an object is a one-shot object that can be accessed by at most m processes. Its power is to solve the ℓ-set agreement problem among m processes. Let us observe that, for $1 \leq m \leq n$, an $[m, m]\_SA$ object is a trivial object that has no coordination power.

Round-based synchrony. The system is *synchronous*. This means that each of its runs consists of a sequence of *rounds*. Those are identified by the successive integers $1, 2$, etc. For the processes, the current round number appears as a global variable r that they can read, and whose progress is given for free: it is managed by an external entity. A round is made up of two main consecutive phases:

- A send phase in which each process sends zero or one message to each other processes. If a process crashes during the send phase of a round, an arbitrary subset of the processes to which it sent messages will receive these messages.
- A receive phase in which each process receives messages. The fundamental property of the synchronous model lies in the fact that a message sent by a process p_i to a process p_j at round r, is received by p_j at the very same round r.

Before or after a phase, a process can execute local computations (e.g., process the messages it received during the current round). It can also invokes an underlying $[m, \ell]\_SA$ base object.

3   A Synchronous $[n, k]$_SA Algorithm

This section presents a simple algorithm that, when at most t processes may crash, builds an $[n, k]$_SA object if the system provides the n processes with round-based synchrony and $[m, \ell]$_SA base objects.

Notation. In all the rest of the paper we are using the following notations:

- $k = \alpha\ell + \beta$ with $\alpha = \lfloor \frac{k}{\ell} \rfloor$ and $\beta = k \bmod \ell$.
- $\Delta = \alpha\,m + \beta$ and $R_t = \lfloor \frac{t}{\Delta} \rfloor + 1 = \lfloor \frac{t}{m\lfloor \frac{k}{\ell} \rfloor + (k \bmod \ell)} \rfloor + 1$.

3.1   The Algorithm

The algorithm is pretty simple. It is described in Figure 1. A process p_i invokes the operation propose$_k(v_i)$ where v_i is the value it proposes. That value is initially stored in the local variable est_i (line 01), that afterwards will contain the current estimate of p_i's decision value (line 10). The process terminates when it executes the return(est_i) statement.

Each process executes R_t rounds (line 02). During any round r, only Δ processes are allowed to send their current estimates. These processes are called the *senders* of round r. When $r = 1$, they are the processes $p_1, \ldots, p_\Delta$, during the second round the processes $p_{\Delta+1}, \ldots, p_{2\Delta}$, and so on (lines 04-05).

The Δ senders of a round r are partitioned into $\lceil \frac{\Delta}{m} \rceil$ subsets of m processes (the last subset containing possibly less than m processes), and each subset uses an $[m, \ell]$_SA object to narrow the set of its current estimates (lines 06-07). After this "narrowing", each sender process sends its new current estimate to all the processes. A process p_i accesses an $[m, \ell]$_SA object by invoking the operation propose(est_i). The $\lceil \frac{\Delta}{m} \rceil$ $[m, \ell]$_SA objects used during a round r are in the array $SA[r, 0..\lceil \frac{\Delta}{m} \rceil - 1]$ [5]. Finally, when during a round, a process p_i receives estimates, it updates est_i accordingly (line 10).

It is important to see that, if during a round, at least one sender process does not crash, at most $k = \alpha\ell + \beta$ estimates are sent during that round, which means that k-set agreement is guaranteed as soon as there is a round during which an active process does not crash.

3.2   Proof of the Algorithm

Lemma 1. *Let $nc[r]$ be the number of processes that crash during the round r. There is a round r such that $r \leq R_t$ and $nc[r] < \Delta$.*

Proof. Let $t = \alpha'\Delta + \beta'$ with $\alpha' = \lfloor \frac{t}{\Delta} \rfloor$ and $\beta' = t \bmod \Delta$. The proof is by contradiction. let us assume that, $\forall\, r \leq R_t$, we have $nc[r] \geq \Delta$. We then have:

$$\sum_{r=1}^{R_t} nc[r] \geq \Delta \times R_t = \Delta(\lfloor \frac{t}{\Delta} \rfloor + 1) = \Delta(\alpha' + \lfloor \frac{\beta'}{\Delta} \rfloor + 1) = \Delta \times \alpha' + \Delta > t.$$

---

[5] Actually, only $R_t \lfloor \frac{\Delta}{m} \rfloor$ base $[m, \ell]$_SA objects are needed. This follows from the following observation: during each round r, if $\beta \neq 0$, the "last" β sender processes do not need to use such an $[m, \ell]$_SA object because $\beta \leq \ell$. (Let us recall that $0 \leq \beta < \ell$ and Δ is defined as $\alpha\,m + \beta$.)

```
Function propose_k(v_i)
(01)   est_i ← v_i;
(02)   for r = 1, 2, . . . , R_t do % r: round number %
(03)   begin round
(04)       first_sender ← (r − 1)Δ + 1; last_sender ← rΔ;
(05)       if first_sender ≤ i ≤ last_sender then % p_i is "sender" at round r %
(06)           let y such that first_sender + ym ≤ i < last_sender + (y + 1)m;
                   % y is index of the [m, ℓ]_SA object used by p_i %
(07)           est_i ← SA[r, y].propose(est_i);
(08)           for each j ∈ {1, . . . , n} do send (est_i) to p_j end do
(09)       end if;
(10)       est_i ← any est value received if any, unchanged otherwise
(11)   end round;
(12)   return(est_i)
```

Fig. 1. $[n, k]$_SA object from $[m, \ell]$_SA objects in a synchronous system (code for p_i)

Consequently, there are more than t processes that crash: a contradiction.   □

Lemma 2. *At any round r, at most k different estimate values are sent by the processes.*

Proof. Let us recall that $k = \alpha \ell + \beta$ (Euclidean division of k by ℓ) and the value Δ is $\alpha m + \beta$.

Due to the lines 04-05, at most Δ processes are sender at each round r. These Δ sender processes are partitioned into $\lfloor \frac{\Delta}{m} \rfloor$ sets of exactly m processes plus a set of β processes. As each underlying $[m, \ell]$_SA object used during the round r outputs at most ℓ estimates values from the value it is proposed, it follows that at most $\alpha \ell + \beta$ estimates values can be output by these objects, which proves the lemma.   □

Lemma 3. *At most k different values are decided by the processes.*

Proof. At any round the number of senders is at most Δ (lines 04-05). Moreover, due to lemma 1, there is at least one round $r \leq R_t$ during which a correct process is a sender. If follows from Lemma 2, line 08 and line 10, that, at the end of such a round r, the estimates of the processes contain at most k distinct values.   □

Theorem 1. *The algorithm described in Figure 1 is a synchronous t-resilient k-set agreement algorithm.*

Proof. The termination property follows directly from the synchrony of the model: a process that does not crash executes R_t rounds. The validity property follows directly from the initialization of the estimate values est_i, the correctness of the underlying $[m, \ell]$_SA objects (line 07), and the fact that the algorithm exchanges only est_i values. Finally, the agreement property is Lemma 3.   □

4   Lower Bound on the Number of Rounds

This section proves that the previous algorithm is optimal with respect to the number of rounds. The proof of this lower bound is based on (1) a deep connection relating synchronous efficiency and asynchronous computability in presence of failures [9], and (2) an impossibility result in asynchronous set agreement [13].

4.1   Notation and Previous Results

- $\mathcal{S}_{n,t}[\emptyset]$ denotes the classical round-based synchronous system model made up of n processes, where up to t processes may crash.
- $\mathcal{S}_{n,t}[m, \ell]$ is the $\mathcal{S}_{n,t}[\emptyset]$ system model enriched with $[m, \ell]$_SA objects. This is the model defined in Section 2 (n processes, at most t process crashes, coordination possible through $[m, \ell]$_SA objects).
- $\mathcal{AS}_{n,t}[\emptyset]$ denotes the classical asynchronous system model (n processes, up to processes t may crash, no additional equipment).
- $\mathcal{AS}_{n,t}[m, \ell]$ denotes the asynchronous system model $\mathcal{AS}_{n,t}[\emptyset]$ enriched with $[m, \ell]$_SA objects. (From a computability point of view, $\mathcal{AS}_{n,t}[\emptyset]$ is weaker than $\mathcal{AS}_{n,t}[m, \ell]$.)

The following theorems are central in proving that R_t is a lower bound.

Theorem 2. (Gafni [9]) *Let $n > t \geq k > 0$. It is possible to simulate in $\mathcal{AS}_{n,k}[\emptyset]$ the first $\lfloor \frac{t}{k} \rfloor$ rounds of any algorithm designed for $\mathcal{S}_{n,t}[\emptyset]$ system model.*

The next corollary is a simple extension of Gafni's theorem suited to our needs.

Corollary 1. *Let $n > t \geq k > 0$. It is possible to simulate in $\mathcal{AS}_{n,k}[m, \ell]$ the first $\lfloor \frac{t}{k} \rfloor$ rounds of any algorithm designed for $\mathcal{S}_{n,t}[m, \ell]$ system model.*

Theorem 3. (Herlihy-Rajsbaum [13]) *Let $J_{m,\ell}$ be the function defined as follows: $u \to \ell \lfloor \frac{u}{m} \rfloor + \min(\ell, u \bmod m) - 1$. There is no algorithm that solves the K-set agreement problem, with $K = J_{m,\ell}(t + 1)$, in $\mathcal{AS}_{n,t}[m, \ell]$.*

4.2   The Lower Bound

Theorem 4. *Let $1 \leq \ell \leq m < n$ and $1 \leq k \leq t < n$. Any algorithm that solves the k-set agreement problem in $\mathcal{S}_{n,t}[m, \ell]$ has at least one run in which at least one process does not decide before the round $R_t = \lfloor \frac{t}{m\lfloor \frac{k}{\ell} \rfloor + (k \bmod \ell)} \rfloor + 1$.*

Proof. The proof is by contradiction. let us assume that there is an algorithm A that solves the k-set agreement problem in at most $R < R_t$ rounds in $\mathcal{S}_{n,t}[m, \ell]$ (this means that any process decides by at most R rounds, or crashes before). We consider two cases.

- $k < \ell$. We have then $R < R_t = \lfloor \frac{t}{k} \rfloor + 1$.

1. As $k < \ell$, the ℓ-set agreement can be solved in in $\mathcal{AS}_{n,k}[\emptyset]$. It follows that, as far as set agreement is concerned, $\mathcal{AS}_{n,k}[\emptyset]$ and $\mathcal{AS}_{n,k}[m, \ell]$ have the same computational power.
2. It follows from the corollary of Gafni's theorem that there is, in $\mathcal{AS}_{n,k}[m, \ell]$, a simulation of the first $\lfloor \frac{t}{k} \rfloor$ rounds of any algorithm designed for the $\mathcal{S}_{n,t}[m, \ell]$ system model. It is consequently possible to simulate in $\mathcal{AS}_{n,k}[m, \ell]$ the $R < R_t = \lfloor \frac{t}{k} \rfloor + 1$ rounds of the algorithm A. It follows that the k-set agreement problem can be solved in in $\mathcal{AS}_{n,k}[m, \ell]$.
3. Combining the two previous items, we obtain an algorithm that solves the k-set agreement problem in $\mathcal{AS}_{n,k}[\emptyset]$. This contradicts the impossibility to solve the k-set agreement problem in $\mathcal{AS}_{n,k}[\emptyset]$ [3,14,23]. This proves the theorem for the case $k < \ell$.

– $k \geq \ell$. Let us recall the definition $\Delta = m \lfloor \frac{k}{\ell} \rfloor + (k \bmod \ell) = \alpha\, m + \beta$.
1. It follows from the corollary of Gafni's theorem that at least $\lfloor \frac{t}{\Delta} \rfloor$ rounds of any algorithm designed for the $\mathcal{S}_{n,t}[m, \ell]$ system model can be simulated in $\mathcal{AS}_{n,\Delta}[m, \ell]$.

   So, as the algorithm A solves the k-set agreement problem in $\mathcal{S}_{n,t}[m, \ell]$, in at most $R < R_t = \lfloor \frac{t}{\Delta} \rfloor + 1$, combining the simulation with A, we obtain an algorithm that solves the k-set agreement problem in $\mathcal{AS}_{n,\Delta}[m, \ell]$.
2. Considering the argument used in Herlihy-Rajsbaum's theorem we have the following:

$$J_{m,\ell}(\Delta + 1) = \ell \left\lfloor \frac{\Delta + 1}{m} \right\rfloor + \min\left(\ell, (\Delta + 1) \bmod m\right) - 1,$$
$$= \ell \left\lfloor \frac{\alpha\, m + \beta + 1}{m} \right\rfloor + \min\left(\ell, (\alpha\, m + \beta + 1) \bmod m\right) - 1,$$
$$= \ell \left(\alpha + \left\lfloor \frac{\beta + 1}{m} \right\rfloor\right) + \min\left(\ell, (\beta + 1) \bmod m\right) - 1.$$

Let us observe that $\ell \leq m$. Moreover, as $\beta = k \bmod \ell$, we also have $\beta < \ell$. To summarize: $\beta < \ell \leq m$. There are two cases to consider.

(a) $m = \beta + 1$. Observe that this implies that $\ell = m$ and $\ell - 1 = \beta$.

$$J_{m,\ell}(\Delta + 1) = \ell\,(\alpha + 1) + \min\left(\ell, m \bmod m\right) - 1,$$
$$= \ell\,\alpha + \ell - 1 = \ell\,\alpha + \beta = k.$$

(b) $m > \beta + 1$:

$$J_{m,\ell}(\Delta + 1) = \ell\,\alpha + \min\left(\ell, (\beta + 1) \bmod m\right) - 1,$$
$$= \ell\,\alpha + \beta + 1 - 1 = k.$$

In both cases, $J_{m,\ell}(\Delta + 1) = k$. It follows from Herlihy-Rajsbaum's theorem that there is no algorithm that solves the $J_{m,\ell}(\Delta + 1)$-set agreement problem (i.e., the k-set agreement problem) in $\mathcal{AS}_{n,\Delta}[m, \ell]$.
3. The two previous items contradict each other, thereby proving the theorem for the case $k < \ell$. □

Function ED_propose$_k(v_i)$
(01) $est_i \leftarrow v_i$;
(02) **for** $r = 1, 2, \ldots, R_t$ **do** % r: round number %
(03) **begin round**
(04) $first\_sender \leftarrow (r - 1)\Delta + 1$; $last\_sender \leftarrow r\Delta$;
(05)   **if** $first\_sender \leq i \leq last\_sender$ **then** % p_i is "sender" at round r %
(06)   let y such that $first\_sender + ym \leq i < last\_sender + (y + 1)m$;
              % y is index of the $[m, \ell]$_SA object used by p_i %
(07) $est_i \leftarrow SA[r, y].\mathsf{propose}(est_i)$;
(08)   **for each** $j \in \{1, \ldots, n\}$ **do** send (est_i) to p_j **end do**
(09)   **end if**;
(A1)   **if** $(p_i$ was a sender at round $r - 1)$ **then**
              for each $j \in \{1, \ldots, n\}$ **do** send (COMMIT) to p_j **end do end if**;
(A2)   **if** (COMMIT received) **then** return(est_i) **end if**;
(10) $est_i \leftarrow$ any est value received if any, unchanged otherwise
(11) **end round**;
(12) return(est_i)

Fig. 2. Early-deciding $[n, k]$_SA object from $[m, \ell]$_SA objects in a synchronous system (p_i)

Corollary 2. *When $k < \ell$, the underlying $[m, \ell]$_SA objects are useless.*

Proof. The corollary follows from the fact that $k < \ell \implies R_t = \lfloor \frac{t}{k} \rfloor + 1$, that is the lower bound when no underlying base object is used.   □

This corollary means that no k-set agreement algorithm can benefit from $[m, \ell]$_SA objects when $k < \ell$.

5   Early Decision

This section extends the algorithm described in Figure 1 in order to obtain an early-deciding algorithm that allows the processes to decide by round $R_f = \min\left(\lfloor \frac{f}{\Delta} \rfloor + 2, \lfloor \frac{t}{\Delta} \rfloor + 1\right)$, where $\Delta = m\lfloor \frac{k}{\ell} \rfloor + (k \bmod \ell)$.

This algorithm is described in Figure 2 (its proof can be found in [21]). It is obtained from the base algorithm in a surprisingly simple way: only two new statements are added to the base algorithm to obtain early decision. These are the new lines, named A1 and A2, inserted between line 09 and line 10. No statement of the base algorithm has to be modified or suppressed.

The design principles of this algorithm are very simple. A process p_i that is a sender during a round r' and participates in the next round $r' + 1$ (so, it has not crashed by the end of r'), sends to all the processes a control message (denoted COMMIT) during the round $r' + 1$ (additional line A1). In that way, p_i informs all the processes that the estimate value it sent during the previous round r' was received by all the processes (this follows from the communication synchrony property). Moreover, as at most k different values are sent during a round (Lemma 2), and at least one process (namely, p_i) sent a value to all during r', it follows from the fact that p_i participates to the round $r' + 1$

that the estimates of all the processes contain at most k different values at the end of r'. Consequently, a process that receives a COMMIT message during a round $r' + 1$ can decide the value of its estimate at the end of the round r' and stops (additional line A2).

It is easy to see that if at least one process in $p_1, \ldots, p_\Delta$ does not crash, the processes decide in two rounds. If all the processes $p_1, \ldots, p_\Delta$ crash and at least one process in $p_{\Delta+1}, \ldots, p_{2\Delta}$ does not crash, the decision is obtained in at most 3 rounds. Etc. It is interesting to observe that, when $m = \ell = k = 1$ we have $\Delta = 1$ and we obtain a remarkably simple uniform early deciding consensus algorithm for the classical round-based synchronous model $\mathcal{S}_{n,t}[\emptyset]$.

References

1. Aguilera, M.K., Toueg, S.: A Simple Bivalency Proof that t-Resilient Consensus Requires $t + 1$ Rounds. Information Processing Letters 71, 155–178 (1999)
2. Aguilera, M.K., Le Lann, G., Toueg, S.: On the Impact of Fast failure Detectors on Real-Time Fault-Tolerant Systems. In: Malkhi, D. (ed.) DISC 2002. LNCS, vol. 2508, pp. 354–369. Springer, Heidelberg (2002)
3. Borowsky, E., Gafni, E.: Generalized FLP Impossibility Results for t-Resilient Asynchronous Computations. In: STOC 1993. Proc. 25th ACM Symposium on Theory of Distributed Computing, pp. 91–100. ACM Press, New York (1993)
4. Chaudhuri, S.: More Choices Allow More Faults: Set Consensus Problems in Totally Asynchronous Systems. Information and Computation 105, 132–158 (1993)
5. Chaudhuri, S., Herlihy, M., Lynch, N., Tuttle, M.: Tight Bounds for k-Set Agreement. Journal of the ACM 47(5), 912–943 (2000)
6. Dolev, D., Reischuk, R., Strong, R.: Early Stopping in Byzantine Agreement. Journal of the ACM 37(4), 720–741 (1990)
7. Fischer, M.J., Lynch, N.A.: A Lower Bound on the Time to Assure Interactive Consistency. Information Processing Letters 14(4), 183–186 (1982)
8. Fischer, M.J., Lynch, N.A., Paterson, M.S.: Impossibility of Distributed Consensus with One Faulty Process. Journal of the ACM 32(2), 374–382 (1985)
9. Gafni, E.: Round-by-round Fault Detectors: Unifying Synchrony and Asynchrony. In: PODC 2000. Proc. 17th ACM Symp. on Principles of Dist. Computing, pp. 143–152. ACM Press, New York (1998)
10. Gafni, E., Guerraoui, R., Pochon, B.: From a Static Impossibility to an Adaptive Lower Bound: The Complexity of Early Deciding Set Agreement. In: STOC 2005. Proc. 37th ACM Symposium on Theory of Computing, pp. 714–722. ACM Press, New York (2005)
11. Herlihy, M.P.: Wait-Free Synchronization. ACM TOPLAS 13(1), 124–149 (1991)
12. Herlihy, M.P., Penso, L.D.: Tight Bounds for k-Set Agreement with Limited Scope Accuracy Failure Detectors. Distributed Computing 18(2), 157–166 (2005)
13. Herlihy, M.P., Rajsbaum, S.: Algebraic Spans. MSCS 10(4), 549–573 (2000)
14. Herlihy, M.P., Shavit, N.: The Topological Structure of Asynchronous Computability. Journal of the ACM 46(6), 858–923 (1999)
15. Lamport, L., Fischer, M.: Byzantine Generals and Transaction Commit Protocols. Unpublished manuscript, pages 16 (April 1982)
16. Mostéfaoui, A., Rajsbaum, S., Raynal, M.: Conditions on Input Vectors for Consensus Solvability in Asynchronous Distributed Systems. Journal of the ACM 50(6), 922–954 (2003)

17. Mostéfaoui, A., Rajsbaum, S., Raynal, M.: The Combined Power of Conditions and Failure Detectors to Solve Asynchronous Set Agreement. In: PODC 2005. Proc. 24th ACM Symposium on Principles of Distributed Computing, pp. 179–188. ACM Press, New York (2005)
18. Mostéfaoui, A., Rajsbaum, S., Raynal, M.: Synchronous Condition-Based Consensus. Distributed Computing 18(5), 325–343 (2006)
19. Mostéfaoui, A., Raynal, M.: k-Set Agreement with Limited Accuracy Failure Detectors. In: PODC 2000. 19th ACM Symp. on Principles of Distributed Computing, pp. 143–152 (2000)
20. Mostéfaoui, A., Raynal, M.: Randomized Set Agreement. In: SPAA 2001. Proc. 13th ACM Symposium on Parallel Algorithms and Architectures, pp. 291–297. ACM Press, New York (2001)
21. Mostéfaoui, A., Raynal, M., Travers, C.: Narrowing power vs efficiency in synchronous set agreement. Tech Report #1836, IRISA, Université de Rennes (France), pages 13 (2007)
22. Raynal, M., Travers, C.: Synchronous Set Agreement: A Concise Guided Tour (with open problems). In: PRDC 2006. Proc. 12th Int'l IEEE Pacific Rim Dependable Computing Symposium, pp. 267–274. IEEE Computer Press, Los Alamitos (2006)
23. Saks, M., Zaharoglou, F.: Wait-Free k-Set Agreement is Impossible: The Topology of Public Knowledge. SIAM Journal on Computing 29(5), 1449–1483 (2000)

Highly-Concurrent Multi-word Synchronization*
(Extended Abstract)

Hagit Attiya and Eshcar Hillel

Department of Computer Science, Technion

Abstract. The design of concurrent data structures is greatly facilitated by the availability of synchronization operations that atomically modify k arbitrary locations, such as k-*read-modify-write* (kRMW). Aiming to increase concurrency in order to exploit the parallelism offered by today's multi-core and multiprocessing architectures, we propose a software implementation of kRMW that efficiently breaks apart delay chains. Our algorithm ensures that two operations delay each other only if they are within distance $O(k)$ in the *conflict graph*, dynamically induced by the operations' data items.

The algorithm uses *double compare-and-swap* (DCAS). When DCAS is not supported by the architecture, the algorithm of Attiya and Dagan [3] can be used to replace DCAS with (unary) CAS, with only a slight increase in the interference among operations.

1 Introduction

Multi-word synchronization operations, like k-*read-modify-write* (kRMW), allow to read the contents of several memory locations, compute new values and write them back, all in one atomic operation. A popular special case is k-*compare-and-swap* (kCAS), where the values read from the memory locations are compared against specified values, and if they all match, the locations are updated. Multi-word synchronization facilitates the design and implementation of concurrent data structures, making it more effective and easier than when using only single-word synchronization operations. For example, removing a node from a doubly-linked list and a right (or left) rotation applied on a node in an AVL tree can easily be implemented with 3CAS and 4CAS, respectively.

Today's multi-core architectures, however, support in hardware only single-word synchronization operations like CAS or at best, *double compare-and-swap* (DCAS). Providing kRMW or kCAS in software has therefore been an important research topic.

It is crucial to allow many operations to make progress concurrently and complete without interference, in order to utilize the capabilities of contemporary architectures. Clearly, when operations need to simultaneously access the same words, an inherent "hot spot" is created and operations must be delayed. A worse and unnecessary situation happens in typical kRMW implementations, when the progress of an operation is hindered also due to operations that do not contend for the same memory words. In these implementations [14, 12, 8, 5, 15], an operation tries to lock all the words it needs,

---

* Supported by the *Israel Science Foundation* (grant number 953/06). The full version of this paper is available from http://www.cs.technion.ac.il/~hagit/publications/

S. Rao et al. (Eds.): ICDCN 2008, LNCS 4904, pp. 112–123, 2008.

one by one; if another operation already holds the lock on a word, the operation is blocked and can either *wait* for the lock to be released (possibly while *helping* the conflicting operation to make progress) or *reset* the conflicting operation and try to acquire the lock.

In these schemes, a *chain* of operations may be created, where each operation in the chain is either waiting for a word locked by the next operation (possibly while helping it), or is being reset by the previous operation in the chain. It is possible to construct *recurring* scenarios where an operation repeatedly waits, helps, or is reset due to each operation along the path. In these scenarios, an operation is delayed a number of steps proportional to the total number of operations in these chains and their length, causing a lot of work to be invested, while only a few operations complete. Evidently, it is necessary to bound the length of the chains, in order to improve the concurrency of a kRMW implementation.

We proceed more precisely, by considering the *conflict graph* of operations that overlap in time; in this graph, vertices represent data items, i.e., memory locations, and edges connect data items if they are accessed by the same operation. The *distance* between two operations in a conflict graph is the length of the path between the operations' data items. Thus, two simultaneous operations contending for a data item have zero distance in the conflict graph. Algorithms of the kind described above guarantee that operations in disconnected parts of the conflict graph do not delay each other; that is, operations proceed in parallel if they access disjoint parts of the data structure; that is, they are *disjoint access parallel* [12].

Even when operations choose their items uniformly at random, it has been shown [7], both analytically and experimentally, that the lengths of such paths depend on the total number of operations, and paths of significant length might be created in the conflict graph. This means that the connected components have non-constant diameter, implying that an operation in the typical multi-word synchronization algorithms can be delayed by "distant" operations, even when an algorithm is disjoint access parallel.

The adverse effect of waiting and delay chains can be mitigated, greatly improving the concurrency, if operations are delayed only due to operations within constant distance. Informally, an implementation is *d-local nonblocking* if whenever an operation *op* takes an infinite number of steps, some operation, within distance d from *op*, completes. This implies that the throughput of the algorithm is localized in components of diameter d in the conflict graph, and they are effectively *isolated* from operations at distance $> d$. This extends the notion of *nonblocking* (also called *lock-free*) algorithms.

Our contribution. We present an algorithm for multi-word synchronization, specifically, kRMW, which is $O(k)$-local nonblocking. The algorithm is flexible and does not fix k across operations. We store a constant amount of information (independent of k), in each data item.

Our main new algorithmic ideas are first explained in the context of a *blocking* implementation (Section 3), in which the failure or delay of an operation may block operations that access *nearby* data items; however, operations that access data items that are farther than $O(k)$ away in the conflict graph are not affected. (This is a slightly weaker property than *failure locality*, suggested by Choy and Singh [6].)

A key insight of our algorithm is that the length of waiting chains can be bounded, yielding better concurrency, if an operation decides whether to wait for another operation or reset it by comparing how advanced they are in obtaining locks on their data items. If the conflicting operation is more advanced, the operation waits; otherwise, the operation resets the conflicting operation and seizes the lock on the item. While a similar approach has been used in many resource allocation algorithms, part of our contribution is in bounding the locality properties of this approach. A particularly intricate part of the proof shows that an operation cannot be repeatedly reset, without some operation in its $O(k)$-neighborhood completing.

Another novelty of our algorithm is in handling the inevitable situation that happens when overlapping operations that has made the same progress, that is, locked the same number of items, create a chain of conflicts. The symmetry inherent in this situation can, in principle, be broken by relying on operation identifiers, so as to avoid deadlocks and guarantee progress. However, this can create delay chains that are as long as the number of operations in this path (which can be n). Instead, we break such ties by having the conflicting operations try to atomically lock the two objects associated with the operations, using *double compare-and-swap* (DCAS). This easily and efficiently partitions the above kind of path into disjoint chains of length 2, ensuring that operations are delayed only due to close-by conflicts.

This scheme is made $3k$-local nonblocking by *helping* a blocking operation that is more advanced, instead of waiting for it to complete; we still reset conflicting operations that are less advanced (see Section 4). In this algorithm, helping chains replace delay chains, which intuitively explains how the $O(k)$ failure locality of the blocking algorithm translates into $O(k)$-local nonblocking. (This intuition is made concrete in the proof of the local nonblocking algorithm.)

Our algorithm demonstrates that DCAS provides critical leverage allowing to implement kRMW, for any $k > 2$, with locality that is difficult, perhaps impossible, to obtain using only CAS. While few architectures provide DCAS in hardware, DCAS is an ideal candidate to be supported by *hardware transactional memory* [10, 13], being a short transaction with static data set of minimal size (two). Alternatively, DCAS can be simulated in software from CAS using the highly-concurrent implementation of Attiya and Dagan [3], which is $O(\log^* n)$-local nonblocking. This yields kRMW implementation from CAS, which is $O(k + \log^* n)$-local nonblocking.

Related work. Afek et al. [1] present a kRMW algorithm, for any fixed k, which can be shown to be $O(k + \log^* n)$-local nonblocking. Their implementation works recursively in k, going through the locations according to their memory addresses, and coloring the items before proceeding to lock them; at the base of the recursion (for $k = 2$), it employs the binary algorithm of Attiya and Dagan [3]. To support the recursion, their implementation stores $O(k)$ information per location. The recursive structure of their algorithm makes it very complicated and infeasible as a basis for practical, dynamic situations, as it requires that k must be hard-wired, uniformly for all operations. In contrast, our algorithm is more flexible, as each operation can access a different numbers of data items. We store a constant amount of information, independent of k. More importantly, our algorithm can be modified not to require all the data items when the operation starts, allowing to extend it to dynamic situations (see Section 5).

Afek et al. [1] define two measures in order to capture the locality of nonblocking algorithm in a more quantitative sense. Roughly, an implementation has *d-local step complexity* if the step complexity of an operation is bounded by a function of the number of operations within distance d of it in the conflict graph; an implementation has *d-local contention* if two operations accessing the same memory location simultaneously are within distance d. Their implementation has $O(k + \log^* n)$-local step complexity and contention,[1] matching the complexities of our algorithm, when the DCAS is implemented as proposed in [3].

The first multi-word algorithms that rely on helping were the "locking without blocking" schemes [5, 15], where operations recursively help other operations, without releasing the items they have acquired. These algorithms are $O(n)$-local nonblocking. The static *software transactional memory* (STM) [14] also provides multi-word synchronization. In this algorithm, operations acquire words in the order of their memory addresses, and help only operations at distance 0; nevertheless, it is $O(n)$-local nonblocking. Harris et al. [8] give an implementation of dynamic multi-word operations with recursive helping, which is $O(n)$-local nonblocking.

2 Preliminaries

We consider a standard model for a shared memory system [4] in which a finite set of *asynchronous processes* $p_1, \ldots, p_n$ communicate by applying *primitive* operations to m shared *memory locations* $l_1, \ldots, l_m$. A *configuration* is a vector describing the states of processes and the values of memory locations. In the (unique) *initial configuration*, every process is in its initial state and every location contains its initial value.

An *event* is a computation step by a process consisting of some local computation and the application of a primitive to the memory. Besides standard READ and WRITE primitives, we employ CAS(l_j, exp, new), which writes the value *new* to location l_j if its value is equal to *exp*, and returns a success or failure flag. We also use a DCAS primitive, which is similar to CAS, but operates on two memory locations atomically.

An *execution interval* α is an alternating sequence of configurations and events, where each configuration is obtained from the previous configuration by applying an event. An *execution* is an execution interval starting with the initial configuration.

An *implementation* of a kRMW operation specifies the data representation of operations and data items, and provides algorithms, defined in terms of primitives applied to the memory locations, that processes follow in order to execute operations. The implementation has to be *linearizable* [11].

The *interval of an operation op*, denoted I_{op}, is the execution interval between the first event and last event (if exists) of the process executing the algorithm for *op*. Two operations *overlap* (in time) if their intervals overlap.

The *conflict graph* of a configuration C, is an undirected graph, in which vertices represent data items and edges represent operations; it captures the distance between operations overlapping in time. If C is a configuration during the execution interval of an operation *op*, and *op* accesses the data items l_i and l_j, the graph includes an

---

[1] Afek et al. [1] state $O(\log^* n)$-local complexities, treating k as a constant.

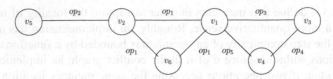

Fig. 1. The conflict graph of five overlapping operations: $op_1 = 3\mathsf{RMW}(v_1, v_2, v_6)$, $op_2 = 2\mathsf{RMW}(v_2, v_5)$, $op_3 = 2\mathsf{RMW}(v_1, v_3)$, $op_4 = 2\mathsf{RMW}(v_3, v_4)$, $op_5 = 2\mathsf{RMW}(v_1, v_4)$

edge, labeled op, between the vertices v_i and v_j. (See Fig. 1.) The conflict graph of an execution interval α is the union of the conflict graphs of all configurations C in α.

The *distance* between two operations, op and op', in a conflict graph, is the length of the shortest path between an item that is accessed by op and an item that is accessed by op'. In particular, if the operations access a common item, then the distance between op and op' is zero; the distance is ∞, if there is no such path. The *d-neighborhood of an operation op* contains all the operations within distance $\leq d$ from op.

We use the following variant on the failure locality definition [6]:

Definition 1. *The* failure locality *of an algorithm is d if some operation in the d-neighborhood of an operation op completes after a finite number of steps by the process that invokes op, unless some operation in the d-neighborhood of op fails.*[2]

The next definition is the nonblocking analogue of failure locality; it grantees progress within every neighborhood of a small diameter, even when there are failures. This property is stronger than requiring the implementation to be *nonblocking* [9].

Definition 2. *An algorithm is* d-local *nonblocking if some operation in the d-neighborhood of an operation op completes after a finite number of steps by the process that invokes op.*

3   A Blocking Algorithm with $3k$ Failure Locality

In this section, we present a general scheme for implementing kRMW with bounded locality; several methods of the scheme are then implemented in a way that yields a *blocking* implementation with $3k$ failure locality. In the next section, these methods are implemented in a way that yields a local nonblocking implementation.

An operation first acquires *locks* on its data items, one item after the other, then applies its changes atomically, and finally, release the locks. A contentious situation occurs when an operation op is blocked since one of its items is locked by another, *blocking* operation op'. Our algorithm uses the number of data items that are already locked to decide whether to *wait* for or *reset* op', i.e., release all the locks acquired by op', and seize the lock on the required item. That is, op waits for op' only if op' is more advanced in acquiring its locks, i.e., op' has locked more items. Otherwise, if op' has locked fewer items than op, op resets op'. Resetting another operation is synchronized

---

[2] Choy and Singh [6] require an operation to complete if no operation fails in its d-neighborhood, while we only guarantee that *some* operation in the neighborhood completes.

through an *operation object* that can be acquired by operations; an operation resets another operation only after acquiring ownership on its object.

The crux of the algorithm is in handling the *symmetric* case, when op and op' have locked the same number of items. In this case, the algorithms breaks the symmetry by applying DCAS to atomically acquire ownership of the two operation objects (op and op'); the operation that acquires ownership, resets its contender. This breaks apart long hold-and-wait chains that would deteriorate the locality as well as hold-and-wait cycles that can cause a deadlock.

Detailed description. Shared memory locations are grouped in contiguous blocks, called *item objects*, which are accessed by the processes. Each item object contains a *data* attribute and a *lock* attribute. For each operation, we maintain an *operation object* containing a *dataset*, referencing the set of items the operation has to modify, a *count keeper*, which is a tuple of a *counter* holding the number of items locked so far (initially 0), and a *lock* referencing the *owner* of the operation object ($\perp$ if the object is released). The object also contains a self pointer, *initiator*.

The psudocode for the general scheme appears in Algorithm 1, while the methods for the blocking implementation appear in Algorithm 2. An operation acquires the lock on its operation object (line 3) before proceeding to acquire the locks on its data items (lines 8-9). When the operation succeeds in locking an additional item (line 10) it increases the counter (line 11); when all the items are locked, i.e., the counter is equal to the number of data items, the operation can apply its changes (line 15), and release the locks on the data items (line 16). When op discovers that it is blocked by another operation op' (line 12), it calls handleContention, which compares the counters of op and op'. If the counter of op is higher than (line 22) or equal to (line 27) the counter of op', op tries to reset op' (lines 24, 29)so as to seize the lock on the item. For this purpose, op needs to hold the locks on the operation objects of both op and op'. When the counter of op is higher than the counter of op', op keeps the lock on its operation object, and tries to acquire the lock on the operation object of op' (line 23), using CAS suffices in this case (line 5 in Algorithm 2). When the counters are equal, op releases the lock on its operation object (line 26)and tries to lock atomically both operation objects (line 28) by applying DCAS (line 8 in Algorithm 2). If the counter of op is lower (line 31), then op releases the lock on its operation object (line 26) and tries again.

Outline of correctness proof: Locks on items are acquired and released and counters are changed either in the locking items loop (lines 9, 11), or during a reset (lines 36, 38, 45). In both cases, locks on data items and counters are modified only after the initiator acquires the lock on its operation object (lines 3, 23, 28). Moreover, the operation holds the lock on its operation object when it has locked all its items and cannot be reset. Thus, changes are applied (line 15) in isolation, implying that the algorithm is linearizable.

Several types of blocking and delay chains might be created during an execution of the algorithm. Some of these chains are created when an operation fails and causes other operations to wait. It is intuitively clear why the length of these chains is in $O(k)$.

More intricate delay chains are created when operations reset other operations. For example, assume an operation op_1 resets another operation op_2, then, a third operation resets op_1. At some later time, op_2 and op_1 can reacquire their locks, and the same

---

Algorithm 1. Multi-location read-modify-write: general scheme

```
 1: run() {
 2:     while (c ← READ(initiator.countKeeper.counter)) < size do
 3:         if initiator.lockOperation(initiator, c) then          // lock this operation object
 4:             initiator.execute()
 5: }

 6: execute() {
 7:     while (c ← READ(initiator.countKeeper.counter)) < size do    // more items to lock
 8:         item ← READ(initiator.dataset[c])
 9:         CAS(item.lock, ⊥, initiator)                          // acquire lock on item
10:         if READ(item.lock) = initiator then
11:             CAS(initiator.countKeeper, ⟨c,initiator⟩, ⟨c+1,initiator⟩)    // increase counter
12:         else                                       // initiator is not the owner of the item
13:             initiator.handleContention(item)
14:             return
15:     write modified values to the memory locations
16:     initiator.unlockDataset()
17: }

18: handleContention(Item item) {
19:     if (conflict ← READ(item.lock)) = ⊥ then return            // no conflict on item
20:     ⟨ic,iowner⟩ ← READ(initiator.countKeeper)
21:     ⟨cc,cowner⟩ ← READ(conflict.countKeeper)
22:     if ic > cc then                         // conflict with an operation with a lower counter
23:         if initiator.lockOperation(conflict, cc) then
24:             initiator.reset(conflict, item)
25:             return
26:     CAS(initiator.countKeeper, ⟨ic,initiator⟩, ⟨ic,⊥⟩)         // release this operation object
27:     if ic = cc then                        // conflict with an operation with an equal counter
28:         if initiator.lockTwoOperations(initiator, ic, conflict, cc) then
29:             initiator.reset(conflict, item)
30:             return
31:     if ic < cc then                        // conflict with an operation with a higher counter
32:         initiator.handleHigherConflict(conflict)
33: }

34: reset(Operation conflict, Item item) {
35:     c ← READ(initiator.countKeeper.counter)
36:     CAS(item.lock, conflict, initiator)                       // seize lock on item
37:     if READ(item.lock) = initiator then
38:         CAS(initiator.countKeeper, ⟨c,initiator⟩, ⟨c+1,initiator⟩)    // increase counter
39:     conflict.unlockDataset()
40: }

41: unlockDataset() {
42:     ⟨c,owner⟩ ← READ(initiator.countKeeper)
43:     for i = 0 to c do
44:         item ← READ(initiator.dataset[i])
45:         CAS(item.lock, initiator, ⊥)                          // release lock on item
46:     CAS(initiator.countKeeper, ⟨c,owner⟩, ⟨0,⊥⟩) // reset counter, release operation object
47: }
```

Algorithm 2. Multi-location read-modify-write: methods for the blocking algorithm

```
1:  handleHigherConflict(Operation conflict) {
2:      nop                                              // (blocking) busy wait
3:  }
4:  boolean lockOperation(Operation op, int c) {
5:      return CAS(op.countKeeper, ⟨c,⊥⟩, ⟨c,initiator⟩)
6:  }
7:  boolean lockTwoOperations(Operation iop, int ic, Operation cop, int cc) {
8:      return DCAS(iop.countKeeper,cop.countKeeper,⟨ic,⊥⟩,⟨cc,⊥⟩,⟨ic,initiator⟩,⟨cc,initiator⟩)
9:  }
```

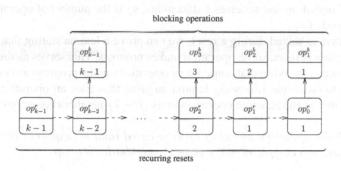

Fig. 2. A recurring resets scenario. The number below an operation indicates its counter; solid arrows indicate blocking and dashed arrows indicate reset.

scenario may happen over and over again. It may even seem as if a livelock can happen due to a cycle of resetting operations.

Since this behavior is the least intuitive, we start with the most delicate part of the proof, bounding the number of times an operation can be reset, before some operation completes in its k-neighborhood.

Fig. 2 presents an example where the superscript r denotes an operation that applies (and suffers from) recurring resets, and b denotes blocking operation that cause the operations in the recurring reset chain to release the locks on their operation objects. In the example, op_0^r is blocked by op_1^b with equal counter, 1, holding the lock on the item t_1. So, op_0^r releases the lock on its operation object (in order to try and reset op_1^b and seize the lock on t_1). op_1^r is blocked by op_0^r holding the lock on the item s_0. op_1^r resets op_0^r, seizes the lock on s_0, and increases its counter to 2. At this point, op_1^r is blocked by op_2^b with equal counter, 2. In a similar way, op_2^r resets op_1^r (holding the lock on the item s_1) after it releases the lock on its operation object, and op_3^r resets op_2^r. Then op_0^r and op_1^r are able to reacquire the locks on s_0 and s_1 respectively. This scenario is repeated with longer chains of resets each time. Inspecting the example reveals that after $k/2$ resets of op_0^r, op_{k-1}^r at distance $k-2$ from op_0^r locks all its data items, and it can complete.

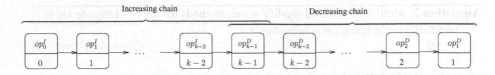

Fig. 3. The operations op_j^I create an increasing chain; each op_j^I operation is blocked by the operation op_{j+1}^I holding the lock on the data item t_{i+1}. The operations op_i^D create a decreasing chain; each op_i^D operation is blocked by the operation op_{i-1}^D holding the lock on its operation object.

Let $c(op)$ be the counter of op in a given configuration. For an operation op, k is the maximal number such that some operation that overlaps op in time, is within the $3k$-neighborhood of op and accesses k data items; n_k is the number of operations in the k-neighborhood of op.

Since an item is seized during a reset, we can prove a lemma stating that after each time an operation is reset, some operation makes progress. This serves as the base case for another lemma, proving that some set of operations make progress after each reset. This is used to prove the following lemma, arguing that after an operation is reset a bounded number of times, some operation in its $(k-1)$-neighborhood completes.

Lemma 1. *If the operation object of op is released (and re-acquired)* $(n_k)^2 k$ *times, then some operation completes in the* $(k-1)$-*neighborhood of op.*

We next describe how to bound the blocking chains created due to failures.

Consider an operation op that fails while holding the lock on its operation object and a data item. Another operation op' needing this item cannot complete without resetting op. If $c(op') > c(op)$, op' continues to hold the lock on its operation object, thus it may block a third operation with higher counter that cannot reset op', and so on. Fig. 3 shows such a chain, called a *decreasing chain*.

A decreasing chain consist of *stuck* operations, either initiated by a failed process or unable to increase their counter beyond some value. An operation op considers another operation op' *stuck at* m in an execution interval α, if in any configuration C during α in which op needs to reset op' (since op' blocks op), $c(op') \leq m$, and some operation (possibly op') has the lock on the operation object of op'.

Consider, for example, the operation op_2^D in Fig. 3 that needs to acquire the lock on a data item s_1, is blocked by another operation op_1^D with a lower counter that has the lock on its operation object. op_1^D does not complete either because it does not take steps or because it is repeatedly being reset by other operations, and always before op_2^D has a chance to acquire the lock on s_1, op_1^D reacquires the lock on its operation object and on s_1. Thus op_2^D considers op_1^D stuck at 1. For every i, $1 < i < k - 1$, the operation op_{i+1}^D in Fig. 3 considers the operation op_i^D stuck at i, since op_i^D holds the lock on its operation object while blocking op_{i+1}^D, leading to the decreasing chain.

Another blocking scenario is when an operation op that needs to acquire a lock on a data item is blocked by another operation whose counter is higher than $c(op)$. Moreover, op may block a third operation with a lower counter, and so on, creating an *increasing chain*, also depicted in Fig. 3. Since each operation in an increasing chain has counter that is strictly higher than the counter of the operation that it blocks, the length of the chain can easily be bounded by k.

Decreasing and increasing chains, together with recurring resets may create a longer delay chain. We show that these are the only ways to combine delay chains. In an *increasing-decreasing chain* of operations, every operation op is blocked either by the next operation in the chain op' with $c(op') > c(op)$ or by a decreasing chain that starts at op' with $c(op') \leq c(op)$. The next lemma bounds the length of increasing-decreasing chains and yields the bound on the failure locality.

Lemma 2. *Let* m, $0 \leq m \leq k$, *be the counter of an operation* op, *and assume no operation on an increasing-decreasing chain* idc *from* op *fails, and all the operations that reset an operation on* idc *complete the reset. Then some operation in the* $(3k - m - 2)$-*neighborhood of* op *completes after a finite number of steps by* op.

Theorem 1. *Algorithm 1 with the methods of Algorithm 2 has* $3k$ *failure locality.*

4   The $3k$-Local Nonblocking Algorithm

A $3k$-local nonblocking implementation is obtained by incorporating a recursive *helping* mechanism, as in other multi-word synchronization algorithms [5,14,15,8]. When a process p, executing an operation op, is blocked by another operation op' with a higher counter, p *helps* op' to complete and release the item, instead of waiting for the process p' executing op' to do so by itself (which may never happen due to the failure of p'). Helping means that p executes the protocol of op' via the helping method (we say that op helps op'). Helping is recursive, thus if while executing op', p discovers that op' is blocked by a third operation op'', then p recursively helps op''. Note that op still resets op' if the counter of op is equal or higher than the counter of op'. Special care is needed since op can also be blocked while trying to lock an operation object; in this case also, op helps the blocking operation.

The methods for the nonblocking algorithm appear in Algorithm 3. The first difference is that an operation op, blocked by another operation op' with higher counter (handleHigherConflict), helps op' to complete and release its data items (line 2).

While trying to acquire the lock on an operation object (lockOperation or lockTwoOperations), an operation op may succeed (line 16) or be blocked by another operation op'. If op' is the initiator of this operation (line 18), then op helps op' to complete, and release the operation object (line 19); otherwise (line 20), op' locked the operation object in order to reset its initiator, so op only helps op' to complete the reset (line 23).

In the helping scheme, several *executing processes* execute an operation. Helping is synchronized with CAS primitives to ensure that only one executing process performs each step of the operation, and the others have no effect.

The execution interval of an operation in the general scheme is divided into disjoint *rounds*, each starting after the lock on its object is released. If an executing process p discovers (while executing some operation op) that it is blocked by op' in its r-th round, it helps op' only in the context of this round. If the round number of op' changes, then op' released its operation lock, and the set of items locked by op' might have

---

Algorithm 3. Multi-location read-modify-write: methods for the nonblocking algorithm

```
 1:  handleHigherConflict(Operation conflict) {
 2:      conflict.execute()                                    // help execute the operation
 3:  }

 4:  boolean lockOperation(Operation op, int c) {
 5:      CAS(op.countKeeper, ⟨c,⊥⟩, ⟨c,initiator⟩)
 6:      return initiator.verifyLock(op)
 7:  }

 8:  boolean lockTwoOperations(Operation iop, int ic, Operation cop, int cc) {
 9:      DCAS(iop.countKeeper, cop.countKeeper, ⟨ic,⊥⟩, ⟨cc,⊥⟩, ⟨ic,initiator⟩, ⟨cc,initiator⟩)
10:      if initiator.verifyLock(iop) then
11:          return initiator.verifyLock(cop)
12:      return FALSE
13:  }

14:  boolean verifyLock(Operation op) {
15:      ⟨c,owner⟩ ← READ(op.countKeeper)
16:      if owner = initiator then
17:          return TRUE                                // succeeded locking the operation object
18:      if owner = op.initiator then    // the initiator of the operation owns the operation object
19:          op.execute()                                      // help execute the operation
20:      else                                    // a third operation owns the operation object
21:          oc ← READ(owner.countKeeper.counter)
22:          item ← READ(owner.dataset[oc])
23:          owner.reset(op,item)                              // help reset the operation
24:      return FALSE                                  // failed locking the operation object
25:  }
```

---

changed. As in the blocking algorithm, we omit details such as round numbers and ABA-prevention tags from the code, for clarity.

By showing that the executing processes are correctly synchronized by the round numbers and ABA-prevention tags, we can prove that the algorithm is linearizable. The locality properties of the algorithm are proved by reduction to the failure locality of the blocking algorithm. The next lemma shows that if a process takes many steps, it will eventually get to help any process that could be blocking it to make progress, thereby alleviating the effect of their failure.

Lemma 3. *If an executing process of an operation op takes an infinite number of steps, then an executing process of each of the operations on any increasing-decreasing chain idc from op takes an infinite number of steps and all the operations that reset an operation on idc complete the reset.*

Lemmas 2 and 3 imply that the algorithm is local nonblocking; similar ideas show that the algorithm has $3k$-local step complexity and $4k + 1$-local contention.

Theorem 2. *Algorithm 1 with the methods of Algorithm 3, is $3k$-local nonblocking.*

5   Discussion

We have presented a kRMW algorithm with improved throughput even when there is contention. Like Afek et al. [1], we can make this algorithm be wait-free by applying a known technique [2] while maintaining the locality properties of the algorithm.

Our algorithm has $O(k)$-locality properties, when using DCAS, and $O(k + \log^* n)$-locality properties, when using only CAS. It is theoretically interesting to obtain locality properties that are independent of n, without using DCAS. Even more intriguing is to investigate whether $O(k)$ is the best locality that can be achieved, even with DCAS.

Our algorithmic ideas can serve as the basis for *dynamic* STM. This is because our algorithm needs to know the identity of a data item only as it is about to lock it and can be adapted to work when data items are given one-by-one. Realizing a full-fledged STM requires to address many additional issues, e.g., handling read-only data, and optimizing the common case, which are outside the scope of this paper.

Acknowledgements. We thank Rachid Guerraoui, David Hay, Danny Hendler, Alex Kogan and Alex Shraer for helpful comments.

References

1. Afek, Y., Merritt, M., Taubenfeld, G., Touitou, D.: Disentangling multi-object operations. In: PODC 1997, pp. 111–120 (1997)
2. Anderson, J.H., Moir, M.: Universal constructions for multi-object operations. In: PODC 1995, pp. 184–193 (1995)
3. Attiya, H., Dagan, E.: Improved implementations of binary universal operations. J. ACM 48(5), 1013–1037 (2001)
4. Attiya, H., Welch, J.: Distributed Computing: Fundamentals, Simulations and Advanced Topics, 2nd edn. John Wiley & Sons, West Sussex (2004)
5. Barnes, G.: A method for implementing lock-free shared-data structures. In: SPAA 1993, pp. 261–270 (1993)
6. Choy, M., Singh, A.K.: Efficient fault-tolerant algorithms for distributed resource allocation. ACM Trans. Program. Lang. Syst. 17(3), 535–559 (1995)
7. Ha, P.H., Tsigas, P., Wattenhofer, M., Wattenhofer, R.: Efficient multi-word locking using randomization. In: PODC 2005, pp. 249–257 (2005)
8. Harris, T.L., Fraser, K., Pratt, I.A.: A practical multi-word compare-and-swap operation. In: Malkhi, D. (ed.) DISC 2002. LNCS, vol. 2508, pp. 265–279. Springer, Heidelberg (2002)
9. Herlihy, M.: Wait-free synchronization. ACM Trans. Program. Lang. Syst. 13(1), 124–149 (1991)
10. Herlihy, M., Moss, J.E.B.: Transactional memory: Architectural support for lock-free data structures. In: ISCA 1993, pp. 289–300 (1993)
11. Herlihy, M.P., Wing, J.M.: Linearizability: A correctness condition for concurrent objects. ACM Trans. Program. Lang. Syst. 12(3), 463–492 (1990)
12. Israeli, A., Rappoport, L.: Disjoint-access-parallel implementations of strong shared memory primitives. In: PODC 1994, pp. 151–160 (1994)
13. Rajwar, R., Goodman, J.R.: Transactional lock-free execution of lock-based programs. In: ASPLOS 2002, pp. 5–17 (2002)
14. Shavit, N., Touitou, D.: Software transactional memory. Dist. Comp. 10(2), 99–116 (1997)
15. Turek, J., Shasha, D., Prakash, S.: Locking without blocking: Making lock based concurrent data structure algorithms nonblocking. In: PODS 1992, pp. 212–222 (1992)

Fault Tolerance in Finite State Machines Using Fusion

Bharath Balasubramanian[1], Vinit Ogale[1], and Vijay K. Garg[2],*

[1] Parallel and Distributed Systems Laboratory
Dept. of Electrical and Computer Engineering
The University of Texas at Austin
[2] IBM India Research Lab (IRL)
Delhi
{balasubr, ogale, garg}@ece.utexas.edu

Abstract. Given a set of n different deterministic finite state machines (DFSMs), we examine the problem of tolerating k faults among them. The traditional approach to this problem involves replication, requiring $n.k$ backup DFSMs. For example, given two state machines, say A and B, to tolerate two faults, this approach maintains two copies each of A and B, thus resulting in a total of six DF-SMs in the system. In this paper, we question the optimality of such an approach and present another approach based on the 'fusion' of state machines allowing for more efficient backups. We introduce the theory of fusion machines and provide an algorithm which can generate fusion machines corresponding to a given set of machines. Further, we have implemented this algorithm and tested it for various examples. It is important to note that our approach requires only k backup DF-SMs, as opposed to the $n.k$ backup DFSMs required by the replication approach.

1 Introduction

In distributed systems, it is often necessary to maintain the execution state of a server in the event of faults. Hence, designing fault tolerant systems remains an interesting avenue for research in this field. Traditional approaches to this problem require some form of replication. One commonly used technique, which forms the basis of the work done in [1,2,3,4,5,6], involves replicating the server DFSMs and sending client requests in the same order to all the servers. Another approach, seen in [7,8], involves designating one of the servers as the primary and all the others as backups. Client requests are handled by the primary server, until it fails, and then one of the backups take over. In both these approaches, given n different DFSMs, in order to tolerate k faults, we need to maintain k extra copies of each DFSM, resulting in a total of $n.k$ backup DFSMs.

We propose an approach called *fusion*, that allows for more efficient backups. Given n different DFSMs, we tolerate k faults by having k backup DFSMs as opposed to the $n.k$ DFSMs required in the replication based approaches. We assume a system model that has infrequent fail-stop faults [9]. The technique discussed in this paper deals with

* Supported in part by the NSF Grants CNS-0509024, Texas Education Board Grant 781, and Cullen Trust for Higher Education Endowed Professorship. A significant portion of the work was performed when the author was at the University of Texas at Austin.

S. Rao et al. (Eds.): ICDCN 2008, LNCS 4904, pp. 124–134, 2008.
© Springer-Verlag Berlin Heidelberg 2008

recovering the *state* of the failed machines and not the entire DFSM (which, in almost all cases, is stored on some form of failure-resistant permanent storage medium).

Figure. 1(i) and Fig. 1(ii) show two mod-3 counters, A and B, acting on different inputs, I_0 and I_1 respectively. For tolerating two failures, traditional approaches would require two more copies of each DFSM requiring 6 DFSMs in all. The machine shown in Fig. 1(iii) is the *reachable cross product* machine (defined formally in Sect. 3) corresponding to the counters. Each state corresponding to this machine is a tuple, in which the first element corresponds to the state of A, and the second element corresponds to the state of B. A simple version of fusion would be to maintain the reachable cross product of A and B.

In general, the reachable cross product may have a large number of states. However, for recovery, along with the backup machines, if we use information from the machines that have not failed, it is often possible to design backup DFSMs that are much smaller than the reachable cross product.

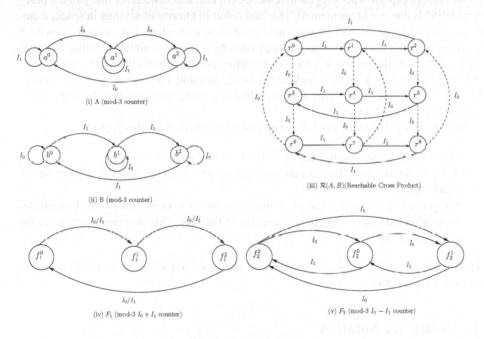

(i) A (mod-3 counter)

(ii) B (mod-3 counter)

(iii) $\mathcal{R}(A, B)$(Reachable Cross Product)

(iv) F_1 (mod-3 $I_0 + I_1$ counter)

(v) F_2 (mod-3 $I_0 - I_1$ counter)

Fig. 1. Mod 3 Counters

In this specific example, we can intuitively see that, instead of two reachable cross product machines (with nine states each), it is sufficient to maintain just two machines that compute $(I_0 + I_1)$ MOD 3 and $(I_0 - I_1)$ MOD 3 in order to tolerate two faults. These two machines are called *fusions* of A and B and are illustrated in Fig. 1(iv) and Fig. 1(v). We will generate the same machines using our algorithm, as shown in Sec. 5.

The work presented in [10] introduces the idea of fusible data structures. In this paper, the authors show that commonly used data structures such as arrays, hash tables, stacks and queues can be fused into a single fusible structure, smaller than the combined size of the original structures. Our idea is similar to this approach, in the sense that we generate a reachable cross product DFSM which contains the information corresponding to all the DFSMs in our system. The work presented in this paper effectively presents an algorithm to compute a fusion operation given a set of specific input machines.

Extensive work has been done [11,12] on the minimization of completely specified DFSMs. In these approaches, the basic idea is to create equivalence classes of the state space of the DFSM and then combine them based on the transition functions. Even though our approach is also focussed on reducing the reachable cross product corresponding to a set of given n machines, it is important to note that the machines we generate need not be equivalent to the combined DFSM. In fact, we implicitly assume that the input machines to our algorithm are reduced a priori using these techniques.

In this paper, we develop the theory and algorithms for computing fusions. Note that, in some cases the most efficient fusion could be the reachable cross product machine. However, our experiments suggest that there exist efficient fusions for many of the practical DFSMs that we implemented. This can result in enormous savings in space, especially when a large number of machines need to be backed up. For example, consider a sensor network with 100 sensors, each running a mod-3 counter counting different inputs (for example, parameters like temperature, pressure, humidity and so on). To tolerate a fault in such a system, replication would demand 100 new sensors for backup. Fusion, on the other hand, can tolerate a fault by using only one new backup sensor with exactly three states.

Summarizing, we make the following contributions through this paper:

- We introduce the idea and theory of the fusion of state machines.
- We present an algorithm to find fusion machines corresponding to a given set of machines.
- We provide an implementation of this algorithm in Java. We have tested the implementation with many practical examples of DFSMs. This program is available for download [13].

The proofs for all the theorems and lemmas presented in the paper, are provided in the technical report [14].

2   Model and Notation

We now discuss in detail, the model and notation used in this paper. The system under consideration consists of deterministic finite state machines (DFSMs) satisfying the following conditions:

- The DFSMs execute independently with no shared state or communication between them. Hence there is no way for one DFSM to independently determine the current state in which any other DFSM is executing.
- The DFSMs act concurrently on the same set of events. If some event e is not applicable for a certain DFSM, we assume that e is ignored by that DFSM.

– The system model assumes fail-stop failures [9]. A failure in any of the DFSMs results in the loss of the current state but the underlying DFSM remains intact. We assume that this failure can be detected. Hence, if the current state can be regenerated, the machine can continue executing.

A DFSM in this system, denoted by A, is a quadruple, (X, Σ, α, a^0), where,

– X is the finite set of states corresponding to A.
– Σ is the finite set of events common to all the DFSMs in the system.
– $\alpha : X \times \Sigma \to X$, is the transition function corresponding to A. If the current state of A is s, and an event σ is applied on it, the next state can be uniquely determined as $\alpha(s, \sigma)$.
– a^0 is the initial state corresponding to A.

A state, $s \in X$, is *reachable* iff there exists a sequence of events, which, when applied on the initial state a^0, takes the machine to state s. Our model assumes that all the states corresponding to the machines are reachable.

The *size* of a machine A, is the number of states in X, and is denoted by $|A|$.

We now define the concept of homomorphism and isomorphism [15] corresponding to two machines.

Definition 1. *(Homomorphism) A homomorphism from a machine* A $(X_A, \Sigma, \alpha_A, a^0)$ *onto a machine* B $(X_B, \Sigma, \alpha_B, b^0)$, *is the mapping,* $\psi : X_A \to X_B$, *satisfying the following relationship:*

– $\psi(a^0) = b^0$
– $\forall s \in X_A, \forall \sigma \in \Sigma, \psi(\alpha_A(s, \sigma)) = \alpha_B(\psi(s), \sigma)$

If such a homomorphism, ψ, exists from X_A onto X_B, B is said to be homomorphic to A and we denote it as $B \preccurlyeq A$. The mapping, ψ, is called an *isomorphsim* if it is both one-one and onto. In this case, B is said to be isomorphic to A and vice-versa. We denote it as $B \cong A$.

Consider the two machines $F_2(X_2, \Sigma, \alpha_2, f_2^0)$ and $\mathcal{R}(\mathcal{A}, \mathcal{B})(X_\mathcal{R}, \Sigma, \alpha_\mathcal{R}, r^0)$ shown in Fig. 1(v) and Fig. 1(iii) respectively. Let us define a mapping, $\psi : X_r \to X_2$, as follows:
$\psi(r^0) = \psi(r^4) = \psi(r^8) = f_2^0$; $\psi(r^2) = \psi(r^3) = \psi(r^7) = f_2^1$; $\psi(r^1) = \psi(r^5) = \psi(r^6) = f_2^2$
For $s = r^0$, $\sigma = I_0$,

$$\psi(\alpha_\mathcal{R}(r^0, I_0)) = \psi(r^3) = f_2^1 \text{ and } \alpha_2(\psi(r^0), I_0) = \alpha_2(f_2^0, I_0) = f_2^1$$

It can be verified that,

$$\forall s \in X_\mathcal{R}, \forall \sigma \in \Sigma, \psi(\alpha_\mathcal{R}(s, \sigma)) = \alpha_2(\psi(s), \sigma)$$

Hence, F_2 is homomorphic to $\mathcal{R}(\mathcal{A}, \mathcal{B})$ or $F_2 \preccurlyeq \mathcal{R}(\mathcal{A}, \mathcal{B})$. Based on the mapping ψ defined above, we can represent the states of machine F_2 as follows:

$$f_2^0 = \{r^4, r^0, r^8\}, \ f_2^1 = \{r^2, r^3, r^7\}, \ f_2^2 = \{r^6, r^1, r^5\}$$

Observation 1. *Consider two machines* $A(X_A, \Sigma, \alpha_A, a^0)$ *and* $B(X_B, \Sigma, \alpha_A, b^0)$, *such that, there exists a homomorphism* ψ *from* X_A *onto* X_B. *Every state,* $b \in X_B$, *can be represented equivalently by a set of states specified by* $\psi^{-1}(b)$.

Consider an event sequence "I_1, I_0" applied on the initial state of $\mathcal{R}(\mathcal{A}, \mathcal{B})$. $\mathcal{R}(\mathcal{A}, \mathcal{B})$ reaches the state $r^4 (r^0 \to r^1 \to r^4)$. On applying the same event sequence on the initial state of F_2, F_2 reaches state $f_2^0 (f_2^0 \to f_2^2 \to f_2^0)$. We know that, $\psi(r^4) = f_2^0$. This property can be generalized for all event sequences.

Lemma 1. *Consider two machines $A(X_A, \Sigma, \alpha_A, a^0)$ and $B(X_B, \Sigma, \alpha_B, b^0)$, such that, there exists a homomorphism ψ from X_A onto X_B. On the application of any r events on a^0 and b^0, if A and B reach states a and b respectively, then, $\psi(a) = b$.*

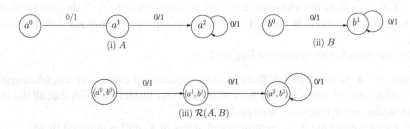

(i) A (ii) B

(iii) $\mathcal{R}(A, B)$

Fig. 2. Reachable Cross Product Machine

3   Reachable Cross Product Machine

In this section, we define the reachable cross product machine corresponding to a set of machines.

Consider a set of n machines, $\mathcal{A} = \{A_1, \ldots, A_n\}$, where machine, $A_i \in \mathcal{A}$, is represented by the quadruple $(X_i, \Sigma, \alpha_i, a_i^0)$. We now define the reachable cross product machine corresponding to $\mathcal{A}$, denoted $\mathcal{R}(\mathcal{A})$. $\mathcal{R}(\mathcal{A})$ is a quadruple $(X_\mathcal{R}, \Sigma, \alpha_\mathcal{R}, r^0)$, where,

- $X_\mathcal{R}$ is the finite set of states corresponding to $\mathcal{R}(\mathcal{A})$. We consider the set X of all tuples as defined:

$$X := \{ \langle a_1, a_2, \ldots, a_n \rangle : a_i \in X_i \}$$

  $X_\mathcal{R}$, is the set of states in X, reachable from the initial state $\langle a_1^0, a_2^0, \ldots, a_n^0 \rangle$.

  Consider machines A, B and their reachable cross product $\mathcal{R}(A, B)$ shown in Fig. 2.

$$X_\mathcal{R} := \{ \langle a^0, b^0 \rangle, \langle a^1, b^1 \rangle, \langle a^2, b^1 \rangle \}$$

- Σ is the finite set of events common to all the machines in our system.
- $\alpha_\mathcal{R} : X_\mathcal{R} \times \Sigma \to X_\mathcal{R}$, is the transition function corresponding to $\mathcal{R}(\mathcal{A})$, defined as follows:

$$\forall \langle a_1, a_2, \ldots, a_n \rangle \in X_\mathcal{R}, \sigma \in \Sigma, \alpha(\langle a_1, a_2, \ldots, a_n \rangle, \sigma) := \langle \alpha_1(a_1, \sigma), \ldots, \alpha_n(a_n, \sigma) \rangle$$

- r^0 is the initial state of $\mathcal{R}(\mathcal{A})$. As mentioned above, $r^0 := \langle a_1^0, a_2^0, \ldots, a_n^0 \rangle$.

Consider machines B and $\mathcal{R}(A, B)$, shown in Fig. 2. We can define a homomorphic mapping ψ from $X_\mathcal{R}$ onto X_B as follows:

$$\psi(\langle a^0, b^0 \rangle) = b^0; \quad \psi(\langle a^0, b^1 \rangle) = b^1; \quad \psi(\langle a^2, b^1 \rangle) = b^1$$

Lemma 2. *Consider a set of n machines, $\mathcal{A} = \{A_1, \ldots, A_n\}$, where machine, $A_i \in \mathcal{A}$, is represented by the quadruple $(X_i, \Sigma, \alpha_i, a_i^0)$. For all $A_i \in \mathcal{A}$, $A_i \preccurlyeq \mathcal{R}(\mathcal{A})$.*

4 Fusion of DFSMs

In this section, we explain the theory of *fusion* of DFSMs along with the relevant results.

Definition 2. *(Fusion) Given a set of n machines, $\mathcal{A} = \{A_1, \ldots, A_n\}$, we call the set of k machines, $\mathcal{F} = \{F_1, \ldots, F_k\}$, as the k-fusion of $\mathcal{A}$ iff the reachable cross product of any n machines from $\mathcal{A} \bigcup \mathcal{F}$ is isomorphic to the reachable cross product of all the machines in $\mathcal{A}$.*

Henceforth, any 1-fusion machine is simply referred to as a *fusion* machine. Note that the reachable cross product of $\mathcal{A}$, $\mathcal{R}(\mathcal{A})$, is always a fusion machine.

Consider the example shown in Fig. 1. Machines $A(X_A, \Sigma, \alpha_A, a^0)$ and $B(X_B, \Sigma, \alpha_B, b^0)$ are mod-3 counters each acting on inputs I_0 and I_1 respectively and $\mathcal{R}(A, B)$ is the reachable cross product machine corresponding to them. The machines $F_1(X_1, \Sigma, \alpha_1, f_1^0)$ and $F_2(X_2, \Sigma, \alpha_2, f_2^0)$ are two independently executing machines computing $(I_0 + I_1)$ MOD 3 and $(I_0 - I_1)$ MOD 3 respectively. It can be verified that,

$$\mathcal{R}(A, F_1) \cong \mathcal{R}(A, F_2) \cong \mathcal{R}(B, F_1) \cong \mathcal{R}(B, F_2) \cong \mathcal{R}(F_1, F_2) \cong \mathcal{R}(A, B)$$

Hence, F_1 and F_2 form a 2-fusion of A and B. Since, $\mathcal{R}(F_1, F_2) \cong \mathcal{R}(A, B)$, from Lemma 2, both F_1 and F_2 are homomorphic to $\mathcal{R}(\mathcal{A})$. We generalize this result in the following lemma.

Lemma 3. *Given a set of n machines, $\mathcal{A} = \{A_1, \ldots, A_n\}$ and a corresponding k-fusion, $\mathcal{F} = \{F_1, \ldots, F_k\}$, every machine in $\mathcal{F}$ is homomorphic to $\mathcal{R}(A)$.*

As explained in Sect. 3, the reachable cross product machine contains information corresponding to all the component machines. Given any two machines A and B, each state corresponding to $\mathcal{R}(A, B)$ is a tuple in which the first state corresponds to the state of A and the second state corresponds to the state of B. Hence, given the state of $\mathcal{R}(A, B)$, we can uniquely determine the state of both A and B. The converse is trivially true.

Lemma 4. *Given a set of n machines, $\mathcal{A} = \{A_1, \ldots, A_n\}$, we can uniquely determine the state of all the machines in $\mathcal{A} \cup \mathcal{F}$, iff we can construct the corresponding state of $\mathcal{R}(\mathcal{A})$.*

The four machines (A, B, F_1, F_2) can tolerate up to two failures. For example, let us assume that both A and B fail. Since $\mathcal{R}(F_1, F_2) \cong \mathcal{R}(A, B)$, the state of $\mathcal{R}(A, B)$ can be determined using the state of F_1 and F_2. From Lemma 4, the state of both A and B can be determined. We now generalize this result to n original machines and k fusion machines.

Theorem 1. *Given a set of n machines, $\mathcal{A} = \{A_1, \ldots, A_n\}$ and a set of k machines, $\mathcal{F} = \{F_1, \ldots, F_k\}$, we can uniquely determine the state of any k failed machines belonging to $\mathcal{A} \bigcup \mathcal{F}$, if $\mathcal{F}$ is a k-fusion of $\mathcal{A}$.*

In the example given in Fig. 1, we saw that,

$$\mathcal{R}(A, F_1) \cong \mathcal{R}(A, F_2) \cong \mathcal{R}(B, F_1) \cong \mathcal{R}(B, F_2) \cong \mathcal{R}(F_1, F_2) \cong \mathcal{R}(A, B)$$

Since, $\mathcal{R}(A, F_1) \cong \mathcal{R}(B, F_1) \cong \mathcal{R}(A, B)$, F_1 is a 1-fusion of A and B. Similarly, F_2 is also a 1-fusion of A and B.

Lemma 5. *Given a set of n machines, $\mathcal{A} = \{A_1, \ldots, A_n\}$, and a corresponding k-fusion, $\mathcal{F} = \{F_1, \ldots, F_k\}$, every subset of $\mathcal{F}$ of size k' is a k'-fusion of $\mathcal{A}$.*

Each state corresponding to $\mathcal{R}(\mathcal{A})$ is a n-tuple $\langle a_1, \ldots, a_n \rangle$, where a_i is a state corresponding to machine A_i. Since every fusion machine is homomorphic to $\mathcal{R}(\mathcal{A})$, it follows from Observation 1 that each state in any of the fusion machines can be represented by a set of n-tuples. We call this the *tuple-set* of a state and denote it as, $T = \{t_1, \ldots, t_m\}$, where t_i $(1 \le i \le m)$ is a n-tuple corresponding to a state in $\mathcal{R}(\mathcal{A})$.

In the example shown in Fig. 1, since $F_2 \preccurlyeq \mathcal{R}(\mathcal{A})$, each state can be represented as follows:

$$f_2^0 = \{r^4, r^0, r^8\}, \ f_2^1 = \{r^2, r^3, r^7\}, \ f_2^2 = \{r^6, r^1, r^5\}$$

Consider a n-tuple set, $T = \{r^0, r^1, r^8\}$, where, $r^0 = \langle a^0, b^0 \rangle$, $r^1 = \langle a^0, b^1 \rangle$ and $r^8 = \langle a^2, b^2 \rangle$. T can never be a state of any fusion machine F, because, given that F is in state T and A is in state a^0, we cannot uniquely determine whether $\mathcal{R}(A, B)$ is in state $\langle a^0, b^0 \rangle$ or $\langle a^0, b^1 \rangle$. From Lemma 4, $\mathcal{R}(A, F) \not\equiv \mathcal{R}(A, B)$. Hence, for $n = 2$, we cannot tolerate even one common element among the states in T.

We now generalize this result to impose a condition on a tuple-set corresponding to any state of a fusion machine. We use this condition in the algorithm to generate the fusion machines by reducing the reachable cross product machine. The intersection of two n-tuples, denoted by $\cap$, is the set containing all the elements common to both the n-tuples. In the example above, $\langle a^0, b^0 \rangle \cap \langle a^0, b^1 \rangle = \{a^0\}$.

Lemma 6. *Let, $\mathcal{A} = \{A_1, \ldots, A_n\}$, be a set of n machines and let $F(X_F, \Sigma, \alpha_F, f^0)$ be a 1-fusion of $\mathcal{A}$.*

For any tuple-set, $T = \{t_1, \ldots, t_m\}$, corresponding to a state from the machine F, for all $t_i, t_j \in X_\mathcal{R}$, the pairwise intersection of any t_i, t_j has less than $n - 1$ elements.

We now see the conditions which need to be imposed on fusion machines.

Theorem 2. *Given a set of n machines, $\mathcal{A} = \{A_1, \ldots, A_n\}$, a machine $F(X_F, \Sigma, \alpha_F, f^0)$ is a 1-fusion of $\mathcal{A}$ iff:*

1. *$F \preccurlyeq \mathcal{R}(\mathcal{A})$.*
2. *For any tuple-set, $T = \{t_1, \ldots, t_m\}$, corresponding to a state from the machine F, for all $t_i, t_j \in X_\mathcal{R}$, the pairwise intersection of any t_i, t_j has less than $n - 1$ elements.*

From Lemma 6, we can obtain an upper bound on the size of the tuple-set, $T = \{t_1, \ldots, t_m\}$, corresponding to the state of any fusion machine. We refer to this size as T_{max}.

Consider the case where $\mathcal{A}$ contains two machines A and B, where, $X_A = \{a^0, a^1\}$ and $X_B = \{b^0, b^1, b^2\}$. Let us assume that a machine $F(X_F, \Sigma, \alpha_F, f^0)$ is a 1-fusion of A and B. From Lemma 6, the number of common elements between any two n-tuples corresponding to any state, $T \in X_F$, is less than one. T can be $\{\langle a^0, b^0 \rangle, \langle a^1, b^1 \rangle\}$ or $\{\langle a^0, b^1 \rangle, \langle a^1, b^0 \rangle\}$. If T contained more than two n-tuples, then, either a^0 or a^1 is repeated more than once. Hence, $|T| \le 2$.

Lemma 7. *Let, $\mathcal{A} = \{A_1, \ldots, A_n\}$, be a set of machines and let $F(X_F, \Sigma, \alpha_F, f^0)$ be a 1-fusion of $\mathcal{A}$.*

Without loss of generality let us assume that the elements of $\mathcal{A}$ are enumerated in increasing order of their sizes.

For any tuple-set, $T = \{t_1, \ldots, t_m\}$, corresponding to a state from X_F, the size of T is bound by the following expression:

$|T| \leq \prod_{i=1}^{n-1} |A_i|.$

We now present a lower bound on the size of the fusion machines.

Theorem 3. *Let, $\mathcal{A} = \{A_1, \ldots, A_n\}$, be a set of machines and let $F(X_F, \Sigma, \alpha_F, f^0)$ be a 1-fusion of $\mathcal{A}$. The size of F is greater than or equal to $\frac{|\mathcal{R}(\mathcal{A})|}{T_{max}}$.*

5 Algorithm to Generate Fusion Machines

Consider a set of n machines, $\mathcal{A} = \{A_1, \ldots, A_n\}$, where, $A_i \in \mathcal{A}$, is represented by the quadruple $(X_i, \Sigma, \alpha_i, a_i^0)$. The reachable cross product corresponding to these machines, $\mathcal{R}(\mathcal{A})$, is represented by the quadruple $(X_{\mathcal{R}}, \Sigma, \alpha_{\mathcal{R}}, r^0)$.

The goal of the algorithm is to generate k-fusion ($1 \leq k \leq n$) machines corresponding to $\mathcal{A}$. The algorithm generates $\mathcal{R}(\mathcal{A})$ and then reduces it to generate machines homomorphic to $\mathcal{R}(\mathcal{A})$ and satisfying Lemma 6.

We first define the following:

- *valid* state: A set of n-tuples, $T = \{t_1, \ldots, t_m\}$, where t_i ($1 \leq i \leq m$) is a n-tuple corresponding to a state in $X_{\mathcal{R}}$, is said to be valid, if it satisfies Lemma 6.
- Set of valid n-tuple sets, V: An element, $T \in V$, can be represented as $T = \{t_1, \ldots, t_m\}$, where t_i ($1 \leq i \leq m$) is a n-tuple corresponding to a state in $X_{\mathcal{R}}$. In addition, T needs to be a valid state and r^0 must belong to T.
- Transition function, next: We define the transition function, next : $2^{X_{\mathcal{R}}} \times \Sigma \rightarrow 2^{X_{\mathcal{R}}}$, as follows:

$$\forall T \in 2^{X_{\mathcal{R}}}, \forall \sigma \in \Sigma, \text{next}(T, \sigma) = \{ \alpha_{\mathcal{R}}(t_1, \sigma), \alpha_{\mathcal{R}}(t_2, \sigma), \ldots, \alpha_{\mathcal{R}}(t_m, \sigma) \}$$

- Set of 1-fusions $\mathcal{B}^1$: Our algorithm generates a set of 1-fusions corresponding to $\mathcal{A}$, denoted by $\mathcal{B}^1$.

The algorithm for generating the 1-fusions is shown in Fig. 3. The input to the algorithm is the set of valid n-tuple sets V. The basic idea is to generate all the n-tuple sets containing r^0 and satisfying Lemma 6. Consider the example shown in Fig. 1. Since $n = 2$, any n-tuple set, T, is valid, if for any two tuples in T, the number of common elements is less than 1.

We first generate $\mathcal{R}(A, B)$. As seen in Fig. 1(iii), it has 9 states. Starting from this, we generate V. Here,

$$V = \{\{r^0\}, \{r^0, r^7\}, \{r^0, r^4\}, \{r^0, r^5\}, \{r^0, r^8\}, \{r^0, r^7, r^5\}, \{r^0, r^4, r^8\}\}$$

Starting with each element, $T \in V$, as the initial state, we generate machines by recursively finding the next state, applying function next. If a machine contains an invalid state, it is discarded. Finally, we add these machines to $\mathcal{B}^1$ if they are homomorphic to $\mathcal{R}(\mathcal{A})$.

```
function Compute_1-Fusion
Input: V; //set of all valid tuple sets containing r⁰
Output: B¹; //set of 1-fusions of A
for all (T ∈ V), do
      initialState = T;
      B = generateMachine(initialState);
      if (B ≠ null) and (B ≼ R(A)), then
          B¹ = B¹ ∪ {B}; //B is a 1-fusion
      end if
end for
end function
```

```
function generateMachine
Inputs: initialState;
Output: fusionMachine;
/*
recursively generate fusionMachine starting from
initialState applying the transition function next
*/
          ⋮
if (all states in fusionMachine are valid), then
      return fusionMachine;
else
      return null;
end function
```

Fig. 3. Algorithm to generate 1-fusions

Referring to the example in Fig. 1, we generate fusions starting from the elements in V. Let us consider an element $T = \{r^0, r^4, r^8\}$.

$$\texttt{next}(T, I_0) = \texttt{next}(\{r^0, r^4, r^8\}, I_0) = \{\alpha_{\mathcal{R}}(r^0, I_0), \alpha_{\mathcal{R}}(r^4, I_0), \alpha_{\mathcal{R}}(r^8, I_0)\} = \{r^2, r^3, r^7\}$$

Since $\{r^2, r^3, r^7\}$ is valid, we continue constructing the machine and finally generate a machine identical to F_2, shown in Fig. 1(v). Similarly, starting from $\{r^0, r^7, r^5\}$, we generate machine F_1, shown in Fig. 1(iv).

Theorem 4. *The algorithm in Fig. 3 generates fusions corresponding to a given set of machines.*

Given a set of 1-fusions, $\mathcal{B}^1$, we now proceed to see if subsets of $\mathcal{B}^1$ form k-fusions $(1 < k \leq n)$. Any k machines, $\mathcal{B}' \subseteq \mathcal{B}^1$, is a k-fusion if for all subsets $A' \subseteq A$, of size $n - k$, $R(A' \cup B') \cong R(A)$. This simply follows from the definition of k-fusion.

Let us assume that the number of states in $R(A)$ is N_r. The time complexity of the algorithm to generate 1-fusions is given by $O(|V|N_r|\Sigma|)$ and that of the algorithm to generate k-fusions is given by $O(^{|V|}C_k \,^nC_{n-k}\, N_r|\Sigma|)$. For a detailed time complexity analysis, refer to the technical report.

It is important to note that the algorithm in Fig. 3 creates only a subset of fusion machines that can be obtained by applying the next transition to all valid initial tuple sets. An exhaustive algorithm to generate all fusions can be found in the technical report.

6   Implementation and Results

We implemented a fusion machine generator in Java (JDK 6) based on the algorithm discussed in this paper. The results are shown in the following table. We compare the number states of the reachable cross product (RCP) with the smallest 1-fusion machine generated by our algorithm.

Original Machines	RCP	Fusion	$|V|$
Divider, One Counter, Zero Counter	27	6	231
Divider, One Counter, Pattern Generator	36	27	33
Even Parity Checker, Odd Parity Checker, Toggle Switch, Shift Register	32	19	13
One Counter, Zero Counter, Shift Register	72	25	155
TCP, MESI(Cache), Shift Register	340	340	1
Even Parity Checker, Odd Parity Checker, MESI	16	16	3

The time complexity of the algorithm is dominated by the size of V. As seen from the results, in many practical examples, the size of V is much smaller than the theoretical complexity. There are many cases in which the smallest fusion machine generated by our algorithm is considerably smaller than the corresponding reachable cross product for the given set of machines. However, there are scenarios in which the algorithm yields no reduction. In such cases replication might be a cheaper approach.

Note that, recovery involves more overhead in our algorithm when compared to replication, since we need the state of all the $n - k$ machines to recover the state of the k missing machines.

7   Conclusion

In this paper, we present a new fusion approach to design fault tolerant systems using a small number of backup machines. In many cases, fusion results in significant space savings compared to traditional replication based approaches. Though the algorithm presented in this paper for computing the fusion is expensive, it is important to note that this needs to be executed only once at design time.

The idea introduced in this paper opens up several interesting avenues for further research. The minimality of fusion machines seems to be an interesting problem. We are currently working on a polynomial time algorithm for generating minimal fusions.

References

1. Lamport, L.: The implementation of reliable distributed multiprocess systems. Computer networks 2, 95–114 (1978)
2. Pease, M., Shostak, R., Lamport, L.: Reaching agreement in the presence of faults. J. ACM 27 (1980)
3. Gafni, E., Lamport, L.: Disk paxos. Distrib. Comput. 16, 1–20 (2003)
4. Tenzakhti, F., Day, K., Ould-Khaoua, M.: Replication algorithms for the world-wide web. J. Syst. Archit. 50 (2004)
5. Schneider, F.B.: Implementing fault-tolerant services using the state machine approach: A tutorial. ACM Computing Surveys 22, 299–319 (1990)
6. Sivasubramanian, S., Szymaniak, M., Pierre, G., van Steen, M.: Replication for web hosting systems. ACM Comput. Surv. 36, 291–334 (2004)
7. Budhiraja, N., Marzullo, K., Schneider, F.B., Toueg, S.: The primary-backup approach, 199–216 (1993)

8. Sussman, J.B., Marzullo, K.: Comparing primary-backup and state machines for crash failures. In: PODC 1996. Proceedings of the fifteenth annual ACM symposium on Principles of distributed computing, p. 90. ACM Press, New York (1996)
9. Schneider, F.B.: Byzantine generals in action: Implementing fail-stop processors. ACM Trans. Comput. Syst. 2, 145–154 (1984)
10. Garg, V.K., Ogale, V.: Fusible data structures for fault tolerance. In: ICDCS 2007. Proceedings of the 27th International Conference on Distributed Computing Systems (2007)
11. Huffman, D.A.: The synthesis of sequential switching circuits. Technical report, Massachusetts, USA (1954)
12. Hopcroft, J.E.: An n log n algorithm for minimizing states in a finite automaton. Technical report, Stanford, CA, USA (1971)
13. Balasubramanian, B., Ogale, V., Garg, V.K.: Fusion generator (implemented in java 1.6). In Parallel and Distributed Systems Laboratory (2007),
   http://maple.ece.utexas.edu
14. Balasubramanian, B., Ogale, V., Garg, V.K.: Fault tolerance in finite state machines using fusion. Technical Report TR-PDS-2007-003, Parallel and Distributed Systems Laboratory, The University of Texas at Austin (2007)
15. Glushkov, V.M.: The abstract theory of automata. RUSS MATH SURV. 16, 1–53 (1961)

Wait-Free Dining Under Eventual Weak Exclusion

Scott M. Pike*, Yantao Song, and Srikanth Sastry

Texas A&M University
Department of Computer Science
College Station, TX 77843-3112, USA
{pike,yantao,sastry}@cs.tamu.edu

Abstract. We present a wait-free solution to the generalized dining philosophers problem under eventual weak exclusion in environments subject to crash faults. Wait-free dining guarantees that every correct hungry process eventually eats, regardless of process crashes. Eventual weak exclusion ($\Diamond\mathcal{WX}$) actually allows scheduling mistakes, whereby mutual exclusion may be violated finitely-many times; for each run, however, there must exist a convergence point after which *live* neighbors never eat simultaneously. Wait-free dining under $\Diamond\mathcal{WX}$ is particularly useful for synchronization tasks where eventual safety is sufficient for correctness (e.g., duty-cycle scheduling, self-stabilizing daemons, and contention managers). Unfortunately, wait-free dining is unsolvable in asynchronous systems. As such, we characterize sufficient conditions for solvability under partial synchrony by presenting a wait-free dining algorithm for $\Diamond\mathcal{WX}$ using a local refinement of the eventually perfect failure detector $\Diamond\mathcal{P}_1$.

Keywords: Dining Philosophers, Failure Detectors, Wait-Freedom.

1   Introduction

The dining philosophers problem (or *dining* for short) is a fundamental scheduling paradigm in which processes (called *diners*) periodically require exclusive access to a fixed subset of shared resources [1,2]. Each diner is either *thinking*, *hungry*, or *eating*. These states correspond to three basic phases of computation: executing independently, requesting resources, and utilizing shared resources in a critical section, respectively. Potential scheduling conflicts are modeled by a conflict graph in which diners with overlapping resource requirements are connected as neighbors. As such, dining is a generalization of the mutual exclusion problem, which corresponds to the special case where the conflict graph forms a clique.

Wait-free dining guarantees that every correct hungry process eventually eats, even if other processes fault by crashing. The solvability of wait-free dining depends on two primary factors: (1) the degree to which concurrency is restricted among eating diners, and (2) the degree to which crash faults can be detected reliably. The former depends on the applicable safety specification for local exclusion, while the latter depends on the degree of synchrony in the system.

---

* This work was supported by the Advanced Research Program of the Texas Higher Education Coordinating Board under Project Number 000512-0007-2006.

S. Rao et al. (Eds.): ICDCN 2008, LNCS 4904, pp. 135–146, 2008.

Safety specifications restrict concurrency among eating diners. For example, *strong exclusion* prohibits any pair of conflicting neighbors from eating simultaneously, even if one of them has crashed. This safety property models resources that can be permanently corrupted by process crashes. Unfortunately, wait-free dining under strong exclusion is vacuously unsolvable. To see why, consider any diner that crashes while eating. Wait-freedom guarantees that every correct hungry neighbor will eventually eat, but strong exclusion prohibits the same. Moreover, this result is independent of whether crashes can be detected reliably.

A less restrictive model called *weak exclusion* prohibits only *live* neighbors from eating simultaneously. This safety property models resources that are recoverable or eventually stateless after crash faults. For example, consider a wireless network where diners broadcast messages over a subset of shared frequencies. If some diner crashes while eating, then the current transmission terminates. As such, the frequency allocated to the crashed diner becomes available for subsequent use by neighboring diners.

Wait-free dining for weak exclusion is actually solvable, but it requires substantial timing assumptions, or, alternatively, access to sufficiently powerful failure detectors. A failure detector can be viewed as a distributed system service that can be queried like an oracle for information about process crashes [3]. Oracle-based algorithms are decoupled from the underlying timing assumptions about partial or even full synchrony necessary to implement such fault-detection capabilities in practice. Recent results on fault-tolerant mutual exclusion indicate that wait-free dining under weak exclusion is solvable in systems augmented with Trusting failure detectors — a relatively powerful class of oracles that can reliably detect certain crashes [4].

Unfortunately, trusting oracles require significant assumptions about network timing parameters to be implemented in practice. By contrast, less powerful oracles that are implementable in more practical models of partial synchrony — such as those for solving fault-tolerant consensus — are too weak to solve wait-free dining under weak exclusion. This problem remains unsolvable even for oracles of intermediate strength. For example, the eventually perfect failure detector $\Diamond \mathcal{P}$ always suspects crashed processes, and eventually stops suspecting correct processes [3]. This oracle, which can make finitely many false-positive mistakes in any run, is more than sufficient to solve fault-tolerance consensus. Still, no $\Diamond \mathcal{P}$-based algorithm can solve wait-free dining for weak exclusion; neighbors of any crashed diner will always be able to starve [5].

Our contribution examines a practical model of exclusion for wait-free dining which is solvable under modest assumptions of partial synchrony. In particular, we explore dining under *eventual weak exclusion*, and show that it is solvable using the aforementioned oracle $\Diamond \mathcal{P}$. Eventual weak exclusion (abbreviated $\Diamond \mathcal{WX}$ hereafter) permits finitely-many scheduling mistakes whereby conflicting diners eat together. *For each run, however, there exists a time after which no two live neighbors eat simultaneously.*

The time to convergence may be unknown, and it may also vary from run to run. Nevertheless, $\Diamond \mathcal{WX}$ is sufficiently powerful to serve as a useful scheduling abstraction. For example, $\Diamond \mathcal{WX}$ models recoverable resources where sharing violations precipitate at worst repairable (transient) faults. $\Diamond \mathcal{WX}$ has received considerable attention recently in the context of shared-memory contention management [6], conflict managers for self-stabilizing systems [7], as well as wait-free eventually fair distributed daemons[8].

2 Background and Technical Framework

Although originally proposed by Dijkstra for a ring topology [1], dining philosophers was later generalized by Lynch for overlapping local exclusion problems on arbitrary graphs [2]. A dining instance is modeled by an undirected conflict graph $DP = (\Pi, E)$, where each vertex $p \in \Pi$ represents a diner, and each edge $(p, q) \in E$ represents a set resource conflicts between neighbors p and q.

Each diner is either *thinking, hungry,* or *eating,* but initially all diners are thinking. Diners may think forever, but they can also become hungry at any time. By contrast, eating is always finite (but not necessarily bounded). Hungry neighbors are said to be in *conflict,* because they compete for shared but exclusive resources. A correct solution to wait-free dining under eventual weak exclusion ($\Diamond \mathcal{WX}$) is an algorithm that schedules diner transitions from hungry to eating, subject to the following two requirements:

Safety: Every run has an infinite suffix where no two live neighbors eat simultaneously.

Progress: Every correct hungry diner eventually eats, regardless of process crash faults.

Progress ensures fairness among hungry diners. In particular, dining solutions are not permitted to *starve* hungry processes by never scheduling them to eat. In the presence of crash faults, a dining algorithm that satisfies progress is called *wait-free* [9]. The safety requirement of eventual weak exclusion permits finitely many scheduling mistakes. A mistake occurs when two live neighbors are scheduled to eat simultaneously.

Computational Model. We consider asynchronous environments where message delay, clock drift, and relative process speeds are unbounded. A system is modeled by a set of n distributed processes $\Pi = \{p_1, p_2, \dots, p_n\}$ which communicate only by asynchronous message passing. We assume that the dining conflict graph is a subgraph of the communication graph, so that each pair of neighboring diners is connected by reliable FIFO channels.

Fault Patterns. Processes may fault only by crashing. A crash fault occurs when a process ceases execution (without warning) and never recovers [10]. A *fault pattern* F models the occurrence of crash faults in a given run. Specifically, F is a function from the global time range $\mathcal{T}$ to the powerset of processes 2^Π, where $F(t)$ denotes the subset of processes that have crashed by time t. Since crash faults are permanent, F is monotonically non-decreasing. We say that p *is faulty in* F if $p \in F(t)$ for some time t; otherwise, we say that p *is correct in* F. Additionally, a process p is *live at time* t if p has not crashed by time t. That is, $p \notin F(t)$. Thus, correct processes are always live, but faulty processes are live only prior to crashing.

Failure Detectors. An unreliable failure detector can be viewed as a distributed oracle that can be queried for (possibly incorrect) information about crashes in Π. Each process has access to its own local detector module that outputs the set of processes currently suspected of having crashed. Unreliable failure detectors are characterized by the kinds of *mistakes* they can make. Mistakes can include false-negatives (*i.e.,* not suspecting a crashed process), as well as false-positives (*i.e.,* wrongly suspecting a correct process). In Chandra and Toueg's original definition [3], each oracle class is defined by two properties: *completeness* and *accuracy.* Completeness restricts false negatives, while accuracy restricts false positives. More precisely, each oracle class is a function (defined by the intersection of a completeness property and an accuracy property), which maps each possible fault pattern to a set of admissible histories.

Our wait-free dining algorithm is based on the eventually perfect failure detector $\Diamond \mathcal{P}$ from the original Chandra-Toueg hierarchy [3]. Informally, $\Diamond \mathcal{P}$ is a convergent oracle that always suspects crashed processes and eventually stops suspecting correct processes. As such, $\Diamond \mathcal{P}$ may commit finitely-many false positive mistakes during any run before converging to an infinite suffix during which the oracle provides reliable information about process crashes. Unfortunately, the time to convergence is not known and it may vary from run to run.

As originally defined, the scope of $\Diamond \mathcal{P}$ is global, insofar as it provides information about all processes. One drawback of global oracles is that communication overhead can limit their practicality for large-scale networks. Accordingly, scope-restricted oracles have been proposed that provide information only about subsets of processes [11,12,13]. Our dining solution uses a variant of $\Diamond \mathcal{P}$ defined in [14,15] for which suspect information is only provided about immediate neighbors. This local refinement, called $\Diamond \mathcal{P}_1$, satisfies the following completeness and accuracy properties:

Local Strong Completeness — Every crashed process is eventually and permanently suspected by all correct neighbors.

Local Eventual Strong Accuracy — For every run, there exists a time after which no correct process is suspected by any correct neighbor.

It is worth noting that $\Diamond \mathcal{P}$ cannot be implemented in purely asynchronous systems. Implementations typically use adaptive time-outs based on modest assumptions about partial synchrony. A simple technique assumes that upper bounds on message delay and relative process speed exist, but are unknown. Such bounds can be adaptively estimated by ping-ack protocols which increase a time-out threshold after each false positive. After finitely-many mistakes, the current time-out will exceed the unknown round-trip message time, after which false positives desist.

There are known implementations of $\Diamond \mathcal{P}$ in several other models partial synchrony as well [3,16,17,18]. The common advantage is that $\Diamond \mathcal{P}$-based algorithms are decoupled from explicit commitments to underlying detection mechanisms and/or specific timing parameters. Additionally, the local refinement $\Diamond \mathcal{P}_1$ can also be implemented efficiently in sparse, large-scale, and even partitionable networks [15].

3 A Wait-Free Dining Algorithm for $\Diamond \mathcal{WX}$

Our solution is based on the classic hygienic dining algorithm [19]. In hygienic dining, a unique fork is associated with each edge in the conflict graph. A hungry process must collect and hold all shared forks to eat. This provides a simple basis for safety, since at most one diner can hold a given fork at any time. Fork conflicts are resolved according to a dynamic partial ordering on process priority. After eating, diners reduce priority below all neighbors; this ensures progress by yielding to previously lower-priority diners.

It is easy to see why hygienic dining is not wait-free. Without fault detection, hungry processes starve whenever missing forks are lost to crashed neighbors. The result is actually much worse: if no process thinks forever, then the crash of any eating diner will eventually precipitate global starvation among all processes (not just neighbors).

In our solution, suspicion by $\Diamond\mathcal{P}_1$ serves as a proxy for permanently missing forks. The completeness property guarantees that every crashed process will be eventually and permanently suspected by all correct neighbors. As such, hungry neighbors of crashed diners can avoid starvation by using suspicion as a proxy for permanently missing forks. Specifically, a hungry diner i can eat if, for every neighbor j, either i holds the fork shared with j, or the $\Diamond\mathcal{P}_1$ oracle at i suspects j.

Unfortunately, suspicion by $\Diamond\mathcal{P}_1$ is an unreliable proxy for missing forks, because the eventual accuracy property also allows false-positive mistakes. For example, if live neighbors falsely suspect each other, they may proceed to eat simultaneously, regardless of the fork. Ideally, scheduling violations should be limited by the finite number of false-positive mistakes per run. It remains to show, however, that $\Diamond\mathcal{W}\mathcal{X}$ will still be satisfied after $\Diamond\mathcal{P}_1$ converges.

A deeper subtlety is the impact of oracular mistakes on maintaining a consistent ordering of process priorities. In hygienic dining, relative process priorities are typically encoded directly in the fork variables. As such, it becomes trivial for diners to reduce their priority below all neighbors after eating, because (1) diners must hold every shared fork while eating, so (2) the current priority of every neighbor is actually known.

The same technique does not work with $\Diamond\mathcal{P}_1$, because false-positive mistakes may enable diners to eat despite missing critical forks. In the worst case, *two neighbors can eat simultaneously even if neither holds the fork*. This can occur if the fork is in transit, but both diners begin eating as the result of mutual suspicion. If the fork is still in transit when both diners complete eating, then neither diner knows the actual priority ordering. Unlike hygienic dining, it is impossible for both diners to reduce their own priority below all neighbors; either one diner will not lower its priority sufficiently, or both priorities will match (which could lead to symmetries resulting in deadlock).

To circumvent this difficulty, we store process priorities explicitly at each diner, and assume unique identifiers to break symmetries. Additionally, we establish wait-free progress even though priorities are reduced by arbitrary values after eating.

3.1 Algorithm Variables

Our algorithm guarantees safety using forks plus the eventual strong accuracy of $\Diamond\mathcal{P}_1$. It guarantees wait-free progress using a dynamic ordering on process priorities, plus the strong completeness of $\Diamond\mathcal{P}_1$. In addition to the local oracle module, each process has the following local variables. A trivalent variable $state_i$ denotes the current dining phase: thinking, hungry, or eating. Each process also has a local integer-valued variable $height_i$ (which can grow negatively without bound), and a unique process identifier id_i. Taken together as an ordered pair, $(height_i, id_i)$ determines the $priority_i$ of process i. Since process identifiers are unique, every pair of priorities, x and y, can be totally ordered lexicographically as follows:

$$x < y \ \stackrel{\text{def}}{=} \ (x.\text{height} < y.\text{height}) \ \vee \ ((x.\text{height} = y.\text{height}) \wedge (x.\text{id} < y.\text{id}))$$

To implement the forks, we introduce two local variables for each pair of neighbors. For process i, we associate a boolean variable fork$_{ij}$ for each neighbor j. Symmetrically, each process j has a boolean variable fork$_{ji}$ corresponding to neighbor i. We interpret these variables as follows: fork$_{ij}$ is true iff process i holds the unique fork that it shares with neighbor j. Alternatively, fork$_{ji}$ is true iff j holds the fork. When the fork is in transit from one neighbor to the other, both local variables are false. Since the fork is unique and exclusive, it is never the case that both variables are true.

In addition to the forks, we also introduce a request token between each pair of neighbors. In general, if process i holds a request token, but needs the corresponding fork from j, then i can request the missing fork by sending the request token to j. Request tokens are implemented and interpreted the same as forks. For process i, we associate a unique boolean variable token$_{ij}$ for each neighbor j. Symmetrically, each process j has a boolean variable token$_{ji}$ corresponding to neighbor i.

3.2   Algorithm Actions

A thinking process can become hungry at any time by executing Action 1 and selecting the corresponding alternative. Action 2 is always enabled while hungry. When executed, it requests every missing fork for which no previous request is currently pending. This is achieved by sending the request token to the corresponding neighbor, including the current priority of the requesting process. As a result, the local token variable becomes false to indicate that a request has been sent.

Action 3 handles fork requests. The requested fork must be sent immediately if the recipient is thinking, but also if the recipient is hungry but has lower priority than the requestor. Otherwise, the fork request is deferred until after eating. Deferred requests are represented by holding both the shared fork and the request token. Note that if a hungry process loses a requested fork to a higher-priority neighbor in Action 3, the relinquished fork will be re-requested by subsequently executing Action 2, which is always enabled while hungry.

Action 4 simply receives forks, and Action 5 determines when a hungry process can begin eating. A hungry process i can begin eating if, for each neighbor j, process i either holds the shared fork, or currently suspects j. This is the only action that utilizes the local oracle $\diamond\mathcal{P}_1$ and it is central to the wait-freedom of the algorithm.

Action 6 exits eating and transits back to thinking. This action reduces the priority of the diner, and sends forks for any requests that were previously deferred while hungry or eating. To reduce priority, Action 6 invokes a local procedure called *Lower* which reduces only the *height* component of the diner's priority by some positive integer. The magnitude of the reduction is up to the algorithm designer, and can be either statically fixed or dynamically chosen at runtime.

Action 6 isolates several subtleties. In hygienic dining, a process must reduce its priority below that of all neighbors after eating. This absolute reduction forms the basis for progress, because it forces high-priority diners to yield to lower-priority neighbors. In our algorithm, oracular mistakes may enable some diners to eat without knowing the priorities of all live neighbors. As such, hygienic reductions cannot be guaranteed. Our proof of progress shows that reducing priority by an arbitrary amount is sufficient, because it still reduces the number of times any diner can overtake its live neighbors.

Code for process i, with unique identifier id_i and local set of neighbors $N(i)$

var	state_i	: {thinking, hungry, eating}	$init,$	state_i	= thinking
	height_i	: integer	$init,$	height_i	= 0
	priority_i	: (height$_i$ × process-id)	$init,$	priority_i	= $(0, \text{id}_i)$
	fork_{ij}	: boolean, for each $j \in N(i)$	$init,$	fork_{ij}	= $(i > j)$
	token_{ij}	: boolean, for each $j \in N(i)$	$init,$	token_{ij}	= $(i < j)$
	$\Diamond \mathcal{P}_1$	: local eventually perfect detector	$init,$	$\Diamond \mathcal{P}_1$	$\subseteq N(i)$

---

1 : $\{\text{state}_i = \text{thinking}\} \longrightarrow$ *Action 1*
2 : $\text{state}_i := (\text{thinking or hungry})$ *Become Hungry*

---

3 : $\{\text{state}_i = \text{hungry}\} \longrightarrow$ *Action 2*
4 : $\forall j \in N(i)$ **where** $(\text{token}_{ij} \wedge \neg \text{fork}_{ij})$ **do** *Request Missing Forks*
5 :   send-request $\langle \text{priority}_i \rangle$ **to** j
6 : $\text{token}_{ij} := \text{false}$

---

7 : $\{\text{receive-request } \langle \text{priority}_j \rangle \text{ from } j \in N(i)\} \longrightarrow$ *Action 3*
8 : $\text{token}_{ij} := \text{true}$ *Send Fork or*
9 :   **if** $(\text{state}_i = \text{thinking} \vee (\text{state}_i = \text{hungry} \wedge (\text{priority}_i < \text{priority}_j)))$ *Defer*
10 :   **then** send-fork$\langle i \rangle$ **to** j
11 : $\text{fork}_{ij} := \text{false}$

---

12 : $\{\text{receive-fork } \langle j \rangle \text{ from } j \in N(i)\} \longrightarrow$ *Action 4*
13 : $\text{fork}_{ij} := \text{true}$ *Obtain Shared Fork*

---

14 : $\{\text{state}_i = \text{hungry} \wedge (\forall j \in N(i) :: (\text{fork}_{ij} \vee j \in \Diamond \mathcal{P}_1))\} \longrightarrow$ *Action 5*
15 : $\text{state}_i := \text{eating}$ *Enter Critical Section*

---

16 : $\{\text{state}_i = \text{eating}\} \longrightarrow$ *Action 6*
17 : $Lower(\text{priority}_i)$ *Exit Critical Section*
18 : $\text{state}_i := \text{thinking}$ *Send Deferred Forks*
19 : $\forall j \in N(i)$ **where** $(\text{token}_{ij} \wedge \text{fork}_{ij})$ **do**
20 :   send-fork$\langle i \rangle$ **to** j
21 : $\text{fork}_{ij} := \text{false}$

---

22 : **procedure** $Lower$ (p : priority) *Reduce Priority*
23 :   **ensures** p' := $Lower$ (p) **where** *Process ID Unchanged*
24 :   (p'.id = p.id) **and** (p'.height < p.height) *Integer Height Lowered*

Algorithm 1. 1. Wait-Free Dining under Eventual Weak Exclusion

4   Proof of Correctness

Lost tokens or forks can compromise progress, while duplicated tokens or forks can compromise safety. First we prove some basic lemmas which assert that each pair of live neighbors share a unique fork and a unique request token.

Lemma 1. *There exists exactly one token between each pair of live neighbors.*

Proof. For each pair of neighbors, the initialization code creates a unique token at the lower-priority process. Since communication channels are reliable, this token is neither lost nor duplicated while in transit. Only Actions 2 and 3 can modify the token variables. No token is lost, because every token received is locally stored (Action 3), and no token is locally removed unless it is sent (Action 2). No token is duplicated, because every token sent is locally removed, and no absent token is ever sent (Action 2). Thus, token uniqueness is preserved.   □

Lemma 2.1. *There exists exactly one fork between each pair of live neighbors.*

Proof. For each pair of neighbors, the initialization code creates a unique fork at the higher-priority process. Since communication channels are reliable, this fork is neither lost nor duplicated while in transit. Only Actions 3, 4, and 6 modify the fork variables. No fork is lost, because every fork received is locally stored (Action 4), and no fork is locally removed unless it is sent (Actions 3 & 6). No fork is duplicated, because every fork sent is locally removed, *and no absent fork is ever sent* * *(Action 3 & 6).* Thus, fork uniqueness is preserved.   □

*Action 3 can send forks (Line 11) without verifying their local presence. If such forks are absent, then this action could compromise $\Diamond \mathcal{WX}$ by duplicating forks. As it turns out, Action 3 is never enabled unless the requested fork is actually present. This result may not be obvious from the program text, because it depends explicitly on the assumption of FIFO channels. Consequently, we prove this assertion separately below.

Lemma 2.2. *Action 3 is never enabled unless the requested fork is present.*

Proof. Suppose for contradiction that Action 3 is enabled at some process i at time t_2, but that the requested fork is absent. This action can only be enabled by i receiving a request token from some neighbor j that executed Action 2 at an earlier time $t_1 < t_2$. The condition in Line 4 asserts that j held the token but not the shared fork at time t_1. Consequently, the fork was already at i or it was in transit at time t_1.

1. Suppose the fork was in transit from j to i. By FIFO channels, the fork had to arrive at i before the request token which enabled Action 3 at time t_2. Only Actions 3 and 6 send forks, but both require the fork and token to be co-located. Thus, the fork remains at i until Action 3 became enabled at time t_2.
2. Suppose the fork was in transit from i to j. Then i must have sent the fork by executing Action 3 or 6 at some earlier time $t_0 < t_1$. As mentioned above, the token must have been co-located with the fork at time t_0. Again, by FIFO channels, j could not execute Action 2 at time t_1, because the token could not have overtaken the fork which was still in transit.   □

Theorem 1. *Algorithm 1 satisfies eventual weak exclusion $\Diamond \mathcal{WX}$. That is, for every execution there exists a time after which no two live neighbors eat simultaneously.*

Proof. The safety proof is by direct construction and uses the local eventually strong accuracy property of $\Diamond\mathcal{P}_1$. This property guarantees that for each run there exists a time t after which no correct process is suspected by any correct neighbor.

We observe that faulty processes cannot prevent $\Diamond\mathcal{W}\mathcal{X}$ from being established. Since faulty processes are live for only a finite prefix before crashing, they can eat simultaneously with live neighbors only finitely many times in any run. Consequently, we can restrict our focus to correct processes only.

Consider any execution α of Algorithm 1. Let t denote the time in α after which $\Diamond\mathcal{P}_1$ never suspects correct neighbors. Let i be any correct process that *begins* eating after time t. By Action 5, process i can only transit from hungry to eating if, for each neighbor j, either i holds the shared fork or i suspects j. Since $\Diamond\mathcal{P}_1$ never suspects correct neighbors after time t in execution α, process i must hold every fork it shares with its correct neighbors in order to begin eating.

So long as i remains eating, Actions 3 and 6 guarantee that i will defer all fork requests. As such, p will not relinquish any forks while eating. From Lemma 2.1, we know that forks cannot be duplicated either. Furthermore, $\Diamond\mathcal{P}_1$ has already converged in α, so no correct neighbor can suspect p. Thus, Action 5 remains disabled for every correct hungry neighbor of i until after i transits back to thinking. We conclude that no pair of correct neighbors can *begin*[1] overlapping eating sessions after time t.   □

Next we introduce some definitions to construct a metric function for the progress proof. First, we measure the priority *distance* between any two processes i and j as:

$$dist(i,j) = \begin{cases} 0, & \text{if } (\text{priority}_i < \text{priority}_j) \\ \text{height}_i - \text{height}_j, & \text{if } (\text{priority}_i > \text{priority}_j) \wedge (\text{id}_i < \text{id}_j) \\ \text{height}_i - \text{height}_j + 1, & \text{if } (\text{priority}_i > \text{priority}_j) \wedge (\text{id}_i > \text{id}_j) \end{cases}$$

Suppose for any pair of processes i and j that $dist(i,j) = d$ in some configuration where j is hungry. While j remains hungry, priority_j remains unchanged. Also, recall from Action 6 that each process reduces the height component of its priority after eating. Consequently, d is an upper bound on the maximum number of times that process i can overtake process j before either j gets scheduled to eat or $\text{priority}_i < \text{priority}_j$.

Now we define a metric function $M : \Pi \rightarrow \mathbb{N}$ for each diner $j \in \Pi$ as follows:

$$M(j) = \sum_{i \neq j} dist(i,j)$$

First, we observe that M is bounded below by 0, and that $M(j) = 0$ iff j currently has the highest priority value among all processes in Π. In general, the value of $M(j)$ depends only on processes that are currently higher-priority than j. This is because

---

[1] As a technical point, diners might forestall $\Diamond\mathcal{W}\mathcal{X}$ by eating with neighbors that began eating *before* $\Diamond\mathcal{P}_1$ converged. For example, consider neighbors i and j, where i holds the shared fork, but j began eating by falsely suspecting i before $\Diamond\mathcal{P}_1$ converged. Since j is already eating, but i holds the shared fork, i might violate exclusion by eating with j even after the oracle has converged. This can happen multiple times, in fact, so long as j continues to eat. The phenomenon is temporary, however, because j is either faulty and crashes, or j is correct and must exit eating within finite time. Thereafter, i and j never eat simultaneously again.

$dist(i, j) = 0$ for any process i with priority$_i$ < priority$_j$. If $M(j) = b$, then b is an upper bound on how many times *any* higher-priority process can eat before either j gets scheduled to eat or priority$_j$ becomes globally maximal.

We also note that the metric value of each process in a given configuration is unique: $(i \neq j) \Rightarrow M(i) \neq M(j)$. Moreover, $M(i) < M(j) \Leftrightarrow$ (priority$_i$ > priority$_j$). These properties follow from the fact that priorities are totally ordered.

Finally, the metric value $M(j)$ never increases while process j is thinking or hungry. $M(j)$ can only increase by reducing the height component of priority$_j$ in Action 6 after eating. Importantly, *this change in relative priority actually causes the metric values of all other processes to decrease*.

We are now prepared to state and prove the following helper lemma for progress:

Lemma 3. Let C be a configuration where some correct process is hungry, and let H denote the set of all hungry processes in C. The correct process $j \in H$ with minimal metric eventually eats, or some correct process i with $M(i) < M(j)$ becomes hungry.

Proof. Let j be the unique correct hungry process with minimal metric value in H. In other words, j is the highest-priority correct hungry process in configuration C. Lemma 3 holds trivially if j eats or if any correct process i with $M(i) < M(j)$ becomes hungry. Otherwise, j remains the highest-priority correct hungry process forever. We will show that this latter case leads to a contradiction.

By definition, every faulty neighbor of j will crash within finite time. By the local strong completeness of $\Diamond\mathcal{P}_1$, process j will permanently suspect such processes by some unknown time t. Thereafter, j must collect forks only from its correct neighbors.

First, j will not lose any such forks. By hypothesis, j is hungry and higher priority than any correct neighbor, so any fork request received by j in Action 3 will be deferred.

Second, j will eventually acquire every fork shared with its correct neighbors. By Lemma 1, j shares a unique request token with each such neighbor. For any missing fork, Action 2 guarantees that j will eventually send the corresponding token. Since j is higher priority than any correct neighbor, these fork requests must be honored unless the recipient is currently eating. In the latter case, the requested fork will be sent when the correct neighbor exits eating in Action 6.

We conclude that if j remains hungry indefinitely, then j eventually suspects each faulty neighbor and eventually holds the shared fork with each correct neighbor. By Line 14, the guard on Action 5 is enabled. So j eats and Lemma 3 is established.   □

Theorem 2: *Algorithm 1 satisfies wait-free progress. That is, every correct hungry process eventually eats.*

Proof: We prove wait-freedom by complete (strong) induction on metric values.

Base Case: Let j be a correct hungry process with $M(j) = 0$.

By definition, the metric value $M(j)$ is minimal, so Lemma 3 applies to j. There are only two outcomes: either j eats, or some process i with $M(i) < M(j)$ becomes hungry. Since metric values are unique and bounded below by 0, no such process i exists. Consequently, j eventually eats.   □

Inductive Hypothesis: Suppose for $k > 0$ that every correct hungry process i with $M(i) < k$ eventually eats. It remains to show that every correct hungry process j with $M(j) = k$ eventually eats as well.

Let C be a configuration, and let j be a correct hungry process in C with $M(j) = k$. Suppose that k is the minimal metric value among all correct hungry processes in C. Then Lemma 3 applies to j, so we conclude that j eventually eats, or some correct process i with $M(i) < M(j)$ becomes hungry. Alternatively, suppose that k is *not* the minimal metric value among all correct hungry processes in C. Then some correct hungry process i with $M(i) < k$ already exists.

Either way, we conclude that j eventually eats or the inductive hypothesis applies to some correct hungry process i with $M(i) < k$. In the latter case, process i eats. As a correct diner, i eventually stops eating by executing Action 6, which thereby lowers the height component of priority$_i$ and decreases $dist(i, j)$ by at least 1. Recall that while j remains hungry, $M(j)$ does not increase. Thus, any decrease in $dist(i, j)$ will cause the metric value of $M(j)$ becomes less than k. Since j is now a correct hungry process with $M(j) < k$, the inductive hypothesis applies directly to j. We conclude that j eventually eats, and that Algorithm 1 satisfies wait-free progress by complete induction.   □

5 Contributions

We have examined the dining philosophers problem under eventual weak exclusion in environments subject to permanent crash faults. Eventual weak exclusion ($\Diamond \mathcal{WX}$) permits conflicting diners to eat concurrently only finitely many times, but requires that, for each run, there exists a (potentially unknown) time after which *live* neighbors never eat simultaneously. This safety property models systems where resources are recoverable or where sharing violations precipitate only transient (repairable) faults. Applications of $\Diamond \mathcal{WX}$ include shared-memory contention management [6], conflict managers for self-stabilizing systems [7], and wait-free eventually fair daemons [8].

Dining under $\Diamond \mathcal{WX}$ is unsolvable in asynchronous environments, where crash faults can precipitate permanent starvation among live diners. The contribution of our work is a wait-free dining algorithm for $\Diamond \mathcal{WX}$ in partially synchronous environments which guarantees that every correct hungry process eventually eats, even in the presence of arbitrarily many crash faults. Our oracle-based solution uses a local refinement of the eventually perfect failure detector $\Diamond \mathcal{P}_1$. This oracle always suspects crashed neighbors, and eventually stops suspecting correct neighbors. $\Diamond \mathcal{P}_1$ provides information only about immediate neighbors, and, as such, it is fundamental to the scalability of our approach, since it is implementable in partially synchronous environments with sparse communication graphs that are partitionable by crash faults.

Our work demonstrates that $\Diamond \mathcal{P}_1$ is *sufficient* for wait-free dining under $\Diamond \mathcal{WX}$. It is an open question, however, whether this oracle is actually *necessary*. This question goes to the minimality of our assumptions and the portability of our solutions to weaker models of partial synchrony. On the one hand, wait-free dining under $\Diamond \mathcal{WX}$ is a harder problem than fault-tolerant consensus; the eventually strong oracle $\Diamond \mathcal{S}$ — which is sufficient for consensus [3] — is not sufficient for wait-free dining [20]. Thus, the search for a weakest failure detector is bounded above by $\Diamond \mathcal{P}_1$ and below by $\Diamond \mathcal{S}$.

References

1. Dijkstra, E.W.: Hierarchical ordering of sequential processes. Acta Informatica 1, 115–138 (1971) Reprinted in Operating Systems Techniques, Hoare, C.A.R., Perrot, R.H. (eds.), Academic Press, pp. 72–93 (1972) (An earlier version appeared as EWD310)
2. Lynch, N.A.: Fast allocation of nearby resources in a distributed system. In: STOC. Proceedings of the 12th ACM Symposium on Theory of Computing, pp. 70–81 (1980)
3. Chandra, T.D., Toueg, S.: Unreliable failure detectors for reliable distributed systems. Journal of the ACM 43, 225–267 (1996)
4. Delporte-Gallet, C., Fauconnier, H., Guerraoui, R., Kouznetsov, P.: Mutual exclusion in asynchronous systems with failure detectors. J. Parallel Distrib. Comput. 65, 492–505 (2005)
5. Pike, S.M., Sivilotti, P.A.G.: Dining philosophers with crash locality 1. In: ICDCS. Proceedings of the 24th IEEE International Conference on Distributed Computing Systems, pp. 22–29. IEEE, Los Alamitos (2004)
6. Guerraoui, R., Kapałka, M., Kouznetsov, P.: The weakest failure detectors to boost obstruction-freedom. In: Dolev, S. (ed.) DISC 2006. LNCS, vol. 4167, pp. 399–412. Springer, Heidelberg (2006)
7. Gradinariu, M., Tixeuil, S.: Conflict managers for self-stabilization without fairness assumption. In: ICDCS. 27th International Conference on Distributed Computing Systems, pp. 46–53. IEEE, Los Alamitos (2007)
8. Song, Y., Pike, S.M.: Eventually k-bounded wait-free distributed daemons. In: DSN. 37th International Conference on Dependable Systems and Networks, pp. 645–655. IEEE, Los Alamitos (2007)
9. Herlihy, M.: Wait-free synchronization. ACM Trans. Program. Lang. Syst. (TOPLAS) 13, 124–149 (1991)
10. Cristian, F.: Understanding fault-tolerant distributed systems. Comm. ACM 34, 56–78 (1991)
11. Anceaume, E., Fernández, A., Mostéfaoui, A., Neiger, G., Raynal, M.: A necessary and sufficient condition for transforming limited accuracy failure detectors. J. Comput. Syst. Sci. 68, 123–133 (2004)
12. Guerraoui, R., Schiper, A.: Γ–accurate failure detectors. In: Babaoğlu, Ö., Marzullo, K. (eds.) WDAG 1996. LNCS, vol. 1151, pp. 269–286. Springer, Heidelberg (1996)
13. Raynal, M., Tronel, F.: Restricted failure detectors: Definition and reduction protocols. Information Processing Letters 72, 91–97 (1999)
14. Beauquier, J., Kekkonen-Moneta, S.: Fault-tolerance and self-stabilization: Impossibility results and solutions using self-stabilizing failure detectors. International Journal of Systems Science 28, 1177–1187 (1997)
15. Hutle, M., Widder, J.: Self-stabilizing failure detector algorithms. In: Fahringer, T., Hamza, M.H. (eds.) PDCN. Parallel and Distributed Computing and Networks, IASTED/ACTA Press, pp. 485–490 (2005)
16. Dwork, C., Lynch, N.A., Stockmeyer, L.: Consensus in the presence of partial synchrony. Journal of the ACM 35, 288–323 (1988)
17. Fetzer, C., Schmid, U., Süsskraut, M.: On the possibility of consensus in asynchronous systems with finite average response times. In: ICDCS. 25th International Conference on Distributed Computing System, pp. 271–280. IEEE, Los Alamitos (2005)
18. Sastry, S., Pike, S.M.: Eventually perfect failure detectors using ADD channels. In: Stojmenovic, I., Thulasiram, R.K., Yang, L.T., Jia, W., Guo, M., de Mello, R.F. (eds.) ISPA 2007. LNCS, vol. 4742, pp. 483–496. Springer, Heidelberg (2007)
19. Chandy, K.M., Misra, J.: The drinking philosophers problem. ACM Transactions on Programming Languages and Systems (TOPLAS) 6, 632–646 (1984)
20. Pike, S.M.: Distributed Resource Allocation with Scalable Crash Containment. PhD thesis, The Ohio State University, Department of Computer Science & Engineering (2004)

On the Inherent Cost of Atomic Broadcast and Multicast in Wide Area Networks[*]

Nicolas Schiper and Fernando Pedone

University of Lugano, Switzerland

Abstract. In this paper, we study the atomic broadcast and multicast problems, two fundamental abstractions for building fault-tolerant systems. As opposed to atomic broadcast, atomic multicast allows messages to be addressed to a subset of the processes in the system, each message possibly being multicast to a different subset. Our study focuses on wide area networks where *groups of processes*, i.e., processes physically close to each other, are inter-connected through high latency communication links. In this context, we capture the cost of algorithms, denoted *latency degree*, as the minimum number of inter-group message delays between the broadcasting (multicasting) of a message and its delivery. We present an atomic multicast algorithm with a latency degree of two and show that it is optimal. We then present the first fault-tolerant atomic broadcast algorithm with a latency degree of one. To achieve such a low latency, the algorithm is proactive, i.e., it may take actions even though no messages are broadcast. Nevertheless, it is quiescent: provided that the number of broadcast messages is finite, the algorithm eventually ceases its operation.

1 Introduction

Distributed applications spanning multiple geographical locations have become common in recent years. Typically, each geographical site, or *group*, hosts an arbitrarily large number of processes connected through high-end local links; a few groups exist, interconnected through high-latency communication links. As a consequence, communication among processes in the same group is cheap and fast; communication among processes in different groups is expensive and orders of magnitude slower than local communication. Data is replicated both locally, for high availability, and globally, usually for locality of access. In this paper we investigate the atomic broadcast and multicast problems, two communication primitives that offer adequate properties, namely agreement on the set of messages delivered and on their delivery order, to implement replication [9].

Ideally, we would like to devise algorithms that use inter-group links as sparingly as possible, saving on both latency and bandwidth (i.e., number of messages). As we explain next, however, atomic broadcast and multicast establish an inherent tradeoff in this context. As opposed to atomic broadcast, atomic multicast allows messages to be sent to a subset of processes in the system. More precisely, messages can be addressed to any subset of the system's groups, each message possibly being multicast

---

[*] The work presented in this paper has been partially funded by the SNSF, Switzerland (project #200021-107824).

S. Rao et al. (Eds.): ICDCN 2008, LNCS 4904, pp. 147–157, 2008.

to a different subset. From a problem solvability point of view, atomic multicast can be easily reduced to atomic broadcast: every message is broadcast to all the groups in the system and only delivered by those processes the message is originally addressed to. Obviously, this solution is inefficient as it implies communication among processes that are not concerned by the multicast messages. To rule out trivial implementations of no practical interest, we require multicast algorithms to be *genuine* [7], i.e., only processes addressed by the message should be involved in the protocol. A genuine atomic multicast can thus be seen as an adequate communication primitive for distributed applications spanning multiple geographical locations in which processes store a subset of the application's data (i.e., *partial replication*).

We show that for messages multicast to at least two groups, no genuine atomic multicast algorithm can hope to achieve a latency degree lower than two.[1] This result is proven under strong system assumptions, namely processes do not crash and links are reliable. Moreover, this lower bound is tight, i.e., the fault-tolerant algorithm $\mathcal{A}1$ of Section 4 and the algorithm in [5] achieve this latency degree ($\mathcal{A}1$ is an optimized version of [5], see Section 4). A corollary of this result is that Skeen's algorithm, initially described in [2] and designed for failure-free systems, is also optimal—a result that has apparently been left unnoticed by the scientific community for more than 20 years.

We demonstrate that atomic multicast is inherently more expensive than atomic broadcast by presenting the first fault-tolerant broadcast algorithm with a latency degree of one. To achieve such a low latency, the algorithm is proactive, i.e., it may take actions even though no messages are broadcast. Nevertheless, we show how it can be made *quiescent*: provided that a finite number of messages is broadcast, processes eventually cease to communicate. In runs where the algorithm becomes quiescent too early, that is, a message m is broadcast after processes have decided to stop communicating, m will not be delivered in a single inter-group message delay, but in two. We show that this extra cost is unavoidable, i.e., no quiescent atomic broadcast algorithm can hope to always achieve a latency degree of one.[2]

These two lower bound results stem from a common cause, namely the *reactiveness* of the processes at the time when the message is cast. Roughly speaking, a process p is said to be *reactive* when the next message m that p sends is in response either to a local multicast event or to the reception of another message. In Section 3, we first show that no atomic broadcast or multicast algorithm can hope to deliver the last cast message m with a latency degree of one if m is cast at a time when processes are reactive. To obtain the lower bounds, we then show that (i) in runs of any genuine atomic multicast algorithm where one message is multicast at time t, processes are reactive at t and (ii) in runs of any quiescent atomic broadcast or atomic multicast algorithm where a finite number of messages are cast, processes are eventually reactive forever.

These results help better understand the difference between atomic broadcast and multicast. In particular, they point out a tradeoff between the latency degree and message complexity of these two problems. Consider a partial replication scenario where each group replicates a set of objects. If latency is the main concern, then every

---

[1] A precise definition of latency degree is given in Section 2.

[2] This result also holds for quiescent (genuine or non-genuine) atomic multicast algorithms. The genuine case is already covered by the first lower bound result and is therefore irrelevant here.

operation should be broadcast to all groups, and only groups concerned by the operation handle it. This solution, however, has a high message complexity: every operation
leads to sending at least one message to all processes in the system. Obviously, this is
inefficient if the operation only *touches* a subset of the system's groups. To reduce the
message complexity, genuine multicast can be used. However, any genuine multicast
algorithm will have a latency degree of at least two.

The rest of the paper is structured as follows. In Section 2, we present our system
model and definitions. Section 3 shows the genuine atomic multicast latency degree
lower bound and investigates the cost of quiescence in a unified way. In Sections 4
and 5, we present the optimal multicast and broadcast algorithms. Finally, Section 6
discusses the related work and concludes the paper. The proofs of correctness of the
algorithms can be found in [12].

2   System Model and Definitions

2.1   Processes and Links

We consider a system $\Pi = \{p_1, ..., p_n\}$ of processes which communicate through message passing and do not have access to a shared memory or a global clock. We assume
the benign crash-stop failure model, i.e., processes may fail by crashing, but do not behave maliciously. A process that never crashes is *correct*; otherwise it is *faulty*. The
system is asynchronous, i.e., messages may experience arbitrarily large (but finite) delays and there is no bound on relative process speeds. Furthermore, the communication
links do not corrupt or duplicate messages, and are quasi-reliable: if a correct process
p sends a message m to a correct process q, then q eventually receives m. We define $\Gamma = \{g_1, ..., g_m\}$ as the set of process groups in the system. Groups are disjoint,
non-empty and satisfy $\bigcup_{g \in \Gamma} g = \Pi$. For each process $p \in \Pi$, $group(p)$ identifies the
group p belongs to. Hereafter, we assume that in each group: (1) there exists at least one
correct process and (2) consensus is solvable (consensus is defined below).

2.2   Specifications of Agreement Problems

We define the agreement problems considered in this paper, namely consensus, reliable
multicast, and atomic multicast/broadcast. Let $\mathcal{A}$ be an agreement algorithm. We define
$\mathcal{R}(\mathcal{A})$ as the set of all admissible runs of $\mathcal{A}$.

Consensus. In the *consensus* problem, processes propose values and must reach agreement on the value decided. Uniform consensus is defined by the primitives propose(v)
and decide(v) and satisfies the following properties [8]: (i) *uniform integrity:* if a process decides v, then v was previously proposed by some process, (ii) *termination:* every
correct process eventually decides exactly one value, (iii) *uniform agreement:* if a process decides v, then all correct processes eventually decide v.

Reliable Multicast. With *reliable multicast*, messages may be addressed to any subset
of the processes in Π. For each message m, $m.dest$ denotes the processes to which
the message is reliably multicast. Non-uniform reliable multicast is defined by primitives *R-MCast(m)* and *R-Deliver(m)*, and satisfies the following properties : (i) *uniform*

integrity: for any process p and any message m, p R-Delivers m at most once, and only if $p \in m.dest$ and m was previously R-MCast, (ii) *validity:* if a correct process p R-MCasts a message m, then eventually all correct processes $q \in m.dest$ R-Deliver m, (iii) *agreement:* if a correct process p R-Delivers a message m, then eventually all correct processes $q \in m.dest$ R-Deliver m.

Atomic Multicast. Atomic multicast allows messages to be addressed to a subset of groups in Γ. For each message m, $m.dest$ denotes the groups to which m is addressed. Let p be a process. By abuse of notation, we write $p \in m.dest$ instead of $\exists g \in \Gamma : g \in m.dest \wedge p \in g$. Hereafter, we denote the sequence of messages delivered by p at time t as S_p^t, and the sequence of messages delivered by p at time t *projected* on processes p and q as $P_{p,q}(S_p^t)$, i.e., $P_{p,q}(S_p^t)$ is the sequence of messages S_p^t restricted to the messages m such that $p, q \in m.dest$. Atomic multicast is defined by the primitives A-MCast and A-Deliver, and satisfies the uniform integrity and validity properties of reliable multicast as well as the two following properties: (i) *uniform agreement:* if a process p A-Delivers m, then all correct processes $q \in m.dest$ eventually A-Deliver m, (ii) *uniform prefix order:* for any two processes p and q and any time t, either $P_{p,q}(S_p^t)$ is a prefix of $P_{p,q}(S_q^t)$ or $P_{p,q}(S_q^t)$ is a prefix of $P_{p,q}(S_p^t)$.

We also require atomic multicast algorithms to be *genuine* [7]: An algorithm $\mathcal{A}$ solving atomic multicast is said to be *genuine* iff for any run $R \in \mathcal{R}(\mathcal{A})$ and for any process p, in R if p sends or receives a message then some message m is A-MCast and either p is the process that A-MCasts m or $p \in m.dest$.

Atomic Broadcast. Atomic broadcast is a special case of atomic multicast. It is defined by the primitives A-BCast and A-Deliver and satisfies the same properties as atomic multicast where all A-BCast messages m are such that $m.dest = \Gamma$, i.e., messages are always A-BCast to all groups in the system.

2.3 Latency Degree

Let $\mathcal{A}$ be a broadcast or multicast algorithm and R be a run of $\mathcal{A}$ ($R \in \mathcal{R}(\mathcal{A})$). Moreover, in run R, let m be a message A-XCast (A-BCast or A-MCast) and $\Pi'(m) \subseteq \Pi$ be the set of processes that A-Deliver m. Intuitively, the latency degree of R is the minimal length of the causal path between the A-XCast of m and the last A-delivery of m among the processes in $\Pi'(m)$, when counting inter-group messages only. To define this latency degree we assign timestamps to process events using a slightly modified version of Lamport's logical clocks [9]. Initially, for all processes $p \in \Pi$, p's logical clock, LC_p, is initialized to 0. On process p, an event e is assigned its timestamp as follows:

1. If e is a local event, $ts(e) = LC_p$
2. If e is the send event of a message m to a process q,

$$ts(e) = \begin{cases} LC_p + 1, \, if \, group(p) \neq group(q) \\ LC_p, \quad otherwise \end{cases}$$

3. If e is the receive event of a message m, $ts(e) = \max(LC_p, ts(send(m)))$

The latency degree of a message m A-XCast in run R is defined as follows:

$$\Delta(m, R) = \max_{q \in \Pi'(m)}(ts(A\text{-}Deliver(m)_q) - ts(A\text{-}XCast(m)_p))$$

where $A\text{-}Deliver(m)_q$ and $A\text{-}XCast(m)_p$ respectively denote the A-Deliver(m) event on process q and the A-XCast(m) event on process p. We refer to the latency degree of an algorithm $\mathcal{A}$ as the minimum value of $\Delta(m, R)$ among all admissible runs R of $\mathcal{A}$ and messages m A-XCast in R.

3   The Inherent Cost of Reactiveness

We establish the inherent cost of the genuine atomic multicast problem for messages that are multicast to multiple groups and we show that quiescence has a cost, i.e., in runs where a message m is cast at a time when the algorithm is quiescent, there exists no algorithm that delivers m with a latency degree of one. As explained in Section 1, we proceed in two steps. We first show that, if processes are reactive when the last message m is cast, then m cannot be delivered with a latency degree of one. We then prove that (i) in runs of any genuine atomic multicast algorithm where one message is multicast at time t, processes are reactive at t and (ii) in runs of any quiescent atomic broadcast or atomic multicast algorithm where a finite number of messages are cast, processes are eventually reactive forever.

The proofs are done in a model identical to the model of Section 2, except that processes do not crash and links are reliable, i.e., they do not corrupt, duplicate, or lose messages.

Definition 1. *In a run R of an atomic broadcast or multicast algorithm, we say that a process p is reactive at time t iff p sends a message m at time $t' \geq t$ only if p A-XCasts m or if p received a message sent in the interval $[t, t']$.*

Proposition 1. *In a system with at least two groups, for any atomic broadcast or any atomic multicast algorithm $\mathcal{A}$, there does not exist runs R_1, R_2 of $\mathcal{A}$ in which processes are reactive at the time the last messages m_1, m_2 are A-XCast to at least two groups, such that $\Delta(m_1, R_1) = \Delta(m_2, R_2) = 1$.*

Proof: Suppose, by way of contradiction, that there exist an algorithm $\mathcal{A}$ and runs R_i of $\mathcal{A}$, $i \in \{1, 2\}$, such that $\Delta(m_i, R_i) = 1$. Consider two groups, g_1 and g_2. In run R_i, process $p_i \in g_i$ A-XCasts message m_i at time t to g_1 and g_2. We first show that (*) in R_i, at or after time t, processes can only send messages m such that for a sequence of events $e_1 = $ A-XCast(m_i), $e_2, ..., e_k = $ send(m), A-XCast(m_i) $\rightarrow e_2 \rightarrow ... \rightarrow$ send(m).[3] Suppose, by way of contradiction, that there exists a process p in R_i that sends a message m at a time $t'_i \geq t$ such that the event send(m) is not causally linked to the event A-XCast(m_i). We construct a run R'_i identical to run R_i except that message

---

[3] Events $e_1, ..., e_k$ can be of four kinds, either send(m), receive(m), A-XCast(m), or A-Deliver(m) for some message m. Moreover, the relation $\rightarrow$ is Lamport's transitive happened before relation on events [9]. It is defined as follows: $e_1 \rightarrow e_2 \Leftrightarrow e_1, e_2$ are two events on the same process and e_1 happens before e_2 or $e_1 = $ send(m) and $e_2 = $ receive(m) for some message m.

m_i is not A-MCast (note that processes are also reactive at time t in R'_i). Since in R_i, there is no causal chain linking the event A-XCast(m_i) with the event send(m), runs R'_i and R_i are indistinguishable to process p up to and including time t'_i. Therefore, p also sends m in R'_i. Hence, since processes are reactive at time t and no message is A-XCast at or after t, p must have received a messag m' sent at or after t by some process q. Applying the same reasoning multiple times, we argue that there must exist a process r that sends a message m'' at time t such that for some events $e_1 = \text{send}(m'')$, $e_2, ..., e_{x-1} = \text{send}(m')$, $e_x = \text{send}(m)$, we have send(m'') $\rightarrow ... \rightarrow$ send(m') $\rightarrow$ send(m). However, r cannot send m'' because no message is A-XCast at or after t, a contradiction.

By the validity property of $\mathcal{A}$ and because there is no failure, all processes eventually A-Deliver m_i. Since $\Delta(m_i, R_i) = 1$, by (*), processes in g_i A-Deliver m_i before receiving any message from processes in g_{3-i} sent at or after time t. Let $t^*_i > t$ be the time at which all processes in g_i have A-Delivered message m_i. We now build run R_3 as follows. As in run R_i, p_i A-XCasts m_i. Runs R_i and R_3 are indistinguishable for processes in group g_i up to time t^*_i, that is, all messages causally linked to the event A-XCast(m_{3-i}) (including A-XCast(m_{3-i}) itself) sent from processes in group g_{3-i} to processes in group g_i are delayed until after t^*_i. Consequently, processes in group g_i have all A-Delivered m_i by time t^*_i. By the uniform agreement of $\mathcal{A}$, processes in g_1 eventually A-Deliver m_2 and processes in g_2 eventually A-Deliver m_1, violating the uniform prefix order property of $\mathcal{A}$. □

Proposition 2. *For any run R of any genuine atomic multicast algorithm $\mathcal{A}$ where one message is A-MCast at time t, processes are reactive at time t.*

Proof: In run R, by the genuineness property of $\mathcal{A}$, for any message m' sent, there exist events $e_1 = \text{A-MCast}(m)$, $e_2, ..., e_x = \text{send}(m')$ such that A-MCast(m) $\rightarrow e_2 \rightarrow ... \rightarrow$ send(m') (otherwise, using a similar argument as in Proposition 1, we could build a run R' identical to run R, except that no message is A-MCast in R', such that a process sends a message anyway, contradicting the fact that in R' no message is A-MCast and $\mathcal{A}$ is genuine).

Consequently, for any process p, if p sends a message m' at $t' \geq t$, then p A-MCasts m' or p received a message in the interval $[t, t']$. □

Proposition 3. *For any run R of any quiescent atomic broadcast or atomic multicast algorithm $\mathcal{A}$ in which a finite number of messages are A-XCast, there exists a time t such that for all $t' \geq t$, processes are reactive at t'.*

Proof: In R, a finite number of messages are A-XCast. Because $\mathcal{A}$ is quiescent, there exists a time t at or after which no messages are sent. It follows directly that for all $t' \geq t$ processes are reactive at t'. □

Although our result shows that if the last message m is cast when processes are reactive, then m cannot be delivered in one inter-group message delay, in practice, multiple messages may bear this overhead. In fact, this might even be the case in runs where an infinite number of messages are cast. Indeed, to ensure quiescence, processes must somehow *predict* whether any message will be cast in the future. Hence, if no message is expected to be cast, processes must stop communicating, and this may happen prematurely.

4   Atomic Multicast for WANs

In this section, we present a latency degree-optimal atomic multicast algorithm which is inspired by the one from Fritzke *et al.* [5], an adaptation of Skeen's algorithm for failure-prone systems. Due to space constraints, we here only present the basic principles of the algorithm, the pseudo-code as well as a detailed explanation can be found in [12].

4.1   Algorithm Overview

The algorithm associates every multicast message with a timestamp. To ensure agreement on the message delivery order, two properties are ensured: (1) processes agree on the message timestamps and (2) after a process p A-Delivers a message with timestamp ts, p does not A-Deliver a message with a smaller timestamp than ts. To satisfy these two properties, inside each group g, processes implement a logical *clock* that is used to generate timestamps—this is g's clock. To guarantee g's clock consistency, processes use consensus to maintain it. Moreover, every message m goes trough the following four stages:

- *Stage s_0:* In every group $g \in m.dest$, processes define a timestamp for m using g's clock. This is g's proposal for m's final timestamp.
- *Stage s_1:* Groups in $m.dest$ exchange their proposals for m's timestamp and set m's final timestamp to the maximum timestamp among all proposals.
- *Stage s_2:* Every group in $m.dest$ sets its clock to a value greater than the final timestamp of m.
- *Stage s_3:* Message m is A-Delivered when its timestamp is the smallest among all messages that are in one of the four stages and not yet A-Delivered.

As mentioned above, our algorithm differentiates itself from [5] in several aspects. First, when a message is multicast, instead of using a uniform reliable multicast primitive, we use a non-uniform version of this primitive while still ensuring properties as strong as in [5]. Second, in contrast to [5], not all messages go trough all four stages. Messages that are multicast to only one group can *jump* from stage s_0 to stage s_3. Moreover, even if a message m is multicast to more than one group, on processes belonging to the group that proposed the largest timestamp (i.e., m's final timestamp), m can skip stage s_2.

4.2   Latency Degree Analysis

Consider a message m that is multicast by a process p. In [12], we show that if m is multicast to one group, the latency degree of the algorithm, denoted as $\mathcal{A}1$, is zero if $p \in g$, and one otherwise. Moreover, if m is multicast to multiple groups, the latency degree is two, which matches the lower bound of Section 3.

Theorem 1. *There exists a run R of algorithm $\mathcal{A}1$ in which a message m is A-MCast to two groups such that $\Delta(m, R) = 2$.*

5   Atomic Broadcast for WANs

In this section, we present the first fault-tolerant atomic broadcast algorithm that achieves a latency degree of one. Together with the lower bound of Section 3, this shows that atomic multicast is more costly than atomic broadcast. Due to space constraints, we here only present an overview of the algorithm, the pseudo-code as well as a detailed explanation can be found in [12].

5.1   Algorithm Overview

To atomically broadcast a message m, a process p reliably multicasts m to the processes in p's group. In parallel, processes execute an *unbounded* sequence of rounds. At the end of each round, processes deliver a set of messages according to some deterministic order. To ensure agreement on the messages delivered in round r, processes proceed in two steps. In the first step, inside each group g, processes use consensus to define g's bundle of messages. In the second step, groups exchange their message bundles. The set of message delivered at the end of round r is the union of all bundles. Note that we also wish to ensure *quiescence*, i.e., if there is a time after which no message is broadcast, then processes eventually stop sending messages. To do so, processes try to predict when no further messages will be broadcast. Our prediction strategy is simple, it consists in checking, at the end of each round, whether any message was delivered or not. If no messages were delivered, processes stop executing rounds. Note that our algorithm is indulgent with regards to prediction mistakes, i.e., if processes become quiescent too early, they can restart so that liveness is still ensured.

5.2   Latency Degree Analysis

In [12], we analyze the latency degree of the algorithm, denoted as $\mathcal{A}2$. We first show that its best latency degree (among all its admissible runs) is one, which is optimal. We then consider runs where processes become quiescent too early, i.e., processes stop executing rounds before a message is broadcast. In these runs, the latency degree of the algorithm is two.

Theorem 2. *There exists a run R of algorithm $\mathcal{A}2$ in which a message m is A-BCast such that $\Delta(m, R) = 1$.*

Theorem 3. *There exists a run R of algorithm $\mathcal{A}2$ in which the last message m is A-BCast when processes are reactive such that $\Delta(m, R) = 2$.*

It is worth noting that the presented broadcast algorithm never becomes reactive if the time between two consecutive broadcasts is smaller than the time to execute a round. Moreover, in this case, all rounds are *useful*, i.e., they all deliver at least one message. For example, in a system where the inter-group latency is 100 milliseconds, a broadcast frequency of 10 messages per second is enough to obtain this desired behavior. In case the broadcast frequency is too low or not constant, to prevent processes from stopping prematurely, more elaborate prediction strategies based on application behavior could be used.

6   Related Work and Final Remarks

The literature on atomic broadcast and multicast algorithms is abundant [3]. We here review the most relevant papers to our protocols.

Atomic Multicast. In [7], the authors show the impossibility of solving genuine atomic multicast with unreliable failure detectors when groups are allowed to intersect. Hence, the algorithms cited below circumvent this impossibility result by considering non-intersecting groups that contain a sufficient number of correct processes to solve consensus. They can be viewed as variations of Skeen's algorithm [2], a multicast algorithm designed for failure-free systems, where messages are associated with timestamps and the message delivery follows the timestamp order. In [10], the addressees of a message m, i.e., the processes to which m is multicast, exchange the timestamp they assigned to m, and, once they receive this timestamp from a majority of processes of each group, they propose the maximum value received to consensus. Because consensus is run among the addressees of a message and can thus span multiple groups, this algorithm is not well-suited for wide area networks. In [4], consensus is run inside groups exclusively. Consider a message m that is multicast to groups $g_1, ..., g_k$. The first destination group of m, g_1, runs consensus to define the final timestamp of m and hands over this message to group g_2. Every subsequent group proceeds similarly up to g_k. To avoid cycles in the message delivery order, before handling other messages, every group waits for a final acknowledgment from group g_k. The latency degree of this algorithm is therefore proportional to the number of destination groups. In [5], to ensure that processes agree on the timestamps associated to every message and to deliver messages according to the timestamp order, every message goes through four stages. In contrast to [5], the algorithm presented in this paper allows messages to skip stages, therefore reducing the number of intra-group messages sent by sparing the execution of consensus instances.

Atomic Broadcast. In [1], the authors consider the atomic broadcast and multicast problems in a publish-subscribe system where links are reliable, publishers *do not crash*, and cast infinitely many messages. Agreement on the message ordering is ensured by using the same deterministic merge function at every subscriber process. Given the cast rate of publishers, the authors give optimal algorithms with regards to the merge delay, i.e., the time elapsed between the reception of a message by a subscriber and its delivery. Both algorithms achieve a latency degree of one.[4] In [13], a time-based protocol is introduced to increase the probability of *spontaneous* total order in wide area networks by artificially delaying messages. Although the latency degree of the *optimistic* delivery of a message is one, the latency degree of its *final* delivery is two. Moreover, their protocol is non-uniform, i.e., the *agreement* property of Section 2 is only ensured for correct processes. In [14], a uniform protocol based on multiple sequencers is proposed. Every process p is assigned a sequencer that associates sequence numbers to the messages p broadcasts. Processes optimistically deliver a message m when they receive m's sequence number. The final delivery of m occurs when the sequence number of

---

[4] Note that this does not contradict the latency degree lower bound of genuine atomic multicast. Indeed, their assumptions are different than ours, i.e., to ensure liveness of their multicast algorithm, they require that each publisher multicast infinitely many messages to *each* subscriber.

Algorithm	latency degree	inter-group msgs.
[4]	$k+1$	$O(kd^2)$
[10]	4	$O(k^2d^2)$
[5]	2	$O(k^2d^2)$
Algorithm $\mathcal{A}1$	2	$O(k^2d^2)$
[1][5]	1	$O(kd)$

(a) Atomic Multicast

Algorithm	latency degree	inter-group msgs.
[13][6]	2	$O(n)$
[14]	2	$O(n^2)$
Algorithm $\mathcal{A}2$	1	$O(n^2)$
[1][5]	1	$O(n)$

(b) Atomic Broadcast

Fig. 1. Comparison of the algorithms (d : nb. of processes per group, k : nb. of destination groups)

m has been validated by a majority of processes. The latency degree of this algorithm is identical to [13].

In Figure 1, we compare the latency degree and the number of inter-group exchanged messages of the aforementioned algorithms. In this comparison, we consider the best-case scenario, in particular there is no failure nor failure suspicion. We denote n as the total number of processes in the system, d as the number of processes in each group, and k as the number of groups to which a message is cast ($k \geq 2$). To compute the latency degree and number of inter-group messages sent, we consider the oracle-based uniform reliable broadcast and uniform consensus algorithms of [6] and [11] respectively (note that [6] can easily be modified to implement reliable multicast). The latency degrees of [6] and [11] are respectively one and two. Furthermore, considering that a process p multicasts a message to k groups (we consider that p belongs to one of these k groups) or that k groups execute consensus, the algorithms respectively send $d(k-1)$ and $2kd(kd-1)$ inter-group messages.

From Figure 1, we conclude that, among uniform fault-tolerant broadcast protocols, Algorithm $\mathcal{A}2$ achieves the best latency degree and message complexity. In the case of the atomic multicast problem, although Algorithm $\mathcal{A}1$ and [5] achieve the best latency degree among fault-tolerant protocols, [4] has a lower message complexity. Deciding which algorithm is best is not straightforward as it depends on factors such as the network topology as well as the latencies and bandwidths of links.

References

1. Aguilera, M.K., Strom, R.E.: Efficient atomic broadcast using deterministic merge. In: PODC 2000. Proceedings of the nineteenth annual ACM symposium on Principles of distributed computing, pp. 209–218. ACM Press, New York (2000)
2. Birman, K.P., Joseph, T.A.: Reliable communication in the presence of failures. ACM Trans. Comput. Syst. 5(1), 47–76 (1987)
3. Défago, X., Schiper, A., Urbán, P.: Total order broadcast and multicast algorithms: Taxonomy and survey. ACM Comput. Surv. 36(4), 372–421 (2004)

---

[5] This paper considers a strong model where links are reliable, *multicaster* processes do not crash, and multicast infinitely many messages to every process.

[6] This algorithm is non-uniform, i.e., it guarantees the agreement property of Section 2 only for correct processes.

4. Delporte-Gallet, C., Fauconnier, H.: Fault-tolerant genuine atomic multicast to multiple groups. In: Proceedings of the 4th International Conference on Principles of Distributed Computing, pp. 107–122 (2000)
5. Fritzke, U., Ingels, Ph., Mostéfaoui, A., Raynal, M.: Fault-tolerant total order multicast to asynchronous groups. In: Proceedings of the 17th IEEE Symposium on Reliable Distributed Systems, pp. 578–585 (1998)
6. Frolund, S., Pedone, F.: Ruminations on domain-based reliable broadcast. In: Malkhi, D. (ed.) DISC 2002. LNCS, vol. 2508, pp. 148–162. Springer, Heidelberg (2002)
7. Guerraoui, R., Schiper, A.: Genuine atomic multicast in asynchronous distributed systems. Theor. Comput. Sci. 254(1-2), 297–316 (2001)
8. Hadzilacos, V., Toueg, S.: Fault-tolerant broadcasts and related problems. In: Mullender, S.J. (ed.) Distributed Systems, Ch. 5, pp. 97–145. Addison-Wesley, Reading (1993)
9. Lamport, L.: Time, clocks, and the ordering of events in a distributed system. Communications of the ACM 21(7), 558–565 (1978)
10. Rodrigues, L., Guerraoui, R., Schiper, A.: Scalable atomic multicast. In: IC3N 1998. Proceedings of the 7th IEEE International Conference on Computer Communications and Networks, Lafayette, Louisiana, USA, pp. 840–847 (1998)
11. Schiper, A.: Early consensus in an asynchronous system with a weak failure detector. Distributed Computing 10(3), 149–157 (1997)
12. Schiper, N., Pedone, F.: Optimal atomic broadcast and multicast algorithms for wide area networks. Technical Report 2007/004 Revision 1, University of Lugano (2007)
13. Sousa, A., Pereira, J., Moura, F., Oliveira, R.: Optimistic total order in wide area networks. In: Proceedings of the 21st IEEE Symposium on Reliable Distributed Systems, pp. 190–199. IEEE CS, Los Alamitos (2002)
14. Vicente, P., Rodrigues, L.: An indulgent uniform total order algorithm with optimistic delivery. In: Proceedings of the 21st IEEE Symposium on Reliable Distributed Systems, p. 92. IEEE Computer Society, Washington, DC (2002)

Detection of Disjunctive Normal Form Predicate in Distributed Systems*

Hongtao Huang[1,2]

[1] State Key Laboratory of Computer Science,
Institute of Software, Chinese Academy of Sciences, Beijing 100080, China
[2] Graduate University, Chinese Academy of Sciences, Beijing 100080, China
hht@ios.ac.cn

Abstract. Predicate detection in a distributed system is an important problem. It is useful in debugging and testing of the distributed system. Two modalities are introduced for predicate detection by Cooper and Marzullo. They are denoted by *Possibly* and *Definitely*. In general, the complexity of detecting predicates in the two modalities is NP-complete and coNP-complete. On detecting conjunctive predicates in *Definitely* modality, Garg and Waldecker proposed an efficient method. In this paper, we extend the notion of the conjunctive predicate to the notion of the disjunctive normal form (DNF) predicate, which is a disjunction of several conjunctive predicates. We are concerned with the problem of detecting DNF predicates in *Definitely* modality. We study two classes of DNF predicates called separation DNF predicates and separation-inclusion DNF predicates, which can be detected in *Definitely* modality using an idea similar to that of Garg and Waldecker.

1 Introduction

Predicate detection in a distributed system is an important problem. It is useful in debugging and testing of the distributed system. A predicate is an interesting property that we want to check in the execution of a distributed system. Two modalities are introduced for predicate detection by Cooper and Marzullo [4]. They are denoted by *Possibly* and *Definitely*. We know that the state space of an execution of a distributed system is a distributive lattice. Given a predicate Φ, $Possibly(\Phi)$ means that there exists one path from the initial state to the final state in the lattice, which passes through a state satisfying Φ. $Definitely(\Phi)$ means that all paths from the initial state to the final state in the lattice pass through a state satisfying Φ. $Possibly(\Phi)$ is usually used to check the property Φ that we want to avoid, such as, the number of tokens in a system is less than a constant. While $Definitely(\Phi)$ is usually used to check the desired property Φ that we want to guarantee, such as, a leader is elected.

---

* Supported by the National Natural Science Foundation of China under Grant No. 60573012 and 60421001, and the National Grand Fundamental Research 973 Program of China under Grant No. 2002cb312200.

S. Rao et al. (Eds.): ICDCN 2008, LNCS 4904, pp. 158–169, 2008.

Predicate detection suffers from the state explosion problem. It has been shown that in general, detection of $Possibly(\Phi)$ is NP-complete [3] and detection of $Definitely(\Phi)$ is coNP-complete [13].

The conjunctive predicate is an important class of predicates. A conjunctive predicate is a conjunction of local predicates. A local predicate is defined on only one process. Thus the truth of it can be easily verified by the process. On detecting conjunctive predicates in $Possibly$ modality, [8] and [9] proposed efficient algorithms. On detecting conjunctive predicates in $Definitely$ modality, Garg and Waldecker proposed an efficient method in [7]. The concept of intervals play an important role in their method. An interval in a process is a sequence of consecutive events satisfying a local predicate of the conjunctive predicate Φ. The essence of the method is choosing one interval from every process and analyzing the relation of these intervals. An similar method was independently proposed in [14] by Venkatesan and Dathan.

In this paper, we extend the notion of the conjunctive predicate to the notion of the disjunctive normal form (DNF) predicate, which is a disjunction of several conjunctive predicates. From [13], we know that in general detection of DNF predicates in $Definitely$ modality is coNP-complete. The purpose of this paper is to discuss two classes of DNF predicates called separation DNF predicates and separation-inclusion DNF predicates, which can be detected efficiently in $Definitely$ modality using an idea similar to that of Garg and Waldecker by analyzing the relation of intervals.

Given a DNF predicate $\Phi = \Phi^1 \vee \Phi^2 \vee \ldots \vee \Phi^m$, where each Φ^i is a conjunctive predicate, for every conjunctive predicate Φ^i we have a set of intervals. The set of intervals with respect to Φ is the union of these sets of intervals. Separation DNF predicates and separation-inclusion DNF predicates put some restrictions on the relationship between these intervals. Informally speaking, both separation DNF predicates and separation-inclusion DNF predicates require that no two intervals are adjacent. Besides, separation-inclusion DNF predicates require that the relation of interval inclusion satisfies certain conditions.

We observe the similarity between the condition on intervals of the method of Garg and Waldecker in [7] and the concept of inevitable states in [5]. For using the concept of inevitable states to prove our results, we use the technique of interval compression. Such ideas were first explored in [1] and [11]. But they concern the problem of detecting predicates in $Possibly$ modality. In [2] Chakraborty and Garg prove such an idea can be used for detecting predicates in $Definitely$ modality.

Then based on the concept of inevitable states, we use a constructive way to obtain the desired result on separation DNF predicates. And we use an indirect way to obtain the desired result on separation-inclusion DNF predicates.

The remainder of the paper is organized as follows: Section 2 discusses the model that we use. In section 3 we introduce the concept of DNF predicates and discuss the interval compression theorem with respect to DNF predicates. Section 4 discusses some properties of inevitable states. Section 5 presents the main results on detection of separation DNF predicates and separation-inclusion DNF predicates. Section 6 concludes the paper.

2   Model

We assume a loosely-coupled message-passing asynchronous system. A distributed system consists of n sequential processes denoted by $P_1, P_2, \ldots, P_n$. The processes do not share a global clock or a global memory. They can communicate with each other only by exchanging messages through communication channels. The system is asynchronous, which means that each process executes at its own speed because of the lack of global clock, and message transition delay is arbitrary but finite. We assume that the communication channels are reliable. No messages are lost, altered or spuriously introduced. We do not assume that the channels are FIFO channels. In this paper, we are concerned with detecting global predicates in a given execution of a distributed system in an off-line manner.

Each process in the distributed system is sequential. For each process $P_i, 1 \leq i \leq n$, the sequence of events in the process is $E_i^1 E_i^2 E_i^3 \cdots$. Let E_i denote the set of events in P_i. Let $E = E_1 \cup E_2 \cup \ldots \cup E_n$. We use Lamport's happened-before relation [10] to give an irreflexive partial order $\rightarrow$ on E. Happened-before relation is defined as the smallest relation satisfying the following conditions: for two events $e, f \in E$, (1) if e and f belong to the same process, and e occurs before f, then $e \rightarrow f$; (2) if e is an event which sends a message and f is an event which receives the message sent by e, then $e \rightarrow f$; (3) if there exists an event $g \in E$ such that $e \rightarrow g$ and $g \rightarrow f$, then $e \rightarrow f$. Based on the induced order, we model the given execution of the system as an irreflexive partial order set $\langle E, \rightarrow \rangle$. We call it a computation.

A global state of a computation $\langle E, \rightarrow \rangle$ is a subset G of E such that for each event e in G, any event f occurring before e in the process that e belongs to, is in G. A global state G is a consistent global state, if for each event e, any event f satisfying $f \rightarrow e$, is in G. The intuitive meaning of consistent global states is that for each event in the global state, all the events that should occur before it have occurred. The set of consistent global states forms a distributive lattice under the relation of $\subseteq$ [12][6]. Let $L(E)$ denote the distributive lattice.

We can represent a global state G by an n-dimension vector $S = (s_1, s_2, \ldots, s_n)$, where for each i, $1 \leq i \leq n$, if $E_i \cap G \neq \emptyset$, then $E_i^{s_i}$ is the greatest element in $E_i \cap G$; otherwise $s_i = 0$. The frontier of a global state S is an n-tuple $H = (E_1^{s_1}, E_2^{s_2}, \ldots, E_n^{s_n})$. For two global states S and S' in $L(E)$, $S \leq S'$ if and only if $s_i \leq s_i'$, for all i, $1 \leq i \leq n$. $S < S'$ if and only if $S \leq S'$ and $S \neq S'$. $S \cap S' = (min(s_1, s_1'), min(s_2, s_2'), \ldots, min(s_n, s_n'))$. $S \cup S' = (max(s_1, s_1'), max(s_2, s_2'), \ldots, max(s_n, s_n'))$.

A run of a computation is a total order of the events in E, which is compatible with $\rightarrow$, that is, if $e \rightarrow f$, then e comes before f in the run. A run is also a chain of states from $\bot$ to $\top$ in the lattice $L(E)$.

When detecting a predicate in a computation, each process has an interesting variable which is used to check some properties of the execution. Given a consistent global state $S = (s_1, s_2, \ldots, s_n)$, the value of the variable on P_i is the value of the variable after the occurrence of the event $E_i^{s_i}$, if $s_i > 0$; otherwise, it is a given initial value. A global predicate is a predicate defined on variables of processes. If a predicate is defined on the variable on a single process, it is called a local predicate. An event e satisfies a local predicate defined on the process that e belongs to, if after the occurrence of e the value of the variable in the process satisfies the local predicate.

Given a predicate Φ, two modalities are usually used in predicate detection [4]:

$Definitely(\Phi)$. It is true if for every run of the computation, there exists a consistent global state satisfying Φ on this run.

$Possibly(\Phi)$. It is true if there exists a run of the computation such that a consistent global state on this run satisfies Φ.

For example, in the computation of figure 1, assume the interesting variables in P_1 and P_2 are x and y respectively and the global predicate we want to detect is $\Phi = x > y$. We can see that $Possibly(\Phi)$ is true, while $Definitely(\Phi)$ is false.

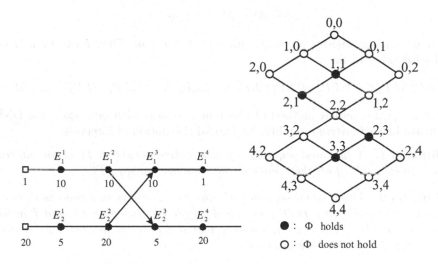

Fig. 1. A computation and its corresponding lattice

3   Interval Compression

In [7] Garg and Waldecker proposed a method to detect $Definitely(\Phi)$, where Φ is a conjunctive predicate. A predicate is conjunctive if it is a conjunction of local predicates. A conjunctive predicate has the form:

$$\Phi = LP_1 \wedge LP_2 \wedge \ldots \wedge LP_n$$

where LP_i is a local predicate defined on P_i, for every i, $1 \le i \le n$.

Now we briefly state their method with a slight modification. The notion of intervals is important in detecting a conjunctive predicate. An interval is a maximal sequence of consecutive events in a process P_i such that LP_i is true for all the events in the sequence. The beginning event of an interval I is denoted by $I.low$ and the ending event is denoted by $I.high$. When there exists only one event in the interval, the beginning event and the ending event are the same. For an event e, the immediately next event of e in the process that e belongs to, is denoted by $e.next$. In the remainder of the paper, we assume that in every process, neither the initial value nor the final event satisfies the local predicate defined on the process.

Theorem 1. *[7] For a conjunctive predicate* $\Phi = LP_1 \wedge LP_2 \wedge \ldots LP_n$, *Definitely($\Phi$) is true if and only if there exist n intervals, $I_1, I_2, \ldots, I_n$, each belonging to a different process such that $I_i.low \rightarrow I_j.high.next$, for all i, j, $1 \le i \le n$, $1 \le j \le n$.*

In this paper we extend the notion of conjunctive predicates to the one of disjunctive normal form (DNF) predicates. A predicate Φ is a disjunctive normal form predicate if it has the form:

$$\Phi = \Phi^1 \vee \Phi^2 \vee \ldots \vee \Phi^m$$

where Φ^i is a conjunctive predicate, for all i, $1 \le i \le m$. Thus Φ can be written in the following form:

$$\Phi = (LP_1^1 \wedge LP_2^1 \wedge \ldots \wedge LP_n^1) \vee (LP_1^2 \wedge LP_2^2 \wedge \ldots \wedge LP_n^2) \vee \ldots \vee (LP_1^m \wedge LP_2^m \wedge \ldots \wedge LP_n^m)$$

For using the similar method of theorem 1 to deal with detection of a DNF predicate in *Definitely* modality, we extend the notion of intervals.

Definition 1. *A maximal sequence of consecutive events in P_i is an interval with respect to Φ^k, if all the events in the sequence satisfy LP_i^k.*

Definition 2. *An maximal sequence of consecutive events in a process P_i is an interval with respect to a DNF predicate Φ, if for any two events e and f in the sequence, for all k, $1 \le k \le m$, we have that if e is in an interval with respect to Φ^k, then f is also in the interval.*

Now we will show that an interval with respect to a DNF predicate can be treated as a single event when we detect the predicate in *Definitely* modality. We call this interval compression. Such an idea was proposed by Chakraborty and Garg in [2].

We collect the beginning events of all intervals with respect to Φ on processes into a set E'. Apparently, we have that $E' \subseteq E$. From the relation $\rightarrow$ we can induce the relation $\rightarrow'$. For every e and f, $e, f \in E'$, $e \rightarrow' f$ if and only if $e \rightarrow f$. From the original computation $\langle E, \rightarrow \rangle$, we can obtain the reduced computation $\langle E', \rightarrow' \rangle$. In $\langle E', \rightarrow' \rangle$ events in each process are also indexed by consecutive natural numbers starting from 1.

The next theorem presents the relation of the two computations.

Theorem 2. *Given a DNF predicate Φ, $Definitely(\Phi)$ is true for the original computation $\langle E, \rightarrow \rangle$, if and only if $Definitely(\Phi)$ is true for the reduced computation $\langle E', \rightarrow' \rangle$.*

This theorem can be derived from [2] (theorem 4).

4   Inevitable States

In a state space $L(E)$, inevitable states are some special states. A state is inevitable if it is on all the runs of the computation. For example, in the lattice of figure 1, (2,2) is an inevitable state. Inevitable states are useful in the detection of certain classes of DNF predicates in $Definitely$ modality. In this section, we give some properties of inevitable states.

In [5] Fromentin and Raynal proposed a method to determine whether a consistent global state is inevitable.

Theorem 3. *[5] $S = (s_1, s_2, \ldots, s_n)$ is an inevitable state if and only if $E_i^{s_i} \rightarrow E_j^{s_j}.next$, for all i, j, $1 \le i \le n$, $1 \le j \le n$.*

Now we use this result to obtain the following lemma, which is useful in the detection of certain classes of DNF predicates in $Definitely$ modality.

For a state S, let $Level(S)$ denote $\sum_{i=1}^{n} s_i$. We call $Level(S)$ the level value of S.

Lemma 1. *If S is not an inevitable state, there exists a state S' such that $Level(S) = Level(S')$, and S and S' are different in only two processes i, j, with $|s_i - s_i'| = 1$ and $|s_j - s_j'| = 1$.*

5   Detection of Two Classes of DNF Predicates

In this section, we will present the main results in this paper on detection of two classes of DNF predicates in $Definitely$ modality. The result can be seen as an extension of theorem 1 to the two classes of DNF predicates. The next two definitions define two classes of DNF predicates which we are interested in.

For two interval I and I' which are on the same process P_i, let a be the index of the event $I.low$ and b be the index of $I.high$, that is, $E_i^a = I.low$ and $E_i^b = I.high$. And let a' be the index of the event $I'.low$ and b' be the index of $I'.high$. If $a = a'$ and $b = b'$, we say that I and I' coincide. If $a > b' + 1$ or $a' > b + 1$, we say that I and I' separate. Intuitively, it means that I and I' have not any same event and they are not adjacent. If $a \le a' \le b' \le b$, and I and I' do not coincide, we say that I includes I'.

Definition 3. *Given a computation $\langle E, \rightarrow \rangle$ and a DNF predicate $\Phi = \Phi^1 \vee \Phi^2 \vee \ldots \vee \Phi^m$. Let A_i be the set of intervals that are with respect to Φ^i, for each i, $1 \le i \le m$. Let $A = A_1 \cup \ldots \cup A_m$. Φ is a separation DNF predicate, if for any two intervals I and I' in A on the same process they coincide or separate.*

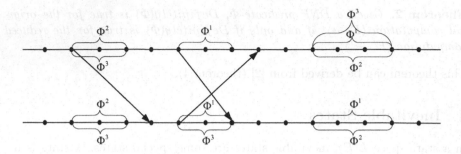

Fig. 2. An example of separation DNF predicate

Figure 2 illustrates an example of the separation DNF predicate.

Definition 4. *Given a computation $\langle E, \rightarrow \rangle$ and a DNF predicate $\Phi = \Phi^1 \vee \Phi^2 \vee \ldots \vee \Phi^m$. Let A_i be the set of intervals that are with respect to Φ^i, for all i, $1 \leq i \leq m$. Let $A = A_1 \cup \ldots \cup A_m$. Let R be a binary relation such that $R = \{(i,j)|$ there exist an intervals I with respect to Φ^i and an interval I' with respect to Φ^j in A such that I and I' are on the same process and I includes $I'\}$. Φ is a separation-inclusion DNF predicate, if the two conditions are satisfied: (1) for any two intervals I and I' in A on the same process they coincide, or they separate, or I includes I', or I' includes I; (2) R is acyclic, that is, there does not exist a sequence $b_1 b_2 \ldots b_l$ such that $b_1 = b_l$ and $(b_k, b_{k+1}) \in R$ for all k, $1 \leq k \leq l - 1$.*

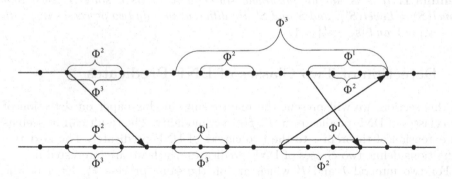

Fig. 3. An example of separation-inclusion DNF predicate

Figure 3 illustrates an example of the separation-inclusion DNF predicate.

From the above two definitions, we can see that the separation DNF predicate is a subclass of the separation-inclusion DNF predicate. Next we will prove that the two classes can be detected in *Definitely* modality using a method similar to that of theorem 1. Both of the proofs are based on inevitable states. We use a constructive way to prove the first theorem on separation DNF predicates. While we use an indirect way to prove the second theorem on separation-inclusion DNF predicates.

First we give a theorem on separation DNF predicates. Given a DNF predicate, a true state is a consistent global state satisfying the predicate.

Before we present the theorem, given a separation DNF predicate Φ, we show a property of $L(E')$. From the definition of separation DNF predicates, any two intervals $I \in A$ and $I' \in A$, which are on the same process, coincide or separate. Thus any $I \in A$ is an interval with respect to Φ. When doing interval compression, it is compressed to an event.

In $\langle E', \rightarrow' \rangle$, in some process P_i, if an event f satisfies a local predicate LP_i^k of some Φ^k, then before interval compression it is the beginning event of an interval with respect to Φ^k. Let $f' \in E'$ is another event in P_i such that $f' \neq f$ and f' satisfies a local predicate of some Φ^j. From the definition of separation DNF predicates, f and f' are not adjacent, that is, $f.next \neq f'$ and $f'.next \neq f$. Thus we have that in $L(E')$ for any $S = (s_1, s_2, \ldots, s_n)$ satisfying Φ and $S' = (s_1', s_2', \ldots, s_n')$ satisfying Φ, $|s_i - s_i'| \geq 2$ or $s_i = s_i'$, for all i, $1 \leq i \leq n$.

The idea of the proof is as follows. After interval compression, we obtain $\langle E', \rightarrow' \rangle$ from $\langle E, \rightarrow \rangle$. Every n intervals with respect to a conjunctive predicate in different processes is transformed to a state of $\langle E', \rightarrow' \rangle$. We can see that the n intervals satisfy the relation stated in theorem 1 if and only if the compressed state is an inevitable state. If one of the compressed states is inevitable, then $Definitely(\Phi)$ is true. Based on the above property, if none of the compressed states is inevitable, we can construct a run which does not pass through any true state. It implies that $Definitely(\Phi)$ is false. Then we can have the next lemma and theorem.

Lemma 2. *Given a separation DNF predicate* $\Phi = \Phi^1 \vee \Phi^2 \vee \ldots \vee \Phi^m$ *and a computation* $\langle E, \rightarrow \rangle$, $Definitely(\Phi)$ *is true for the reduced computation* $\langle E', \rightarrow' \rangle$, *if and only if there exists an inevitable state satisfying* Φ *in* $L(E')$.

Theorem 4. *For a separation DNF predicate* $\Phi = \Phi^1 \vee \Phi^2 \vee \ldots \vee \Phi^m$, $Definitely(\Phi)$ *is true if and only if there exist* n *intervals,* $I_1, I_2, \ldots, I_n$, *each belonging to a different process, such that all are intervals with respect to the same* Φ^k, *and* $I_i.low \rightarrow I_j.high.next$, *for all* $i, j, 1 \leq i \leq n, 1 \leq j \leq n$.

Next we will show theorem 4 can be extended to the case of separation-inclusion DNF predicates. The case for separation-inclusion DNF predicates is more complex than the one of separation DNF predicates. For separation-inclusion DNF predicates, when doing interval compression, not all intervals with respect to some Φ^k can be compressed to an event (because it maybe include other intervals with respect to other Φ^j). Thus $L(E')$ for separation-inclusion DNF predicates does not have the property of $L(E')$ for separation DNF predicates as stated above.

The next definition introduces the concept of zones for depicting basic units of $L(E)$ for separation-inclusion DNF predicates.

Definition 5. *A zone* $Z[(a_1, b_1), (a_2, b_2), \ldots, (a_n, b_n)]$ *is a set of states. A state* $S = (s_1, s_2, \ldots, s_n) \in Z$ *if and only if* $a_i \leq s_i \leq b_i$ *for all* $i, 1 \leq i \leq n$.

We can see that the states (not restricted to consistent global states) satisfying $\Phi = \Phi^1 \vee \Phi^2 \vee \ldots \vee \Phi^m$ must be a set of zones $\mathbf{Z} = \{Z_1, Z_2, \ldots\}$. For example, let $I_1, I_2, \ldots, I_n$ be n intervals with respect to the same Φ^k, where I_i is on process P_i. Let a_i be the index of $I_i.low$ on P_i and b_i be the index of $I_i.high$ on P_i, for all i, $1 \le i \le n$. Then we get a zone $Z[(a_1, b_1), (a_2, b_2), \ldots, (a_n, b_n)]$. Any state $S = (s_1, s_2, \ldots, s_n) \in Z$ must satisfy Φ^k, because $E_i^{s_i}$ satisfies LP_i^k for all i, $i \le i \le n$.

Given two zones Z and Z'. Let $I_1, I_2, \ldots, I_n$ be the corresponding intervals for Z and $I_1', I_2', \ldots, I_n'$ be the corresponding intervals for Z'. From the definition of separation-inclusion DNF predicates, we have that there does not exist such case that I_j includes I_j' in process P_j, and I_k' includes I_k in process P_k. Thus if $I_i \cap I_i' \ne \emptyset$ for all i, $1 \le i \le n$, there only exist two cases: (1) I_i includes I_i' or I_i coincide with I_i', for all i, $1 \le i \le n$. In this case $Z' \subseteq Z$; (2) I_i' includes I_i or I_i' coincide with I_i, for all i, $1 \le i \le n$. In this case $Z \subseteq Z'$. Otherwise there exist I_k and I_k' such that they separate. In this case, $Z_i \cap Z_j = \emptyset$.

Thus there are only three cases for Z and Z': (1) $Z_i \cap Z_j = \emptyset$; (2) $Z' \subseteq Z$; (3) $Z \subseteq Z'$.

Let $\mathbf{Z} = \{Z_1, Z_2, \ldots\}$ be the set of zones corresponding to $\Phi = \Phi^1 \vee \Phi^2 \vee \ldots \vee \Phi^m$. We say a zone Z is a top zone, if no zone Z' satisfies $Z \subseteq Z'$. Let $\mathbf{Z}'$ be a set of top zones in $\mathbf{Z}$ such that $\bigcup_{Z' \in \mathbf{Z}'} Z' = \bigcup_{Z \in \mathbf{Z}} Z$.

Some states in the zones are not consistent global states. In predicate detection, these states are meaningless. Therefore, the zone where none of the states is consistent, is meaningless. In $\mathbf{Z}'$, such zones can be deleted. Now we redefine $\mathbf{Z} = \{Z | Z \in \mathbf{Z}' \text{ and } Z \cap L(E) \ne \emptyset\}$.

Definition 6. *A set $\mathbf{S}$ of states in $L(E)$ is definite if every run of the computation $\langle E, \rightarrow \rangle$ passes through a state S such that $S \in \mathbf{S}$ and $S \in L(E)$. If a set of states $\mathbf{S}$ is definite, we denote it by $Definitely(\mathbf{S})$.*

Because all the true states in $L(E)$ are in $\mathbf{Z}$, we have that $Definitely(\Phi)$ is true if and only if $Definitely(\bigcup_{Z \in \mathbf{Z}} Z)$ is true.

In the previous part of this paper, we define predicates on the interesting variables on processes. Now we will define predicates on the indices of events. If $e = E_i^{s_i}$, the index of e is s_i. At this time, we can treat the value of the interesting variable after executing an event e in a process P_i is the value of the index of e in P_i. For example, if $e = E_i^{s_i}$, then after executing e, the value of the interesting variable in P_i is s_i.

Now we rewrite the separation-inclusion DNF predicate Φ in a new form $\tilde{\Phi}$ based on indices. For every $Z_k[(a_1, b_1), (a_2, b_2), \ldots, (a_n, b_n)] \in \mathbf{Z}$, a corresponding conjunctive predicate $\tilde{\Phi}^k$ is defined as $\tilde{\Phi}^k = \bigwedge_{i=1}^n Z_k.a_i \le s_i \le Z_k.b_i$. Then $\tilde{\Phi} = \bigvee_{k=1}^q \tilde{\Phi}^k$, where q is the number of zones in $\mathbf{Z}$. Because a state S(not restricting to consistent global states) satisfies $\tilde{\Phi}$ if and only if $S \in \bigcup_{Z \in \mathbf{Z}} Z$, and $Definitely(\Phi)$ is true if and only if $Definitely(\bigcup_{Z \in \mathbf{Z}} Z)$ is true, we have the next lemma.

Lemma 3. *$Definitely(\Phi)$ is true if and only if $Definitely(\tilde{\Phi})$ is true.*

Because any interval with respect to some $\tilde{\Phi}^k$ must be an interval with respect to some Φ^j, it is easy to obtain the next lemma.

Lemma 4. *If Φ is a separation-inclusion DNF predicate, $\tilde{\Phi}$ is also a separation-inclusion DNF predicate.*

The next two lemmas show an interesting property of separation-inclusion DNF predicates.

Lemma 5. *Suppose that in $\mathbf{Z}$ there exists a zone $Z[(s_1, s_1), (s_2, s_2), \ldots, (s_n, s_n)]$ containing only one state $S = (s_1, s_2, \ldots, s_n)$, and S satisfies that there does not exist any true state $S' = (s'_1, s'_2, \ldots, s'_n)$ such that $S' \neq S$, and for all i, $1 \leq i \leq n$, $|s_i - s'_i| \leq 1$. If there exists a path from $\perp$ to S which does not pass through any other true state than S, and $S'' = (s''_1, s''_2, \ldots, s''_n)$ is a consistent global state such that for all i, $1 \leq i \leq n$, $s''_i = s_i$ or $s''_i = s_i - 1$, then there exists a path from $\perp$ to S'' which does not pass through any true state.*

Lemma 6. *Suppose that in $\mathbf{Z}$ there exists a zone $Z[(s_1, s_1), (s_2, s_2), \ldots, (s_n, s_n)]$ containing only one state $S = (s_1, s_2, \ldots, s_n)$, and S satisfies that there does not exist any true state $S' = (s'_1, s'_2, \ldots, s'_n)$ such that $S' \neq S$, and for all i, $1 \leq i \leq n$, $|s_i - s'_i| \leq 1$. If S is not an inevitable state and $Definitely(\mathbf{Z})$, then $Definitely(\mathbf{Z} - \{Z\})$ is true.*

Now we show that after interval compression, in $L(E')$ there actually exists such a zone that satisfies the conditions stated in lemma 5 and lemma 6.

Lemma 7. *In $\mathbf{Z}'$ there exists a zone $Z'[(s_1, s_1), (s_2, s_2), \ldots, (s_n, s_n)]$ containing only one state $S = (s_1, s_2, \ldots, s_n)$, and in $L(E')$ S satisfies that there does not exist any true state $S' = (s'_1, s'_2, \ldots, s'_n)$ such that $S' \neq S$, and for all i, $1 \leq i \leq n$, $|s_i - s'_i| \leq 1$.*

Theorem 5. *For a separation-inclusion DNF predicate $\Phi = \Phi^1 \vee \Phi^2 \vee \ldots \vee \Phi^m$, $Definitely(\Phi)$ is true if and only if there exist n intervals, $I_1, I_2, \ldots, I_n$, each belonging to a different process, such that all are intervals with respect to the same Φ^k, and $I_i.low \rightarrow I_j.high.next$, for all i, j, $1 \leq i \leq n$, $1 \leq j \leq n$.*

Proof. ($\Rightarrow$): Assume that $Definitely(\Phi)$ is true and there do not exist n intervals, $I_1, I_2, \ldots, I_n$, each belonging to a different process, such that all are intervals with respect to the same Φ^k, and $I_i.low \rightarrow I_j.high.next$, for all i, j, $1 \leq i \leq n$, $1 \leq j \leq n$. We can get $\mathbf{Z}$ from $L(E)$, and $\tilde{\Phi}$ from $\mathbf{Z}$. From lemma 3, we know that $Definitely(\tilde{\Phi})$ is true. From lemma 4, we know that $\tilde{\Phi}$ is also a separation-inclusion DNF predicate.

We derive the reduced computation $\langle E', \rightarrow' \rangle$ from the original computation $\langle E, \rightarrow \rangle$. We obtain $\mathbf{Z}'$ from $\mathbf{Z}$ and $\tilde{\Phi}'$ from $\tilde{\Phi}$. From theorem 2, we can prove that $Definitely(\tilde{\Phi})$ is true for the original computation $\langle E, \rightarrow \rangle$, if and only if $Definitely(\tilde{\Phi}')$ is true for the reduced computation $\langle E', \rightarrow' \rangle$. Then $Definitely(\tilde{\Phi}')$ is true for the reduced computation $\langle E', \rightarrow' \rangle$. Then $Definitely(\mathbf{Z}')$ is true in $L(E')$.

From lemma 7 we know that there exists a zone $Z'_u[(s_1, s_1), (s_2, s_2), \ldots, (s_n, s_n)]$ satisfying the conditions stated in lemma 5 and lemma 6 after interval compression. From the assumption and theorem 3 we can conclude that S is not an inevitable state.

Then from lemma 6, we have that $Definitely(\mathbf{Z}' - \{Z'_u\})$ is true. Then Z'_u can be deleted. Let Ψ be a formula obtained by deleting Φ^u from the formula of $\tilde{\Phi}'$. Let $\tilde{\mathbf{Z}} = \mathbf{Z}' - \{Z'_u\}$.

Let a new original computation $\langle E, \rightarrow \rangle$ be $\langle E', \rightarrow' \rangle$, a new $\tilde{\Phi}$ be Ψ, a new $\mathbf{Z}$ be $\tilde{\mathbf{Z}}$.

Continue the above process until $\mathbf{Z} = \emptyset$. We know that $Definitely(\tilde{\Phi})$ is true, which implies that $Definitely(\mathbf{Z})$ is true. Then $Definitely(\emptyset)$ is true. It leads to a contradiction.

($\Leftarrow$): From theorem 1, we have that $Definitely(\Phi^k)$ is true. Then $Definitely(\Phi)$ is true.   □

Now we give the complexity results on separation-inclusion DNF predicates.

According to theorem 5, we know that $Definitely(\Phi)$ is true if and only if there exists a Φ^k such that $Definitely(\Phi^k)$ is true. As shown in [7] the time complexity of detection of $Definitely(\Phi^k)$ is $O(n^2 p)$, where $p = \max\{|E_i|\}$, we have that the time complexity of using theorem 5 to detection separation-inclusion DNF predicates in $Definitely$ modality is at most $O(mn^2 p)$.

6   Conclusion

In this paper we extend the notion of conjunctive predicates to the one of DNF predicates. In general, detecting DNF predicates in $Definitely$ is coNP-complete. In this paper, we find two classes of DNF predicates named separation DNF predicates and separation-inclusion DNF predicates, which can be detected in $Definitely$ modality in a similar method of Garg and Waldecker's method for detecting conjunctive predicates in $Definitely$ modality. We prove the results based on the concept of inevitable states.

References

1. Alagar, S., Venkatesan, S.: Techniques to Tackle State Explosion in Global Predicate Detection. Proceedings of the IEEE Transactions on Software Engineering 27(8), 704–714 (2001)
2. Chakraborty, A., Garg, V.K.: On Reducing the Global State Graph for Verification of Distributed Computations. In: MTV 2006. Proceedings of 7th International Workshop on Microprocessor Test and Verification Common Challenges and Solutions (2006)
3. Chase, C., Garg, V.K.: Efficient Detection of Restricted Classes of Global Predicates. In: Helary, J.-M., Raynal, M. (eds.) WDAG 1995. LNCS, vol. 972, pp. 303–317. Springer, Heidelberg (1995)
4. Cooper, R., Marzullo, K.: Consistent Detection of Global Predicates. In: Proceedings of ACM/ONR workshop on Parallel and Distributed Debugging, pp. 163–173 (1991)

5. Fromentin, E., Raynal, M.: Inevitable global states: A concept to detect unstable properties of distributed computations in an observer independent way. In: Proceedings of Sixth IEEE Symposium on Parallel and Distributed Processing, pp. 242–248 (1994)
6. Garg, V.K., Mittal, N.: On Slicing a Distributed Computation. In: Proceedings of IEEE International Conference on Distributed Computing Systems, pp. 322–329 (2001)
7. Garg, V.K., Waldecker, B.: Detection of Strong Unstable Predicates in Distributed Programs. IEEE Transactions on Parallel and Distributed Systems 7(12), 1323–1333 (1996)
8. Garg, V.K., Waldecker, B.: Detection of Weak Unstable Predicates in Distributed Programs. IEEE Transactions on Parallel and Distributed Systems 5(3), 299–307 (1994)
9. Hurfin, M., Mizuno, M., Raynal, M., Singhal, M.: Efficient detection of conjunctions of local predicates. IEEE Transactions on Software Engineering 24(8), 664–677 (1998)
10. Lamport, L.: Time, Clocks and the Ordering of Events in a Distributed System. Communications of the ACM 21(7), 558–564 (1978)
11. Marzullo, K., Neiger, G.: Detection of Global Stable Predicates. In: Proceedings of the Fifth Workshop on Distributed Algorithms and Graphs, pp. 254–272 (1991)
12. Mattern, F.: Virtual Time and Global States of Distributed Systems. In: Proceedings of the International Workshop on Parallel and Distributed Algorithms, pp. 120–131 (1989)
13. Tarafdar, A., Garg, V.K.: Predicate Control for Active Debugging of Distributed Programs. In: SPDP. Proceedings of IEEE 9th Symposium on Parallel and Distributed Processing, pp. 763–769 (1998)
14. Venkatesan, S., Dathan, B.: Test and Debugging Distributed Programs Using Global Predicates. IEEE Transactions on Software Engineering 21(2), 163–177 (1995)

Solving Classic Problems in Distributed Systems: The Smart-Message Paradigm

Sandip Dey

Project Lead, IBM Business Unit
Persistent Systems Ltd., Pune - 411016, India
sandip_dey@persistent.co.in

Abstract. In this paper, I have presented a paradigm based on Smart-Messages. A Smart-Message is a message that carries intelligence in the form of a program element. The paper discusses the anatomy of a Smart-Message along-with its application in solving two of the important problems in distributed systems: Leader election problem and Mutual exclusion problem.

1 Introduction

Distributed computing systems are subjects of great academic and research interests. Messages in a distributed algorithm simply carry data or state information of a node or information computed from the local states of n different computing nodes. These messages can trigger a computation at a node, but they themselves can not be executed. A Smart-Message is an executable message that contains a program element and one or more data elements. A Smart-Message typically contains a program section that help the message to route itself to a designated node. A Smart-Message keeps on forwarding itself along a path (or a cycle) in a connected graph that contains all nodes of the graph. A Smart-Message while executed at a node can collect node information that is *public*, update node information that is *public*, aggregate local state data elements from multiple nodes, perform an algorithm that is encoded in the message (and triggered on certain inputs) and route itself to the next desired node based on a routing procedure.

2 System Model and Assumptions

A set of nodes (or processes) are connected over a graph and nodes communicate only by means of message passing. A node has sufficient computing power to carry a local computation.

Nodes do not fail and links between nodes do not crash. Messages may get delayed finitely but they do not get lost. Message send primitives are non-blocking in nature. Message receive buffer at a node never overflows.

S. Rao et al. (Eds.): ICDCN 2008, LNCS 4904, pp. 170–175, 2008.

3 Anatomy of a Smart-Message

A Smart-Message is different from a normal data message in the sense that it carries a program element that is executable at a site that has sufficient computational power to carry an execution. A Smart-Message typically consists of a program element and n number of data elements stored in a local data structure as required by the program element.

3.1 Program Element

A program element of a Smart-Message typically consists of the following three program sections.

- *Interaction with Local State of a Node:* In this program section a Smart-Message can read values of node state variables and update node state variables. A node may decide to enforce an access control policy by exposing only a subset of its state variables as *public*. A public state variable can be read by a message or any other node in the network graph. If a node decides not to expose a node variable as public, it may define it as *private*. Private variables can only be accessed in a computation that is local to a node i.e., private variables can not be accessed in a distributed computation that requires exchange of state information between nodes. A public state variable at a node may depend on a private node variable that is generated using a local computation specific to a node. A Smart-Message reads publicly accessible variables at a node and copies values of these variables to a local data structure internal to the message.

- *A Smart Algorithm:* This program section is the heart of a Smart-Message. This is typically an algorithm that takes the local data structure of the message as input and performs a computation that often produces new data elements. These data elements generated from the execution of a Smart Algorithm can be written to local node state. In essence, the execution of a Smart Algorithm often happens at a node when the Smart-Message has a fairly complete global view of all local node states collected in its local data structure and the Smart-Message is in a position to deduce a solution or to generate a set of new data elements that represent the solution of a distributed problem.

- *Routing Section:* The routing information, i.e. how a Smart-Message propagates itself to the next desirable node in the system is often encoded as a routing procedure in this program section. In many cases, the Smart-Message needs a global view of the local node states to arrive at a conclusion about a distributed problem. Consequently, a Smart-Message is required to visit all the nodes of a connected graph at least once. Typically, the Smart-Message travels along a network path (or cycle) that originates at a node and goes through all the nodes in the network. A particular node may appear in the Smart-Message path more than once depending upon the network topology. Finding such a network path (or cycle) for a connected network graph is outside the scope of the paper and standard graph-theoretic algorithms exist that can find such a path. The Routing section of a Smart-Message however should contain this path information. It is not required for a Smart-Message to travel along a cycle that goes through all nodes. Depending upon specific requirements of a distributed problem, routing procedure can be encoded appropriately for a Smart-Message.

3.2 Local Data Structure

A Smart-Message has a local data structure where it can store a number of data elements. *Public* state variables are often read by a Smart-Message (when executed) and copied as data elements into the local data structure of the Smart-Message. A Smart-Message thrives to collect relevant local state information from various nodes and constructs a global view of the system, before the execution of its Smart Algorithm. The execution of a Smart Algorithm may not produce the desired solution of a distributed problem, if the constructed global view is not reliable enough. So, for proper construction of its local data structure and a global view of the system, a Smart-Message may need to visit the relevant nodes (or all nodes) of the network graph more than once.

4 Execution of a Smart-Message

The Smart-Message paradigm extents the existing distributed framework of networked nodes communicating via explicit message passing. In Smart-Message paradigm, communication between nodes is still by means of message passing. It is just that messages now carry intelligence in the forms of executable program elements.

The successful usage of the Smart-Message framework relies on the execution of a Smart Algorithm, as mentioned in Section 3.1. The algorithm tries to find a solution of a given distributed problem by collecting sufficient local state information from various nodes in the network graph.

Usually, there is an initiator node in the network graph that starts solving a distributed problem (e.g., a leader election problem) by generating a Smart-Message. The design of a Smart-Message (specifically the Smart Algorithm) depends on the distributed problem that is being solved. The initiator node has a copy of the Smart-Message. For the sake of simplicity, we may assume that all nodes in the network know how the Smart-Message for the given distributed problem looks like. So any node, can initiate a computation by generating a Smart-Message, if required. Smart-Messages typically get forwarded from one node to the next node (along a cycle as described in Section 3.1) when they are executed. Whenever a node receives a Smart-Message, it executes it. As part of the execution of a Smart-Message, the program element in the Smart-Message gets executed.

The three program sections of the program element of a Smart-Message will be executed at a node. The first program section will collect local node state information (*public* node variables) and copy this information to its local data structure. Depending upon whether the local data structure is complete in terms of relevance or not (a complete local data structure of a Smart-Message represents a global state view of the system), the Smart Algorithm (second program section) can be triggered and this Smart Algorithm can compute new data elements which can then be copied back to local node state. The execution of the Smart Algorithm is often conditional and is driven by the constructed global state view of the system. The third program section contains a routing procedure which when executed simply forwards the Smart-Message to the next logical node (can be the next node in the network cycle as mentioned in Section 3.1).

The Smart Algorithm of a Smart-Message can generate other ordinary messages (that carry data elements only) that can be sent by the node that is executing the Smart-Message. Depending upon the routing procedure, a Smart-Message may be forwarded to only one node at a time (e.g., the Smart-Message moves in a cycle of all nodes). This routing mechanism is often more than adequate for a leader-election algorithm or a token-based mutual exclusion algorithm as described in Section 5.

5 Application of Smart-Message Paradigm

5.1 A Leader Election Algorithm

A solution using a Smart-Message for leader election in a circular configuration of nodes $(i_1, i_2... i_n)$ [1] is proposed in this section. The local node state is consisted of two *public* variables ($Node_{ID}$, *Current-Leader$_{ID}$*). The Smart-Message that is executed for this problem has the following anatomy:

Local Data Structure of the Smart-Message

- $Node_{ID}$ [ ]: This is a set that stores the node IDs of various nodes.
- *Leader-decided:* Boolean which is FALSE until a new leader has been chosen.
- *Leader$_{ID}$:* This variable holds the identity of the elected leader. Initially it may be undefined.
- *Message-Pass-Number:* The pass that the Smart-Message is making. Initially this is 0.

Program Element

Interaction with Local State of a Node

```
If Not Leader-decided

Then

        Read node ID iₖ and insert iₖ to Node_ID [];

Else

        Copy Leader_ID to local state of the node;
```

Smart Algorithm

```
If the Smart-Message is getting executed at the initia-
tor node

Then

        Increment Message-Pass-Number by 1;
```

```
If (Message-Pass-Number = 2) and Node_ID [] contains all
the node IDs of all nodes and Not Leader-decided
Then
            Choose the maximum element of set Node_ID [];
            Set Leader_ID = Maximum element chosen above;
            Set Leader-decided as TRUE;
```

Routing Section

```
If (Message-Pass-Number <= 2)
Then
            Forward the Smart-Message to the next logical
node in the network cycle going through all nodes;
```

Execution of the Smart-Message

The Smart-Message gets forwarded to all nodes in the network cycle starting from an initiator node and it gets executed at all nodes. An execution of a program element executes all three program sections one after the other. The message makes two passes along the network cycle. In the first pass it collects all the node identities and in the second pass it distributes the identity of the newly elected leader to all nodes in the cycle. The Smart-Algorithm contains the logic for finding the maximum identifier from a set of node identifiers and it typically gets executed at the node that had initiated an election round.

5.2   A Mutual Exclusion Algorithm

Mutual exclusion among a set of communicating processes is a well-known problem in distributed systems [2]. This section illustrates a simplistic variation of token-based mutual exclusion using a Smart-Message.

Local Data Structure of the Smart-Message

- *Token:* This variable indicates a token.

Program Element

Interaction with Local State of a Node

```
Copy Token from Smart-Message to a local node variable;
Set Has-token in node local state to TRUE;
```

Smart Algorithm

```
If (Has-token of a node is TRUE)
Then
            Enter Critical Section (CS) of process;
```

Routing Section

```
Once CS execution is over, forward the Smart-Message to
the next node in a logical ring of all nodes;
```

Execution of the Smart-Message

Whenever a node receives the Token (included in the Smart-Message) it sets a local variable *Has-token* to TRUE and enters a Critical Section (CS). Once the execution of CS at a node is over, the node forwards the Smart-Message (along-with the Token) to the next node in the logical ring. This ensures only one of the nodes has the Token at a time and can enter a CS.

6 Conclusions and Future Works

In this idea paper, a Smart-Message paradigm has been proposed. As illustrated in Section 5, only one node in the network executes the Smart-Message at a time. Also there are no unnecessary exchanges of data messages between nodes. The Smart-Message paradigm thus promises significant potential over the traditional approach of arriving at a consolidated global view by means of considerable number of data message exchanges between participating nodes. Also, instead of the (same) program residing in every node, the program now resides in the message.

Future work includes applying the Smart-Message methodology in developing distributed algorithms that can tolerate node crash, link crash and timing failures. Smart-Message paradigm can be extended to support routing in dynamic networks. A number of possibilities will arise when we decide to allow a Smart-Algorithm to be modified along a network path. A Smart-Message can be made more sophisticated by introducing additional program sections that deal with various specific aspects of a particular distributed problem. One can define appropriate formats for a Smart-Message to make it transmission-efficient. Smart-Messages themselves should be made fault-tolerant and this is important because Smart-Messages carry intelligence.

References

[1] Chang, E., Roberts, R.: An improved Algorithm for Decentralized Extrema Finding in Circular Configuration of Processes. Communications of the ACM 22(5), 281–283 (1979)
[2] Ricart, G., Agrawala, A.K.: An optimal algorithm for mutual exclusion in computer networks. Communications of the ACM 24(1) (1981)

Design of Concurrent Utilities in Jackal: A Software DSM Implementation

Pradeep Kumar Nalla[1], Rajeev Wankar[2], and Arun Agarwal[2]

[1] Cavium Networks (India) Pvt Ltd, 203 Ashoka MyHome Chambers,
SP Road, Secunderabad 500 003, India
[2] Department of Computer and Information Sciences,
University of Hyderabad, Hyderabad, 500 046, India
pnalla@caviumnetworks.com, {wankarcs, aruncs}@uohyd.ernet.in

Abstract. A Distributed Shared Memory (DSM) system logically implements the shared-memory model on a physically distributed-memory system. Jackal is an open source [2] fine grained distributed shared memory implementation of the Java programming language. Java inherently supports parallel programming with the use of multi-threading. Jackal exploits this property and allows users to run multi-threaded programs unmodified on a distributed memory environment such as a cluster. Since the built-in language support for threads is insufficient for many programming tasks, Java-1.5 introduces concurrent utilities [4]. Concurrent utilities of Java are classes that are designed as building blocks in making concurrent classes or applications. These utilities provide reduce programming effort, increase performance, increase reliability, improve maintainability and increase productivity. In this work we implement a subset of these utilities in Jackal.

Keywords: DSM, concurrent utilities, Jackal, ReentrantLock, Atomic variable and ThreadPoolExecutor.

1 Introduction

A Distributed Shared Memory system is implemented either in hardware or in software. There are three ways to build a DSM system in software: Runtime-system centric, Programming-language centric and Compiler-technology centric. Jackal (Section 3) is a Compiler-technology centric DSM that involves shipping data to the machine requesting memory. As an optimization, it uses function shipping whenever possible.

Jackal is a fine-grained DSM implementation of Java programming language. Java inherently supports parallel programming with the use of multi-threading. In practice it became apparent that writing high-performance multithreaded applications using only Java's limited built-in functionality was difficult. Since Jackal doesn't have support for concurrent utilities, our work focuses to provide these packages efficiently in Jackal. Concurrent utilities are made for building efficient concurrent applications. Main constituents of concurrent utilities are Locks, Thread Pool Executor, and Atomic Variables.

S. Rao et al. (Eds.): ICDCN 2008, LNCS 4904, pp. 176–181, 2008.
© Springer-Verlag Berlin Heidelberg 2008

2 Java Memory Model

Original Java Memory Model (JMM) contained certain unintended side effects and drawbacks. These drawbacks of JMM are addressed in Java Specification Request 133 (JSR-133) [5]. JSR-133 does not retain the concept of a single main memory but instead uses a more distributed approach that allows the use of hierarchical caches. This allows some threads to observe updates to main memory made by other threads earlier than others. Jackal implements JSR-133 and it does not comply with the original Java Memory. Jackal only violates the JMM when the programs are not properly synchronized.

3 Brief Introduction to Jackal

Jackal consists of a compiler and runtime system that together provide an object-based DSM. It uses a native compiler rather than a JIT compiler or byte-code interpreter. Jackal uses compiler to add access checks to a program and implements aggressive optimizations [3] to reduce the number of messages sent over the network. If the object about to be accessed is not present or not in the correct read or write mode, the access check calls the runtime system to cache it.

Jackal communicates by using Upcalls, these are remote procedure calls and are similar to active messages. Since in active messages there is only one buffer, only one of the threads or processes can send RPC at a time. In Jackal this buffer is protected by the lock namely 'MANTA_RTS_LOCK', so before performing any RPC one needs to obtain this lock.

4 Design and Implementation of Concurrent Utilities

This section presents algorithms and the design optimizations used in implementing a subset of Concurrent Utilities. Following are the descriptions of the key words used

Allocation-home is the node where the object is first allocated.
Logical-home is the node maintaining the master copy of the object.

4.1 Implementation of ReentrantLock

Ticketing lock mechanism is used in implementing ReentrantLock. Logical-home of the lock object is used to gain or release the lock. A synchronization queue for each lock is maintained at the lock object's Allocation-home. The thread that needs a lock sends request to the lock object's Logical-home for a ticket and waits on synchronization queue for its turn. Whenever a thread's turn comes it is removed from the queue and resumed. Since the synchronization queue can be large, it is not moved across the network to avoid the network bandwidth consumption.

Since locking and unlocking makes synchronization points, the thread that encounters these points must flush the cached objects to their respective Logical-home nodes and should make local copies invalid. By the time the lock request arrives at Logical-home the protocol action might have taken and Logical-home might have migrated. To avoid this we use the runtime system lock 'MANTA_RTS_LOCK', that is also required by the runtime system to perform protocol specific action, before sending lock request.

Atomic library developed by HP [6] is used for atomically updating a variable. The functions in this library allow us to atomically swap the contents of a variable, and atomically add a value to a variable.

Ex: to swap AO_compare_and_swap_full(reference to a variable, current, update).

4.1.1 Description of Methods in the ReentrantLock Class

lock(): This method is used to acquire the ReentrantLock.

- Since lock method is a synchronization point, according to JMM thread's local memory is flushed. We perform upcall to lock object's allocation home to see whether the requesting thread is already the owner of the lock. If yes, the *state* (indicates how many times the lock has been taken) of the lock object at Logical-home will be incremented and the thread is allowed to continue through the critical section. *Otherwise* following step is executed.
- At the Logical-home of the lock object a ticket (counter) will be generated for the thread. Using the current turn of the object it is checked whether the lock can be taken. If the ticket of the thread is equal to the current turn then the state is incremented and the thread is allowed to continue through the critical section. *Otherwise* the following step is executed.
- If the lock is in use then an upcall will be generated to the Allocation-home of the lock object, where this request is queued, and the thread will be blocked. A queue entry includes information such as thread pointer, lock object pointer, thread's ticket and how many times it wants to acquire the lock (used in condition variables).

unlock(): This method is used to release the ReentrantLock.

- Since this is also a synchronization point, first we need to flush the thread's cached data before performing any Upcall (according to JMM).
- Perform an Upcall to lock object's allocation home then we see whether the current thread is the owner of the lock or not.
- If yes, we perform an Upcall to the logical home and decrement the state of the object, *otherwise* the method exits.
- If the state is decremented to zero then object's current_turn is incremented and an Upcall is performed to Allocation-home to dequeue the request, which has a ticket equal to the current_turn, from the synchronization queue.
- A signal is generated to the thread corresponding to the dequeued request and this thread will continue through the critical section.

await(): Check whether the thread is the owner of the lock. If yes the lock's *state* is saved along with pointer to thread and the node id on which this thread is being executed on the corresponding condition queue (maintained at condition objects home node). Lock is released using the unlock() method.

notify(): Signals the longest waiting thread on a condition. This method will dequeue the first node from the condition queue and enqueues it to the corresponding lock objects synchronization queue.

*notifyAll():*Same as *notify()* except it signals all threads waiting on a condition.

All above modules are implemented in C language using Java Native Interface (JNI).

4.1.2 Optimization

- Since the Synchronization queue is maintained at the Allocation-home of the object, all enqueue and dequeue requests are forwarded to this node making it a bottleneck. We maintain the queue at every node in the cluster. We use only the Logical-home to acquire or release the lock. Even if Logical-home migrates, a synchronization queue will be available locally thus avoiding the bottleneck.

- Also we tried better optimization by registering the number of acquires from different nodes. This optimization depends on the assumption that the node that mostly acquired the lock may also acquire it mostly in future.

4.2 Implementation of Atomic Variable

Atomic variable is maintained at a single node in the cluster. All updates to the variable are forward to that node where these updates are done atomically. Node assignment to the atomic variables is done in a round robin fashion.

4.2.1 Methods in Atomic Class

Following are few methods which performs an RPC to the atomic integer home

int get(), int getAndSet(newvalue), boolean compareAndSet(int expect, int update), int getAndIncrement(), int decrementAndGet(), int getAndDecrement(), int getAndAdd(int delta), int incrementAndGet(), int addAndGet(int delta)

4.3 Implementation of NonBlocking Queue

Operations on this queue are atomic and non-blocking. Even though it is not part of Concurrent Utilities, we make use of NonBlocking Queue in ThreadPoolExecutor. Since there are no synchronization points in Non Blocking queue implementation, we need to explicitly broadcast the *diffs* whenever the queue is modified.

4.4 Implementation of ThreadPoolExecutor

ThreadPoolExecutor is implemented using Random work stealing [1]. A pool of threads is created on each node and each thread will have two phases: execution phase and steal phase. Local thread pool size depends on the number of processors available in the node. We use a Non Blocking queue of works at each node in a cluster to increase the cache locality. With the use of a work queue at each node, there is high probability that most of the computation is local.

Thread Pool size has two user-imposed limits: *core pool size* and *maximum pool size*. The following steps show what happens when a job is submitted:

- If the thread pool is shutdown no new job can be submitted.
- If the pool size (number of threads) is less than core pool size a new thread will be created and the submitted job is assigned to it.
- If the pool size is greater than the core pool size, the job is submitted to the work pool for later execution.
- If the submission to the work pool fails because of the limits imposed on the work queue, and if the pool size is less than the maximum pool size, a new thread is created and the submitted job is assigned to it.
- In rest of the cases the job is rejected.

4.4.1 Methods in ThreadPoolExecutor Class

ThreadPoolExecutor(): is a constructor which takes core pool size and maximum pool size and *keep-alive-time* as some of its parameters. It is the time until which the thread waits for the job to be available, if failure, terminates. *execute():* submit the job to the Thread Pool. Other methods are *shutdown(), getTask() and workerDone().*

4.5 Experimental Results

We ran following standard Benchmark programs using the developed lock package with optimized and unoptimized versions of lock utility:

- Watermaster: Simulation of water molecule for splash benchmark.
- Cholesky factorization:
- Asp: All-pair shortest Path problem.

Table 1. Experimental results of Watermaster and Cholesky

Application	Parameter	On 2 CPUs (seconds)	On 4 CPUs (seconds)
WaterMaster	1728 mols	24.262	21.549
Cholesky	2080 cells	16.826	22.492

Table 2. Optimized and unoptimized versions of lock utility using Watermolecule simulation

No. of Iterations	Un-optimized (seconds)		Optimized (seconds)	
25	284.107	271.038	234.884	211.436
50	560.746	541.898	526.203	509.167
100	1124.508	1083.562	920.128	881.303

5 Conclusion and Future Work

We implemented ReentrantLock, Atomic variable and ThreadPoolExecutor in Jackal. The results obtained prove that these utilities are efficient. There are numerous directions to extend the work. Work is in progress to optimize ThreadPoolExecutor, using hierarchical work queues instead of Random work stealing.

References

1. Blumofe, R.D., Leiserson, C.E.: Scheduling Multithreaded Computations by Work Stealing. In: Proceedings of the 35th Annual Symposium on Foundations of Computer Science, Santa Fe and New Mexico, pp. 356–368 (November 1994)
2. Veldema, Ronald, Hofman, et al.: Source-Level Global Optimizations for Fine- Grain Distributed Shared Memory Systems. In: ACM SIGPLAN Symposium on Principles and Practice of Parallel Programming, PPoPP, Snowbird, Utah/USA, pp. 83–92. (June 18-20, 2001)
3. Veldema, R., Hofman, R.F.H., Bhoedjang, R.A.F., Bal, H.E.: Runtime Optimizations for a Java DSM Implementation. ACM Concurrency: Practice and Experience 15, 299–316 (2003)
4. Java-1.5 concurrent utilities homepage, http://java.sun.com/j2se/1.5.0/docs/api/java/util/concurrent/packagesummary.html
5. Java Specification Request 133, http://today.java.net/pub/n/JSR133PR
6. Atomic library by hp, http://www.hpl.hp.com/research/linux/atomic_ops

Anonymous Daemon Conversion in Self-stabilizing Algorithms by Randomization in Constant Space

W. Goddard, S.T. Hedetniemi, D.P. Jacobs, and Pradip K. Srimani

School of Computing, Clemson University, Clemson, SC 29634-0974

Abstract. We propose a generalized scheme that can convert any algorithm that self-stabilizes under an unfair central daemon into a randomized one that self-stabilizes under a distributed daemon, using only constant extra space and without IDs. If the original algorithm is anonymous the resulting self-stabilizing algorithm is also anonymous. We provide a detailed complexity analysis that show that the expected slowdown is upper bounded by $O(n^3)$.

1 Introduction

A self-stabilizing algorithm is a distributed algorithm designed to converge to a desired global system state without any external coordination or global system initialization. Each node participates in the distributed algorithm based on local knowledge: its own state and the states of its immediate neighbors. The goal is to achieve some global objective – a predicate defined on the states of all the nodes in the network – based on local actions where individual nodes have no global knowledge about the network. Self-stabilizing algorithms are robust (fault tolerant) in the *optimistic* sense that the distributed system may temporarily behave inconsistently but a return to correct system behavior is guranteed in finite time while traditional robust distributed algorithms follow a *pessimistic* approach in that it protects against the worst possible scenario which demands an assumption of the upper bound on the number of faults.

A self-stabilizing algorithm is usually written as a collection of production *rules* at each node: each rule specifies a condition and an action. The **condition** is a boolean predicate on the state of the node and the states of its neighbors; the action or **move** is a change in the state of the node executing the action. A node is **privileged** at a particular time if the condition of one or more of its rules is satisfied. Note that a node might stop being privileged if a neighbor moves. We work in the **shared-variable** model in which a node can directly read its neighbors' variables. We restrict attention to undirected, bidirectional links. All computation by a node is completed in one atomic step.

In order to analyze the correctness and time complexity of a self-stabilizing algorithm, a daemon or an execution model(run time environment) is assumed:

S. Rao et al. (Eds.): ICDCN 2008, LNCS 4904, pp. 182–190, 2008.

the daemon plays the role of both scheduler and adversary. In the literature, there are several daemons, and several possible attributes of those daemons. The **central daemon** (or serial daemon) chooses or **taps** exactly one privileged node to move at each step. In contrast, the **distributed daemon** taps a nonempty subset of the privileged nodes to move at each step. These daemons are considered adversarial. A daemon can be fair or unfair. For a (weakly) **fair daemon**, every node that is continuously privileged is tapped eventually; for an **unfair** daemon, there is no such restriction.

In general, algorithms and protocols are designed (and analyzed) assuming a specific daemon; and, an algorithm designed for one daemon may not work with another daemon in a straightforward way. In order to simplify algorithm development, it would be useful to have mechanisms or procedures to convert an algorithm, designed for one daemon to work with other daemons. These procedures are sometimes called transforms [6]. The concept of daemon can be thought of as two parts: The central daemon promises exclusivity (local mutual exclusion), while the fair daemon promises each processor gets its turn (fairness or clock synchronization). Most of the work on local mutual exclusion, fairness or daemon conversion assumes IDs. This includes the ULME algorithm of [2], the alternator of [4], the conversions of [11] based on the dining philosophers problem, the fairness enhancements of [9], the timestamp-based transforms of [10], and algorithms in the book [3]. Awerbuch et al. [1] provided algorithms for clock synchronization for both anonymous and ID-based networks.

Randomization can be used to ensure local mutual exclusion, and hence to convert a central-daemon algorithm to a distributed-daemon one. One approach is to use randomness to obtain "approximate" IDs (such as a **neighborhood-unique numbering** [5]) for the nodes. However, this requires a stabilization period to establish the node IDs and non-constant additional space. Shukla et al. [12] provided a method using randomness that can be used to convert some specific central-daemon algorithms to run under a distributed daemon.

In this paper, we propose a general algorithm, that converts any arbitrary algorithm (stabilizing under an unfair central daemon) randomization We show that, by using randomness but not to one that self-stabilizes under a distributed daemon. The proposed algorithm has three distinct advantages: (1) it is applicable to *all* self-stabilizing algorithms in central daemon; (2) it does not assume that the nodes in the network have unique **IDs**—it works for **anonymous** algorithms (using node identifiers for reference purpose only). The resulting algorithm is scalable (especially suitable for dynamic networks; deaprture and arrival of new nodes are most efficient); and (3) the conversion is achieved with a single additional bit at each node (so that if the original algorithm ran in constant space the transformed one does too). The trade-off is a slow-down. We measure the running time of the algorithms in terms of the maximum number of **steps** needed for the algorithm to converge to a stable legitimate state in the worst case. We provide the correctness and convergence analysis of the proposed algorithm and an upperbound of the resulting slowdown.

2   The Conversion Algorithm

Let S be a given arbitrary self-stabilizing algorithm that works for an unfair, central daemon. We want to design a general conversion algorithm that transforms S to a new self-stabilizing algorithm S', that works for a distributed daemon.

The algorithm/transform is presented as the code for a node i. For the new algorithm S', we add to each node i a boolean flag $b(i)$ in addition to the S-variables (the variables that are used by the algorithm S at each node i). The design approach is to make this flag $b(i)$ true if the node i is privileged for the underlying algorithm S <u>and</u> is the only node in its neighborhood that has its b-flag set; when two (or more) adjacent nodes are simultaneously S-privileged and have their flags set, the nodes randomly determine a new value of their flag bits. A node i can execute the underlying algorithm S only if it is indeed privileged for S and is the only node in its neighborhood that has its b-flag set. We define the boolean predicate $p_S(i)$ (in terms of S-variables at node i) as true iff node i is privileged for algorithm S in a given system state. The notation $N(i)$ denotes the set of neighbors of node i. The new algorithm S' is shown as Algorithm 1 [we use Algorithm 1 and Algorithm S' interchangeably].

Algorithm 1. *Using randomness for exclusivity*

Variables: binary $b(i)$ (and variables needed for S)
BitClear: if $b(i) = 1$ and not $p_S(i)$
    then set $b(i) = 0$
BitSet: if $p_S(i)$ and $b(i) = 0$ and $\forall j \in N(i) : b(j) = 0$
    then set $b(i) = 1$
BitToss: if $p_S(i)$ and $b(i) = 1$ and $\exists j \in N(i)$ with $b(j) = 1$
    then set $b(i) = $ RANDOM (toss a fair coin to determine the new value of $b(i)$)
Step: if $p_S(i)$ and $b(i) = 1$ and $\forall j \in N(i) : b(j) = 0$
    then execute one step of S at i

Note: In Rule BitToss, setting $b(i)$ to RANDOM means tossing a fair-coin to determine the new value of $b(i)$ (either 0 or 1).

2.1   Correctness Analysis

Lemma 1. *Under a distributed daemon, Algorithm 1 (Algorithm S')*

- *achieves local exclusivity for S, i.e., no two adjacent nodes execute the underlying algorithm S (executing Rule Step) concurrently;*
- *cannot terminate while there is an S-privileged node (i.e., Algorithm 1 terminates only when Algorithm S terminates).*

Proof.   – For node i to be able to execute Rule Step, at the point it is tapped it must have its b-bit set, and none of its neighbors can have their b-bit set. Thus, if node i is privileged for Rule Step of Algorithm 1 in a given system state, no neighbor j of node i can also be privileged for Rule Step. Thus two adjacent nodes cannot execute Rule Step simultaneously.

– Assume Algorithm 1 terminates. Then, if a node has its b-bit set, it must be privileged for one of Rules BitClear, BitToss and Step (since their hypotheses are exhaustive). So, when Algorithm 1 terminates, each node i has $b(i) = 0$. But then there cannot be a $\mathcal{S}$-privileged node, since any such node would be privileged for Rule BitSet. So, when algorithm $\mathcal{S}'$ terminates, there is no $\mathcal{S}$-privileged node.

2.2   Convergence Analysis

Thus it remains to show that, no matter what the distributed daemon does, there is progress on $\mathcal{S}$. That is, we need to show that the expected time between two consecutive steps of $\mathcal{S}$ is bounded. So, define:

> T is a maximal interval (sequence of steps executed by the distributed daemon) such that Rule Step is not executed.

The steps within T are denoted by an integer variable t, $t \geq 0$. If the daemon is perpetually lucky, T can be infinite; but we now argue that the expected length of T is bounded.

Definition 1. *The set of $\mathcal{S}$-privileged nodes during the interval T is denoted by P; by the definition of T, the set P does not change during T. The set of nodes that have their b-bit set at the start of step t is denoted by $B(t)$ and the set of those with their b-bit clear is denoted by $C(t)$ [$B(t) \cup C(t) = V$, V is the set of nodes in the graph].*

Definition 2. *We define a node i of P as* **stuck** *if $b(i) = 1$ and $b(j) = 0$ for each neighbor j of node i. We define a node i in $C(t) - P$ as* **dead** *[a dead node cannot make any move while it is dead].*

This terminology is motivated by the following lemma:

Lemma 2. *During the interval T:*

(a) a stuck or dead node cannot move;
(b) a node in $B(t) - P$ can move only to become dead.

Proof. (a) A stuck node is privileged only for Rule Step of Algorithm 1 and by definition the Rule Step is not executed during the interval T.

(b) Since P does not change during T, the only move a node in $B(t) - P$ can make is to clear its b-bit; this places it in $C(t+1) - P$, i.e., it becomes dead.

Note: A node in $C(t) \cap P$ ($= P - B(t)$) can execute only Rule BitSet; by doing so, the node either becomes a stuck node or it enters the set $\$ = P \cap B - stuck$. A node in $B(t) \cap P - stuck$ can execute only Rule BitToss: depending on the result of the coin, this puts it in $C(t+1)$ or $B(t+1)$ — the node either becomes stuck, or remains in the set $B(t+1) \cap P - stuck$ or enters the set $P - B(t+1)$. The possible movement of a node from set to set is depicted in Figure 1.

The intuition behind the subsequent analysis is that if the interval T is to continue for a long time, then the daemon must keep on tapping the non-stuck $\mathcal{S}$-privileged nodes, clearing and setting their bits, without creating stuck nodes. This we formalize using a potential function argument.

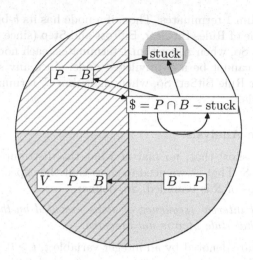

Fig. 1. Set changes without a Step

Intervals Without Stuck Or Dead Nodes Arising

Define a maximal subinterval $T^{\#}$ of T such that no new stuck or dead node is created.

Observation 3. *By Lemma 2, T is divided into at most n such intervals.*

We now bound the expected length of $T^{\#}$.

Definition 3. *(a) $H(t)$ is defined to be the subgraph induced by the nodes in the set $B(t)$, and $m(t)$ denotes the number of components of $H(t)$ that contain only nodes of P ($\mathcal{S}$-privileged).*
(b) $q(t)$ denotes the number of nodes in $B(t)$ that are $\mathcal{S}$-privileged, i.e., $q(t) = |B(t) \cap P|$.
(c) We define a potential function $\phi(t)$ as follows:

$$\phi(t) = q(t) - (n+1) \times m(t).$$

It is obvious that $-n^2 - n \leq \phi(t) \leq n$. We will now focus on the potential function. It is sufficient to bound how long before the potential function runs out, since that is a bound on the length of $T^{\#}$. If it were the case that $\phi(t)$ always decreased, then one would immediately have an $O(n^2)$ bound on the length of $T^{\#}$. Unfortunately, though $\phi(t)$ mostly decreases, the daemon can get lucky. But we will show that in order for the daemon to get the potential function to increase, the daemon must run the risk that $T^{\#}$ ends.

Definition 4. *Let $A(t)$ denote the subset of nodes tapped by the daemon at time t.*

Note that at time t, each node in $A(t)$ is privileged for $\mathcal{S}'$. We may assume that no node of $A(t)$ is in $B(t) - P$, since that node would become dead, thus terminating $T^{\#}$.

Observation 4. *We may assume that the subgraph induced by $A(t)$ is connected.*

Proof. Since the daemon is trying to make the interval $T^{\#}$ as long as possible, one may assume that if one step can be split into two independent steps that are equivalent, the daemon does so. So if the subgraph induced by $A(t)$ were not connected, the daemon would tap the different components in consecutive steps.

If all nodes in $A(t)$ execute Rule BitToss, then it is possible for there to be no change (all coins come up 1). However:

Observation 5. *We may assume that every step results in a change in the global state.*

Proof. Recall that the daemon is adversarial. It follows that if $A(t)$ was the correct choice for the daemon the first time, and nothing changed, it is the correct choice the next time. And if nothing changes then, it is the correct choice again. Since the probability of nothing changing is at most $\frac{1}{2}$ (actually it is smaller), the expected number of steps before there is a global change is 2. So, for a constant factor of 2 in the analysis, we may assume that every step results in a change in the global state.

Lemma 6. *If $A(t) \subseteq B(t)$ but not all of a component of $H(t)$, then the potential function ϕ decreases.*

Proof. Every node of $A(t)$ executes Rule BitToss. Since $A(t)$ is not all of a component of $H(t)$, $m(t)$ cannot decrease. On the other hand, $q(t)$ decreases unless every node has its coin come up 1; that possibility is taken care of by Observation 5. The result follows.

Lemma 7. *If $A(t) \not\subseteq B(t)$, then the potential function ϕ decreases.*

Proof. Then $A(t)$ contains a node i of $P - B(t)$. The node i has $b(i) = 0$ and such a node is privileged only if all its neighbors have a clear b-bit. Since the subgraph induced by $A(t)$ is connected, it follows that every node in $A(t)$ and all their neighbors have clear bits. Further, in the step, each node in $A(t)$ sets its b-bit, and thus $A(t)$ forms a new component of $H(t+1)$. It follows that $m(t)$ increases while $q(t)$ increases by at most n; thus ϕ decreases.

If the hypotheses of the above two lemmas do not hold, then $A(t)$ is all of a component of $H(t)$. In this case, all of $A(t)$ execute Rule BitToss. Note that $|A(t)| \geq 2$, since otherwise the single tapped node would be stuck.

Lemma 8. *Suppose $A(t)$ is all of a component of $H(t)$. Suppose $|A(t)| = y$ and that z nodes' coin tosses come up so that they remain with bit set. (We assume $z = y$ does not occur, by Observation 5.)*

(a) If $2 \leq z < y$, then ϕ decreases.
(b) If $z = 0$, then ϕ increases by less than n.
(c) If $z = 1$, then $T^{\#}$ ends.

Proof. Note that $q(t+1) = q(t) - (y - z)$.

(a) Assume $2 \leq z < y$. In this case, no component disappears, and indeed, the component $A(t)$ might split; it follows that $m(t)$ does not decrease while $q(t)$ does decrease. Thus ϕ decreases.

(b) Assume $z = 0$. In this case, $q(t)$ decreases by y, but the component $A(t)$ of $H(t)$ disappears, so that $m(t+1) = m(t) - 1$. It follows that ϕ increases by less than n.

(c) Assume $z = 1$. In this case, the node which remains with bit set becomes stuck, and $T^\#$ ends.

We call the three cases of Lemma 8 Events (a), (b) and (c).

Lemma 9. *The probability of Event (c) is at least twice the probability of Event (b).*

Proof. Since the coin tosses are independent, in any one step, the chance of Event (c) is $y2^{-y}$, while the chance of Event (b) is 2^{-y}. If we adjust for excluding the possibility of $z = y$, both probabilities are divided by $1 - 2^{-y}$, so their ratio remains y. The result follows since $y \geq 2$.

Finally, before we are able to bound the length of $T^\#$, we need to introduce a simple gambling game.

A Gambling Game

Consider a *gambling game* defined as follows. Let ψ_0 and x be positive integers, and α a number between 0 and 1. Consider a person Damon who starts a gambling game with ψ_0 chips. At each step Damon pays 1 chip and has two choices:

- He can choose to not gamble. In this case the step ends.
- He can choose to gamble. In this case he tosses a coin: if the coin comes up heads, he gains $x + 1$ chips; but if it comes up tails, the game ends. The coin comes up heads with probability α.

The game ends when either the coin comes up tails or Damon runs out of money. Damon's goal is to maximize the length of the game.

Lemma 10. *Under optimal strategy by Damon, the expected length of the gambling game is $\psi_0 + x\alpha/(1 - \alpha)$.*

Proof. Suppose that if Damon were to take the coin and toss it repeatedly, then it would come up heads L times before coming up tails. Then, no matter what Damon does, the game will last at most $\psi_0 + Lx$ steps. On the other hand, there is a simple strategy that guarantees the game lasts this long: Damon should wait until having only 1 chip left each time to gamble.

Since L is a geometric random variable, the expected value of L is $\alpha/(1 - \alpha)$. It follows that the expected length of the game is at most $\psi_0 + x\alpha/(1 - \alpha)$, and Damon can achieve this by gambling only when he has 1 chip left.

Lemma 11. *For Algorithm 1, consider a maximal interval $T^{\#}$ such that Rule Step is not executed and no node becomes dead or stuck. Then the expected length of $T^{\#}$ is at most $O(n^2)$ steps, no matter the daemon's choices.*

Proof. By Lemmas 6 and 7, the potential function ϕ always decreases unless $A(t)$ is a component of $H(t)$. Call such a choice of $A(t)$ a **component choice**. Say $y = |A(t)|$ and z nodes keep their bit set.

Now, suppose we give the daemon further powers; this can only make the daemon's job easier. We give the daemon the power to partially choose the future with a component choice. Specifically, the daemon can choose whether Event (a) occurs or not; that is, he can choose whether $z \geq 2$ or not. We define a **gamble** as the event that the daemon chooses that z is to be less than 2. (Note that if $y = 2$ then a component choice is automatically a gamble.)

It follows that the expected length of $T^{\#}$ is at most the expected length of the gambling game for Damon playing optimally, with the following parameters. The total number of coins is $\psi_0 = n^2 + 2n$, the difference between the upper and lower extremes of the potential function. The chance of success α is the conditional probability of Event (b) given that it is not Event (a), which is at most

$$\max_{y \geq 2} 2^{-y}/(2^{-y} + y2^{-y}) = \max_{y \geq 2} 1/(1+y) = 1/3.$$

And the increase if lucky is (at most) $x = n$.

So by Lemma 10, the expected length of $T^{\#}$ is at most $n^2 + O(n)$.

Theorem 1. *Any algorithm S that self-stabilizes under an unfair central daemon can be converted to a randomized one S' that self-stabilizes under an unfair distributed daemon, using constant extra space, without IDs, and with at most $O(n^3)$ expected slowdown.*

Proof. Since T is divided into at most n such intervals $T^{\#}$ (see Observation 3), it follows that the expected length of T is at most $O(n^3)$. This establishes the theorem.

We suspect that the above analysis can be improved to show that the slowdown is at most $O(n^2)$.

2.3 Conclusion

These results reaffirm that in the deterministic ID-based shared-variable model, all daemons are equally powerful. The same result holds in link-registers, since link-registers and shared-variable are equivalent in ID-based networks.

The interesting question is of comparing the power of daemons in deterministic anonymous networks. A distinguished node (root) and link-registers suffice to allow leader election and thus the assigning of IDs, and hence daemons are equally powerful. However, without a root, in both the link-register and uniform shared-variable case, the results of [8,7] and others on rings show that the distributed and central daemon have different powers.

Acknowledgement

This work has been supported by NSF grant # ANI-0218495.

References

1. Awerbuch, B., Kutten, S., Mansour, Y., Patt-Shamir, B., Varghese, G.: Time optimal self-stabilizing synchronization. In: STOC 1993. Proceedings of the 25th Annual ACM Symposium on Theory of Computing, pp. 652–661 (1993)
2. Beauquier, J., Datta, A.K., Gradinariu, M., Magniette, F.: Self-stabilizing local mutual exclusion and daemon refinement. In: Herlihy, M.P. (ed.) DISC 2000. LNCS, vol. 1914, pp. 223–237. Springer, Heidelberg (2000)
3. Dolev, S.: Self-Stabilization. MIT Press, Cambridge (2000)
4. Gouda, M.G., Haddix, F.: The alternator. In: Proceedings of the Fourth Workshop on Self-Stabilizing Systems (published in association with ICDCS 1999), pp. 48–53. IEEE Computer Society, Los Alamitos (1999)
5. Gradinariu, M., Johnen, C.: Self-stabilizing neighborhood unique naming under unfair scheduler. In: Sakellariou, R., Keane, J.A., Gurd, J.R., Freeman, L. (eds.) Euro-Par 2001. LNCS, vol. 2150, pp. 458–465. Springer, Heidelberg (2001)
6. Herman, T.: Models of self-stabilization and sensor networks. In: Das, S.R., Das, S.K. (eds.) IWDC 2003. LNCS, vol. 2918, pp. 205–214. Springer, Heidelberg (2003)
7. Hoepman, J.H.: Uniform deterministic self-stabilizing ring-orientation on odd-length rings. In: Tel, G., Vitányi, P.M.B. (eds.) WDAG 1994. LNCS, vol. 857, pp. 265–279. Springer, Heidelberg (1994)
8. Israeli, A., Jalfon, M.: Uniform self-stabilizing ring orientation. Information and Computation 104, 175–196 (1993)
9. Karaata, M.H.: Self-stabilizing strong fairness under weak fairness. IEEE Transactions on Parallel and Distributed Systems 12, 337–345 (2001)
10. Mizuno, M., Kakugawa, H.: A timestamp based transformation of self-stabilizing programs for distributed computing environments. In: Babaoğlu, Ö., Marzullo, K. (eds.) WDAG 1996. LNCS, vol. 1151, pp. 304–321. Springer, Heidelberg (1996)
11. Nesterenko, M., Arora, A.: Stabilization-preserving atomicity refinement. Journal of Parallel and Distributed Computing 62(5), 766–791 (2002)
12. Shukla, S., Rosenkrantz, D., Ravi, S.: Developing self-stabilizing coloring algorithms via systematic randomization. In: Proceedings of the International Workshop on Parallel Processing, pp. 668–673 (1994)

Snap-Stabilizing Waves in Anonymous Networks*

Christian Boulinier, Mathieu Levert, and Franck Petit

LaRIA/CNRS
Université de Picardie Jules Verne, France

Abstract. We propose the first snap-stabilizing wave algorithm for anonymous networks. In the worst case, a process decides in $O(n + D)$ time
units, where n and D are the number of process and the diameter of
the network, respectively. The proposed algorithm uses a self-stabilizing
underlying unison protocol. If the underlying unison is stabilized when
a process request a wave, then a decide event occurs in an optimal time,
i.e., $O(D)$ time units. The proposed solution is generic in the sense that,
it can be used for any static or dynamic scheme which is feasible in
an anonymous network. In particular, as an application of our scheme,
we provide a snap-stabilizing causal atomic broadcast for anonymous
networks, which can be used as a pipeline of messages.

1   Introduction

Wave algorithms (or, Total algorithms) [16] are widely used as the basis to solve
many network control problems. A wave algorithm is a distributed algorithm
where the participation of all processes in the network is required before a particular event, called a *decision*, is taken. Wave algorithms include well-know and
basis schemes of distributed systems such as Spanning Tree Construction (STC),
Token Circulation (TC), Propagation of Information with Feedback (PIF), etc.
Wave algorithms are also related to message broadcasting [13]. They are often
designed to be executed either only once or infinitely often. In the former case,
they leads the whole system toward a fixed point and are said to be *static*. They
mainly refer to STC algorithms. In the latter case (TC and PIF) are said to be
dynamic. Solutions to these basic problems can then be used as the basis for the
solution to a wide class of problems in distributed computing, mainly in order to
improve the coordination of the processes. So, designing efficient fault-tolerant
wave algorithms is an important task in the distributed computing research.

The concept of self-stabilization [9] is a general technique to design a system
to tolerate arbitrary *transient faults*. A self-stabilizing system, regardless of the
initial states of the processors and initial messages in the links, is guaranteed
to converge to the intended behavior in finite time. *Snap-stabilization* was first
introduced in [4]. A *snap-stabilizing protocol* guarantees that the system always

---

* This research is supported in part by Région Picardie (France), Project "APREDY".

maintains the desirable behavior. In other words, a snap-stabilizing algorithm is also a self-stabilizing algorithm that stabilizes in 0 steps. Obviously, any snap-stabilizing protocol is optimal in terms of the worst-case stabilization time.

Related Works. Many self-stabilizing wave algorithms for arbitrary networks have been proposed in the literature, *e.g.*, [1,7,10,14,15]. Snap-Stabilizing wave algorithms for arbitrary networks are given in [5,6]. All the above solutions assume the existence of a particular process called the *root*. Waves algorithms and their applications in anonymous networks are discussed in [16,17]. Among the numerous results in [16,17], the author shows that there exists no wave algorithm for anonymous arbitrary networks with no bound on the diameter. The solutions in [16,17] are not stabilizing. In [11], the author propose the first self-stabilizing wave algorithms for anonymous networks. The waves algorithms in [11] are based on *r*-operators which are general tools ensuring the global convergence of the system toward a fixed point. Such protocols for anonymous networks are also proposed in [12,8]. None of the above solution is snap-stabilizing.

Contributions. In this paper, we propose the first *snap-stabilizing wave algorithm for anonymous networks*. Our solution is based on the fundamental algebraic properties which were used in the design of the unison developed in [3]. In the worst case, a process decides in $O(n + D)$ time units, where n and D are the number of process and the diameter of the network, respectively. If the underlying unison is stabilized when a process request a wave, then a decide event occurs in optimal time, *i.e.*, $O(D)$ rounds[1].

The proposed solution is generic in the sense that, it can be used for any static or dynamic scheme which is feasible in an anonymous network. In particular, as an application of our scheme, we provide a *snap-stabilizing causal atomic broadcast for anonymous networks*. Our broadcast protocol can be used as a *pipeline* (or, *stream*) of messages, *i.e.*, several messages can be launched at each clock pulse, and thereby, minimize the *latency*, *i.e.*, the time required between the sending of two successive messages. It also keeps the order in which the messages are sent.

Paper Outline. The remainder of the paper is organized as follows. We formally describe notations, definitions, and the execution model in Section 2. In the same section, we also state what it means for a protocol to be snap-stabilizing. The problem considered in this paper followed by the solution and its correctness proof are given in Section 3. The snap-stabilizing causal atomic broadcast is the purpose of Section 4. Finally, we make some concluding remarks in Section 5.

2   Preliminaries

Distributed System. A *distributed system* is an undirected connected graph, $G = (V, E)$, where V is a set of nodes—$|V| = n$, $n \geq 2$—and E is the set

---

[1] We use the term of *round* in order to compute the time complexity — refer to [6,10] for its definition.

of edges. Nodes represent *processes*, and edges represent *bidirectional communication links*. A communication link (p, q) exists iff p and q are neighbors. D denote the diameter of the network. The distributed system is considered to be arbitrary and anonymous, *i.e.*, we consider no particular topology nor unique identifiers on processes. The set of neighbors of every process p is denoted as $\mathcal{N}_p$. The *degree* of p is the number of neighbors of p, *i.e.*, equal to $|\mathcal{N}_p|$. The distance between two processes p and q, denoted by $d(p, q)$, is the length of the shortest path between p and q.

The program of a process consists of a set of registers (also referred to as variables) and a finite set of guarded actions of the following form: $< label >::$ $< guard > \rightarrow < statement >$. Each process can only write to its own registers, and read its own registers and registers owned by the neighboring processes. The guard of an action in the program of p is a boolean expression involving the registers of p and its neighbors. The statement of an action of p updates one or more registers of p. An action can be executed only if its guard evaluates to true. The actions are atomically executed, meaning the evaluation of a guard and the execution of the corresponding statement of an action, if executed, are done in one atomic step.

The *state* of a process is defined by the values of its registers. The *configuration* of a system is the product of the states of all processes. Let a distributed protocol $\mathcal{P}$ be a collection of binary transition relations denoted by $\mapsto$, on Γ, the set of all possible configurations of the system. $\mathcal{P}$ describes an oriented graph $S = (\Gamma, \mapsto)$, called the *transition graph* of $\mathcal{P}$. A sequence $e = \gamma_0, \gamma_1, \ldots, \gamma_i, \gamma_{i+1}, \ldots$ is called an *execution* of $\mathcal{P}$ iff $\forall i \geq 0, \gamma_i \mapsto \gamma_{i+1} \in S$. A process p is said to be *enabled* in a configuration γ_i ($\gamma_i \in \Gamma$) if there exists an action A such that the guard of A is true in γ_i. We consider that any enabled processor p is *neutralized* in the computation step $\gamma_i \mapsto \gamma_{i+1}$ if p is enabled in γ_i and not enabled in γ_{i+1}, but does not execute any action between these two configurations. (The neutralization of a processor represents the following situation: At least one neighbor of p changes its state between γ_i and γ_{i+1}, and this change effectively made the guard of all actions of p false.) We assume an *unfair and asynchronous distributed daemon*. *Unfairness* means that even if a processor p is continuously enabled, then p may never be chosen by the daemon unless p is the only enabled processor. The *asynchronous distributed* daemon implies that during a computation step, if one or more processors are enabled, then the daemon chooses at least one (possibly more) of these enabled processors to execute an action.

Events, Causal DAG's and Cuts.

Definition 1 (Events). *Let $\gamma_0 \gamma_1 \ldots$ be a finite or infinite execution. For all $p \in V, (p, 0)$ is an event. Let $\gamma_t \mapsto \gamma_{t+1}$ be a transition. If the process p executes a guarded action during this transition, we say that p executes an action at time $t + 1$. The pair $(p, t + 1)$ is said to be an event (or a p-event). Events so that the guard does not depend on the shared registers of any neighbor are said to be internal.*

Definition 2 (Causal DAG). *The causal DAG associated is the smallest relation $\leadsto$ on the set of events such that the following two conditions hold: (1) Let (p, t) and (p, t') be two events such that $t > t_0$, t' is the greatest integer such that $t_0 \leq t' < t$. Then, $(p, t') \leadsto (p, t)$; (2) Let (p, t) and (q, t') be two events such that (p, t) is not an internal event, $q \in \mathcal{N}_p$, $t > t_0$, and t' is the greatest integer such that $t_0 \leq t' < t$. Then, $(q, t') \leadsto (p, t)$.*

Denote the *causal order* on the sequence $\gamma_0 \gamma_1 \ldots$ by $\preceq$. Relation $\preceq$ is the reflexive and transitive closure of the causal relation $\leadsto$. The *past cone* of an event (p, t) is the causal-*DAG* induced by every event (q, t') such that $(q, t') \preceq (p, t)$. A past cone involves a process q iff there is a q-event in the cone. We say that a past cone *covers* V, iff every process $q \in V$ is involved in the cone. The *cover* of an event (p, t), denoted by $Cover(p, t)$, is the set of processes q covered by the past cone of (p, t).

Definition 3 (Cut). *A cut C on a causal DAG is a map from V to $\mathbb{N}$, which associates a process p with a time t_p^C. We mix this map with its graph: $C = \{(p, t_p^C), p \in V\}$.*

The *past* of C, denoted by $]\leftarrow, C]$, is the set of events (p, t) such that $t \leq t_p^C$. Similarly, we define the *future* of C, denoted by $[C, \rightarrow[$, as the set of events (p, t) such that $t_p^C \leq t$. A cut is said to be *coherent* if $(q, t') \preceq (p, t)$ and $(p, t) \preceq (p, t_p^C)$, then $(q, t') \preceq (q, t_q^C)$. A cut C_1 is less than or equal to a cut C_2, denoted by $C_1 \preceq C_2$, if the past of C_1 is included in the past of C_2. If C_1 and C_2 are coherent cuts such that $C_1 \preceq C_2$, then $[C_1, C_2]$ is the *induced* causal DAG defined by the events (p, t) such that $(p, t_p^{C_1}) \preceq (p, t) \preceq (p, t_p^{C_2})$. A *sequence of events* is any segment $[C_1, C_2]$ where C_1 and C_2 are coherent cuts satisfying $C_1 \preceq C_2$. Any event of C_1 is called an *initial event*.

Snap-Stabilization. Let $\mathcal{X}$ be a set. $x \vdash P$ means that an element $x \in \mathcal{X}$ satisfies the predicate P defined on the set $\mathcal{X}$.

Definition 4 (Snap-stabilization). *The protocol $\mathcal{P}$ is snap-stabilizing for the specification $\mathcal{SP_P}$ on $\mathcal{E}$ if and only if the following condition holds: $\forall \gamma \in \mathcal{C}$: $\forall e \in \mathcal{E}_\gamma :: e \vdash \mathcal{SP_P}$.*

Remark 1. To prove that an algorithm is a snap-stabilizing wave algorithm, we need to show that: (1) Starting from any arbitrary configuration, if a process p needs to initiate a wave, then p initiates it in a finite time; (2) Starting from a configuration where a process p initiates a wave, then the protocol works according to its specification.

3   Snap-Stabilizing Waves in Anonymous Networks

3.1   Problem Definition

The problem is formally defined in [16,17]. It is specified for non-faulty environments, implying that *at least one process initiates* the algorithm. The following definition is similar as in [16,17], except that the initialization is formally stated.

Definition 5 (Wave). *A computation* $e = \gamma_0, \ldots, \gamma_i, \gamma_{i+1}, \ldots$ *is a wave iff the following condition holds:*

If a process p requests a decision in $\gamma_0 \mapsto \gamma_1$, then:

[DECISION] *there exists $t > 0$ and a process p' such that p' decides in the transition $\gamma_{t-1} \mapsto \gamma_t$, and*
[TERMINATION and DEPENDENCY] *for each process q, there is a finite number of transitions $\gamma_{i-1} \mapsto \gamma_i$ ($i \in [0,t]$) of e in which q executes an action of which the decision made by p' depends on.*

3.2   Algorithm

Algorithm SWT is formally described in Algorithm 3.1. According to the result in [16,17], each process knows D, an upper bound of the actual diameter. Let us consider the overall system architecture of our solution. The system is made of three layers: The lower layer is the unison in [3], the middle layer is the Wave Toolbox (Algorithm SWT, described in this paper), and the upper layer is an application. Note that it is not required for the application layer to have the knowledge of the underlying unison. The toolbox being snap-stabilizing, it must guarantee that each requested wave computation eventually receives the correct result.

The description of Algorithm 3.1 requires that we first borrow some definitions and basic properties from [3]. Let $\mathbb{Z}$ be the set of integers and K be a strictly positive integer. Two integers a and b are said to be *congruent modulo K*, denoted by $a = b[K]$ if and only if $\exists \lambda \in \mathbb{Z}$, $b = a + \lambda K$. Denote $\bar{a}$ the unique element in $[0, K-1]$ such that $a = \bar{a}[K]$. Define $\min(\overline{a-b}, \overline{b-a})$ as the *distance* on the torus $[0, K-1]$ denoted by $d_K(a, b)$. Two integers a and b are said to be *locally comparable* if and only if $d_K(a, b) \leq 1$. We then define the *local order relationship* $\leq_l$ as follows: $a \leq_l b \overset{\text{def}}{\Leftrightarrow} 0 \leq \overline{b-a} \leq 1$. If a and b are two locally comparable integers, we define $b \ominus a$ as follows: $b \ominus a \overset{\text{def}}{=}$ if $a \leq_l b$ then $\overline{b-a}$ else $-\overline{a-b}$.

Let $\mathcal{X}$ be the set $\{-\alpha, \ldots, 0, \ldots, K-1\}$, where α is a positive integer. Let φ be the function from $\mathcal{X}$ to $\mathcal{X}$ defined by: $\varphi(x) \overset{\text{def}}{=}$ if $x \geq 0$ then $\overline{x+1}$ else $x+1$. The pair $(\mathcal{X}, \varphi)$ is called a *finite incrementing system*. Let $tail_\varphi = \{-\alpha, \ldots, 0\}$ and $ring_\varphi = \{0, \ldots, K-1\}$ be the sets of "extra" values and "expected" values, respectively. The set $tail_\varphi^*$ is equal to $tail_\varphi \setminus \{0\}$. A *reset* on $\mathcal{X}$ consists in enforcing any value of $\mathcal{X}$ to $-\alpha$.

In Algorithm 3.1, each process p maintains a clock register $p.r$ using an incrementing system $(\mathcal{X}, \varphi)$ such that:

1. α is greater than or equal to T_G (upperbounded by n) to ensure the stabilization of the underlying unison [3], where T_G is the *size of the greatest hole* of G, i.e., the length of the longest chordless cycle of G if G contains cycle, 2 otherwise (G is acyclic);
2. K is greater than $3D + 5$ — this lowerbound is explained later. Note that K must be greater than C_G to ensure the liveness of the underlying unison [3], where C_G is the *cyclomatic characteristic* of G, i.e., the smallest length of the longest cycle in the set of all the cycle basis of G, 3 otherwise (G is

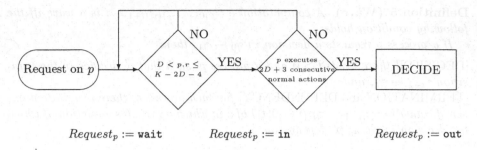

$Request_p := \texttt{wait}$ $Request_p := \texttt{in}$ $Request_p := \texttt{out}$

Fig. 1. Principle of Algorithm 3.1

acyclic). Note that C_G is upperbounded by $min(n, 2D)$. So, $K > 3D + 5$ ensures the liveness of the unison.

Let us refer to Figure 1 to informally describe our main idea. Given a process p, the underlying unison ensures that after p has successively executed $2D + 3)$ times Action NA, every process q ($\neq p$) successively executed at least D times Action NA — shown in Subsection 3.3. So, to make sure that a decide event causally depends on at least one event of each process, Process p is required to execute at least $2D + 3$ normal actions. However, there are two cases leading Process p to sets its register $p.r$ to 0: Process p sets $p.r$ to 0 by executing either (1) Action NA ($p.r := \varphi(p.r)$ s.t. $p.r = K$), or (2) Action CA ($p.r := \varphi(p.r)$ s.t. $p.r = -1$). So, some neighbors of a process p with $p.r = 0$ can be confused to know whether or not p participates to a normal computation — *i.e.*, either p ends (or masks) a reset propagation or p participates to a normal computation. To avoid ambiguity and to make sure that p sets $p.r$ to 0 by executing Action NA only, the above counting ($2D + 3$ normal actions) starts only when $p.r > D$ and $p.r \leq K - 2D - 4$. This explains why K is required to be greater than $3D + 5$.

In order to handle the scheme described in Figure 1, we use the variable $Counter_p \in \{0 \dots 2D + 2\}$. Since the countdown is initialized executing Action NA, it is enough to set it to $2D + 2$ to count $2D + 3$ normal actions.

We also need an extra variable, $Request_p$. Combined with $Counter_p$, $Request_p$ is used to implement the synchronization interface between the application layer and the Wave Toolbox. $Request_p$ takes its value in $\{\texttt{wait}, \texttt{in}, \texttt{out}\}$. When the application layer needs to launch a wave, the process running the application layer sets $Request_p$ to $\texttt{wait}$. Then, Algorithm SWT changes $Request_p$ from $\texttt{wait}$ to $\texttt{in}$ once the condition $D < p.r \leq K - 2D - 4$ holds, *i.e.*, the countdown of normal action is initiated. Eventually, the application layer is granted to decide when $Counter_p$ is equal to 0. On completion of the decision, the application layer process sets $Request_p$ to $\texttt{out}$.

Note that the resets do not disrupt this scheme: When a reset occurs (Action RA), $Resquest_p$ is reset to $\texttt{wait}$. This has no effect on the application layer, except that the process has to wait longer for the decide event. In the worst case (*i.e.*, resets are still propagated in the network), a process decides in $\alpha + K$ rounds. Since α and K are of the order of n and D, respectively, the service time

---

Algorithm 3.1. (SWT) Snap-Stabilizing Wave for any process p

Constants and Variables:

$\mathcal{N}_p$: the set of neighbors of process p; $p.r \in \chi$; $Counter_p \in \{0 \ldots 2D+2\}$;

Uses:

$Request_p \in \{\texttt{wait}, \texttt{in}, \texttt{out}\}$;

Boolean Functions:

$ConvergenceStep_p \equiv p.r \in tail_\varphi^* \wedge (\forall q \in \mathcal{N}_p : (q.r \in tail_\varphi) \wedge (p.r \leq_{tail_\varphi} q.r))$;

$LocallyCorrect_p \quad \equiv p.r \in ring_\varphi \wedge (\forall q \in \mathcal{N}_p, q.r \in ring_\varphi \wedge ((p.r = q.r)$

$\qquad \vee (p.r = \varphi(q.r)) \vee (\varphi(p.r) = q.r)))$;

$NormalStep_p \qquad \equiv p.r \in ring_\varphi \wedge (\forall q \in \mathcal{N}_p : (p.r = q.r) \vee (q.r = \varphi(p.r)))$;

$ResetInit_p \qquad\quad \equiv \neg LocallyCorrect_p \wedge (p.r \notin tail_\varphi)$;

$Ready_p \qquad\qquad \equiv (p.r > D) \wedge (p.r \leq K - 2D - 4)$;

Actions:

$NA : NormalStep_p \qquad \rightarrow p.r := \varphi(p.r)$;

$\qquad\qquad\qquad\qquad\quad$ **if** $((Request_p = \texttt{wait}) \wedge (Ready_p))$

$\qquad\qquad\qquad\qquad\quad$ **then** $Counter_p := 2D+2;\ Request_p = \texttt{in}$;

$\qquad\qquad\qquad\qquad\quad$ **elseif** $((Request_p = \texttt{in}) \wedge (Counter_p > 0))$

$\qquad\qquad\qquad\qquad\quad$ **then** $Counter_p := Counter_p - 1$;

$CA : ConvergenceStep_p \rightarrow p.r := \varphi(p.r)$;

$RA : ResetInit_p \qquad\quad \rightarrow p.r := -\alpha$ (reset); $Request_p := \texttt{wait}$;

Application layer (external rules):

$Req : (Request_p = \texttt{out}) \wedge (Requested\ Wave) \rightarrow Request_p := \texttt{wait}$;

$Res : (Request_p = \texttt{in}) \wedge (Counter_p = 0) \quad \rightarrow\ < DECIDE > ;\ Request_p := \texttt{out}$;

(*i.e.*, the time to complete a requested wave) is in the worst case $O(n + D)$. If the underlying unison is stabilized when a process request a wave, then a decide event occurs in optimal time, *i.e.*, $O(D)$ rounds.

3.3   Correctness Proof

In this subsection, we prove that Algorithm SWT is snap-stabilizing for the wave specification. The proof outline is as follows: Using the notions of causal DAG's coherent cuts, we first show that each process can locally detect coherent cuts, by the way, allowing detection of decide events. This result leads to the prove the correctness of Algorithm SWT. Due to the lack of space, some of the formal proofs are omitted.

Local detection of coherent cuts. In this subsection, we show that, given a process p, starting from a configuration such that $p.r$ is equal to any u greater than D, if p executes $2D + 3$ consecutive normal actions without setting $p.r$ to 0, then the cut C_{u+D+1} is well-defined and coherent.

Definition 6 (Normal Dependance Relation). *Let (p, t) and (q, t') be two events. (q, t') normally depend on (p, t) if $(p, t) \rightarrow (q, t')$, and q executes Action NA at time t'. We denote this normal dependency relation as follows: $(p, t) \xrightarrow{N} (q, t')$. Denote $(p, t) \leq_N (q, t')$ if there is a normal actions path from (p, t) to (q, t').*

Definition 7 (N-Sequence). *When a process p consecutively executes several normal actions* $\xrightarrow{N} (p, t_0) \xrightarrow{N} (p, t_1) \xrightarrow{N} \ldots \xrightarrow{N} (p, t_x)$, *it executes an N-sequence.*

In the sequel, we describe process behaviors in terms of N-sequence, and we assume that no process sets its clock register to 0 — 0 can nevertheless be the initial value.

Lemma 1. *Let p and q be two neighboring processes. If p executes an N-sequence* $\xrightarrow{N} (p, t_0) \xrightarrow{N} (p, t_1) \xrightarrow{N} (p, t_2)$ *such that p.r is equal to u, u + 1, u + 2 in* t_0, t_1, t_2, *respectively, with* $\forall i \in \{1, 2\} : u + i \neq 0$, *then between* t_0 *and* t_2, *q executes a normal action* (q, t_1') *such that q.r = u + 1, and* $(p, t_0) \leq_N (q, t_1') \leq_N (p, t_2)$.

Proof. At time t_0, $q.r$ is equal to $\overline{u-1}$ or u. Let us assume by contradiction that (q, t_1') does not exist. It means that at time t_2, $q.r = u + 2$ although $q.r$ is equal to at most u. A contradiction. □

The following theorem directly follows by induction of Lemma 1 on the length of an N-sequence:

Theorem 1. *Let p and q be two neighboring processes. If p executes an N-sequence* $\xrightarrow{N} (p, t_0) \xrightarrow{N} (p, t_1) \xrightarrow{N} \ldots \xrightarrow{N} (p, t_x)$ *with* $x \geq 3$ *and such that p.r is successively equal to u, u+1, ..., u+x with* $\forall i \in \{1, x\}$, $u+i \neq 0$, *then between* t_0 *and* t_x, *q also executes an N-sequence* $\xrightarrow{N} (q, t_1') \xrightarrow{N} (q, t_2') \xrightarrow{N} \ldots \xrightarrow{N} (q, t_{x-1}')$ *such that q.r is successively equal to u+1, ..., u+x−1, and* $(p, t_0) \leq_N (q, t_1') \leq_N (q, t_{x-1}') \leq_N (p, t_x)$.

Theorem 1 establishes the link between the behavior of two neighboring processes. By induction on the distance between p and any other process, Corollary 1 follows from Theorem 1:

Corollary 1. *Let p and q be two processes, such that* $d(p, q) = k \leq 1$. *If p executes an N-sequence* $\xrightarrow{N} (p, t_0) \xrightarrow{N} (p, t_1) \xrightarrow{N} \ldots \xrightarrow{N} (p, t_x)$ *of length x with* $x \geq 1 + 2k$ *and such that p.r is successively equal to u, u + 1, ..., u + x with* $\forall i \in \{1, x\}$, $u + i \neq 0$, *then between* t_0 *and* t_x, *q also executes an N-sequence* $\xrightarrow{N} (q, t_k') \xrightarrow{N} (q, t_{k+1}') \xrightarrow{N} \ldots (q, t_{x-k}')$ *of length x − 2k such that q.r is successively equal to u + k, ..., u + x − k, and* $(p, t_0) \leq_N (q, t_k') \leq_N (q, t_{x-k}') \leq_N (p, t_x)$.

Now, let us prove that if p executes a particular N-sequence, then every process reaches once the same clock value, designing a coherent cut. Lemma 2 follows from Corollary 1:

Lemma 2. *Let p and q be two processes. If p executes an N-sequence* $\xrightarrow{N} (p, t_0) \xrightarrow{N} (p, t_1) \xrightarrow{N} \ldots \xrightarrow{N} (p, t_{2D+3})$ *such that p.r is successively equal to u, u+1, ..., u+ 2D+3 with* $\forall i \in \{1, 2D + 3\}$, $u+i \neq 0$, *then between* t_0 *and* t_{2D+3}, *there exists* $t \in]t_0, t_{2D+3}[$ *such that* (q, t) *is a normal action. At this time t, q.r = u + D + 1, and* $(p, t_0) \leq_N (q, t) \leq_N (p, t_{2D+3})$.

Informally, if a process executes a normal action sequence of length $2D + 3$, every process reaches at least once the same value. Now, let us show that in a particular case, this value is reached only once.

Lemma 3. *In Lemma 2, if $D < u \leq K - 2D - 4$, then there exists a single $t \in]t_0, t_{2D+3}[$ such that: (1) (q,t) is a normal action, (2) at time t, $q.r = u+D+1$, and $(p,t_0) \leq_N (q,t) \leq_N (p,t_{2D+3})$.*

Proof. Assume by contradiction, that there exists two events (q,t) and (q,t') holding the 3 conditions. Assume that $t' < t$. So, $(q,t') < (q,t)$, and during the action sequence $(q,t') \rightarrow \ldots \rightarrow (q,t)$, $q.r$ necessarily reaches at least once 0 (following a reset, or by incrementation). Thus, in this actions sequence, there exists an N-sequence $(q,t_0') \rightarrow \ldots \rightarrow (q,t)$ such that $q.r$ is successively equal to $0, 1, \ldots, u+D+1$. Since $u > D$, this N-sequence is longer than $2D+1$, meaning from Corollary 1 that in $]t_0', t[\subset]t_0, t_{2D+3}[$, $p.r$ reaches D. This contradicts the fact that $p.r$ is successively equal to $\{u, u+1, \ldots, u+2D+3\}$ in $]t_0, t_{2D+3}[$. $\square$

In the sequel, we assume that p executes an N-sequence $\xrightarrow{N} (p,t_0) \xrightarrow{N} (p,t_1) \xrightarrow{N} \ldots \xrightarrow{N} (p,t_{2D+3})$ such that $p.r$ is successively equal to u, $u+1, \ldots$, $u+2D+3$ with $\forall i \in \{1, 2D+3\}$, $u+i \neq 0$ and $D < u \leq K - 2D - 4$ — recall that $K > 3D + 5$. Now, let us define a coherent cut, according to the behavior of p.

We are now able to define a coherent cut as follows: For each $q \in V$, we denote the event (q, t_q^{D+1}) as the single normal action (by Lemmas 2 and 3) executed by q such that: (1) At time t_q^{D+1}, $q.r = u + D + 1$, and (2) $(p,t_0) \leq_N (q, t_q^{D+1}) \leq_N (p, t_{2D+3})$.

Since p executes an N-sequence of length $2D+3$, by Corollary 1, each process q executes an N-sequence $\xrightarrow{N} (q, t_q^D) \xrightarrow{N} (q, t_q^{D+1}) \xrightarrow{N} (q, t_q^{D+2})$ of length equal to at least 3 such that $(p,t_0) \leq_N (q, t_q^D) \xrightarrow{N} (q, t_q^{D+1}) \xrightarrow{N} (q, t_q^{D+2}) \leq_N (p, t_{2D+3})$. Denote $C_{p,D+1}$ the cut $\{(q, t_q^{D+1}), p \in V\}$.

We now show that the cut $C_{p,D+1}$ is coherent for each couple of neighboring processes. Next, we generalize that $C_{p,D+1}$ is coherent for any couple of processes.

Lemma 4. *Let p_1 and p_2 be two neighbors. The cut $C_{p,D+1}$ is coherent for p_1 and p_2, which means that if $(p_2, t_2) \leq (p_1, t_{p_1}^{D+1})$ then $(p_2, t_2) \leq (p_2, t_{p_2}^{D+1})$.*

Proof. If $t_{p_1}^{D+1} \leq t_{p_2}^{D+1}$, then the lemma trivially holds. Assume that $t_{p_1}^{D+1} > t_{p_2}^{D+1}$. By definition of $(p_1, t_{p_1}^{D+1})$, the following N-sequence exists: $(p_1, t_{p_1}^D) \xrightarrow{N} (p_1, t_{p_1}^{D+1}) \xrightarrow{N} (p_1, t_{p_1}^{D+2})$. So, p_2 executes a normal action denoted (p_2, t') with $t' \in]t_{p_1}^D, t_{p_1}^{D+2}[$ such that $q.r$ reaches value $u + D + 1$. By Lemmas 2 and 3, $(p_2, t') = (p_2, t_{p_2}^{D+1})$. So, there exists: $(p_2, t_{p_2}^D) \xrightarrow{N} (p_2, t_{p_2}^{D+1}) \xrightarrow{N} (p_2, t_{p_2}^{D+2})$. Obviously, $t_{p_2}^{D+2} > t_{p_1}^{D+1}$. So, $(p_2, t_2) < (p_2, t_{p_2}^{D+2})$. Thus, $(p_2, t_2) \leq (p_2, t_{p_2}^{D+1})$. $\square$

The following theorem follows by induction of Lemma 4:

Theorem 2. *The cut $C_{p,D+1} = \{(q, t_q^{D+1}), q \in V\}$ is coherent, which means for each pair (q_0, q), if $(q_0, t_0) \leq (q, t_q^{D+1})$ then $(q_0, t_0) \leq (q_0, t_{q_0}^{D+1})$.*

It follows from Theorem 2 that every process is able to detect any coherent cut by executing an N-sequence which is long enough, possibly after many resets.

Algorithm SWT is Snap-Stabilizing. We first need the predicate WU over the set of configurations, Γ, as follows: $WU(\gamma) \overset{\text{def}}{\equiv} \forall p \in V, \forall q \in \mathcal{N}_p : (p.r \in ring_\varphi) \wedge (|p.r - q.r| \leq 1)$ in γ. In the sequel, we abuse notation, referring to the corresponding set of configurations simply by WU. Since $\alpha \geq T_G$ and $K > 3D + 5$, the following lemma holds:

Lemma 5 ([3]). *The following properties are true in every execution of Algorithm SWT starting from any arbitrary configuration γ:*

Closure: *In every execution starting from a configuration γ such that $WU(\gamma)$ holds, then in every γ' of any execution starting from γ, $WU(\gamma')$ holds.*

Convergence: *In every execution starting from an arbitrary configuration γ, there exists a configuration γ' such that $WU(\gamma')$ holds.*

Liveness: *In every execution starting from a configuration γ such that $WU(\gamma)$ holds, then every process p executes $p.r := \varphi(p.r)$ infinitely often.*

If $a_0, a_1, a_2, \ldots a_{p-1}, a_p$ is a sequence of integers such that $\forall i \in \{0, \ldots, p-1\}$, a_i is locally comparable to a_{i+1}, then $S = \sum_{i=0}^{p-1} (a_{i+1} \ominus a_i)$ is the *local variation* of this sequence. In WU, the clock registers of neighboring processes are locally comparable. Define the *delay* on a path $\mu = p_0 p_1 \ldots p_k$, denoted by δ_μ, as the local variation of the sequence $p_0.r, p_1.r, \ldots, p_k.r$, *i.e.*, $\delta_\mu = \sum_{i=0}^{k-1} (p_{i+1}.r \ominus_l p_i.r)$ if $k > 0$, 0 otherwise ($k = 0$). The delay between two processes p and q is said to be *intrinsic* if it is independent on the choice of the path from p to q. The delay is *intrinsic* iff it is *intrinsic* for every p and q in V. It is shown in [3] that if $K > C_G$, then the delay is intrinsic. In that case, the intrinsic delay defines a *total preordering* on the processes in V, so called *precedence relation*. Given a configuration in WU, the absolute value of the delay between two processes p and q is equal to or less than the distance $d(p, q)$ in the network. Let $\gamma_0 \gamma_1 \ldots$ be an infinite execution starting in WU. Let p_0 be a maximal process, according to the precedence relation for γ_0. Let $\perp_0 = p_0.r$ at time 0.

We now borrow the following theorem from [2]:

Theorem 3 ([2]). *Let $u \geq \perp_0 + D$. If $C_{u+\delta}$ is a set of decide events, then $[C_u, C_{u+\delta}]$, $\delta \geq D$, is a wave.*

We are now ready to prove our final result w.r.t. Remark 1. From the algorithm and Lemma 5, we can easily show the following lemma:

Lemma 6. *In every execution starting from any arbitrary configuration γ, $\forall p \in V$, $Request_p$ is infinitely often equal to out.*

From Theorem 3, Theorem 2, Lemma 6, Lemma 5 and Remark 1, the following theorem holds:

Theorem 4. *Algorithm 3.1 (SWT) is a snap-stabilizing Wave Protocol.*

4   Snap-Stabilizing Causal Atomic Broadcast

In this section, we show how to use Algorithm 3.1 as a basis to build a snap-stabilizing causal atomic broadcast protocol for anonymous arbitrary networks. We first define the problem to be solved, and then, we describe our solution.

Problem Statement
The Causal Atomic Broadcast (CAB) is to design a protocol so that the following properties are true in every execution [13]:

Total Order: If two processes p and q both deliver two messages m_1 and m_2, then p delivers m_1 before m_2 if and only if q delivers m_1 before m_2.
Causal Order: If the broadcast of a message m_1 causally precedes the broadcast of a message m_2, then no process deliver m_2 unless it has previously delivered m_1.

Snap-Stabilizing CAB Protocol. The principle of our solution, in the remainder referred to as Algorithm $SCAB$, is as follows: In addition of the registers used by Algorithm 3.1, each process p maintains a set of messages into the register $p.M$. When a process p needs to *broadcast* a message m (requested by the application using the broadcast protocol), p adds m to $p.M$ — $p.M := p.M \cup \{m\}$. Each time p executes its normal action, while getting the values of its neighbor phase clocks, p stores the (new) messages received from its neighbors into $p.M$ — $p.M := p.M \bigcup_{q \in \mathcal{N}_p} q.m$. During a transition $\gamma_t \mapsto \gamma_{t+1}$, p *delivers* the messages to the application layer belonging to the message sets of its neighbors which are not in its own message set, *i.e.*, messages in $\bigcup_{q \in \mathcal{N}_p} q.m \setminus p.m$.

Clearly, the above simple principle provides an efficient message broadcasting. However, since messages are infinitely often added to the message sets, each process requires an infinite amount of memory. A straightforward solution to deal with this problem is that each process p removes the delivered messages from $p.M$. But an earlier elimination of messages could caused loss of messages and multiple delivering. Notice that Algorithm 3.1 ensures that between two coherent cuts $[C_u, C_{u+D}]$, any broadcasted messages has been received by every process of the system. In other words, each process must remain each message during at least two coherent cuts. This can be achieved by marking each message with the phase number when the broadcast is initiated.

So, we modify the above principle by marking each message m added to $p.M$ with a stamp x_m equal to $p.r$. This allows each p to remove every messages m in $p.M$ such that x_m satisfies $\overline{x_m - p.r} > D$. Note that, due to the unpredictable initial configurations and transient errors, $p.M$ may contains incorrect messages. Since the range of $x_m \in ring_\varphi$, this mechanism also ensures that after having executed D normal action, the set of messages is cleaned up of incorrect messages.

Clearly, properties of both causal and total order are guaranteed by the underlying unison. Furthermore, since our protocol is based on Algorithm 3.1, from Theorem 3, Theorem 2, and Theorem 4, the following theorem holds:

Theorem 5. *Algorithm $SCAB$ is a snap-stabilizing Causal Atomic Broadcast protocol.*

5   Conclusion

We proposed two snap-stabilizing protocols for anonymous networks. The former is a generic wave algorithm. It can be used for any static or dynamic schemes which is feasible in an anonymous network. The latter protocol is a causal atomic broadcast, which can be used as a pipeline of messages.

References

1. Arora, A., Gouda, M.G.: Distributed reset. IEEE Transactions on Computers 43, 1026–1038 (1994)
2. Boulinier, C., Petit, F.: Self-stabilizing wavelets and ϱ-hops coordination. Technical Report TR07-05, LaRIA, University of Picardie Jules Verne, France (2007), https://hal.ccsd.cnrs.fr/hal-00157946
3. Boulinier, C., Petit, F., Villain, V.: When graph theory helps self-stabilization. In: PODC 2004. Proceedings of the twenty-third annual ACM symposium on Principles of distributed computing, pp. 150–159 (2004)
4. Bui, A., Datta, A.K., Petit, F., Villain, V.: State-optimal snap-stabilizing PIF in tree networks. In: WSS 1999. Proceedings of the Forth Workshop on Self-Stabilizing Systems, pp. 78–85. IEEE Computer Society Press, Los Alamitos (1999)
5. Cournier, A., Datta, A.K., Petit, F., Villain, V.: Snap-stabilizing PIF algorithm in arbitrary networks. In: ICDCS 2002. IEEE 22nd International Conference on Distributed Computing Systems, pp. 199–206. IEEE Computer Society Press, Los Alamitos (2002)
6. Cournier, A., Devismes, S., Petit, F., Villain, V.: Snap-stabilizing depth-first search in arbitrary networks. The Computer Journal 49(3), 268–280 (2006)
7. Datta, A.K., Johnen, C., Petit, F., Villain, V.: Self-stabilizing depth-first token circulation in arbitrary rooted networks. Distributed Computing 13(4), 207–218 (2000)
8. Delaët, S., Ducourthial, B., Tixeuil, S.: Self-stabilization with r-operators in unreliable directed networks. Technical Report TR 1361, LRI, Orsay, France (2003)
9. Dolev, S.: Self-Stabilization. The MIT Press, Cambridge (2000)
10. Dolev, S., Israeli, A., Moran, S.: Self-stabilization of dynamic systems assuming only read/write atomicity. Distributed Computing 7, 3–16 (1993)
11. Ducourthial, B.: New operators for computing with associative nets. In: SIROCCO 1998. The 5th International Colloquium On Structural Information and Communication Complexity Proceedings, pp. 51–65. Carleton University Press, Ottawa (1998)
12. Ducourthial, B., Tixeuil, S.: Self-stabilization with r-operators. Distributed Computing 14, 147–162 (2001)
13. Hadzilacos, V., Toueg, S.: A modular approach to fault-tolerant broadcasts and related problems. Technical Report TR94-1425 (1994), http://citeseer.ist.psu.edu/hadzilacos94modular.html
14. Huang, S.T., Chen, N.S.: A self-stabilizing algorithm for constructing breadth-first trees. Information Processing Letters 41, 109–117 (1992)
15. Johnen, C.: Memory-efficient self-stabilizing algorithm to construct BFS spanning trees. In: Third Workshop on Self-Stabilizing Systems, pp. 125–140. Carleton University Press, Ottawa (1997)
16. Tel, G.: Total algorithms. In: Vogt, F.H. (ed.) Concurrency 1988. LNCS, vol. 335, pp. 277–291. Springer, Heidelberg (1988)
17. Tel, G.: Introduction to Distributed Algorithms, 2nd edn. Cambridge University Press, Cambridge (2000)

Self-stabilizing Distributed Protocol Switching

Sushanta Karmakar and Arobinda Gupta

Department of Computer Science and Engineering,
Indian Institute of Technology, Kharagpur - 721 302, India
{sushantak,agupta}@cse.iitkgp.ernet.in

Abstract. Switching between protocols based on environment is an elegant idea of enabling adaptation in distributed systems. Also self-stabilizing algorithms have been proposed as a mechanism to handle transient failures in distributed systems. In this work we illustrate self-stabilizing distributed protocol switching by proposing a self-stabilizing algorithm for dynamically switching between a BFS tree and a DFS tree. At low network load, the BFS tree may be used for broadcasting messages since it also minimizes delay. At higher network load, the DFS tree may be used to reduce the load on any one node. Both trees are rooted at the common broadcast source. Different properties relating to the delivery of broadcast messages under different failure conditions are investigated.

Keywords: self-stabilization, protocol switching, BFS tree, DFS tree, broadcast.

1 Introduction

The performance of a distributed system depends on its environment. However, the environment may change with time. So it is necessary for a distributed system to be adaptive under changing environments. Adaptation can be achieved in various ways, by modifying the runtime parameters of the algorithm [1] or by incorporating the ability to adapt directly into a system [2]. However these techniques are less general and often application specific. In many distributed systems, it may happen that the same problem has multiple protocols, each of which performs differently under different environments. In such cases adaptation can be achieved by dynamically switching between them as the environment changes.

A self-stabilizing system [3] can start in an arbitrary initial state and still converge to some desired legitimate state in finite time. Such a property is desirable for any distributed system, because after any unexpected perturbation such as a transient failure, the system eventually recovers and returns to a legitimate state without any outside intervention.

In this paper, we illustrate self-stabilizing distributed protocol switching by proposing a self-stabilizing distributed algorithm for switching from a BFS tree to a DFS tree. The switching from a DFS tree to a BFS tree is similar and is omitted in this paper. Topology of a distributed system is often used by various applications like routing, broadcasting etc. BFS tree and DFS tree are two well known topologies. At low network load, a BFS tree may be used for broadcast as it reduces the broadcast delay since the path length from the root of the BFS tree to any other node is always minimum.

S. Rao et al. (Eds.): ICDCN 2008, LNCS 4904, pp. 203–208, 2008.

However at higher load, a DFS tree may be used to reduce the load on any one node since the degree of a node in a DFS tree is generally lower than that in a BFS tree. Therefore the system can adapt to the network load, which is dynamically changing, by dynamically switching between a BFS tree and a DFS tree. In fact, the algorithm will work for switching between any two spanning trees of the network. Also the different guarantees that can be provided on the delivery of broadcast messages during switching and under different failure conditions are investigated. More specifically we show that under no failure, each broadcast message is correctly delivered to all the nodes in spite of switching. For arbitrary failure, the switching eventually completes with the proper tree as the output. The broadcast properties that can be guaranteed under limited transient failure (single fault) are also investigated.

Bar-Noy et al. [4] proposed a method of dynamically changing between different byzantine agreement protocols. Arora et al. [5] proposed a method to switch from one state to another in a distributed system without requiring a global freeze. Liu et al. [6] described a method to build a hybrid protocol which adapts by dynamically mapping the state of a process in one protocol to the state in another. Mocito and Rodrigues [7] proposed an algorithm that dynamically switches between different total order algorithms with negligible interference to the data flow. Jain et al. [8] proposed a method of switching between two connected dominating sets while always maintaining some connected dominating set of the network. Karmakar and Gupta [9] proposed a distributed algorithm for dynamically switching between a BFS tree computation protocol and a DFS tree computation protocol. They also ensured that each broadcast message is correctly delivered to all the nodes in spite of switching. However the algorithm proposed in [9] is not fault-tolerant. In [10], they proposed a fault-tolerant version of the protocol that can tolerate arbitrary crash faults. This paper discusses the self-stabilizing aspect of distributed protocol switching, and investigates the effect of transient failures on the delivery of broadcast messages under protocol switching.

The rest of the paper is organized as follows. Section 2 contains the system model. Section 3 describes the self-stabilizing algorithm for distributed protocol switching and presents an outline of the proof of correctness of the protocol and its properties.

2   System Model

The system is modeled as a connected graph $\mathcal{G}(V, E)$ where V is the set of nodes and E is the set of edges. Each node has a unique identifier. For ease of exposition it is assumed that each node can read from each neighbor in its 2-hop neighborhood, but can modify only its own variables. The algorithm can be easily changed (using the scheme proposed in [11]) to work in a model in which a node can only read the state of its 1-hop neighbors. Each node i maintains a FIFO buffer B_i for sending messages. Whenever node i intends to send a broadcast message it places the message in the buffer. Similarly whenever node i wants to receive the broadcast messages sent by its parent j, it reads B_j. This simulates the broadcast of a message. For simplicity, the buffer size is assumed to be infinite in this paper. The buffer may become corrupted due to a transient failure. The fault model assumes the transient failure of a node. Three different time parameters are defined for such failures. T_s is the time when the faulty behavior of a node starts,

T_{ss} is the time when the faulty behavior of the node stops, and T_r is the time when the faulty node recovers from the failure (i.e. legitimate state is reached). The behavior of the faulty node between T_s and T_{ss} can be arbitrary. Each node executes a program. The program for a node is specified using guarded statements of the form $G \rightarrow A$ where G is the guard, and A is the action. The action A is executed if and only if G is true. So the program at any node i contains a sequence of statements $\{S_1, S_2, \ldots, S_n\}$ where each S_j is of the form $G \rightarrow A$. The j-th statement of the program at node i is denoted by $S_j(i)$. The guard corresponding to $S_j(i)$ is denoted by $G_j(i)$ and the action corresponding to $S_j(i)$ is denoted by $A_j(i)$.

3   Self-stabilizing Distributed Protocol Switching

Let N_i denote the neighbors of each node $i \in V$. Each node i maintains a binary variable b_i and an integer variable T_M^i. Both b_i and T_M^i may become corrupted due to transient failure. Let $max(B_i)$ denote the index of the last message placed in the message buffer of i. When node i wants to read n broadcast messages from the message buffer of j, node i executes a function $read(B_j, n)$. The function reads n topmost messages from the buffer of j.

Let T be a BFS tree of $\mathcal{G}$ rooted at a node r. Let T' be a DFS tree of $\mathcal{G}$ rooted at the same node r. Also let there exist a third spanning tree T'' of $\mathcal{G}$ rooted at r. T'' can be any spanning tree of $\mathcal{G}$ including T and T'. These spanning trees are assumed to be fixed and known apriori. If $b_i = 1$ then node i uses T for broadcast. Similarly if $b_i = 0$ then i uses T' for broadcast. Ideally each node i in the graph should have the same b_i so that each node uses the same tree for broadcast of messages. At root node r, b_r is assigned as a function of the overall load on the network which is monitored using the spanning tree T''. Let this function be defined by $f(L)$. Based on the overall load of the system, the root node r initiates the use of a particular tree. The spanning tree T'' is used to propagate b_r to all other nodes. Let p_i denote the parent of i in the spanning tree T''. Let $U(i)$ denote the predicate $b_i \neq b_{p_i}$. Let C_i denote the set of children of node i in the spanning tree T''. Let $X(i) \equiv U(i) \wedge [(\forall j \in C_i)\neg U(j)] \wedge \neg U(p_i)$. For root node $X(i) \equiv U(i) \wedge [(\forall j \in C_i)\neg U(j)]$ whereas for leaves $X(i) \equiv U(i) \wedge \neg U(p_i)$. Let i be a node such that $X(i) = true$. Clearly $X(i) = true$ at a node i if i is about to switch from one protocol to another. Such switches must be controlled so that in the absence of any failure, each broadcast message is correctly delivered to all the nodes. To ensure this, each broadcast message transmitted using protocol $\mathcal{P}_1$ at each $j \in \{i\} \cup N_i$ should happen before the switching at i from $\mathcal{P}_1$ to $\mathcal{P}_2$. Similarly messages transmitted using protocol $\mathcal{P}_2$ at each $j \in \{i\} \cup N_i$ should happen after the switching at i from $\mathcal{P}_1$ to $\mathcal{P}_2$. In this work, $\mathcal{P}_1$ is the BFS tree and $\mathcal{P}_2$ is the DFS tree. Let $Y(i) \equiv (\forall j \in N_i)[(T_M^j \geq T_M^i)]$. Let $p(b_i)$ denote the parent of i according to the current value of b_i. The protocol for any node i is given in Figure 1. Let this protocol be denoted by Q. Statement S_1 and S_2 along with S_5 and S_6 control the flow of broadcast messages under no failure. However an error in b_i at i may propagate along the spanning tree T''. So in an intermediate state some of the nodes will use T for broadcast whereas some other nodes will use T', and therefore some nodes may send broadcast messages erroneously. To reduce the number of messages broadcast erroneously, it is necessary to contain the

$$(S_1) \quad X(r) \wedge Y(r) \rightarrow b_r = f(L)$$

$$(S_2) \quad X(i) \wedge Y(i) \rightarrow b_i = b_{p_i}$$

$$(S_3) \quad \neg X(r) \wedge b_r \neq f(L) \rightarrow b_r = f(L)$$

$$(S_4) \quad \neg X(i) \wedge U(i) \wedge \neg U(p_i) \rightarrow b_i = b_{p_i}$$

$$(S_5) \quad \neg U(i) \wedge T_M^i \neq max(B_i) \rightarrow T_M^i = max(B_i)$$

$$(S_6) \quad \neg U(i) \wedge (\forall j \in N_i)(b_j = b_i) \wedge T_M^i = max(B_i)$$
$$\wedge \, T_M^{p(b_i)} = max(B_{p(b_i)}) \wedge (T_M^i < T_M^{p(b_i)})$$
$$\rightarrow read(B_{p(b_i)}, T_M^{p(b_i)} - T_M^i)$$

Fig. 1. Protocol Q: fault-containing self-stabilizing distributed protocol switching

propagation of faults. In this paper we contain the propagation of a single fault. This is done by statement S_3 and S_4. The fault is repaired by the faulty node itself and in this process only the faulty node and its neighbors make a constant number of moves. The legitimate state of the protocol is given by the following definition.

Definition 1. *At legitimate state, the protocol Q is in a state where $U(i)$ is false at each i and $Y(i)$ is true at each i.*

It can be proved that the protocol is self-stabilizing and satisfies the property that under no failure each broadcast message is correctly delivered to all the nodes. Also some additional broadcast properties can be guaranteed under single transient failure.

3.1 Outline of Proof of Correctness

Lemma 1. *If no guard of Q is enabled then for all i, $U(i)$ is false.*

Proof. Since no guard of Q is enabled, $G_2(i)$ and $G_4(i)$ are both false at each node i. Now $X(i)$ can be either true or false. Let $X(i) = true$ at some i. If $Y(i) = true$ then $G_2(i) = true$, which is a contradiction. Again if $Y(i) = false$ then $\exists j \in N_i : T_M^j < T_M^i$. There can be the following subcases.

Subcase 1: j has not switched and $b_j = b_i$. In this case, if $T_M^j = T_M^i$ then obviously this is a contradiction. If $T_M^j \neq T_M^i$ then $T_M^j < T_M^i$ and j must be a descendant of i in T''. Suppose $k \in C_i$ in T'' and $T_M^k < T_M^i$. By $G_5(k)$, $T_M^k = max(B_k)$. Also by $G_5(i)$, $T_M^i = max(B_i)$. So by $G_6(k)$, k will read each broadcast message from $p(b_k)$ when none of the neighbors of k have switched (i.e. $\forall x \in N_k : b_k = b_x$). So eventually $T_M^k = T_M^i$. Applying similar argument for x where $x \in C_k$ in T'', we can argue that eventually $T_M^j = T_M^i$ where j is a descendant of i in the spanning tree T''. This is again a contradiction.

Subcase 2: j has switched and $b_j = b_{p_i}$. So j must have executed $A_2(j)$. So $Y(j)$ must have been true. So $(\forall k \in N_j) T_M^k \geq T_M^j$. Since $i \in N_j$, $T_M^i \geq T_M^j$. But before switching of j, $b_j = b_i$. Hence $T_M^i = T_M^j$. Since T_M^j increases monotonically based on the receive of a message, therefore after switching of j, $T_M^j \geq T_M^i$. This is a contradiction.

So eventually $Y(i) = true$. If $Y(i) = true$ then $G_2(i) = true$, which is a contradiction. So $X(i)$ cannot be true at any i. So $X(i)$ must be false at each i. So $U(i) \wedge (\forall j \in C_i)\neg U(j) \wedge \neg U(p_i)$ is false at each i. Hence $U(i)$ must be false at each i. $\square$

Lemma 2. *If no guard of Q is enabled then for all i, $Y(i)$ is true.*

Proof. By Lemma 1, $U(i) = false$ at each i. Let there be a node i such that $Y(i) = false$. So $\exists j$ such that $G_5(j) = true$ or $G_6(j) = true$. This is a contradiction. Hence by $S_5(i)$ and $S_6(i)$, eventually $Y(i) = true$ at each i. $\square$

Theorem 1 (Partial Correctness). *If no guard is enabled in the system, then the system is in a legitimate state.*

Proof. The proof follows from Lemma 1, Lemma 2, and Definition 1. $\square$

Lemma 3. *From any arbitrary state, eventually $U(i)$ is false at each i.*

Proof. At each node i, either $X(i) = true$ or $X(i) = false$. If $X(i) = false$ then by $S_3(i)$ or $S_4(i)$, $U(i)$ eventually becomes false. Let $X(i) = true$. Now $Y(i) = true$ or $Y(i) = false$. If $Y(i) = true$ then by $S_1(i)$ or $S_2(i)$, $U(i) = false$ at each i. Again if $Y(i) = false$, then by arguments given in Lemma 1, eventually $Y(i) = true$. Hence by $S_1(i)$ or $S_2(i)$, $U(i) = false$ at each i. $\square$

The following theorem follows easily from Lemma 3.

Theorem 2 (Termination). *From any arbitrary state, the algorithm Q eventually terminates.*

Lemma 4. *Under no failure each broadcast message m is eventually correctly read by all the nodes.*

Proof. There can be two cases.

Case 1: There is no failure and no switching is in progress. So for each i, $X(i) = false$. So by S_3 and S_4, $\forall i, j : i \neq j$, $b_i = b_j$. Hence $U(i) = false$ for each i. So if $T_M^i \neq max(B_i)$ then by $S_5(i)$, eventually $T_M^i = max(B_i)$ for each i. Let i has not yet read a message m from $p(b_i)$ and thus $T_M^i < T_M^{p(b_i)}$. By $S_6(i)$, i will eventually read the broadcast message m from $p(b_i)$ and thus eventually $T_M^i = T_M^{p(b_i)}$ will hold. Since $\forall i, j : i \neq j$, $b_i = b_j$, each node i will read m from $p(b_i)$ using the same b_i. So each broadcast message m is correctly read by all the nodes.

Case 2: There is no failure but switching is in progress. So $\exists i, X(i) = true$. So $U(i) = true$. So $G_5(i) = false$ and $G_6(i) = false$. So i stops reading any broadcast message. However by $S_2(i)$, until $X(i) \wedge Y(i) = true$, i does not switch. If $Y(i) = false$ then by arguments similar to that in Lemma 1, eventually $Y(i) = true$.

However by $S_6(i)$, i has already stopped reading any broadcast message. Let m be the last broadcast message read by i from $p(b_i)$ before i switches. Now after i switches, it will read each broadcast message using $p(\neg b_i)$. Since the message buffer at each i is FIFO therefore each message read earlier to m is read by each node i using $p(b_i)$. Similarly each message read after m is read by each node i using $p(\neg b_i)$. Hence each message is read by each i using the same b_i. So each broadcast message is correctly read by all the nodes.   □

The following lemmas can be proved.

Lemma 5. *Under single transient failure, each broadcast message read by a child of the faulty node i before time T_s is eventually correctly read by all the non-faulty nodes.*

Lemma 6. *Under single transient failure, each broadcast message m that has not yet been read by the faulty node i before T_{ss} is eventually correctly read by all the nodes.*

It is easy to see that under single transient failure, irrespective of whether switching is in progress or not, any broadcast message m that is at the faulty node i between T_s and T_{ss} may be lost. So unless rebroadcast is allowed, the delivery of these messages is not guaranteed.

References

1. Jacobson, V.: Congestion avoidance and control. In: ACM SIGCOMM Symp. on Communications Architectures and Protocols (1988)
2. Anderson, J., Kim, Y.J.: Adaptive mutual exclusion with local spinning. In: Herlihy, M.P. (ed.) DISC 2000. LNCS, vol. 1914, Springer, Heidelberg (2000)
3. Dijkstra, E.W.: Self-stabilizing systems in spite of distributed control. Communications of the ACM 17 (1974)
4. Bar-Noy, A., Dolev, D., Dwork, C., Strong, R.: Shifting gears: Changing algorithms on the fly to expedite byzantine agreement. Information and Computation 97, 205–233 (1992)
5. Arora, A., Gouda, M.: Distributed reset. IEEE Transactions on Computers 43 (1994)
6. Liu, X., van Renesse, R.: Brief announcement: Fast protocol transition in a distributed environment. In: ACM PODC (2000)
7. Mocito, J., Rodrigues, L.: Run-time switching between total order algorithms. In: Proceedings of the Euro-Par (2006)
8. Jain, A., Karmakar, S., Gupta, A.: Adaptive connected dominating set – an exercise in distributed output switching. In: Chaudhuri, S., Das, S.R., Paul, H.S., Tirthapura, S. (eds.) ICDCN 2006. LNCS, vol. 4308, pp. 88–93. Springer, Heidelberg (2006)
9. Karmakar, S., Gupta, A.: Adaptive broadcast by distributed protocol switching. In: SAC. Proceedings of ACM Symposium on Applied Computing, pp. 588–589 (2007)
10. Karmakar, S., Gupta, A.: Fault-tolerant topology adaptation by localized distributed protocol switching. In: HiPC. Proceedings of IEEE International Conference on High Performce Computing (2007)
11. Ghosh, S., Gupta, A.: An exercise in fault-containment: Self-stabilizing leader election. Information Processing Letters 59, 281–288 (1996)

A Self-stabilizing Algorithm for the Minimum Color Sum of a Graph

Huang Sun, Brice Effantin, and Hamamache Kheddouci

Université de Lyon, F-69003, France
Laboratory LIESP, Université Lyon 1
Bâtiment Nautibus (ex.710), 43 bd du 11 Novembre 1918
69622 Villeurbanne Cedex, France
serge_sun@yahoo.fr,{beffanti, hkheddou}@bat710.univ-lyon1.fr

Abstract. The chromatic sum of a graph G is the minimum sum of colors in a vertex coloring of G. This problem has many interests like in networks, where it models the minimization of the total charge of a network. As systems are more and more large and dynamic, distributed approaches are needed to manage them. In this paper we present a self-stabilizing algorithm to determine a minimal sum of colors for a graph. Such a coloring is determined with at most $O(n\Delta^2)$ changes of colors, where Δ is the maximum degree of the graph.

1 Introduction

In a distributed system, a node exchanges information only with its neighborhood. Every node has a set of local variables to determine a local state of the node. The state of the entire system, called *global state*, is the union of the local states of all the nodes in the system. Thus, each node has a partial view of the global state. The objective in a distributed system is to obtain automatically a desirable global final state (called *legitimate state*) from an illegitimate state. These illegitimate states are due to malfunctions or perturbations which bring the system in an undesirable state. One of the goals of a distributed system is so to bring back (and keep) the system in a legitimate state if malfunctions perturb it, without the interference of an external agent. Such systems, able to reach a legitimate state in a finite number of steps, are called *self-stabilizing* systems, first introduced by Dijkstra [4] in 1974. Several graph problems arise naturally in distributed systems. For example, self-stabilizing algorithms for finding spanning trees, matchings, independent sets have been studied [1,10,17]. Graph coloring is also a very attractive field in which self-stabilizing algorithms are studied. In 1993, Ghosh and Karaata [6] proposed a self-stabilizing algorithm to color planar graphs with six colors by transforming it in a directed acyclic graph. Sur and Srimani [20] presented a vertex coloring algorithm for bipartite graphs. Shukla et al. [18] gave a randomized self-stabilizing coloring of several classes of bipartite graphs and trees. In 2000, Gradinariu and Tixeuil [7] showed algorithms to color the arbitrary networks. Their algorithms use at most $\Delta + 1$ colors and stabilize in $O(n\Delta)$. More recently, Hedetniemi et al. [9] presented two self-stabilizing

S. Rao et al. (Eds.): ICDCN 2008, LNCS 4904, pp. 209–214, 2008.
© Springer-Verlag Berlin Heidelberg 2008

algorithms which use at most $\Delta + 1$ colors. In 2005, Huang et *al.* [11] exhibed a self-stabilizing algorithm to color planar graphs with six colors, but, in comparison to [6], they do not construct a directed acyclic graph and decrease the quantity of memory required for the algorithm.

In our study, we are interested in a particular graph coloring. We consider graphs without self loops or multiple edges. Let G be a graph with a vertex set V and an edge set E. A k-*coloring* of G is defined as a function c on $V(G) = \{x_1, x_2, \ldots, x_n\}$ into a set of colors $C = \{1, 2, \ldots, k\}$ such that for each vertex x_i, with $1 \leq i \leq n$, we have $c(x_i) \in C$. A *proper k-coloring* is a k-coloring satisfying the condition $c(x_i) \neq c(x_j)$ for every pair of adjacent vertices $x_i, x_j \in V(G)$. The *chromatic number* $\chi(G)$ is the minimum number of colors in a proper coloring of G. Instead of considering the number of colors in a proper coloring, we study in this paper, the sum of these colors. The *chromatic sum*, denoted $\Sigma(G)$, is the minimum sum of colors among all proper colorings of G. The minimum number of colors used in a coloring with the minimum sum of colors is called the *strength*, $s(G)$, of G (note that $s(G) \geq \chi(G)$).

The concept of chromatic sum was introduced independently by Kubicka [13] and Supowit [19]. Chromatic sum problem has many important applications in scheduling ([2]), VLSI routing ([19]),... Thus, a lot of authors were interested in this parameter. In [14], Kubicka and Schwenk proved the NP-completeness of the chromatic sum problem. Then the problem was studied for restricted families of graphs. Thus, in [14] authors gave a polynomial time algorithm to find the chromatic sum of trees. In [3], Bar-Noy and Kortsarz were interested in the minimum color sum problem for bipartite graphs. They proved that this problem admits no polynomial approximation scheme, unless $P = NP$, and they presented a 10/9-approximation algorithm. Jiang and West presented in [12] a method to construct for each integer $k \geq 1$, a tree T with $s(T) = k$ that has maximum degree $2k - 2$. In [8], Hajiabolhassan et *al.* proposed an upper bound for the strength of a graph G depending on the maximum degree of G and an invariant based on linear orderings of the vertices. More recently, Salavatipour [16] proved the NP-hardness of finding the strength for graphs with $\Delta(G) = 6$ and gave polynomial algorithms for the sum coloring of chain bipartite graphs and k-split graphs. In 2004, Nicoloso [15] showed an upper bound for the strength of any interval graph: $s(G) \leq \min\{n, 2\chi(G) - 1\}$. And in 2005, Effantin and Kheddouci [5] studied the chromatic sum for several classes of distance and circulant graphs.

This coloring initiated several studies because its fields of application are vast like network environments where the chromatic sum can be used to minimize (or to limit) the total charge of the network. Thus, in this article, we propose a self-stabilizing algorithm to compute a minimal color sum in a proper coloring of a graph. A self-stabilizing approach enables to make the system entirely autonomous. The idea is to minimize locally the sum of colors of a node and its neighbors. Thus, we define a *local coloring* of a node i as the coloring of i and its neighborhood $N(i)$. We let $d(i) = |N(i)|$, the number of neighbors of vertex i, or its *degree*, and we let $\Delta = \max\{d(i) | i \in V\}$. Note that $\mathcal{C}(S)$ defines the set of colors of the vertex set S.

2 Algorithm

In a self-stabilizing algorithm, a node can change its local state by making a *move*. In our work, a move represents the color change of a node. In the algorithm, a *privileged* node is defined as a node able to move its color and that of its neighborhood. In our approach, we consider a serial model where no two privileged nodes run simultaneously. A *central daemon* selects, among all privileged nodes, the next to consider. Thus, if several nodes are privileged, we cannot predict which node will be selected next. Moreover, we consider a synchronous model where every node executes the same action at the same time.

The principle of the algorithm is as follows. We consider the local coloring of a node i. Suppose that i has no color. What are the minimum colors of its neighbors, to keep a proper coloring ? Thus, we define for each node i, a table T_{new}^i of size at most Δ containing the smallest possible color of the node when each of its neighbor has no color (*i.e.* $T_{new}^i[j] = \min\{q|q \notin C(N(i)\backslash\{j\})\}$), for any $j \in N(i)$). Thus, $T_{new}^i[j]$ contains the color of the node i if the color of its neighbor j is not considered. Then, any node i will be able to evaluate a new coloring for it and its neighborhood (by considering the colors of $T_{new}^j[i]$ for its neighbors $j \in N(i)$). Consequently, we can compare the current local coloring of i with this possible new local coloring. If the color sum of this new local coloring of i is lower than the color sum of its current local coloring, then i becomes a privileged node and the current local coloring of i can be replaced by the new local coloring found.

We then propose a first procedure used by the main procedure to compute the table T_{new}^i. A particular case must be distinguished. Suppose that two (or more) neighbor nodes, j and j', are adjacent to the same node i. When j and j' compute their tables T_{new}^j and $T_{new}^{j'}$, they may find a same color for $T_{new}^j[i]$ and $T_{new}^{j'}[i]$ (which can bring a non proper color). To keep a proper coloring, only one of them will be able to compute $T_{new}[i]$ (that with the highest color).

Procedure 1. *FindNewColors() (applied on the node i)*
BEGIN
Let $L = \bigcup_{j \in N(i)} c(j)$.
Let $c = \min\{q|q \notin L\}$.
For all $j \in N(i)$ **do**
    if there exists a node k adjacent to i and j such that $c(k) > c(i)$ **then**
    //i.e. to find a new color for $T_{new}^i[j]$ and to avoid a non proper coloring,
    //i must not be adjacent to a neighbor of j with a highest color.
        $T_{new}^i[j] = c(i)$.
    else
    //else $T_{new}^i[j]$ takes the smallest possible value.
        if $c(j) > c$ **then** $T_{new}^i[j] = c$. **else** $T_{new}^i[j] = c(j)$. **endif.**
    endif.
endfor.
END.

Proposition 1. *For a node i, the table T_{new}^i is computed in time $O(\Delta^2)$.*

Proof. Since the node i has at most Δ neighbors, the data L and c are computed in time $O(\Delta)$. Then, for every neighbor of i, the determination if it is adjacent to another neighbor of i can be done in $O(\Delta)$ and a new color is determined in $O(1)$. Therefore the time needed is $O(\Delta^2)$. $\qquad\square$

Next, we can present the main procedure. This procedure runs continuously on each node to detect any perturbation of the system. When a node i executes the following procedure, we distinguish three steps. The first step is the computation of its table T_{new}^i (done by Procedure 1). The second step is the evaluation of the color sums of the current and the new local colorings. Finally the third step is the affectation of the new coloring if i is the privileged nodes elected by the central daemon. Nevertheless, since the first condition to have a legitimate state is the property of the coloring, a step 0 is proposed to verify this property. Thus, during the first execution of the procedure, this step enables to find a proper coloring of the graph (if it is not) and for the others, this step maintains a proper coloring (although the Procedure 1 generates only proper colorings).

Procedure 2. *(applied on the node i)*
BEGIN
//step 0: verify the property of the coloring
if $c(i) \neq \min\{q \geq 1 | q \notin \mathcal{C}(N(i))\}$ **then** $c(i) \neq \min\{q \geq 1 | q \notin \mathcal{C}(N(i))\}$.**endif.**
//step 1: compute a new possible coloring
$FindNewColors()$.
//step 2: compare the current coloring with the possible coloring found
Let $Q = \min\{q | \forall j \in N(i), q \notin T_{new}^j[i]\}$.
Let $\Sigma_{current} = c(i) + \sum_{j \in N(i)} c(j)$.
Let $\Sigma_{new} = Q + \sum_{j \in N(i)} T_{new}^j[i]$.
//step 3: determine the privileged nodes
if $\Sigma_{new} < \Sigma_{current}$ **then**
    i becomes privileged.
endif.
if i is the privileged node elected by the central daemon **then**
    $c(i) = Q$.
    $\forall j \in N(i), c(j) = T_{new}^j[i]$.
endif.
END.

The last action (where neighbors of i get new colors) can be done by a sending of a message to inform these nodes to change their color. Then, the procedure can start again when this step is done.

Now, we study this algorithm to determine if it self-stabilizes. Firstly, we can see that the algorithm gives a legitimate state for the graph.

Proposition 2. *Procedure 2 gives a legitimate state for the graph.*

Proof. A legitimate state consists in a proper coloring where we search to decrease the sum of colors. The step 0 of the Procedure 2 gives a proper coloring.

Thus Procedure 1 is applied only on a proper coloring. Moreover, in the Procedure 1, for two neighbors adjacent to a same node, only one can change its color (to maintain the property of the coloring). Nevertheless, while the local coloring of a node i can be decreased, i becomes privileged and the central daemon selects only one privileged node to change its local coloring. The final coloring is then a legitimate state for the graph. □

Secondly, we bound the number of privileged nodes that can appear.

Lemma 1. *At most $n\Delta$ privileged nodes can be selected by the central daemon.*

Proof. If every node was colored with the smallest color (*i.e.* 1), then the color sum would be n. By the same way, if every node was colored with the highest color (*i.e.* $\Delta+1$), the color sum would be $n\Delta+n$. Moreover, to have a privileged node i, the color sum of the new local coloring of i must be strictly lower than that of its current local coloring. Thus, for each privileged node, the total sum of colors decreases by at least 1. Thus, at most $(n\Delta + n) - n = n\Delta$ privileged nodes change their local coloring. □

Thus, we can evaluate the time and the number of moves used by the algorithm.

Theorem 1. *A legitimate state is reached in $O(n\Delta^2)$ moves.*

Proof. If a privileged node changes its local coloring, it can modify the coloring of at most $\Delta + 1$ nodes. By Lemma 1, at most $n\Delta$ privileged nodes are selected by the central daemon, which implies $O(n\Delta^2)$ changes of colors. □

Theorem 2. *A minimal sum of colors of the graph is computed in time $O(n\Delta^3)$.*

Proof. In Procedure 2, the step 0 (to have a proper coloring) is done in time $O(\Delta)$, while the computation of new local coloring (step 1) is proved in time $O(\Delta^2)$ (Proposition 1). Since the computation is synchronous, all the nodes have executed Procedure 1 before running the remaining of the Procedure 2. Thus, the step 2 is done in time $O(\Delta)$, and since the algorithm is distributed, the color change of a node and its neighborhood can be done in $O(1)$ (step 3). Thus, for each node elected by the central daemon, a new local coloring is found in time $O(\Delta^2)$. By Lemma 1, there are at most $n\Delta$ privileged nodes selected by the central daemon. Thus, the algorithm converges in time $O(n\Delta^3)$. □

Thus, the algorithm determines a legitimate state for G in a finite number of moves without external intervention. It is a self-stabilizing algorithm.

3   Conclusion

The color sum given by this algorithm is an upper bound for the chromatic sum. As we saw, we use a serial model where only one privileged node is selected at the same time. It is possible for the central daemon to choose several privileged nodes to be computed in parallel, but to avoid a non proper coloring, two selected nodes must be at distance at least 4 in the graph. Thus, two neighbors of two distinct privileged nodes are not neighbors. The color change of these nodes then enables to keep the coloring proper.

References

1. Antonoiu, G., Srimani, P.K.: A self-stabilizing distributed algorithm for minimal spanning tree problem in a symmetric graph. Computer & Mathematics with Application 35(10), 15–23 (1998)
2. Bar-Noy, A., Bellare, M., Halldórsson, M., Shashnai, H., Tamir, T.: On Chromatic Sums and Distributed Resource Allocation. Information and Computation 140, 183–202 (1998)
3. Bar-Noy, A., Kortsarz, G.: Minimum color sum of bipartite graphs. Journal of Algorithms 28(2), 339–365 (1998)
4. Dijkstra, E.W.: Self-stabilizing systems in spite of distributed control. Communications of ACM 17(11), 643–644 (1974)
5. Effantin, B., Kheddouci, H.: Sum coloring of distance and circulant graphs. In: 7th International Colloquium on Graph Theory. Electronic Notes in Discrete Mathematics, vol. 22, pp. 239–244 (2005)
6. Ghosh, S., Karaata, M.H.: A self-stabilizing algorithm for coloring planar graph. Distributed Compututing 7(1), 55–59 (1993)
7. Gradinariu, M., Tixeuil, S.: Self-stabilizing vertex coloring of arbitrary graphs. In: OPODIS 2000. Proceedings of the International Conference on Principles of Distributed Systems, pp. 55–70 (2000)
8. Hajiabolhassan, H., Mehrabadi, M.L., Tusserkani, R.: Minimal Coloring and Strength of Graphs. Discrete Mathematics 215(1-3), 265–270 (2000)
9. Hedetniemi, S.T., Jacobs, D.P., Srimani, P.K.: Linear time self-stabilizing colorings. Information Processing Letters 87, 251–255 (2003)
10. Hsi, S-C., Huang, S-T.: A self-stabilizing algorithm for maximal matching. Information Processing Letters 43(2), 77–81 (1992)
11. Huang, S.-T., Hung, S.-S., Tzeng, C.-H.: Self-stabilizing coloration in anonymous planar networks. Information Processing Letters 95, 307–312 (2005)
12. Jiang, T., West, D.B.: Coloring of Trees with Minimum Sum of Colors. Journal of Graph Theory 32, 354–358 (1999)
13. Kubicka, E.: The chromatic sum of a graph, Ph.D. Dissertation. Western Michigan University, Kalamazoo, MI (1989)
14. Kubicka, E., Schwenk, A.J.: An introduction to chromatic sums. In: Proceedings of the seventeenth annual ACM conference on Computer science, pp. 39–45 (1989)
15. Nicoloso, S.: Sum coloring and interval graphs: A tight upper bound for the minimum number of colors. Discrete Mathematics 280, 251–257 (2004)
16. Salavatipour, M.: On Sum Coloring of Graphs. Discrete Applied Mathematics 127(3), 477–488 (2003)
17. Shi, Z., Goddard, W., Hedetniemi, S.T.: An anonymous self-stabilizing algorithm for 1-maximal independant set in trees. Information Processing Letters 91, 77–83 (2004)
18. Shukla, S., Rosenkrantz, D., Ravi, S.: Development self-stabilizing coloring algorithms via systematic randomization. In: Proceedings of the International Workshop on Parallel Processing, pp. 668–673 (1994)
19. Supowit, K.J.: Finding a maximum planar subset of nets in a channel. IEEE Transactions on Computer Aided Design 6(1), 93–94 (1987)
20. Sur, S., Srimani, P.K.: A self-stabilizing algorithm for coloring bipartite graphs. Information Science 69, 219–227 (1993)

Global Fixed-Priority Scheduling of Arbitrary-Deadline Sporadic Task Systems[*]

Sanjay Baruah[1] and Nathan Fisher[2]

[1] The University of North Carolina at Chapel Hill
baruah@cs.unc.edu
[2] Wayne State University
fishern@cs.wayne.edu

Abstract. Fixed Task Priority (FTP) scheduling algorithms are priority-driven scheduling algorithms in which all jobs generated by each recurrent task are restricted to have the same priority. The multiprocessor FTP scheduling of sporadic task systems is studied in this paper. A new sufficient schedulability test is presented and proved correct. It is shown that this test offers non-trivial quantitative guarantees, including a processor speedup bound.

1 Introduction

A real-time system is often modelled as a finite collection of independent recurring tasks, each of which generates a potentially infinite sequence of *jobs*. Every job is characterized by an arrival time, an execution requirement, and a deadline, and it is required that a job complete execution between its arrival time and its deadline. Different formal models for recurring tasks place different restrictions on the values of the parameters of jobs generated by each task. One of the more commonly used formal models is the *sporadic task model* [15,6], which is described in Section 2.

In this paper, we consider real-time systems that are modeled by the sporadic task model and implemented upon a platform comprised of several identical processors. We assume that the platform

- is fully *preemptive*: an executing job may be interrupted at any instant in time and have its execution resumed later with no cost or penalty.
- allows for *global* inter-processor migration: a job may begin execution on any processor and a preempted job may resume execution on the same processor as, or a different processor from, the one it had been executing on prior to preemption.
- forbids *intra-task parallelism*: each task may have at most one job executing on at most one processor at each instant in time, regardless of how many jobs of the task are awaiting execution and how many processors are idle.

---

[*] Supported in part by NSF Grant Nos. CNS-0408996, CCF-0541056, and CCR-0615197, ARO Grant No. W911NF-06-1-0425, and funding from the Intel Corporation.

S. Rao et al. (Eds.): ICDCN 2008, LNCS 4904, pp. 215–226, 2008.

We study the behavior of a particular class of scheduling algorithms, known as *Fixed Task Priority* (FTP) scheduling algorithms [3] when scheduling systems of sporadic tasks upon such preemptive platforms. We discuss FTP scheduling algorithms in greater detail in Section 2; due to various pragmatic considerations, FTP scheduling algorithms are widely favored by real-time systems designers.

Our results, and their significance. First, we present, and prove the correctness of, a new test for determining whether a given sporadic task system is guaranteed to meet all deadlines upon a specified computing platform, when scheduled using a specified FTP scheduling algorithm. Next, we demonstrate that the *Deadline Monotonic* FTP scheduling algorithm is optimal from the perspective of this test: if a task system is deemed by this test to meet all deadlines for any FTP scheduling algorithm, then the Deadline Monotonic scheduling algorithm is also deemed to meet all deadlines. Furthermore, we provide several different quantitative characterizations of the performance of this test; for instance, we show that any sporadic task system that is feasible (i.e., can be scheduled using an optimal clairvoyant algorithm) is identified by our test as being scheduled to meet all deadlines by the Deadline Monotonic algorithm upon a platform in which each processor is approximately four times as fast.

Previous tests for determining whether sporadic task systems can be successfully scheduled using FTP scheduling algorithms have only been applicable to task systems in which every sporadic task generates a job after the deadline of its previous job has elapsed (such task systems are called constrained-deadline task systems – see Section 2). Since, as stated above, our machine model forbids the simultaneous execution of multiple jobs of the same task, getting rid of this restriction turns out to be surprisingly challenging. We believe that one of the major contributions of the research presented in this paper is a general technique for dealing with task systems that do not observe this restriction, thereby enabling the analysis of the behavior of scheduling algorithms on sporadic task systems that are not constrained-deadline.

Organization. The remainder of this paper is organized as follows. In Section 2, we formally define the task and processor models used in this research, and provide some additional useful definitions. In Section 3, we briefly describe some related research. In Section 4, we derive some technical results that are used in later sections. In Section 5, we present, and prove the correctness of, a new schedulability test for FTP scheduling. In Section 6, we apply this test to the well-known Deadline Monotonic [13] FTP priority assignment scheme. In Section 7, we provide a quantitative characterization of the efficacy of this new schedulability test for Deadline Monotonic priority assignment.

2   Model and Definitions

§1. *Task model.* A sporadic task $\tau_i = (C_i, D_i, T_i)$ is characterized by a *worst-case execution requirement* C_i, a *(relative) deadline* D_i, and a *minimum inter-arrival separation* parameter T_i, also referred to as the *period* of the task. Such a sporadic task generates a potentially infinite sequence of jobs, with successive job-arrivals separated by at least T_i time units. Each job has a worst-case execution requirement equal to C_i and a deadline that occurs D_i time units after its arrival time. We refer to the interval, of size D_i, between a job's arrival instant and deadline as its *scheduling window*. A *sporadic task system* is comprised of several such independent sporadic tasks. Task system τ is said to be an *implicit-deadline* sporadic task system if it is guaranteed that each task has its relative deadline parameter equal to its period, and a *constrained-deadline* sporadic task system if it is guaranteed that it has its relative deadline parameter no larger than its period. A task system that may not be constrained-deadline is said to be an *arbitrary-deadline* sporadic task system.

Throughout this paper, τ denotes an arbitrary-deadline sporadic task system comprised of n tasks: $\tau = \{\tau_1, \tau_2, \dots \tau_n\}$, with $\tau_i = (C_i, D_i, T_i)$ for all $i, 1 \leq i \leq n$.

§2. Processor model. In this paper, we study the scheduling of sporadic task systems upon a platform comprised of m identical processors, where m is an integer ≥ 1. For the most part (except, e.g., in Lemmas 4 and 5), we assume that all processors are of unit computing capacity: a job completes one unit of execution by executing upon a processor for one unit of time. We assume that the platform is fully *preemptive*, and allows for *global* inter-processor migration. However, each task may have at most one job executing on at most one processor at each instant in time.

§3. Fixed Task Priority (FTP) scheduling. Priority-driven scheduling algorithms operate as follows: at each instant in time they assign a priority to each job that is awaiting execution, and choose for execution the jobs with the greatest priority. *Fixed Task Priority (FTP)* scheduling algorithms are a subclass of the class of priority-driven algorithms for scheduling systems of recurring tasks, in which it is required that *there is a unique priority associated with each task, and all the jobs generated by the task are assigned this priority.* The *Deadline Monotonic* (DM) scheduling algorithm [13] is an example of a FTP scheduling algorithm. The DM scheduling algorithm assigns priority to jobs according to the relative-deadline parameter of the task that generates them: the smaller the relative deadline, the greater the priority. On the other hand, the Earliest Deadline First scheduling algorithm [14,9] is not an FTP algorithm, since different jobs generated by the same task generally have different priorities.

We adopt the convention of representing task priorities by positive integers, with lower numbers denoting greater priority. Under this convention, a FTP scheduling algorithm on a given sporadic task system τ is completely specified by specifying the *priority assignment* on τ:

Definition 1 (priority assignment). *A priority assignment $\pi : \{1, 2, \dots, n\} \rightarrow \{1, 2, \dots, n\}$ is a one-one function denoting which task is assigned what priority, with the interpretation that task $\tau_{\pi(i)}$ is assigned priority i.*   □

As stated above, deadline monotonic priority assignment assigns priorities in inverse order of the relative deadline parameter: the smaller the relative deadline parameter, the greater the priority (with ties broken arbitrarily). We will abuse notation somewhat, and let DM denote both the deadline monotonic scheduling algorithm, and the deadline monotonic priority assignment on τ: $i < j \Rightarrow$ $D_{DM(i)} \leq D_{DM(j)}$.

§4. *Processor speedup bounds.* A given sporadic task system is said to be *feasible* upon a particular platform if there exists a schedule meeting all deadlines, for every collection of jobs that may be generated by the task system. A given sporadic task system is said to be *(global) π-schedulable* if FTP scheduling of the task system with priority assignment π meets all deadlines for every collection of jobs that may be generated by the task system. A *schedulability test* for a priority assignment π determines whether the given system is π-schedulable. Such a test is *exact* if is correctly identifies all π schedulable systems, and *sufficient* if it identifies some, but not necessarily all, π-schedulable systems (however, it must not incorrectly declare some non π-schedulable system to be π schedulable).

Processor speedup bounds are one metric that may be used for quantifying the quality of sufficient schedulability tests. A sufficient schedulability test is said to have a processor speedup bound of c ($c \geq 1$) if

- Any task system deemed schedulable by the test is guaranteed to actually be so; and
- For any task system that is not deemed schedulable by the test, it is the case that the task system is actually not schedulable upon a platform in which each processor is $\frac{1}{c}$ times as fast.

Intuitively speaking, a processor speedup bound of c for a sufficient schedulability test implies that the inexactness of the test penalizes its user by at most a speedup factor of c when compared to an exact test. The smaller the processor speedup bound, the better the sufficient schedulability test: a processor speedup bound of 1 would mean that the test is in fact an exact one.

3   Related Work

FTP scheduling is widely used in real-time systems design and implementation. A comprehensive design methodology — the *Rate-Monotonic Analysis* (RMA) Methodology [12] — that is based upon FTP scheduling upon uniprocessor platforms has been developed. It has been shown [13] that the Deadline Monotonic priority assignment (DM) is optimal for constrained-deadline sporadic task systems upon uniprocessors: if any FTP scheduling algorithm guarantees to meet all deadlines for such a task system, then so can DM.

Upon multiprocessors, FTP scheduling of implicit-deadline sporadic task systems has been studied in [1]. The FTP scheduling of constrained-deadline sporadic task systems using Deadline Monotonic (DM) priorities was studied in [2,7], and the results obtained were subsequently extended to arbitrary-deadline task systems in [4].

In [11], a sufficient test very different from the ones in [2,7,4] was derived for determining whether a given constrained-deadline sporadic task system is deadline monotonic schedulable upon a preemptive multiprocessor platform comprised of m unit-capacity processors. Unlike the tests in [2,7,4], the test in [11] comes with an associated processor speedup bound. *One of the results in this paper is to demonstrate that this speedup bound holds for the more general arbitrary-deadline sporadic task model as well.*

4   Some Task and System Properties

For any sporadic task $\tau_i = (C_i, D_i, T_i)$, the **density** δ_i of task τ_i denotes the ratio $(C_i / \min(D_i, T_i))$ of its execution requirement to the smaller of its relative deadline and its period.

For any priority assignment π and any integer k, $1 \leq k \leq n$, $\delta_{\max}(\pi, k)$ and $D_{\max}(\pi, k)$ denote the **largest density** and the **largest relative deadline** from among the k highest-priority tasks in τ:

$$D_{\max}(\pi, k) \overset{\text{def}}{=} \overset{k}{\underset{j=1}{\max}}(D_{\pi(j)}); \quad \delta_{\max}(\pi, k) \overset{\text{def}}{=} \overset{k}{\underset{j=1}{\max}}(\delta_{\pi(j)})$$

The concepts of *demand bound function* and *load* find widespread use in real-time schedulability analysis. We provide formal definitions below; for further detail, consult, e.g., [8].

Definition 2 (DBF). *For any interval length t, the* **demand bound function** DBF(τ_i, t) *of a sporadic task τ_i bounds the maximum cumulative execution requirement by jobs of τ_i that both arrive in, and have deadlines within, any interval of length t.* □

It has been shown [6] that $\text{DBF}(\tau_i, t) = \max\left(0, \left(\left\lfloor \frac{t - D_i}{T_i} \right\rfloor + 1\right) C_i\right)$.

Definition 3 (load). *For any priority assignment π and any k, a* **load** *parameter is defined as follows:*

$$\text{LOAD}(\pi, k) \overset{\text{def}}{=} \underset{t>0}{\max}\left(\frac{\sum_{j=1}^{k} \text{DBF}(\tau_{\pi(j)}, t)}{t}\right)$$

□

Efficient algorithms have been designed for computing LOAD both exactly in pseudo-polynomial time, and approximately to any arbitrary desired degree of accuracy in polynomial time — see, e.g., [5,10].

In constrained-deadline task systems — those in which $D_i \leq T_i \ \forall i$ — a job becomes eligible to execute upon arrival, and remains eligible until it completes execution[1]. In systems with $D_i > T_i$ for some tasks τ_i, we require that at most

---

[1] Or its deadline has elapsed, in which case the system is deemed to have failed.

one job of each task be eligible to execute at each time instant. We assume that jobs of the same task are considered in order of arrival; hence, a job only becomes eligible to execute after both these conditions are satisfied: *(i)* it has arrived, and *(ii)* all previous jobs generated by the same task that generated it have completed execution. This gives rise to the notion of an active task: briefly, a task is active at some instant if it has some eligible job awaiting execution at that instant. More formally,

Definition 4 (active task). *A task is said to be* active *in a given schedule at a time-instant t if some job of the task is eligible to execute at time-instant t. That is,* (i) *t ≥ the greater of the job's arrival time and the completion time of the previous job of the same task, and* (ii) *the job has not completed execution prior to time-instant t.*   □

The following Lemma relating density and DBF will be used later in this paper.

Lemma 1. *For all tasks τ_i and for all $t \geq 0$, $t \times \delta_i \geq \mathrm{DBF}(\tau_i, t)$.*

Proof Sketch: This lemma is easily validated informally by sketching $\mathrm{DBF}(\tau_i, t)$ as a function of t, and comparing this with the graph for $t \times \delta_i$, a straight line of slope $(C_i / \min(D_i, T_i))$ through the origin. $\mathrm{DBF}(\tau_i, t)$ is a step function comprised of steps of height C_i, with the first step at $t = D_i$ and successive steps exactly T_i time units apart. The graph of δ_i lies above the plot for $\mathrm{DBF}(\tau_i, t)$, for all t. (For $D_i < T_i$, the graph for δ_i touches the plot for $\mathrm{DBF}(\tau_i, t)$ at $t = D_i$; for $D_i = T_i$, the two touch at all integer multiples of T_i; and for $D_i > T_i$ the two plots never touch.)   □

Recall that $D_{\max}(\pi, k)$, $\delta_{\max}(\pi, k)$ and $\mathrm{LOAD}(\pi, k)$ respectively denote the largest relative deadline, largest density, and maximum possible normalized cumulative execution requirement, of the k highest-priority tasks. Not surprisingly, therefore, they are all monotonically non-decreasing with the number of tasks considered; this is formally asserted by the following lemma.

Lemma 2. *For a given priority assignment π, $D_{\max}(\pi, k)$, $\delta_{\max}(\pi, k)$ and $\mathrm{LOAD}(\pi, k)$ are all monotonically non-decreasing in k:*

$$D_{\max}(\pi, k) \leq D_{\max}(\pi, k+1) \bigwedge \delta_{\max}(\pi, k) \leq \delta_{\max}(\pi, k+1) \bigwedge \mathrm{LOAD}(\pi, k) \leq \mathrm{LOAD}(\pi, k+1)$$
$$(1)$$
□

5   An FTP Schedulability Test

In this section, we derive (Theorem 1) a sufficient schedulability test for the FTP scheduling of arbitrary-deadline sporadic task systems upon multiprocessors. As can be seen from the statement of Theorem 1, this test determines schedulability of a task system τ under a priority assignment π based upon the values of the densities, relative deadlines, and loads of τ.

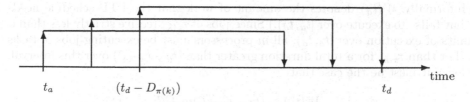

Fig. 1. Example: defining t_a for the case $D_{\pi(k)} \geq T_{\pi(k)}$. Three jobs of $\tau_{\pi(k)}$ are shown. Task τ_k is not active prior to the arrival of the first of these 3 jobs, the first job completes execution only after the second job arrives, and the second job completes execution only after the third job arrives. Thus, the task is continuously active after the arrival of the first job shown, and t_a is hence set equal to the arrival time of this job.

Let $\tau = \{\tau_1, \tau_2, \ldots, \tau_n\}$ denote a collection of sporadic tasks, to which priorities have been assigned according to the FTP priority-assignment scheme π. Consider any legal sequence of jobs of task system τ, on which a deadline miss occurs. Suppose that a job of the k'th-highest priority task — i.e., a job of task $\tau_{\pi(k)}$ — is the one to first miss a deadline, and that this deadline miss occurs at time-instant t_d. Discard from this sequence of jobs all those jobs that have priority lower than $\tau_{\pi(k)}$'s priority. Consider the FTP schedule of this new – "reduced"– sequence of jobs. Since jobs of priority lower than $\tau_{\pi(k)}$'s have no effect whatsoever on the scheduling of jobs of priority $\geq \tau_{\pi(k)}$'s, this schedule, too, will see a deadline miss of a job of $\tau_{\pi(k)}$ at time-instant t_d, and this will be the first deadline miss in the schedule. *Henceforth in this section, we will consider this FTP schedule of the reduced sequence of jobs.*

Let t_a denote the earliest time-instant prior to t_d, such that $\tau_{\pi(k)}$ is active[2] throughout the interval $[t_a, t_d]$. We can make the following assertions about t_a:

- t_a is the arrival time of some job of $\tau_{\pi(k)}$.
- $t_a \leq t_d - D_{\pi(k)}$. This follows from the observation that the job of $\tau_{\pi(k)}$ that misses its deadline at t_d arrives at $t_d - D_{\pi(k)}$. If $D_{\pi(k)} < T_{\pi(k)}$, then t_a is equal to this arrival time of the job of $\tau_{\pi(k)}$ that misses its deadline at t_d. If $D_{\pi(k)} \geq T_{\pi(k)}$, however, t_a may be the arrival-time of an earlier job of $\tau_{\pi(k)}$— see Figure 1. In either case, we have

$$t_d - t_a \geq D_{\pi(k)}. \tag{2}$$

- Let $\mathcal{C}$ denote the cumulative execution requirement of all jobs of $\tau_{\pi(k)}$ that arrive $\geq t_a$, and have deadline $\leq t_d$. (In the example of Figure 1, $\mathcal{C} = 3C_{\pi(k)}$.) By definition of DBF and Lemma 1, we have

$$\mathcal{C} \leq \text{DBF}(\tau_{\pi(k)}, t_d - t_a) \leq \delta_{\pi(k)} \times (t_d - t_a). \tag{3}$$

Let $W(t_a)$ denote the total amount that all jobs, other than those generated by task $\tau_{\pi(k)}$, that have deadline $\leq t_d$ execute over the interval $[t_a, t_d)$, plus $\underline{\mathcal{C}}$.

---

[2] See Definition 4 to recall the definition of *active task*.

(Informally, $W(t_a)$ denotes the amount of work that the FTP schedule needs –but fails– to execute over $[t_a, t_d)$.) Since jobs of $\tau_{\pi(k)}$ receive strictly less than C units of execution over $[t_a, t_d)$, all m processors must be executing jobs of tasks other than $\tau_{\pi(k)}$ for a total duration greater than $(t_d - t_a - C)$ over this interval. Hence it must be the case that

$$W(t_a) > (t_d - t_a - C)m + C \tag{4}$$

Since all this work is to execute over $[t_a, t_d)$, all the jobs contributing to it must have scheduling windows that overlap with $[t_a, t_d)$. In order for these scheduling windows to overlap with $[t_a, t_d)$, all such jobs must arrive no earlier than $D_{\max}(\pi, k)$ time units prior to t_a (i.e., after $t_a - D_{\max}(\pi, k)$), and have their deadlines no later than $D_{\max}(\pi, k)$ time units after t_d (i.e., before $t_d + D_{\max}(\pi, k)$). In other words, all these jobs have their arrival times and deadlines within the $(2D_{\max}(\pi, k) + (t_d - t_a))$-sized interval $[t_a - D_{\max}(\pi, k), t_d + D_{\max}(\pi, k))$. By definition of LOAD, we therefore have

$$W(t_a) \leq (t_d - t_a + 2D_{\max}(\pi, k)) \times \text{LOAD}(\pi, k)$$
$$\Rightarrow \text{(By Inequality 4)} \ (t_d - t_a - C)m + C < (t_d - t_a + 2D_{\max}(\pi, k)) \times \text{LOAD}(\pi, k)$$
$$\equiv m(t_d - t_a) - (m-1)C < (t_d - t_a + 2D_{\max}(\pi, k)) \times \text{LOAD}(\pi, k)$$
$$\equiv m - (m-1)\frac{C}{t_d - t_a} < \left(1 + 2\frac{D_{\max}(\pi, k)}{t_d - t_a}\right) \times \text{LOAD}(\pi, k)$$
$$\Rightarrow \text{(By Inequality 3)} \ m - (m-1)\delta_{\pi(k)} < \left(1 + 2\frac{D_{\max}(\pi, k)}{t_d - t_a}\right) \times \text{LOAD}(\pi, k)$$
$$\Rightarrow \text{(By Inequality 2)} \ m - (m-1)\delta_{\pi(k)} < \left(1 + 2\frac{D_{\max}(\pi, k)}{D_{\pi(k)}}\right) \times \text{LOAD}(\pi, k) \tag{5}$$

Thus, we see that Condition 5 is necessary for a deadline miss to occur; equivalently, the negation of Condition 5 is sufficient for all deadlines to be met:

Theorem 1. *A sufficient condition for arbitrary-deadline sporadic task system $\{\tau_1, \tau_2, \ldots, \tau_n\}$ to be global FTP schedulable under priority assignment π is*

$$\forall k : 1 \leq k \leq n : \left[\text{LOAD}(\pi, k) \leq \frac{m - (m-1)\delta_{\pi(k)}}{1 + 2(D_{\max}(\pi, k)/D_{\pi(k)})}\right] \qquad \square$$

The following corollary immediately follows, based on the trivial observation that $\delta_{\pi(k)}$ is, by definition, $\leq \delta_{\max}(\pi, k)$:

Corollary 1. *A sufficient condition for arbitrary-deadline sporadic task system $\{\tau_1, \tau_2, \ldots, \tau_n\}$ to be global FTP schedulable under priority assignment π is*

$$\forall k \ : \ 1 \leq k \leq n \ : \ \left(\text{LOAD}(\pi, k) \leq \frac{m - (m-1)\delta_{\max}(\pi, k)}{1 + 2(D_{\max}(\pi, k)/D_{\pi(k)})}\right) \tag{6}$$

$$\square$$

6   The Optimality of DM

We now prove that any sporadic task system deemed schedulable for some FTP priority assignment scheme by the test of Corollary 1, is also deemed schedulable for the DM priority assignment scheme by the test of Corollary 1.

Let π_1 denote a priority assignment such that τ with priority assignment π_1 is deemed schedulable by the schedulability test of Corollary 1, in which the tasks at the ℓ'th and $(\ell + 1)$'th priorities are not in deadline-monotonic order, i.e.. $D_{\pi_1(\ell)} > D_{\pi_1(\ell+1)})$. We will demonstrate that the priority assignment obtained from π_1 by swapping the priorities of these two tasks is also deemed schedulable by the schedulability test of Corollary 1.

Lemma 3. *Let π_1 denote a priority assignment such that τ with priority assignment π_1 is deemed schedulable by the schedulability test of Corollary 1, in which $D_{\pi_1(\ell)} > D_{\pi_1(\ell+1)}$. Let π_2 denote a priority assignment identical to π_1, except that the tasks at the ℓ'th and $(\ell + 1)$'th priority levels are swapped. Task system τ with priority assignment π_2 is also deemed schedulable by the test of Corollary 1.*

Proof: Let $\pi_1(\ell) = a$ and $\pi_1(\ell + 1) = b$. It is readily verified that for $k = 1, 2, \ldots, \ell - 1$, and for $k = \ell + 2, \ldots, n$, Equation 6 evaluates identically for $\pi \leftarrow \pi_1$ and for $\pi \leftarrow \pi_2$. Below, we show that if Equation 6 is satisfied for $k = \ell$ and $k = \ell + 1$ for $\pi \leftarrow \pi_1$, then it is satisfied for $k = \ell$ and $k = \ell + 1$ for $\pi \leftarrow \pi_2$ as well.

Suppose that Equation 6 is satisfied for $k = \ell$ and $k = \ell + 1$ for $\pi \leftarrow \pi_1$.

- To see that Equation 6 is satisfied for $\pi \leftarrow \pi_2$ for $k = \ell$, consider task τ_b, which is the task at priority level ℓ in π_2. Observe that
    1. $\text{LOAD}(\pi_2, \ell + 1) = \text{LOAD}(\pi_1, \ell + 1)$, since both loads are computed over exactly the same set of tasks.
    2. By Lemma 2, $\text{LOAD}(\pi_2, \ell) \leq \text{LOAD}(\pi_2, \ell + 1)$.
    These two facts together yield the fact that $\text{LOAD}(\pi_2, \ell) \leq \text{LOAD}(\pi_1, \ell+1)$. By a similar argument, it can be shown that $D_{\max}(\pi_2, \ell) \leq D_{\max}(\pi_1, \ell + 1)$. Also, $\delta_{\max}(\pi_2, \ell) \leq \delta_{\max}(\pi_1, \ell + 1)$ and $D_{\pi_2(\ell)} = D_{\pi_1(\ell+1)}$. It immediately follows that since Equation 6 is satisfied for $k = (\ell + 1)$ for $\pi \leftarrow \pi_1$, it is satisfied for $k = \ell$ for $\pi \leftarrow \pi_2$.
- To see that Equation 6 is satisfied for $\pi \leftarrow \pi_2$ for $k = \ell + 1$, consider task τ_a, which is the task at priority level $(\ell + 1)$ in π_2. Observe that the set of $(\ell+1)$ highest-priority tasks in π_2 is equal to the set of $(\ell+1)$ highest-priority tasks in π_1. Hence, $\text{LOAD}(\pi_2, \ell + 1) = \text{LOAD}(\pi_1, \ell + 1)$. For the same reason, $D_{\max}(\pi_2, \ell + 1) = D_{\max}(\pi_1, \ell + 1)$, and $\delta_{\max}(\pi_2, \ell + 1) = \delta_{\max}(\pi_1, \ell + 1)$. However, $D_{\pi_2(\ell+1)} > D_{\pi_1(\ell+1)}$ by choice of ℓ and $\ell + 1$ as priorities violating deadline monotonic order. It follows that since Equation 6 is satisfied for $k = (\ell + 1)$ for $\pi \leftarrow \pi_1$, it is satisfied for $k = \ell + 1$ for $\pi \leftarrow \pi_2$.   □

Theorem 2 immediately follows, by repeated applications of Lemma 3:

Theorem 2. *Any task system that is deemed schedulable by the schedulability test of Corollary 1 for any priority assignment is also deemed schedulable for the DM priority assignment.*

7   A Processor Speedup Bound for DM

For the DM priority assignment, Corollary 1 may be specialized as follows:

Theorem 3. *Sporadic task system τ is global-DM schedulable upon a platform comprised of m unit-capacity processors, provided*

$$\text{LOAD}(\text{DM}, k) \leq \frac{1}{3}\left(m - (m-1)\delta_{\max}(\text{DM}, k)\right) \tag{7}$$

for all k, $1 \leq k \leq n$.

Proof Sketch: Immediately follows from the statement of Corollary 1, by observing that $D_{\max}(\text{DM}, k)$ is exactly equal to $D_{\text{DM}(k)}$ for all k, by very definition of deadline monotonic scheduling.   □

We will obtain a processor speedup result for the DM schedulability test of Theorem 3. But first, a lemma on *necessary* conditions for DM schedulability:

Lemma 4. *Any sporadic task system τ that is DM-schedulable upon a multiprocessor platform comprised of m speed-x processors must satisfy*

$$\delta_{\max}(\text{DM}, k) \leq x \quad \text{and} \quad \text{LOAD}(\text{DM}, k) \leq mx \tag{8}$$

for all k, $1 \leq k \leq n$.

Proof Sketch: Suppose that task system τ is DM-schedulable upon m speed-x processors. We first prove that $\delta_{\text{DM}(k)} \leq x$, for each task τ_i:

- In order to be able to meet all deadlines of τ_i if τ_i generates jobs exactly T_i time units apart, it is necessary that $C_i/T_i \leq x$.
- Since any individual job of τ_i can receive at most $D_i \times x$ units of execution by its deadline, we must have $C_i \leq D_i \times x$; i.e., $C_i/D_i \leq x$.

Putting both conditions together, we get $(C_i/\min(T_i, D_i)) \leq x$. Taken over all tasks in τ, this observation yields the condition that $\delta_{\max}(\text{DM}, k) \leq x$.

To prove that $\text{LOAD}(\text{DM}, k) \leq mx$, recall the definition of $\text{LOAD}(\text{DM}, k)$ from Section 1. Let t' denote some value of t which defines $\text{LOAD}(\text{DM}, k)$: $t' \stackrel{\text{def}}{=} \text{argmax}_{t>0}\left((\sum_{i=1}^{k}\text{DBF}(\tau_i, t))/t\right)$. Suppose that all tasks in $\{\tau_1, \tau_2, \ldots, \tau_k\}$ generate a job at time-instant zero, and each task τ_i generates subsequent jobs exactly T_i time-units apart. The total amount of execution that is available over the interval $[0, t')$ on this platform is equal to mxt'; hence, it is necessary that $\text{LOAD}(\text{DM}, k) \leq mx$ if all deadlines are to be met.   □

Using Theorem 3 and Lemma 4, we obtain below a bound on the processor speedup that is sufficient in order for the test of Theorem 3 to identify DM-schedulability:

Lemma 5. *Any sporadic task system that is feasible upon a multiprocessor platform comprised of m speed-x processors platform is determined to be global-DM schedulable on m unit-capacity processors by the DM-schedulability test of Theorem 3, provided*

$$x \leq \frac{m}{4m-1} \tag{9}$$

Proof: Suppose that τ is DM schedulable upon a platform comprised of m speed-x processors. From Lemma 4, it must be the case that $\text{LOAD}(\text{DM}, k) \leq mx$ and $\delta_{\text{DM}(k)} \leq x$. For τ to be determined to be DM-schedulable upon m unit-capacity processors by the test of Theorem 3, it is sufficient that:

$$\text{LOAD}(\text{DM}, k) \leq \frac{1}{3}(m - (m - 1)\delta_{\max}(\text{DM}, k))$$

$$\Leftarrow mx \leq \frac{1}{3}(m - (m - 1)x)$$

$$\equiv x \leq m/(4m - 1) \qquad \qquad \square$$

Lemma 5 above bounds from above the values of x such that task systems feasible on speed-x processors are correctly identified as being DM-schedulable by the test of Theorem 3. The processor speedup bound of Corollary 2 is obtained by taking the multiplicative inverse of this x:

Corollary 2. *The* DM-*schedulability test of Theorem 3 has a processor speedup bound of* $(4 - \frac{1}{m})$. $\qquad \qquad \square$

Corollary 2 expresses the processor speedup bound as a function of the number of processors m in the platform. The bound increases with increasing m, approaching 4 as $m \to \infty$.

We already know that global DM is not an optimal scheduling algorithm. It is also easy to show that the schedulability test of Theorem 3 is not optimal. The significance of this processor speedup result lies in what it tells us about the "goodness" of both global DM and of our schedulability test: in essence, it is asserting that a processor speedup of $(4 - \frac{1}{m})$ (which is always < 4) compensates for *both* the non-optimality of global DM *and* the inexactness of our schedulability test.

8   Conclusions

We have derived a new sufficient schedulability test for determining whether a given sporadic task system is FTP schedulable for a given priority assignment upon a preemptive multiprocessor platform, when global inter-processor migration is permitted. To our knowledge, this is the first non-trivial FTP schedulability test that may be be applied to the analysis of arbitrary-deadline sporadic task systems.

We have proved that the well-known Deadline Monotonic (DM) FTP priority assignment scheme is optimal from the perspective of our schedulability test. We have obtained a processor speedup bound for our test when applied to DM: This speedup bound of $(4 - \frac{1}{m})$ tells us that any arbitrary-deadline sporadic task system that is feasible upon a multiprocessor platform is correctly identified by our test as being DM-schedulable upon a platform in which each processor is no more than four times as fast.

References

1. Andersson, B., Baruah, S., Jansson, J.: Static-priority scheduling on multiprocessors. In: Proceedings of the IEEE Real-Time Systems Symposium, pp. 193–202. IEEE Computer Society Press, Los Alamitos (2001)
2. Baker, T.: Multiprocessor EDF and deadline monotonic schedulability analysis. In: Proceedings of the IEEE Real-Time Systems Symposium, pp. 120–129. IEEE Computer Society Press, Los Alamitos (2003)
3. Baker, T., Baruah, S.: Schedulability analysis of multiprocessor sporadic task systems. In: Son, S.H., Lee, I., Leung, J.Y.-T. (eds.) Handbook of Real-Time and Embedded Systems, Chapman Hall/ CRC Press (2007)
4. Baker, T.P.: An analysis of fixed-priority schedulability on a multiprocessor. Real-Time Systems: The International Journal of Time-Critical Computing 32(1-2), 49–71 (2006)
5. Baker, T.P., Fisher, N., Baruah, S.: Algorithms for determining the load of a sporadic task system. Tech. Rep. TR-051201, Department of Computer Science, Florida State University (2005)
6. Baruah, S., Mok, A., Rosier, L.: Preemptively scheduling hard-real-time sporadic tasks on one processor. In: Proceedings of the 11th Real-Time Systems Symposium, Orlando, Florida, pp. 182–190. IEEE Computer Society Press, Los Alamitos (1990)
7. Bertogna, M., Cirinei, M., Lipari, G.: New schedulability tests for real-time tasks sets scheduled by deadline monotonic on multiprocessors. In: Proceedings of the 9th International Conference on Principles of Distributed Systems, Pisa, Italy, December 2005, IEEE Computer Society Press, Los Alamitos (2005)
8. Buttazzo, G.C.: Hard Real-Time Computing Systems: Predictable Scheduling Algorithms and Applications, 2nd edn. (2005)
9. Dertouzos, M.: Control robotics: The procedural control of physical processors. In: Proceedings of the IFIP Congress, pp. 807–813 (1974)
10. Fisher, N., Baker, T., Baruah, S.: Algorithms for determining the demand-based load of a sporadic task system. In: Proceedings of the International Conference on Real-time Computing Systems and Applications, Sydney, Australia, August 2006, IEEE Computer Society Press, Los Alamitos (2006)
11. Fisher, N., Baruah, S.: Global static-priority scheduling of sporadic task systems on multiprocessor platforms. In: Proceeding of the IASTED International Conference on Parallel and Distributed Computing and Systems, Dallas, TX, November 2006 (2006)
12. Klein, M., Ralya, T., Pollak, B., Obenza, R., Harbour, M.G.: A Practitioner's Handbook for Real-Time Analysis: Guide to Rate Monotonic Analysis for Real-Time Systems. Kluwer Academic Publishers, Boston (1993)
13. Leung, J., Whitehead, J.: On the complexity of fixed-priority scheduling of periodic, real-time tasks. Performance Evaluation 2, 237–250 (1982)
14. Liu, C., Layland, J.: Scheduling algorithms for multiprogramming in a hard real-time environment. Journal of the ACM 20(1), 46–61 (1973)
15. Mok, A.K.: Fundamental Design Problems of Distributed Systems for The Hard-Real-Time Environment. PhD thesis, Laboratory for Computer Science, Massachusetts Institute of Technology, Available as Technical Report No. MIT/LCS/ TR-297 (1983)

Scalable and Distributed Mechanisms for Integrated Scheduling and Replication in Data Grids

Anirban Chakrabarti and Shubhashis Sengupta

Software Engineering and Technology Laboratory, Infosys Technologies Ltd.,
Bangalore 560 100, India
{anirban_chakrabarti, shubhashis_sengupta}@infosys.com

Abstract. Data Grids seek to harness geographically distributed resources for large-scale data-intensive problems. The issues that need to be considered in the Data Grid research area include resource management for computation and data. Computation management comprises scheduling of jobs, load balancing, fault tolerance and response time; while data management includes replication and movement of data at selected sites. As jobs are data intensive, data management issues often become integral to the problems of scheduling and effective resource management in the Data Grids. Therefore, integration of data replication and scheduling strategies is important. Such an integrating solution is either non-existent or work in a centralized manner which is not scalable. The paper deals with the problem of integrating the scheduling and replication strategies in a distributed manner. As part of the solution, we have proposed a Distributed Replication and Scheduling Strategy (DistReSS) which aims at an iterative improvement of the performance based on coupling between scheduling and replication, which is achieved in distributed and hierarchical fashion. Results suggest that, in the context of our experiments, DistReSS performs comparable to the centralized approach when the parameters are tuned properly in addition to being more scalable to the centralized approach.

Keywords: Data Grids, Scheduling, Replication, Clustering.

1 Introduction

Today's scientific as well as industrial world requires processing of vast amount of distributed data. Collaborative scientific experiments, in domains as diverse as global climate change high energy physics, and computational genomics generate petabytes of laboratory data [1]. Data management is also important in high volume and transaction-oriented enterprise application domains of Energy, Utilities, Finance and Retail, where large volume of data related to sales, customers and products reside in remote corporate data centers. Such data is routinely touched for transactional and analytic (data mining) purposes. The combination of large data sizes, geographic distribution of users and resources, diverse data sources, and computationally intensive analysis results in complex and stringent performance demands that are not satisfied by any existing data management infrastructure. A large scientific

S. Rao et al. (Eds.): ICDCN 2008, LNCS 4904, pp. 227–238, 2008.

collaboration may generate many queries that involve supercomputer-class computations on gigabytes or terabytes of data. Similarly, distributed analytical query for real-time enterprise would require complex materialized views and data cubes to be built and are very performance intensive [2]. The current research on Data Grid is motivated by these considerations, and effort is on to design and produce an integrated architecture of computer systems, storages and networks with advanced data discovery, transport and scheduling protocols in wide area, multi-institutional, heterogeneous environments. Efficient and reliable execution of queries in Data Grid requires proper placement and replication of data assets at different sites as well as scheduling of the query jobs on the data taking the replication and other system properties (such as processor speeds and network latency) into consideration. The problem, though referred in a few recent literature (e.g., see [3,4,5]), has not been addressed adequately yet. In this work, we have proposed an integrated scheduling and replication strategy which works in a distributed and hierarchical manner.

2 Motivation

In a Data Grid the total time to execute a job depends on the computation time to execute a job and the latencies involved in bringing the data files to the execution site from the remote locations. Therefore, the total time depends on the computing resource chosen for job execution and the location of the data file(s) the job needs to access. Therefore data locality needs to be taken into account in any scheduling decisions and data management strategies like data replication would reduce the overall latency of data access and job completion considerably. Hence, there should be a coupling between data locality achieved through data replication mechanisms and scheduling. Again, because of the inherent distributed nature of the grid, a centralized replication and scheduling strategy will incur a huge cost and may not be feasible in many cases. Therefore, there is a need for integration of replication and scheduling needs to be done in a distributed and scalable manner. In this paper a distributed interaction approach between scheduling and replication called **Dist**ributed **Re**plication and **S**cheduling **S**trategies (DistReSS) is provided.

Most of the works in this field have concentrated either on replication or scheduling aspects of the problem. Work on scheduling algorithms, which considered data locality/storage issues as secondary to job placement are [5], [6], [7]. Work on data replication strategies for Grids includes [8] and [9]. An economy based replication strategy had been proposed in [10] and a detailed implementation of replication strategies in European Data Grid (EDG) has been published in [11]. Recently, some work has been carried out which combines the scheduling and replication strategies to provide better overall performance in Data Grids [12], [13]. Real effort to combine scheduling and reapplication was undertaken by Ranganathan et al. [14]. An efficient centralized replication and scheduling strategy that addresses these issues has been proposed by us in [15] and performance of the scheduling has been evaluated in [16].

The centralized way of integrating scheduling and replication as proposed in [15] will not be efficient because of the inherent distributed nature of the grid. In this paper, we propose a replication-scheduling algorithm which iteratively improves the performance of the Data Grids in a distributed and hierarchical manner. The key contribution of the paper lies in the idea of the possible integration between scheduling and replication in a hierarchical and distributed manner. The main objectives of the paper include: (a) Developing distributed and hierarchical replication strategy called DistReSS which takes help of the traffic history information to replicate data at specific sites. (b) Developing distributed and hierarchical scheduling strategies to schedule jobs at each site so that the latency between job submission and job execution is minimized. (c) Evaluating the algorithms through simulation studies.

The rest of the paper is organized as followed. In the next sub-section, we list out the DistReSS architecture and some assumptions made. In Section 3, we define the scheduling and replication problems in a Data Grid. Section 4 outlines our DistReSS algorithm in detail with suitable examples. In Section 5, we present and discuss the performance test results vis-à-vis some other approaches. We conclude in Section 6 by pointing out the salient contributions and future work.

2.1 DistReSS Architecture

Figure 1 shows the architecture of DistReSS system. DistReSS architecture allows users to submit a job to the Global Scheduler (GS). The sites are arranged in a Virtual Clusters (VC). The algorithm for creating and maintaining VCs will be discussed later in the paper. The GS has information about the VCs and submit the jobs to the head of the VC called the VC Core (VCC). It is to be noted that VCC is a site which performs the VC level scheduling. Any site can claim to be a VCC, and VCC election can be carried out in a random manner or based on some heuristics Once the job reaches a VCC, it schedules the job to the corresponding site based on the information exchanged within the VC. Within a site there are Local Scheduler (LS) and a data set scheduler (DS). LS determines in which order the jobs will be executed within a site and DS determines which files will be replicated within the site.

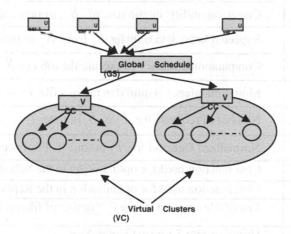

Fig. 1. DistReSS Architecture

The assumptions made throughout the paper are: (a) The Data Grid is considered to be an undirected graph. Hence, the transfer cost is same both ways. (b) Each site has a local scheduler and the scheduling policy can vary from site to site. (c) Jobs are non-preemptable and times to execute the jobs are considered to be proportional to the size of the data required for the job. (d) Data files are transferred into or out of a site in a sequential manner through a single port.

3 Distributed Replication and Scheduling Strategies (DistReSS)

Please note the symbols defined in Table 1. We model a job request as a 3-tuple $J = <\tilde{F}, \tilde{C}_p>$, where $\tilde{F}$ is the list of files needed by the job and $\tilde{C}_p$ is the computation time required by the job J at a site having processing power P and which possesses all the files in $\tilde{F}$. A site is modeled as a 3-tuple $S = <\hat{F}, V, P_s>$, where $\hat{F}$ is the set of files stored in the site S, V is the storage capacity at that site and P_s is the computation capacity at that site. It is to be noted that P_s is expressed in sec/GB. In [14], the authors have stated that P_s varies between 10 sec/GB to 50 sec/GB. The *Job Scheduling (JS)* problem states that: Let $\hat{J} = \{J_1, J_2 \ldots J_n\}$ be a set of jobs, and $\hat{S} = \{S_1, S_2 \ldots S_n\}$ be the set of sites, then the problem is to schedule the jobs $\hat{J}$ to the sites $\hat{S}$, such that the average latency between submitting the jobs and execution of the jobs is minimized. $D_{F_i S_j}{}^T$ $\forall i = 1 \ldots n, j = 1 \ldots m$, a Demand Matrix, is created based on

Table 1. List of Symbols

SYM	DEFINITION
S_i F_i τ_i	Site i, File i, Size of F_i
P_i q_i V_i	Comp. capability, queue size of S_i, storage capacity of S_i
δ_{ij}	Expected latency to transfer F_i from S_j to other sites
ω_{ij}	Computational latency to execute the job i in S_j
Δ_{ij}	Minimum latency required to move a file F_i to site S_j
$D_{F_i S_j}{}^T$	Number of requests for F_i in S_i in time T
η_{F_i} $\tilde{F}_i$	Normalized Demand for F_i in time T, Files needed by job i
$C^s{}_{ij}$	Cost function used for optimization in the Scheduling Problem
$C^R{}_{ij}$	Cost function used for optimization in the Replication Problem
$\hat{F}_j$ ϕ	List of files present in site j Number of files in the system
U_S λ	Utility of Site S Lowest Utility Site
O_F β_F	Owner of the File F, Called Frequency of the File F
L_{ij}	Latency of Job i in site j

a set of jobs J within a time interval T. The replication involves creation of identical copies of data files and their distribution over the nodes in a Grid. The *Data Replication (DR) problem* states that: Let $D_{F_iS_j}{}^T$ be a demand matrix and $\hat{S}$ be a set of sites; the aim is to distribute a set of files to the sites, so that the latency is minimized based on the demand matrix and the volume constraint at each site is maintained.

3.1 Solution Overview

DistReSS strategy integrates the replication and scheduling strategies in a scalable manner. As mentioned earlier, scheduling and replication work hand-in-hand to provide better overall performance in terms of overall latency. By employing better replication strategies the latency in bringing the files to the scheduled sites in reduced, while scheduling takes this replication information through a History Table to do more efficient scheduling. However, maintaining a History Table for all the files in a large and dynamic grid is not a trivial problem, and results in scalability issues. To deal with this scalability problem DistReSS defines Virtual Cluster (VC) which will be used extensively in this paper. A group of grid sites form a Virtual Cluster (VC) to take the responsibility of the replication and scheduling within the group. The VC elects a cluster leader called the Virtual Cluster Core (VCC). A virtual cluster conducts all communications to another virtual cluster only through VCC. VCC takes care of the replication and scheduling strategies in a cluster as it maintains the local cluster information. Replication can happen across the VCs also. The process is illustrated in Figure 2. Replication strategy involves two strategies: while Intra-VC replication is essentially based on the information available within a VC, the inter-VC replication depends on broad VC level information exchange. Scheduling, similarly, has two components: Intra-VC and inter-VC scheduling. In addition to scheduling and replication, there is also cluster management which influences both scheduling and replication. Therefore, the strategies to integrate these three components form the basis of the DistReSS approach. The different components of the DistReSS approach are: (i) Scheduling, (ii) Replication (iii) VC Management.

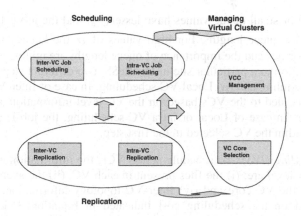

Fig. 2. Interaction between different components of DistReSS

3.2 Scheduling in DistReSS

Before describing the scheduling approaches, let us define some terms which will be used in the description.

Multiplicative Factor (M): This factor is used to estimate the effect of queue on the latency of jobs. α is a configurable constant. The expression of M is provided below. q_i in the expression indicates the queue size of the site where the job is scheduled. $\overline{q}$ indicates the average queue of the system.

$$M_i = \frac{q_i + \alpha.\overline{q}}{q_i + \overline{q}} \tag{1}$$

Job Latency (L_{ij}): Let $f_{i1}, f_{i2}....f_{ik}$ be the set of files required initially by a job J_i to be scheduled at site S_j. Then the total time required to execute the job J_i is

$$L_{ij} = \sum_{r=1}^{k} \Delta_{i,j} + \omega_{ij} \tag{2}$$

It is to be noted that in Equation (2) the assumption made is that all the files are required by the job at the start of the execution.

Scheduling Cost (C^s_{ij}): This indicates the cost of scheduling a job i onto a site j. If not otherwise stated, the scheduling cost is given by:

$$C^s_{ij} = L_{ij}.M_i \tag{3}$$

The multiplicative factor M is able to capture the effect of queue on the scheduling decisions. From Equation 3 it is clear that scheduling cost is dependent on the cost latency of job execution in the scheduled site as well as the job queues at that site. Through the selection of α importance is either given to the queue latency or the current job latency. When $\frac{q_i}{\overline{q}} = 0$, the C^s_{ij} becomes equal to $L_{ij}.\alpha$. Therefore, for low α sites having 0 or small queue values have lesser C^s_{ij}, and the job gets scheduled to sites having lesser queue lengths. For high values of α the latency of the jobs are given higher priorities and the importance of queue lengths are minimized.

To schedule a job to a particular site in DistReSS, two different steps are involved: (i) Inter-VC scheduling and (ii) Local VC scheduling. In case of Inter-VC scheduling, the jobs are scheduled to the VCs based on the VC level information available at the global scheduler. In case of Local or intra-VC scheduling, the job is scheduled to a particular site within the VC selected in the first step.

Inter-VC Scheduling (IVS): To schedule across VCs, the information available at the global scheduler level are: (i) the files present in each VC, (ii) the average queue size of the VC, (iii) the VC core and (iv) Inter-VC topology information. The jobs are scheduled based on the scheduling cost indicated in Equation 3. Let us take an example. Let there are three virtual clusters and each of them has 4 sites. The file distribution in each site is also shown. The information available to the global scheduler is the queue information and the file information (mentioned in boxes above each VC). Let the job be J=<D1, D4, D6, D12>. The numbers by the side of the lines joining the VCs indicate the latency to move a unit file across the clusters. The values are calculated with the VC Core as the reference. The latencies to schedule jobs at VC1, VC2 and VC3 are 30, 20 and 30 seconds respectively. Now, assuming $\alpha = 0.1$ (using Equation 1), the cost of scheduling at VC1, VC2 and VC3 are 13.8, 18 and 9.75 respectively. Therefore, in this case, the job is scheduled at the VC3, which is also the VC having the least queue. However, it is to be noted that when $\alpha = 0.5$, the job is scheduled at VC2. Therefore, the performance of the scheduling algorithm depends on the value of alpha. In the simulation section, the simulation studies are carried out for different values of α.

Intra-VC or Local VC Scheduling (LVS): Within a VC, a cost based job scheduling strategy is proposed [15]. Cost (c_{ij}^s) of scheduling a job J_i onto a site s_j is defined as the combined cost of moving the data into the site s_j, latency to compute the job J_i in the site s_j and the wait time in the queue in the site s_j. The job is scheduled onto the site which has the minimum c_{ij}^s.

3.3 Replication in DistReSS

We start by defining some operational terms.

Normalized Demand (η_{F_i}): η_{F_i} is defined as the ratio of the demand for the file F_i to the demand of all files. Normalized demand for the file F_i within VC VC_j is defined as the sum of normalized demand of all sites within the VC and is represented as $\eta_{F_i}^{VC_j}$.

Called Frequency ($\beta_{F_i}^j$): $\beta_{F_i}^j$ is defined as the number of times the file F_i is called from different sites from the current site j. This determines the usefulness of the file within the site.

Expected Latency: Expected file latency (δ_{ij}) of a file F_i to be replicated in site S_j is defined as the average latency of moving the file from site S_j to any other site where the job will be scheduled. Let the probability of a job scheduled in site S_k requiring the file F_i be p_{ik}.

File Owner (O_F): A site is called the owner of a file F if a site stores a file which is never replaced.

Similar to scheduling, replication in DistReSS can also be of two types: (i) Inter-VC Replication and (ii) Intra-VC Replication. In case of Inter-VC replication, the replication is done based on the information collected as part of the IVS scheduling strategy. On the other hand, intra-VC replication (or Local Replication) is done based on the History Table collected as part of the LVS strategy.

Inter-VC Replication (IVR): IVR strategy has three phases – Seek, Capture and Replace. In the Seek phase, each VCC seeks to capture a new file by probing the other VCCs. In the capture phase, a file is captured from a VC and in the replace phase the captured file replaces one of the files stored inside the VC. A file is said to be captured if the VCC can find a file stored in some other VC (VC_j) having a non-zero $\eta_{F_i}^{VC_j}$. When the file has been captured, the VCC instructs all the sites within its VC to look for a site where the file can be stored. Each site within the VC sends the value of η_{F_i} where F_i is the file which has been captured. The site having the maximum η_{F_i} is selected because the site has the maximum normalized demand for the captured file. The file is then immediately stored in the selected site if there is space. However, if there is no space a replacement file within the site is searched. The file which has the lowest $\beta_{F_i}^j$ (unless the site is the file owner) is selected as the replacement file because the file which is replaced has the least usefulness among all the files within the site.

Local VC Replication (LVR): Similar to the IVR strategy, LVR strategy also has three phases – Seek, Capture and Replace. All the files stored within a site are sorted in terms of their Expected Latency. In the seek phase, each site probes the other sites within a VC if there is a site which has a file whose Expected Latency is lower than the file having the Expected Latency stored in the VC. For example, let a site S1 has files F1, F2, and F3 with Expected Latencies 1, 2 and 3 seconds respectively. S1 sends a PROBE message to S2 mentioning the maximum Expected latency is 3 secs. If S2 has a file F4 with lower Expected latency, it replies. S1 replaces the file F3 with F4. This has been explained in detail in [15].

3.4 Virtual Clustering in DistReSS

Based on the scheduling and replication information, Virtual Clusters are created and maintained. Before going into details about the clustering approaches we define some terms which will be used in discussing the clustering approaches.

Utility (U): Utility of a site S in a VC is defined as the files transferred from the site to the rest of the VC, multiplied by the ratio of the number of jobs scheduled to that site by the total number of jobs within the VC. A low utility indicates that the files stored in the site has very little utility to the rest of the VC and also the number of jobs scheduled in that site in the VC is very low.

Lowest Utility Site (λ): The site within a VC having the lowest utility.

Inter-VC Relation: A VC (VC1) is said to be stronger than the other VC (VC2) if the sum of the demands for the file in the VC1 is greater than VC2.

Min and max site Limit: Each VC has a minimum and maximum number of sites it can contain. This is determined in advance by the grid administrator based on the number of clusters in the system.

The different steps of the clustering process are: (i) VC Initialization, (ii) VCC Selection and (iii) VC Maintenance. For the cluster initialization, a K-means cluster approach can be used. A VCC can be selected as the center of the cluster thus formed. In this section, we will discuss about the VC Maintenance in detail.

VC Initialization: This can be done using a random algorithm, or a sophisticated K-means approach can be applied. The center created as a result of the K-means algorithm can result in VCC selection. It is to be noted any other algorithm can be selected to solve this problem.

VC Maintenance: In this step, each VC tries to add a site from the other VCs in a greedy manner. A VC (VC1) tries to add a site from another VC (VC2) if both the conditions take place: (a) VC1 is **stronger** than VC2, (b) The maximum limit of VC1 is not attained, (c) The minimum limit of VC2 is not attained.

Let the utility of λ_{VC2} be U_1 and the utility of λ_{VC2} when added to VC2 be U_2. Once the above three conditions are satisfied, λ_{VC2} is added to VC1 if $U_2 > U_1$.

Let us now look at the running times and storage complexity of DistReSS vis-à-vis the centralized algorithm.

Running time for Scheduler: The worst case running time for the scheduler in case of the non-hierarchical centralized approach is O($n^2 f$), where n is the number of sites and f is the number of files in the grid system. In case of DistReSS, the worst case running time is O($c^2 f + (n/c)^2 f$), where c is the number of clusters. If $c = \sqrt{n}$, then the worst case running time for DistReSS becomes O(nf), which is O(n) less than the centralized non-hierarchical approach.

Storage Requirements: In case of DistReSS, storage required at the VC level is the list of files present in each cluster. The storage size required to store such information is O(cf) or O($\sqrt{n}f$). To maintain the history table and called frequency information, the storage size required is O($n/c.f$) or O($\sqrt{n}.f$). In case of centralized algorithm, O(nf) storage is required in addition to queue information for each site.

4 Performance Studies

Extensive simulations were conducted using Network Simulator (NS-2) [17] to evaluate the effectiveness of the distributed mechanism proposed in this paper. The DistReSS mechanism is compared with a centralized scheduling/replication approach.

For the experiments, the various inputs were generated as follows: (a) Random grid topologies were generated based # nodes, # links. (b) The processing speed at the nodes is considered constant at 10 second/Gb of data. (c) Number of jobs requesting a particular file is distributed exponentially. This gives an elliptical file distribution per job with an average of 7 and total files in the system (ϕ) as 20. The initial file distribution in the Grid is random. We also consider no background traffic in the Grid networks and the average bandwidth simulated is 20 Mbps. (d) Other default parameters: Number of sites = 100, Number of links = 200, Storage limit at each node = 10 GB, number of clusters = 10.

4.1 Selection of α

In this set of experiments, latency is calculated and plotted for different values of α_{VC} and α_{site}. In Figure 3, a variation of latency is plotted against α_{VC} and α_{site} (x and z axes respectively). It is a 3-D figure. For low values of α_{VC} and α_{site}, the jobs are dispersed off to different sites, resulting in low queues at each site during scheduling. This can be seen from Figure 4, which shows the variation of AMQ with α_{VC} and α_{site}. For high values of α_{VC} and α_{site} the jobs are scheduled to sites which has the least latency ignoring the queues resulting in increase in queue length. Figure 6 confirms this observation. From the figures, a value of α_{VC} = 0.1 and α_{site} = 0.3 results in lowest latency, though α_{VC} = 0.1 and α_{site} = 0.1 results in lowest queue. For the subsequent experiments, we choose α_{VC} = 0.1 and α_{site} = 0.3 as the choice results in the lowering of latency.

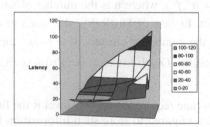

Fig. 3. Variation of Latency with α_{VC} **Fig. 4.** α_{site}, (b) Variation of AMQ with α_{VC}, α_{site}

4.2 Comparison with Centralized Approach

In the next set of experiments, the DistReSS approach is compared with the centralized scheme. Centralized scheme, with cost based scheduling, has all the queue information and performs centralized replication.

In Figures 5, 6 and 7, average latency is varied with bandwidth, number of nodes and storage limit respectively. In all these cases, the average latency decreases with the increase in the different parameters. When bandwidth increases, the time required to bring the number of files across sites decreases, resulting in the trend shown in Figure 7. The performance of the DistReSS approach (mentioned as Distributed in the Figure) is 5-7% worse than the centralized scheme.

When the number of sites to schedule jobs increases, there are multiple options to schedule jobs. Therefore, the queue size at each site decreases resulting in the decrease in average latency. The trend is shown in Figure 6. The difference between

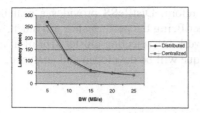

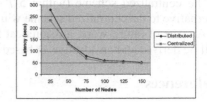

Fig. 5. Variation of Latency with bandwidth   **Fig. 6.** Variation of Latency with #sites

the DistReSS approach and the centralized scheme reduces as the number of sites increases. This is because with more sites, the queues decrease and the effect of the scheduling and replication algorithm reduces. This can also be observed when the increase in the number of sites do not reflect in the same decrease in average latency (when number of sites >75).

With the increase in the storage limit of the sites the average latency shows a similar trend. After the storage limit reaches a certain limit (10GB in Figure 7), the average latency more of less become static. This is because most of the commonly used files are present in all the sites resulting in a low average latency. In this case, the average latency for DistReSS does not go above 5% of the centralized scheme.

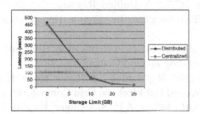

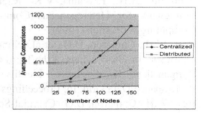

Fig. 7. Variation of Latency with storage Limit   **Fig. 8.** Variation of scheduling time with size

Figure 8 shows the variation of computation overhead at the scheduler with the number of nodes. Computation overhead is measured by the number of comparisons the scheduler performs before coming to a scheduling decision. The distributed approach (DistReSS) requires significantly less computation than its centralized counterpart.

5   Conclusions

In this paper, a distributed and scalable replication and scheduling approach called DistReSS has been proposed. The DistReSS approach provides a technique of integrating scheduling and replication techniques in a distributed and hierarchical manner. The technique is O(n) times faster than the centralized scheme and requires $O(\sqrt{n})$ less storage than the centralized scheme. Several experiments have been conducted to evaluate the effectiveness of the centralized scheme vis-à-vis the centralized scheme. The performance of the DistReSS approach is comparable to that of the centralized scheme (within 5-7%). Therefore, DistReSS provides a scalable alternative to the centralized scheme without sacrificing the performance too much.

As part of future work, a theoretical framework for selecting cluster size of a VC will be derived and an adaptive α based technique will be developed and analyzed.

References

1. Chervenak, I., Foster, C., Kesselman, C., Salisbury, S.: The Data Grid: Towards an Architecture for the Distributed Management and Analysis of Large Scientific Datasets. Journal of Network and Computer Applications 23, 187–200 (2001)
2. Beck, M., Moore, T.: The Internet2 distributed storage infrastructure project: An architecture for internet content channels. In: Comp. Net. and ISDN Systems (1998)
3. Foster, Kasselman, C.: The Grid 2: Blueprint for a new Computing Infrastructure. Morgan Kaufman, San Francisco (2004)
4. Foster, Kesselman, C.: The Globus Project: A Status Report. In: Proc. IPPS/SPDP 1998 Heterogeneous Computing Workshop, pp. 4–18 (1998)
5. Casanova, H., Obertelli, G., Berman, F., Wolski, R.: The AppLeS Parameter Sweep Template: User-Level Middleware for the Grid. In: Proc. of SuperComputing (2000)
6. Banino, O., Beaumont, L., Carter, J., Ferrante, A.: Scheduling Strategies for Master-Slave tasking for Heterogeneous Processor Platforms. IEEE Trans. On Parallel and Distributed Systems 15(4) (April 2004)
7. Alhusaini, A.H., Prasanna, V.K., Raghavendra, C.S.: A Unified Resource Scheduling Framework for Heterogeneous Computing Environments. In: Eighth Heterogeneous Computing Workshop (1999)
8. Bell, W.H., Cameron, D.G., et al.: Simulation of Dynamic Grid Replication Strategies in OptorSim. In: Proceedings of the Third Int'l Workshop on Grid Computing (2002)
9. Ranganathan, K., Foster, I.: Identifying Dynamic Replication Strategies for a High Performance Data Grid. In: Proceedings of the Second Intl Work. on Grid Comp. (2001)
10. Bell, W.H., Cameron, D.G., Carvajal-Schiaffino, R., Millar, A.P., Stockinger, K., Zini, F.: Evaluation of an Economy-Based File Replication Strategy for a Data Grid. In: Proc. CCGrid (May 2003)
11. Cameron, D., Casey, J., Guy, L., Kunszt, P., Lemaitre, S., McCance, G., Stockinger, H., Stockinger, K., Andronico, G., Bell, W., Ben-Akiva, I., Bosio, D., Chytracek, R., Domenici, A., Donno, F., Hoschek, W., Laure, E., Lucio, L., Millar, P., Salconi, L., Segal, B., Silander, M.: Replica Management in the EU DataGrid Project. International J. of Grid Computing 2(4), 341–351 (2004)
12. Thain, J., Bent, A., Arpaci-Dusseau, R.: Gathering at the Well: Creating Communities for Grid I/O. In: Proc. of SuperComputing (2001)
13. Basney, J., Livny, M., Mazzanti, P.: Harnessing the Capacity of Computational Grids for High Energy Physics. In: CHEP 2000. Proceedings of the International Conference on Computing in High Energy and Nuclear Physics (2000)
14. Ranganathan, K., Foster, I.: Simulation Studies of Computation and Data Scheduling Algorithms for Data Grids. J. of Grid Computing 1(2), 53–62 (2003)
15. Chakrabarti, A., Dheepak, R.A.: Integration of Scheduling and Replication in Data Grids. In: Proc. IEEE HiPC (December 2004)
16. Dheepak, R.A., Ali, S., Chakrabarti, A., Sengupta, S.: Study of Scheduling Strategies in Dynamic Data Grid Environment. In: Sen, A., Das, N., Das, S.K., Sinha, B.P. (eds.) IWDC 2004. LNCS, vol. 3326, Springer, Heidelberg (2004)
17. UCB/LBNL/VINT Network Simulator – ns (version 2), http://www.isi.edu/nsnam/ns

DGDCT: A Distributed Grid-Density Based Algorithm for Intrinsic Cluster Detection over Massive Spatial Data

Sauravjyoti Sarmah[1], Rosy Das[2], and Dhruba Kumar Bhattacharyya[3]

Dept. of Comp Sc & Engg., Tezpur University, Napaam 784 028, India
{sjs, rosy8, dkb}@tezu.ernet.in

Abstract. This paper presents a distributed Grid-based Density Clustering using Triangle-subdivision (DGDCT), capable of identifying arbitrary shaped embedded clusters as well as multi density clusters over large spatial datasets. Experimental results are presented to establish the superiority of the technique in terms of scale-up, speedup as well as cluster quality.

1 Introduction

Clustering is the process of division of a data set into subsets or clusters, so that the similarity of points in each partition is as high as possible, while points in different partitions are dissimilar [1]. It is very effective in discovering hidden patterns of data sets and is an important research topic. Major clustering techniques have been classified into partitional, hierarchical, density based, grid based and model based. Among these techniques, the density-based approach is famous for its capability of discovering arbitrary shaped clusters of good quality even in noisy datasets [2]. Grid-based clustering approach is well known for its fast processing time especially for large datasets. In this paper, an efficient distributed intrinsic cluster detection algorithm (DGDCT) is presented, which can handle massive spatial datasets with better cluster quality. The method exploits a grid based technique to group the data points into blocks and the density of each grid cell calculated. The blocks are then clustered by a topological search algorithm. For finer clustering result, a triangle-subdivision method is used. The algorithm finds quality clustering even over variable density space.

2 Related Works

This section reports a selected review on some of the relevant density based, grid based and parallel and distributed clustering techniques.

The idea behind density based clustering approach is that the density of points within a cluster is higher as compared to those outside of it. DBSCAN [2] is a density-based clustering algorithm capable of discovering clusters of various

S. Rao et al. (Eds.): ICDCN 2008, LNCS 4904, pp. 239–250, 2008.

shapes even in presence of noise. However, due to the use of the global density parameters, it fails to detect embedded or nested clusters.

Grid based methods are computationally efficient which divide the data space into a finite number of cells that form a grid structure on which the clustering operations are performed. It has many advantages such as the total number of the grid cells is independent of the number of data points and is insensitive to the order of input. Among the popular grid based clustering techniques, STING [3] uses a multi-resolution approach, which is query-independent and easy to parallelize. However the shapes of clusters have horizontal or vertical boundaries but no diagonal boundary is detected. WaveCluster [4] is capable in detecting outliers and is very fast. However, it is not suitable for high dimensional data sets. CLIQUE [5] automatically finds subspaces of the highest dimensionality and is insensitive to the order of input. pMAFIA [6] an improved version of CLIQUE, uses the concept of adaptive grids for detecting the clusters. It is not scalable w.r.t. dimension.

Real life datasets have a skewed distribution and may also contain nested cluster structures, the discovery of which is very difficult. Chameleon [7] can handle multi-density datasets at the cost of time complexity. SNN [8] finds clusters of varying shapes, sizes over multi-density datasets, however, the degree of precision is low in finding outliers. In [9], clusters are found based on the idea of density-isoline, however, each cluster cannot be separated efficiently. Density-grid based algorithm [10] uses a uniform density threshold which causes the low density clusters to be lost. OPTICS [11] and EnDBSCAN [12] can identify embedded clusters over varying density space. However, these are very sensitive to the input parameters. EnDBSCAN [12] can detect embedded clusters, however, with the increase in the volume of data, it's performance degrades.

Parallel and distributed computing is expected to relieve current clustering methods from the sequential bottleneck, providing the ability to scale massive datasets and improving the response time. Such algorithms divide the data into partitions, which are processed in parallel. The results from the partitions are then merged. The distributed DBSCAN algorithm [13]based on low cost distributed memory multi-computers can be found to be scalable both in terms of speedup and scale-up. The parallel k-means algorithm [13] is based on shared nothing architecture. PDBSCAN [13], also uses a shared-nothing architecture which offers nearly linear speedup and has excellent scale-up and size-up behavior. DBDC [14] is scalable to large datasets and gives clusters of good quality. In [13], a parallel version of the AutoClass system, P-AutoClass is described. In [13], a Collective Hierarchical Clustering (CHC) algorithm for analyzing distributed and heterogeneous data was presented.

Based on our selected survey and experimental analysis, it has been observed that most of the techniques are incapable in handling multi-density datasets as well as multiple intrinsic or nested clusters over massive datasets qualitatively. To overcome these shortcomings, this paper presents a grid-density based clustering algorithm which can effectively find clusters according to the structure of the embedding space over massive datasets.

3   Theoretical Background of the Work

In a grid-density based clustering approach, the data space is divided into grid cells and the grid cells whose densities are similar are merged. The adaptive grid cell represents the maximal space that can be covered by the similar dense grid cells. Here, we introduce some definitions which are used in DGDCT.

Definition 1. *Cell Density: The number of spatial point objects within a particular grid cell.*

Definition 2. *Useful Cell: Only those cells which are populated i.e., which contain data points will be treated as useful cell.*

Definition 3. *Neighbor Cell: Those cells which are edge neighbors or vertex neighbors of a current cell are the neighbors of the current cell.*

Definition 4. *Density Confidence of a cell: If the ratio of the densities of the current cell and one of its neighbors is greater than or equal to some β (user input) then β is the density confidence between them. Two cells P_1 and Q_1 will be merged into the same cluster if $\beta \leq d_n (P_1) / d_n (Q_1)$ where d_n represents the density of that particular cell.*

Definition 5. *Reachability of a cell: A cell p is reachable from a cell q if p is a neighbor cell of q and cell p satisfies the density confidence condition w.r.t. cell q.*

Definition 6. *Triangle Density: The number of spatial point objects within a particular triangle of a particular grid cell.*

Definition 7. *Useful Triangle: Only those triangles which are populated i.e., which contain data points will be treated as useful triangle.*

Definition 8. *Neighbor Triangle: Those triangles which have a common edge to the current triangle are the neighbors of the current triangle. Figure 1 shows the neighbor triangles (shaded) of the current triangle P.*

Fig. 1. Neighbor triangles of the triangle P

Definition 9. *Density Confidence of a triangle: Two triangles can be merged into the same cluster, if the ratio of the densities of the current triangle and one of its neighbors is greater than or equal to $\beta/4$ i.e. $\beta / 4 \leq d_n (T_{P_1}) / d_n (T_{Q_1})$, where d_n represents the density of the particular triangle.*

Definition 10. *Reachability of a triangle: A triangle p is reachable from a triangle q if p is a neighbor triangle of q and triangle p satisfies the density confidence condition w.r.t. triangle q.*

Definition 11. *Cluster: A cluster is defined to be the set of points belonging to the set of reachable cells and triangles i.e. if $p \in C$ and q is reachable from p w.r.t. β, then $q \in C$, where p and q are cells or triangles.*

Definition 12. *Noise: Noise is simply the set of points belonging to the cells (or triangles) not belonging to any of its clusters. Let C_1, C_2, ...C_k be the clusters w.r.t. β, then noise = $\{no\_p \mid p \in n \times n, \forall i : no\_p \notin C_i\}$, where no_p is the set of points in cell p and C_i (i=1,...,k).*

Both cell-reachability and triangle-reachable relation follows symmetric and transitive property within a cluster C.

3.1 Density Confidence

The density confidence for a given set of cells or triangles reflects the general trend of that set. If the density of one cell (or triangle) is abnormal from the others it will not be included in the set. Similarly, each useful cell has a density confidence with each of its neighbor cells. If the density confidence of a current cell with one of its neighbor cell does not satisfy the density confidence condition than that neighbor cell is not included into the local dense area. On the contrary, if it satisfies the condition than the neighbor cell is treated as a part of the local dense area and merged with the dense area. In comparison to other methods of setting a global threshold, this method has the ability to recognize the local dense areas in variable density space.

3.2 Use of Triangle-Subdivision

Triangle is a special form of a quadrilateral i.e. triangles are degenerated quadrilaterals with two of the vertices merged together. Triangle-subdivision is adopted for interpolation of data with better accuracy as compared to that in rectangle. This is because of the fact that partitioning of the data set can be performed more efficiently in triangular shape than in rectangular shape due to its smaller space dimension.

4   The Proposed Technique

The proposed architecture adopts shared nothing architecture. It considers a system having k-nodes where the entire dataset D is located in any of the nodes (say node 1). Node 1 executes a fast partitioning technique to generate the k initial partitions. The partitions are then sent to k nodes (including itself) for cluster detection using a grid-density based clustering technique (GDCT) which can operate over variable density space. Finally, the local cluster results are received from the nodes at the initiator node (node 1) and a merger module is used to obtain the final cluster results. Basically the technique works in *three phases* and the output of each phase becomes the input of the subsequent phase.

Phase I

Phase I of the architecture is executed in one of the nodes (node 1). The dataset is spatially divided into equal size square grid cells and density of each grid cell is computed. The square mesh is then partitioned with some overlap between adjacent partitions and distributed over k available computers (nodes). No subsequent movement of data between partitions will take place.

Initially, the data space is divided into $n \times n$ non-overlapping square grid cells, where n is a user input, and maps the data points to each cell. It then calculates the density of each cell.

Assuming, the grid mesh D contains the set of $n \times n$ objects say, $D = O_0, O_1, O_2, ..., O_{(n \times n)-1}$. Suppose, $O_j = (a_{0j}, a_{1j}, a_{2j}, ..., a_{(d-1)j}; d_n)$ represents a grid cell with d real-valued attributes a_i, $i=0,..,d-1$ and density d_n. The ith attribute value of object O_j is drawn from domain a_j. If there are k clients, the grid mesh D is partitioned into k subsets $D_0, D_1, ..., D_{(k-1)}$ ordered in sequence. We refer the clients by the corresponding partition D_j that it receives for processing.

$$D = D_0 \cup D_1 \cup D_2 \cup \cdots \cup D_{k-1}$$
$$D_i \cap D_j \neq \phi \ for \ i, j = 0, \cdots, (n \times n) - 1$$
$$= \phi \ for \ |i, j| \geq 2, i = 0, \cdots, (n \times n) - 1, j = 0, \cdots, (n \times n) - 1$$

The partially overlapped partitions are shown in Fig. 2 for 2D case. An overlap of one grid cell occurs between two adjacent partitions. The overlapped regions are much smaller than the partitions. The grid cells in the overlapped regions are locally clustered in both the adjacent partitions. Thus they provide the information for merging together the local clustering results of two adjacent partitions. The overlapped width should be at least one cell width because adjacent cells are neighbors according to *Definition* 3. The grid mesh D is partitioned in this manner based on the values of a selected attribute of the data objects say a_s. The values of as have a range of $[min\_a_s, max\_a_s]$. We need to select $(k + 1)$ constants in the given range. Let c_i, $i = 1, \cdots, k+1$ represent the constants such that $c_i = min\_a_s$, $c_{k+1} = max\_a_s$ and $c_i < c_{i+1}$. Therefore the overlapped region can be represented as,

$$D_i = \{\exists j (O_j \in D) \mid c_i - cell\_width \leq a_{sj} \leq c_{i+1}\}, i = 2, \cdots, k - 1$$
$$D_i = \{\exists j (O_j \in D) \mid c_i \leq a_{sj} \leq c_{i+1} + cell\_width\}, i = 1$$
$$D_i = \{\exists j (O_j \in D) \mid c_i - cell\_width \leq a_{sj} \leq c_{i+1}\}, i = k$$

Load Balancing. Partition D_i is sent to processor P_i, $i=1,\cdots,k$ for concurrent clustering. Since no data movement takes place after the partitions are created, care has been taken so that each processor receives nearly equal number of data objects for processing. We assume that the processing speeds of the processors

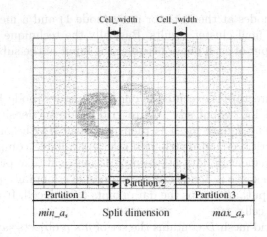

Fig. 2. Overlapped spatial partitioning of a 2D data set

are equal. The range of a_s is divided into intervals of width of one *cell_width* and the frequencies of data in each interval is counted. The load balancing is done in a manner similar to [13] which ensures that each partition gets number of objects nearly equal to N/k.

Phase II

This phase is executed in each of the k nodes and plays the actual role of clustering. Here, each node executes GDCT over the partition of data received from the initiator node. The cells of the partition received are sorted according to their density values and the cell with the highest density becomes the cluster initiator. The remaining cells are then clustered iteratively in order of their densities. A neighbor search is conducted, starting at the highest density cell and inspecting adjacent cells. If a neighbor cell is found which satisfies the density confidence condition of a cell, then the neighbor cell is merged with the current cell to form the adaptive grid, and the search proceeds recursively with this neighbor cell. This search is similar to a graph traversal where the nodes represent the cells and an edge between two nodes exists if the respective cells are adjacent and satisfies the density confidence condition of a cell. When this process stops, the first adaptive grid is formed which is an approximation of the innermost cluster or the cluster with the maximum density, minus the boundary region. The cells falling inside a particular adaptive grid are classified with the same cluster_id. The adaptive grid will reflect the rough cluster formed.

The cluster shape in the boundary region varies more since there is a transition from denser region to sparser region when we are considering intrinsic or variable density clusters. Therefore, this region needs special analysis. So, after the adaptive grid is formed, there might still be some points of the approximate clusters that lie outside the adaptive grid as shown by the red ellipse (black color ellipse for gray scale images) in Fig. 3. These points have been excluded because the cells in which they reside have not satisfied the density confidence

of a cell with its neighbor belonging to the adaptive grid so formed. This is because only a small portion of that part of the cluster has fallen in a different cell. Therefore the density of that cell is much less than its adaptive grid neighbor. Therefore, for finding the finer clustering, a cell is triangulated i.e. the cell is divided into four triangles. Those cells in the adaptive grid having at least one of its useful neighbor cells as unclassified are triangulated. The useful unclassified cells which have at least one of its neighbor cells belonging to the most recently formed adaptive grid are also triangulated. The data points of the cells that have been triangulated are mapped to the respective triangles in which they fall using the Barycentric coordinates [15]. Once the first adaptive grid has been formed,

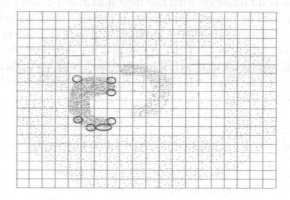

Fig. 3. Example grid approximation for a dataset ($n = 20$)

the cells falling inside that particular adaptive grid are classified with the same cluster_id . The process then checks the neighbors of the last formed adaptive grid cells. If any one of the neighbors is an unclassified useful cell then both the adaptive grid cell as well as the unclassified neighbor cell is triangulated. Suppose P_m is a cell of the adaptive grid last formed and cell P_i is one of its unclassified useful neighbor cell where $P_i \in P_{i1}, P_{i2}, \cdots, P_{i8}$. Then P_i and P_m is triangulated in a manner as shown in Fig. 4. During Triangle-subdivision, a particular grid cell is divided into four triangles. Each of the triangles T_{ki} inside the cell P_i is verified for the following cases:

Case 1: T_{ki} has a neighbor triangle T_{mi} which is part of adaptive grid cell P_m, then the two triangles T_{ki} and T_{mi} are merged if their densities satisfy the density confidence condition of a triangle and triangle T_{ki} obtains the cluster_id of T_{mi}.
Case 2: T_{ki} has a neighbor triangle T_{ji} which has already been classified and the densities of T_{ki} and T_{ji} satisfy the density confidence condition of triangles, then T_{ki} will be merged with T_{ji} and T_{ki} will be classified with the same cluster_id as T_{ji}.

The process of triangle merging stops when no more triangles satisfy the density confidence condition of a triangle. When the process of triangle merging

Fig. 4. Triangle-subdivision of grid cells (red polygon shows the adaptive grid or a rough cluster)

stops the cluster with the maximum density is obtained. The process then starts the next adaptive cell formation with the next maximum density cell from the set of unclassified cells. The process continues recursively merging neighboring cells that satisfy the density confidence condition of a cell. Therefore, the adaptive grid formation and triangle-subdivision method are repeated alternately till all the useful cells have been classified. The classified cells and triangles represent the distinct clusters and finally the data points are assigned the cluster_id of the respective cells and triangles.

Procedure of GDCT
The execution of the algorithm includes the following 9 steps:

1. Create the grid structure
2. Compute the density of each cell
3. Sort the cells according to their densities
4. Identify the maximum dense cell from the set of unclassified cells
5. Traverse the neighbor cells starting from the dense cell and form the adaptive grid (rough cluster)
6. Triangle-subdivision of the border cells of the adaptive grid which have at least one of its neighbors as a useful cell
7. Triangle-subdivision of the unclassified neighbor cells of those border cells
8. Merge the triangles and assign cluster_id
9. Repeat steps 4 through 9 till all cells are classified

The cluster expansion based on the grid cells detects embedded and nested cluster structures since after expansion of a cluster the algorithm searches for the next candidate cell which reflects a variation in density in the dataset. The process starts expanding the new density region till there is again a density variation. This process iterates till all the cells have been classified. The triangle expansion gives a finer clustering result since the cluster expansion based on cells misses some border points as can be seen in Fig. 3. The expansion based on triangle-subdivision detects the border points which have been left out by cell based expansion. Therefore, the quality of the clusters becomes highly accurate in addition to detecting intrinsic and multi-density clusters.

During clustering, the algorithm considers only the grid cells to identify the possible global and embedded clusters and assigns cluster_id accordingly. For the partition D_i in node i, the grid cells in it will be assigned cluster_id according to the clusters formed in that partition. The cluster_id will be used during the server based merging process.

The cluster expansion based on grid cells reduces the computation time as all the data points are not considered for cluster expansion only the density information of each cell is used. Moreover, the cluster_id information is used during Phase III merging process. It saves the cost of merging to a great extent. Finally, Phase II transmits the cluster objects to the server along with the cluster_id information.

Phase III

In Phase III, the cluster results received from the k nodes undergo a simplified, yet faster merging procedure to obtain the final clusters. Since the Phase II process in a node may yield more than one cluster along with the embedded clusters, so there are always possibilities for merging during Phase III operation. The Merger module works as follows:

1. Join the partitions received from the k nodes according to their overlapping marks.
2. Consider the marked grid cells (overlapping cells) of the candidate clusters.
3. If any of the marked grid cells is identified by different cluster_ids by different partitions (say l, m), then assign any one of the ids (say l) to that cell.
4. Assign all those cells having the same cluster_id as that of the replaced id (m) with l.

4.1   Complexity Analysis

Since the proposed technique is executed in three phases and each phase is independent of each other, therefore, the total complexity will be the sum of the complexities due to these three phases. The first phase, partitions the dataset into $n \times n$ cells resulting in a complexity of $O(N)$ where N is the total number of data points and then partitioning the grid mesh into k partitions results in a complexity of $O(n \times n)$, where $n << N$. Therefore $(N/k) + t$ points will be sent, where t is the average number of points present in an overlapped region. Transmitting these $(N/k) + t$ points to each node requires a communication time of $O((N/k) + t)$. The second phase is dedicated to sorting of the cells according to density as well as clustering, which results in a complexity of $O((n \times r)$ log $(n \times r)) + O(n_c \times m \times (p + q))$, where m is the number of cells in an adaptive grid formed, n_c is the number of clusters obtained, p and q are the average number of border and neighbor cells that undergo triangle subdivision. The clusters detected in this phase are re-transmitted to the initiator node with a transmission cost of $O((N/k) + t))$. The third phase is responsible for merging of the clusters resulting in $O(N+k.t)$ time. The overall time complexity of distributed GDCT will be $O(N) + O(n \times n) + O((N/k) + t)) + O((n \times r)$ log $(n \times r)) + O(n_c \times m \times (p + q)) + O((N/k) + t))$. Now, since $O(N)$ dominates the other terms, therefore, the time complexity becomes $O(N)$.

5   Performance Evaluation

To evaluate the technique in terms of quality of clustering, we generated the synthetic data set as shown in Fig. 5. The results are shown in Fig. 6. The results obtained when the algorithm was applied on the Chameleon t4.8k.dat, t7.10k.dat and t5.8k.datdatasets [8] are shown in Fig. 7 (a), 7(b) and 8 respectively. From our experiments it has been found that the clustering result is dependent on the threshold β which varies in the interval [0.5, 0.7]. From the experimental results

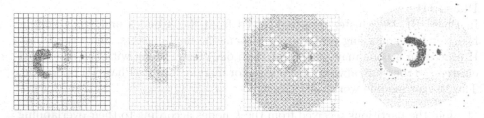

Fig. 5. Synthetic Dataset   **Fig. 6(a).** Formation of first cluster   **Fig. 6(b).** After full expansion   **Fig. 6(c).** The final five clusters

obtained, we can conclude that DGDCT is highly capable of detecting intrinsic as well as multi-density clusters qualitatively. In the next section, we empirically study the performance of the proposed DGDCT algorithm.

5.1   Performance and Scalability Analysis

Since there is no inter-processor communication except for a single processor communicating with each of the remaining processors. Each processor has the same specification i.e. PIV with 1 GHz speed and 128 MB RAM and the processors are connected through Ethernet LAN of speed 10/100 Mbps. To smooth out any variation, each experiment was carried out for five times and the average result were taken and each reported data point is to be interpreted as an average over five measurements. Our implementation is in C in Linux environment. Next, we generated several synthetic datasets containing arbitrary number of arbitrary shaped clusters having 2,00,000, 4,00,000, 6,00,000, 8,00,000 and 10,000,000 objects respectively and experimentation was carried out.

Parallel Execution Time: The parallel execution time, denoted by $T(k)$, of a program is the time required to run the program on a k-processor parallel computer. When $k = 1$, $T(1)$ denotes the sequential run time of a program on a single processor. Our experiments reveal that the execution time decreases significantly with the increase in the number of processors.

Speedup: Speedup is a measure of relative performance between a multiprocessor system and a single processor system, defined as, $S(k) = T(1)/T(k)$. On

Fig. 7(a). t4.8k.dat dataset   **Fig. 7(b).** t7.10k.dat dataset

Fig. 8. Clusters obtained from t5.8k.dat dataset

experimenting it has been found that the speedup factor increases with the increase in the number of processors. Figure 9 shows relative speedup curves for two data sets with points $N = 8 \times 10^5$ and 6×10^5. The number of dimensions and the number of clusters are fixed for both the data sets. The solid line represents "ideal" linear relative speedup. For each data set, a dotted line connects observed relative speedups.

Efficiency: The efficiency of a program on n processors, i.e. $E(k)$ is defined as the ratio of speedup achieved and the number of processors used to achieve it. $E(k) = S(k)/k = T(1)/k.T(k)$. In case of the proposed technique we observed that too many processors does not ensure the efficiency.

Scale-up: The scale-up characteristic of the proposed technique has been found to be satisfactory with the increase in the number of processors as can be seen from Fig. 10. Here the number of data points is scaled by the number of processors while dimensions and number of clusters are held constant.

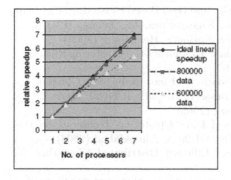

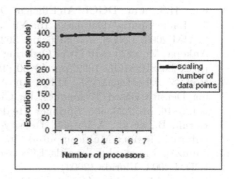

Fig. 9. Relative Speedup curves   **Fig. 10.** Scale-up curve

While comparing to DBSCAN, OPTICS, EnDBSCAN, GDLC and Density-isoline, the proposed DGDCT requires the number of grid cells, i.e. n and threshold β as input parameters. However, from our experiments it has been observed that the threshold β does not vary significantly with different datasets. GDCT can effectively detect embedded clusters over variable density space as well as multiple nested clusters.

6   Conclusions and Future Work

A distributed grid-density based clustering technique that can detect global as well as embedded clusters qualitatively has been presented. Experimental results are reported to establish the superiority of the algorithm in terms of scale-up and speedup. However, there are scopes for scaling DGDCT to detect clusters over high dimensional space.

References

1. Han, J., Kamber, M.: Data Mining: Concepts and Techniques. Morgan Kaufmann Publishers, San Francisco (2004)
2. Ester, M., Kriegel, H.P., et al.: A Density-Based Algorithm for Discovering Clusters in Large Spatial Databases with Noise. In: KDD 1996, Portland, pp. 226–231 (1996)
3. Wang, W., et al.: STING: A Statistical Information Grid Approach to Spatial data Mining. In: VLDB 1997, Athens, pp. 186–195 (1997)
4. Sheikholeslami, G., et al.: Wavecluster: A Multi- resolution Clustering approach for very large spatial database. In: SIGMOD 1998, Seattle (1998)
5. Agrawal, R., et al.: Automatic subspace clustering of high dimensional data for data mining applications. In: SIGMOD 1998, pp. 94–105 (1998)
6. Nagesh, H.S., et al.: A scalable parallel subspace clustering algorithm for massive data sets. In: Proc. of Intnl. Conf. on Parallel Processing, p. 477 (2000)
7. Ertoz, L., et al.: Finding Clusters of Different Sizes, Shapes, and Densities in Noisy, High Dimensional Data. In: SDM 2003. SIAM Intnl. Conf. on Data Mining (2003)
8. Karypis, G., et al.: CHAMELEON: A hierarchical clustering algorithm using dynamic modeling. IEEE Computer 32(8), 68–75 (1999)
9. Yan-chang, Z.: Clustering Datasets Containing Clusters of Various Densities. Journal of Beijing University of Posts and Telecomm 26(2), 42–47 (2003)
10. Kim, H.S., et al.: DGCL: An Efficient Density and Grid Based Clustering Algorithm for Large Spatial Database. In: Yu, J.X., Kitsuregawa, M., Leong, H.V. (eds.) WAIM 2006. LNCS, vol. 4016, pp. 362–371. Springer, Heidelberg (2006)
11. Ankerst, M., et al.: OPTICS: Ordering Points To Identify the Clustering Structure. In: ACM-SIGMOD 1999, pp. 49–60 (1999)
12. Roy, S., Bhattacharyya, D.K.: An Approach to Find Embedded Clusters Using Density Based Techniques. In: Chakraborty, G. (ed.) ICDCIT 2005. LNCS, vol. 3816, pp. 523–535. Springer, Heidelberg (2005)
13. Borah, B., et al.: A Parallel Density-Based Data Clustering Technique on Distributed Memory Multicomputers. In: ADCOM 2004, Ahmedabad (2004)
14. Januzaj, E., et al.: Towards Effective and Efficient Distributed Clustering. In: ICDM 2003, Florida (2003)
15. Retrieved from, http//steve.hollasch.net/cgindex/math/barycentric.html

An Abstraction Based Communication Efficient Distributed Association Rule Mining

P. Santhi Thilagam[1] and V.S. Ananthanarayana[2]

[1] Sr. Lecturer, Dept. of Computer Engineering, NITK-Surathkal, India-575 025
santhi_soci@yahoo.co.in
[2] Professor, Dept. of Information Technology, NITK-Surathkal, India-575 025
anvs@nitk.ac.in

Abstract. Association rule mining is one of the most researched areas because of its applicability in various fields. We propose a novel data structure called Sequence Pattern Count, SPC, tree which stores the database compactly and completely and requires only one scan of the database for its construction. The completeness property of the SPC tree with respect to the database makes it more suitable for mining association rules in the context of changing data and changing supports without rebuilding the tree. A performance study shows that SPC tree is efficient and scalable. We also propose a Doubly Logarithmic-depth Tree, DLT, algorithm which uses SPC tree to efficiently mine the huge amounts of geographically distributed datasets in order to minimize the communication and computation costs. DLT requires only $O(n)$ messages for support count exchange and it takes only $O(\log \log n)$ time for exchange of messages, which increases its efficiency

Keywords: Association rule mining, Distributed databases, Sequence Pattern Count Tree, Incremental mining, Doubly Logarithmic-depth Tree.

1 Introduction

Due to the explosive growth in the number, size and complexity of databases, many geographically distributed organizations, the ever-growing number of applications and the high scalability of distributed systems, there is a need for mining distributed databases [4]. Association Rule Mining (ARM), the mining of frequent patterns in large transaction databases and many other types of databases has been studied popularly in data mining research. The most important component affecting the performance of any ARM algorithm is the number of disk accesses required [1]. Recently alternative data structures were employed in order to improve the efficiency of existing and new algorithms [5]. This motivated us to propose an approach that employs an abstraction called Sequence Pattern Count, SPC, tree which is more compact and complete, and suitable for incremental mining and changing support [10]. A SPC tree is constructed using a single database scan and can be updated dynamically. Algorithm based on this structure does not require any more database scans to generate frequent itemsets [6].

S. Rao et al. (Eds.): ICDCN 2008, LNCS 4904, pp. 251–256, 2008.

All proposed algorithms for mining association rules in distributed databases focus on reduction of communication [3], efficient usage of memory, processing power, ability to scale up the number of processors and associated data, ability to increase the size of the database, decrease in response time with addition of processors[4][8]. However, the majority of the parallel mining algorithms suffer from high communication and synchronization overhead [2][7]. In this work, a new distributed association rule mining approach is proposed that decreases communication costs by introducing a new message exchange procedure and a new computational efficient technique that reduces computation time. Our main contributions reported in this paper are:

1. Communication optimization: Doubly Logarithmic-depth Tree algorithm is used to minimize the communication costs in terms of number of messages for support count exchange and time taken for exchange of these messages.
2. Minimization of the number of database scans: SPC tree structure is used to make the mining process more efficient in terms of database scans in the distributed environment, which requires only one scan of the database for mining frequent itemsets.

2   Distributed Association Rule Mining

Let 'DB' be a database and 'n' be the processors of nodes namely $P_1, P_2, \ldots, P_n$ which are connected over a computer network. Each processor has a local memory and a local disk. The processor can communicate only by passing messages and we assume that there is no loss of message during communication and network is completely reliable. Let the database DB be partitioned into n non-overlapping blocks $DB^1, DB^2, \ldots, DB^n$ where n is the number or processors available and each partition DB^i has the same schema. Let the size of DB and the partitions DB^i be D and D^i respectively. For a given itemset X, let $X.sup$ and $X.sup^i$ be the respective support counts of X in DB and DB^i. The problem is to find all frequent itemsets in DB[9].

2.1   Solution Approach

Distributed Association Rule Mining is explained in Algorithm 1 which consists of the following phases:

SPC tree Construction – This preprocessing step allows us to store the DB^i compactly in main memory. The frequent-1 itemsets can be generated during the construction of the SPC tree which will be used in mining process later. SPC tree construction is explained in Algorithm 2. *SPC tree Growth* – This algorithm adopts pattern-growth approach to mine all frequent itemsets from the SPC tree which requires no more database scans. *Communication between processors* – It uses DLT algorithm to exchange the local counts between the processors in order to calculate the global count of each itemsets which is explained in Algorithm 3.

Algorithm 1: Distributed Association Rule Mining using SPC Tree

Input: Database DB partitioned into n non-overlapping blocks
$D^1, \ldots, D^n$
Output: Frequent itemsets with respect to Database DB.
Steps:
1. Each processor P_i makes a pass over its database partition DB^i
   and builds a local SPC tree and local frequent-1 itemset with
   respect to DB^i.
2. All the processors synchronize after this step to exchange
   their local frequent-1 itemset with all other processors using
   Doubly Logarithmic-depth Tree (DLT) algorithm to get global
   frequent-1 Itemset. Now all the processors have the same
   global frequent-1 itemset.
3. Each processor P_i now computes the locally large frequent
   itemset for each item in global frequent-1 itemset using DB^i
   and removes infrequent items from its SPC tree.
4. All the processors synchronize again at this point and exchange
   their SPC trees(excluding infrequent items) with other nodes
   using DLT algorithm and accumulate the total frequent itemsets
   for each item in global frequent-1 itemset for
   DB $(DB^1 \cup DB^2 \cup \ldots \cup DB^n)$.
5. Association rules are obtained by mining on this global
   frequent count obtained after the second synchronization.

2.2   Sequence Pattern Count Tree

Node Structure: Each node in the SPC tree consists of five fields: *start* represents
the start of a partial sequence, *end* represents the end of a sequence, *count*
registers the number of transactions represented by the portion of the sequence,
child pointer - a pointer to the left most child from the node and *sibling pointer*
- a pointer to the right sibling of a node.

Definition 1. Sequence. A Sequence in a transaction is a non-empty succes-
sion of itemset(s) which form a subset in a given transaction.

Algorithm 2: Construction of SPC Tree

Input: A transaction Database DB
Output: SPC Tree for the given database DB
Steps:
  Let DB be the transaction database.
  Let T be the root of the SPC Tree.
    for each transaction $t_i \in DB$,
    BEGIN
      Let k_i and k_j be the start and end of a sequence S_i in m_i.
      If no branch of T with start index k_i exist,

> Create a new node for each $S_i, S_j, \ldots$ in m_i with count value
> set to 1 for all nodes. Add this branch to T as child node.
> Else
> > Increment the count of the node T if $S_{node} = S_{m_i}$ or if the
> > sequence matches partially, split the node accordingly and
> > create a new node for unmatched S and rest of m_i and insert
> > into T.
> End if
> END

Properties of the SPC tree: Given a transaction database, the corresponding SPC tree stores all the information of the database completely. SPC tree representation of the transaction database is compact. The maximum height of SPC tree is half of the length of the transaction. SPC tree supports change of data and allows mining with multiple minimum support values.

2.3   Analysis and Results

Datasets are generated with the data generator by IBM QUEST [11]. Experiments are performed on a Pentium IV 1.6 GHz PC with 512MB RAM running on Window 2000 server. We implemented the SPC tree using the IBM Quest Database file which has a total of 2, 94,846 transactions having 1000 items. Our experiments show that a small SPC tree is created by compressing quite large database. Scalability of the SPC tree is tested against different datasets. The Fig. 1 shows the time required to construct SPC tree, PC tree and memory requirements of both the trees. The time required to mine is proportional to the time required to traverse the SPC Tree. The Fig. 1 also shows the time required to mine all the frequent itemsets from Table 1 Data Set_4.

Table 1. Datasets used

Data Set	Size of database(MB)	Number of items
Set_1	16.7	1000
Set_2	33.4	1000
Set_3	66.9	1000
Set_4	98.5	1000

2.4   Doubly Logarithmic-Depth Tree Algorithm (DLT)

DLT algorithm is used to exchange support count messages efficiently in a distributed environment. The time complexity required by this algorithm is minimized and turns out to be $O(log\ log\ n)$. The number of message transfers required by this algorithm is minimized and turns out to be $O(n)$ at every synchronization point, where 'n' is the total number of nodes.

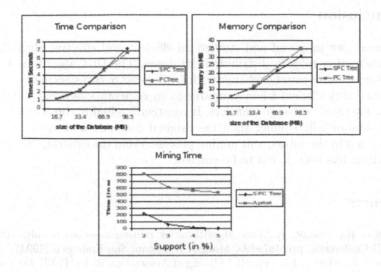

Fig. 1. Space and Time graph

Algorithm 3: Doubly Logarithmic-depth Tree for message exchange

Input: Configuration file containing ADDR: Internet address,
  PORT: port number, MYNUM: node number, num: number of items,
  sup: minimum support, n: total number of nodes,
  level: number of levels in the doubly logarithmic tree.
Output: Globally frequent patterns.
Steps:
  1. Start from level 'k'. Every processor P_i where $i = 2 * j + 1$
     for $j = 0, 1, \ldots, n/2$ sends its support count to the processor
     P_{i+1} which is its parent.
  2. P_{i+1} compute the sum of support counts from its local set and
     the set received through the message.
  3. For levels $d = k - 1$ to 0, do the following:
     a. Consider the processors that were parents at $(d+1)^{th}$ level.
     b. Partition them into groups of $2^{2^{(k-d-1)}}$ children in order of
        their numbering.
     c. All the processors in a group send their computed support
        counts to the processor P_i with the highest value of i.
        P_i becomes their parent.
  4. The sole parent P_i at the level $d = 0$ is the root of the
     doubly logarithmic-depth tree and contains the computed
     global count.
  5. The global count is back propagated to all the other
     processors by going down the path traversed in the steps 1-3.
     The parent node at each stage sends the global count to each
     of its children.

3   Conclusion

In this paper, we proposed and studied an efficient and effective algorithm for mining association rules in distributed databases. The DLT algorithm for message passing achieves count exchange with $O(n)$ message transfers in $O(log\ log\ n)$ time which is very efficient when compared to implementations using polling sites which require $O(n^2)$ message transfers. It constructs a highly compact SPC Tree which is substantially smaller than the original database and saves the costly database scans in the subsequent mining process. From the experimental studies, our algorithm has been found to be efficient.

References

1. Agrawal, R., Srikant, R.: Fast algorithms or mining association rules. In: 20th VLDB Conference, pp. 487–499. Morgan Kaufman, San Francisco (1994)
2. Agrawal, R., Shafer, J.C.: Parallel Mining of Association Rules. IEEE Transactions on Knowledge and Data Engineering 8(6), 962–969 (1996)
3. Cheung, D.W., Han, J., Ng, V.T., Fu, A.W., Fu, Y.: A Fast Distributed Algorithm for Mining Association Rules. In: PDIS 1996 International Conference on Parallel and Distributed Information Systems, Miami, FL, pp. 31–44 (1996)
4. Zaki, M.: Parallel and Distributed Association Mining: A Survey. IEEE Concurrency, 14–25 (1999)
5. Han, J., Pei, J., Yiwen, Y.: Mining Frequent Patterns without Candidate Generation. In: ACM-SIGMOD International Conference on Management of Data, pp. 1–12. ACM Press, New York (2000)
6. Ananthanarayana, V.S., Subramanian, D.K., Murty, M.N.: Scalable, Distributed and Dynamic Mining of Association Rules. In: Prasanna, V.K., Vajapeyam, S., Valero, M. (eds.) HIPC 2000. LNCS, vol. 1970, pp. 559–566. Springer, Heidelberg (2000)
7. Zaiane, M., El-Hajj, Lu, P.: Fast: Parallel Association Rules Mining without Candidacy Generation. In: ICDM 2001. IEEE 2001 International Conference on Data Mining, pp. 665–668 (2001)
8. Schuster, A., Wolff, R., Trock, D.: A High-Performance Distributed Algorithm for Mining Association Rules. In: 3rd IEEE International Conference on Data Mining, Florida, USA (2003)
9. Schuster, Wolff, R.: Communication-Efficient Distributed Mining of Association Rules. Data Mining and Knowledge Discovery 8(2) (2004)
10. Tsai, P.S.M., Lee, C.C., Chen, A.L.P.: An Efficient Approach for Incremental Association Rule Mining, Technical Report (1998)
11. Srikant, R.: Synthetic data generation code for association and sequential patterns, Available from the IBM Quest web site at (1993),
http://www.almaden.ibm.com/cs/quest/

List Heuristic Scheduling Algorithms
for Distributed Memory Systems
with Improved Time Complexity

Maruf Ahmed[1], Sharif M.H. Chowdhury[2], and Masud Hasan[1]

[1] Department of Computer Science and Engineering
Bangladesh University of Engineering and Technology, Dhaka-1000, Bangladesh
marufahmeds@gmail.com, masudhasan@cse.buet.ac.bd
[2] Department of Computer Science and Engineering
Shah Jalal University of Science and Technology, Sylhet, Bangladesh
sharif2day@yahoo.com

Abstract. We present a compile time list heuristic scheduling algorithm called *Low Cost Critical Path algorithm (LCCP)* for the distributed memory systems. LCCP has low scheduling cost for both homogeneous and heterogeneous systems. In some recent papers list heuristic scheduling algorithms keep their scheduling cost low by using a fixed size heap and a FIFO, where the heap always keeps fixed number of tasks and the excess tasks are inserted in the FIFO. When the heap has empty spaces, tasks are inserted in it from the FIFO. The best known list scheduling algorithm based on this strategy requires two heap restoration operations, one after extraction and another after insertion. Our LCCP algorithm improves on this by using only one such operation for both the extraction and insertion, which in theory reduces the scheduling cost without compromising the scheduling performance. In our experiment we compare LCCP with other well known list scheduling algorithms and it shows that LCCP is the fastest among all.

1 Introduction

Parallel computers are getting faster by using more and more processors and the processors are becoming very complex day by day. But it is not long before the transistors would reach their physical boundaries, thus making further improvements impossible. So, the distributed memory systems will become most important in the field of fast parallel processing systems.

The problem of scheduling tasks in a large scale system during the compilation is costly. It has been proven that the optimal solution of the scheduling of the tasks on the bounded number of processors is NP-complete [6,8,11]. There are many types of scheduling algorithms like the list scheduling algorithms [5,7,10,12,13,14,15], clustering algorithms [16], and duplication based algorithms [1,3,9]. But the algorithms other than the list scheduling ones have the drawback of high time complexity. On the other hand, list scheduling algorithms have low scheduling cost with acceptable scheduling performance [5].

S. Rao et al. (Eds.): ICDCN 2008, LNCS 4904, pp. 257–262, 2008.

This paper presents a list heuristic scheduling algorithm called *Low Cost Critical Path algorithm (LCCP)* for the distributed memory systems with improved time bounds for both homogeneous and heterogeneous processors. Homogeneous processors means all the processors must operate at the same speed, whereas heterogeneous processors do not have such restriction. LCCP uses a fixed size heap and a FIFO to store the tasks and the heap size is same as the number of processors in the system. The LCCP outperforms all the other algorithms that use fixed size heap by using less number of heap restoration operation. Theoretically LCCP achieves an $O(|V| \log |P|)$ improvement over those algorithms over the set of $|V|$ tasks and we also show this in practice.

2   Preliminaries and Related Work

A parallel program can be modeled as a directed acyclic graph $G = (V, E)$, called the *task graph*, where V is the set of nodes and E is the set of edges Fig. 1 shows the miniature structure of task graphs representing *LU decomposition, laplace equation solver, stencil,* and *fast fourier transformation* problems. Actual task graphs has more nodes but same structure. Each *task* (node) represents a group of instructions that can be executed sequentially without any interruption and is associated with a *task computation cost*. Each edge is associated with a *message communication cost*. When a task is scheduled, a processor, a *start time* and a

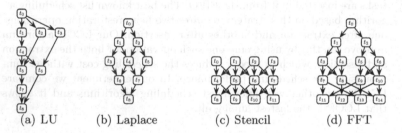

    (a) LU   (b) Laplace   (c) Stencil   (d) FFT

Fig. 1. Miniature task graphs for (a) LU decomposition, (b) laplace equation solver, (c) stencil algorithm, (d) fast fourier transform

finish time is assigned to it. A task is said to be *ready* if all of its parents have already been scheduled. Note that parents of a task may be scheduled on different processors. The Processor from which the last message arrives to a ready task is called the *enabling processor*. A new task can start to execute on a processor only after all the previously scheduled tasks on that processor have finished their execution. The processor that can finish executing the tasks already scheduled on it earliest, is called the *processor become idle the earliest*. The time at which a task can start execution on a processor is called the *execution start time* of that task on that processor. The processors are connected in a *clique* topology, that is the inter-processor communication is contention free.

An *entry task* has no incoming edges, hence no parents. An *exit task* has no outgoing edges, hence no children. The *earliest starting time* of a node v is the length of the longest path from an entry node to v. The *latest starting time* of v is the length of longest path from v to an exit node. Since by definition entry tasks can be scheduled before other tasks, the earliest and latest starting time of entry tasks are set to be zero. In contrary, since exit tasks must be scheduled after the other tasks have been scheduled, for an exit task the earliest starting time needs to be calculated and the latest starting time is set equal to that. One or more of the above attributes of a task is used as the task priority.

The *scheduling cost* of an scheduling algorithm means the algorithm's own time complexity. The *make-span* or the *scheduling length* of G is the time from the starting of execution of the very first task(s) and the ending of the last task(s). The *scheduling performance* of an algorithm means how much it can optimize the make-span. The *scheduling problem* is to schedule V tasks on P processors in such a way that the make-span of the tasks is optimized.

Related work. We will compare LCCP with *fast critical path algorithm (FCP)* [13,14] and some other well known list heuristic scheduling algorithms such as *modified critical path algorithm (MCP)* [12], *highest level first with estimated time algorithm (HLFET)* [10], *earliest time first algorithm (ETF)* [7] and *dynamic level schedule algorithm (DLS)* [15]. So far FCP has the lowest scheduling cost. FCP is based on MCP. It maintains a min heap of fixed size $|P|$ and a FIFO, where $|P|$ is the number of processors. Among all ready tasks, only $|P|$ tasks are in the heap and the remaining ready tasks are in FIFO. The priority task selection criteria in FCP is the latest starting time. At each iteration the ready task with the highest priority is extracted from the heap for scheduling and another task is inserted in the heap from the FIFO. Two heap restoration operations are used here, one after extraction and another after insertion. The processor selection criteria is the minimum among the earliest execution start time on the enabling processor and the processor become idle the earliest.

3   The LCCP Algorithm

The LCCP is based on FCP algorithm. Like FCP, LCCP uses a min heap of fixed size and a FIFO. Processor selection steps are also similar to that of FCP. But LCCP improves over FCP in the task selection steps. Each time a ready task is extracted from the heap (to schedule), a new task is inserted in the heap from the FIFO to keep the heap size fixed. Instead of using two heap restoration operations, LCCP uses a *combined restoration operation*, thus saving an $O(\log|P|)$-time operations, where $|P|$ is the size of the heap as well as the number of processors. Over all tasks, the saving is $|V| * O(\log|P|)$.

The combined operation first extracts the highest priority key of the (binary) heap from the root in $O(1)$ time (Fig. 2(b)). Then a new task from the FIFO is inserted in the root of the heap (which is now empty)(Fig. 2(c)), and then heap property is restored (Fig. 2(d)). Fig. 2(e) shows the final heap. The combination of those two operations work perfectly here. This reduces time complexity by using only one $O(\log|P|)$-time operation instead of two, and hence LCCP has

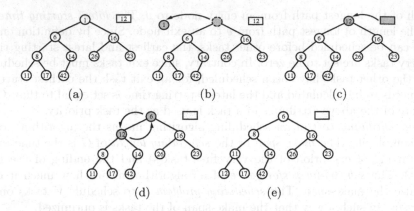

$$(a) \qquad\qquad (b) \qquad\qquad (c)$$

$$(d) \qquad\qquad (e)$$

Fig. 2. A combined heap restoration operation: highest priority key is extracted and a new key 12 is inserted followed by a heap restore operation. Note that if we insert any key less than 12, this would take only $O(1)$ time.

the lowest scheduling cost among all the list heuristic scheduling algorithms. In the heterogeneous system, where the processor speed may vary, the execution time of a task is proportional to the speed of the processor on which it is being executed. So, now the priority criterion of the LCCP for selecting the processors is changed and estimated finish time of a task is used as the priority.

4 Performance Results

The scheduling cost and performance of LCCP is compared with other best known list scheduling algorithms on the task graphs of Fig. 1. Each graph is made large enough to hold about 122,000 nodes. A Pentium centrino duo 1.66

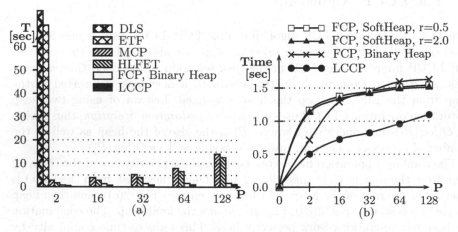

Fig. 3. Comparison of Scheduling cost of LCCP with other list scheduling algorithms

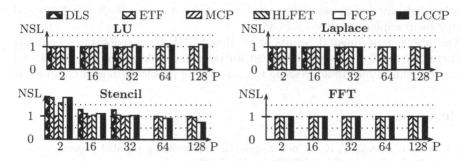

Fig. 4. Comparison of NSL for homogeneous system: ETF, HLFET, DLS, FCP and LCCP

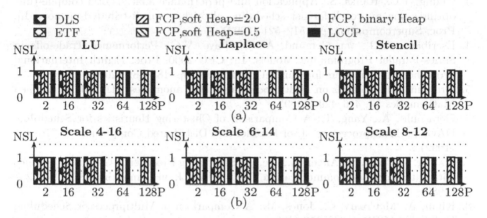

Fig. 5. Comparison of NSL for heterogenous system: (a) comparison of performance with respect to problem (b) comparison of performance with respect to heterogeneity

GHz processor PC with 1 GB RAM is used. Following experimental results show that LCCP has lower scheduling cost and its scheduling performance is better (in most cases) or equal to other list scheduling algorithms for both homogeneous systems and heterogeneous systems. Fig. 3(a) shows that the scheduling costs of LCCP is better than any other algorithm for any number of processors. Fig. 3(b) closely compares LCCP with FCP. LCCP has the lower scheduling cost even when the soft heap [2] is used as priority queue in FCP. So, the scheduling cost of the LCCP is less than any other scheduling algorithm and 29.5% to 41.8% better (less) than that of FCP. *Normalized Scheduling Length(NSL)* is a measure of scheduling performance, it is the ratio between the scheduling length from an algorithm and that of a reference algorithm. Fig 4 shows the Scheduling Performance of LCCP for homogeneous system, where MCP is used as the reference algorithm. Fig. 5(a)compares scheduling performance of LCCP with other list scheduling algorithms for heterogeneous system. Fig. 5(b) compares scheduling performance of LCCP for three processor speed ranges for heterogeneous system. In summary, the scheduling performance of LCCP is comparable to that of other list scheduling algorithms and always better than both soft heap and binary heap implementation of FCP.

The above experimental results show that LCCP has acceptable scheduling performance and lowest scheduling cost for large size task graphs. So, LCCP can be a promising choice in addressing the scheduling problems in grid computing.

References

1. Ahmed, I., Kwok, Y.-K.: A new approach to scheduling parallel programs using task duplication. In: Proc. ICCP, pp. 47–55 (1994)
2. Chazelle, B.: The Soft Heap: An Approximate Priority Queue with Optimal Error Rate. J. of the ACM 47, 1012–1027 (2000)
3. Chung, Y.C., Ranka, S.: Application and performance analysis of a compile-time optimization approach for list scheduling algorithms on distributed-memory. In: Proc. Supercomputing, pp. 512–521 (1992)
4. Escribano, A.G., van Gemund, A.J.C., Payo, V.C.: Performance Trade-offs in Series-Parallel Programming Models. In: CPC 2000. Proc. Eighth International Workshop on Compilers for Parallel Computers, pp. 183–189 (2000)
5. Graham, R.L.: Bounds on Multiprocessing timing anomalies. SIAM J. on Applied Mathematics 17, 416–429 (1969)
6. Gerasoulis, A., Yang, T.: A Comparison of Clustering Heuristics for Scheduling DAGs on Multiprocessors. J. of Parallel and Distributed Computing 16, 276–291 (1992)
7. Hwang, J., Chow, Y., Anger, E., Lee, C.: Scheduling Precedence Graphs in Systems with Interprocessor Communication Times. SIAM J. on Computing 18(2), 244–257 (1989)
8. Khan, A., McCreary, C., Jones, M.: A Comparison of Multiprocessor Scheduling Heuristics. ICPP 2, 243–250 (1994)
9. Kruatrachue, B., Lewis, T.G.: Grain size determination for parallel processing. IEEE Software, 23–32 (1988)
10. Kwok, Y., Ahmed, I.: Benchmarking the Task Graph scheduling Algorithms. In: Proc. IPPS/SPDP (1998)
11. Liou, J., Palis, M.: A Comparison of General Approaches to Multiprocessor Scheduling. In: Proc. Int'l Parallel Processing Symp, pp. 152–156 (1997)
12. Min-You, W., Gajski, D.: Hypertool: A Programming aid for Message-Passing Systems. IEEE Trans. Parallel and Distributed Systems 1(3) (1990)
13. Radulescu, A., van Gemund, A.J.C.: On the Complexity of List Scheduling Algorithms for Distributed-Memory Systems. In: ICS 1999. Proc. Int'l ACM Conf. on Supercomputing, Rhodes Greece (1999)
14. Radulescu, A., van Gemund, A.J.C.: Fast and Effective Task Scheduling in Heterogeneous Systems. In: Proc. HCW 2000, pp. 229–238. IEEE CS, Cancun (2000)
15. Sih, G., Lee, E.: A Compile-Time Scheduling Heuristic for Interconnection-Constrained Heterogeneous Processor Architecture. IEEE Trans. In Parallel and distributed Systems 4(2), 75–87 (1993)
16. Yang, T., Gerasoulis, A.: DSC: Scheduling parallel tasks on an unbounded number of processors. IEEE Trans. on Parallel and Distributed Systems 5(9), 951–967 (1994)

CG-Cell: An NPB Benchmark Implementation on Cell Broadband Engine

Dong Li, Song Huang, and Kirk Cameron

Department of Computer Science
Virginia Tech
{lid,huangs,Cameron}@cs.vt.edu

Abstract. The NAS Conjugate Gradient (CG) benchmark is an important scientific kernel used to evaluate machine performance and compare characteristics of different programming models. CG represents a computation and communication paradigm for sparse linear algebra, which is common in scientific fields. In this paper, we present the porting, performance optimization and evaluation of CG on Cell Broadband Engine (CBE). CBE, a heterogeneous multi-core processor with SIMD accelerators, is gaining attention and being deployed on supercomputers and high-end server architectures. We take advantages of CBE's particular architecture to optimize the performance of CG. We also quantify these optimizations and assess their impact. In addition, by exploring distributed nature of CBE, we present trade-off between parallelization and serialization, and Cell-specific data scheduling in its memory hierarchy. Our final result shows that the CG-Cell can achieve more than 4 times speedup over the performance of single comparable PowerPC Processor.

1 Introduction

The NAS Conjugate Gradient (CG) benchmark is often used to evaluate computer machine performance and compare characteristics of different programming models. It uses a conjugate gradient method to compute an approximation to the smallest eigenvalue of a large, sparse, symmetric positive definite matrix. CG is one of the memory intensive benchmark in NAS kernels and is typical of unstructured grid computations, which tests irregular long distance communication by employing unstructured matrix vector multiplication [1].

The recent developments in semiconductor technology lead to the debuts of multi-core processors in the computing industry, such as IBM's Cell, Sun Microsystems' Niagara and AMD's Opteron. The multi-core helps multi-programmed workloads which could contain a mix of independent sequential tasks. It presents a chance to study new or existing parallel programming models. However many questions for programming on multi-core are still open, such as how to efficiently handle specific communication and computation patterns. Cell Broadband Engine (CBE), developed jointly by Sony, Toshiba and IBM, is a new heterogeneous multi-core platform. The Cell is a general-purpose microprocessor which offers a rich palette of thread-level and data-level parallelization options to the programmer.

S. Rao et al. (Eds.): ICDCN 2008, LNCS 4904, pp. 263–273, 2008.
© Springer-Verlag Berlin Heidelberg 2008

The NPB CG presents a communication and computing pattern seen in sparse linear algebra [11]. It would be helpful to see how CG can be implemented on Cell, the new distributed and parallel scenario. Implementing CG on this special multi-core is a challenging topic. Firstly the essences of heterogeneous cores require careful consideration of task schedules while improving execution efficiency. Secondly Cell architecture shows an explicit and special memory hierarchy to users. On one hand, it presents a shared/global view of data to its nine cores through main memory. On the other hand, it presents a distributed view of data since eight of its nine cores have local memory. To achieve good performance on Cell, people need to carefully handle the data distribution and locality of references. Thirdly, due to its unusual architecture, unconventional Cell-specific code optimization approaches should be considered.

In this paper, we present how we solve the above problems in the implement CG on a real Cell multi-core. The main contributions of this paper include:

- We port NAS CG onto CBE. We present an example of how the communication and computation pattern of CG could be implemented on Cell and how we take advantage of the Cell's distributed multi-core nature. The result shows that CBE as a new architecture has good potential for this programming pattern with limited working data sets.
- We quantify Cell-specific code optimizations and assess their impacts using CG. These quantified results are beneficial for application developments on the Cell.
- We explore the parallelization methods on the Cell. We find that sometimes merely exposing task level parallelism is insufficient for high performance computing. We also find that parallelization on the Cell does not always mean performance speedup. Other factors, like overhead for creating threads and Direct Memory Access (DMA) communication, should be considerable when making decisions on parallelization.

The rest of this paper is organized as follows. Section 2 summarizes related works on programming support for Cell and studies of implementing CG using different programming models. Section 3 introduces kernel CG algorithm and section 4 outlines the Cell architecture. Section 5 presents step by step our CG porting and optimization process. In Section 6, we present the performance of parallel CG on Cell. In the end, we conclude the paper in Section 7.

2 Related Work

As a brand-new multi-core architecture, Cell has attracted many attentions in various research communities. Some researches focus on how to develop applications and speedup their performances. These include exploring new programming models and developing compiler supports. Other researches focus on analyzing the performance of the processor in terms of chip architecture.

Pieter et. al. [4] presents a simple and flexible programming model for Cell. It requires the input application source code to follow a certain paradigm. Then based on the paradigm annotation, a source to source compiler builds a task dependency graph of functions calls and schedules these calls in the SPEs. A locality-aware scheduling algorithm was also implemented to reduce the amount of data that is transferred to and from the SPEs. Eichenberger et. al [5] present several compiler techniques targeting automatic generation of highly optimized Cell code. The techniques include compiler-assisted memory alignment, branch prediction, SIMD parallelization, and OpenMP task level parallelization. They present the user with a single shared memory image through compiler mediated partitioning of code and data and the automatic orchestration of data movement implied by the partitioning. However, we didn't use their compilers in this paper, because some optimizations, such as the communication optimization and the parallelism decision, may be hard to derive automatically in a compiler due to application complexities. Filip et al. [6] [7] designs a multigrain parallelism scheduler to automatically exploit the task level and loop level parallel in response to workload characteristics. The scheduler oversubscribes the PowerPC Processor Element (PPE) to strive for higher utilization of Synergistic Processor Elements (SPE). In addition, he explored the conditions under which loop-level parallelism within off-loaded code can be used. He ported a bio-informatics code (RAxML) with inherent multigrain parallelism as a case study.

Williams et al. [9] present an analytical framework to predict performance of program code written for Cell. They apply it to several key scientific computing kernels, including dense matrix multiply, sparse matrix vector multiply, stencil computation and 1D/2D FFTs. Driven by their observation, they propose modest micro-architectural modification to increase the efficiency of double-precision calculations. Kistler et. al [8] analyze the Cell processor's communication network, using a series of benchmarks involving DMA traffic patterns and synchronization protocols.

CG benchmark has attracted considerable attentions from high-performance computing community, due to its random communication in computation. Zhang et. al [12] parallelizes the CG using the global arrays shared memory programming model. Mills et. al [13] satisfices the CG memory access by introducing a remote memory access capability based on MPI communication of cached memory blocks between compute nodes and designated memory servers.

3 Kernel CG Description

The Conjugate Gradient Method (CG) is the most prominent iterative method for solving sparse systems of linear equations. The NAS CG benchmark uses the inverse power method to find an estimation of the largest eigenvalue of a symmetric positive definite sparse matrix with a random pattern of non-zeros. The inverse power method involves solving a linear system of equation $Az = x$ using the conjugate gradient method. The size of the system n, number of outer iteration as "niter" in Figure 1, and the shift λ for different problem sizes in the benchmark are clearly specified in its official document [2]. Figure 1 illustrates the main iteration in NAS CG benchmark.

```
Initialize random number generator
Use Makea() to generate sparse matrix
```

$$x = [1,1,...,1]^T$$

```
DO it =1, niter    # For CLASS A, niter=15
     Running the function conj_grad to solve the
     system Az = x and return‖r‖,
```

$$\zeta = \lambda + 1/(x^T z)$$

$$x = z / \| z \|$$

ENDDO

Fig. 1. The main iteration in CG benchmark

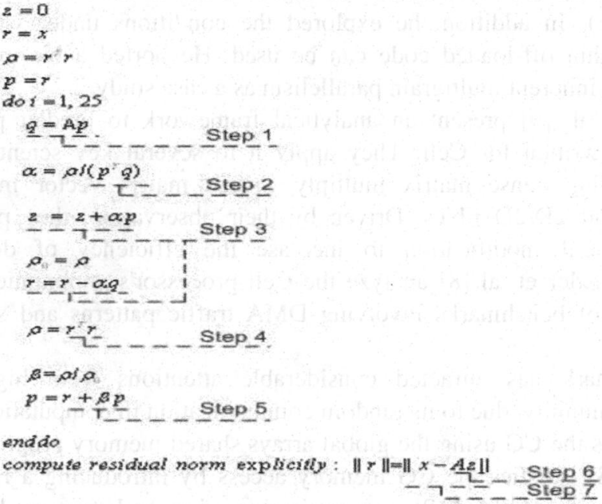

$$z = 0$$
$$r = x$$
$$\rho = r^T r$$
$$p = r$$
$$do\ i = 1, 25$$
$$q = Ap \qquad \text{Step 1}$$
$$\alpha = \rho/(p^T q) \qquad \text{Step 2}$$
$$z = z + \alpha p \qquad \text{Step 3}$$
$$\rho_0 = \rho$$
$$r = r - \alpha q$$
$$\rho = r^T r \qquad \text{Step 4}$$
$$\beta = \rho/\rho_0$$
$$p = r + \beta p \qquad \text{Step 5}$$
$$enddo$$
$$compute\ residual\ norm\ explicitly:\ \| r \| = \| x - Az \| \qquad \text{Step 6}$$
$$\text{Step 7}$$

Fig. 2. Conjugate Gradient Method

The solution z to the linear system of equations $Az = x$ is to be approximated using the conjugate gradient (CG) method, which is implemented as in Figure2. In this paper, we use NPB2.3 OpenMP version as our start point.

4 Cell Broadband Engine

CBE is the first incarnation of a new family of microprocessors extending the 64-bit PowerPC architecture. It is a single-chip multiprocessor with nine processors operating on a shared, coherent memory. These nine processors are specified as one *PowerPC Processor Element (PPE)*, and eight *Synergistic Processor Elements (SPE)*. The PPE is a 64-bit, dual-thread PowerPC processor, while the SPE is the high-end computing engines optimized for running compute-intensive applications. The designation *synergistic* for the SPE was chosen carefully because there is a mutual dependence between the PPE and the SPEs. The SPEs depend on the PPE to run the operating system, and, in many cases, the top-level control thread of an application; the PPE depends on the SPEs to provide the bulk of the application performance.

The PPE supports both the PowerPC instruction set and the Vector/SIMD multimedia extension instruction set [10]. In our current Play Station 3 (PS3) Cell, the PPE doesn't support the vectorization of double precision float point data (the data type of matrix element in CG).

Each SPE contains a RISC core (SPU), 256-KB, software-controlled Local Store (LS) for instructions and data, and a large (128-bit, 128-entry) unified register file. The SPEs support a special SIMD instruction set which could lead to computation vectorization. SPEs rely on asynchronous DMA transfers to move data and instructions between main storage and their LS. Data transferred between local storage and main memory must be 128-bit aligned and the size of each DMA transfer can be at most 16KB. The Memory Flow Controller (MFC), which handles DMA transfer, supports only DMA transfer sizes that are 1, 2, 4, 8 or multiples of 16 bytes long. Note that the LS in SPE has no memory protection, and memory access wraps from the end of LS back to the beginning. An SPU program is free to write anywhere in LS including its own instruction space. We need to avoid the corruption of the SPU program text when the stack area overflows into the program area.

The PPE and SPEs communicate coherently with each other and with main memory and I/O through the Element Interconnect Bus (EIB). The EIB is a 4-ring structure for data, and a tree structure for commands. The EIB's internal bandwidth is 96 bytes per cycle, thus achieving a peak bandwidth of 204.8GB/s. It can support more than 100 outstanding DMA memory requests between main storage and the SPEs.

5 Design and Analysis

In our implementation we ported CG to Cell in four steps: (i) porting the CG on the PPE; (ii) offloading the most time-consuming parts on one SPE; (iii) parallelizing the SPE code to run on multiple SPEs; (iv) optimizing the SPE code. These steps are outlined in the following sections.

The results reported in this section are obtained from a Cell multi-processor in a PS3. It has 256MB XDR RAM. The PPE have a 32KB L1 instruction cache, a 32 KB L1 data cache, and a 512KB unified L2 cache. The system runs Fedora Core 5 (Linux kernel 2.6.16), including Cell-Specific kernel patches. We compile our code using ppuxlc and spu-gcc in the Cell SDK 2.1 for ppu and spu respectively.

5.1 Porting CG on PPE

As our first step, we port CG onto PPE, which is actually a single Power 970 architecture compliant core. To port CG on PPE, we collect all functions distributed in several source files and move them into one source file. In original OpenMP implementation, the header files used to be automatically generated by the NPB script. We manually write the header files according to our input CLASS. These works simplify both the program directory hierarchy and its build process. We call the current work the version 0.1.

In this version, we run the CG on one PPE thread with an input of CLASS A. The system matrix size for CLASS A is 14,000×14,000. It has 15 iteration, i.e. 15 conj_grad function calls as in Figure 1, which has total 1.50×10^9 FLOPs., The time for the 15 conj_grad function calls running on PPE is 14.90 seconds. We treat this result as our performance baseline for later sections.

5.2 Function Off-Loading

Our next step is to offload the computation intensive function conj_grad into SPE. We create one SPE thread to be in charge of the total 15 conj_grad function calls. To observe the initial speedup, it is better to use a small input matrix, which can be completely loaded into SPE 256KB LS. We shrink the input matrix size to 256×256, which occupies 30KB memory space. This mini-matrix allows us not to involve into the communication complexity of dividing data sets and focus only on the computation optimization. We will talk about dividing data sets later in Section 5.3.

Our initial computation optimization is to vectorize all the matrix data. Vector operations eliminate the overhead for scalar formatting and thus reduce the long latency caused by scalar load and store. The Vector/SIMD Multimedia Extension intrinsic and SPE SIMD operation provide supports to vector operation for PPE and SPE respectively. We could depend on auto-vectorizing compiler to do the vectorization by merging scalar data into a parallel-packed SIMD data structure. However such compiler must handle all the high-level language constructs and do not always produce optimal code. Therefore, we choose to do vectorization manually in our program. In addition, we only vectorize the function conj_grad running on the SPE, because PPE doesn't support SIMD operation for double precision floating point matrix data in CG.

Generally speaking, there are two methods for organizing data in SIMD vectors: Array-of-Structure (AOS) and Structure-of-Array (SOA) [3]. In this paper, we use SOA for vectorizing matrix data, i.e. across the vector both the data types and data interpretation are the same. This conforms to most data operations requirements in the algorithm and execute more efficiently than AOS organization. Although AOS produces small code sizes, it requires significant loop-unrolling to improve its efficiency and executes poorly. Note that here we don't vectorize step1 and step6 shown in Figure 2. The reason lies that these two steps do sparse matrix-vector multiplication. The data for computation in vector p and z are scattered around in the memory space (Figure 3). To vectorize the computing, we need to gather vector data into address-aligned continuous memory space. This requires extra memory copy operations which are proved to have big overhead by our experiences.

Based on the above work, our result shows that the new CG takes 35 milliseconds with mini-array as input, while the version 0.1 with the same input takes 8.1 milliseconds. This new CG's performance is even worse. Obviously the optimization with only data vectorization is not enough for performance improvement. This is because the vectorization can only happen on the SPE in our case and thus has limited benefits. Meanwhile for function off-loading we have to pay for the costs of transferring data between the main memory and SPE's LS, which counteracts the gains of vectorization.

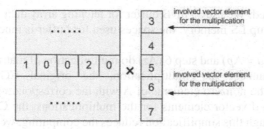

Fig. 3. An example of spare matrix-vector multiplication. One matrix row is doing multiplication with the vector. Only non-zero matrix data are considered. The involved vector elements for multiplication are not in continuous memory address.

5.3 Parallel Execution across Multiple SPEs

To fully take advantage of CBE multi-core architecture, we want to parallelize the program on 8 SPEs. An obvious method is to regard each conj_grad function call as a task and distribute 15 tasks across 8 SPEs. However due to data dependency on vector x, this task-level parallelization doesn't work. Due to the same reason (the data dependency on vector p in Figure 2), distribution of 25 iterations in the conj_grad function across 8 SPE doesn't work either.

As an alternative, we deliberately divide each loop into 5 steps and parallel them as shown in Figure 2. We also parallel two "residual norm" computing steps outside of conj_grad loops, as step 6 and step 7 in Figure 2. We create seven SPE modules corresponding to these steps and move the conj_grad loop into the PPE. Whenever the PPE program flow meets a step, it will load SPE program image corresponding to this step into each SPE LS and create threads to execute it. Then each SPE will fetch part of total matrix data from the main memory to the LS, do computing and/or update data in the main memory.

CG uses three arrays ("*rowstr*", "*colidx*" and "*a*") to record the sparse matrix in a compact way. The array *a* stores non-zero data elements of the matrix and put them in a row. The array *rowstr* records the position of first non-zero element in each matrix row. The array *colidx* records the column number for each non-zero data elements in the matrix. For CLASS A, the total size of these three array data is 4.41MB, which cannot be fitted into the LS (256KB) of a SPE.

The way we distribute the data is described in the following. The conj_grad function does computation row by row, so we distribute the data among SPEs at the granularity of row. In particular, each SPE processes 1/8 of the total rows and needs data for its 1/8 share of the total rows. For the array *rowstr*, we just evenly divide it into eight parts and copy them from the main memory to SPE LS. For the array *colidx* and *a*, even distribution doesn't work, because the number of nonzero elements varies from one row to the others. We need to locate the starting and the ending position for each 1/8 row block. This could be done with the help of *rowstr* array. The *rowstr* array data for 1/8 rows with CLASS A as input is 6.8KB and can be totally put in the LS.

However even though we distribute the array data in the above way, the array data for 1/8 row could still be bigger than the 256KB LS size. Therefore we strip-mine each 1/8 rows data by fetching a few row elements to local storage, and execute the corresponding loop iterations on this batch of elements. This operation continues until all data are processed. We use an 8KB buffer for fetching array data. It should be noted that to avoid using up LS memory, the spaces used for buffer is much smaller than the size of the LS.

Both the step 1 ($q = Ap$) and step 6 (Az) do multiplication of matrix A with a vector. To reduce the unnecessary multiplication, the original CG only computes multiplications of the nonzero elements of A with the corresponding vector elements. To locate the needed vector elements for the multiplications, the CG depends on the array *colidx*. Although this simplification reduces the computing, we may have to copy the *colidx* and the vector from the main memory to the LS, as far as the parallel implementation is concerned. Since the *colidx* is too big to be totally placed in the LS, we could process it in the same way as we do to the array *a*. However for the vector *p* or *z*, the needed elements for the multiplication are scattered around the memory. It is highly inefficient to copy these elements one by one from the main memory to LS.

There are two ways to solve this problem. One is to ignore the unnecessary vector elements and firstly copy the needed vector elements into an address-aligned new array in the main memory. We call this array as "compressed vector". Then only the compressed vector is copied to the SPE and the SPE doesn't care about *colidx* at all. Although this method sounds promising, it has big overhead of copying. Since the vector *p* is updated each time at the step 5, we need to re-produce the compressed vector at each loop. According to our experiences this overhead easily beats the gains of parallelization. The second way is to completely put the vector *p* in the SPE LS and process the *colidx* in the same way as we do to the array *a*. This method needs to reserve enough LS space for the vector. In our implementation we manage to limit the data (three arrays) in the LS within 30KB (The section 5.4.2 describes how we use the double buffer to limit the size of array *a* and array *colidx* in the LS. The array *rowstr* is 6.8KB and totally placed in the LS. This sums up to 30KB) and the program image is less than 8KB, so the rest LS space can hold the whole vector *p* under the case of input CLASS A. For larger CLASS, there is a chance the vector can't be totally placed in the LS. We have to divide it into data blocks. The size of data blocks is determined by the available LS space. We leave this case as our future work.

After the parallelization in this step, we got the current version 0.2. This version takes 21.62 seconds with CLASS A as input. This result is even worse than our baseline (14.90 seconds). The next section will describe how we reduce the execution time by optimization.

5.4 Performance Optimization

We consider performance optimization from two aspects. One is to balance the tradeoff between parallelization and serialization based on the profiling results. The other is to take into consideration Cell architecture characters.

5.4.1 Parallel or Not

To figure out the reason why version 0.2(parallel version) does not gain performance speedup over version 0.1(serial version), we profile the conj_grad for both versions at the granularity of step. To make things simpler, we only run one loop for the conj_grad main iteration. The profiling results are shown in Figure 4. It is clear that step1 and step 6 gain great performance improvements from the parallelization, while other steps do the opposite. Further analysis reveals that step1 and step6 have O (n^2) multiplication while other steps have O (n), where n is the matrix size. This means that step1 and step 6 take up a predominant percentage of computation if n is large. Larger computation intensiveness means more computing on each data movement (DMA transmission) between SPE LS and main memory. Only after the parallelization gains counteract the overhead of data movement could we get the performance improved. Thus, the overhead of data movement for parallelization should be considered. In addition, creating SPE threads is not free. Our experiment shows that the overhead of creating a single SPU thread costs 1.81 milliseconds, which is comparable to running 10 times of step 2 in one loop. Furthermore, more threads also mean more scheduling tasks and more competition in DMA bus. Due to those various factors, parallelization is not always beneficial to performance. Therefore, we have to carefully consider the balance between parallelization and serialization.

Based on the analysis above, we don't parallel steps 2-5 and 7. Results show (Figure 4 and Figure 6) that this optimization (we call it the version 0.3 hereafter) improves a factor of 6.093 over version 0.2, and a factor of 4.519 over the baseline (version 0.1).

5.4.2 Branch Reducing and Communication Optimization

The Cell SPE hardware assumes linear structure flow and produces no stall penalties from sequential instruction execution. A branch instruction has the potential of disrupting the assumed sequential flow. Specifically, a mispredicted branch incurs a penalty of approximately 18-19 cycles in the SPE. Branches also create scheduling barriers, reducing the opportunity of dual issue and covering up dependency stalls. Our next optimization is to reduce branches in SPE as much as possible. In step1 and step6, we need to use a function called getNextBlockSize, which deals with address alignment for DMA transfer and controls transfer block size within the limits of available SPE LS. This function employs several conditional branches. Moreover, considering the popularity of this function, these branches would be rather expensive for SPE. Therefore we move this function to PPE and use DMA-List to determine each transfer size before SPE takes over computation tasks. Each SPE gets its DMA-list after it starts new thread and uses the list to determine each transfer size.

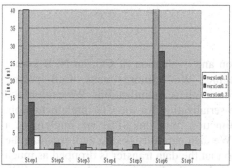

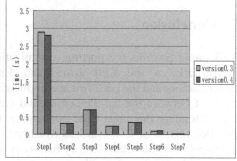

Fig. 4. conj_grad function profiling. The time for each step is for one loop in the function.

Fig. 5. Performance profiling of 15 times of the conj_grad function call

Another optimization we employ is to use double buffering in SPE. We allocate two buffers for array *a* and *colidx* respectively and each buffer holds 1024 array elements. When the SPE is working on one buffer, the other buffer is for data transferring. In this way, we can pipeline computation time with data transferring time. The total buffer size is 24KB, which is much smaller than the size of LS. This double buffering scheme maximize the time spent in the compute phase of a program and minimize the time spent waiting for DMA transfer to complete.

With the above two optimizations, our performance improves more than four times over the baseline. We call the current CG-Cell after optimization version 0.4, which is also our final version. Figure 5 depicts the profiling of the paralleled conj_grad at the granularity of step for version 0.3 and version 0.4.

6   Performance Evaluation

As a performance comparison, Figure 6 evaluates the total execution time for several important versions in CG_Cell. It shows that our version 0.4 has been improved a lot over version 0.1. Version 0.2, although fully paralleled, costs the most time. Since we eliminate the parallelization in the step 2 to step 5, version 0.3 is improved greatly. In version 0.4, since we have used the specific optimization for the Cell, the total execution time is less than 1/4.

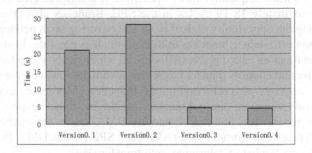

Fig. 6. Total running time of four versions

7   Conclusion

This paper presents the porting, optimization and evaluation of CG, an NPB kernel benchmark on the Cell Broadband Engine. We explore many Cell-specific optimizations and the performance implications of these optimizations. We explore the tradeoff between the parallelization and the serialization for the CG implementation. By offloading the most time-consuming function onto the SPE, we implement a parallel version of CG with less overhead. We also carefully divide and organize the data sets to fit into Cell memory hierarchy so that the data transfer is dropped as much as possible. We vectorize the computation, reduce the branches instructions on SPE program and use double buffer to hide memory access delay. Starting from a less optimized CG implementation on PPE, we were able to boost performance on Cell by more than a factor of four.

References

[1] Bailey, D., Barszcz, E., et al.: The NAS Parallel Benchmarks—Summary and Preliminary Results. In: Proceedings of the 1991 ACM/IEEE Conference on SuperComputing (1991)

[2] Bailey, D., Harris, T., Saphir, W., Van der Vijingaart, R., Woo, A., Yarrow, M.: The NAS Parallel Benchmarks 2.0, Technical Report NAS-95-020, NASA Ames Research Center (1995)

[3] IBM Systems and Technology Group. Cell Broadband Engine Programming Tutorial Version 2.1, http://www.ibm.com/developerworks/power/cell/documents.html

[4] Bellens, P., Perez, J.M., Badia, R.M., Labarta, J.: Memory—CellSs: a programming model for the cell BE architecture. In: Proceedings of the 2006 ACM/IEEE conference on Supercomputing, Tampa, Florida (November 11-17, 2006)

[5] Eichenberger, A.E., et al.: Optimizing Compiler for a Cell processor. In: 14th International Conference on Parallel Architectures and Compilation Techniques, St. Louis, MO (September 2005)

[6] Blagojevic, F., Stamatakis, A., Antonopoulos, C., Nikolopoulos, D.S.: RAxML-CELL: Parallel Phylogenetic Tree Construction on the Cell Broadband Engine. In: Proceedings of the 21st IEEE/ACM International Parallel and Distributed Processing Symposium, IEEE Computer Society Press, Los Alamitos (2007)

[7] Blagojevic, F., Stamatakis, A., Antonopoulos, C., Nikolopoulos, D.S.: Dynamic Mulitgrain Parallelization on the Cell Broadband Engine. In: Proceedings of the 2007 ACM SIGPLAN Symposium on Principles and Practice of Parallel Programming, San Jose, California, pp. 90–100 (March 2007)

[8] Kistler, M., Perrone, M., Petrini, F.: Cell Multi-processor Interconnection Network: Built for Speed. IEEE Micro, 26(3), (May-June 2006), http://hpc.pnl.gov/people/fabrizio/papers/ieeemicro0cell.pdf

[9] Williams, S., Shalf, J., Oliker, L., Kamil, S., Husbands, P., Yelick, K.: The potential of the Cell Processor for Scientific Computing. In: ACM International Conference on Computing Frontiers (May 3-6, 2006)

[10] PowerPC Microprocessor Family: Vector/SIMD Multimedia Extension Technology Programming Environments Manual, http://www-306.ibm.com/chips/techlib

[11] Asanovic, K., Bodik, R., et al.: The Landscape of Parallel Computing Research: A View from Berkeley, http://www.eecs.berkeley.edu/Pubs/TechRpts/2006/EECS-2006-183.htm

[12] Zhang, Y., Tiparaju, V., Nieplocha, J., Hariri, S.: Parallelization of the NAS Conjugate Gradient Benchmark Using the Global Arrays Shared Memory Programming Model. In: IPDPS 2005. Proceedings of the 19th IEEE International Parallel and Distributed Processing Symposium - Workshop 4 - Volume 05 (2005)

[13] Mills, R., Yue, C., Stathopoulos, A., Nikolopoulos, D.S.: Runtime and Programming Support for Memory Adaptation in Scientific Applications via Local Disk and Remote Memory.Journal of Grid Computing, 5(2):213-234, ISSN 1570-7873, 1572-9184. Springer Verlag (June 2007)

Parallel Algorithm for Conflict Graph on OTIS-Triangular Array

Keny T. Lucas[1], Dheeresh K. Mallick[2], and Prasanta K. Jana[3]

[1] Department of Information Management
Xavier Institute of Social Service, Ranchi – 834001, India
kennylucas@xiss.ac.in
[2] Department of Computer Science and Engineering Birla Institute of Technology, Mesra,
Ranchi – 835 215, India
dkmallick@gmail.com
[3] Department of Computer Science and Engineering, Indian School of Mines University,
Dhanbad – 826 004, India
prasantajana@yahoo.com

Abstract. The algorithms dealing with the galled tree problem mostly use a conflict graph as the major tool and the construction of the conflict graph has been the central computation in these algorithms. In this paper, we present a parallel algorithm for the construction of a conflict graph. Given a set of n binary sequences, each of size m, our algorithm is mapped on an OTIS-Triangular array and requires $4m + 2n/k - 7$ electronics moves + 2 OTIS moves, where $k = m (m-1)/2$. The algorithm is shown to be scalable with respect to n.

Keywords: Conflict graph, phylogenetic network, galled tree.

1 Introduction

A phylogenetic network that represents the evolutionary history of living organisms is biologically more complete than a phylogenetic tree as it takes care both the evolutionary and recombination phenomena. In the recent years, much attention has been drawn to construct a special case of phylogenetic network, called a galled tree. Many algorithms [1], [2], [3], [4], [5], [6], [7] have been developed for galled tree problem in which the conflict graph is used as the major tool and its construction is the major computation that dominates the overall time complexity of the algorithms. However, it requires $O(nm^2)$ time for given a set of n binary sequences, each of size m and therefore it is not encouraging in the sequential environment for massive biological data. Parallel construction of the conflict graph is, therefore, called for research to solve the galled tree problem.

In this paper, we propose a parallel algorithm for building the conflict graph. Our algorithm is mapped on an OTIS-Triangular array in $4m + n/k - 7$ electronic moves + 2 OTIS moves, where k is the number of processors within each group of the OTIS-Triangular array. An OTIS (optical transpose interconnection system) proposed by Marsden [8] is an interconnection network that benefits from electronic and optical links. In such systems, the processors are partitioned into groups (also called blocks). The processors within each group are connected by usual electronic links and the

S. Rao et al. (Eds.): ICDCN 2008, LNCS 4904, pp. 274–279, 2008.
© Springer-Verlag Berlin Heidelberg 2008

processors of two different groups are connected by optical links following the OTIS rule: P^{th} processor of Gth group is linked to the Gth processor of the Pth group. The choice of an interconnection pattern among the processors within each group yields a specific model of OTIS parallel computer. Several parallel algorithms have been mapped on different OTIS models such as matrix multiplication [9], image processing [10], numerical algorithms [11], prefix computation [12], BPC permutation [13].

2 Conflict Graph and Computation Model

Let the set of n binary sequences be represented by a binary matrix M where

$$M = \begin{bmatrix} a_{11} & a_{12} & \cdots & a_{1m} \\ a_{21} & a_{22} & \cdots & a_{2m} \\ \vdots & \vdots & & \vdots \\ a_{n1} & a_{n2} & \cdots & a_{nm} \end{bmatrix}$$

Given M, two columns are said to conflict each other if and only if they have at least three rows with the combinations 01, 10 and 11. A column is called conflicted if it has conflict with at least one other column. A conflict graph C_G is formed with all the columns in M where each node is labelled by a distinct column and there exists an undirected edge $<\alpha, \beta>$ if and only if the columns α and β conflict. As an example the conflict graph with four columns is shown in Fig. 1. A connected component in C_G is the maximal subgraph of C_G such that for any pair of nodes in C_G there is at least one path between those nodes in C_G. A trivial connected component has only one node and the column associated with that node is unconflicted. Note that the conflict graph shown in Fig. 1(b) has a single nontrivial connected component that consists of all the columns and there is no trivial connected component. In other words, there is no unconflicted column. It is shown in [4] that the construction of the conflict graph is central to solve the galled tree problem in which only the non-trivial connected components play the major role.

$$M = \begin{bmatrix} 1 & 0 & 1 & 0 \\ 0 & 1 & 0 & 0 \\ 1 & 0 & 1 & 1 \\ 0 & 1 & 1 & 0 \\ 0 & 0 & 1 & 1 \\ 1 & 0 & 0 & 1 \end{bmatrix}$$

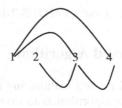

(a) A set of binary sequences   (b) Conflict graph

Fig. 1. Conflict graph

In the construction of the conflict graph, we need to compare each column with all its subsequent columns requiring $O(nm^2)$ time. Our computational model is an OTIS-Triangular array in which k^2 processors are organized into k groups; each group is basically a triangular array of $k = m(m-1)/2$ processors. As an example, for $m = 4$ the model is shown in Fig. 2 in which smaller rectangles represent the processors and the bigger ones represent the groups. The groups are indexed in increasing order from left to right and from bottom to top fashion. The processors within a group are also indexed in the similar fashion in which the 1st index gives the group number and the 2nd index, the processor number within that group. The processors within a group are connected by electronic links in the form of a triangular mesh and the processors of two different groups are connected via optical links following OTIS rule: P^{th} processor of the Gth group is connected to the Gth processor of the Pth group. The electronic and optical links can be essentially differentiated as follows: i) optical links have much larger bandwidth than electronic links and ii) transfer times including latency is different along optical and electronic links. While analyzing our proposed algorithms, we count the data moves along the electronic links (i.e., electronic moves) and that on optical links (i.e., optical moves) separately.

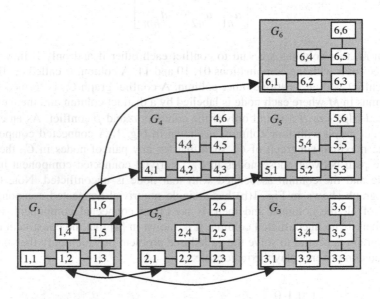

Fig. 2. Topology of OTIS-Triangular array (All optical connections are not shown)

3 Proposed Algorithm

For simplicity and without any loss of generality, we assume here $n = kr$. The basic idea of our algorithm is to divide each column of the binary matrix M into k sub-columns of length r, which are then suitably fed row wise and column wise into the blocks (triangular array). We then check the patterns 01, 10 and 11 on each block with the corresponding rows and columns and store the results locally. These results are then combined using suitable OTIS and electronic moves to obtain the final conflict result. We illustrate the initial inputs to the individual blocks with an example for $n = 30$, $r = 5$ and $m = 4$ as shown in Fig. 3 in which a single '*' indicates one unit delay.

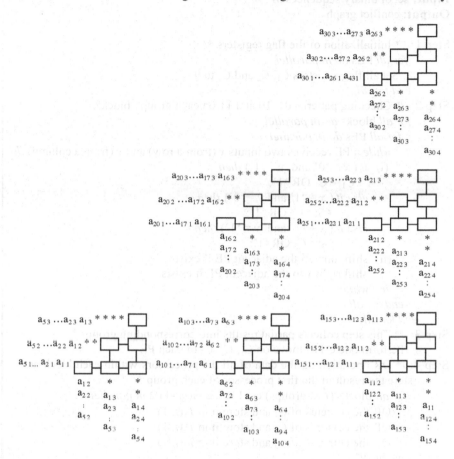

Fig. 3. Initial input in each group

The data is fed to the blocks row wise as follows: The sub-columns of column 1 are inputted to the 1st row of the groups in left to right and bottom to top fashion; the sub-columns of the column 2 are fed to 2nd row and so on. The sub-columns are also inputted column wise in the similar fashion, i.e, the sub-columns of the 2nd column are fed to the 1st column, those of the column 3 to the 2nd column and so on. We assume that each processor has three flag registers namely C_1, C_2 and C_3 to indicate the patterns 01, 10 and 11 respectively, one temporary register T and one status register S. At the end of the algorithm, the final conflict result is stored in the status register S, which is basically an adjacency matrix that represents the conflict graph. The algorithm is formally given stepwise as follows.

Algorithm Con-Graph(M)

Input: set of binary sequences M
Output: conflict graph

Step 1: /* Initialization of the flag registers */
    for all PEs *do in parallel*
        Set all flag registers C_1, C_2 and C_3 to 0
    end for all
Step 2: /* Checking patterns 01, 10 and 11 on each group / block*/
    for all blocks *do in parallel*
      for all PEs *do in parallel*
        while a PE receives two inputs x (from a row) and y (from a column) *do*
        (i) *if* (x = '0' and y = '1') *then*
            $C_1 := C_1$ OR '1';
          else if (x = '1' and y = '0') *then*
            $C_2 := C_2$ OR '1';
          else if (x = '1' and y = '1') *then*
            $C_3 := C_3$ OR '1';
        (ii) shift up y to the adjacent PE if exists
           shift right x to the adjacent PE if exists
        end while
      end for all
    end for all
Step 3: /* This step collects partial results into corresponding groups */
    Perform one OTIS move on C_1, C_2, C_3 of each PE
Step 4: /* OR operation on the data of all the processors within each block and
    store the result in the first processor of each group */
    for all blocks (i.e., groups) G_i, $1 \le i \le m(m-1)/2$ *in parallel*
    OR the contents of C_1 and store it in $T_1(i, 1)$
    OR the contents of C_2 and store it in $T_2(i, 1)$
    OR the contents of C_3 and store it in $T_3(i, 1)$
    end for all
Step 5: Perform one OTIS move on $T_1(i, 1)$, $T_2(i, 1)$, $T_3(i, 1)$, $1 \le i \le m(m-1)/2$
Step 6: /* Obtain final conflict result from the Group 1*/
    for all PE$(1, j)$, $1 \le j \le m(m-1)/2$ *do in parallel*
        $S(1, j) := T_1(1, j)$ AND $T_2(2, j)$ AND $T_3(3, j)$
    end for all
Step 7: Stop

Time Complexity: Step 1 requires constant time. Step 2 is performed in $2m + r - 4$ electronic moves. Each of the steps 3 and 5 require one OTIS move. Step 4 requires $2m - 3$ electronic moves and Step 6 requires constant time. Therefore, the above algorithm requires $4m + r - 7$ electronics moves + 2 OTIS moves, i.e., $4m + n/k - 7$ electronic moves + 2 OTIS moves, where $k = m (m - 1)/2$.

    This is important to note that the algorithm can work for any value of n assuming that n is multiple of k, i.e., $n = kr$.

4 Conclusions

We have presented a parallel algorithm for constructing conflict graph towards the solution of the galled tree problem. Given a set of n binary sequences, each of size m, our algorithm has been mapped on an OTIS-Triangular array. We have shown that the algorithm requires $4m + n/k - 7$ electronics moves $+ 2$ OTIS moves where $k = m$ $(m-1)/2$, i.e., the number of processors within each group of the OTIS-Triangular array. The algorithm has been shown to be scalable with respect to n with the assumption that n is multiple of k.

References

[1] Wang, L., Zhang, K., Zhang, L.: Perfect phylogenetic networks with recombination. Journal of Computational Biology. 8, 69–78 (2001)

[2] Myers, S.R., Griffths, R.C.: Bounds on the minimum number of recombination events in a sample history. Genetics 163, 375–394 (2003)

[3] Gusfield, D., Satish, E., Langley, C.: Efficient reconstruction of phylogenetic networks (of SNPs) with constrained recombination. In: Proceedings of 2nd CSB Bioinformatics Conference, Los Alamitos, CA (2003)

[4] Gusfield, D., Satish, E., Langley, C.: Optimal efficient reconstruction of phylogenetic networks with constrained recombination. Journal of Bioinformatics and Computational Biology 2, 173–213 (2004)

[5] Gusfield, D.: Optimal, efficient reconstruction of root-unknown phylogenetic networks with constrained recombination, Technical Report, Department of Computer Sc., University of California, Davis, CA

[6] Gusfield, D., Satish, E., Langley, C.: The fine structure of galls in phylogenetic networks. Informs Journal on Computing 16, 459–469 (2004)

[7] Bafna, V., Bansal, V.: The number of recombination events in a sample history conflict graph and lower bounds. IEEE Ttrans. on Computational Biology and Bioinformatics 1, 78–90 (2004)

[8] Marsden, G., Marchand, P., Harvey, P., Esner, S.: Optical transpose interconnection system architectures. Optics Letters 18, 1083–1085 (1993)

[9] Wang, C.-F., Sahni, S.: Matrix Multiplication on the OTIS-Mesh optoelectronic computer. IEEE Transactions on Computers 50(7) (July 2001)

[10] Wang, C.-F., Sahni, S.: Image processing on the OTIS-Mesh optoelectronic Computer. IEEE Transactions on parallel and Distributed Systems 11(2), 97–109 (2000)

[11] Jana, P.K.: Polynomial Interpolation and Polynomial Root Finding on OTIS- Mesh. Parallel Computing 32(4), 301–312 (2006)

[12] Jana, P.K., Sinha, B.P.: An Improved parallel prefix algorithm on OTIS-Mesh. Parallel Processing Letters 16(4), 429–440 (2006)

[13] Wang, C.-F., Sahni, S.: BPC permutations on the OTIS-Mesh optoelectronic computer. In: MPPOI 1997. Proc. of 4th Int'l Conference on Massively Parallel Processing Using Optical Transpose Interconnection, pp. 130–135 (1997)

A Deadlock Free Shortest Path Routing Algorithm for WK-Recursive Meshes

Mostafa Rezazad[1,2], M. Hoseiny Farahabady[1], and Hamid Sarbazi-Azad[1,2]

[1] Sharif University of Technology, Terhan, Iran
[2] IPM school of computer sceince, Tehrn, Iran
{Rezazad,hoseiny,azad}@ipm.ir,sharif.edu

Abstract. In this paper, we investigate an efficient deadlock-free shortest path routing algorithm for WK-recursive mesh networks which has been shown that possess several advantages like suitable to be manufactured by VLSI technology and easy to be expanded. It will be shown that the proposed algorithm requires $O(\sqrt{n})$ routing steps (where N is the network size) to route the entire network by exploiting either the self-routing or second order routing scheme.

Keywords: WK-recursive, Deadlock Free Routing Algorithm, shortest path routing.

1 Introduction

In a network-based parallel/distributed system, the underlying interconnection network is used by the processing nodes to exchange data and to operate simultaneously with each other. Two of main design and fundamental challenges of interconnection networks are their topology and routing algorithm. Among the various complex topologies proposed in the literature for the design and implementation of interconnection networks, the WK-Recursive mesh topology [1] has received much attention in the last decade [2-5]. Previous works relating to WK-Recursive topology have shown that this network has the following advantages. First of all, it is suitable to be manufactured by VLSI technology and easy to be expanded as a result of its recursive structure. As well, its recursive structure provides high performance communication at low cost by exploring the locality that exists in the transfer patterns of massively parallel computers. Second, the small diameter and small average internode distance enables WK-recursive meshes to pose short and cost-effective transmission latency when transmitting messages from the source nodes to the destination nodes within the network leading to high performance inter-node communications [3]. Almost all previous studies [1-5] on WK-recursive meshes focus on topological properties and algorithmic issues. In this paper, we investigate an efficient deadlock-free shortest path routing algorithm that is a basic requirement of all interconnection networks. It will be shown that the proposed algorithm requires $O(\sqrt{n})$ routing steps (where N is the network size) to route the entire network by exploiting either the self-routing or second order routing scheme which will be later defined in section 2. It is

S. Rao et al. (Eds.): ICDCN 2008, LNCS 4904, pp. 280–285, 2008.

noteworthy that the existing routing algorithms proposed for this network does not guarantee freedom from deadlock [4]. Our focus is to make a comprehensive comparison between different aspects of the proposed routing algorithms and introduce a new algorithm to overcome drawbacks of previous ones, i.e. to propose a minimal (shortest-path) wormhole routing algorithm which is deadlock-free and requires a minimum number of virtual channels to ensure deadlock freedom and adaptively.

2 The WK-Recursive Mesh

In this section, we formally define the WK-recursive mesh network and investigate its important properties.

Definition 1. An L-level WK-recursive mesh network $WK_{(t,L)}$, with amplitude t and expansion level L, consists of a set of nodes $V(WK_{(t,L)})=$ $\{a_L a_{L-1}...a_1 | 0 \le a_i < t \ for \ 1 \le i \le L\}$. The node with address schema $A = (a_L a_{L-1}...a_1)$ is connected to (1) all nodes with address type $(a_L a_{L-1}...a_2 k)$ for $k \in \{0,1,...,t-1\}, k \ne a_1$, as brother nodes and (2) node $(a_L a_{L-1}...a_{j+1} a_{j-1}(a_j)^j)$ if for one j, $1 \le j \le L-1$, we have $a_{j-1} = a_{j-2} = ... = a_1$ and $a_j \ne a_{j-1}$, as cousin node (notation $(a_j)^j$ denotes j consecutive a_j's). The links of type (1) are called *substituting links* and are labeled 0. The link of type (2) is called *j-flipping link* and is labeled j. It is apparent that the node with address $(a_L)^L$ has not any cousin; we call such a node an *extern node*. Consequently, any $WK_{(t,L)}$ has exactly t extern nodes. The degree of extern nodes for all $WK_{(t,L)}$ is t-1 and the degree of other nodes is t. As a result, the number of nodes in a $WK_{(t,L)}$ is calculated by $|V(WK_{(t,L)})|=t^L$. The number of edges in $WK_{(t,L)}$ is $|E(WK_{(t,L)})|=t^{L+1}-t$ [3]. As well, the diameter of $WK_{(t,L)}$, denoted by D_L, is $2^{L+1}-1$ [5].

Definition 2 [2]. Define $(a_L a_{L-1}...a_{m+1}.WK_{t,m})$ to be the sub-network of $WK_{(t,L)}$ induced by all nodes with address schema $\{(a_L a_{L-1}...a_{m+1} a_m a_{m-1} \cdots a_1 a_0) | 0 \le a_j \le t-1\}$ for all $0 \le j \le m-1$. That is, $(a_L a_{L-1}...a_{m+1}.WK_{t,m})$ is an embedded $WK_{(t,m)}$ with the identifier $a_L a_{L-1}...a_{m+1}$. For example, $(1.WK_{4,1})$ is the sub-network of $WK_{(4,2)}$ induced by nodes $\{10, 11, 12, 13\}$.

Definition 3 [2]. Node $(a_L a_{L-1}...a_1)$ is a k-frontier if $(a_k = a_{k-1} = ... = a_1)$, $1 \le k \le t$.

In the reminder of this section, we introduce two routing schemes between two nodes belonging to different $(a_L.WK_{(t,L)})$ sub-networks to be able to devise the shortest path routing algorithm in a WK-recursive mesh network.

2.1 Routing in WK-Recursive Meshes

Self-Routing Algorithm. Suppose that the source and destination nodes in a $WK_{(t,L)}$ are identified with $S=(s_L s_{L-1}...s_1)$ and $T=(t_L t_{L-1}...t_1)$, respectively. The *Self-routing* schema, proposed in [1], can be recursively realized as follows.

(1) If $S=(s_1)$ and $T=(t_1)$, route directly the message from S to T.

(2) Else If $s_L \neq t_L$, determine recursively both the routing path from S to the node $W=(s_L(t_L)^{L-1})$, namely a bridge of level $L-1$, and the routing path from $X=(t_L(s_L)^{L-1})$ to T. The self-routing algorithm from S to T is the concatenation of the path from S to W, the link (W,X), and the routing path from X to T.

(3) If $s_L = t_L$, determine the routing path from $S'=(s_L s_{L-1}...s_1)$ to $T'=(t_L t_{L-1}...t_1)$ within the sub-network $(s_L.WK_{(t,L-1)})$, recursively.

In [5], it has been proved that the length of self-routing path within the $WK_{(t,)}$ is upper bounded by 2^L-1. The following lemmas give the exact length of the path given by the above-mentioned routing algorithm between two nodes.

Lemma 1. [8] The length of self-path routing algorithm between nodes $S=(s_L s_{L-1}...s_1)$ and $T=((t_L)^L)$ could be obtained by $\ell_{(S,T);SP} = |S \oplus T|$, where operator $\oplus$ performs bitwise *exclusive-or* on two input digit expressions represented in the numeric base L.

Lemma 2. The length of self-routing path between nodes $S=(s_L s_{L-1}...s_1)$ and $T=(t_L t_{L-1}...t_1)$, could be obtained as $\ell_{(S,T);SP} = |S \oplus W| + |X \oplus T| + 1$ when $s_L \neq t_L$; if $s_L=t_L$, the length can be determined recursively.

Proof. According to the definition of self-routing algorithm and recalling Lemma 1, the proof is trivial.

Note that, despite its simplicity, the self-routing algorithm is unable to deliver a message over a minimal length path. For example, in a $WK_{(4,3)}$, the length of self-routing path between nodes (133) and (033) is equal to 6, while the minimal path between them has a length 5.

Considering the substantial limitation of self-routing algorithm to find the minimal path in a WK-recursive network, we introduce a new routing algorithm, namely *second-routing algorithm*, which is able to overcome this shortage.

Second-Routing Algorithm. Suppose that $S=(s_L s_{L-1}...s_1)$ and $T=(t_L t_{L-1}...t_1)$, $L>1$, present the source and destination nodes in a $WK_{(t,L)}$, respectively. The second-routing algorithm could be stated as follows.

(1) if $s_L=t_L$, identify the second-routing path between $S'=(s_{L-1}...s_1)$ and $T'=(t_{L-1}...t_1)$ within the $(s_L.WK_{(t,L-1)})$ network as the second-routing path between S and T.

(2) If $s_L \neq t_L$, two second-routing paths can be created between these two nodes, as follow.

    1. ScndPth$_{(s_L s_{L-1}...s_1),(t_L t_{L-1}...t_1)}$ = <SelfR$_{(S,V)}$||(V,V')|| SelfR$_{(V',U')}$||(U',U)||SelfR$_{(U,T)}$>

    2. ScndPth$_{(t_L t_{L-1}...t_1),(s_L s_{L-1}...s_1)}$ = <SelfR$_{(T,Y)}$||(Y,Y')|| SelfR$_{(Y',Z')}$||(Z',Z)||SelfR$_{(Z,S)}$>.

where $V = (s_L(t_{L-1})^{L-1})$, $V' = (t_{L-1}(s_L)^{L-1})$, $U' = (t_{L-1}(t_L)^{L-1})$ and $U = (t_L(t_{L-1})^{L-1})$ in the first case as well as $Y = (t_L(s_{L-1})^{L-1})$, $Y' = (s_{L-1}(t_L)^{L-1})$, $Z' = (s_{L-1}(s_L)^{L-1})$ and $Z=(s_L(s_{L-1})^{L-1})$ in the second case. In fact, the second-path has been constructed to decrease one step of the distance between two nodes in each phase of the algorithm, based on the second bit of their addresses, i.e. (t_{L-1}) and (s_{L-1}).

It is worth mentioning that calculation of the length of the second-routing path could be done in $O(1)$ time, as it depends on the calculation of two Self-routing paths.

It can be easily observed that the second-routing path crosses an intermediate WK-sub-network of $(t_{L-1}.WK_{(t,L-1)})$. At the first glance, it seems that this extra path can not decrease the length of routing path in comparison with self-routing. But there is some scenario where the second-routing path is shorter than that of a self-routing path. In the reminder, we complete our discussion by presenting the shortest path routing algorithm within a $WK_{(t,L)}$.

The Shortest-path Routing Algorithm. We can now propose a shortest-path routing algorithm simply by finding the minimum length between Self-Routing and Second-routing algorithms. So, it can be stated as:

$$ShrtPth_{(s_L s_{L-1} \ldots s_1)(t_L t_{L-1} \ldots t_1)} = min(SelfR_{(S,T)}, ScndPth_{(S,T)}, ScndPth_{(T,S)}).$$

Theorem 1. [8] The above-mentioned routing algorithm gives the shortest path between any arbitrary source and destination nodes in the $WK_{(t,L)}$. □

2.2 Deadlock-Free Routing Algorithm

A great deal of research has been devoted to creating efficient deadlock-free routing algorithms in wormhole-switched interconnection networks. In [6], it has been shown that a routing algorithm is deadlock free if and only if there are no cycles in its channel buffer dependency graph. Dally [6] proposed a hardware solution to the deadlock problem that divided each physical channel into a number of "virtual channels" to remove the cycles of channel dependency graph in a torus network. In the same way, for WK-recursive mesh networks, we propose a methodology to split each physical link into 3 virtual channels. That is, for each sub WK-recursive mesh like $(a_L.WK_{(t,L-1)})$, the label number of the next virtual channel to be used must be increased. Precisely, in the case of $s_L \neq t_L$, we could exploit a deadlock free routing algorithm within intra- $WK_{(t,L-1)}$ routing, since the self-routing algorithm is deadlock free. But cyclic buffer dependencies may occur when one or two *L-1-flipping* links are traversed by messages which have been routed according *ScndPth* routing. Therefore, to prevent the occurrence of such cyclic buffer dependencies, messages that enter a sub- $WK_{(t,L-1)}$ network, through an *L-1-flipping* channel, must traverse that subgroup through a separate set of virtual channels from those of messages originating in that subgroup. As a result, we suggest that the virtual channels of each channel be split into three equal sets, i.e. each physical link may be split into three virtual groups, v_1, v_2, and v_3. After being injected into the network, a message with address schema $S=(s_L s_{L-1} \ldots s_1)$ traverses the source sub-network $(s_L.WK_{(t,L-1)})$ through v_1. Once an *L-1-flipping* link has been taken and the message has entered another sub-network, the new group is traversed using virtual channels in class v_2, and so forth.

Theorem 2. [8] Let $S=(s_L s_{L-1} \ldots s_1)$ and $T=(t_L t_{L-1} \ldots t_1)$ be the source and destination nodes, consequently. Moreover, assume that S and T have a largest common sub-WK-Recursive group like $(s_L s_{L-1} \ldots s_{j+1}.WK_{(t,j)})$, i.e. $s_j \neq t_j$ and for all $k > j$; $s_k = t_k$. A sufficient condition for *ShrtPth-Routing* algorithm to be deadlock-free is that within sub-network $(s_L s_{L-1} \ldots s_{j+1}.WK_{(t,j)})$, at least one channel buffer (i.e. virtual channel) of each *j-1-flipping* channels be reserved for messages traversing either their first or second *j-1-flipping link*, along with a different set of channel buffers be allotted to messages that are traversing their first $(s_L s_{L-1} \ldots s_{j+1} s_j.WK_{(t,j-1)})$ source group, and a

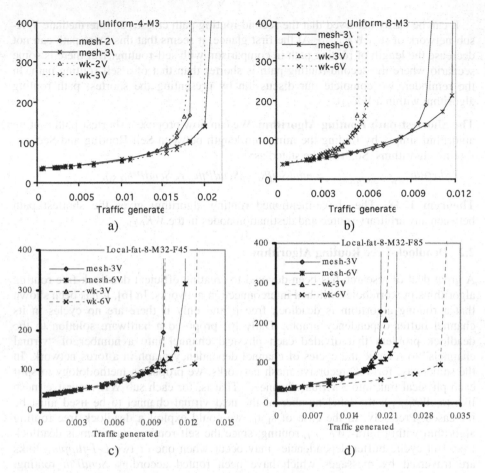

Fig. 1. Average message latency in the mesh and WK-recursive network, for uniform traffic a) 4x4, b) 8x8 networks, and 8x8 network with local traffic c) 45%, d) 85% of locality traffic

separate set to those that are traversing either their second or third, $(s_L s_{L-1} \ldots s_{j+1} \, s_{j-1} (t_{j-1}).WK_{(t,j-1)})$ or $(s_L s_{L-1} \ldots s_{j+1} \, t_j.WK_{(t,j-1)})$ consequently, intermediary or target groups. $\square$

3 Empirical Performance Evaluations

To evaluate the operation of the WK-recursive network under different working conditions, a discrete-event simulator has been developed that mimics the behavior of the described routing algorithm at the flit level in the WK-recursive network. In what follows we assume that messages are generated at each node according to a Poisson process with a mean inter-arrival rate of λ_g messages per cycle. All messages have a fixed length of M flits. The destination node of each message has been determined using a uniform random number generator to form either uniform or local destination distributions. According to the uniform traffic pattern the source node sends messages to any other node in the network with an equal probability of $1/(N-1)$, with N being the network size. Network traffic locality is a special case of the locality phenomenon commonly seen in computer systems. The local traffic pattern enforces a source node with address schema $S=(s_L s_{L-1}\ldots s_1)$ to generate messages for destination nodes in the $(s_L s_{L-1}\ldots s_{j+1}.WK_{(t,j)})$ sub-network with probability $p^j(1-p)$ where p is the locality factor. In the following subsections, we analyze and compare the performance of the mesh and WK-recursive networks obtained under both the uniform and the local traffic distribution patterns. Numerous simulation experiments have been performed for several combinations of network sizes, message lengths, and number of virtual channels to predict the network performance. Figure 1 reports on the average message latency of mesh and WK-recursive networks with 16, 64 nodes and for the two mentioned traffic patterns. For a comprehensive performance evaluation between these two networks, see [8].

4 Conclusions

WK-recursive mesh is a recursively-defined hierarchical interconnection network with excellent properties such as small diameter, small network cost, and high degree of expandability which well idealize it as an attractive alternative for the mesh interconnection topology. In this paper, we proposed a shortest-path deadlock free routing algorithm for WK-recursive networks by finding the minimum length between Self-Routing and Second-routing algorithm and using 3 virtual channels for each physical channel. We also examined the performance issues of WK-recursive network in comparison to the mesh network under different workload choices including traffic pattern, network size, and message length.

References

1. Della Vecchia, G., Sanges, C.: A Recursively Scalable Network VLSI Implementation. Future Generation Computer Systems 4(3), 235–243 (1988)
2. Fu, J.-S.: Hamiltonicity of the WK-Recursive Network with and without Faulty Nodes. IEEE TPDS 16(9) (2005)
3. Hoseiny Farahabady, M., Sarbazi-Azad, H.: The WK-Recursive Pyramid: An Efficient Network Topology. In: ISPAN 2005. 8th International Symposium on Parallel Architectures, Algorithms and Networks, pp. 312–317 (2005)
4. Chen, G.H., Duh, D.R.: Topological Properties, Communication, and Computation on WK-Recursive Networks. Networks 24, 303–317 (1994)
5. Verdoscia, L., Vaccaro, R.: An Adaptive Routing Algorithm for WK-Recursive Topologies. Computing 63(2), 171–184 (1999)
6. Dally, W., Seitz, C.: Deadlock free message routing in multiprocessor interconnection networks. IEEE Transactions on Computers, 547–553 (1987)
7. Hoseiny Farahabady, M., Sarbazi-Azad, H.: The RTCC-pyramid: a versatile hierarchical network for parallel computing. In: Proc. 8th International Conference on High Performance Computing in Asia Pacific Region (HPC Asia), China, pp. 493–498 (2005)
8. Rezazad, M., Hoseiny Farahabady, M., Sarbazi-Azad, H.: Shortest Path Routing Algorithm and performance evaluation for WK-Recursive Meshes, Technical Report, IPM school of computer science (2007)

Proving Distributed Algorithms for Mobile Agents: Examples of Spanning Tree Computation in Anonymous Networks

M.A. Haddar[1,3], A. Hadj Kacem[2], Y. Métivier[3], M. Mosbah[3], and M. Jmaiel[1]

[1] ReDCAD Research Unit
École Nationale d'Ingénieurs de Sfax, Tunisie
[2] MIRACL Laboratory
Faculté des Sciences Economiques et de Gestion de Sfax, Tunisie
[3] LaBRI UMR 5800
ENSEIRB - Université Bordeaux 1, 351 Cours de la Libération
33405 - Talence France
{haddar,mosbah}@labri.fr

Abstract. This paper present a framework for describing distributed algorithms for mobile agents in an anonymous network. We make use of the high level encoding of these algorithms as transitions rules. The main advantage of this uniform and formal approach is the proof correctness of the distributed algorithms. We illustrate this approach by giving examples of distributed computations of a spanning tree by mobile agents in anonymous network.

Keywords: mobile agents, spanning tree, distributed algorithms, proofs.

1 Introduction

1.1 Background

Nowadays, distributed systems are solicited in potential life services (such as banks, railway stations, airports, trade companies , etc). All of them need reliable applications to propose secure services to their clients. This aim can be realized by proposing powerful models which simplify the design and the proof of distributed algorithms. To formally describe distributed algorithms, several works have tried to propose a "standard" model for distributed systems. But, unlike sequential algorithms, there is no "universal" model of computations for the distributed ones. Indeed, designing and proving distributed algorithms is still a hard task and they depend closely on the considered model. The mathematical *tool-box* provided by local computation model proposed an exciting proof approach for distributed algorithms [1]. Nevertheless, with the success of mobile agent based applications, regards are switched from classical systems (message passing, shared memory, remote procedure call, etc) towards this new paradigm.

Mobile agents are programs that can move through a network under their own control and interact with resources and local environments. This technology,

S. Rao et al. (Eds.): ICDCN 2008, LNCS 4904, pp. 286–291, 2008.

a profound revolution in computer software technology, is a brand new computing technique promoted for solving a large scale of problems in computer science [2]. Among many others, the distributed computing community is presenting an increasing interest into mobile agents due to their considerable reduction of network load and their overcoming of the network latency . There are also new trends to use this technology in faulty distributed systems for which mobile agents can intuitively give a promoting solution for arising problems.

1.2 Related Works

Stationary process models are the most used computational models for distributed systems. A distributed system is modeled by a graph where the vertices denote processes and the edges denote the communication links between processes. In these models, computational activities are done by concurrent execution of the *stationary* sequential processes. A panoply of mechanisms exists for interprocess communication. In the message passing mechanism, processes communicate via messages added and removed in a *messages-queue*. In the shared memory mechanism, processes communicate via global shared variables. In *stationary process models* computations are full synchronous, full asynchronous, quasi asynchronous, etc. A diversity of models are then adopted for distributed systems depending on the choice of the timing model, the communication model, the architectural model ,etc.

A well known *stationary processes model* is the local computation one. This model was intensively studied after the pioneer work of Angluin [3]. An elementary computation is made by changing the state of a process. The new state depends on the state of the process and its neighbors. Several results and tools are proposed within this model [3,4,5].

Mobile agent paradigm propose a new vision of distributed systems. This paradigm allows to separate computations from network topology. The vertices of a graph representing the distributed system denote the execution places (or places for short). Computations are carried by mobile agents which does on every visited place some computations. This new vision of the distributed system requires new models (*mobile process models*).

1.3 Motivations and Contributions

Our work is motivated by the increasing needs to develop distributed algorithms executed by mobile agents. Traditional distributed algorithms are based on the classical model of distributed systems, composed of permanently active processes communicating through established links. This model of distributed systems is no longer valid when dealing with mobile agents. Surprisingly, a recent result [6] proves the equivalence of computations between a mobile agent system and a message passing distributed system.

To illustrate the expression power of our model [7], we have developed three distributed algorithms to compute a spanning tree of a graph (see [7]). Such a problem is among the important problems in distributed computing. Trees are essential structures in various communication protocols (routing, information broadcasting). We expose, in this paper, an unique algorithm to solve the spanning tree problem. We describe it as a transition system and we outline its correctness proof. More precisely, using a high-level encoding of mobile agent distributed algorithms, as presented in [7], we show that we can benefit from mathematical properties of *transition systems* to obtain rigorous and formal proofs of our algorithms. We already used rewriting systems to encode distributed algorithms [4,5,8]. In these latter solutions, based on message passing systems, the complexity is calculated by means of needed messages or required time, we express the complexity of our solution by means of *move* made by mobile agents to compute trees which is an intuitive way to focus on complexity of computations carried by mobile agents.

Proposed solutions, in addition to benefits obviously inherited from the use of mobile agent paradigm, and unlike classical models based on *stationary process models*, do not require active processes in each host. The resources, on a given host, are solicited when a mobile agent arrives on it. Another important benefit, at the implementation phase, comes from the omission of the synchronization [9] needed to implement several algorithms using the classical models in asynchronous networks. In fact, computations are encapsulated within mobile agents. Another important and intuitive benefit of mobile agent comes from the separation between computations and the network topology. In fact, this separation make easy to overcome dynamic changes of network topology while computations are carried by these mobile entities. If we look to a mobile agent move as a message sent, we can intuitively conclude that proposed solutions are as efficient as those proposed in classical models. We simulated our solutions in the VISIDIA platform [10].

Due to lack of space we omit, in this paper, the model presentation. A detailed explanation of our model can be found in [7]. We present in the next section a mobile agent based solution to the problem of the spanning tree calculation. We outline, in the same section, the correctness, complexity and termination proofs. The last section gives a conclusion and some prospects.

2   Spanning Tree Computation by Mobile Agents

Spanning tree construction is a classical problem in computer science. In a distributed computing environment, the solution of this problem has many practical motivations. It also has distinct formulations and requirements [11].

In a mobile agent system ($\mathcal{M}a\mathcal{S}$), the construction of a spanning tree of $\mathbb{S}$ means to move the system from an initial system configuration ($\mathbf{C}_0$), where each place is just aware of its local state, to a system configuration where

1. Each place knows its neighbors in the tree (father and sons)
2. All the channels, but those which ports are in the state E (means excluded), constitute the spanning tree of $\mathbb{S}$

The mobile agent systems we deal with for the spanning tree problem consider undistinguishable places. There is no knowledge of the size or the topology of the navigation subsystem.

We have developed three solutions for the spanning tree problem. Due to lack of space, we will present in this paper only one solution with a detailed proof. A complete explanation of all the proposed solutions (together with detailed proofs) can be found in [7].

In the algorithm below, we present a solution for the spanning tree problem using the DFS technique (Depth First Search). In this solution, the system contains a unique mobile agent. Its *home* is in the state V and all others places are in the state N.

The mobile agent starts the computation in the state $Child?$, this state permits to the mobile agent to explore unvisited places and to mark them. Reaching a visited place, the mobile agent changes its state to $Back$ to indicate that it will return back from a visited place. When a mobile agent notices that it has finished the exploration of all ports incident to a given place, it changes its state to $Finished$ and moves from a specific port (in the state Fa) incident to this place.

The mobile agent system describing the algorithm above is defined as follow:

Let $\mathcal{M}a\mathcal{S} = (\mathbb{A}, \mathbb{P}, \mathbb{S}, \pi_0, \lambda)$ be a mobile agent system and $\mathbf{C}_0 = (state_0, \mathbb{D}_0, \mathbb{A}_0)$ its initial configuration such that:

- $\exists! \ p \in \mathbb{P}$, p is the *home* and $state_0(p) = (V, Ny, \ldots, Ny)$,
- $\forall p \in \mathbb{P} \setminus \{home\}, state_0(p) = (N, Ny, \ldots, Ny)$,
- $\mathbb{A} = \{a\}, \pi_0(a) = home$ and $state_0(a) = ("Child?", \emptyset)$,
- $\mathbb{D}_0 = \{\emptyset\}$.

The transition system $\mathbb{T}a$ describing the mobile agent algorithm is the following :

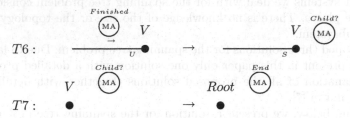

$T6:$

$T7:$

With the following priorities: $T1 > T5$ and $\{T1, T5\} > \{T7\}$

In the following, we prove that the defined system solves the spanning tree problem in an ananymous network:

Lemma 2.1. *The system $\mathbb{T}a$ is noetherian.*

Lemma 2.2. *Let $(\mathbf{C}_i)_{i\geq0}$ be an execution sequence, $\forall i$ $\mathbf{C}_i$ verifies:*

$\Im1$ *There is a unique mobile agent in $\mathcal{M}aS_1$.*
$\Im3$ *A place in the state N has all the incident ports in the state Ny.*
$\Im2$ *All the places which are in the state V, but the home, have a unique port in the state Fa.*
$\Im4$ *A channel containing a port in the state S, has the other port in the state Fa.*
$\Im5$ *The sub-graph induced by channels, which contain a port in the state Fa, is a tree.*

Lemma 2.3. *The mobile agent leaves a place from the port in the state Fa when all incident ports are already visited.*

Lemma 2.4. *In a given direction, a channel is traversed exactly one time.*

Lemma 2.5. *$\mathcal{M}aS$ reaches a final configuration when the mobile agent reaches the state End.*

Lemma 2.6. *When the system reaches a final configuration all the places are already visited.*

With all these properties, we have the following results:

Theorem 2.1. *In a final configuration, the sub-graph induced by channels, which ports are in the state S or Fa, is a spanning tree of $\mathbb{S}$.*

Let n be the number of channels in $\mathcal{M}aS$.

Theorem 2.2. *The mobile agent needs $2 * n$ moves to compute the spanning tree.*

The solution proposed below is as efficient as those proposed in [1] if we consider that applying a rule is equivalent to an agent move. Beyond, our solutions do not need synchronization which is essential for the solutions proposed in [1] in asynchronous networks.

3   Conclusion

This paper aim was to highlight our model [7] expression power and proof simplicity by proposing a catalog of solutions to the spanning tree problem in anonymous networks. We spotlight also facilities and simplicity, supplied by our model, to design distributed algorithms carried by mobile agents. The proposed solutions are implemented and tested within the VISIDIA platform.

We plan, in the near future, to attack other problems from the distributed computing theory (such as election, synchronization, consensus). Later, we plan to design and implement a framework which offers an easy-to-use graphical interface for programming and running distributed algorithms carried by mobile agents.

References

1. Litovsky, I., Métivier, Y., Sopena, E.: Handbook of graph grammars and computing by graph transformation, vol. 3, pp. 1–56. World Scientific, Singapore (1999)
2. Shiao, D.: Mobile agents: A new model of intelligent distributed computing. Technical report, IBM DeveloperWorks, China (2004)
3. Angluin, D.: Local and global properties in networks of processors (extended abstract). In: STOC 1980: Proceedings of the twelfth annual ACM symposium on Theory of computing, pp. 82–93. ACM Press, New York (1980)
4. Derbel, B., Mosbah, M.: Distributed graph traversals by relabeling systems with applications. In: Workshop on Graph Transformation for Verification and Concurrency, San Francisco, California, USA. ENTCS, pp. 79–94 (August 2005)
5. Chalopin, J., Métivier, Y.: Election and local computations on edges. In: Walukiewicz, I. (ed.) FOSSACS 2004. LNCS, vol. 2987, pp. 90–104. Springer, Heidelberg (2004)
6. Chalopin, J., Godard, E., Métivier, Y., Ossamy, R.B.: Mobile agent algorithms versus message passing algorithms. In: Shvartsman, A.A. (ed.) OPODIS 2006. LNCS, vol. 4305, pp. 187–201. Springer, Heidelberg (2006)
7. Haddar, M.A., Kacem, A.H., Mosbah, M., Métivier, Y., Jmaiel, M.: Distributed algorithms for mobile agents. Technical Report RR-1435-07, Université Bordeaux1 (2007)
8. Chalopin, J., Métivier, Y., Zielonka, W.: Election, naming and cellular edge local computations. In: Ehrig, H., Engels, G., Parisi-Presicce, F., Rozenberg, G. (eds.) ICGT 2004. LNCS, vol. 3256, pp. 242–256. Springer, Heidelberg (2004)
9. Szymanski, B.K., Shi, Y., Prywes, N.S.: Terminating iterative solution of simultaneous equations in distributed message passing systems. In: PODC 1985: Proceedings of the fourth annual ACM symposium on Principles of distributed computing, pp. 287–292. ACM Press, New York (1985)
10. Bauderon, M., Gruner, S., Metivier, Y., Mosbah, M., Sellami, A.: Visualization of distributed algorithms based on graph relabelling systems. ENTCS 50(3), 227–237 (2001)
11. Santoro, N.: Design and Analysis of Distributed Algorithms (Wiley Series on Parallel and Distributed Computing). Wiley-Interscience, Chichester (2006)

Mobile Agent Rendezvous in a Ring Using Faulty Tokens

Shantanu Das

School of Information Technology and Engineering, University of Ottawa, Canada
shantdas@site.uottawa.ca

Abstract. We consider the rendezvous problem which requires k mobile agents that are dispersed in a ring of size n, to gather at a single node of the network. The problem is difficult to solve when the agents are identical (i.e. indistinguishable), they execute the same deterministic algorithm, and the nodes of the ring are unlabelled (i.e. anonymous). In this case, rendezvous can be achieved by having each agent mark its starting location in the ring using a token. This paper focusses on fault tolerant solutions to the problem when tokens left by an agent may fail unexpectedly. Previous solutions to the problem had several limitations—they either assumed a completely synchronous setting or were restricted to few specific instances of the problem where the value of n is such that $\gcd(n, k') = 1 \ \forall k' \leq k$. We improve on these results, solving rendezvous in asynchronous rings for arbitrary values of n and k, whenever it is solvable.

1 Introduction

Overview: The *Rendezvous* problem is the most fundamental problem in computing with autonomous mobile agents. The typical setting is when there is a communication network represented by a graph of n nodes and there are k mobile entities, called *agents*, that are dispersed among the nodes of the network. The objective of the *rendezvous* problem is to make all the agents gather together at a node. When the nodes of the network are labelled with unique identities, it is possible to gather at a predetermined location, for instance, the node having the smallest label. The problem is however more interesting when such unique labels are not present, i.e. when the network is anonymous. In this case, the agents have to reach an agreement among themselves about the node where to meet.

The problem of rendezvous in an anonymous network has been studied both for synchronous and asynchronous systems—we focus on the latter case. In such systems, rendezvous can be achieved under certain conditions, by using a simple marking device called a *token* (or sometimes, *pebble* or *marker*). Under this model, each agent has a token that can be released at a node to mark the node. The tokens of all agents are identical however, so nodes marked by one agent may not be distinguished from those marked by another agent.

S. Rao et al. (Eds.): ICDCN 2008, LNCS 4904, pp. 292–297, 2008.

In [6] it was shown how to achieve rendezvous in an anonymous ring network, when every agent puts its token in its starting location. Flocchini *et al.* [7] consider the case when some of the tokens are faulty i.e. a token may suddenly disappear after an agent leaves it on a node. The solutions given in the above paper are applicable either in completely synchronous networks or when tokens may fail only at the time of their release (and not at any other time during the algorithm). Another very strong assumption made in that paper (for the asynchronous case), was that the values of n and k are such that $\gcd(n, k') = 1$, $\forall k' \leq k$. The objective of this paper is to show that this assumption is not necessary for solving rendezvous with faulty tokens. In fact we determine the conditions for solving the rendezvous problem with faulty tokens in asynchronous rings for arbitrary values of n and k. We then give an algorithm that solves the problem for all instances that are solvable.

Our Model: We consider an un-oriented ring network consisting of n nodes with bi-directional channels connecting each node to its two neighbors. The nodes of the network are anonymous (i.e. without any identifiers). There are k mobile agents (or, robots) initially located in distinct nodes of the network. The node in which an agent initially resides is called its homebase. The initial configuration can be represented by a bi-colored ring (where black nodes are the homebases and other nodes are white). The agents are identical and they follow the same algorithm. Each agent has a token which is a simple marking device that can be released at a node in order to mark it. Two agents can communicate (exchange information) with each-other, only when they are at the same node. However, agents may not communicate or even see each-other, while traversing an edge. The agents must gather at a single node called the Rendezvous-point whose location is not predetermined. In our model, some of the tokens may be faulty. A faulty token is one that disappears after it is released and it never re-appears again. We assume that at most $k - 1$ tokens may fail.

Related Work: The *Rendezvous* problem has been studied under many different scenarios, mostly using probabilistic or randomized algorithms (see [1] for a survey). Deterministic solutions for rendezvous have been proposed by Dessmark et al.[4] and Yu and Yung [12] both for rings and arbitrary graphs, assuming a synchronous setting. A solution to rendezvous in the asynchronous graphs was provided by De Marco et al. in [11]. All the above results are for agents having distinct labels and but having no ability to mark the nodes of the graph.

The idea of performing rendezvous search (in unlabelled graphs) using marks on the starting places was explored first by Baston and Gal [2]. Kranakis *et al.* [9] and Flocchini *et al.*[6] gave solutions for the rendezvous of two (resp. multiple) agents, on a ring networks using (unmovable) tokens to mark the starting nodes. Gasieniec et al.[8] gave an optimal memory solution for the same setting. Kranakis et al.[10] studied the problem for a synchronous torus using both fixed and movable tokens.

Among fault-tolerant solutions to rendezvous, Dobrev et al.[5] and Chalopin et al. [3] solved the rendezvous problem, in the whiteboard model, in presence of faulty nodes and faulty edges, respectively. For the token model, the only previous study that considers faulty tokens is that of Flocchini et al. [7] as mentioned before. We improve on those results in the present paper.

2   Conditions for Solvability

It was shown in [6] that there does not exist any terminating algorithm for solving the *Rendezvous* problem in an anonymous ring, if neither the value of n nor k is known to the agents. When solving rendezvous using tokens that may fail, we have a more stronger condition:

Lemma 1. *In presence of token failures, there is no terminating algorithm for solving the rendezvous problem in an asynchronous anonymous ring, if the value of k is unknown to the agents.*

In the following, we shall assume that the value of k is known to the agents. For solving the *Rendezvous* problem using tokens, each agent would put its token at its starting location before traversing the ring. While traversing the ring (in the absence of failures), an agent can obtain a sequence S of inter-token distances, of the form $(d_1, d_2, d_3, \ldots d_k)$ where for $1 \leq i < k$, d_i is the distance between ith and $(i+1)$th token and d_k is the distance between kth and the first token. For $1 \leq i \leq j \leq |S|$, we define $S(i,j)$ as the subsequence $(d_i, d_{i+1}, \ldots d_j)$.
    We define the following two operations on the sequence $S = (d_1, d_2, d_3, \ldots d_k)$

  (i) The reversal operation gives us the sequence $Rev(S) = (d_k, d_{k-1}, \ldots d_1)$,
 (ii) For any $1 \leq i < k$, the rotation operation gives the sequence $Rot_i(S) = (d_{i+1}, d_{i+2}, \ldots d_k, d_1, \ldots d_i)$ which is called the i-th rotation of S.

The sequence $S = (d_1, d_2, d_3, \ldots d_k)$ is called rotation-reversal free (or RR-free) if for every $0 < i < |S|$, $Rot_i(S) \neq S$ and $Rev(Rot_i(S)) \neq S$. Notice that if $Rot_i(S) = S$ for some $1 \leq i < |S|$, then the sequence is periodic with period i and thus i divides both $k = |S|$ and n. On the hand if $Rev(Rot_i(S)) = S$ for some $1 \leq i < |S|$, then the (bi-colored) ring is symmetrical. For any $1 \leq i \leq |S|$, we define $Sum_i(S)$ as the sum of the first i elements of S.

Theorem 1. *If there are k agents in a ring of n nodes with the initial location of each agent marked by a token, and S is the sequence of inter-token distances, then the rendezvous problem is solvable if and only if one of the following holds:*

(1) S is RR-free, or,
(2) S is aperiodic and $S = Rev(Rot_i(S))$ for some $1 \leq i < |S|$ such that $Sum_i(S)$ or $n - Sum_i(S)$ is even.

Proof. If S is RR-free then each agent would have computed a distinct sequence and thus it is easy to break the symmetry between agents; the agents can gather at the location of the ith token such that $Rot_i(S)$ is lexicographically smaller than $Rot_j(S)$ $\forall j \neq i$ and $1 \leq j \leq |S|$. On the other hand, if S is periodic then we already know that rendezvous is not solvable. So, we are left with the case when S is aperiodic but the bi-colored ring is symmetrical. In this case, we can solve rendezvous if and only if the axis of symmetry passes through at least one node of the ring. This will be satisfied if at least one of $Sum_i(S)$ or $n - Sum_i(S)$ is even.

The above conditions are necessary and sufficient for solving rendezvous in a ring when the tokens do not fail. However, we shall show that even when f tokens fail for $0 \leq f < k$, the above conditions are still sufficient for solving rendezvous. In the next section we present an *effective* algorithm (i.e. one which solves rendezvous whenever the conditions of Theorem 1 are satisfied) for rendezvous in a ring when tokens fail only at the beginning.

If we allow for the presence of multiple tokens at a node, then we can get a weighted sequences of inter-token distances of the form $S_W = ((c_1, d_1), (c_2, d_2), \ldots (c_r, d_r))$ where the c_i's are counts of the number of tokens at the respective locations, such that $c_1 + c_2 + \cdots + c_r = k$. We can show that the above result holds also for the weighted sequence of inter-token distances. Since, some of the tokens may disappear, we shall use the following strategy. When an agent loses its token (we shall call such an agent 'LOSER'), it shall itself stand stationary at a node, functioning as a 'virtual' token. We define the *agent-count* of a node v, as the number of tokens plus the number of LOSER agents present at the node v. Thus, in the weighted inter-token sequence S_W, the weights (i.e. c_i's) would represent the agent-counts of the respective nodes. The agent-count of the whole sequence S_W would be the sum of these weights, denoted by Agent-Count(S_W). Similarly, Edge-Count(S_W) would denote the sum of the inter-token distances (i.e. d_i's) in S_W. Notice that Edge-Count$(S_W)= n$.

Definition 1. *Given a sequence S of inter-token distances in a ring, we define the* rendezvous-point *or,* RV-point(S) *as follows. If S is RR-free, then RV-point(S) is the Min-Point—the location of the ith token such that $Rot_i(S)$ is lexicographically smaller than $Rot_j(S)$ $\forall j \neq i$ and $1 < j \leq |S|$. Otherwise, if S satisfies the conditions of Theorem 1 clause-(2), then RV-point(S) is the middle node in the largest[1] even segment among the two segments defined by $S(1, i)$ and $S(i + 1, k)$. In all other cases, RV-point(S) is undefined.*

The following result immediately follows from the above definition.

Lemma 2. *If the sequence S satisfies the conditions of Theorem 1, then RV-point(S) returns the same location as RV-point($Rot_i(S)$) for all $i \in [1, k]$.*

3   Algorithm for Rendezvous When Tokens Fail

As mentioned before we consider the case where failures occur only at the beginning, when a token is released at a node (i.e. a token either disappears immediately on release or never fails at all). This assumption simplifies the design of an algorithm for rendezvous. For the algorithm given below, each agent knows the

---

[1] Largest in terms of edge-count and then agent-count.

value of both n and k at the beginning. The algorithm can be easily modified to work also for the case when only k is known, using a similar technique as in [7].

Algorithm *RVring*

1. Put Token at the homebase, travel for n steps in any choosen direction to compute the sequence of inter-token distances S and return to homebase.
2. If Token at homebase has disappeared, then become LOSER and go to the next node having a token. A LOSER agent remains at this node until it receives instructions from another agent. A LOSER agent also remembers the distance to its original homebase.
3. Else if $|S| = k$, then go to RV-point(S) and stop;
4. Else re-traverse the ring to compute the weighted sequence of inter-token distances S_W, returning to homebase and then execute the following steps.
5. While (Agent-Count(S_W) < k),
   Wait at homebase until another LOSER agent arrives at this node, then recompute S_W by traversing the ring again.
6. When Agent-Count(S_W) = k, compute the sequence S of original inter-token distances, by going round the ring and gathering information from LOSER agents about their original locations.
7. If your homebase is guarded by a LOSER agent, then become an ACTIVE agent. Otherwise wait at the homebase.
8. If ACTIVE, go to RV-point(S) (say, node v) and wait for all other ACTIVE agents to arrive at v. (Note that there are exactly $k_1 = |\{c_i \in S_W : c_i > 1\}|$ ACTIVE agents.) Once all ACTIVE agents have arrived at v, one of them (or, maybe two of them), is(are) chosen as LEADER, depending on the distance to the agent's homebase. (If there are two LEADER agents, they stick together for the rest of the algorithm acting as single unit.)
9. If LEADER, then go round the ring to collect all waiting agents (agents that are not LOSER or ACTIVE). At each node u that contains a token but no LOSER agent, the LEADER waits for the token-owner to return, and collects it before moving to the next node.
10. When $(k - f = |S_W|)$ agents have gathered at the rendezvous-point, the LEADER goes round the ring again to collect all LOSER agents.

4   Proof of Correctness

Assuming that the conditions in Theorem 1 are true, the following results hold. (The proofs have been omitted due to the space constraint.)

Lemma 3. *If no tokens fail, then algorithm RVring terminates correctly after Step 3, achieving rendezvous of all the k agents.*

Lemma 4. *When $1 \leq f < k$ tokens fail, the algorithm RVring correctly solves rendezvous, after no more than $(f + 5) \cdot n$ moves by any agent.*

Theorem 2. *For algorithm RVring, the total number of moves made by the agents is $O(k \cdot n)$ and the memory requirement for each agent is $O(k \log n)$.*

5   Conclusions

We presented solutions to the *Rendezvous* problem for k mobile agents in asynchronous ring networks of size n, using identical tokens which are prone to failure. We first determined the conditions necessary for achieving rendezvous in an anonymous ring and then we showed that even if $0 \leq f \leq k - 1$ tokens fail, it is still possible to solve rendezvous under the same conditions (that are necessary for rendezvous in fault-free situations). These solutions work only if the tokens fails only at the beginning. In the general case (i.e. when tokens may fail anytime during the algorithm), the solution to rendezvous is much more complicated and requires additional assumptions. These solutions would appear in the full paper.

References

1. Alpern, S., Gal, S.: The Theory of Search Games and Rendezvous. Kluwer, Dordrecht (2003)
2. Baston, V., Gal, S.: Rendezvous search when marks are left at the starting points. Naval Research Logistics 38, 469–494 (1991)
3. Chalopin, J., Das, S., Santoro, N.: Rendezvous of Mobile Agents in Unknown Graphs with Faulty Links. In: Pelc, A. (ed.) DISC 2007. LNCS, vol. 4731, pp. 108–122. Springer, Heidelberg (2007)
4. Dessmark, A., Fraigniaud, P., Pelc, A.: Deterministic rendezvous in graphs. In: Di Battista, G., Zwick, U. (eds.) ESA 2003. LNCS, vol. 2832, pp. 184–195. Springer, Heidelberg (2003)
5. Dobrev, S., Flocchini, P., Prencipe, G., Santoro, N.: Multiple agents rendezvous in a ring in spite of a black hole. In: Papatriantafilou, M., Hunel, P. (eds.) OPODIS 2003. LNCS, vol. 3144, pp. 34–46. Springer, Heidelberg (2004)
6. Flocchini, P., Kranakis, E., Krizanc, D., Santoro, N., Sawchuk, C.: Multiple mobile agent rendezvous in a ring. In: Farach-Colton, M. (ed.) LATIN 2004. LNCS, vol. 2976, pp. 599–608. Springer, Heidelberg (2004)
7. Flocchini, P., Kranakis, E., Krizanc, D., Luccio, F.L., Santoro, N., Sawchuk, C.: Mobile Agents Rendezvous When Tokens Fail. In: Kralovic, R., Sýkora, O. (eds.) SIROCCO 2004. LNCS, vol. 3104, pp. 161–172. Springer, Heidelberg (2004)
8. Gasieniec, L., Kranakis, E., Krizanc, D., Zhang, X.: Optimal memory rendezvous of anonymous mobile agents in a unidirectional ring. In: Wiedermann, J., Tel, G., Pokorný, J., Bieliková, M., Štuller, J. (eds.) SOFSEM 2006. LNCS, vol. 3831, pp. 282–292. Springer, Heidelberg (2006)
9. Kranakis, E., Krizanc, D., Santoro, N., Sawchuk, C.: Mobile agent rendezvous in a ring. In: ICDCS 03. Int. Conf. on Distibuted Computing Systems, pp. 592–599 (2003)
10. Kranakis, E., Krizanc, D., Markou, E.: Mobile Agent Rendezvous in a Synchronous Torus. In: Correa, J.R., Hevia, A., Kiwi, M. (eds.) LATIN 2006. LNCS, vol. 3887, pp. 653–664. Springer, Heidelberg (2006)
11. De Marco, G., Gargano, L., Kranakis, E., Krizanc, D., Pelc, A., Vaccaro, U.: Asynchronous deterministic rendezvous in graphs. Theoretical Computer Science 355(3), 315–326 (2006)
12. Yu, X., Yung, M.: Agent rendezvous: A dynamic symmetry-breaking problem. In: Meyer auf der Heide, F., Monien, B. (eds.) ICALP 1996. LNCS, vol. 1099, pp. 610–621. Springer, Heidelberg (1996)

A New Key-Predistribution Scheme for Highly Mobile Sensor Networks

Abhijit Das[1] and Bimal Kumar Roy[2]

[1] Department of Computer Science and Engineering
Indian Institute of Technology, Kharagpur 721 302, India
abhij@cse.iitkgp.ernet.in
[2] Applied Statistics Unit
Indian Statistical Institute, Calcutta 700 035, India
bimal@isical.ac.in

Abstract. In this paper, we propose a new deterministic key predistribution scheme for secure communication in wireless sensor networks. Our scheme provides better trade-off among scalability, computation overhead, connectivity and resilience against node captures than existing key predistribution schemes, particularly in situations where the nodes in the network are highly mobile.

1 Introduction

Secure communication in a network of resource-constrained sensor nodes has been an important area of research in the recent past. In a network where the nodes are static (or have only very limited mobility), deployed nodes establish secure links with neighboring nodes using predistributed keys by a process called shared key discovery. In this paper, we address the situation where the nodes in the sensor network are highly mobile. The nodes may reestablish secure links by carrying out the shared key discovery phase periodically. The resulting overhead becomes unacceptably high under most of the existing schemes. In view of this, we look for a key predistribution scheme with modified requirements. We assume that the nodes are aware of their movements. If not, a node may periodically probe its neighborhood and invokes a key reestablishment procedure if it finds a significant change in its neighborhood. Suppose that a node u attempts to reestablish keys in a new neighborhood, and v is an arbitrary neighbor of u. The reestablishment process should meet the following desirable properties.

- The reestablishment process is initiated by u and requires the cooperation of each neighboring node v.
- The node u is allowed to perform some reasonable amount of computation. If m is the number of nodes in the neighborhood of u, then a computation of amount $O(m)$ is the absolute minimum.
- Each neighboring node v must not be subject to too much computation and/or communication overhead. A good algorithm corresponds to this overhead to be of an amount $O(1)$ per neighbor.

S. Rao et al. (Eds.): ICDCN 2008, LNCS 4904, pp. 298–303, 2008.

The basic scheme [5] and its variants [3], the polynomial-pool scheme [7] and the matrix-based scheme [4] incur sufficiently more overhead than this desirable minimum. Several deterministic and hybrid schemes [1,2,6,10] are available in the literature. These schemes do not make it clear how u can quickly compute the key ring of v, often without invoking the entire key predistribution procedure. The scheme of [8] addresses the issue of the essential asymmetry in the key reestablishment phase as mentioned above. However, the computation overhead of u in this scheme is very high. Ruj and Roy propose a scheme [9] which seems to be the most appropriate for mobile networks, but has small maximum supported network sizes and poor resilience against node captures.

In this paper, we improve Ruj and Roy's scheme and obtain a trade-off among scalability, security and connectivity, which appears acceptable in most practical applications. Our scheme achieves the lower bounds on computation overhead for both u and v. A matrix-layout based scheme (henceforth referred to as the ML scheme) is at the heart of our modification (Section 2). The ML scheme achieves high connectivity, but suffers from somewhat poor resilience, particularly against selective node captures (Sections 3 and 4).

2   Our Matrix-Layout Based (ML) Scheme

2.1   Construction of the Layout Matrix

Let t denote the maximum number of symmetric keys that each sensor node can store in its memory. We assume that t is even. We take $d = t + 2$ and construct a $d \times d$ matrix as follows. We first fill the main diagonal of the matrix by a special symbol which does not stand for the id of any key or node. We then fill out the triangular region below (and excluding) the main diagonal and above (and including) the reverse main diagonal in the column-major order by the integers $1, 2, 3, \ldots, \left(\frac{t+2}{2}\right)^2$. Subsequently, we fill out the triangular region above (and excluding) the main diagonal and above (and including) the reverse main diagonal in the row-major order by the integers $\left(\frac{t+2}{2}\right)^2 + 1, \left(\frac{t+2}{2}\right)^2 + 2, \ldots, 2\left(\frac{t+2}{2}\right)^2$. Finally, we reflect about the reverse main diagonal the entries above this diagonal in order to fill the region below this diagonal, and make the matrix symmetric with respect to the reverse main diagonal. For example, for $t = 4$, the layout matrix is constructed as follows.

$$
\begin{pmatrix}
* & & & & & \\
1 & * & & & & \\
2 & 6 & * & & & \\
3 & 7 & 9 & * & & \\
4 & 8 & & & * & \\
5 & & & & & *
\end{pmatrix}
\rightarrow
\begin{pmatrix}
* & 10 & 11 & 12 & 13 & 14 \\
1 & * & 15 & 16 & 17 & \\
2 & 6 & * & 18 & & \\
3 & 7 & 9 & * & & \\
4 & 8 & & & * & \\
5 & & & & & *
\end{pmatrix}
\rightarrow
\begin{pmatrix}
* & 10 & 11 & 12 & 13 & 14 \\
1 & * & 15 & 16 & 17 & 13 \\
2 & 6 & * & 18 & 16 & 12 \\
3 & 7 & 9 & * & 15 & 11 \\
4 & 8 & 7 & 6 & * & 10 \\
5 & 4 & 3 & 2 & 1 & *
\end{pmatrix}
$$

For easy future references, we call the triangular region in the layout matrix storing $1, 2, \ldots, \left(\frac{t+2}{2}\right)^2$ as the left triangle (LT), and the triangular region storing $\left(\frac{t+2}{2}\right)^2 + 1, \left(\frac{t+2}{2}\right)^2 + 2, \ldots, 2\left(\frac{t+2}{2}\right)^2$ as the top triangle (TT). Their reflections about the reverse main diagonal are respectively called the bottom triangle (BT) and the right triangle (RT).

We assume that matrix indexing is zero-based. Thus, the top-left element of the layout matrix has index $(0,0)$, and the bottom-right element has index $(t+1, t+1)$. The following formula converts an index (i, j) to the entry of the layout matrix at the (i, j)-th location.

$$
f(i,j) = \begin{cases}
* & \text{if } i = j, \\
-j^2 + (t+1)j + i & \text{if } i > j \text{ and } i \leq t+1-j, \\
f(t+1-j, t+1-i) & \text{if } i > j \text{ and } i > t+1-j, \\
\left(\frac{t+2}{2}\right)^2 + f(j,i) & \text{if } i < j.
\end{cases}
$$

Given (i, j), one can compute $f(i, j)$ in O(1) time (using a few single-precision operations only).

2.2   Key Predistribution

Before deployment of the sensor nodes, the key-ring of each node is loaded with t symmetric keys (like AES keys). These keys are selected from a pool of $T = 2\left(\frac{t+2}{2}\right)^2$ randomly chosen keys having the ids $1, 2, 3, \ldots, T$. The maximum number of nodes supported by our scheme is also $N = 2\left(\frac{t+2}{2}\right)^2$. The nodes in the network are also given ids in the range $1, 2, 3, \ldots, N$.

For each position (i, j) in the triangle LT in the layout matrix, one first computes $u = f(i, j)$. All the entries in the j-th column in the matrix are then considered, except u itself and the special symbol $*$. The t keys with ids equal to these t elements are loaded in the key-ring of u along with the respective key ids. In addition, the location (i, j) is also stored in the memory of u.

Subsequently, for each position (i, j) in the triangle TT, one computes $u = f(i, j) = \left(\frac{t+2}{2}\right)^2 + f(j, i)$. The key-ring of u is loaded with the keys whose ids are the elements of the i-th row of the matrix (except u and $*$).

2.3   Shared Key Discovery

Suppose that a node u wants to establish a key with a node v. Let (u_i, u_j) and (v_i, v_j) denote the locations of the nodes u and v in the layout matrix.

Assume that u is located in the triangle LT in the layout matrix. Figures 1 and 2 explain this situation. First consider the case that (v_i, v_j) too is in the triangle LT. If $u_j = v_j$, then u and v share the $t - 1$ keys with ids $f(i, u_j)$ for $i \neq u_i, v_i, u_j$ (Figure 1(c)).

If u and v are both in the triangle LT and $u_j \neq v_j$, we have a situation described in Figure 1(a). By construction, the v_j-th column of the layout matrix is identical to its $(t + 1 - v_j)$-th row. The u_j-th column and the $(t + 1 - v_j)$-th row intersect at the unique location $(t + 1 - v_j, u_j)$. If this location is distinct from (u_i, u_j), then u and v share the unique key with id $f(t + 1 - v_j, u_j)$. If, on the other hand, $u_i = t + 1 - v_j$, then u and v do not share a key (Figure 2(a)).

Finally, suppose that (v_i, v_j) is in the triangle TT of the layout matrix. In this case, u and v share the unique key with id $f(v_i, u_j)$ (Figure 1(b)), unless $v_i = u_i$ (Figure 2(b)) or $v_i = u_j$ (Figure 2(c)).

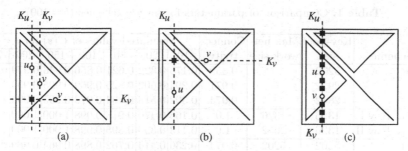

Fig. 1. Two nodes u, v sharing keys

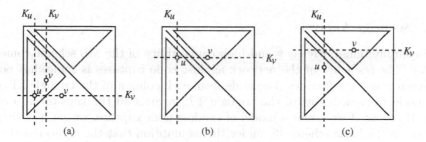

Fig. 2. Two nodes u, v not sharing keys

To sum up, the node u identifies in $O(1)$ time a key shared with v (provided that such a key exists). If m denotes the number of neighbors of u in its new neighborhood, then using only $O(m)$ computation and communication overhead u can reestablish its key connectivity records, whereas each new neighbor of u incurs only $O(1)$ computation and communication overhead. No key predistribution schemes proposed earlier achieve such a high efficiency.

3   Analysis of the ML Scheme

3.1   Connectivity

Figure 2 shows the three situations in which two nodes u and v do not share a key. The number of such ordered pairs (u, v) is $(t + 1)(t + 2)(2t + 3)/3 = \Theta(t^3)$. The total number of ordered pairs (u, v) is $N(N - 1) = \Theta(t^4)$, where $N = 2 \left(\frac{t+2}{2} \right)^2$.

Proposition. The connectivity of the ML scheme is $p = 1 - \Theta \left(\frac{1}{t} \right)$. More precisely, $p \approx 1 - \frac{8}{3t}$ except for very small values of t. In particular, p is very close to 1 for all practical values of t. Moreover, the number of ordered pairs of nodes sharing $t - 1$ common keys is $t(t + 2)(2t + 5)/6 = \Theta(t^3)$, i.e., most pairs of connected nodes share unique keys.

Table 1. Comparison of parameters for several schemes ($t = 100$)

Scheme	Key-pool size	Max network size	Connectivity	Simulated values of $C(s)$ for $s =$						
				10	20	50	100	150	200	250
Basic	5202	–	0.859	0.176	0.322	0.621	0.856	0.946	0.979	0.992
	2922	–	0.971	0.294	0.502	0.825	0.969	0.995	0.999	1.000
	2832	–	0.974	0.302	0.513	0.834	0.973	0.995	0.999	1.000
Ruj & Roy I	1326	1326	1.0	0.166	0.470	0.918	0.998	1.000	1.000	1.000
Ruj & Roy II	1326	2652	1.0	0.113	0.393	0.898	0.998	1.000	1.000	1.000
ML I	5202	5202	0.974	0.236	0.414	0.702	0.898	0.964	0.989	0.993
ML II	5202	10404	0.971	0.176	0.324	0.612	0.863	0.945	0.979	0.991

3.2   Security Analysis

The computational efficiency and high connectivity of the ML scheme come at a cost. The resilience of the network against node captures is somewhat poor. Capturing only $t + 2$ nodes (one node from each column of the triangle LT and one node from each row of the triangle TT) reveals all the keys to an adversary. However, if we adopt a model of random node capture, we get a resilience similar to the basic scheme [5] under the assumption that the deterministically distributed keys behave as randomly distributed keys. This assumption is, however, not very accurate, and we obtain a resilience slightly smaller than that of the basic scheme with the same pool size.

3.3   Doubling the Maximum Supported Network Size

The key-rings of the nodes in the triangle LT (resp. TT) are based on the columns (resp. rows) of the matrix. We now distribute the same keys to a new set of $N = 2 \left(\frac{t+2}{2} \right)^2$ nodes. In this case the key rings of the nodes in the triangle LT (resp. TT) are based on the rows (resp. columns) of the layout matrix. The connectivity among the new nodes remains identical with that among the old nodes. The cross connectivity among the old nodes and the new nodes continues to remain $1 - \Theta(1/t)$. The maximum supported network size now becomes $4 \left(\frac{t+2}{2} \right)^2 \approx t^2$. This extended scheme is called the ML Scheme II.

4   Comparison with Other Schemes

In Table 1, we compare our schemes with the basic scheme [5] and Ruj and Roy's schemes [9]. We take the capacity of the key-ring in each sensor node to be $t = 100$ keys. By $C(s)$, we denote the fraction of compromised links among uncaptured nodes, when s randomly chosen nodes are captured.

Let us first compare our scheme with Ruj and Roy's scheme. By reducing the amount of overlap between key rings, we have increased both the key-pool size and the maximum supported network size by a factor of nearly 4. This gain comes at the cost of some marginal loss of connectivity. For $t = 100$, the loss of connectivity is less than 3%. When the number of captured nodes is quite small, Ruj and Roy's schemes provide better resilience than our schemes because of larger overlaps of key rings of the nodes. However, as the number of captured nodes increases, a smaller key-pool size in Ruj and Roy's schemes makes their resilience noticeably poorer than that of ML schemes.

The basic scheme supports networks of any size. When we use the same key-pool size as the ML schemes, the basic scheme yields poorer connectivity but higher resilience against node captures. On the other hand, if we reduce the key-pool size for the basic scheme so as to achieve the same connectivity as the ML schemes, its resilience becomes poorer than that for the ML schemes.

5   Conclusion

In this paper, we propose the matrix-layout (ML) scheme for deterministic key predistribution in a sensor network. Our scheme is very suitable for mobile networks, since it optimizes the computation and communication overhead of key reestablishment. However, poor resilience of our scheme against node captures (particularly selective captures) is expected to attract further research attention. Several ad hoc techniques (like using multiple copies of the ML scheme) can increase resilience at the cost of decreased connectivity.

References

1. Camtepe, S.A., Yener, B.: Combinatorial design of key distribution mechanisms for wireless sensor networks. In: Samarati, P., Ryan, P.Y.A., Gollmann, D., Molva, R. (eds.) ESORICS 2004. LNCS, vol. 3193, pp. 293–308. Springer, Heidelberg (2004)
2. Chakrabarti, D., Maitra, S., Roy, B.K.: A key pre-distribution scheme for wireless sensor networks: merging blocks in combinatorial design. Intl. Jl. Inf. Sec. 5(2), 105–114 (2006)
3. Chan, H., Perrig, A., Song, D.: Random key predistribution for sensor networks, IEEE Symposium on Security and Privacy, pp. 197–213 (2003)
4. Du, W., Deng, J., Han, Y.S., Varshney, P.K.: A pairwise key pre-distribution scheme for wireless sensor networks. In: CCS 2003, pp. 42–51 (2003)
5. Eschenauer, L., Gligor, V.D.: A key management scheme for distributed sensor networks. In: CCS 2002, pp. 41–47 (2002)
6. Lee, J., Stinson, D.R.: Deterministic key predistribution schemes for distributed sensor networks. In: Handschuh, H., Hasan, M.A. (eds.) SAC 2004. LNCS, vol. 3357, pp. 294–307. Springer, Heidelberg (2004)
7. Liu, D., Ning, P.: Establishing pairwise keys in distributed sensor networks. In: CCS 2003, pp. 52–61 (2003)
8. Mehta, M., Huang, D., Harn, L.: RINK-RKP: A scheme for key predistribution and shared-key discovery in sensor networks. In: IPCCC 2005, pp. 193–197 (2005)
9. Ruj, S., Roy, B.: Key predistribution using partially balanced designs in wireless sensor networks. In: Stojmenovic, I., Thulasiram, R.K., Yang, L.T., Jia, W., Guo, M., de Mello, R.F. (eds.) ISPA 2007. LNCS, vol. 4742, pp. 431–445. Springer, Heidelberg (2007)
10. Sánchez, D.S., Baldus, H.: A deterministic pairwise key pre-distribution scheme for mobile sensor networks. In: Securecomm 2005, pp. 277–288 (2005)

Alternative Protocols for Generalized Oblivious Transfer

Bhavani Shankar[1], Kannan Srinathan[1], and C. Pandu Rangan[2]

[1] Center for Security, Theory and Algorithmic Research (C-STAR),
International Institute of Information Technology,
Hyderabad, 500032, India
shankar@research.iiit.ac.in, srinathan@iiit.ac.in
[2] Department of Computer Science and Engineering,
Indian Institute of Technology, Madras,
Chennai, 600036, India
rangan@iitm.ernet.in

Abstract. Protocols for Generalized Oblivious Transfer(GOT) were introduced by Ishai and Kushilevitz [10]. They built it by reducing GOT protocols to standard 1-out-of-2 oblivious transfer protocols based on private protocols. In our protocols, we provide alternative reduction by using secret sharing schemes instead of private protocols. We therefore show that there exist a natural correspondence between GOT and general secret sharing schemes and thus the techniques and tools developed for the latter can be applied equally well to the former.

1 Introduction

The notion of *Oblivious transfer* (OT) was introduced by Rabin [13] which has proved to be useful tool in the construction of various cryptographic protocols like bit commitment, zero-knowledge proofs, multi-party computations etc [12]. In Rabin's OT protocol, Alice has a list of n strings $x_1, x_2 \ldots x_n$ and Bob wishes to learn about the string x_i. But, Bob does not want to reveal the value of index i and at the same time Alice does not want to reveal any of the x_j for which $j \neq i$. Later, several variations of OT were proposed in the literature [4,8,5,6,9] and some of them were proved to be equivalent by Brassard et. al. [3]. 1-out-of-2 OT introduced by Even et. al. [9] is one among them where Bob is allowed to securely choose a single secret out of a pair of secrets held by Alice. Crepeau [7] showed that Rabin's OT is equivalent to 1-out-of-2 OT.

Direct extensions that followed 1-out-of-2 OT are 1-out-of-n OT [1,16] and m-out-of-n OT [14]. To state informally, in an m-out-of-n OT, Bob can receive only m messages out of n messages $(n > m)$ sent by Alice; and Alice has no idea about which ones have been received. Thus, for Alice all messages are equally likely possible for Bob to receive. 1-out-of-n OT is a special case of m-out-of-n OT where $m = 1$. All the above mentioned variations of OT are analogous to the threshold secret sharing schemes where the number of secrets to be transmitted obliviously is defined by a threshold function. Thus, all the limitations

S. Rao et al. (Eds.): ICDCN 2008, LNCS 4904, pp. 304–309, 2008.
© Springer-Verlag Berlin Heidelberg 2008

of a threshold schemes used in secret sharing schemes hold here, i.e. there exist access structures that cannot be realized by the above mentioned variations of OT. GOT protocol introduced by Ishai and Kushilevitz[10] is thus a natural generalization of all these variations of OT.

In GOT protocol, Alice has n secrets, and wishes to obliviously transfer to Bob a qualified subset $A \subseteq [n]$ of the secrets as per Bob's choice, where n is a positive integer denoting the number of 1-bit secrets held by Alice. Ishai and Kushilevitz[10] implement GOT by means of parallel invocation of simple 1-out-of-2 OT primitive while making use of private protocols. Their model of private protocols consists of n players $P_1, P_2, \ldots, P_n$ where each player holds a secret input x_i. All the players have access to a common random string. Messages are sent by all the n players to a special player *Carol* depending upon its input and the common random string. *Carol* computes a predetermined function using messages received from all the players without learning any additional information about the secret values $x_1, x_2, \ldots, x_n$. We too implement our GOT protocol by parallel invocations of 1-out-of-2 OT, but we greatly reduce the overhead of private protocols by using secret sharing schemes instead of private protocols.

Papers that have close resemblance to our work are Kawamoto and Yamamoto's [11] work on secret function sharing schemes(SFSS) and Tzeng's [17] work on 1-out-of-n OT. Kawamoto and Yamamoto [11] have shown that an unconditionally secure distributed oblivious transfer protocol can be constructed by combining the SFSS with multi-groups secret sharing scheme [15]. On the other hand, Tzeng [17] work showed how to construct OT protocols using any secret sharing scheme. His schemes are based on computational guarantee (based on decisional Diffie-Hellman problem), whereas our scheme's guarantee is dependent on the security guarantee of the underlying secret sharing scheme. Thus by using secret sharing schemes with different security guarantees, our schemes can provide different security guarantees.

Rest of the paper is organized as follows: section 2 covers the required background. In section 3 we give our protocol and its proof of correctness and we conclude the paper in section 4.

2   Preliminaries

Definition 1. Access structure [2]
Let $\mathcal{P} = \{P_0, P_1, \ldots, P_{n-1}\}$ be a set of parties. A collection $\mathcal{A} \subseteq 2^{\{P_1, P_2, \ldots, P_n\}}$ is monotone if $B \in \mathcal{A}$ and $B \subseteq C$ imply $C \in \mathcal{A}$. An access structure is a monotone collection $\mathcal{A}$ of non-empty subsets of $\{P_1, P_2, \ldots, P_n\}$ (that is, $\mathcal{A} \subseteq 2^{\{P_1, P_2, \ldots, P_n\}}$). The sets in $\mathcal{A}$ are called the authorized sets. A set B is called a minimal set of $\mathcal{A}$ if $B \in \mathcal{A}$, and for every $C \subsetneq B$ it holds that $C \notin \mathcal{A}$. The minimal sets of an access structure uniquely define it. Finally, we freely identify an access structure with its monotone characteristic function $f_A : \{0,1\}^n \longrightarrow \{0,1\}$, whose variables are denoted $x_0, \ldots, x_n$.

Definition 2. Complement of an access structure
Let $\mathcal{P} = \{P_0, P_1, \ldots, P_{n-1}\}$ be a set of parties. A collection $\mathcal{B} \subseteq 2^{\mathcal{P}}$ is called as a complement of a collection $\mathcal{A}$ if $\{\exists B \in \mathcal{B} | B = \mathcal{P} - A, \forall A \in \mathcal{A}\}$.

Note: Complement of an access structure is uniquely defined by its maximal basis[1] $\overline{\mathcal{B}}$ instead of minimal basis. Also, there can exist common subsets between both access structure $\mathcal{A}$ and its complement access structure $\mathcal{B}$. For example, consider $\mathcal{P} = \{1, 2, 3, 4\}$, $\overline{\mathcal{A}} = \{\{1, 2\}, \{2, 3\}, \{3, 4\}\}$. Its complement access structure uniquely defined by its maximal basis $\overline{\mathcal{B}} = \{\{1, 2\}, \{1, 4\}, \{3, 4\}\}$. Observe that the subsets $\{1, 2\}$ and $\{3, 4\}$ are common to both the structures.

Definition 3. Secret Sharing [2]
Let S be a finite set of secrets, where $|S| \geq 2$. An n-party secret-sharing scheme Π with secret-domain S is a randomized mapping from S to a set of n-tuples $S_0 \times S_1 \times \ldots \times S_{n-1}$, where S_i is called the share-domain of P_i. A dealer distributes a secret $s \in S$ according to Π by first sampling a vector of shares $(s_0, \ldots, s_{n-1})$ from $\Pi(s)$, and then privately communicating each share s_i to the party P_i. We say that Π realizes an access structure $\mathcal{A} \subseteq 2^{\{P_1, P_2, \ldots, P_n\}}$ (or the corresponding monotone function $f_{\mathcal{A}} : \{0, 1\}^n \longrightarrow \{0, 1\}$) if the following two requirements hold:

1. **Correctness.** *The secret s can be reconstructed by any authorized subset of parties. That is, for any subset $B \in \mathcal{A}$ (where $B = \{P_{i_1}, \ldots, P_{i_{|B|}}\}$), there exists a reconstruction function $Rec_B : S_{i_1} \times \ldots \times S_{i_{|B|}} \longrightarrow S$ such that for every $s \in S$,*
$$Pr[Rec_B(\Pi(s)_B) = s] = 1,$$
   where $\Pi(s)_B$ denotes the restriction of $\Pi(s)$ to its B-entries.
2. **Privacy.** *Every unauthorized subset cannot learn anything about the secret (in the information theoretic sense) from their shares. Formally, for any subset $C \notin \mathcal{A}$, for every two secrets a, $b \in S$, and for every possible shares $\langle s_i \rangle_{P_i \in C}$:*
$$Pr[\Pi(a)_C = \langle s_i \rangle_{P_i \in C}] = Pr[\Pi(b)_C = \langle s_i \rangle_{P_i \in C}].$$

Definition 4. Generalized Oblivious protocol
A Generalized oblivious protocol $\mathcal{P}$ between two players Alice and Bob is said to realize an access structure $\mathcal{B}$ if:

1. *Bob is able to recover all the secrets chosen from any one of the qualified subsets specified by an access structure.*
2. *Bob doesn't recover any set of secrets which is not qualified according to the given access structure.*

3   Protocol

Let $\sigma_1, \sigma_2, \ldots \sigma_n$ be the n messages of the (generalized) OT protocol. The qualified set of messages that receiver can receive is specified by an access structure $\mathcal{A}$.

---

[1] The maximal basis of $\mathcal{B}$ is defined as the collection $\{B | B \in calB, \nexists X \in \mathcal{B}, X \supset A\}$.

Let $\mathcal{B}$ be a complement access structure to $\mathcal{A}$. SHARE and RECOVER are the sharing and reconstruction algorithms of a secret sharing scheme respectively for an access structure $\mathcal{B}$. We give an information theoretic reduction from oblivious transfer on an access structure $\mathcal{A}$ to 1-out-of-2 oblivious transfer using a secret sharing scheme on access structure $\mathcal{B}$. Our protocol is as follows:

1. Alice selects n random values $x_1, x_2, \ldots x_n$ uniformly chosen from a finite field and computes $y_i = \sigma_i \oplus x_i$.
2. Alice chooses a random secret s uniformly chosen from a finite field and applies the SHARE algorithm to get n shares $s_1, s_2, \ldots s_n$.
3. Alice and Bob execute 1-out-of-2 OT protocol n times, with the messages $(s_1, y_1), (s_2, y_2), \ldots (s_n, y_n)$ respectively.
4. Let $A \in \mathcal{A}$ be the set of messages that Bob wishes to receive. For each i, if $i \in A$ then Bob picks y_i, else he picks the share s_i.
5. Bob executes RECOVER algorithm to obtain secret s and sends it back to Alice.
6. Alice verifies whether Bob has correctly computed the secret s. If it is correct, she sends $x_1, x_2, \ldots x_n$ to Bob else she aborts the protocol.
7. Bob computes $\sigma_i = x_i \oplus y_i$ for each i in A.

Theorem 1. *Bob can recover any of the qualified subsets defined by the access structure $\mathcal{A}$.*

Proof. We prove by contradiction. For the rest of the proof, we assume i to be some positive value less than or equal to n. Suppose Bob is unable to recover a valid secret σ_i defined accordingly by a qualified set $A \in \mathcal{A}$. It is either due to x_i or y_i missing or both. Consider each of the cases individually:

1. x_i *is missing:* This implies that Bob has send an invalid secret s to Alice for Alice to refuse to send the values $x_1, x_2, \ldots, x_n$. By the correctness of the RECOVER algorithm, it implies that Bob recovers unqualified set of shares to construct the secret s. But from the security of the underlying 1-out-of-2 OT, we know that Bob recovers a valid set of shares $A \in \mathcal{A}$, if and only if he recovers a valid set of shares $B \in \mathcal{B}^2$. Therefore, Bob cannot posses share y_i. Hence a contradiction.
2. y_i *is missing:* This contradicts the basic assumption of 1-out-of-2 OT that Bob would be able to recover either of the secret s_i or y_i as per his choice. Hence a contradiction.
3. *Both x_i and y_i are missing:* By the similar argument as before, one can vacuously prove that it can occur only when the underlying 1-out-of-2 OT is incorrect. Hence a contradiction.

Theorem 2. *Bob cannot recover any subset of secrets that is not qualified according to the access structure $\mathcal{A}$.*

---

[2] In third step of the protocol, Bob would be able to recover either y_i or s_i for $\forall i, 1 \leq i \leq n$ but not both.

Proof. We prove by contradiction. Suppose that Bob's algorithm is a probabilistic polynomial time that outputs $\{\sigma_i\}_{i \in A}$ for any $A \in \mathcal{A}$ with non-negligible probability. To correctly reconstruct the secret s of Alice, Bob requires all $\{s_i\}_{i \in B}$ for any $B \in \mathcal{B}$. Otherwise it is infeasible to know the value of secret s, whose security follows from the security of underlying secret sharing scheme. The only way in which Bob can get $\{\sigma_i\}_{i \in B}$ for any $B \notin \mathcal{B}$ is to get both the input of Alice in the third step of the above protocol, which is infeasible since it depends on the underlying 1-out-of-2 OT protocol.

Theorem 3. *Alice has no information of which qualified set of secrets defined by $\mathcal{A}$ is recovered by Bob.*

Proof. In the third step of the protocol, Alice and Bob execute 1-out-of-2 OT for n rounds. From the security of the underlying 1-out-of-2 OT protocol, for each round i Alice has no information whether s_i or y_i is been recovered by Bob. Thus, even at the end of the n invocations, Alice has no idea about the set of shares s_i and y_i recovered by Bob. Thus, the privacy of Bob follows from the secrecy of which set of shares he recovers.

4   Conclusion

Oblivious Transfer proved to be very useful tool in the construction of the cryptographic protocol. Similarly, *generalized oblivious transfer* (GOT) is also expected to be very useful in the construction of cryptographic protocols. For instance, GOT has important applications in E-Commerce. Suppose that Alice wants to buy some goods from a shopkeeper, but does not want to reveal to the shopkeeper what set of goods he intends to buy. Whereas the shopkeeper wants to make sure that total cost of the goods that Alice buys is no more than what Alice claims. This can be easily implemented using GOT, where the GOT's access structure contains all possible combinations of goods whose total price does not exceed a specified value. GOT has many other such useful applications. Characterizing the exact lower bounds for GOT in terms of communication and computation is an interesting open problem.

Acknowledgements

We thank the anonymous reviewers for their useful feedback.

References

1. Aiello, B., Ishai, Y., Reingold, O.: Priced oblivious transfer: How to sell digital goods. In: Pfitzmann, B. (ed.) EUROCRYPT 2001. LNCS, vol. 2045, Springer, Heidelberg (2001)
2. Beimel, Ishai.: On the power of nonlinear secret-sharing. In: SCT: Annual Conference on Structure in Complexity Theory (2001)

3. Brassard, G., Crépeau, C., Robert, J.M.: Information theoretic reduction among disclosure problems. In: 27th IEEE Symposium on Foundations of Computer Science, Toronto, Ontario, pp. 168–173 (1986)
4. Cachin, C.: On the foundations of oblivious transfer. In: Nyberg, K. (ed.) EURO-CRYPT 1998. LNCS, vol. 1403, Springer, Heidelberg (1998)
5. Cachin, C., Crepeau, C., Marcil, J.: Oblivious transfer with a memory-bounded receiver. In: IEEE Symposium on Foundations of Computer Science, pp. 493–502 (1998)
6. Cachin, C., Crepeau, C., Marcil, J.: Oblivious transfer in the bounded storage model. In: Kilian, J. (ed.) CRYPTO 2001. LNCS, vol. 2139, pp. 493–502. Springer, Heidelberg (2001)
7. Crepeau, C.: An equivalence between two flavors of oblivious transfer. In: Pomerance, C. (ed.) CRYPTO 1987. LNCS, vol. 293, Springer, Heidelberg (1988)
8. Crepeau, C.: Quantum oblivious transfer. Journal of Modern Optics 41(12), 2455–2466 (1994)
9. Even, S., Goldreich, O., Lempel, A.: A randomized protocol for signing contracts. In: Advances in Cryptology: Proceedings of Crypto 1982, pp. 205–210 (1982)
10. Ishai, Y., Kushilevitz, E.: Private simultaneous messages protocols with applications. In: Israel Symposium on Theory of Computing Systems, pp. 174–184 (1997)
11. Kawamoto, Y., Yamamoto, H.: Secret function sharing schemes and their applications to the oblivious transfer. In: IEEE International Symposium on Information Theory, 2003, IEEE, Los Alamitos (2003)
12. Kilian, J.: Founding crytpography on oblivious transfer. In: Proceedings of the twentieth annual ACM symposium on Theory of computing, pp. 20–31 (1988)
13. Rabin, M.O.: How to exchange secrets by oblivious transfer. In: Technical Report TR-81, Harvard University (1981)
14. Mu, Y., Zhang, J., Varadharajan, V.: m out of n oblivious transfer. In: Batten, L.M., Seberry, J. (eds.) ACISP 2002. LNCS, vol. 2384, pp. 3–5. Springer, Heidelberg (2002)
15. Naor, M., Pinkas, B.: Distributed oblivious transfer. In: Lai, X., Chen, K. (eds.) ASIACRYPT 2006, pp. 205–219. Springer, Heidelberg (2000)
16. Santis, A.D., Persiano, G.: Public-randomness in public-key cryptography. In: Damgård, I.B. (ed.) EUROCRYPT 1990. LNCS, vol. 473, Springer, Heidelberg (1991)
17. Tzeng, W.-G.: Efficient 1-out-of-n oblivious transfer schemes with universally usable parameters. IEEE Trans. Comput. 53(2), 232–240 (2004)

The Crossroads Approach to Information Discovery in Wireless Sensor Networks

Robin Doss, Gang Li, Shui Yu, Vicky Mak, and Morshed Chowdhury

School of Engineering and Information Technology, Deakin University,
221 Burwood Highway, Vic 3125, Australia
(robin.doss,gang.li,shui.yu,vicky,muc)@deakin.edu.au

Abstract. Wireless sensor networks (WSN) are attractive for information gathering in large-scale data rich environments. In order to fully exploit the data gathering and dissemination capabilities of these networks, energy-efficient and scalable solutions for data storage and information discovery are essential. In this paper, we formulate the information discovery problem as a load-balancing problem, with the combined aim being to maximize network lifetime and minimize query processing delay resulting in QoS improvements. We propose a novel information storage and distribution mechanism that takes into account the residual energy levels in individual sensors. Further, we propose a hybrid push-pull strategy that enables fast response to information discovery queries.

Simulations results prove the proposed method(s) of information discovery offer significant QoS benefits for global as well as individual queries in comparison to previous approaches.

1 Introduction

In order to fully exploit the data gathering and dissemination capabilities of wireless sensor networks (WSNs), energy-efficient and scalable solutions for data storage and information discovery are essential. Traditionally, the communication pattern in WSNs has been assumed to be many-to-one; i.e., numerous sensors gather information which is routed to a central point commonly referred to as the *sink*. However, many emerging applications for WSNs require dissemination of information to interested clients within the network requiring support for differing traffic patterns. Military applications where the soldiers in a battlefield "query" for enemy presence or fire-fighters in a building querying for areas of high temperature are some examples. Further, the time and/or life critical nature of these applications place more stringent quality of service (QoS) requirements on the discovery process. This need is the main motivation for our work.

Strategies for information discovery can be proactive or reactive. Sensors that gather information or detect an event can "push" this information out to every sensor in the network or wait for a sensor to "pull" this information through querying. While pure push or pull based methods are possible, the efficiency of the two methods varies and depends on the demand for information [1].

S. Rao et al. (Eds.): ICDCN 2008, LNCS 4904, pp. 310–321, 2008.

In this paper, we formulate the information discovery problem as a load-balancing problem, with the combined aim being to maximize network lifetime and minimize query processing delay. We have developed a novel information storage and distribution mechanism that takes into account the residual energy levels in individual sensors. Further, we propose a hybrid push-pull strategy that enables fast response to information discovery queries. The proposed information storage and dissemination model uses a distributed algorithm to construct multiple energy-rich trees rooted at the information producing node. Our work differs from other recent developments within this space [2],[3],[4] in that we do not employ greedy mechanisms for information dissemination, depend on topological constraints or require knowledge of information location.

2   Related Work

Early research into optimal structures for information discovery in large-scale sensor networks can be traced back to directed diffusion [5] and rumor routing [6]. More recently Liu et al. [1] proposed a hybrid push-pull approach to simulate a comb-needle for data dissemination and retrieval. In a sensor grid as in Fig. 1, a node that generates data pushes its data vertically above and below its location to build a vertical needle of length l. When a sensor has a query, the query is then pushed out horizontally every s vertical hops with the resulting routing structure representing a comb. The main drawback of the approach is the lack of any attempt to balance the load in the network. A node generating a large number of events will always replicate its data along the same path using the same nodes. Apart from the storage limitations of sensor nodes, such a static approach will impact negatively on the network lifetime.

Ratnasamy et al. [2] proposed the use of a geographic hash table (GHT) for data-centric storage. When a node generates data or an event this information

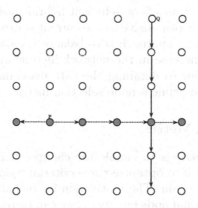

Fig. 1. A simple scheme on a $n \times n$ grid network where a information producer P replicates its data along the horizontal and the query from a node Q traverses the vertical to discover the information. The information discovery cost is therefore $O(n)$.

is stored by name at a location within the sensor network. This location is identified based on the value of a key that hashes to geographic coordinates within the network. Sarkar et al. [3] proposed the Double Rulings (DR) scheme for information brokerage as an extension to the basic GHTs hashing. The DR scheme improves on the GHT method in that it allows for distance sensitive query resolution. However, the choice of nodes in the replication and retrieval curves are not energy-sensitive and hence it suffers from the same drawbacks as the previous methods. Fang et al.[4], proposed an interesting landmark-based strategy that combines the GHT with a DR scheme without the requirement for sensor nodes to be location-aware. In a pre-processing stage the landmark Voronoi complex (LVC) and its dual the combinatorial Delaunay graph (CDG) are computed in order to capture the global topology of the sensor field. The global topology is abstracted using a subset of well-chosen sensor nodes that are referred to as "landmarks". Nodes are then partitioned into regions (or tiles) in such a manner that within each tile greedy routing mechanisms can succeed. Data generated by a node is hashed to a tile based on the data type and routed using a shortest path tree that rooted on the originating tile. Data is replicated at each tile enroute to the hashed tile. When a node issues a query the query is routed towards the hashed tile, until it rendezvous on a tile along the replication path. At the lower-level, DR is employed for information retrieval within each tile. The main drawback of the scheme is the heavy dependency on the global topology abstraction.

3   Our Approach

We note that current approaches for information dissemination in WSNs adopt a data-centric approach that is not responsive to the current state of individual sensors. As stated earlier, the data replication strategies employed are based on distance based greedy methods. These routing strategies are energy-inefficient [7].

We propose the use of an energy-efficient hybrid push-pull information discovery mechanism that is responsive to the current state of the individual sensor nodes. The aim of such an approach is to balance the data load across the network with a resulting increase in the network lifetime and decrease in the cost of query resolution. Prior to detailing the data dissemination and information retrieval mechanisms we define a node selection metric.

3.1   Node Selection Metric

The purpose of the metric is to enable the energy-efficient choosing of a data replication node. We seek to optimize three criteria: residual node energy, occupied buffer and distance gain. The motivation for including these three criteria are: by maximizing residual node energy ε_x, we can increase network lifetime; by minimizing the occupied buffer space b_x, we can increase the persistence of data which can decrease the query resolution cost and by maximizing the distance gain d_x, we can achieve a larger network coverage in terms of data dissemination.

We therefore define the metric $M_x[t]$ as

$$M_x[t] = C.\frac{\varepsilon_x.d_x}{b_x}, \tag{1}$$

where C is a constant. The data replication node X is then added to the tree based on the following condition,

$$X = \arg\max M_x[t] \tag{2}$$

3.2 Node Selection Algorithm

The node selection algorithm is built on the underlying MAC protocol that is assumed to be CSMA with RTS/CTS. A node that has data to send initiates an RTS broadcast that contains the ID of the data packet. All neighbours of the node that receive this RTS packet are potential replication nodes. We initiate a distributed algorithm (similar to [7]) where these nodes contend with each other to serve as a data replication node. On receiving the RTS packet each node calculates a metric and starts a timer that is inversely proportional to the value of the metric. On the expiry of this timer, the node will send out a CTS packet provided it has not overheard another CTS packet with the same packet ID. This simple and elegant process ensures that the node with the best metric will send the CTS first.

We recognize that RTS/CTS mechanisms suffer from hidden terminal problems. While this is considered to be a negative effect we exploit it to achieve data dissemination in the network. In a dense network that is interference-limited, multiple hidden nodes are bound to exist. These nodes can be exploited to construct multiple energy-rich trees along which data replication can be completed. Since these hidden nodes are spatially separated the data replication along the branches of the tree will increase network coverage. The information producing node then sends out the DATA packet after it has received at least one CTS response. However, this DATA packet is not unicast to a particular node. Instead, all nodes that have responded with a CTS packet will receive this DATA packet and store it. Data is then propagated towards the edge of the network either using a TTL value or until a boundary node is reached. However, in order to increase the speed of data dissemination we place a positive distance constraint on the selection of all non-first hop data replication nodes. Nodes contend using a similar process as the first hop nodes but are required to offer a positive geographic advance.

4 The Crossroads Approach to Information Discovery

The crossroads approach is based on perimeter aggregation of events and the construction of energy-efficient query paths for information discovery. We present the details below.

4.1 Perimeter Aggregation

We propose a method of data dissemination where the data in the network is pushed towards the edges of the network. As will be shown later, this serves to significantly reduce the delay involved in resolving global type queries. The branches of the data replication tree that is being constructed terminate when the branches reach the edge of the network. In a grid type network, once the first-hop replication nodes are chosen, they route the data towards their closest edge. This decision is easily computed based on their relative position to the information producing node P. If we assume a node $P(i, j)$ as the information producer and the first-hop replication nodes to be at locations, $(i - 1, j),(i + 1, j),(i, j + 1)$ and $(i, j - 1)$ then the termination points of the four branches will be at $(0, j),(n, j),(i, n)$ and $(0, n)$ respectively. This ensures that all data that is produced in the network can be replicated and aggregated along the perimeter of the network. Periodically, the nodes along each edge execute a data aggregation process where the aggregation point is chosen dynamically based on energy-levels. Once aggregation has been performed along each edge, a global type query has to be simply routed towards the nearest edge and towards the aggregation point. This can reduce the query resolution cost quite significantly.

4.2 Static Crossroads

In the static crossroads approach the replication tree is constructed using a static rule base similar to other approaches [2],[3],[4]. The closest approach to our method is the comb-needle approach. As shown in Fig. 2(a), a node that has information constructs a replication tree that resembles a crossroad centered on itself. The four branches of the crossroad terminate at the four edges of the network as described in the previous section. The use of multiple branches enables a greater data spread across the network.

4.3 Adaptive Crossroads

In the adaptive crossroads approach we construct the replication tree based on the metric presented in Section 2. The result of this construction of the replication tree is a non-regular crossroad that is centered on the information producing node. At each point along the replication tree the nodes contend to act as a replication point resulting in the construction of an energy-rich tree that is dynamic and adapts to the current state of the network. To the best of our knowledge this is the first attempt at energy-efficient information dissemination in a wireless sensor network. A snapshot of an adaptive crossroad is presented in Fig. 2(b).

4.4 Information Discovery

An efficient information discovery mechanism needs to efficiently support different query types. The QoS requirements of many real world applications require the latency of query resolution to be as small as possible. The flooding of all data

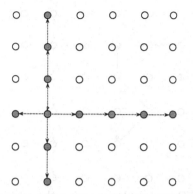
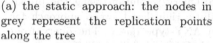
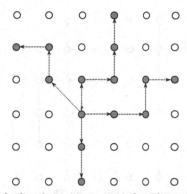

(a) the static approach: the nodes in grey represent the replication points along the tree

(b) the dynamic approach: The nodes in grey represent the replication points along the tree chosen based on the metric. They represent the best next-hop neighbour of each branch node.

Fig. 2. Replication crossroads in a $n \times n$ grid network

that is produced in the network to every node within the network can minimize the query resolution cost but it is an inefficient solution. The query resolution cost in comb-needle can be as high as $O(n^2)$ for global type queries. We show that using the proposed data dissemination mechanisms the query resolution cost of queries can be reduced.

In sensor network different types of queries can be identified. We refer to a query type as global if a node is requiring all instances of the occurrence of an event. An example in a battlefield application is, "Where are all the tanks in the network?" or in the fire-fighting example, "Which locations in the building have a temperature that is > 60 degrees?" To resolve such a query the query needs to collect information form all nodes in the network that have detected the presence of a tank. Global type queries are also referred to as ALL-type queries in literature. ANY-type queries are those where interest is restricted to a/any occurrence of the event. In battlefield situations an ANY-type query can be "Are there any tanks in the network?". The resolving of such a query can be terminated as soon as the presence of a tank has been detected. We propose two methods for query resolution depending on the type of the query. For ALL-type queries we propose the *nearest perimeter* approach that exploits perimeter aggregation. For resolving ANY-type queries we propose the *probabilistic right-hand sweep*.

Nearest Perimeter Approach. When a node issues an ALL-type query we direct the query towards the nearest perimeter. Since the nodes along the perimeter replicate all events in the network and perform aggregation along each edge the cost of query resolution is equivalent to the cost of reaching the edge and the cost of reach of the aggregation point. Since all nodes are location aware it is trivial to determine the nearest edge. In Fig. 3(a), node Q issues an ALL-type query, that requires information to be collected from all nodes that have detected this

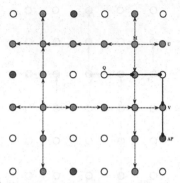 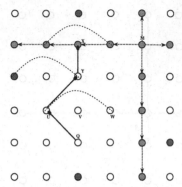

(a) Query resolution using the nearest perimeter approach for an ALL-type query. The query from node Q is routed first to the nearest perimeter and then along the edge to the aggregation point (AP).

(b) Query resolution using the probabilistic right-hand sweep approach for an ANY-type query. The query from node Q is probabilistically forwarded to node U and to node Y and resolved by node X. The dotted curves represents the sweep areas for node Q, node W and node Y.

Fig. 3. Query resolution for ALL-type query and for ANY-type query in a $n \times n$ grid network. The grey nodes represent the replication points along the tree, the red nodes represent the perimeter aggregation points.

specific event. Nodes L and M have detected this event and constructed in this case, a static replication tree. The query from node Q is sent towards the nearest edge which in this case is the right-hand side edge. On reaching the edge, the query is forwarded to the aggregation point (AP) which can resolve the query. The required data can then be sent to the requesting node using reverse path forwarding or any other location-based mechanism.

Probabilistic Right-hand Sweep. To resolve ANY-type queries we use a probabilistic method. Since ANY-type queries do not require aggregated information, we seek to resolve them in-network rather than directing the query towards the nearest edge. However, if a query cannot be resolved in-network then it is sent towards the AP. This is done in a decentralized manner when the query arrives at a network edge.

A node that generates an ANY-type query sends it to one of its neighbours chosen probabilistically. The choice of neighbour is determined by the node facing the major part of the network (i.e., away from the nearest edge), and choosing a node. Node Q with the query faces away from its nearest edge and chooses a next-hop node. As shown in Fig. 3(b), the candidate nodes are U, V and W. The query is forwarded following a similar process at each hop until it reaches a branch of the replication tree or an edge node. If the query reaches an edge node then it is sent towards the AP and is either resolved along the path to the AP or as a last resort at the AP.

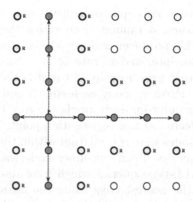

Fig. 4. Information dissemination through opportunistic overhearing in a $n \times n$ grid network. The R nodes (darker circle) represent the replication points adjacent to the replication tree that "overhear" transmissions. The event from node P is disseminated as always along the main replication tree (grey nodes).

4.5 Optimization through Opportunistic Information Dissemination

A further optimization can be achieved by exploiting the broadcast nature of the wireless medium. Information can be opportunistically stored at multiple locations for the same dissemination cost. This can provide a further improvement in the QoS offered to discovery messages. As shown in Fig. 4, when a cross-road is constructed from the *producer* node, the nodes that are adjacent to the crossroad overhear the transmissions. By opportunistically storing these transmissions the number of locations at which information relating to a particular event is available can be increased (in a regular $n \times n$ grid this can be upto a three-fold increase). In Fig. 4, we show the *replicated* crossroad for the static crossroads approach. The same principle can be applied to adaptive crossroads as well. Such an approach can significantly decrease the query resolution time for ANY-type queries as the number of locations at which an ANY-type query can be resolved is increased. The benefit is two-fold: by decreasing the query resolution cost in terms of the required number of transmissions the network lifetime is also increased.

5   Performance Evaluation

Performance evaluation of the proposed approach was carried out using network simulations with OPNET Modeler 12.0. The focus of the evaluations at the first instance was to study the QoS improvements offered by the proposed approach in comparison to earlier work. We compare our work with the comb-needle approach that was detailed in section 2. All results are averaged over 30 simulation runs (with random seeds) with each run of duration 180 secs.

The network topology used in the simulations was a regular $n \times n$ grid with a normalized grid spacing of 1 similar to the figures in the previous sections. For our simulations of the crossroads approach during each simulation run an information producer was chosen at random from within the *core* nodes (i.e., nodes that were not edges). This producer node generated events following a Poisson distribution with a mean inter-arrival rate of λ. λ was set to be 2 secs. The events that were generated were forwarded towards the edge using the metric introduced in section 3. Further, along each edge a node was randomly chosen to act as the aggregation point for each simulation run. Events generated by the producer node were collected at this aggregation point. During each simulation run multiple consumer nodes were chosen from within the core nodes to generate information discovery queries. Each consumer node was capable of generating two types of queries: ALL-type queries which were resolved at one of the aggregation points along the nearest edge using the nearest perimeter approach and ANY-type queries which were resolved where possible in-network using the right-hand sweep approach. Discovery queries were generated following an Exponential or Poisson distribution with a mean inter-arrival rate of λ. λ was varied from 1 to 10 secs. In our simulations of the comb-needle approach the size of the needle l was set to be 3 with an inter-comb spacing s of 1. The opportunistic crossroads approach was also studied. The communication range of each sensor node was set to a normalized range of $\sqrt{2}$. The MAC protocol in use was CSMA with RTS/CTS, a random back-off and delayed sends.

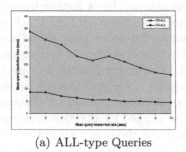   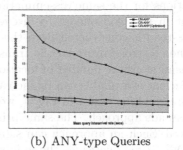

(a) ALL-type Queries   (b) ANY-type Queries

Fig. 5. Query resolution delay for ANY-type queries observed and ALL-type queries in a 8×8 grid network with the comb-needle (CN) scheme and the crossroads (CR) approach to information discovery. Queries arrive according to an Exponential distribution with a mean inter-arrival rate of λ. λ is varied from 1 to 10.

We identified two main performance metrics that were studied for both ALL-type queries and ANY-type queries using the crossroads approach and the comb needle approach. The metrics of interest were:

- Query resolution delay: The average time taken to resolve a particular query; and
- Query discovery ratio: The ratio between the number information discovery queries generated and the number of queries that were successfully resolved.

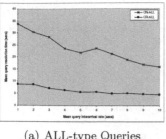
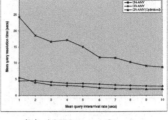

(a) ALL-type Queries   (b) ANY-type Queries

Fig. 6. Query resolution delay for ANY-type queries observed and ALL-type queries in a 8×8 grid network with the comb-needle (CN) scheme and the crossroads (CR) approach to information discovery. Queries arrive according to a Poisson distribution with a mean inter-arrival rate of λ. λ is varied from 1 to 10.

These two metrics taken together provide information on the effectiveness and completeness of the proposed approach in improving QoS (specifically latency).

The simulation results are presented in Fig. 5(a) - Fig. 8(b). Fig. 5(a) presents the query resolution delay for the comb-needle and the crossroads approach for ALL-type queries when the information discovery queries arrive according to an Exponential distribution. It can be observed that the Crossroads scheme outperforms the comb-needle scheme quite significantly. The mean query resolution time is reduced by almost 75% at both high and low query inter-arrival rates. Fig. 5(b) presents the results for query inter-arrival following a Poisson distribution and similar performance gains can be observed. The performance results for ANY-type query resolution is presented for the comb-needle, crossroads and optimised crossroads methods of information discovery is presented in Fig. 6(b) for queries arriving according to an exponential distribution. Significant performance gains can be observed. We observe that at a high query frequency (i.e. with $\lambda = 1$) the query resolution delay for an ANY-type query is reduced by more than 80% using the crossroads approach. At lower inter-arrival rates, for instance $\lambda = 10$ the delay is reduced by almost 65%. We can also note that the optimized crossroads approach offers comparable if not even better performance. We note that at lower inter-arrival rates such as $\lambda = 10$ the optimized crossroads approach outperforms the standard crossroads approach by 35% and the comb-needle approach by almost 80%. Similar trends are observed for inter-arrival rates following a Poisson distribution and is presented in Fig. 6(a).

The performance gains offered by the crossroads approach in reducing the query resolution delay is only significant if the crossroads approach can resolve more or an equivalent number of queries in comparison to the comb-needle approach. Performance results for query discovery ratio (QDR) are presented in Fig. 7(a) - Fig. 8(b). Fig. 7(a) presents the QDR results for ALL-type queries following an Exponential distribution. We observe that at very high inter-arrival rates say $\lambda = 1$ the QDR is quite low for both schemes. However, the crossroads approach outperforms the combneedle approach quite significantly at lower inter-arrival rates. For instance it can be observed that at $\lambda = 5$ comb-needle has a

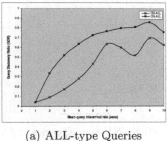
(a) ALL-type Queries

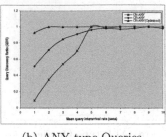
(b) ANY-type Queries

Fig. 7. Query discovery ratio observed for ANY-type queries and ALL-type queries in a 8×8 grid network with the comb-needle (CN) scheme and the crossroads (CR) approach to information discovery. Queries arrive according to an Exponential distribution with a mean inter-arrival rate of λ. λ is varied from 1 to 10.

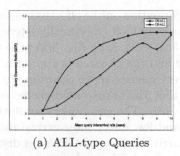
(a) ALL-type Queries

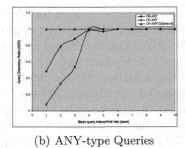
(b) ANY-type Queries

Fig. 8. Query discovery ratio observed for ANY-type queries and ALL-type queries in a 8×8 grid network with the comb-needle (CN) scheme and the crossroads (CR) approach to information discovery. Queries arrive according to a Poisson distribution with a mean inter-arrival rate of λ. λ is varied from 1 to 10.

QDR of 40% while the QDR using the crossroads approach is more than 70%. Similar trends are easily observable when queries arrive according to a Poisson distribution as in Fig. 8(a). However, it can be observed that the performance of all schemes are better for a Poisson distribution of query arrivals as compared to an Exponential arrival rate. This impact of the type of query arrival distribution is along expected lines. In Fig. 7(b) and Fig. 8(b) we present the QDR results for ANY-type queries using the three schemes for Exponential and Poisson inter-arrival rates respectively. We observe that all three schemes exhibit very high QDR values (QDR=1) for lower inter-arrival rates. However, at high inter-arrival rates the crossroad schemes outperform the comb-needle approach quite significantly with the optimized approach giving us the best performance. It is to be noted that the query resolution cost for an ALL-type query using the crossroads approach is significantly less than the cost of an ANY-type query using the comb-needle approach. This augurs very well for the crossroads approach to information discovery.

6 Conclusion and Future Work

In this paper, we have formulated the information discovery problem as a load-balancing problem, with the combined aim being to maximize network lifetime and minimize query processing delay. We have proposed a novel information storage and distribution mechanism that takes into account the residual energy levels in individual sensors. Further, we have also proposed a hybrid push-pull strategy that enables fast response to information discovery queries. Simulations results prove the the proposed method(s) of information discovery offer significant QoS benefits for both ALL-Type and ANY-type queries in comparison to previous approaches. We are currently working on extending the proposed approach to random sensor network deployments in mobile/vehicular platforms.

References

1. Liu, X., Huang, Q., Zhang, Y.: Balancing Push and Pull for Efficient Information Discovery in Large-Scale Sensor Networks. IEEE Trans. on Mobile Computing 6(3), 241–251 (2007)
2. Ratnasamy, S., et al.: A Geographic Hash Table for Data-Centric Storage. In: Proc. of first ACM workshop on wireless sensor networks and applications (2002)
3. Sarkar, R., Zhu, X., Gao, J.: Double Rulings for Information Brokerage in Sensor Networks. In: Proc. of ACM Mobicom 2006 (2006)
4. Fang, Q., Gao, J., Guibas, L.J.: Landmark-Based Information Storage and Retrieval in Sensor Networks. In: Proc. of 25th conference of the IEEE communications society (2006)
5. Braginsky, D., Estrin, D.: Rumor routing algorithm for wireless sensor networks. In: Wireless Sensor Networks and Applications (2002)
6. Intanagonwiwat, C., Govindan, R., Estrin, D.: Directed diffusion: a scalable and robust communication paradigm for sensor networks. In: Mobile Computing and Networking, pp. 56–67 (2000)
7. Coronel, P., Doss, R., Schott, W.: Location-based cooperative relaying in wireless sensor networks. In: IEEE Sensorware (2007)

Tree-Based Anycast for Wireless Sensor/Actuator Networks

Michal Koziuk and Jaroslaw Domaszewicz

Institute of Telecommunications, Warsaw University Of Technology
ul. Nowowiejska 15/19, 00-665 Warsaw, Poland
{mkoziuk,domaszew}@tele.pw.edu.pl

Abstract. This paper presents a tree-based anycast (TBA) protocol designed for wireless sensor/actuator networks. Contrary to existing work, TBA allows forming an anycast address from multiple attributes which describe the destination node. TBA uses spanning trees for query propagation. The usefulness of such a solution is validated by simulations, which show that under certain conditions significant energy gain compared to flooding can be expected.

1 Introduction

Anycast is a service which allows communications with any single node out of the set of nodes satisfying a certain criterion. In this paper these criteria (which can be called *anycast addresses*) are formed as follows. We assume that each node is characterized by a number of binary attributes. Let A be a set of all possible node attributes. Let V denote the set of all nodes in the network, and let V_a be the set of all nodes that have the attribute $a \in A$ ($V_a = \{v \in V : v$ has the attribute $a\}$). An anycast address is given by any subset of attributes $B \subset A$. Specifically, for $B \subset A$, let V_B be the set of all the nodes that have all the attributes in B, i.e.,

$$V_B = \bigcap_{a \in B} V_a \tag{1}$$

The anycast service as explored in this paper can be described by the primitive `ConnectAny(AnycastAddress)`, where `AnycastAddress` is the set B. Its semantics is that communications should be established between the node invoking the primitive and exactly one node $v \in V_B$. The choice of the node is up to the implementation of the anycast service. An important assumption is that the primitive should be available to each node in the network.

The anycast service as described above can be useful, for example, in heterogeneous sensor/actuator networks (such as the one described in [1]), to deliver software agents to nodes offering a required combination of resources. In such networks every node can become a service provider by sharing some of its resources with other nodes, and can be located by means of the anycast service.

This paper contains a description of a protocol implementing the anycast service. The protocol, called tree-based anycast (TBA), is targeted for energy

S. Rao et al. (Eds.): ICDCN 2008, LNCS 4904, pp. 322–331, 2008.

constrained environments such as wireless sensor/actuator networks. Contrary to existing anycast solutions, TBA does not limit the expressiveness of the anycast address, allowing the usage of multiple attributes in descriptions of a destination node.

The paper is organized as follows. In section 2 we present a number of existing anycast solutions, while in section 3 we present the TBA protocol. Section 4 contains experimental results. Conclusions are presented in section 5.

2   Related Work

The concept of anycast was researched in multiple contexts, including network type, communications model, and purpose of usage. For example, anycast can be found deep in the roots of TCP/IP networks, as it is used for directing DNS queries to the closest root nameserver [2]. It is also used for server selection in distributed systems [3]. Anycast will gain further importance, as it will be used to access gateways which interconnect IPv6 with IPv4 networks.

An anycast mechanism has been used to solve the issue of providing distributed services in the MANET environment. A minor change in some existing routing protocols (such as OSPF, RIP, or TORA) suffices for multiple hosts to be reached with a single address in an anycast fashion [4]. The idea is to assign an anycast address to a virtual node, to which all nodes providing a certain service are virtually connected.

Lifetime of heterogeneous wireless sensor networks can be increased in networks with more than one data sink, when access to the sinks is provided by an anycast protocol [5]. Such a network could consist of two types of devices - resource rich (information sinks) and resource-constrained (sensors generating new data) [6]. A similar concept of improving the energy efficiency of WSNs has been proposed in the HAR [7] protocol.

All the above anycast solutions differ from TBA. In each of them, B (the set of attributes used as the anycast address) is a singleton, i.e., it consists of only one element, $B = \{a\}$ for some $a \in A$ (even though A, the set of all existing attributes, need not be a singleton). This happens, for example, when A is a set of available services and an anycast address is used to access only one of them at a time. In some solutions (e.g., when data sources transmit information to sinks) A is itself a singleton (a node is either a sink or not).The main innovation of the TBA protocol, is that it allows establishing communications with a node matching a set of multiple attributes. Thus in TBA, contrary to the above solutions, the number of possible anycast addresses is not $|A|$, but $2^{|A|}$. The potentially huge number of anycast addresses makes it impossible to set up dedicated routes to each individual address.

Another type of anycast, which can be found in the WSN environment, is anycasting to a region. Solutions such as SPEED[8] and HLR [9] assume a situation where it is sufficient to deliver a packet to any node in a specified area. Algorithms for region-targeted anycast rely on the strong spatial correlation of the attributes used for addressing, which is not the case in TBA.

Note that the anycast primitive proposed in this paper is designed for addresses composed of a set of multiple attributes, and it may be applicable to various attribute-based (or context-based) addressing schemes such as [10] [11].

3   TBA Architecture

3.1   Assumptions

TBA assumes that a wireless sensor/actuator network consists of stationary nodes positioned randomly and connected in an ad-hoc mode. As the nodes are battery powered, they can disappear from the network at random. At the same time, new nodes can appear when they are added to the network. Therefore, despite the assumption of nodes being stationary, the TBA protocol can not assume that the network topology is fixed.

TBA further assumes the existence of an efficient data link layer protocol which assures bidirectional packet delivery between two nodes within radio range. We take it for granted that each packet sent to a neighbor node is (eventually) successfully received.

3.2   Protocol Overview

The main requirement for TBA is that it needs to find exactly one node in response to an anycast query. With this in mind we focus on making it possible to stop a query from propagating to the whole network. This is achieved by propagating queries along a spanning tree structure.

TBA starts by creating a number of spanning trees. This is achieved by flooding the network with the first few queries. Each spanning tree is rooted at the node which issued a corresponding query. Then, the protocol stops creating new spanning trees (hence stops flooding the network) and starts using these trees for query propagation. An anycast query is transported along the most fitting spanning tree. That makes it possible to prevent the query from reaching certain parts of the network once a node matching the address is found.

A response to the query is propagated along a route created during query propagation. Since it is still possible that multiple nodes matching the address receive the query, only the first received response is forwarded by each node along the way. The same happens at the query source, which treats the first incoming response as the only valid one.

3.3   Using a Spanning Tree as a Search Basis

The TBA protocol consists of three major mechanisms. The first two mechanisms are used to handle an anycast query, while the third one controls the choice of which of the first two to use for a specific query.

Mechanism 1: Forming a spanning tree. A wireless network can be represented as an undirected graph $G(V, E)$, where the set of vertices V corresponds

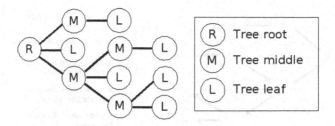

Fig. 1. Sample spanning tree with node positions

to network nodes, and the set of edges E represents bi-directional radio links. Each created spanning tree is a structure $G'(V' = V, E' \subset E)$ located on top of graph G.

Using the Breadth First Search algorithm, a shortest path spanning tree (Fig. 1) for the whole network is created. The root of this tree is the node which invoked the anycast primitive, while its leaves can be determined relying on confirmations sent during the tree creation process (each node receives a confirmation from all of its children; if no confirmations are received, it is a leaf). All remaining nodes are said to be in the middle of the tree, as presented in Fig. 1. Each node preserves information regarding its position in the tree.

Note that during the process of creating a tree, TBA places an anycast query in packets exchanged by network nodes. This means that the anycast query is propagated in the network, at the same time as a spanning tree is created.

Mechanism 2: Using an existing spanning tree for query propagation.
An anycast query propagated according to Mechanism 1 created a spanning tree. The following anycast queries may use this tree for their propagation, even if they do not originate from the original root of the tree. The propagation of a query issued at node Q is shown in Fig. 2. Note that the query moves both up and down the tree.

The actions performed to forward the query depend on the direction of its propagation in the tree structure. If the query is received from a child node, the recipient node sends it to its parent and to all its other children. If the query was received from a parent node, it is sent to all of the children.

While the anycast query is propagated along the chosen spanning tree structure, routes leading to the query's source are created. When a destination node $(v \in V_B)$ is found, it sends a response along those routes, and the query does not have to be sent further. As the query propagates along a predefined tree structure, stopping it from propagation in a single node actually results in preventing the query from reaching a number of nodes placed further along the tree (see Fig. 2). This is not the case when flooding the network. On the other hand the created routes are sub-optimal (the number of hops need not be minimal).

As indicated, each node is aware of its position in the tree and benefits from the knowledge when propagating queries. Nodes that are leaves in a spanning tree do not have to forward a received query to their children as they have none

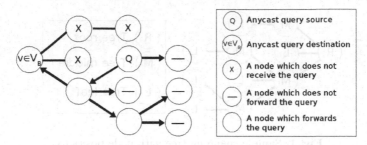

Fig. 2. Propagating a query using an existing spanning tree

(Fig. 2). Depending on the structure of the spanning tree (i.e. the number of its leaves) the obtained energy gain can be very significant or almost none at all.

The algorithm of forwarding a query according to a spanning tree structure is presented in Fig. 3.

```
QUERY-RECEIVED(receivedFrom, usedTree)

1.  if (thisNode ∈ V_B)
2.     then SEND-RESPONSE(receivedFrom)
3.  else
4.     if receivedFrom ∈ CHILDREN
5.        then FORWARD-QUERY(CHILDREN\{receivedFrom})
6.           if treePosition ≠ root
7.              then FORWARD-QUERY(parent)
8.        else
9.           if receivedFrom = parent && treePosition ≠ leaf
10.             then FORWARD-QUERY(CHILDREN)
```

Fig. 3. The algorithm for query propagation along an existing tree. The *treePosition*, *parent* and *CHILDREN* variables are acquired from the *usedTree* input parameter.

Mechanism 3: Determining whether to form a new spanning tree.

Mechanism 1 propagates the query by creating a new spanning tree, Mechanism 2 by using an existing tree. TBA alternates between these two mechanisms, as shown in Fig. 4.

The USABLE-TREE-EXISTS() procedure evaluates if an existing spanning tree should be used or a new one needs to be created. A number of rules can be applied to make the decision. A simple solution is to keep adding new spanning trees until some predefined number of them is reached (Mechanism 3a). Another solution is to evaluate the distance from the node issuing the query to the root for each existing tree and to create a new one only when all of the existing trees are too distant (Mechanism 3b). Both of these solutions are used in the performed experiments.

If a new tree has to be created, the CREATE-TREE() procedure is invoked, which sends out a query according to Mechanism 1. Otherwise, a tree which minimizes the distance from its root to the node issuing the query is selected by the GET-BEST-SPANNING-TREE() procedure (the distance to the root is a part of the tree structure). Then, the query is propagated according to Mechanism 2, along the structure of the selected tree.

```
SEND-ANYCAST-QUERY()

1. if USABLE-TREE-EXISTS()                    //mechanism 3
2.      then t ← GET-BEST-SPANNING-TREE()     //mechanism 3
3.            FORWARD-QUERY-ALONG-TREE(t)      //mechanism 2
4.      else CREATE-TREE()                     //mechanism 1
```

Fig. 4. The algorithm for invoking the anycast primitive

3.4 Protocol Optimization

TBA includes some enhancements, beyond the major mechanisms described above. The enhancements are denoted by OPTx for easier reference.

OPT1: Delaying query packets. When the query propagates through the network, each node deliberately delays its forwarding for a short period of time. If a destination node ($v \in V_B$) is discovered, it sends out a 'Clear Buffer' message to the node from which the query was received. That node in turn sends 'Clear Buffer' to nodes which are its neighbours in the spanning tree. If the 'Clear Buffer' message is received, the buffered query is not forwarded. For example, if a node p sends the query to its children, and one of them happens to be a destination node, then none of the siblings forwards the query (the destination node sends 'Clear Buffer' to p, which in turn sends it to the siblings).

OPT2: Short range flood. Before Mechanism 2, TBA performs an initial short range (two hop) flood with the new query. If a node matching the anycast address is found, the anycast query does not have to be propagated along the tree structure.

OPT3: Route optimization. Propagation along a tree does not guarantee a shortest path if the node that issued the query is not at the root of that tree. During the initial short range flood (OPT2), temporary shortest path routes to the issuing node are established. These are used during response propagation to direct it straight to the query source, once the response reaches a node which was subject to the initial short range flood.

4 Evaluation

As data transmission is the key factor responsible for energy usage, we count the number of bytes sent due to TBA's operation. As every transmitted byte is received by other nodes, we also count the number of received bytes, which we assume to cost approximately 1/3 of the cost of transmitted ones [12][1]. (We do not include media access and synchronization overhead.)

The byte count BC_x for a tested solution x can be evaluated using (2), where BT_x is the total number of bytes transmitted during the simulation, and BR_x is the number of bytes received.

$$BC_x = BT_x + \frac{BR_x}{3} \tag{2}$$

We apply this measure to test the efficiency of each algorithm used in the test scenarios. For comparison we use the simplest bottom line solutions, namely flooding and expanding ring search. The byte count value for each algorithm is compared against the lower bound value which corresponds to flooding, f. We use the ratio in (3) to describe the relative byte count for algorithm x.

$$RBC_x = \frac{BC_x}{BC_f} \tag{3}$$

The test scenario assumes a network of nodes positioned randomly in a pre-defined area. During the tests, eight anycast queries are sent from random nodes in the network. This number is chosen based on an assumption that on average after 8 queries have been sent, links forming spanning trees break, and all the tree structures have to be rebuilt. This means that if a real network happens to be more stable than this, or the node activity is more intense, the gain achieved by TBA will be higher than what follows from our simulation. On the other hand we can imagine a network with lower stability, and in such case it is very probable that the energy gain will significantly decrease.

We tested two versions of TBA, which we define by the mechanisms used: 'Basic TBA'$=< Mechanism1, Mechanism2, Mechanism3a >$ and 'Optimized TBA'$=< Mechanism1, Mechanism2, Mechanism3b, OPT1, OPT2, OPT3 >$. We compare these two algorithms with flooding and with expanding ring search (which floods the network in a limited range, gradually increasing that range until a matching node is found). All the overhead resulting from the optimizations is included in the simulation results.

Variable parameters for the simulations are: network size N (N=40,90,160), the size of the V_B set ($|V_B|$=1,3,5), and the size of transmitted data DT (a specified amount of data is sent on a route established between the query source and the destination node, following the node discovery by the anycast service), (DT=200,...,20000). For each possible combination of these parameters, a test on 50 randomly created network topologies was carried out. The results are shown in Fig. 5. The presented values are averages of the results obtained for all possible settings of the other two parameters.

In the first test we analyzed protocol performance as a function of N (Fig. 5a). For small values of N the performance of basic TBA is close to that of flooding,

---

[1] For radio chips newer than TR1000 (the one assumed in our simulations), the ratio of power consumption for transmission and reception is around 1.0.

while 'Optimized TBA' shows a nearly 25% reduction of RBC. As N increases, both versions of TBA achieve a similar reduction in RBC (approximately 20%).

The good performance of 'Optimized TBA' in small networks is caused by the usage of Mechanism 3b (in small networks a spanning tree rooted close to the query source is likely to exist). As the network size grows, Mechanism 3a and Mechanism 3b start performing in a similar way. Note that 'Optimized TBA' is always better than 'Basic TBA'.

In the second test we analyzed protocol performance as a function of $|V_B|$ (Fig. 5b). For small values of $|V_B|$, the both versions of TBA achieve a similar reduction in RBC (approximately 10%). As $|V_B|$ increases 'Optimized TBA' outperforms 'Basic TBA' and shows a nearly 35% reduction of RBC.

For small values of $|V_B|$, it is in general hard to find the destination node, especially in big networks. As the query propagates along a spanning tree structure, both versions of TBA manage to perform better than flooding. As $|V_B|$ grows, the expanding ring search algorithm achieves results much better than flooding, and even better than 'Basic TBA'. However, due to the optimization mechanism OPT2, 'Optimized TBA' manages to outperform all the other three solutions.

In the third test we analyzed protocol performance as a function of DT (Fig. 5c). For small values of DT both versions of TBA achieve a similar reduction in RBC (approximately 30%). As DT increases 'Optimized TBA' performs better than 'Basic TBA' and keeps its RBC at a similar level as flooding.

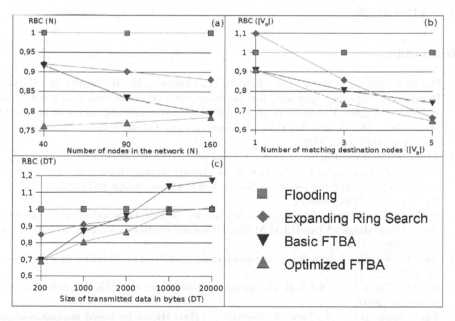

Fig. 5. Simulation results: (a) RBC as a function of the network size, N, (b) RBC as a function of the size of V_B set (the number of matching destination nodes), (c) RBC as a function of the size of transmitted data, DT

For small values of DT, sub-optimality of routes created by TBA is not critical. As DT increases, the number of hops over which the data is transmitted becomes very important. By applying the OPT3 mechanism, routes created by 'Optimized TBA' are usually not much longer than the ones created by flooding. Thus it is possible to keep RBC value close to 1.0.

5   Conclusions

The results show that significant energy gain can be expected when TBA is used for finding anycast destinations in small networks, especially when the resources we are searching for are highly available (large size of the V_B set). For small volumes of transmitted data, or in cases of high availability of resources, the byte count factor is reduced even by 30% as compared to flooding.

A limitation that severely constrains this protocol is that data is transmitted over possibly sub-optimal routes. The more data is transmitted, the more impact can be expected from route sub-optimality. This means that TBA is a good solution for resource discovery. Once a matching node is found, an optimal route could be established with a unicast routing protocol.

Acknowledgements

This work was supported in part by the Polish Ministry of Science, project no. 3 T11D 011 28.

References

1. Domaszewicz, J., Roj, M., Pruszkowski, A., Golanski, M., Kacperski, K.: Rovers: Pervasive computing platform for heterogeneous sensor-actuator networks. In: WOWMOM 2006: Proceedings of the 2006 International Symposium on on World of Wireless, Mobile and Multimedia Networks, pp. 615–620. IEEE Computer Society, Los Alamitos (2006)
2. Abley, J.: Hierarchical Anycast for Global Service Distribution (2003)
3. Michael, J., Freedman, K.L., Mazieres, D.: Oasis: Anycast for any service. In: Proceedings of the 3rd Symposium on Networked Systems Design and Implementation, San Jose, CA (May 2006)
4. Park, V.D., Macker, J.P.: Anycast routing for mobile networking. In: MILCOM 1999. Proceedings of the IEEE Military Communications Conference, vol. 1, pp. 1–5 (1999)
5. Hu, W., Bulusu, N., Jha, S.: A communication paradigm for hybrid sensor/actuator networks (2004)
6. Hu, W., Chou, C.T.: S.J.N.B: Deploying long-lived and cost-effective hybrid sensor networks (2004)
7. Thepvilojanapong, N., Tobe, Y., Sezaki, K.: Har: Hierarchy-based anycast routing protocol for wireless sensor networks. In: SAINT 2005: Proceedings of the The 2005 Symposium on Applications and the Internet (SAINT 2005), pp. 204–212. IEEE Computer Society, Los Alamitos (2005)

8. He, T., Stankovic, J.A., Lu, C., Abdelzaher, T.F.: A spatiotemporal communication protocol for wireless sensor networks. IEEE Transactions on Parallel and Distributed Systems 16, 995–1006 (2005)
9. Bian, F., Govindan, R., Schenker, S., Li, X.: Using hierarchical location names for scalable routing and rendezvous in wireless sensor networks. In: SenSys 2004: Proceedings of the 2nd international conference on Embedded networked sensor systems, pp. 305–306. ACM Press, New York (2004)
10. Loke, S.W., Padovitz, A., Zaslavsky, A.B.: Context-based addressing: The concept and an implementation for large-scale mobile agent systems. In: DAIS, pp. 274–284 (2003)
11. Cutting, D., C.D., A., Q.: Context-based messaging for ad hoc networks. In: The 3rd International Conference on Pervasive Computing Adjunct Proceedings, Pervasive 2005, Munich Germany (May 8-13, 2005)
12. Monolithics, R.F.: Inc (ASH Transceiver TR1000, Data Sheet), http://www.rfm.com/

A Distributed Algorithm for Load-Balanced Routing in Multihop Wireless Sensor Networks

Punyasha Chatterjee[1] and Nabanita Das[2]

[1] Govt. College of Engg. & Textile Technology, Serampore
tachical@gmail.com
[2] Indian Statistical Institute, Kolkata
ndas@isical.ac.in

Abstract. For multi-hop wireless sensor networks, this paper presents a simple, loop-free, distributed algorithm to select path for data gathering from each sensor node to the sink node that attempts to balance the load in terms of power dissipation in communication at individual nodes with 100% data aggregation to enhance the lifetime of the network as a whole. It requires just a one-time computation during the initialization of the network, and the paths remain static unless the routing tree gets partitioned due to faults etc. The performance of the proposed scheme has been compared with some conventional centralized routing techniques, namely the minimum hop routing, the shortest power path routing and the minimum spanning tree routing by simulation. In all the cases, the proposed algorithm results improved lifetime.

1 Introduction

A typical multi-hop Wireless Sensor Network (WSN) consists of a large number of sensor nodes, densely deployed over a field to gather information about the surroundings. The basic operation of such a network is the periodic sensing, gathering and transmission of data by individual sensor nodes to a final sink, which acts as the final data aggregation point, via some intermediate nodes. The *lifetime* of such a sensor network is the time during which all the sensor nodes remain alive and send data to the sink. Besides sensing and data gathering, the sensor nodes mainly deplete energy in the process of data communication. According to the conventional communication model widely used for WSN's [1], for fixed-size packets, the transmission energy depends on the distance between the two communicating nodes, whereas the energy dissipated in receiving a packet is constant. Hence, if it is assumed that the sensor nodes are capable of adjusting transmission power depending on the distance of the receiving node, it is a challenging issue to determine the data gathering paths for the WSN, so as to maximize the *lifetime* of the network.

Extensive research has been done so far on this issue [1-4] that primarily attempts to conserve power at each node by selecting the nearest neighbor as its data-forwarding node. But, since the sensor nodes deplete energy not only in transmission but also for reception, this may create some congested nodes receiving too many packets, and draining out its energy at a faster rate, causing poor *lifetime*. However,

S. Rao et al. (Eds.): ICDCN 2008, LNCS 4904, pp. 332–338, 2008.
© Springer-Verlag Berlin Heidelberg 2008

routing with load balancing in terms of power demand at each individual node may be another efficient approach to enhance *lifetime* of the network.

Various load-balancing schemes for sensor networks have already been proposed in the literature [5-10]. In all these works, either the algorithm is centralized, or it needs much information about the neighbors, such as location, load, remaining power etc., and the most severe limitation is that often before each packet transmission the recent information is required for path computation. Obviously, this increases the message overhead and power usage in nodes, and hence reduces the network *lifetime*.

In this paper, for a multi-hop sensor network, a distributed energy-balanced routing algorithm is proposed by which each individual node selects its next node in an attempt to distribute the load in terms of energy dissipation in its neighborhood evenly. No knowledge about the physical position of the nodes is required. It requires just a one-time computation during the initialization of the network, and the paths remain static unless the routing tree gets partitioned by faults etc. Simulation studies have been done to compare the performance of the proposed algorithm with the centralized algorithms for shortest-power path routing, minimum hop routing, and the minimum spanning tree routing. In spite of being a distributed one, the proposed algorithm shows improvement in *lifetime* over all the three.

The rest of the paper is organized as follows: section 2 describes the system model, section 3 presents the routing algorithm, section 4 shows the simulation results and section 5 concludes the paper.

2 System Model

This paper assumes that a WSN consists of a set of n homogeneous static sensor nodes, $V = \{1, 2,..., n\}$ and a sink node $(n+1)$ distributed over a region. The positions of the sensor nodes and also the sink node are fixed, but not known globally. Each sensor generates one data packet of fixed length per time unit, referred as round, to be sent to the sink node. Each sensor starts with an initial energy E that is depleted at each time the node transmits or receives. The sink has unlimited amount of energy.

The energy model for the sensor nodes assumed here is based on the *first order radio model* as mentioned in [1]. Here, the energy consumed by a sensor i in receiving a k-bit message is $Rx = \varepsilon_{elec} . k$. The energy consumed by sensor i to transmit a k-bit message to node j is $Tx_{i,j} = Rx + \varepsilon_{amp} . k . d_{i,j}^{2}$, where ε_{elec} is the energy required by the transmitter or receiver circuit and ε_{amp} is that for the transmitter amplifier to transmit single bit, and $d_{i,j}$ the Euclidean distance between nodes i and j.

It is assumed that the radio channel is symmetric. Each sensor can transmit with a maximum power P_{max}, and can reach a subset of nodes in single hop. However, each sensor node is capable of controlling its transmission power.

Definition 1. *Given a WSN with a set of n homogeneous static sensor nodes, $V = \{1, 2,..., n\}$ and a sink node $(n+1)$, where the sensor node i transmits with a power $P_i \leq P_{max}$ the network topology is represented by a graph $G (V, E)$, where $E = \{(i, j)| i, j \in V\}$ and $Tx_{i,j} \leq Pi$. $G (V, E)$ is defined as the topology graph of the given sensor network.*

Definition 2. *The set of nodes $N_i \subset V$ is called the 1-hop neighbor set of node i, if i can reach any node $j \in V$ directly.*

Definition 3. *The number of hops along the shortest path from any node i to the sink node (n+1) is termed as the hop-count of node i.*

In this paper, a data aggregation technique same as that followed in [1] is assumed. By this model, the size of a data packet is fixed, say k bits. A node may receive a number of packets from its *1-hop neighbors*, but it fuses all incoming data along with its own sensed data, and forwards a single data packet of k bits towards the sink. This is termed as 100% data aggregation.

With the system model described above, the objective of this paper is to determine data gathering paths to aggregate sensed data from all nodes into the sink in such a way that the power requirements of the nodes are balanced.

3 Distributed Load-Balanced Routing Algorithm

The proposed scheme presents an algorithm for load-balanced data gathering. The algorithm is distributed by nature. For the execution, each node only requires the information about its *1-hop neighbors*. During the initialization of the network, it is assumed that each sensor node individually discovers its *1-hop neighbors* by broadcasting some control packets at its maximum transmission power P_{max}. Also, in this phase, by measuring the received signal strength, each node estimates the required transmission energy for each link. It is assumed that the communication protocol ensures collision-free and reliable message communication.

Therefore, at the end of this phase, each node i knows N_i, the set of its *1-hop neighbors*, and also the required transmission energy $Tx_{i,j}$ for any neighbor $j \in N_i$, and starts the next phase described below.

3.1 Hop-Count Discovery Phase

In this phase, each node finds its *hop-count* from the sink via the shortest path, and broadcasts this information to all of its *1-hop neighbors*. This phase continues for a pre-defined time T_h.

Hop-Count-Discovery Algorithm
For each node-i, $1 \le i \le n$

Input: N_i the set of *1-hop neighbors;* T_h duration of the phase
Output: h_i hop-count of node- i; and h_j hop count of each $j \in N_i$
Each node-i, initializes $h_i = maxnum$ // *maxnum* is an arbitrarily large number
While time $< T_h$ Do
  { if $(n+1) \in N_i$ then   // sink node $(n+1)$ is a neighbor
          $h_i \leftarrow 1$; broadcast hop-count message M with *hop-count* $c = 1$;
      else if received M from node j then
          $h_j \leftarrow c; c = c +1$, if $c < h_i$ then $h_i \leftarrow c$ and broadcast M with h_i}

At the end of time T_h, each node-i, starts to execute the last phase of the proposed algorithm, described in the next subsection.

3.2 Next Node Selection Phase

On completion of the *hop-count-discovery phase*, each node-i selects one of its neighbors $j \in N_i$, with $h_j \leq h_i$ as its next node to forward its aggregated data packet, such that the estimated load remains balanced as far as possible in its *1-hop neighborhood*. Each node-i will start the next node selection procedure, only when all its neighbors with *hop-count* (h_i +1), have completed their *next node selection process*. Based on the information from its *1-hop neighbors* who have already selected the next node, node-i computes the maximum load L_{max} in its neighborhood, and attempts to select its next node-j with $h_j \leq h_i$ so that load on each node i and j either remains below L_{max}, or exceeds L_{max} by the minimum amount.

Next-Node-Selection Algorithm
For each node-i with:

Input : N_i the set of *1-hop neighbors* ; h_i ; h_j and $Tx_{i,j}$ for each $j \in N_i$
Output : *next node (i)* $\in N_i$

Each node-i with hop-count h_i
Initializes *next-node(i)* =0; $S(h_i +1)$:{ $j|j \in N_i$ and $h_j = (h_i +1)$}; $S(h_i) \leftarrow \phi$;
            $P(i) \leftarrow median\ of\ \{\ Tx_{i,j},\ \forall\ j\ with\ h_j \leq\ h_i\ \}$; $Q_i \leftarrow 0$;
1. If receives 'SELECTED' message from $j \in N_i$ then
          if *next-node(j)* = i, then $Q_i \leftarrow Q_i+1$;
          if $h_j = (h_i +1)$ delete j from $S(h_i +1)$; if $S(h_i +1)= \phi$ broadcast a 'REQ' message
          else if $h_j = h_i$ then add j in $S(h_i)$;
2. If receives a 'REQ' massage from $j \in N_i$ and if $h_j =(h_i +1)$, or
   { $h_j = h_i$ and *next-node(i)* $\neq 0$} then send 'REPLY' message to j with Q_i, and $P(i)$;
3. If receives a 'REPLY' message from $j \in N_i$,
          $L_i = (Q_i* Rx + Tx_{i,j})$, $L_j = ((Q_j+1)* Rx + P(j))$;
          $L_{max} (j) = max\ \{(L_i, L_j),\ for\ \forall j \in S(h_i) \cup\{ j|j \in N_i$ and $h_j = (h_i -1)\}\}$;
          $L_{max} = max\ \{L_j\}\ for\ \forall j \in S(h_i) \cup\{ j|j \in N_i$ and $h_j = (h_i +1)\}$
          if $L_{max} (j)< L_{max}$ find $L_{max} (k) = min\{ L_j, \forall j \in S(h_i) \cup\{ j|j \in N_i$ and $h_j = (h_i -1)\}\ \}$
          else find $L_{max} (k) = min\{ L_{max} (j)\}$
          next-node(i) = k;
          broadcast 'SELECTED' message with *next-node(i)* and $P(i)= Tx_{i,k}$

This process terminates when all the nodes-j with $h_j = 1$ completes the *Next-Node-Selection* Procedure. On receiving all the 'SELECTED' messages from its *1-hop neighbors*, the sink broadcasts a 'TERMINATE' message. All sensor nodes then start their normal functions.

Theorem 1. The *next-node-selection algorithm* results a rooted tree with root at sink.

Proof: For details see [11].

4 Performance Evaluation

For performance evaluation, simulation studies have been done on random connected topology graphs. A *100m×100m* deployment region is considered. Number of nodes (*n*) has been varied from *100* to *500*. The maximum range R_{max} = *15m*. The sink node is located at the mean position of the deployment region. Each sensor node starts with the same initial energy of *0.25 Joules*. Energy is dissipated according to the energy model described in section 2. Packets are of length *k* = *2000 bits*; ε_{elec} = *50 nJ/bit*, ε_{amp} = *100 pJ/bit/m²*. Fig. 1 shows the load distribution for a typical sensor network with *500* nodes, achieved by the proposed algorithm. It shows about *85%* nodes are load-balanced.

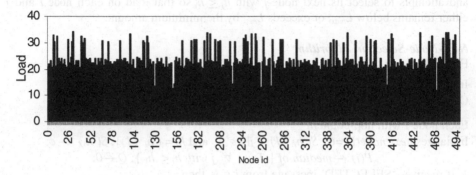

Fig. 1. Load distribution of individual nodes by proposed algorithm

For a typical graph with *n* = *100*, Fig. 2 shows the variation of maximum, minimum and average loads on the network as resulted by the four routing algorithms. Fig. 3 shows the variation of network lifetime following the four routing algorithms under consideration. It shows that the proposed algorithm results about 200% improvement over the least-hop and least-power routing, and about 15% improvement

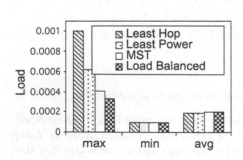

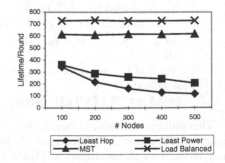

Fig. 2. Comparison of maximum, minimum and average load

Fig. 3. Comparison of system lifetime

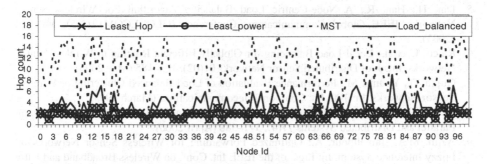

Fig. 4. Comparison of hop count for different routing algorithms

over MST algorithm. Finally, Fig. 4 shows the variation of number of hops in the routing paths from each individual node, for a typical network with $n = 100$. It shows that the proposed algorithm outperforms the MST algorithm, but the other two algorithms perform marginally better than the proposed one.

5 Conclusion and Future Work

For multihop sensor networks, this paper presents a simple distributed static data routing algorithm with load balancing assuming *100%* data aggregation. No information about the location of the sensor nodes is required. It is assumed that nodes are capable of estimating the transmission power required for a link from the received signal strength in the initialization phase. We have compared the performance by simulation, in terms of load (energy dissipation per round), *lifetime* and delay, to three conventional centralized routing techniques, namely the shortest power path routing, least hop routing and routing on minimum spanning tree (MST). Simulation results show that the proposed algorithm outperforms all three in terms of network *lifetime* and load balancing. Also, in terms of number of hops it is better than MST routing, and is comparable with the other two. Its performance is to be studied on different traffic conditions, and under different data aggregation schemes.

References

1. Heinzelman, W.R., Chandrakasan, A., Balakrishnan, H.: Energy-Efficient Communication Protocols for Wireless Microsensor Networks. In: Proc. of the Hawaii Int. Conf. on Systems Sciences, pp. 1–10 (January 2000)
2. Lindsey, S., Raghavendra, C.S.: PEGASIS: Power-Efficient Gathering in Sensor Information Systems. In: Proc. of the IEEE Aerospace Conf., pp. 1–6 (March 2002)
3. Cardei, M., Du, D.Z.: Improving Wireless Sensor Network Lifetime through Power Aware Organization. ACM Wireless Networks 11(3), 333–340 (May 2005)
4. Bhardwaj, M., Garnett, T., Chandrakasan, A.P.: Upper Bounds on the Lifetime of Sensor Networks. In: Proc. of the IEEE Int. Conf. on Communications, pp. 785–790 (June 2001)

5. Dai, H., Han, R.: A Node-Centric Load Balancing Algorithm For Wireless Sensor Networks. IEEE Global Communications Conference (GLOBECOM) 1(1-5), 548–552 (2003)

6. Raicu, I., et al.: Local Load Balancing for Globally Efficient Routing in Wireless Sensor Networks. Int. J. of Distributed Sensor Networks 01(02), 163–185 (May 2005)

7. Gupta, G., Younis, M.: Performance Evaluation of Load-Balanced Clustering of Wireless Sensor Networks. In: 10th Int. Conf. on Telecommunications (March 2003)

8. Gao, J., Zhang, L.: Load-Balanced Short-Path Routing in Wireless Networks. IEEE Tr. on Parallel and Distributed Systems 17(4), 377–388 (April 2006)

9. Azim, M.A., Jamalipour, A.: Optimized Forwarding for Wireless Sensor Networks by Fuzzy Inference System. In: Proc. of the IEEE Int. Conf. on Wireless Broadband and Ultra Wideband Communications, Sydney, pp. 13–16 (March 2006)

10. Jamalipour, A., Azim, M.A.: Two -Layer Optimized Forwarding for Cluster-Based Sensor Networks. In: The 17th Annual IEEE Int. Symp. PIMRC 2006 (2006)

11. Chatterjee, P., Das, N.: On Load-Balanced Routing in Multihop Wireless Sensor Networks. Tech. Rep., No. Tech-rep. ACM/ISI/002-2007 (August 2007)

Using Learned Data Patterns to Detect Malicious Nodes in Sensor Networks

Partha Mukherjee and Sandip Sen

Department of Mathematical and Computer Science
University of Tulsa
{partha-mukherjee,sandip}@utulsa.edu

Abstract. As sensor network applications often involve remote, distributed monitoring of inaccessible and hostile locations, they are vulnerable to both physical and electronic security breaches. The sensor nodes, once compromised, can send erroneous data to the base station, thereby possibly compromising network effectiveness. We consider sensor nodes organized in a hierarchy where the non-leaf nodes serve as the aggregators of the data values sensed at the leaf level and the Base Station corresponds to the root node of the hierarchy. To detect compromised nodes, we use neural network based learning techniques where the nets are used to predict the sensed data at any node given the data reported by its neighbors in the hierarchy. The differences between the predicted and the reported values is used to update the reputation of any given node. We compare a Q-learning schemes with the Beta reputation management approach for their responsiveness to compromised nodes. We evaluate the robustness of our detection schemes by varying the members of compromised nodes, patterns in sensed data, etc.

1 Introduction

Sensors in wireless sensor networks are used to cooperatively monitor physical and environmental conditions specially in regions where human access is limited. Current research on sensor networks propose data aggregation protocol where the sensor nodes reside at the leaf level and the non-leaf nodes act as the aggregator nodes. If a large number of nodes become damaged or compromised, the entire data gathering process may be jeopardized. Hence, the detection of faulty nodes and protecting the security and integrity of the data is a key research challenge.

In our work, the sensor nodes assumed to be deployed in a terrain where the data being sensed follows a time varying pattern over the entire sensed area. In such scenarios standard outlier detection mechanisms will fail as the data values sensed may vary widely over the sensor field. We propose a neural net learning based technique where regional patterns in the sensor field can be learned offline from sufficient number of observations and thereafter used online to predict and monitor data reported by a node from data reported by neighboring nodes.

We assume that the nodes and the network will function without error for an initial period of time after deployment (provides data for offline training of

S. Rao et al. (Eds.): ICDCN 2008, LNCS 4904, pp. 339–344, 2008.

the net). Next the trained neural nets are used online to predict the output of the nodes given the reported values of the neighboring sensors. The difference between the predicted and reported values is used to measure error. Such errors are used by a couple of incremental reputation update mechanisms, Q-learning and Beta reputation scheme,which take sequence of errors to decide if a node is compromised or not. If the updated reputation falls below a specified threshold, the node is reported to be faulty. We have successfully used these reputation schemes to quickly detect erroneous nodes for different network sizes and data patterns over the sensor field without any false positives and false negatives.

2   Experimental Framework

We assume a sensor network with n nodes, where the nodes are distributed over a region with (x_i, y_i) representing the physical location of the sensing node i^1. The n nodes are arranged in a tree hierarchy with the base station as the root node. Each non-leaf node in the L-level[2] hierarchy aggregates data reported to it by its k children and forwards it to its own parent in turn.

We model fluctuations of the sensed data in the environment by adding noise to the function value $f(x_i, y_i, t)$ for the i−th node at time interval t. So, the sensed value at position (x, y) at time t is given by $f(x, y, t) = g(x, y) + h(t) + N(0, \sigma)$, where h maps a time to the range $[l, h]$ and $N(0, \sigma)$ represents a 0 mean, σ standard deviation Gaussian noise. We have used two different g functions, $e^{-(x^2+y^2)}$ and $\frac{(x+y)}{2}$ and refer to these two environments as E1 and E2 respectively. In our experiments, we assume that each sensor node adds a randomly generated offset in the range $[0, \epsilon]$ to the data value it senses and vary the number of compromised nodes only at the leaf level,though our mechanism, is capable of detecting faulty nodes at any position in the hierarchy except the root node, assumed as base station. The initial error-free data reporting interval is assumed to be D and the threshold for malicious node detection is taken as a fraction $p = 0.03$ of the maximum reputation a sibling possesses at a particular iteration. E stands for the entire data set including offline and online data.

2.1   Learning Technique

To form the predictor for a given node i in the sensor network, we use a three-level feed-forward neural network with $k - 1$ nodes in the input layer which receives data reported by the siblings of this node. Each such neural network has one hidden layer with H nodes and the output layer has one node that corresponds to the predicted value for this sensor node. A back-propagation training algorithm, of learning rate η and momentum term γ is used with sigmoid activation function

---

[1] The index of node i is calculated as $index_i = c * k + i$, c is the index of the parent node and k is the number of its children. c $0 \le c \le \lfloor \frac{n}{k} \rfloor$.

[2] There are k^{l-1} nodes in level l and $n = \sum_{l=1}^{L} k^{l-1}$ where k^{L-1} leaf-level nodes are sensing nodes.

$f(y) = \frac{1}{1+e^{-y}}$ for the neural network units. The outputs are restricted to the $[0, 1]$ range.

We experiment with two representative sensor networks, each organized in an m-ary tree:

Network 1 (N1): The smaller network with $m = 3$ has a total of $n = 40$ nodes, of which 27 leaf level nodes sense data from the environment. The neural networks used for learning node predictors have the following parameters: $\eta = 1.0, \gamma = 0.7$, $H = 6$, $D = 4500$, and $E = 5000$. The output of each node is predicted by taking inputs from two of its siblings. The prediction efficiencies of the net for the functions $e^{-(x^2+y^2)}$ and $\frac{(x+y)}{2}$ are 94.45% and 92.6% respectively. We ran experiments with 3, 5 and 7 malicious nodes for this network.

Network 2 (N2): The larger network with $m = 4$ has a total of $n = 85$ nodes, of which 64 leaf level nodes sense data from the environment. The neural networks used for learning node predictors have the following parameters: $\eta = 0.8$, $\gamma = 0.7, H = 8, D = 4500$, and $E = 5000$. The output of each node is predicted by taking inputs from three of its siblings. In this case the prediction efficiencies of the net for the functions $e^{-(x^2+y^2)}$ and $\frac{(x+y)}{2}$ are 93.30% and 90.6% respectively. We ran experiments with 5, 10, and 15 malicious nodes for this network. Algorithm 1 is used online to update the reputation for each node i at each data reporting time interval based on relative error $\varepsilon_i^t = \left| 1 - \frac{reported_i^t}{predicted_i^t} \right|$, where $predicted_i^t$ and $reported_i^t$ are the values predicted for and the actual output by the node i at time t respectively. From this relative error, an error statistic $\aleph_i^t = e^{-K*\varepsilon_i^t 3}$ is computed for updating node reputation. Reputation updates are performed by the Q-learning and Beta-reputation schemes. As performance metric, we use the iterations taken by these mechanisms to detect the first and last erroneous nodes. The latter value corresponds to the time taken to detect all faulty nodes.

Q-Learning Framework: The reputation of every node i is updated as follows: $Reputation_{QL_i}^t \leftarrow (1-\alpha)*Reputation_{QL_i}^{t-1} + \alpha*\aleph_i^t$. We use a learning rate, α, of 0.2 and an initial reputation, $Reputation_{QL_i}^0 = 1, \forall i$.

RFSN Framework: In Reputation Based Framework for Sensor Networks (RFSN) [1] framework the corresponding reputation update equation is given by $Reputation_{\beta_i^t} = \frac{\gamma_i^t+1}{\gamma_i^t+\beta_i^t+2}$, where γ_i^t and β_i^t are the cumulative cooperative and non-cooperative responses received from node i until time t. We assume $\gamma_i^0 = \beta_i^0 = 0$ and these values are subsequently updated as $\gamma_i^t \leftarrow \gamma_i^{t-1} + \aleph_i^t$ and $\beta_i^t \leftarrow \beta_i^{t-1} + (1 - \aleph_i^t)$.

---

[3] We have used $K = 10$. The results are robust to K values of this order but too high or too low K value would respectively be inflexible or will not sufficiently penalize errors.

Algorithm 1: DetectMalicious(n, N)

Data: The trained neural net N with set of given parameters, number of nodes n
Result: Detection of malicious nodes
initialization: $Reputation\_Threshold = 0.03$, $\forall i, Reputation^0_{QL_i} = 1$,
$Reputation^0_{\beta_i} = 0$;
for $t=0;;t++$ **do**
    for *each sensor node $node_i$* **do**
        Compute relative_error: ε;
        Compute error_statistic: $f(\varepsilon)$;
        Update $Reputation^t_{QL_i}$;
        Update $Reputation^t_{\beta_i}$;
        if $Reputation^t_{QL_i} \leq$
        $Reputation\_Threshold * \max_{k \in Neigh_i} Reptutation^t_{QL_k}$ **then**
            $node_i$ is malicious according to Q-learning based reputation
            mechanism;
        end
        if $Reputation_{\beta_i} \leq Reputation\_Threshold * \max_{k \in Neigh_i} Reptutation^t_{\beta_k}$
        then
            $node_i$ is malicious according Beta-Reputation mechanism;
        end
    end
end

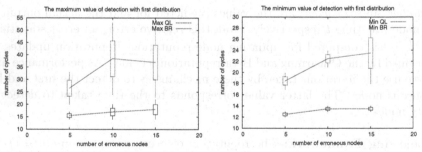

(a) Maximum time to detect malicious (b) Minimum time to detect malicious
nodes   nodes

Fig. 1. Maximum and minimum number of cycles required to detect compromised
nodes by the Q-learning (QL) and RFSN (BR) approaches in environment E1 ($n = 85$)
for distribution $e^{-(x^2+y^2)}$

2.2   Observations

We ran experiments with 10 random orderings of data reporting sequences and
average our results over these runs. Figures 1, 2 show the average time taken
to detect the first and last malicious node taken by these reputation schemes
for the two problem sizes. We omit the figures for distribution $\frac{x+y}{2}$ for both
the networks due to space constraints. The result for $\frac{x+y}{2}$ corroborates the view

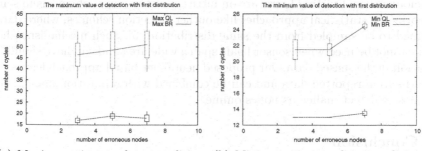

(a) Maximum time to detect malicious nodes

(b) Minimum time to detect malicious nodes

Fig. 2. Maximum and minimum number of cycles required to detect compromised nodes by the Q-learning (QL) and RFSN (BR) approaches in environment E2 ($n = 40$) for distribution $e^{-(x^2+y^2)}$

observed for $e^{-(x^2+y^2)}$. The standard deviations of these metrics, centered around the mean, are also shown. We highlight the following observations:

Observation 1: For both environments and problem sizes, the time taken to detect the first malicious node is less for the Q_Learning based approach than that of the RFSN based approach. This value remains between 12 to 15 iterations irrespective of the environment and number of erroneous nodes in the network. We have experimented with at most 15 and 7 faulty nodes respectively for the 85 and 40 node networks.

Observation 2: The plots show that the mean values of the time taken to detect the last erroneous node is again significantly less for the Q_Learning based reputation scheme compared to the RFSN based approach irrespective of network size and the number of malicious nodes (see Figures 1(a),and 2(a)).

Observation 3: We did not observe any false positives (normal nodes identified as malicious) or false negatives (undetected malicious nodes) in our experiments.

We conclude that for the class of environments that we have considered, the Q-Learning scheme detects malicious nodes in the network more expediently compared to the Beta-reputation approach. The significance of the past reputation values are exponentially discounted in the Q-Learning scheme whereas the Beta-reputation scheme gives equal weight to early and recent experiences.

3 Related Work

Recent work on securing sensor networks use techniques like key establishment, authentication, secure routing, etc. Symmetric key cryptography is preferred for protecting confidentiality, integrity and availability [2,3]. Intrusion Tolerant secure routing protocols in wireless Sensor Networks (INSENS) [4] tries to bypass malicious nodes and nullifies the effect of compromised nodes in the vicinity of malicious nodes. Existing literature on intrusion detection mechanisms in sensor networks use statistical approaches like outlier detection schemes, where data is assumed to be sampled from the same distribution [5]. Such mechanisms, however, cannot be used when sensor fields span a wide area and can have significant variation in the sensed data.Our proposed neural net based approach learns such patterns from reported data and can be combined with reputation management schemes to detect malicious nodes online.

4   Conclusion

For the environments, where standard outlier detection mechanisms are ineffective, we propose a combination of a neural network based offline learning approach and online repuation update schemes to identify nodes reporting inconsistent data. We experimentally evaluate our scheme for two different network sizes and two different data patterns over the sensor field. Results show that our approach is successful in identifying multiple colluding malicious nodes without any false positives and false negatives. The approach scales well and is robust against attacks even when as much as 25% of the sensor nodes are corrupted. The Q-learning based approach is found to detect malicious nodes faster than the Beta-repuation based scheme. In the future we plan to extend our work to incorporate the analysis of more sophisticated collusion, and prevent malicious nodes from using false identities to report spurious, multiple false data.

Acknowledgement.   Research supported in part by a DOD-ARO Grant #W911NF-05-1-0285.

References

1. Ganeriwal, S., Srivastava, M.B.: Reputation-based framework for high integrity sensor networks. In: SASN 2004. Proceedings of the 2nd ACM workshop on Security of ad hoc and sensor networks, pp. 66–77. ACM Press, New York (2004)
2. Eschenauer, L., Gligor, V.D.: A key-management scheme for distributed sensor networks. In: Proceedings of the 9th ACM conference on Computer and communications security, pp. 41–47 (November 2002)
3. Perrig, A., Szewczyk, R., Tygar, J.D., Wen, V., Culler, D.E.: Spins: security protocols for sensor networks. Wirel. Netw. 8(5), 521–534 (2002)
4. Deng, J., Han, R., Mishra, S.: Insens: Intrusion-tolerant routing in wireless sensor networks (2002)
5. Yang, Y., Wang, X., Zhu, S., Cao, G.: Sdap: A secure hop-by-hop data aggregation protocol for sensor networks. In: MobiHoc 2006. Proceedings of the 7th international symposium on Mobile ad hoc networking and computing, pp. 356–367. ACM Press, New York (2006)

An Efficient Key Establishment Scheme for Self-organizing Sensor Networks

Yong Ho Kim*, Kyu Young Choi, Jongin Lim, and Dong Hoon Lee

Center for Information Security Technologies (CIST),
Korea University, Seoul, Korea
{optim,young,jilim,donghlee}@korea.ac.kr

Abstract. In this paper, we propose an efficient authenticated key establishment scheme for self-organizing sensor networks. The proposed scheme has low communication cost and eliminates expensive operations required by most ID-based schemes, such as sensor nodes calculating bilinear maps. Additionally, the proposed scheme provides perfect forward secrecy.

Keywords: security, sensor network, elliptic curve cryptography.

1 Introduction

There has been a common perception that traditional public key infrastructure (PKI) is too complex, slow and power hungry to be used in sensor networks. For this reason, the most research is primarily based on symmetric key cryptography [4,5]. While symmetric mechanisms can achieve low computation overhead, they typically require significant communication overhead or a large amount of memory for each node. For these reasons, many researchers [6,9] have recently begun to challenge those old beliefs about PKI by showing that it is indeed viable in sensor networks.

Huang et al. [7] proposed two efficient key establishment schemes where a Full-Functional Device (FFD) and a Reduced-Functional Device (RFD) can achieve key exchange and mutual authentication. An FFD takes the role of a coordinator, a router or a security manager, while an RFD takes on the role of an end device, such as a low-power sensor. These schemes are based on elliptic curve cryptography where each device can authenticate other devices through its certificate [8].

In this paper, we propose an efficient ID-based scheme for key establishment in self-organizing sensor networks. The proposed scheme was devised after comparing the advantages and disadvantages of certificate-based and ID-based systems. The main contributions of our approach can be summarized as follows.

* "This research was supported by the MIC(Ministry of Information and Communication), Korea, under the ITRC(Information Technology Research Center) support program supervised by the IITA(Institute of Information Technology Advancement)" (IITA-2007-(C1090-0701-0025)).

S. Rao et al. (Eds.): ICDCN 2008, LNCS 4904, pp. 345–349, 2008.
© Springer-Verlag Berlin Heidelberg 2008

First, when compared with Huang et al.'s schemes [7], the proposed scheme eliminates the communication overhead required to transmit public-key certificates. In wireless sensor networks, the advantage is significant because wireless transmission of a single bit consumes several orders of magnitude more power than a single 32-bit computation [1]. Furthermore, a sensor need not perform the Weil/Tate pairing and Map-To-Point operations required in most ID-based schemes [10,11]. Additionally, the proposed scheme provides perfect forward secrecy [3] where the the exposure of each device's long-lived secret key does not compromise the security of previous session keys.

2   Bilinear Map

In this subsection, we review bilinear maps and some assumptions related to the proposed scheme. Let $\mathbb{G}_1$ be a cyclic additive group of prime order q and $\mathbb{G}_2$ be a cyclic multiplicative group of same order q. We assume that the discrete logarithm problems (DLP) in both $\mathbb{G}_1$ and $\mathbb{G}_2$ are intractable. We call $e : \mathbb{G}_1 \times \mathbb{G}_1 \longrightarrow \mathbb{G}_2$ an *admissible bilinear* map if it satisfies the following properties:

1. Bilinearity: $e(aP, bQ) = e(P,Q)^{ab}$ for all $P, Q \in \mathbb{G}_1$ and $a, b \in \mathbb{Z}_q^*$.
2. Non-degenerancy: There exists $P \in \mathbb{G}_1$ such that $e(P,P) \neq 1$.
3. Computability: There exists an efficient algorithm to compute $e(P,Q)$ for all $P, Q \in \mathbb{G}_1$.

3   Proposed Scheme

We denote the proposed scheme by SN-AKE. Before network deployment, a trusted authority (TA) performs the following operations.

1. TA constructs two groups $\mathbb{G}_1, \mathbb{G}_2$, and a map e as described above.
2. TA chooses two cryptographic hash functions $H : \{0,1\}^\ell \longrightarrow \mathbb{Z}_q^*$ and $H_1 : \{0,1\}^* \longrightarrow \mathbb{Z}_q^*$, where ℓ is the bit length of a node ID.
3. TA computes $g = e(P,P)$, where P is a random generator of $\mathbb{G}_1$.
4. TA picks a random integer $\kappa \in \mathbb{Z}_q^*$ as the network master secret and sets $P_{pub} = \kappa P$.
5. For each device A with identification information ID_A, TA calculates $Q_A = H(ID_A)P + P_{pub}$ and $D_A = (H(ID_A) + \kappa)^{-1}P$.

Next, each device A is preloaded with the public system parameters (p, q, $\mathbb{G}_1$, $\mathbb{G}_2$, e, h, P, P_{pub}, g), its identification information ID_A, and its key pair (Q_A, D_A).

When a sensor node U and a security manager V first communicate to each other, they perform an efficient authenticated key establishment as shown in Figure 1.

1. After V obtains ID_U, V chooses a random number r' in $\mathbb{Z}_q^*$ and sends (ID_V, X') to U where $X' = r'Q_V$.

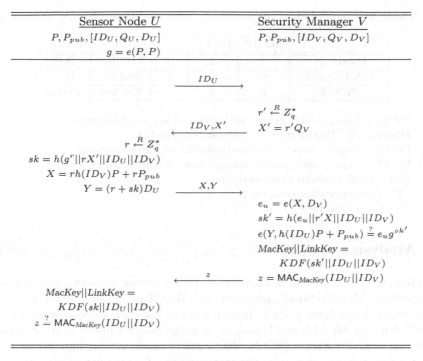

Fig. 1. SN-AKE

2. After U obtains (ID_V, X'), U chooses a random number r in Z_q^* and computes $sk = h(g^r||rX'||ID_U||ID_V)$. Next, U sends (X, Y) to V where $X = rh(ID_V)P + rP_{pub}$ and $Y = (r + sk)D_U$.
3. V calculates $e_u = e(X, D_V)$ and $sk' = h(e_u||r'X||ID_U||ID_V)$. Once deriving e_u and sk', it verifies that the following equation holds:

$$e(Y, h(ID_U)P + P_{pub}) = e_u g^{sk'}.$$

If the equality holds, the security manager V believes that the sensor node U has the knowledge of its private key, $D_U = (h(ID_U) + \kappa)^{-1}P$. Also, it computes $MacKey||LinkKey = KDF(sk||ID_U||ID_V)$ and sends $z = \text{MAC}_{MacKey}(ID_U||ID_V)$ to U, where KDF is the specified key derivation function.
4. After U computes $MacKey||LinkKey = KDF(sk||ID_U||ID_V)$, it verifies $z = \text{MAC}_{MacKey}(ID_U||ID_V)$, where MAC is a message authentication code function. If the equality holds, the sensor node U believes that the security manager V has the knowledge of its private key, $D_V = (h(ID_V) + \kappa)^{-1}P$.

SN-AKE suitable for wireless sensor networks is a simplified adaptation of the ID-based AKE [2]. The previous scheme provides implicit key authentication if a participant is assured that no other participants except its intended partner can possibly learn the value of a particular secret key. However, SN-AKE provides explicit key authentication. Also, it has the property of perfect forward secrecy while the previous schemes [2,7] provide half forward secrecy.

Table 1. Comparison of the proposed scheme and Huang et al.'s schemes

	EC-RP	EC-FP	EXP	CC	FS
Hybrid [7]	1	2	0	1437 bits	Half
MSR-Hybrid[7]	0	3	1	3682 bits	Half
SN-AKE	2	2	1	736 bits	Perfect

Hybrid : Huang et al.'s hybrid authenticated key establishment
MSR-Hybrid : Huang et al.'s MSR-combined Hybrid
EC-RP : elliptic curve scalar multiplication of a random point
EC-FP : elliptic curve scalar multiplication of a fixed point
EXP : small modular exponentiation
CC : communication complexity
FS : forward secrecy

4   Analysis

Efficiency. Unlike ID-based schemes [10,11] for sensor networks, a sensor need not perform Map-To-Point operation and Weil/Tate pairing which is several times more costly than a scalar multiplication. For each sensor, we summarize the efficiency of SN-AKE and Huang et al.'s schemes in Table 1. When compared to Huang et al.'s schemes [7], SN-AKE features remarkable communication efficiency since it does not require the transmission of public-key certificates.

Key Confidentiality. After performing the key establishment, an adversary can obtain $h(ID_V)$, P, $P_{pub} = \kappa P$, and $r(h(ID_V) + \kappa)P$. However, she cannot compute $e_u = g^r = e(P, P)^{\frac{1}{\kappa + h(ID_V)}} r(h(ID_V) + \kappa)$ and $sk = sk'$ since there is no polynomial time algorithm solving mBIDH problem [2] with non-negligible.

Authentication and Key Confirmation. In SN-AKE, if $e(Y, h(ID_U)P + P_{pub}) = e_u g^{sk'}$ holds, the security manager V has verified that the sensor node U has the knowledge of sk' and its private key D_V. Also, if $z = \mathsf{MAC}_{MacKey}$ $(ID_U \| ID_V)$ holds, the sensor node U has verified that the security manager V has the knowledge of sk and its private key D_U.

Forward Secrecy. In SN-AKE and Huang et al.'s schemes[7], compromise of the sensor node's private key does not appear to allow an adversary to recover any past session keys. However, in Huang et al.'s schemes, compromise of the security manager's private key induces that all previous session key can be recovered from the transcripts. Thereby, the schemes have the property of half forward secrecy. On the other hand, in SN-AKE, even if the security manager's private key is compromised, data protected with a previous session key is still secure because derivation of the key requires the knowledge of previous random integer r'. Therefore, SN-AKE provides perfect forward secrecy while the previous schemes [2,7] provide half forward secrecy.

5 Conclusion

In SN-AKE, a sensor need not transmit public-key certificates and perform expensive computation such as Weil/Tate pairing and Map-To-Point operation. Particulary, SN-AKE guarantees perfect forward secrecy and thereby is suitable for some weaker security manager applications.

References

1. Barr, K., Asanovic, K.: Energy aware lossless data compression. In: 1st Int. Conf. Mobile Syst., Applicat., Services, pp. 231–244 (May 2003)
2. Choi, K.Y., Hwang, J.Y., Lee, D.H.: ID-based Authenticated Key Agreement for Low-Power Mobile Devices. In: Boyd, C., González Nieto, J.M. (eds.) ACISP 2005. LNCS, vol. 3574, pp. 494–505. Springer, Heidelberg (2005)
3. Carman, D.W., Kruus, P.S., Matt, B.J.: Constraints and approaches for distributed sensor network security, NAI Labs Technical Report 00-010 (September 2000)
4. Chan, H., Perrig, A., Song, D.: Random key predistribution schemes for sensor networks. In: IEEE Symposium on Security and Privacy, pp. 197–213 (May 2003)
5. Eschenauer, L., Gligor, V.D.: A key-management scheme for distributed sensor networks. In: ACM CCS 2002, pp. 41–47 (November 2002)
6. Gaubatz, G., Kaps, J., Sunar, B.: Public keys cryptography in sensor networks-revisited. In: Castelluccia, C., Hartenstein, H., Paar, C., Westhoff, D. (eds.) ESAS 2004. LNCS, vol. 3313, pp. 2–18. Springer, Heidelberg (2005)
7. Huang, Q., Cukier, J., Kobayashi, H., Liu, B., Zhang, J.: Fast authenticated key establishment protocols for self-organizing sensor networks. In: ACM WSNA 2003, pp. 141–150 (2003)
8. Menezes, A.: Elliptic Curve Public Key Cryptosystems. Kluwer Academic Publishers, Dordrecht (1993)
9. Watro, R., Kong, D., fen Cuti, S., Gardiner, C., Lynn, C., Kruus, P.: Tinypk: Securing sensor networks with public key technology. In: ACM SASN 2004, pp. 59–64 (October 2004)
10. Zhang, Y., Liu, W., Lou, W., Fang, Y.: Location-based compromise-tolerant security mechanisms for wireless sensor networks. IEEE JSAC, Special Issue on Security in Wireless Ad Hoc Networks 24(2), 247–260 (2006)
11. Zhang, Y., Liu, W., Lou, W., Fang, Y., Wu, D.: Secure localization and authentication in ultra-wideband sensor networks. IEEE JSAC, Special Issue on UWB Wireless Communications - Theory and Applications 24(4), 829–835 (2006)

SuperTrust – A Secure and Efficient Framework for Handling Trust in Super Peer Networks

Tassos Dimitriou[1], Ghassan Karame[2], and Ioannis Christou[1]

[1] Athens Information Technology
Athens, Greece
[2] ETH Zürich
Zürich, Switzerland
tdim@ait.edu.gr, karameg@inf.ethz.ch, ichr@ait.edu.gr

Abstract. In this paper, we describe SuperTrust, a novel framework designed to handle trust relationships in Super peer networks. What distinguishes SuperTrust from other contributions is that trust reports remain *encrypted* and are never opened during the submission or aggregation processes, thus guaranteeing privacy and anonymity of transactions. As reputations of peers influence their future interactions, we argue that such systems must have properties like fairness and soundness, persistence, eligibility and unreusability of reports, similar to the properties of current electronic voting systems.

SuperTrust is a *decentralized* protocol, based on K-redundant Super peer networks, that guarantees the aforementioned properties and is in some sense complementary to the models proposed for building trust among peers. Additionally the framework is very efficient and minimizes the effects of collusion of malicious Super peers/aggregators. We have tested the framework on a large subset of peers and demonstrated via simulations its superior performance when compared to the other proposed protocols.

1 Introduction

Peer-to-peer (P2P) systems have recently become a popular medium that facilitates sharing huge amounts of data (e.g: KaZaA[1], Gnutella[2]). These incentives behind peer-to-peer architectures derive from their ability to function and scale in the presence of high dynamism and in spite of failures without the need of a central authority.

The wide success of KaZaA has driven the attention towards a promising P2P architecture: *Super Peer systems*. The latter combines the advantages of pure and hybrid P2P systems as a mean of addressing the problems induced in both architectures by offering increased scalability and promises for enhanced security.

Although P2P architectures provide for anonymity when searching for content (e.g. pseudonymes), sharing files with anonymous and unknown users challenges the very notion of systems security. Genuine looking files may contain viruses or self-replicating software which can destroy data and cause massive damage. This lack of accountability opens the door to malicious users abusing the network and hinders the promotion of P2P systems in more useful settings. Due to the absence of methods to convince a peer that another node is malicious, the need for trust in P2P systems emerges as one of few available mechanisms to keep malicious nodes from damaging the network.

S. Rao et al. (Eds.): ICDCN 2008, LNCS 4904, pp. 350–362, 2008.

These facts lead to a widespread use of reputation management systems, e.g. eBay[3]. In fact, many researchers ([4,5,6,7,8]) have proposed the use of reputation mechanisms as a tool to evaluate the trustworthiness of peers.

In this work, we are *not concerned with developing a new reputation system or model for building trust among peers*. Instead, we focus on developing an efficient and secure framework for distributing and accessing the trust ratings in a way that preserves the peers' *privacy* and *anonymity* of transactions by taking advantage of Super Peer architectures. This suggests that peers who rate other peers must remain anonymous and the actual ratings must remain secure. Furthermore, we argue that nothing must affect the submission process: Peers must not be able to affect the system if they submit wrong values, colluding peers must not be able to alter the resulting ratings and the contents of the ballots must not be visible even by trust handling peers.

Our contribution in this work is threefold: First, we introduce SuperTrust, a novel framework that ensures the security of trust handling issues in Super Peer networks as opposed to any previous work in this area. SuperTrust takes advantage of the peers' heterogeneity and the increased scalability and fault tolerance featured by such networks in order to manage and distribute trust values across peers. In addition, we make sure that properties like *anonymity, privacy and integrity of reports, fairness and soundness*, etc., are preserved. Second, we analyze SuperTrust against a multitude of attacks that seem important in designing new protocols for submitting trust reports and we identify anonymity and protection against collusion as one of the key challenges in the area. Finally, we evaluate the efficiency of our approach derived from a Java-based implementation of SuperTrust. This assessment relates to the system's responsiveness, performance, resilience to malicious behavior and network stress and demonstrates SuperTrust's superior performance.

2   Design Goals

In this work, we present the first precise definition of design properties that *any* protocol for handling trust values must satisfy. We also present a protocol that can be shown to fulfill this list of desired properties.

Anonymity: The system should support the peers' right to secrecy of their reporting ratings. Hence peers should not lose their identities because their expressed opinions have been revealed, accidentally or not. When this happens, a malicious node may try to eliminate these peers by mounting denial of service attacks against them.

Privacy and Integrity of reports: An opinion expressed by some peer in the form of a report should be protected from disclosure and modification. A malicious node or a *collusion* of such nodes should not be able to eavesdrop or modify these ratings.

Persistence: All trust reports should be accounted in building the reputation of a peer even when these reporting peers are no longer in the network. Any other option could be potentially exploited by a set of malicious peers who are always in the system, sending the same bad votes or masking legitimate peers from expressing authentic opinions.

Fairness and Soundness: No one should be able to change, add, or delete trust reports without being discovered.

Eligibility: Only peers legitimate to express an opinion about some other peer should be able to do so. This protects from malicious nodes giving poor ratings for peers that have never interacted with. So, we require that when a peer u interacts with a peer v, there should be some *proof* of this interaction. It is only then that u can submit a report for the service offered by v.

Unreusability and Verifiability: The system should prevent report stuffing. A peer eligible to express an opinion should be able to do this only *once* for a particular interaction it had with v. Further submissions should be detected and not be used to update the trust value of another peer. In addition, we require verifiability to be a system property so that trust values reflect the actual reputation of any peer and that reports are never left out of consideration, accidentally or not.

Efficiency: The entire process should be as efficient as possible. This includes the overhead in computation and submission of the a trust report.

3   Related Work

While there are many papers that deal with models and architectures for building reputation and trust among peers (see for example [4,5,6,7,8]), there have been only a few works that attempt to secure the process of submitting or retrieving trust reports. An even *smaller* subset of these contributions were proposed for Super peer networks. Furthermore, it is worth emphasizing that while these works use voting terminology, they fail to provide all the requirements mentioned in the previous section.

Kamvar *et al.*[6] attempt to secure the computed reputation values by having the trust value of a peer v be computed by a set of *mother peers* which are selected by a *deterministic* process based on the identity of v. A peer u, requesting the trust value of peer v, first queries all of v's mother peers and then takes a majority vote. Unfortunately, this system lacks anonymity, it can fall prey to peers presenting multiple identities, and its transactions between a querying peer and the mother peers are not secured.

TrustMe, presented by Singh and Liu [10], follows a similar approach in the sense that trust values for v are stored in *trust-holding agent (THA)* peers that are randomly distributed in the network and not known to v. When peer u submits a trust rating to one of the THA peers of v, its rating of the interaction with v is revealed, which is a serious weakness of the protocol since trust reports are protected from disclosure and modification attacks only by *outside* attackers and not by malicious THAs.

PeerTrust[11] is a framework that includes an adaptive trust model for quantifying and comparing the trustworthiness of peers based on a transaction-based feedback system over a structured P2P overlay network. This framework focuses on providing confidentiality and integrity but lacks many of the other required properties mentioned in the previous section.

Cornelli *et al.*[12] propose to base reputation sharing on distributed polling whereby a requestor u can assess the reliability of perspective providers by polling its peers. The votes issued by the various peers are then forwarded to u, giving it the opportunity to choose the most reputable peer. In [13], this work has been extended to cover Super peer networks. In both works u must individually contact *each* voter and ask for confirmation

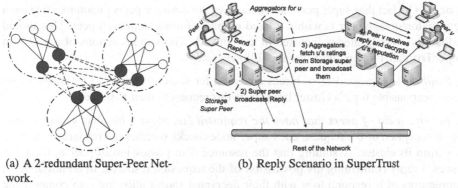

(a) A 2-redundant Super-Peer Network.   (b) Reply Scenario in SuperTrust

Fig. 1.

in order to rule out faked votes (loss in efficiency). It is also exactly at this point where peers lose their anonymity since a malicious peer can query for its own trust value in order to identify the voters who give poor trust ratings.

4   The SuperTrust Framework

We start by presenting an outline of our framework: SuperTrust is designed for *K-redundant* Super peer networks. In traditional Super peer networks, each peer can be either a super node (SN) or an ordinary node (ON). The SN tracks the content of its designated ONs. In this way, Super Peer networks are well suited to scalable designs and present fault tolerant aspects due to the presence of many Super nodes. Because of these various qualities, many applications have migrated towards the Super Peer paradigm (KaZaA [1], Gnutella 0.6). Additionally, K-redundant Super peer networks take benefit of having K-super peers working in a round robin fashion for each cluster (a cluster is the grouping of the leaf nodes of each super peer) in order to ameliorate the performance of Super peer networks. Figure 1(a) depicts a 2-redundant super peer network. Dark nodes represent Super peers, white nodes represent ordinary peers and the three clusters are marked by dashed lines. Super peer redundancy decreases the load on super peers and tolerates more failures[14]. Our framework will make use of such benefits for the purpose of enhancing security in the voting process.

Associated with each peer v is a chosen set of n Super peers (*aggregators*) that are responsible for "collecting" the votes/reports of other peers that have interacted with v and aggregate the results. The aggregators for each peer are chosen amongst the K super peers responsible for the various clusters. Furthermore, in each cluster, a *storage*[1] node is chosen amongst the K super peers as a storage facility for the reputations of the peers/resources located in the corresponding cluster.

Such a semi-centralized, semi-distributed approach reduces the stress in the network, thus improving the overall performance and reducing the probability of failures in the

---

[1] For the sake of a cleaner presentation, we present the protocol in terms of this storage peer, notice however, that its role can be maintained by the aggregators as well, thus improving robustness to failures.

system. The fact that super peers are the aggregators/storage peers guarantees that each aggregator/storage peer is within a fixed number of hops from each peer. This should reduce the overall latency incurred in the network. The various actions of a peer v in SuperTrust are broken down into the following steps:

1. *Send a file request:* Peer v issues a request for some resource r. One of the super peers responsible for v's cluster broadcasts this request to their neighbors.

2. *Receive a list of peers that have the requested file, along with their global rating:* Upon reception of v's request, each super node checks whether the resource requested is within its cluster. Assuming that the resource is in possession of peer u, the latter issues a reply confirming his possession of the requested resource. In addition, the n aggregators of u respond to v with their decrypted *shares* allowing v to compute the final trust value, as shown in Figure 1(b) and explained further in Section 4.6.

3. *Select a peer or a set of peers, based on a reputation metric in order to download the resource:* Upon reception of the replies and the decrypted shares from *a sufficient number* t of aggregators, peer v calculates the global trust value of the replying peers (Section 4.5) and chooses to download the resource from the most reputable peer.

4. *Send Vote:* Then, peer v rates the interaction it had with peer u. It first encrypts the report encapsulating its rating for both peer u and its resource and then submits it to the designated Super peer. The latter forwards the encrypted vote to its neighbors. This process is explained further in Section 4.4. Upon reception of the encrypted vote, and using appropriate cryptographic schemes, *the global trust value of v is updated by v' aggregators* without *decrypting the intermediate reports*, thus ensuring privacy and integrity of votes. At this point, the global trust value remains *encrypted* in the system.

The feature that most distinguishes SuperTrust from other contributions is that trust reports remain encrypted and are never opened during the submission or aggregation processes. In the rest of the section, we present the details of our scheme.

4.1 Threat Model and Assumptions

We start by discussing the threat and trust models we expect to encounter in trust handling applications.

In an outsider attack, the attacker is not an authorized participant of the network. As peers exchange messages, a passive attacker can easily eavesdrop in an attempt to steal private or sensitive information. The adversary can also alter, spoof or replay messages, trying to create erroneous trust values. The use of proper cryptographic primitives helps defend against these types of attackers.

The existence of inside attackers is more important from a security point of view. These are malicious peers who are authorized participants in the network and come equipped with the right cryptographic material so that they can participate in the various phases of the protocol. Despite this fact, we make sure that privacy and anonymity of benign peers is guaranteed. However, there always exists the possibility that such *malicious peers can rate other peers with poor ratings* in spite of good performance. We *don't deal with this type of behavior* as this should be tackled by the underlying trust model or architecture.

Our protocol relies on the existence of some authority or mechanism that can generate or certify special purpose keys, assign groups of aggregators, etc. when a peer joins the network. Since we will be relying on the use of public key cryptography, this entity can be viewed as a certifying authority (CA) and its public key can be trusted as authentic. We also assume that the underlying Super peer system provides for anonymity of information providers as long as these providers do not reveal themselves any identifying information. Thus we rely on the message forwarding mechanism of the Super peer system to provide for anonymity of broadcasted messages (see [10] for a similar assumption). Finally, we use trust functions that rely on simple aggregations. While such trust functions does not capture the full generality of trust in reputation systems, we assume that these values take into consideration more general transactions contexts, histories, credibility of issuers, etc.[16]

4.2 Definitions and Cryptographic Tools

We are assuming basic familiarity with the concept of public key cryptography.

Definition 1. *We say that an encryption function $E()$ is (additive) homomorphic if it allows computations with encrypted values. More precisely, if $E(M_i)$ are the encryptions of messages M_i, $i = 1, 2, \ldots, k$, then the product of the encryption messages M_i is equal to the encryption of their sum.*

This property is necessary to achieve anonymity since the aggregated trust value can be computed *without* the decryption of individual reports submitted by interested parties. The decryption is performed only on the *final sum*, guaranteeing privacy of voters. In [17], Paillier proposed an RSA-type public key cryptosystem based on computations in the group $Z_{N^2}^*$ (the set of numbers relatively prime to N^2), where N is the product of two large primes p and q. This scheme is additive homomorphic and allows for efficient decryption (details omitted). However, in order to prevent authorities from learning the contents of the submitted reports and to ensure the privacy of the voters a *threshold* version of the Paillier cryptosystem is needed.

Definition 2. *[18] A (t, n) threshold secret sharing scheme distributes a secret among n participants so that any t of them can recreate the secret, but any $t - 1$ or fewer gain no information about it. The piece held by each participant is called the secret share.*

In our case, instead of having a single authority decrypt the encrypted tally, n authorities share the decryption key, so that at least t are needed to perform the decryption operation. Such versions of the Paillier cryptosystem have been presented in [19]. Below we give a general description of the threshold decryption model. The participants is a set of n players (our aggregators) that share the decryption key and users (peers that submit confidential reports).

Initialization: The players run a a key generation protocol to create the public key PK and the secret shares SK_i of the private key SK. This is done securely[20] so that no player can find anything about shares other than its own.

Encryption and Decryption: The user uses PK to encrypt a message. To decrypt a ciphertext c, each player uses its share SK_i to produce a partial decryption c_i together with a *proof of validity* for the partial decryption. These proofs allow interested parties to verify that the partial decryption is valid even without knowing the underlying secret SK_i. Thus malicious players cannot submit erroneous results. The final decryption of c can be produced, if t or more valid decryptions are collected.

4.3   Initial Setup

When a peer v joins the network, the CA assigns a random set of the Super peers pertaining to its cluster to be the n *aggregators* for v. These will be responsible for decrypting the aggregated trust value of v that remains encrypted in the system. This group's public key PK_A^v is used by other peers u to rate their interactions with v and submit their encrypted reports into the system. The authenticity of the public key can be verified as it is equipped with a *certificate* carrying the signature of the CA and an indication that this is the key used to submit reports only for v. The decryption key is *shared* among the aggregators using the threshold cryptosystem.

Additionally, the CA assigns a storage Super peer for each cluster chosen from the most reputable and trusted Super peers. The storage Super peer serves as a storage repository for the *encrypted* ratings of the peers lying within its cluster. We stress at this point that the storage peer *is not able to decrypt* any rating it possesses; its sole function is to store the rating advertised and accumulated by the various aggregators (this is why its role may also be assumed by the aggregators).

In case of some supernode failure, a secure supernode selection process ensuring that the substitute super peers are chosen amongst the highly trusted and the least vulnerable nodes is needed (details omitted due to space constraints).

4.4   Submitting a Trust Report

When a peer u has interacted with peer v, it can file a report indicating the rating of this interaction. We assume here that u has acquired the public key PK_A^v through a previous reply received from v. Given the public key, u constructs the following message m:

$$m = < \text{``Report for } v\text{''} \mid E_A^v(Value) \mid \; < T_i, u, v, Sig_v(T_i, u, v) > \; \mid T > .$$

Then it transmits:

$$m \mid Sig_u(m) \mid PK_u \mid Cert_u \mid PK_v \mid Cert_v,$$

where the various parts are described below:

- $E_A^v(Value)$: The *encrypted* rating of the interaction using the public key PK_A^v.
- A *proof of the interaction* with v, $< T_i, u, v, Sig_v(T_i, u, v) >$: This proof is needed in order to prevent the replay of trust reports. When two peers u and v interact, they exchange such proofs with each other. This makes them eligible to vote and protects them from malicious peers submitting bad reports. Any report containing this proof outside some reasonable time frame Δt, is discarded. In addition, all duplicate reports but *one* in the interval Δt carrying the same proof of interaction are discarded by the system.
- A timestamp T: The use of the timestamp ensures that the report cannot be replayed and resubmitted at a later time by a malicious peer.

- A *signature* $Sig_u(m)$ of the whole message by u: The signature binds all the parts together so that nobody can alter or replace parts of the message.
- The public keys PK_u of u and PK_v of v: the latter key can be obtained after interacting with v and is included in the message so that during the aggregation process the proof of interaction $< T_i, u, v, Sig_v(T_i, u, v) >$ can be verified as authentic.

4.5   Aggregating Trust Reports

Trust reports for peer v get aggregated by its designated aggregators that subsequently submit the updated value to the cluster's storage Super peer, *replacing* previous reports for v. The invariant that is maintained at any moment is that the current aggregate value resides encrypted in the system. When a new report for v is issued, the format and the validity of the report is checked in reverse order from the generation process described in Section 4.4. Then using the homomorphic property of the encryption scheme the new aggregated value is computed simply by multiplying the encrypted value in the report with the current aggregate for v.

This approach aims at enforcing the consistency of the aggregation process and protecting from malicious aggregators. In fact, and upon receiving the trust report for v, the aggregators fetch from the storage Super peer v's previous ratings, update it using the homomorphic property, and submit the aggregation result back to the storage Super peer in order to guarantee the durability of the ratings in the system. In turn, the storage Super peer receives the various aggregation results, and *only* stores the encrypted value that was advertised by the majority of the aggregators. Such a scheme protects against up to $n/2$ suspicious aggregators (where n is the total number of aggregators in some cluster) that are trying to cheat the system by submitting erroneous aggregation results. Furthermore, in such a case, an alarm can be triggered notifying about the malicious behavior of these super-peers.

4.6   Reporting Back Trust Values

When a peer u issues a request for a resource r, it should wait to receive a reply indicating the availability of the resource in addition to the decrypted aggregators' shares that will allow it to construct the global rating for r and its possessor v.

Peer u first transmits a request message about r into the system. Such a query is broadcasted anonymously by the various Super peers in the network using the message forwarding mechanism so that the identity of u is protected.

Upon receiving the request for resource r, the various Super peers identify its availability within their cluster, and transmit a reply message containing the ID v of r's holder . Then after sniffing the reply message, v's aggregators automatically access the encrypted aggregated value stored in the storage Super peer (Section 4.5) and produce their partial decryptions. Then they respond back with a message of the form:

$$\text{"Partial decryption for } v\text{"} \mid D_i \mid Proof_{Valid}(D_i) \mid PK_A^v \mid Cert_A^v \mid T,$$

where D_i is a partial decryption value of v's reputation and $Proof_{Valid}(D_i)$ is a *proof of validity* ensuring that the decryption is correct.

Once peer u collects at least t shares, it can compute the final decrypted result. Then upon satisfaction of the reputation of v, it can decide whether or not to interact with v. The use of a (t, n) threshold cryptosystem protects against malicious aggregators submitting erroneous decryptions. Additionally, our approach offers protection against replay attacks since the timestamp ensures that the partial decryption is up to date.

5   Security Analysis of SuperTrust

Privacy and Anonymity: The privacy of the peers' reports is guaranteed even if up to $t - 1$ aggregators (where t represents the threshold cryptography) collude with each other. The use of a threshold cryptosystem guarantees that no faulty or malicious aggregator can decrypt the report submitted by a peer. Additionally, SuperTrust uses the homomorphic property of the cryptosystem in order to compute the final tally *without* decrypting individual reports. This strengthens peer's privacy and anonymity since at no point in the submission process will a report be decrypted[2]. Finally, an external attacker or eavesdropper can infer no information about the contents of a report since these are are sent encrypted using public key cryptography.

Fairness and Soundness: A malicious node cannot affect the submission process by submitting invalid reports or by not following the protocol. If a peer tries to submit an invalid report or if there is no associated proof of interaction, the report will be discarded by the system. This prevents malicious peers from rating other peers when they have no such right. Notice, however, that two malicious cooperating peers may interact with each other (thus having valid proofs of interaction) in order to elevate their own ratings. We don't deal with this type of behavior in this work as this should handled by the underlying trust model.

Persistence: Persistence of submitted reports is guaranteed by the character of the aggregation process. When a peer submits a trust report, its contents are securely stored in the designated Storage super peer. If this peer ever leaves the system, its role will be assigned to a new super peer, thus guaranteeing maintenance of votes.

Eligibility and Unreusability: SuperTrust ensures that only eligible peers are allowed to cast a report. This is achieved by the incorporation of proofs of interaction in the reports. The inclusion of timestamps in the reports and the proofs of interaction guarantee that reports can be submitted only once, thus preventing report duplication.

Verifiability: In SuperTrust, the nature of the aggregation process and the use of majority by the storage Super peer guarantees that all reports are taken into consideration when computing a peer's global trust value. Additionally, the aggregators may check the Storage peer for *consistency* since after performing the homomorphic multiplication they can test whether the storage peer has updated the global trust value with the values they submitted.

---

[2] However, peer v may query for its trust value, before and after, an interaction with peer u, thus recovering the vote of u. This attack applies to *all* systems and can be reduced if the aggregators "batch" or "mix" the votes.

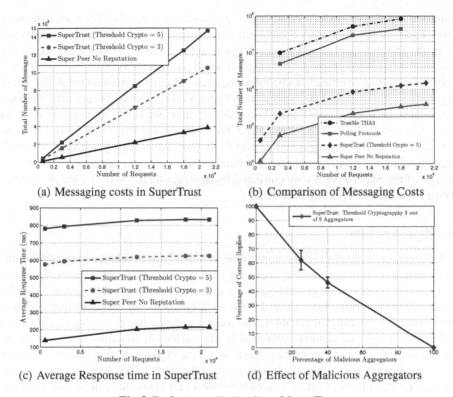

(a) Messaging costs in SuperTrust   (b) Comparison of Messaging Costs

(c) Average Response time in SuperTrust   (d) Effect of Malicious Aggregators

Fig. 2. Performance Evaluation of SuperTrust

6   Experimental Results

We have implemented SuperTrust in Java. Our implementation is mutlithreaded and relies on Jade agents [21] as the main infrastructure for exchanging messages between the various peers. Our framework was evaluated on a moderately connected network consisting of various networked computers connected to a 100 Mbit LAN where up to two different processes reside on each machine. We have simulated a total of 1200 peers, 2400 different resources and at least 18 superpeers/aggregators pertaining to six different clusters of 200 peers each. At the beginning of the simulations, each peer has a number of random resources (with replication index of 1.43).

To evaluate the effectiveness of our framework, we conducted our experiments aiming at analyzing three main performance metrics: response time, messaging costs and the effect of malicious aggregators. These scenarios were run in two modes: SuperTrust mode and no reputation mode, the latter representing a non-reputation based Super peer network. In what follows, we present an analysis of our simulations results.

6.1   Messaging Costs

In order to assess the messaging costs induced in our framework, we have evaluated three models: SuperTrust with threshold cryptography of 3 and 5 aggregators, and no reputation super-peer model. Figure 2(a) illustrates the obtained results. Each data point in this figure is averaged over 6 times the total number of requests. These results are due to the fact that each issued request triggers at least 5 to 7 additional messages, per reply, in the threshold cryptography cases of 3 and 5 respectively.

Such messaging overhead can be tolerated even in highly congested networks, when compared to the overhead induced in other proposed protocols. Figure 2(b) shows a comparison between SuperTrust, TrustME[10] and SupRep[13], with respect to messaging costs. As it can be seen, SuperTrust achieves much lower overhead when compared to these aforementioned protocols. In fact, SuperTrust guarantees that each aggregator/storage peer is within a fixed number of hops from each peer by taking advantage of the Super-Peer architecture and by aggregating the votes *on the fly* without relying on distributed polling protocols.

6.2 Response Time

We have measured the average response time in SuperTrust in relation to the total number of requests. Our measurements were done for various number of requests sent at the fixed rate of 15 per second per cluster (90 requests per second in the network), for the threshold cryptography cases of 3 and 5. Figure 2(c)depicts our findings (averaged over 10000 runs). Our findings incorporate the time to encrypt/decrypt a vote plus the time to verify the proofs of validity submitted by the various aggregators according to the findings in [19]. As a matter of fact, the time for encryption (or decryption) is almost 0.3ms (0.18ms) *per bit* of plaintext message on a Pentium 2.4GHz. In our case, and assuming that the submitted rating ranges between 1 and 1000, one can see that the time for encryption/decryption is negligible.

Our results (Figure 2(c)) show an advantage of 500ms, per request for the no reputation scheme over SuperTrust. This is mainly due to the overhead induced by the use of threshold cryptography: one modular exponentiation consumes almost 70 ms for a 1024 bit exponent. Nevertheless, our studies have demonstrated that SuperTrust is the most efficient system to date since almost all contributions in this area neglect to provide response time. For example, although SupRep[13] is expected to have less cryptographic overhead, since it does not make use of threshold cryptography, it induces more stress in the network because of its requirement to poll for *all* available opinions. Similar performance can be observed in the other polling protocols (Figure 2(b)).

6.3 Effect of Malicious Aggregators

In SuperTrust, the requestor peer must have a sufficient number of valid partial decryptions from some aggregators, in order to correctly retrieve the global rating of another peer. Although malicious aggregators cannot cheat the system by inserting invalid votes, they might not allow a correct decryption of a global rating if they send invalid decryption shares. Fortunately, the use of threshold cryptography helps to minimize such a malicious behavior. Our simulation results show that even if we assume the presence of 30% malicious aggregators in the network, almost 60% of the requests will have sufficient partial decryption from the aggregators in order for the requestor peer to fully decrypt the advertised rating (Figure 2(d)).

7   Conclusions

In this paper, we have presented SuperTrust, a framework that manages trust ratings of peers in a way that preserves the privacy and anonymity of transactions, in the context of Super peer networks. SuperTrust achieves these properties by ensuring that *trust reports remain encrypted and are never opened* during the submission or aggregation process. The use of *threshold* cryptography allows the aggregators to have access to such ratings and compute a global trust value without the need to see the individual reports. Each aggregator produces a partial value, and when enough of these shares are collected, the final trust value can be computed in a simple and mechanical way. Thus, SuperTrust is resistant to attacks by colluding Super peers. Furthermore, SuperTrust exploits the benefits of Super peer networks to reduce messaging overhead in the network, while providing robust and efficient security. We hope that SuperTrust, along with this first precise definition of properties that *any* protocol for handling trust values must satisfy, will stimulate further research in this area.

References

1. KaZaA: http://www.kazaa.com/us/index.htm
2. The Gnutella Protocol Specifications, http://www.clip2.com
3. eBay, http://www.ebay.com
4. Dutta, D., Goel, A., Govindan, R., Zhang, H.: The Design of a Distributed Rating Scheme for Peer-to Peer Systems. In: Workshop on Economics of Peer-to-Peer Systems (2003)
5. Aberer, K., Despotovic, Z.: Managing trust in a peer-to-peer information system. Proceedings of IKE (2001)
6. Kamvar, S., Schlosser, M., Garcia-Molina, H.: Eigenrep: Reputation management in p2p networks. In: Proceedings of WWW (2003)
7. Wand, Y., Vassileva, J.: Trust and Reputation model in Peer-to-peer Networks. In: Proceedings of P2P (2003)
8. Xiong, L., Liu, L.: A reputation-based trust model for peer-to-peer e-commerce communities. In: IEEE International Conference on Electronic Commerce (2003)
9. Baudron, O., Fouque, P.-A., Pointcheval, D., Pouparde, G., Stern, J.: Practical Multi-Candidate Election System. In: PODC (2001)
10. Singh, A., Liu, L.: TrustMe: Anonymous Management of Trust Relationships in Decentralized P2P Systems. In: Proceedings of P2P (2003)
11. Xiong, L., Liu, L.: PeerTrust: Supporting Reputation-Based Trust for Peer-to-Peer Electronic Communities. In: IEEE Transactions on Knowledge and Data Engineering (2004)
12. Cornelli, F., Damiani, E., di Vimercati, S.D.C., Paraboschi, S., Samarati, P.: Choosing Reputable Servents in a P2P Network. In: Proceedings of WWW (2002)
13. Chhabra, S., Damiani, E., De Capitani di Vimercati, S., Paraboschi, S., Samarati, P.: A Protocol for Reputation Management in Super-Peer Networks. In: Galindo, F., Takizawa, M., Traunmüller, R. (eds.) DEXA 2004. LNCS, vol. 3180, Springer, Heidelberg (2004)
14. Yang, B., Garcia Molina, H.: Designing a Super-Peer Network. In: ICDE (2003)
15. Damiani, E., De Capitani di Vimercati, S., Paraboschi, S.: A Reputation Based Approach for Choosing Reliable Resources in Peer to Peer Networks. In: CCS (2002)
16. Jøsang, A., Ismail, R., Boyd, C.: A Survey of Trust and Reputation Systems for Online Service Provision. Decision Support Systems (2006)

17. Paillier, P.: Public-Key Cryptosystems Based on Discrete Logarithm Residues. In: Stern, J. (ed.) EUROCRYPT 1999. LNCS, vol. 1592, Springer, Heidelberg (1999)
18. Shamir, A.: How to share a secret. Comm. of the ACM 22, 612–613 (1979)
19. Damgård, I., Jurik, M.: A Generalization, a Simplification and some Applications of Paillier's Probabilistic Public-Key System. In: Kim, K.-c. (ed.) PKC 2001. LNCS, vol. 1992, Springer, Heidelberg (2001)
20. Damgård, I., Koprowski, M.: Practical Threshold RSA Signatures Without a Trusted Dealer. In: Pfitzmann, B. (ed.) EUROCRYPT 2001. LNCS, vol. 2045, Springer, Heidelberg (2001)
21. Jade: Java Agent DEvelopment Framework, http://jade.tilab.com/

A Highly Flexible Data Structure for Multi-level Visibility of P2P Communities[*]

Debmalya Biswas[1] and Krishnamurthy Vidyasankar[2]

[1] IRISA/INRIA, Campus Universitaire de Beaulieu, Rennes, France 35042
dbiswas@irisa.fr
[2] Dept. of Computer Science, Memorial University of Newfoundland, St. John's, NL,
Canada A1B 3X5
vidya@cs.mun.ca

Abstract. Peer to Peer (P2P) communities (or "interest groups") are referred to as nodes that share a common interest. Each peer in the system claims to have some interests and, accordingly, would like to become a member of these groups. The available interest groups are arranged according to a hierarchical semantics ontology, and managed with a semantic overlay network. P2P community structure is highly dynamic: a peer may be added to or deleted from a community; communities may be added or deleted; communities may be merged or split; and sub-communities may become parent-level communities and vice versa. In this paper, we propose a highly flexible multi-level data structure to capture the visibility aspect of P2P communities. The data structure is simple, facilitates dynamic changes easily and efficiently in a decentralized fashion, and is highly scalable.

1 Introduction

Over the past few years, Peer to Peer (P2P) systems have gained widespread acceptance as a result of their decentralized control, high scalability and availability. However, their commercial use has been mostly restricted to information/file sharing systems. As a result, work has already been initiated towards the use of P2P systems for collaborative work [1,2]. A related application area where we also need to consider "groups" of peers is that of Interest Groups, e.g., Yahoo Groups [3]. Basically, the peers in an interest group share some common interests. The notion of P2P Communities [4] has been proposed to model such interest groups. We generalize P2P communities as an abstraction for a group of peers, which work collaboratively to perform a specific task or share some common interests.

By default, each peer has knowledge of (visibility over) the rest of the peers in its own community. Now, for a community to grow, it needs visibility over other

---

[*] D. Biswas's work is supported by the ANR DOCFLOW and CREATE ACTIVEDOC projects. K. Vidyasankar's work is supported in part by the Natural Sciences and Engineering Research Council of Canada Discovery Grant 3182.

S. Rao et al. (Eds.): ICDCN 2008, LNCS 4904, pp. 363–374, 2008.

communities and their peers. Similarly, a peer would like to have information about communities catering to "related" interests. Current P2P systems either function as independent entities (peers/communities) or assume that each peer is aware of all the other peers and communities ([8]). Allowing each peer to have full information, about all the other communities and their peers, is not a practical solution. For dynamic and heterogeneous environments such as P2P systems, trust and anonymity issues may force a peer (or community) to be restrictive in the visibility it allows to others. Thus, a fundamental issue to address in P2P communities is how to capture the visibility a peer (or community) has over the other peers and communities.

Towards this end, we introduce a visibility graph formalism for P2P communities. The communities are often organized hierarchically corresponding to a hierarchical semantics ontology, for example, as shown in Fig. 1. Our formalism is a multi-level graph to facilitate community visibility at different levels of the hierarchy. Note that the P2P community structure is highly dynamic: a peer may be added to or deleted from a community; communities may be added or deleted; communities may be merged into bigger ones or split into smaller ones; and sub-communities may become parent-level communities and vice versa. The multi-level visibility graphs facilitate performing query evaluation and structural updates in a decentralized and scalable fashion to accommodate the inherent dynamism.

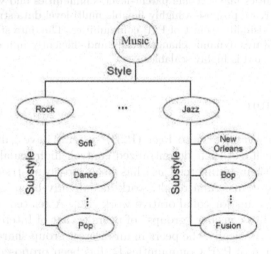

Fig. 1. A sample hierarchical ontology

The rest of the paper is organized as follows: The visibility graph formalism is introduced in section 2. Sections 3 and 4 outline algorithms for query evaluation and for performing structural updates on visibility graphs, respectively. In section 5, we discuss some implementation details of visibility graphs. Section 6 presents some related work. Section 7 concludes the paper and provides some directions for future work.

2   Visibility Graph

2.1   Multi-level Visibility

We present a graph model to represent the visibilities of the peers and communities in a P2P system. Let $\mathcal{P}$ be the set of peers and $\mathcal{C}$ be the set of communities in a P2P system S. Peers are represented by nodes. We use the same notation to refer to the nodes as well as the peers they represent. An edge between peers P_1 and P_2 indicates that P_1 is visible to P_2, and vice versa. The visibility is assumed to be symmetric in this paper. Peers are grouped into communities, which may further be grouped into higher level communities, and so on. The communities are usually arranged according to one or more hierarchical semantics ontologies. Fig. 1 shows a sample hierarchy of music related interests (as given in [5]). Fig. 2 illustrates a hierarchical organization. At the bottom level, there are several communities. We call them level-1 communities. We use single (solid, and different dotted and broken) lines for the intra-community edges. The communities are grouped into three higher level communities. In each group, connections between communities are shown in double line edges. These are level-2 communities. All these groups of communities belong to an even higher level (level-3) community shown in triple line edges. For example, Fig. 2 may correspond partly to Fig. 1, with level-1 communities of Soft, Dance, Pop, etc., level-2 communities of Rock, Jazz, etc., and level-3 community of Music.

In our model, we represent a parent-level community through certain peers of its children communities called *seers*. The seers are connected by edges identifying the community. In Fig. 2, the double line edges connect seers of level-1 communities, and similarly, triple line edges connect seers of level-2 communities. Thus, the actual connections will be as shown in Fig. 3. We note that each node will be incident to single line edges (as long as its community has at least two peers). Then, some nodes may be incident to other (double line, triple line, etc.) edges too. In Fig. 3, there are nodes incident to (i) single line and double line edges, (ii) single, double, and triple line edges, and also (iii) single and triple line edges. That is, a peer may be a seer for a higher level (e.g., level-3) community, and not for a lower level (e.g., level-2) community. Thus, the edges of the visibility graph are of different level communities in the hierarchy.

2.2   Data Structure

Let $\mathcal{H}$ be a set of hierarchies that may exist in a P2P system S. We confine our initial discussion and the graph formalism to one hierarchy $H \in \mathcal{H}$. Fig. 4 shows the hierarchy used in our previous example. We use Fig. 4 to illustrate some notations and concepts. Each node in the figure represents a community at some level of the hierarchy. We assume that each peer forms its own *unit community*. We call this level-0 community. The nodes, and the corresponding communities, are named locally (within that level) and globally with the sequence of local labels of nodes in the path from the root to that node. For example, e is the local name and $a/b/e$ is the global name of a node in the figure. We use the

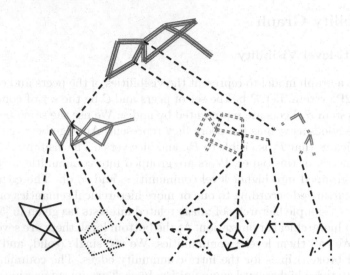

Fig. 2. Hierarchical visibility

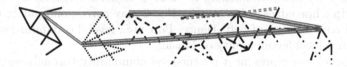

Fig. 3. Actual connections of the hierarchy in Fig. 2

global name to indicate the corresponding path also. We define a prefix α^p of a global name α as the sequence of labels of the nodes in a prefix of the path corresponding to α. On the same lines, we define an extension α^s of a global name α as the sequence of labels of the nodes of a global name β which contains α as one of its prefixes, that is, $\exists \beta, \beta^p = \alpha$. For example, for α equal to $a/b/e$, a/b and a are the prefixes, and $a/b/e/P_1$ and $a/b/e/P_2$ are extensions. We also denote the *immediate* prefix by α^I and an immediate extension by α^E. For $a/b/e$, the immediate prefix is a/b, and both the extensions in Fig. 4 are immediate extensions. Finally, for a global name α, we use $^*\alpha$ and α^* to denote the set of its prefixes and extensions, respectively.

We note that only the leaf nodes in H (Fig. 4) correspond to peers in S. They have labels as in the figure. (Labels of only some nodes are shown for easy readability.) All non-leaf nodes are virtual. Essentially, H describes all (lower and higher level) communities in S. Each peer belongs to several, hierarchically related, communities. To be precise, a peer with label α is a member of all the communities with labels in $^*\alpha$.

For each node (with local or global name) α in the hierarchy, we define two communities. The first one is the α-*full-community*, denoted with α in square brackets as [α]-community. This consists of all the peers in the subtree rooted at α. For example, [b]-community membership is $\{P_1, P_2, P_3, P_4, P_5\}$. The

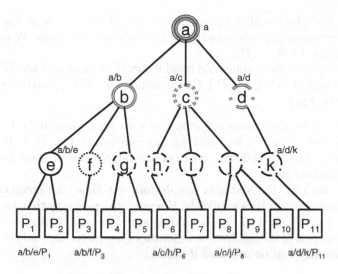

Fig. 4. Complete hierarchy with peers

second is α-*seer-community*, denoted with α in parentheses as (α)-community. For non-leaf nodes α, this will contain one or more peers from *each* of its children communities, that is from those of each immediate extension of α; these peers will be *seers* of the respective communities *for* [α]-community. For example, (b)-community membership could be $\{P_1, P_3, P_5\}$. For leaf nodes α, the local name will be that of the respective peer, say P_i, and both the full and the seer communities will consist of just that peer. Note that each level-1 community is a full as well as a seer community. Now, a peer can be a seer for several ancestral communities. For a community C, we define a C-*graph* as the graph with node set consisting of members of C and edges, called C-edges, depicting the visibility among the members. When C is a seer community, we refer to the graph as C-*seer-graph* also. In our model, we require that each seer graph is connected.

Definition. For a P2P system S, with peers $\mathcal{P}$, hierarchy H, and related set of (full) communities $\mathcal{C}$, a *global visibility graph* is the union of C-seer-graphs of all communities C in $\mathcal{C}$ such that each seer graph is connected.

Example: A visibility graph for the P2P system in Fig. 4 is shown in Fig. 5. Here:

- $\mathcal{P}$ is $\{P_1, P_2, ..., P_{11}\}$;
- $\mathcal{C}$ is $\{[a], [b], ..., [k], [P_1], [P_2], ..., [P_{11}]\}$;
- $[P_2]$ is the unit community containing peer P_2, and the corresponding seer community (P_2) also contains P_2;
- Both $[e]$- and (e)-communities have peers P_1 and P_2; Similarly, for each of $\{f, g, ..., k\}$, their full and seer communities have all their children shown in the figure;

– Each of $\{[a]\text{-},[b]\text{-},[c]\text{-},[d]\text{-}\}$ communities have all the peers in the leaf level of the corresponding sub-trees in the hierarchy; For example, $[b]$-community membership is $\{P_1, ..., P_5\}$.
– The seer community membership is as follows: (b)-community has $\{P_1, P_3, P_5\}$, (c)-community has $\{P_6, P_7, P_8\}$, (d)-community has $\{P_{11}\}$, and (a)-community has $\{P_3, P_9, P_{11}\}$.

In this example, the connected graph of each seer community is a tree, in fact, a path. Note that P_8 is a seer for (c)-community but P_9 is the seer for (a)-community. That is, different peers of a sub-tree may be seers for different ancestral communities.

We point out that the visibility graph does not show the member peers of higher level full communities explicitly. However, the property that for every full community at every level its corresponding seer community must have at least one peer from each of its children communities guarantees that all the members of that community can be accessed if needed.

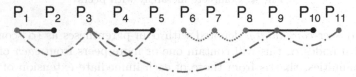

Fig. 5. Complete visibility graph of Fig. 4

3   Searching the Visibility Graph

Any search involves searching one or more communities. Search within a community typically involves flooding, that is, searching each peer in the community. Common search methods, when the peers within a community are arbitrarily connected, are Breadth First and Depth First Searches, with or without using a spanning tree. A search may be initiated from any node. It may also be initiated, in parallel, from several nodes. In each case, the search results may be forwarded to one or more initiating nodes, to some other nodes, or even to all the nodes. In this paper, we will neither be concerned with the actual search method nor with any specific way of forwarding the results. We denote searching a community C as C-search.

We explain a general search procedure with the graph in Fig. 5. Any query is initiated at a peer. Suppose a query q is initiated at P_2. Then, first, the (P_2)-search and, if necessary, an (e)-search will be performed. If q cannot be evaluated within (e)-community, then P_1 (which is the seer of $[e]$-community for (b)-community, will initiate a (b)-search. This will involve the graph consisting of P_1, P_3 and P_5. Then, P_5 may suggest that a (g)-search is appropriate, involving peers P_4 and P_5. On the other hand, P_3 may suggest that (the higher level) (a)-search, involving P_3, P_9 and P_{11} may be appropriate. Taking up one or more suggestions and continuing the search can be done either in a centralized or distributed fashion.

Thus, in comparison to traditional query resolution via flooding, our method provides the following benefits: Privacy and security constraints are maintained as queries are only forwarded to visible (trusted) peers. On the other hand, each peer may be a member of different seer communities at different levels. And, based on the information it has on each of these communities, it may be able to direct the search to any of these levels. For example, in the above search process, P_3 will be involved in the searches of (P_3)-, (f)-, (b)- and (a)-communities. Suppose (P_3)-search is the first one. The next search could be (a)-search, then (f)-search, etc. This allows the searches to be mixed rather than being strictly top-down or bottom-up. In (P_3)-search, its role is an individual peer; in (a)-search, its role is a seer for $[b]$-community, and in that capacity it is supposed to utilize some summary information of the $[b]$-community; and so on.

3.1   A Specific Example

We consider simple hierarchical path queries having the following syntax:

$I :=$ An area of interest in the underlying (hierarchical) ontology O.
$Path := \epsilon | I / Path$
$Query := (n)Path | (Query \wedge Query) | (Query \vee Query)$

where n refers to the *number of nodes* to retrieve satisfying the *Path* criterion. $I/(sub\text{-})I$ refers to a pair of parent-child interests in O. A sample query is given below:

Query q. $(1)music/classic \wedge ((1)music/jazz/fusion \vee (2)music/rock/soft)$.

Query q can be interpreted as follows: Find a peer interested in *music/classic* and a peer interested in *music/jazz/fusion*, or a peer interested in *music/classic* and two peers interested in *music/rock/soft*.

Given this, a search to evaluate query q over the global visibility graph (Fig. 5) would be as follows. (We assume that a, b, c and d correspond to the *music*, *music/rock*, *music/jazz* and *music/classic* communities, respectively.) We assume that q is submitted at peer P_3.

1. P_3 initiates an (a)-search, that is, evaluates q within the (a)-community.
2. If unsuccessful, P_3 chooses nodes in the (a)-community (peers P_9, P_{11}, and peer P_3 itself) for propagating (the entire query or parts of) q for further evaluation. Peer P_3 makes this decision based on the "similarity" between the path criteria in q and the global names of the nodes in the (a)-community. Here, P_3 would choose itself for the (sub)query $(2)music/rock/soft$, while P_9 would be chosen for $(1)music/jazz/fusion$ and P_{11} for $(1)music/classic$.
3. The nodes P_3, P_9 and P_{11} initiate a (b)-search, (j)-search and (d)-search, respectively. In the course of (j)-search, P_9 might find a need for, and initiate, a (c)-search.
4. This continues until the appropriate peers are found, or all the peers in H have been explored (in which case, there may not exist peers satisfying the query).

4   Visibility Structure Changes

P2P systems are highly dynamic in nature, with peers being added to or deleted from communities, communities being added to or deleted from higher level communities, merging and splitting of the communities, etc. All these operations change the visibility graph. Our formalism facilitates these changes easily. We outline the general procedures in the following, with examples from the hierarchy of Fig. 4, and Fig. 5.

I. Basic operations

(a) *Adding a peer P to a community C.* Add the node P and a C-edge between P and some node already in C. Note that the addition of this single edge is sufficient to keep the new C-graph connected. Of course, additional edges can be added too. We restrict our description to the minimum requirements.

(b) *Deleting a peer P from a community C.* This may require several operations: (i) P is deleted from the C-graph; (ii) If this disconnects the C-graph, then additional C-edges, between other peers in C, are added to keep the C-graph connected; (iii) Suppose P is a seer of a sub-community C' of C for C. If P is the only such seer, then some other peer P' of C'-community should be designated as a seer for C and added to C.

(c) *Deleting a peer P from the P2P system S.* Then P must be deleted from every community it is part of (as a seer).

II. Other structural changes

Some of the other structural changes are:

- adding a community C to a higher level community C';
- deleting a community C from a higher level community C';
- merging two same level communities;
- splitting a community to two communities under the same parent community;
- merging two different level communities; etc.

These, and several other operations involving combinations of those considered above, can be executed. All these involve essentially some generic operations like adding a node to a graph, deleting a node from the graph but keeping the graph connected after the deletion, etc. Depending on how the graph (C-graph for community C) is maintained (as a tree, arbitrary connected graph, complete graph, etc.), these operations can be implemented efficiently. The key property of our formalism is that a node may be incident to C-edges of several communities C, and so the node may have to be deleted from some C-graphs and not from some others.

5   Implementation and Discussion

As we know, P2P systems are very highly decentralized. Peers are far apart, they are highly autonomous, they may join the system and drop out in an ad hoc manner, their storage and processing capacities may be varied and limited, their availability and accessibility may be different at different times, communication between them may not be reliable, and so on. Therefore, implementation of the algorithms for both searching the peers for query evaluation and for modifying the structure of the visibility graph, outlined in the previous two sections, requires special attention. For instance, in any distributed implementation, the algorithms will be executed only lazily, that is, asynchronously. The algorithms can be fine tuned for "safe" execution. For example, when a community is deleted from another, and added to a different community, the addition part can be done first, and then the deletion. This may result, in the worst case, in a concurrent execution exploring more peers than necessary, but without loss of visibility.

We note that peers can execute their part of the algorithms autonomously. For example (as discussed in section 3), a peer which is a seer for several (higher level) communities could employ its own heuristics to decide on which order to explore the various communities. The selection strategy could be different for a different peer even for the same set of choices.

The core element of the implementation is the manipulation of C-graph for each community C in the hierarchy. Depending on the type of connectivity maintained, the amount of work in the manipulation will be different. Searching could be more systematic and efficient with tree structure. On the other hand, updates on the hierarchical structure may be implemented more efficiently with graphs which are not trees.

With our model, several C-graphs have to be manipulated. However, each can be manipulated independent of the others. So, the complexity of the implementation will not increase very much with the increase in the number of communities. With proper extensions to the underlying hierarchy, an increase in the number of peers in the P2P system can be accommodated by increasing the number of communities without substantially increasing the size of the corresponding seer-communities. Thus, our data structure and the algorithms are highly *scalable*.

At an abstract level, multi-level visibility seems close to the notion of database views [6]. For a set of relational tables in a database, a view allows us to summarize their data based on some characteristics. Here, the peers can be considered as data. The information on the various peers in a community can be summarized and kept in the seers of that community. However, since a peer can be a seer of a higher level ancestral community without being a seer of a lower level one, hierarchical relationships of the communities cannot be represented directly.

Having said this, there is also sufficient overlap between the two concepts, for a lot of the existing work for database/views to be used here, especially, with respect to query optimization and rewriting. Also, we have not considered *concurrent* query and update of the visibility graph which is very relevant, especially, for collaborative P2P systems. Database solutions [7] appear very attractive for the above as well.

Finally (as mentioned earlier), we consider visibility graphs as an abstraction to capture the visibility aspect of P2P communities, and we expect other middleware aspects, e.g., security, monitoring, etc. to build on this abstraction. In the sequel, we briefly show how visibility graphs facilitate P2P security. Security for P2P communities is usually provided with the help of a Trust Management scheme [8]. In this scheme, each peer maintains the trust rating of all the other members in its own group (group-mates), based on its own dealings with them. For inter-community accesses, "when a member p requests to acquire resources from a member q of another community, it sends a request to q. q checks with the group-mates of p if p is trustable and what kind of access privileges it has. q then accepts or rejects the transaction with p". The above can be modeled using visibility graphs as follows: The underlying assumption, that the seer graph of each community is connected, allows a peer to monitor the activities of its group-mates (that is, to maintain their trust ratings). Inter-community access between peers $P_1 \in C_1$ and $P_2 \in C_2$ may only occur via an access path from a C_1-seer to a C_2-seer. Further, recall that visibility is symmetric. Thus, given such an inter-community access, P_2 can backtrack along the access path, and retrieve the trust rating of P_1 from the C_1-seer.

6   Related Works

The notion of P2P communities was introduced in [4]. They also represent visibility using intra-community and inter-community edges. They use only one type of inter-community edges. Our formalism uses different edges for (seer communities at) different levels of the hierarchy.

Further works [8], [9] and [10] have extended the P2P community notion as follows: [8] presents a Trust Management scheme for P2P communities. [9] discusses efficient discovery for P2P communities based on the "type" of communities, e.g., co-operative, goal oriented, ad hoc communities, etc. [10] presents a gossip based discovery mechanism for P2P communities. However, none of them consider the visibility aspect with respect to P2P systems.

No other work (that we are aware of) has attempted to formalize the visibility aspect for P2P systems. Some of the works which have touched upon this aspect are the following: [11] identifies real-life scenarios where there might be a need to deviate from the inheritance of access rights upwards through the hierarchy in a role-based access control system. [12] considers the visibility aspect with respect to sending publish/subscribe notifications for event based systems. [13] identifies the need for visibility across levels of a supply chain management system as follows: "The information required by downstream entities are mainly material and capacity availability information from their suppliers. The information acquired by an upstream entity is information about customer demand and orders. The depth of information penetration can be specified in various degrees, e.g., isolated, upward one tier, upward two tiers, downward one tier, downward two tiers, and so forth".

In previous works [14] and [15], we have studied the visibility aspect for hierarchical systems, especially, hierarchical Web Services compositions. In [14], we introduced the notion of Sphere of Visibility (SoV) to capture the visibility aspect, and showed its application in the context of performing compensation under visibility constraints. However, [14] only considered vertical visibility (that is, visibility over ancestors and descendants) as compared to the more generalized notion of visibility presented in [15] (visibility over siblings, uncles, cousins, etc.). In [15], we also studied some inherent relationships which might exist among the SoV's of a group of providers, e.g., coherence, correlation, etc.

7   Conclusion and Future Work

In this paper, we have proposed a multi-level visibility graph formalism to capture the visibility of peers and communities in P2P systems. The formalism caters to the grouping of peers in a hierarchical community organization. The graph model accommodates, with equal ease, any number of levels in the hierarchy and any number of communities in each level.

In this paper, we have assumed that at a level of the hierarchy, the node sets of the children components are disjoint. When we consider multiple attributes, the resulting components (at the same level) may be overlapping. This can be accommodated in our model though the search and update algorithms would become more complicated. For instance, in the event of such overlapping it may no longer be sufficient to use the hierarchical path as the global name of a peer.

Further, the visibility graph formalism, and the search and update algorithms in this paper have been defined for a single underlying hierarchy. The scenario becomes more interesting as soon as we allow for multiple overlapping hierarchies. For example, in Fig. 1, in addition to the hierarchical classification by type, the peers may also be chronologically (again, hierarchically) classified by the interest in decades, years and months. Given this, a query evaluation, after some initial search with respect to the type hierarchy and determining the year of production, might switch to a search by the chronological hierarchy. Our formalism can easily be extended for multiple hierarchies. We leave this extension and the above issues as directions for future work.

References

1. Grid Computing, http://www.ogf.org/
2. Active XML (AXML) Systems, http://www.activexml.net
3. Yahoo Groups, http://groups.yahoo.com/
4. Khambatti, M., Ryu, K., Dasgupta, P.: Peer-to-Peer Communities: Formation and Discovery. In: PDCS. Proceedings of the 14th IASTED Intl. Conf. Parallel and Distributed Computing Systems, pp. 161–166 (2002)
5. Crespo, A., Garcia-Molina, H.: Semantic Overlay Networks for P2P Systems. Technical report, Stanford University, USA (2002)
6. Database Views, http://en.wikipedia.org/wiki/View_(database)
7. Abiteboul, S., Amann, B., Cluet, S., Eyal, A., Mignet, L., Milo, T.: Active Views for Electronic Commerce. In: VLDB. Proceedings of the 25th International Conference on Very Large Data Bases, pp. 138–149 (1999)

8. In, H.-P., Meintanis, K.A., Zhang, M., Im, E.-G.: Kaliphimos: A Community-Based Peer-to-Peer Group Management Scheme. In: Yakhno, T. (ed.) ADVIS 2004. LNCS, vol. 3261, pp. 533–542. Springer, Heidelberg (2004)
9. Akram, A., Rana, O.F.: Structuring Peer-2-Peer Communities. In: P2P. Proceedings of the 3rd International Conference on Peer-to-Peer Computing, pp. 194–195 (2003)
10. Khambatti, M.S., Ryu, K.D., Dasgupta, P.: Push-pull gossiping for information sharing in peer-to-peer communities. In: PDPTA. Proceedings of the IASTED International Conference on Parallel and Distributed Processing Techniques and Applications, pp. 1393–1399 (2003)
11. Moffet, J.D.: Control principles and role hierarchies. In: RBAC. Proceedings of the 3rd ACM Workshop on Role-Based Access Control, pp. 63–69 (1998)
12. Fiege, L.: Visibility in Event-Based Systems. Ph.D. Thesis, Department of Computer Science, Darmstadt University of Technology, Darmstadt, Germany (2005)
13. Lin, F.-R, Tan, G.W., Shaw, M.J.: Modeling Supply-Chain Networks by a Multi-Agent System. In: HICSS. Proceedings of the 31st Annual Hawaii International Conference on System Science, pp. 105–114 (1998)
14. Biswas, D., Vidyasankar, K.: Spheres of Visibility. In: ECOWS. Proceedings of the 3rd IEEE European Conference on Web Services, pp. 2–13 (2005)
15. Biswas, D., Vidyasankar, K.: Modeling Visibility in Hierarchical Systems. In: Embley, D.W., Olivé, A., Ram, S. (eds.) ER 2006. LNCS, vol. 4215, pp. 155–167. Springer, Heidelberg (2006)

Mathematical Performance Modelling of Stretched Hypercubes

Sina Meraji[1,2] and Hamid Sarbazi-Azad[1,2]

[1] Sharif University of Technology, Terhan, Iran
[2] IPM school of computer sceince, Tehrn, Iran
{meraji,azad}@ipm.ir, sharif.edu

Abstract. The stretched hypercube has recently been introduced as an attractive alternative to the well-known hypercube. Previous research on this network topology has mainly focused on topological properties, VLSI and algorithmic aspects of this network. Several analytical models have been proposed in the literature for different interconnection networks, as the most cost-effective tools to evaluate the performance merits of such systems. This paper proposes an analytical performance model to predict message latency in wormhole-switched stretched hypercube interconnection networks with fully adaptive routing. The analysis focuses on a fully adaptive routing algorithm which has been shown to be the most effective for stretched hypercube networks. The results obtained from simulation experiments confirm that the proposed model exhibits a good accuracy under different operating conditions.

Keywords: stretched hypercube, analytical model, performance evaluation, wormhole routing.

1 Introduction

A large number of interconnection networks have been proposed and studied for highly parallel distributed-memory multicomputers [2, 3, 7, 8, 11, 14, 15, 17, 18, 19, 26, 29]. Among them the hypercube has been one of the most famous ones which has many desirable properties such as logarithmic diameter and fault-tolerance. It is not, however, scalable from hardware cost point of view, i.e. when adding some few nodes to it, we have to duplicate the network size to reach the next specified network size. Other drawback with hypercubes was reported by Patel et al. [28] when considering VLSI layout. They showed that the minimum number of tracks for VLSI layout of an n-cube (n-dimensional hypercube) using a one-dimensional implementation has an order of network size. Their investigation revealed that for an example network of 1k processors (a 10-cube), at least 687 tracks are required for VLSI implementation.

The *stretched hypercube,* introduced in [23], is a new interconnection network based on the hypercube network. While preserving most of properties of the hypercube, it has some other desirable properties such as hardware scalability and efficient VLSI layout that make it more attractive than an equivalent hypercube network [23].

S. Rao et al. (Eds.): ICDCN 2008, LNCS 4904, pp. 375–386, 2008.

There are three main approaches for performance evaluation of interconnection networks. The first one is monitoring the behavior of the actual system; it can capture the effects of low-level design choices, but restricts experimentation with different router policies since it can be prohibitively expensive and time-consuming to change these features. Simulation is the second approach for performance evaluation of interconnection network. We may implement different routing algorithms, different switching methods, and different interconnection topologies with simulation environments, but simulation is time consuming especially when we study large networks. The last way is to using mathematical approaches for performance analysis of interconnection networks. Mathematical models are cost-effective and versatile tools for evaluating system performance under different design alternatives. The significant advantage of analytical models over simulation is that they can be used to obtain performance results for large systems and their behaviour under network configurations and working conditions which may not be feasible to study using simulation on conventional computers.

Several researchers have recently proposed analytical models of popular interconnection networks, e.g. k-ary n-cubes, tori, hypercubes, and meshes [1, 4, 6, 24]. The most difficult part in developing any analytical model of adaptive routing is the computation of the probability of message blocking at a given router due to the number of combinations that have to be considered when enumerating the number of paths that a message may have used to reach its current position in the network. Almost all studies on stretched hypercube interconnection networks focus on topological properties and algorithmic issues. There has been hardly any study on performance evaluation of such networks and no analytical model has been proposed for stretched hypercubes. In this paper, we discuss performance issues of stretched hypercube graphs by introducing a reasonably accurate mathematical model to predict the average message latency in wormhole stretched hypercubes using a high-performance routing algorithm proposed in [22].

2 The Stretched Hypercube Graph

Among the various classes of interconnection networks, scalable symmetric (or even partially symmetric) graphs with lower average node degree and lower diameter are of great interest (for their lower cost) to the designers of multiprocessor systems. On the other hand, most of the well-known interconnection networks like the hypercube, star graph, and the pyramid, suffer greatly from not being scalable; for example, in the case of the hypercube, the network size is such quantized that, for adding a single node to the network, the network size must be duplicated. Stretched hypercube [23] tried to overcome the scalability problem by placing some processor nodes on edges of hypercube graph, thus achieving a far more scalable interconnection network. Stretched hypercube networks possess lower average degree than the same size hypercube networks. Accordingly, stretched hypercube networks are of lower average node degree in comparison with hypercube networks when equal network degree is considered.

Definition 1. Let $G = (V_G, E_G)$ be a hypercube graph, the *Regular Stretched* hypercube network, $RS_rH = (V_{RS}, E_{RS})$, is an undirected graph based on G, where each edge of G is replaced by an array of r nodes. That is

$$V_{RS} = \{ (b,b',i) \mid (b=b' \ \& \ i=0) \ \text{or} \ (b<b' \ \& \ < label^{-1}(b), label^{-1}(b') >\in E_G \\ \& \ 0 < i \leq r)\},$$

where *label* is a bijective function as *label*: $V_G \rightarrow [\, |V_G| \,] = \{ 1, 2, ..., |V_G| \}$.

From now on, we shall refer to every label value as a base graph node. For each $u = (b,b',i) \in V_{RS}$, b (base vertex) and b' (last vertex) are two adjacent nodes in the base hypercube, and i, $0 \leq i \leq r$, represents the index of node u in the array. Conventionally, we apply zero to the index of the base graph nodes and we set $b'=b$ for such nodes; as a result, the base graph vertices can be addressed uniquely. The edge-set of the stretched hypercube can be defined as $E_{RS} = \{\langle u,v \rangle \mid u = (b_1,b_1',i_1), v = (b_2,b_2',i_2) \in V_G \}$, where nodes u and v must satisfy one of the following conditions: *Array edges* where: $b_1 = b_2$, $b_1' = b_2'$, $|i_1 - i_2| = 1$, and *Junction edges* where $b_1 = b_2$, $i_1 = 0$, $i_2 = 1$; or $b_1' = b_2$, $i_1 = r, i_2 = 0$.

Definition 2. The *irregular stretched hypercube network*, denoted as $IS_{r_1, r_2, ..., r_{|E(G)|}} H$, (with r_k, $k = 1,2,...,|E(G)|$ representing the length of the corresponding array), is defined similarly (to the regular stretched hypercube). The difference is that each array has its own length.

The numbering order of the arrays is as follows. Starting with a base graph node that has the least label value, we number the array that connects the mentioned node to another node of the base graph with the next least label value, as 1. Then, the next array that connects the mentioned node to a node of the base graph with the next least label value is numbered as 2, and so on. After numbering all of such arrays, we do the same starting with the next base graph node that has the next least label value; at last, the base graph node with the greatest label value would not be used for numbering any array. Fig. 1 presents such a numbering in the RS_4H_3 *and* $IS_{4,3,4,0,2,2,3,2,0,3,4,4}H_3$. The gray numbered rectangles show the numbering order of the arrays.

3 Adaptive Routing in Stretched Hypercubes

In this section, we introduce a fully adaptive routing algorithm for the stretched hypercube. The algorithm can be used with both packet switching and wormhole switching techniques. To define a fully adaptive routing algorithm, we must first define a deadlock-free routing (with any level of adaptivity). We can then use the deadlock-free routing algorithm as described in [22] to construct a fully adaptive routing algorithm.

In order to have a deadlock-free routing algorithm in the stretched hypercube, we use three classes of virtual channels A, B and C. Virtual channels of class A are used when the message is at the source stretched edge; we use virtual channels of this class until we reach the first base vertex of the source stretched edge. Virtual channels of class C are used in the destination stretched edge; it means that when we enter the destination stretched edge, we use this class of virtual channels until we reach to the destination node. Finally, virtual channels of class B are used for a deadlock-free routing algorithm in the base hypercube, e.g. e-cube routing. The minimum number of virtual channels in each class is 1. Thus, we need at least 3 virtual channels per physical channel to implement a deadlock-free routing algorithm in stretched hypercubes.

According to Duato's methodology, since the base deadlock-free routing algorithm requires 3 virtual channels, we can have a fully adaptive deadlock-free routing algorithm in the stretched hypercube using at least 4 virtual channels, three of which used by the base routing algorithm and the remaining one used in any possible way that can brings the message closer to the destination node.

We call the virtual channels used for base deadlock-free routing as the *base virtual channels* and the remaining virtual channels as the *adaptive virtual channels*.

When there are more than 4 virtual channels per physical channel, the network performance is maximized when the extra virtual channels are added to adaptive virtual channels. Thus, with V virtual channels per physical channel, the best performance is achieved when we have V-3 adaptive virtual channels and three base virtual channels.

The proposed routing algorithm contains three main steps: 1) Move towards the nearest base neighbor using any of the V-3 adaptive virtual channels. If all V-3 adaptive virtual channels are busy use the virtual channel of class A from base virtual channels to move toward the nearest base neighbor in the source stretched edge. 2) Move towards the nearest base node of the destination node using fully adaptive routing algorithm in the hypercube with V-3 adaptive virtual channels [13]. If all V-3 virtual channels are busy use the virtual channel of class B with e-cube routing in the base hypercube. 3) Now the current node is one of the base vertices of the destination stretched edge. Move towards the destination node using any of the V-3 adaptive virtual channels. If all V-3 adaptive virtual channels are busy use the virtual channel of class C from base virtual channels to move toward the destination node in the destination stretched edge.

4 The Analytical Model

In this section, we derive an analytical performance model for wormhole adaptive routing in a stretched hypercube. Our analysis focuses on the routing algorithm which was introduced in previous section (described in [22]) but the modelling approach used here can be equally applied for other routing schemes after some few changes.

The measure of interest in our model is the *average message latency* as a representative for network performance. The following assumptions are made when developing the proposed performance model. These assumptions have been widely used in similar modelling studies [1, 5, 6, 9, 12, 16, 20, 24, 27].

a) Messages are broken into some packet of fixed length of M flits which are the unit of switching. The flit transfer time between any two neighbouring nodes is assumed to one cycle.
b) Message destinations are uniformly distributed across the network nodes.
c) Nodes generate traffic independently of each other, which follow a Poisson process, with a mean rate of λ_g messages/cycle.
d) Messages are transferred to the local processor through the ejection channel once they arrive at their destination.

e) V virtual channels per physical channel are used. These virtual channels are used according to the routing algorithm described in the previous section.

In order to compute the mean message latency in each of the three sub-networks (the network parts used in the three steps listed above), we must consider three parameters: the mean network latency, $\overline{S}$, that is the time to cross the network, the mean waiting time seen by a message in the source node to be injected into the network, $\overline{W}_s$. To model the effect of virtual channels multiplexing effects, the mean message latency is then scaled by a factor, $\overline{V}$, representing the average degree of virtual channels multiplexing that takes place at a given physical channel [10]. Therefore, the mean message latency in each sub-network can be approximated as

$$Latency = (\overline{S} + \overline{W}_s)\overline{V} \tag{1}$$

The average number of hops that a message makes across the network, $\overline{d}$, can be computed as follows [23]:

$$\overline{d} = \left(\frac{n}{2} + 1\right) \times k \tag{2}$$

where $k\frac{n}{2}$ is the average number of hops that must be crossed in the main hypercube and k is the average number of hops that must be crossed in the source and destination stretched edges.

Fully adaptive routing in the stretched hypercube allows a message to use any available channel that brings it closer to its destination node, resulting in an evenly distributed traffic rate over all channels. Since each message travels, on average, $\overline{d}$ hops to cross the network, the rate of messages received by each channel, λ_c, can be approximated as

$$\lambda_c = \frac{N \times \lambda_g \times \overline{d}}{L} \tag{3}$$

where N is the number of nodes in the stretched hypercube which is equal to $2^{n-1}(nk+2)$ and L is the total number of links which is equal to $n2^{n-1}(k+1)$ [23].

Let us follow a typical message which makes $\overline{d}$ hops to reach to its destination. The average network latency, $\overline{S}$, seen by the message crossing from the source to the destination node consists of two parts: one is the time due to the actual message transmission, and the other is due to the blocking time in the network. Therefore, $\overline{S}$, can be expressed as

$$\overline{S} = M - 1 + \overline{d} + \overline{d}T_b \tag{4}$$

where M is the message length, and T_b is the average blocking time seen by the message at each hop. The term T_b is given by

$$T_b = P_{block}w \tag{5}$$

with P_{Block} being the probability that a message is blocked at the current channel and w is the mean waiting time to acquire a channel in the event of blocking. A message is blocked at a given channel in the stretched edge sub-network when all adaptive and deterministic virtual channels of the current physical channel are busy. Let P_a be the probability that all adaptive virtual channels of a physical channel are busy and $P_{a\&d}$ denote the probability that all adaptive and deterministic virtual channels of a physical channel are busy. In stretched edge sub-networks, we have only one path for the messages, so no adaptivity exists for messages moving across a stretched edge.

In order to compute $P_{a\&d}$, we must consider three cases: (a) The probability that all of V virtual channels of a physical channel are busy, P_V. (b) When V-1 virtual channels of the V virtual channels associated to a physical channel are busy. In this case, if the free virtual channel is the channel of class B or C when in source stretched edge, class A or C when in the base network, and class A or B when in the destination stretched edge, then all adaptive and the base virtual channel that can be used by the message are busy. Thus, at any step, only two combinations can result in blocking out of all possible combinations that V-1 virtual channels of the total V virtual channels are busy. (c) When V-2 virtual channels of the V virtual channels associated to a physical channel are busy. In this case, the message is blocked if virtual channels of class B and C are free when routing in the source stretched edge, or if virtual channels of class A and C are free when routing in the hypercubic part, or if virtual channels of class A and B are free when routing in the destination stretched edge. Thus, at any step only one combination out of all possible combinations that V-2 virtual are busy can result in blocking.

Therefore, the probability that all of the adaptive and base virtual channels of a physical channel are busy can be expressed as

$$P_{a\&d} = P_V + \frac{2P_{V-1}}{\binom{V}{V-1}} + \frac{P_{V-2}}{\binom{V}{V-2}}. \tag{6}$$

In order to compute P_a, we must consider 4 cases: (a) The probability that all of V virtual channels of a physical channel are busy, P_V. (b) When V-1 virtual channels of the V virtual channels associated to a physical channel are busy. In this case, if the free virtual channel is one of the base virtual channels we end up with blocking. Thus only 3 combinations out of all possible combinations that V-1 virtual channels are busy can result in blocking. (c) When V-2 virtual channels of the V virtual channels associated to a physical channel are busy. In this case, 3 combinations of two free channels from virtual channels in class A, B and C may result in blocking out of all possible $\binom{V}{V-2}$ combinations. (d) When V-3 Virtual channels of a physical channel are busy. In this case, only one combination of the $\binom{V}{V-3}$ total possible combinations results in having all adaptive virtual channels being busy.

Thus, we have

$$P_a = P_V + \frac{3P_{V-1}}{\left(\dfrac{V}{V-1}\right)} + \frac{3P_{V-2}}{\left(\dfrac{V}{V-2}\right)} + \frac{P_{V-3}}{\left(\dfrac{V}{V-3}\right)} \tag{7}$$

In order to compute the probability of blocking, P_{block}, we calculate the average of all the probabilities that a message may be blocked crossing $\overline{d}$ hops in the network. $\overline{d}$ hops can be divided into two parts: a) $n/2$ hops when we are in the main hypercube nodes and we have adaptivity, and b) the remaining $n/2(k-1)+k$ hops are made in stretched edges without any adaptivity. A message is blocked at a given channel in the main hypercube nodes when all the adaptive virtual channels of class B of the remaining dimensions to be visited and also the deterministic virtual channel of class B for the current dimension are busy. A message is blocked in the stretched nodes when all virtual channels of class A are busy (for a message leaving the source and not yet visited a hypercubic node), or when all virtual channels of class B are busy (for a message that has already visited its first hypercubic node), or when all virtual channels of class C are busy (for a message that has visited the last hypercubic node along its path to the destination node). Considering all above mentioned cases, we can write

$$P_{block} = \frac{\frac{n}{2}}{(\frac{n}{2}+1)k}\left(\frac{\sum\limits_{i=0}^{n/2-1}(P_a)^{n/2-i-1}P_{a\&d}}{\frac{n}{2}}\right) + \frac{(\frac{n}{2}+1)k-\frac{n}{2}}{(\frac{n}{2}+1)k}P_{a\&d} \tag{8}$$

where $\dfrac{\frac{n}{2}}{(\frac{n}{2}+1)k}$ is the probability that the current node is a hypercubic node, and

$\dfrac{(\frac{n}{2}+1)k-\frac{n}{2}}{(\frac{n}{2}+1)k}$ is the probability that it is not a hypercubic node.

To determine the mean waiting time, w, to acquire a virtual channel when a message is blocked, a physical channel is treated as an M/G/1 queue with a mean waiting time of [21]

$$w = \frac{\rho\overline{S}(1+C_{\overline{S}}^2)}{2(1-\rho)}, \quad \rho = \lambda_c\overline{S}, \quad C_{\overline{S}}^2 = \frac{\sigma_{\overline{S}}^2}{\overline{S}^2} \tag{9-11}$$

where λ_c is the traffic arrival rate on the channel, $\overline{S}$ is its service time calculated by equation 4, and $\sigma_{\overline{S}}^2$ is the variance of the service time distribution. Since the minimum service time at a channel is equal to the message length, M, following a suggestion given in [12], the variance of the service time distribution can be approximated as $\sigma_{\overline{S}}^2 = (\overline{S}-M)^2$. Hence, the mean waiting time becomes

$$w = \frac{\lambda_c\overline{S}^2(1+(1-M/\overline{S})^2)}{2(1-\lambda_c\overline{S})} \tag{12}$$

Similarly, modelling the local queue in the source node as an M/G/1 queue, with the mean arrival rate of λ_g / V and service time $\overline{S}$ with an approximated variance $(\overline{S} - M)^2$ yields the mean waiting time seen by a message at the source node as [21]

$$W_s = \frac{\dfrac{\lambda_g}{V}\overline{S}^2(1+(1-M/\overline{S})^2)}{2(1-\dfrac{\lambda_g}{V}\overline{S})} \tag{13}$$

The probability, P_v, that v virtual channels are busy at a physical channel can be determined using a Markovian model. State P_v ($0 . v . V$) corresponds to v virtual channels being busy. The transition rate out of state P_v to state P_v+1 is the traffic rate λ_c (given by equations 3) while the rate out of state P_v to state P_{v-1} is $1/\overline{S}$ ($\overline{S}$ is given by equation 4). The transition rates out of state P_v are reduced by λ_c to account for the arrival of messages while a channel is in this state.

The Markovian model results in the following steady state probability [21], in which the service time of a channel has been approximated as the network latency of that channel, as

$$P_v = \begin{cases} (1-\lambda_c\overline{S})(\lambda_c\overline{S})^v, & 0 \le v < V \\ (\lambda_c\overline{S})^v, & v = V. \end{cases} \tag{14}$$

When multiple virtual channels are used per physical channel, they share the physical bandwidth in a time-multiplexed manner. The average degree of multiplexing of virtual channels, that takes place at a given physical channel, can then be estimated by [10]

$$\overline{V} = \frac{\sum_{v=1}^{V} v^2 P_v}{\sum_{v=1}^{V} v P_v}. \tag{15}$$

The above equations reveal that there are several inter-dependencies between the different variables of the model. For instance, Equations 4 and 5 reveal that $\overline{S}$ is a function of w while equation 9 shows that w is a function of $\overline{S}$. Given that closed-form solutions to such inter-dependencies are very difficult to determine, the different variables of the model are computed using an iterative technique.

5 Validation of the Model

The proposed analytical model has been validated through a discrete-event simulator (Xmulator [25]) that mimics the behaviour of the described routing algorithms in the stretched hypercube network at flit level. The simulator uses the same assumptions as the analysis, and some of these assumptions are detailed here with a view to making the network operation clearer. The network cycle time is defined as the transmission time of a single flit from one router to the next. Messages are generated at each node according to a Poisson process with a mean inter-arrival rate of λ_g messages/cycle.

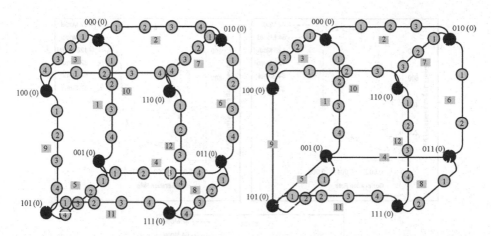

Fig. 1. a) A regular stretched hypercube with $n=3$ and $k=4$ b) An irregular stretched hypercube

Message length is fixed at M flits. Destination nodes are determined using a uniform random number generator. The mean message latency is defined as the mean amount of time from the generation of a message until the last data flit reaches the local processor at the destination node. The other measures include the mean network latency, the time taken to cross the network, the mean queuing time at the source node, and the time spent at the local queue before entering the first network channel. Numerous validation experiments have been performed for several combinations of network sizes, message lengths, and number of virtual channels to validate the model.

Figures 2 depict latency results predicted by the model explained in the previous section, plotted against those provided by the simulator for different sized stretched hypercubes. The horizontal axis in the figure shows the traffic generation rate at each node while the vertical axis shows the mean message latency. In figure 2-a, we consider a large network (about 1000 nodes) with $V=10$ virtual channels per physical channel, and three different message lengths of $M=32$, 64 and 128 flits. Figure 2-b represents the same results for a medium sized network (about 256 nodes); here we have $V=8$ virtual channels per physical channel and messages of length $M=32$, 64 and 128 flits. Finally, in figure 2-c, we have shown a comparison between the results given by the model and those gathered from the simulation experiments for a small network (about 100 nodes); here the number of virtual channels is $V=6$ per physical channel and message length is $M=32$, 64 and 128 flits.

The figure reveals that in all cases the analytical model can predict the mean message latency with a good degree of accuracy. However, some discrepancies around the saturation point are apparent. These can be accounted for by the approximations made to ease the derivation of different variables of the model, e.g. the approximation made to estimate the variance of the service time distribution at a channel.

Such an approximation simplifies the model as it allows us to avoid computing the exact distribution of the message service time at a given channel, which is not a straightforward task due to inter-dependencies between service times at successive channels as wormhole routing relies on a blocking mechanism for flow control.

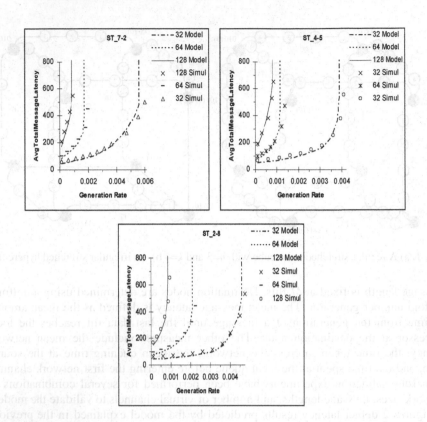

Fig. 2. The average message latency predicted by the model against simulation results for different sized networks

6 Conclusion

The stretched hypercube network has recently been introduced as an attractive alternative to the well-known hypercube. However, most of studies reported in the literature have focused on topological properties and algorithmic aspects of these networks. In this paper, we introduced the first mathematical performance model of adaptive wormhole routing in stretched hypercubes and validated it through simulation experiments. We saw that the proposed model manages to achieve a good degree of accuracy while maintaining simplicity, that make it a practical evaluation tool that can be used by the researchers in the field to gain insight into the performance behaviour of fully adaptive routing in wormhole-switched stretched hypercube.

References

1. Abraham, S., Padmanabhan, K.: Performance of the direct binary n-cube networks for multiprocessors. IEEE Trans. on Computers 37(7), 1000–1011 (1989)
2. Agarwal: Limits on interconnection network performance. IEEE Transactions on Parallel and Distributed Systems 2(4), 398–412 (1991)

3. Berthome, P., Ferreira, A., Perennes, S.: Optimal Information Dissemination in Star and Pancake Networks. IEEE Trans. on Parallel and Distributed Systems 7(12), 1292–1300 (1996)
4. Boppana, R.V., Chalasani, S.: A Comparison of Adaptive Wormhole Routing Algorithms. In: ISCA 1993. Proceedings of the 20th Annual International Symposium on Computer Architecture, pp. 351–360 (1993)
5. Boppana, R.V., Chalasani, S.: A Framework for Designing Deadlock-Free Wormhole Routing Algorithms. IEEE Transactions on Parallel and Distributed Systems 7(2), 169–183 (1996)
6. Boura, Y., Das, C.R., Jacob, T.M.: A performance model for adaptive routing in hypercubes. In: Proceedings of the International Workshop on Parallel Processing, pp. 11–16 (1994)
7. Chen, C., Chen, J.: Optimal Parallel Routing in Star Networks. IEEE Trans. Computers 46(12), 1293–1303 (1997)
8. Chen, C., Chen, J.: Nearly Optimal One-to-many Parallel Routing in Star Networks. IEEE Trans. on Parallel and Distributed Systems 8(12), 1196–1202 (1997)
9. Ciciani, B., Colajanni, M., Paolucci, C.: An accurate model for the performance analysis of deterministic wormhole routing. In: Proceedings of the 11th International Parallel Processing Symposium, pp. 353–359 (1997)
10. Dally, W.J.: Virtual channel flow control. IEEE Transactions on Parallel and Distributed Systems 3(2), 194–205 (1992)
11. Day, K., Tripathi, A.: A Comparative Study of Topological Properties of Hypercubes and Star Graphs. IEEE Transactions on Parallel and Distributed Systems 5(1), 31–38 (1994)
12. Draper, J.T., Ghosh, J.: A Comprehensive analytical model for wormhole routing in multicomputer systems. Jour. of Parallel and Distributed Computing 23(2), 202–214 (1994)
13. Duato, J., Yalamanchili, C., Ni, L.: Interconnection Networks: an engineering approach. IEEE computer society press, Los Alamitos (1997)
14. Fujita, S.: Neighborhood Information Dissemination in the Star Graph. IEEE Trans. on Computers 49(12), 1366–1370 (2000)
15. Graham, S.W., Seidel, S.R.: The Cost of Broadcasting on Star Graphs and k-ary hypercubes. IEEE Trans. Computers 42(6), 756–759 (1993)
16. Greenberg, R., Guan, L.: Modelling and comparison of wormhole routed mesh and torus networks. In: Proceedings of the 9th IASTED International Conference on Parallel and Distributed Computing and Systems, pp. 501–506 (1997)
17. Jwo, J.S., Lakshmivarahan, S., Dhall, S.K.: Embedding of Cycles and Grids in Star Graphs. Journal of Circuits, Systems and Computers 1(1), 43–74 (1991)
18. Lee, J.I., Chang, H.: Embedding Complete Binary Trees in Star Graphs. Journal of the Korea Information Science Society 21(2), 407–415 (1994)
19. Kessler, R.E., Schwarzmeier, J.L.: CRAY: T3D: A new dimension for Cray Research. CompCon, 176–182 (1993)
20. Kim, J., Das, C.R.: Hypercube communication delay with wormhole routing. IEEE Transactions on Computers 43(7), 806–814 (1994)
21. Kleinrock, L.: Queueing Systems, vol. 1. John Wiley, New York (1975)
22. Meraji, S., Sarbazi-Azad, A.: Deterministic routing in stretched hypercubes, Technical Report, School of Computer Science, IPM, Tehran, Iran (2006)
23. Shareghi, P., Sarbazi-Azad, H.: Topological Properties of Stretched Graphs. In: Proc. of the 4th ACS/IEEE International Conference on Computer Systems and Applications, Dubai/Sharjah, UAE, March 18-20, pp. 123–126 (2006)

24. Najafabadi, H.H., Sarbazi-Azad, H., Rajabzadeh, P.: Performance Modeling of Fully Adaptive Wormhole Routing in 2-D Mesh-Connected Multiprocessors. In: MASCOTS 2004. 12th Proc. of the IEEE ACM International Symp. on Modeling, Analysis, and Simulation of Computer and Telecommunication Systems, pp. 528–534 (2004)
25. Nayebi, S.M., shamaei, A.: Using listener-based integration to develop a simulation platform for interconnection networks - Xmulator, Sharif university of Technology, http://www.xmulator.com
26. Nigam, M., Sahni, S., Krishnamurthy, B.: Embedding Hamiltonians and Hypercubes in Star Interconnection Graphs. In: Proc. Intl. Conf. Parallel Processing, vol. 3, pp. 340–343 (1990)
27. Patel, A., Kusalik, A., McCrosky, C.: Area-Efficient VLSI Layout for Binary Hypercubes. IEEE Trans. on Computers 49(2) (2000)
28. Rezazad, M., Sarbazi-Azad, H.: A Constraint-Based Performance Comparison of Hypercube and Star Multicomputers with Failures. In: AINA 2005. 19th International Conference on Advanced Information Networking and Applications, pp. 841–846 (2005)
29. Sheu, J.P., Liaw, W., Chen, T.: A Broadcasting Algorithm in Star Graph Interconnection Networks. Information Processing Letters 48(5), 237–241 (1993)

A Family of Collusion Resistant Symmetric Key Protocols for Authentication

Bruhadeshwar Bezawada and Kishore Kothapalli

Center for Security, Theory, and Algorithmic Research
International Institute of Information Technology
Gachibowli, Hyderabad 500 032, India
Tel.: +91-40-23001967; Exts:143,151
bezawada@iiit.ac.in, kkishore@iiit.ac.in

Abstract. We address the problem of message authentication in communication networks which are resource constrained or are performance bound. Recent research has focused on development of symmetric key protocols for authentication in such networks. In these protocols, the sender generates a pool of keys -used to sign the messages, and distributes a different subset of keys -used to verify the signatures, to each user. However, in these protocols, users can collude to combine their keys and impersonate the sender by generating the sender signatures. In this work, we describe a family of collusion resistant symmetric key distribution protocols for authentication which address the problem of collusion. We show that the collusion resistance achieved using our protocols is practical (and hence, sufficient) for networks whose communication diameter is known or is within fixed bounds. Furthermore, we show that some existing protocols in literature are members of our family of protocols.

Keywords: Authentication, Collusion resistance, Key Distribution.

1 Introduction

In communication networks, many critical tasks require regular exchange of information among the nodes in the network. In such scenarios, motivated by economic gains or other malicious intent, the data may be manipulated by a single node or by a group of such intermediate nodes. The propagation of such incorrect data can lead to instability of networks, loss of service, loss of revenue and damage the reputation of service providers. In particular, data manipulation by a group of colluding nodes is a serious problem as the extent of damage possible is higher than that is possible by attacks launched by a single malicious node. Thus, protecting the integrity of the data against attacks launched by a group of colluding users is an important problem in communication networks.

A standard solution to achieve collusion resistant message authentication is to employ digital signatures using public-key cryptography. A sender signs the message with its private key and the receiver can check the authenticity of the

S. Rao et al. (Eds.): ICDCN 2008, LNCS 4904, pp. 387–392, 2008.

signature using the public key of the sender. However, the cost of signature generation and verification in public-key crypto systems is relatively high for network devices and can slow down per-packet processing considerably.

To address the computational overhead in public-key crypto systems, several works [1,2,3] have proposed using symmetric key protocols for achieving message authentication. The sender uses a shared symmetric key to sign the message and the receiver verifies the signature using the same key. As most protocols [1,4] rely on multiply shared keys for reducing sender and user storage, collusion is likely in such protocols. However, in earlier works, the issue of collusion resistance has not been studied in detail.

In this paper, we address the issue of collusion resistance in symmetric key distribution protocols such as those in [1]. Towards this, we propose a family of collusion resistant symmetric key distribution protocols for message authentication in a communication network. Our contributions are as follows:

- We show that our key distribution protocols provide sufficient collusion resistance against message tampering for networks whose communication diameter is known to be within certain bounds, say, $O(\log N)$. Higher collusion resistance can be achieved by increasing the sender storage marginally. Although, our protocols require higher storage at the sender, the storage at the receivers is still $O(\log N)$ as in [1]. Furthermore, we show that, the currently known solution [1] is a member of our family of protocols.
- We show that, for most practical networks, the sender can choose to store a smaller number of keys and hence, reduce the signature cost per packet.

Organization. In Section 2, we describe the problem in detail, outline our network model and assumptions. In Section 3, we describe our family of collusion resistant symmetric key distribution protocols and provide a detailed analysis of their collusion resistance. In Section 4, we present the experimental results of applying our protocols to networks with different diameters. Finally, in Section 5, we conclude the paper and outline some future work.

2 Problem Description

We address the problem of message authentication in communication networks. As an example, consider the link state routing protocol on the Internet (e.g., OSPF) that requires a router to broadcast link updates in its neighborhood to the entire network. This information is critical as other routers recompute their routing tables using this information. Since the information passes through different routers, one or more malicious routers can manipulate the information for selfish gains. Hence, there is a need for message integrity preserving mechanisms that are able to withstand a wide variety of falsification attacks particularly, those that are launched by a group of colluding malicious routers.

In [1], the authors describe a logarithmic keying protocol for achieving authentication in communication networks. In this scheme, a sender maintains $2 \log N$ keys for a set of N receivers. The sender assigns a unique $\log N$ bit identifier to each receiver and gives each receiver a unique subset of $\log N$ keys using the bit-values in the receiver's identifier. The authentication technique is that, the sender signs each message with all its keys and each receiver verifies those signatures for which it has the corresponding signing key. Since, by construction, each receiver maintains a different subset of the sender keys it is not possible for any single receiver to replace all the sender signatures. However, in this scheme, a select pair of users i.e., users who have complementary binary identifiers can collude and compromise all the keys of the sender.

In this work, we describe a family of key distribution protocols that use the same authentication techniques from [1]. We show that the collusion resistance of our protocols depends on the number of keys stored by the sender. For practical purposes, we assume that the sender storage is directly proportional to the communication network diameter and hence, is logarithmic in size. The network diameter assumption can be justified by the fact that most well-known network topologies including the class of hypercubic graphs [5], random graphs in the $G(n,p)$ model with $p = O(1/\log n)$, the Internet, and most peer-to-peer networks [6] have a small diameter.

Threat Model and Assumptions. Our threat model considers a group of malicious nodes that can falsify data and impersonate as the sender. We assume a communication network where critical data is exchanged among the nodes for network related tasks. We do not assume any support from the underlying network other than best effort message delivery. A node can be a router or an end-host and is capable of symmetric key signature generation and verification. We assume that the nodes follow the semantics of communication i.e., the nodes do not drop packets or launch denial of service attacks. These problems are orthogonal to the issues addressed in this current work.

Related Work. In [2], the authors describe a collaborative shared key technique for authentication which has low storage and signature cost. However, it can be shown that this technique can compromised by an arbitrary number of routers. In [4], the authors propose a scheme where the number of keys stored by users is equivalent to the probability of compromise. The only drawback in this scheme is that a large number of keys need to be stored by users. In [3,7], the authors describe one-way hash chain based techniques for message authentication. In [3], the protocol requires loose synchronization of routers which cannot be guaranteed in most real-time applications. In [7], the authentication approach requires complex setup and protocol state overhead making it more expensive than the protocol from [1]. In the next section, we describe our protocols which improve upon the collusion resistance properties of the protocol described in [1].

3   Our Approach

We describe our family of key distribution protocols in Section 3.1 and give a detailed analysis of their collusion resistance in Section 3.2.

3.1   Key Distribution Protocols

Initially, the sender assigns a unique kl-bit identifier to each receiver where k and l are chosen according to network parameters. The identifier is viewed as k pieces of length ℓ bits. For each piece, a sender maintains 2^ℓ keys, one key for each possible value of ℓ bits. A key is represented as $K_i^{b_1 b_2 \cdots b_\ell}$ for the ith piece, $1 \le i \le k$ and $b_j \in \{0,1\}$ for $1 \le j \le \ell$. The values of k and ℓ are chosen depending on the desired collusion resistance or the corresponding network diameter.

Now, if the identifier of a receiver t is $t_1 t_2 \cdots t_k$ then, $t_1, t_2 \ldots t_k$ are each l-bit values. For each of these t_i's in the receiver's identifier, the sender gives the receiver the key that corresponds to the l-bit value from the 2^ℓ keys that it stored in i^{th} position. For example, if $t_1 = 001$, then the sender gives the receiver the key, K_1^{001} from the $K_1^{2^\ell}$ keys that are associated with the first identifier location. Thus, in this key distribution protocol, the user stores k keys per-sender and the sender stores $k2^\ell$ keys. When $k = \log N$ and $l = 1$, then, the above protocol is the same that is described in [1]. Furthermore, for different values of k and l we get a different member from this family of key distribution protocols.

Using our protocols, we achieve authentication using an approach that is similar to that described in [1]. We describe the authentication approach for unicast and multicast communication. For unicast, the sender computes an XOR of the all keys held by the user and uses this combined secret to compute the message authentication code, e.g., by using SHA-1, for the message. For multicast, the sender computes several message authentication codes using each of the keys that are in the union of all keys held by the multicast receivers. A user verifies those signatures for which it has the corresponding signing keys to detect message tampering. In the next section, we analyze the collusion resistance of these protocols and show that they perform well in most practical scenarios.

3.2   Collusion Resistance of Our Protocols

Suppose that a message M from source s to destination t is traversing a path P with $u_1, u_2, \cdots, u_d$ as the intermediate nodes in the path. We wish to guarantee that M cannot be tampered with even if all the d intermediate nodes collude. For this we will compute the desired value of ℓ. We use K_{st} to denote the set of keys used by a sender s to sign the message for a receiver t.

Let X_i denote the random variable that the intermediate node u_i can tamper the signature with respect to key K_{st}^j where j denotes the jth key from K_{st}. From our key distribution protocol described in Section 3.1, we have: $E[X_i] = 1/2^\ell$.

Now, let $X = \sum_{i=1}^d X_i$, then, X denotes the random variable that any of the d intermediate nodes have success in tampering with the signature of key K_{st}^j. Assuming independence, it also holds that using Chernoff bounds, that, $E[X \ge 1] \le e^{\frac{-2^\ell}{2d}}$. Let E_π be the event that all the signatures can be tampered along a path π. Then, $\Pr[E_\pi] \le \exp\{-\frac{2^\ell k}{2d}\}$.

Let E be the event that there exists some path of length d over signatures can be tampered. The number of paths of length d can be at most n^{d+1} since any node of the path can be chosen in n ways. Thus, applying the union bound of probability we have: $\Pr[E] = \Pr[\cup_\pi E_\pi] \leq \sum_\pi \Pr[E_\pi] \leq n^{d+1} \cdot \exp\{-\frac{2^\ell k}{2d}\}$.

Choosing ℓ and k: From the above analysis, the value of ℓ and k depend on d. A cursory glance reveals that in fact d should be the diameter of the network. Considering logarithmic-diameter networks, for the event E to have a low probability, we require that $n^{d+1} \cdot \exp\{-\frac{2^\ell k}{2d}\} \leq n^{-c}$ for some constant $c > 1$. Simplifying, we require that $(d+1)\log n - 2^\ell k/2d < -c\log n$ or $2^\ell k > O(d^2 \log n)$. By letting $k = O(\log n)$, we can choose $\ell = O(\log d)$. With these values of k and ℓ, it now implies that for an n-node network, nodes have to choose identifiers of length at most $O(\log n \log d)$ bits.

4 Results

We analyze the performance of our proposed family of key distribution protocols with respect to the protocol from [1]. We show that the collusion resistance in our protocols, for most practical networks with a given diameter, is better than the protocol from [1]. Our results aid a system designer in choosing an appropriate protocol based on the network diameter and/or the probability of collusion among nodes.

Our experiments were simulated on random network sizes with different diameters and averaged over 1000 trials. In Figure 1, we show the percentage of the signatures that are compromised for networks with diameters: $\log N/2$, $\log N$ and $2\log N$ for a total of N users. This percentage represents the number of forged signatures that can be generated by the colluding users. For this comparison, we chose the value of $2^l = \log N$, i.e., the number of keys stored by the sender as $\log^2 N$. We compare the performance of our scheme (termed, "Our Scheme") with the scheme from [1] (termed, "Gouda"). In Figure 1(a), the number of sender signatures that are compromised along a diameter are shown. We see that our protocol exhibits better collusion resistance even when the network

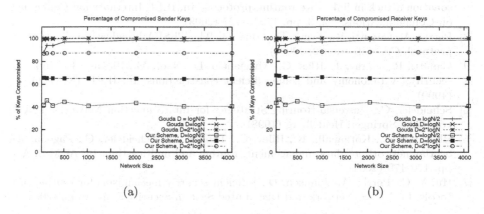

Fig. 1. Percentage of Keys Compromised for, (a) Sender (b) Receiver

diameter is as large as $2 \log N$. In Figure 1(b), we show the scenario where the keys held by an individual receiver are compromised by nodes that are along the path from the sender to the receiver. We observe that, even for large network diameters, the receiver still has some keys that are not compromised and hence, signature verification by the receiver can detect falsification attempts. Hence, these results show that for most practical situations our protocols provide the necessary collusion resistance.

We have compared the collusion resistance of different members of our family of protocols. Our results show that, by progressively choosing smaller/larger values of 2^l we are able to trade off collusion resistance with cost of signing the messages. Due to lack of space we do not present those results.

5 Conclusion and Future Work

In this work, we have addressed the issue of collusion resistance in symmetric key distribution protocols for authentication. Towards this, we have described a family of collusion resistant protocols where the desired collusion resistance can be achieved by choosing appropriate values for the parameters. Using probabilistic analysis and experimental evidence we have shown that our protocols offer the required collusion resistance for most practical network diameters. Currently, we are investigating the exact level of collusion resistance of different members of our protocols. This analysis will aid a system designer in choosing an appropriate member from our family of key distribution protocols.

References

[1] Gouda, M.G., Kulkarni, S.S., Elmallah, S.E.: Logarithmic keying of communication networks. In: 8th International Symposium on Stabilization, Safety, and Security of Distributed Systems, SSS-06 (2006)
[2] Huang, D., Sinha, A., Medhi, D.: A double authentication scheme to detect impersonation attack in link state routing protocols. In: IEEE International Conference on Communications, vol. 3, pp. 1723–1727 (2003)
[3] Perrig, A., Canetti, R., Tygar, D., Song, D.: The TESLA broadcast authentication protocol. Cryptobytes 5(2) (2002)
[4] Canetti, R., Garay, J., Itkis, G., Micciancio, D., Naor, M., Pinkas, B.: Multicast security: A taxonomy and some efficient constructions. In: IEEE INFOCOMM (1999)
[5] Scheideler, C.: Universal Routing Strategies for Interconnection Networks. LNCS, vol. 1390. Springer, Heidelberg (1998)
[6] Bhargava, A., Kothapalli, K., Riley, C., Thober, M., Scheideler, C.: Pagoda: An overlay network for data management, routing and multicasting. In: ACM SPAA, pp. 170–179 (2004)
[7] Hu, Y.-C., Perrig, A., Johnson, D.: Efficient security mechanisms for routing protocols. In: NDSS. Network and Distributed System Security Symposium (2003)

An Escalated Approach to Ant Colony Clustering Algorithm for Intrusion Detection System

L. Prema Rajeswari, A. Kannan, and R. Baskaran

Dept. of Computer Science and Engineering
College of Engineering
Anna University
Chennai-25
jlprema@cs.annauniv.edu, kannan@annauniv.edu,
baaski@cs.annauniv.edu

Abstract. Intrusion detection systems are increasingly a key part of systems defense. Various approaches to intrusion detection are currently being used, but they are relatively ineffective. Constructing and maintaining a misuse detection system is very labor-intensive since attack scenarios and patterns need to be analyzed and categorized, and the corresponding rules and patterns need to be carefully hand-coded. Thus data mining can be used to ease this inconvenience. This paper proposes a multiple level hybrid classifier for an intrusion detection system that uses a combination of tree classifiers which rely on labeled training data and applies an Ant colony clustering algorithm for mixed data. The main advantage of this approach is that the system can be trained with unlabelled data and is capable of detecting previously "unseen" attacks. Verification tests have been carried out by using the 1999 KDD Cup data set. From this work, it is observed that significant improvement has been achieved from the viewpoint of both high intrusion detection rate and reasonably low false alarm rate.

Keywords: Intrusion Detection, Data Mining, Multiple-level decision tree, Ant colony Clustering.

1 Introduction

As network-based computer systems play increasingly vital role in modern society, security of network systems has become more important than before. It is difficult to keep the system safe by static safeguards like firewall. As an active defense technology, an Intrusion Detection System (IDS) attempts to identify existing attack patterns and recognize new intrusion, and hence becomes an indispensable component in security architecture.

However, the existing intrusion detection methods, including misuse detection and anomaly detection [1][2], are generally incapable of adapting detection systems to the change of circumstance, which causes a high false positive rate. Moreover traditional Intrusion Detection methods can only detect known intrusion since they classify instances by what they have learned. However, the necessity to build an adaptive IDS with self-learning abilities has become a hot spot in security field [3]. In this paper, a

S. Rao et al. (Eds.): ICDCN 2008, LNCS 4904, pp. 393–400, 2008.

multiple level hybrid classifier for an intrusion detection system that uses a combination of tree classifier and an Ant colony clustering algorithm for mixed data to distinguish intrusions from legal behaviors effectively. At the first level, the data are split into normal, DOS, PROBE and "others" (a new class label containing both U2R and R2L). The second level splits the "others" into its corresponding U2R and R2L, while the third level classifies the attacks into its individual specific attacks.

The subsequent sections are organized as follows. In Section 2, we first present a general survey in the field of misuse detection and anomaly detection in network intrusion detection. Section 3, describes the systems architecture of the new multiple level hybrid classifier. Section 4, gives a brief introduction on both decision tree [4] and enhanced fast heuristic clustering algorithm [5]. In Section 5, we discuss the results and its possible implications. Conclusions and plans for future works are given in Section 6.

2 Literature Survey

The research on IDS carried out many of the current researchers who are interested in network security. A Data Mining based Adaptive Intrusion Detection Model (DMAIDM) is presented in [5] with several data mining techniques. This DMAIDM applies a Fast Heuristic Clustering Algorithm for mixed data (FHCAM) to distinguish intrusions from legal behaviors efficiently and an Attribute - Constrained based Fuzzy Mining Algorithm (ACFMA) to construct intrusion Pattern-database automatically. However, some parameters of DMAIDM are still based on limited statistic data and knowledge of domain experts.

There are many clustering algorithms that are found in the literature [6][7][8]. However these classical clustering algorithms, whether based on K-means or K-medoids have two shortcomings in clustering large network data sets namely number of clusters dependency and lacking of the ability of dealing with the character attributes in the network transactions. Among these the number of clusters dependency suggests that the value of K is very critical to the clustering result and should be fixed before clustering and the lacking of the ability to deal with the character attributes is focuses on the similarity of character attribute.(e.g. Protocol) is difficultly computed by K-means or K-medoids. Hence it is necessary to propose a new clustering technique that provides a solution to these problems.

MADAM ID [9] is another work which utilized data mining for adaptive and automatic construction of intrusion detection models. The key idea in that paper is the use of auditing programs to extract an extensive set of features that describe each host session or network connection, and to apply data mining programs to learn rules that accurately capture the characteristics of normal activities and intrusions. In MADAM ID, the goal of constructing a classification model is to apply a serial of attribute tests so that the dataset can be divided into "pure" subsets, i.e., each in a target class. This target class can be normal/abnormal judgment, different intrusion categories or specific intrusion types. In particular, MADAM ID used C4.5 algorithm [4] to construct one decision tree where each node of the tree specifies a test on an attribute, and each branch of the node corresponds to one of its values. The leaves are the classification results. In contrast to using only a single tree classifier to classify intrusions, as that in MADAM ID, a multiple level tree classifier was recently proposed in [10][11][12] to design an IDS, which contains 3 levels of decision tree classification. At the first level, the data are split into normal, DOS, PROBE and "others" (a new class label containing both U2R and R2L). The second level splits the others" into its corresponding U2R and R2L, while the third level classifies the attacks into its individual specific attacks. It was shown to be easy to design and very efficient in detecting old attacks. However, serious shortcoming of this approach is its high false alarm rate as well as low detection rate for new attacks.

In this paper, we propose a new multiple level hybrid classifier for an intrusion detection system that uses a combination of tree classifier that uses enhanced C4.5 algorithm and applies an ant colony clustering algorithm for mixed data to distinguish intrusions from legal behaviors efficiently to further reduce the false alarm rate to an industrially acceptable level while maintaining the low false negative rate.

3 System Architecture

The multi level hybrid IDS architecture proposed in this paper is presented schematically in figure 1. In this hybrid approach, classification is done in multiple levels and KDD cup 1999 data set is used. Enhanced C4.5 algorithm is used for classification. In the first level DoS and PROBE types of attacks are classified from the data set. U2R, R2L and normal connections are grouped as 'OTHERS'. This is because U2R and R2L attacks have close resemblance with the normal connections. This step helps to reduce the false alarm rate and improve the detection rate. In the next level normal connections are separated from the data set and grouped as normal and abnormal connections.

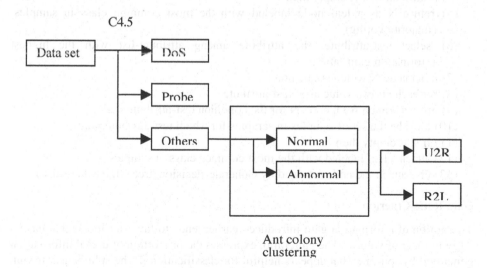

Fig. 1. System Architecture

This is done using the ant colony-clustering algorithm as explained in section 3.2. The clustering algorithm groups the new types of attacks into the abnormal category. This module performs the anomaly detection. In the next level, the abnormal group is classified into U2R and R2L using the classifier. Enhanced C4.5 algorithm is used for classification.

3.1 Enhanced C4.5 Algorithm

A classifier, which is a function (or model) that assigns a class label to each data item described by a set of attributes, is often needed in these classification tasks. There are quite a few machine-learning approaches for generating classification models, among which decision tree learning [4] is a typical one. Figure 2 pictorially represents the misuse detection module. In this paper, an Enhanced C4.5, a later version of the ID3 algorithm, has been used to construct the decision trees for classification. The specific algorithm is given below

Algorithm: Generate_decision_tree. Generate a decision tree from the given training data.

Input: training samples, represented by discrete/continuous attributes; the set of candidate attributes, attribute-list.

Output: a decision tree

Method:

    (1) create a node N;

    (2) if samples are all of the same class, C, then

    (3) return N as a leaf node labeled with the class C;

    (4) if attribute-list is empty then

    (5) return N as a leaf node labeled with the most common class in samples; (majority voting)

    (6) select test-attribute, the attribute among attribute-list with the highest information gain ratio ;

    (7) label node N with test-attribute;

    (8) for each known value ai of test-attribute

    (9) grow a branch from node N for the condition test-attribute = ai;

    (10) let si be the set of samples in samples for which test-attribute = ai;

    (11) if si is empty then

    (12) attach a leaf labeled with the most common class in samples;

    (13) else attach the node returned by Generate_decision_tree (si, attribute-list).

Gain Ratio Criterion

The notion of information gain introduced earlier tends to favor attributes that have a large number of values. The gain ratio, expresses the proportion of useful information generated by split, i.e. that appears helpful for classification. If the split is near trivial, split information will be small and this ratio will be unstable. To avoid this, the gain

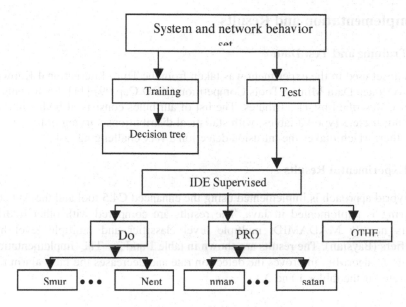

Fig. 2. Misuse Detection Component

ratio criterion selects a test to maximize the ratio above, subject to the constraint that the information gain must be large, at least as great as the average gain over all tests examined.

3.2 Ant Colony Clustering Algorithm

Ants are model organisms for bio-simulations due to both their relative individual simplicity and their complex group behaviors. Colonies have evolved for collectively performing tasks that are far beyond the capacities of individual ants. They do so without direct communication or centralized control. Given points in some space, often a high-dimensional space, group the points into a small number of clusters, each cluster consisting of points that are "near" in some sense.

Ant colony algorithm

- Initialize randomly the ant positions
- Repeat
- For each ant (i) do
- Move ant (i)
- If ant (i) does not carry any object Then look at 8-cell neighborhood and pick up object according to pick-up algorithm
- Else (ant (i) is already carrying an object O) look at 8-cell neighborhood and drop O according to drop-off algorithm
- Until stopping criterion

4   Implementation and Results

4.1   Training and Test Data

The dataset used in the experiment was taken from the Third International Knowledge Discovery and Data Mining Tools Competition (KDD Cup 99) [11]. Each connection record is described by 41 attributes. The list of attributes consists of both continuous-type and discrete type variables, with statistical distributions varying drastically from each other, which makes the intrusion detection a very challenging task.

4.2   Experimental Results

The hybrid approach is implemented using the enhanced C4.5 tool and the Ant colony clustering is implemented in Java. The results are compared with other traditional models namely MADAMID, multiple level classifier and multiple level hybrid classifiers (Baysian). The results are shown in table 1 and 2. The implementation of ant colony algorithm improves the detection rate and decreases the false alarm rate as interpreted in the tables 1 and 2.

Table 1. Comparison of Old Attacks Detection Rates (%)

	MADAM ID	Multiple level classifier	Multiple level Hybrid Classifier (Bayesian)	Multiple level Hybrid Classifier (Ant Colony)
DoS	79.9	99.11	99.19	99.35
PROBE	97.0	96.76	99.71	99.7
U2R	75.0	76.92	66.67	73.2
R2L	60.0	65.46	69.50	71.1
Normal	N/A	42.73	90.89	95.42

Table 2. Comparisons of New Attacks Detection Rates (%)

	MADAM ID	Multiple level classifier	Multiple level Hybrid Classifier (Bayesian)	Multiple level Hybrid Classifier (Ant Colony)
DoS	24.3	37.44	83.59	83.32
PROBE	96.7	88.54	70.60	70.81
U2R	81.8	41.94	28.06	35.93
R2L	5.9	9.10	28.53	51.04

It was shown that this new approach is very efficient in detecting intrusions with a extremely low false negative rate of 3.37%, while keeping an acceptable level of false-alarm rate of 9.1%. Such an excellent intrusion detection performance with appropriate trade-off of false negative and false positive rates has never been reported in the literature, to the authors' knowledge.

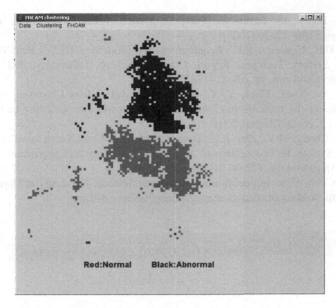

Fig. 3. Snapshot of the ant colony clustering

5 Conclusion and Future Work

A multiple-level hybrid classification model combining decision trees and ant colony clustering has been proposed. The novel feature of this approach is the combination of both supervised learning (tree classifier design) and unsupervised learning (clustering analysis). Application of data mining technology in anomaly detection is a hot spot in research of IDS. To facilitate adaptability and extensibility, ant colony clustering is used to classify the normal and abnormal. Experimental results with this new scheme on KDD Cup 1999 Data were compared with other popular approaches such as MADAM ID and multiple-level tree classifier. However further works may be done to improve the detection rate of U2R and R2L.

However, a weakness observed is that it did not perform so well for detecting U2R attacks. This is the trade off for the high detection rate of other attack types. Furthermore the low number of instances for U2R connections in the training and testing data makes the detection rate of U2R negligible compared to other attacks. • Detection rates of U2R attack may be further increased by focusing more research on the U2R training data.

References

1. Yu, Z.-x., Chen, J.-R., Zhu, T.-Q.: A Novel Adaptive Intrusion Detection System Based on Data Mining. In: Proceedings of the fourth international Conference on Machine learning and Cybernetics, Guangzhou, pp. 2390–2395 (August 2005)
2. Axelsson, S.: Intrusion Detection Systems: A Survey and Taxonomy. Technical Report No 9, Dept. of Computer Engineering, Chalmers, University of Technology, Sweden, pp. 9–15 (2000)

3. Denning, D.E.: An Intrusion Detection Model. IEEE Transactions on Software Engineering 51(8), 12–26 (2003)
4. Denning, D.E., Neumann, P.G.: Requirements and Model for IDES-A Real-Time Intrusion Detection System, Technical Report, Computer Science Laboratory, SRI International, Menlo Park, California, pp. 58–63 (1985)
5. Chen, L., Xu, X.-H., Chen, Y.-X.: An Adaptive Ant Colony Clustering Algorithm. In: Proceedings of the third international conference on Machine Learning and Cybernetics, Shanghai, pp. 26–29 (August 2004)
6. Xiang, C., Chong, M.Y., Zhu, H.L.: Design of Multiple-Level Tree Classifier for Intrusion Detection System. In: Proceedings of 2004 IEEE Conference on Cybernetics and Intelligent Systems, Singapore, pp. 872–877 (December 2004)
7. KDD Cup 1999 Data, Information and Computer Science, University of California, Irvine (1999), http://kdd.ics.uci.edu/databases/kddcup99/kddcup99.html

Interplay of Processing and Routing in Aggregate Query Optimization for Sensor Networks

Niki Trigoni, Alexandre Guitton, and Antonios Skordylis

Computing Laboratory, University of Oxford, Oxford OX1 3QD, UK

Abstract. This paper presents a novel approach to processing continuous aggregate queries in sensor networks, which lifts the assumption of tree-based routing. Given a query workload and a special-purpose gateway node where results are expected, the query optimizer exploits query correlations in order to generate an energy-efficient distributed evaluation plan. The proposed optimization algorithms identify common query sub-aggregates, and propose common routing structures to share the sub-aggregates at an early stage. Moreover, they avoid routing sub-aggregates of the same query through long-disjoint paths, thus further reducing the communication cost of result propagation. The proposed algorithms are fully-distributed, and are shown to offer significant communication savings compared to existing tree-based approaches. A thorough experimental evaluation shows the benefits of the proposed techniques for a variety of query workloads and network topologies.

1 Introduction

Recent advances in micro-electro-mechanical systems (MEMS) have enabled the inexpensive production and deployment of nodes with communication, computation, storage and sensing capabilities. Sensor nodes can be deployed in large areas to monitor the ambient environment, and they communicate their readings to one or more basestations (referred to as *gateways*) in a wireless multihop manner.

A typical way of extracting information from a sensor network is to disseminate declarative aggregate queries from a gateway node to sensor nodes, asking them to periodically monitor the environment, and return aggregate results in regular rounds. An example of such long-running queries is *"select avg(temperature) from Sensors where loc in Region every 10 min"*. Since nodes are battery-powered, energy preservation is a major consideration in system design, as it directly impacts the lifetime of the network. Recent studies have shown that radio communication is significantly more expensive than computation or sensing in most existing sensor node platforms. Hence, the main consideration in designing query processing algorithms is to minimize the communication overhead of forwarding query results from the sources to the gateway node. The cost of disseminating query information into the network is assumed to have a secondary role for long-running queries, since query dissemination occurs once, whereas result propagation occurs repeatedly at regular rounds. Moreover, many monitoring scenarios apply a pure push model, in which nodes are programmed to proactively send

S. Rao et al. (Eds.): ICDCN 2008, LNCS 4904, pp. 401–415, 2008.

specific information to the gateway. The communication cost of result propagation thus dominates the communication cost of query dissemination.

Tree-based routing has been proposed as an energy-efficient mechanism for processing aggregate queries in sensor networks [6,8]. Tree construction is performed using simple flooding algorithms [8], data-centric reinforcement strategies [6] or energy-aware route selection schemes [13,16]. After a tree is constructed, sensor nodes forward their readings along the paths of the tree, evaluating partial query results at intermediate nodes. The aforementioned research focused on processing a *single aggregate query given a routing tree*; the tree is generated using a tree selection scheme and is thereafter used for result propagation. More recent research has focused on *optimizing multiple aggregate queries given a routing tree* [12]. Query commonalities are taken into account to reduce the communication cost of result propagation, but without making any attempt to select suitable tree routes [12].

Unlike previous approaches, this paper considers the more general problem of multi-query optimization lifting the assumption of an existing aggregation tree. The objective is to find efficient routes that minimize the communication cost of executing multiple aggregate queries, by studying the interplay between the processing and routing aspects of query evaluation. Unlike previous work, there is no limitation for the selected routes to form a tree structure. The only requirement is that the optimizer must operate in a distributed manner, and should scale gracefully with the network size. In summary, the contributions of this paper are as follows:

- A demonstration of the interplay between the processing and routing aspects of single- and multi-query optimization (Section 2).
- A formal definition of the multi-query optimization problem for aggregate queries which lifts the assumption of a communication tree used in [6,8,12].
- Two novel heuristic algorithms, SegmentToGateway (STG) and SegmentToSegment (STS), for optimizing multiple aggregate queries (Section 4), by carefully interweaving routing and processing decisions at each node. Existing query evaluation algorithms use tree routes constructed independent of the query workload. Given a tree, they focus on in-network partial processing of one query [8,6] or multiple queries [12]. STG and STS are the first algorithms that select suitable routes for a workload of multiple queries, and carefully interweave routing and processing in the optimization process.
- Experimental results that compare the performance of the proposed algorithms with the most efficient existing algorithm for multi-query optimization [12] (Section 5). The benefits of STG and STS are demonstrated under a variety of query workloads and network topologies, both in terms of network-wide communication cost and in terms of local communication cost in the critical area around the gateway.

2   Illustrative Examples

The potential advantages of carefully selecting a routing and processing plan for executing aggregate queries are shown in the following examples. Figure 1 shows an example of processing a single aggregate query, which asks for the sum of all readings in

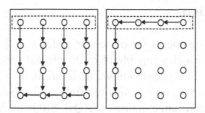

Fig. 1. Example with one query

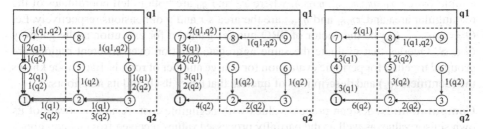

Fig. 2. Example with two queries: (i) the left plan is based on a randomly selected tree, (ii) the middle plan is the output of STG, and (iii) the right plan is the output of STS

the dotted rectangular area. Notice that a total number of 15 messages are sent along the left minimum-hop tree of Figure 1, whereas only 6 messages are forwarded along the carefully selected right tree of the same figure. The right routing tree is better not only in terms of total communication cost, but also in terms of communication cost in the critical area around the gateway. Informally, the benefit of the second plan is that it aggregates all readings of a query early and avoids sending different subaggregates through disjoint paths.

Figure 2 illustrates the benefits of building a suitable execution plan in the case of processing multiple *count* queries. For ease of understanding the graphs also include node IDs and messages forwarded through network links. Messages have the format $v(q_1, \ldots, q_n)$, which denotes that value v contributes to queries $q_1, \ldots, q_n$. The left plan does not exploit query commonalities, and therefore fails to aggregate together readings (of nodes 8 and 9) within the intersection area. The middle plan incurs smaller communication cost, because it exploits query commonalities, but still forwards the subaggregate of the intersection area separately all the way to the gateway. This behavior is similar to the first heuristic proposed in this paper called SegmentToGateway (STG). The right plan has an optimal behavior because it exploits query commonalities and it avoids sending partial aggregates through long disjoint paths. Notice that the optimal plan does not follow a tree structure, as node 8 sends the partial aggregate of the intersection area to two parents. The intersection partial aggregate is thus merged immediately with the other two query subaggregates and, eventually, only two partial results are sent to the gateway. This would be the plan identified by the second proposed algorithm, called SegmentToSegment (STS). Although the examples above use a grid topology, both STG and STS are designed to work well for random topologies with potential empty areas (or holes).

3   Problem Definition

Sensors and queries: Consider a set of sensor nodes $S = \{s_1, \ldots, s_n\}$ with known location coordinates. Two nodes capable of bi-directional wireless communication are referred to as *neighbors*. Every node knows its location, as well as the identifiers and locations of its neighbors. We consider a commonly used subclass of aggregate queries, which we refer to as spatial range queries (SRQs). SRQs evaluate the aggregate *aggr* of all sensors in a rectangular area, where *aggr* is a distributive or algebraic aggregate function (*e.g. sum, count, avg, max, min* but not *median*) [8,4]. A query is denoted by a tuple $(aggr, x_0, y_0, x_{dim}, y_{dim})$, where x_0 and y_0 are bottom left coordinates of the rectangular area and x_{dim} and y_{dim} are the area's x and y dimensions respectively. Let $Q = [q_1, \ldots, q_m]$ be the vector of SRQ queries gathered for execution at the gateway $G \in S$. Queries that evaluate the same aggregate function over different regions are grouped together for periodic evaluation for a large number of rounds. Each node knows the identifiers (q_i) and descriptions of queries that *cover* itself and its neighbors.

Computation: Nodes can process values with negligible cost. A node is aware of its own sensor value, as well as the partially processed values received from its neighbors. We refer to these values as input values. A node processes the input values taking into account how they contribute to the query results, and converts them into output values. The contribution of a value (either input or output) to the query results is referred to as *semantics*. In this paper, the propagation of data across an edge will be represented as a directed edge, labeled with the pair (value,semantics). For uniformity, the generation of a reading locally at a node is also represented as a directed edge (pointing to the node, but with a dangling starting point). Such dangling edges are referred to as *initial directed edges* and will be drawn in bold.

Computation and communication: Nodes receive input values from their neighbors and the local sensors, and generate output values at a negligible cost. One-hop data propagation is represented as a directed edge, labeled with the pair *(value, semantics)*, where the *semantics* denotes how the *value* contributes to each one of the queries. For uniformity, the generation of a reading locally at a node is also represented as a directed edge with a dangling starting point. Such edges are called *initial directed edges*.

Let u_i be the sensor reading generated locally at a node s_i. The semantics of u_i consists of the set of queries that access the particular node, and is represented as a bit vector of size m (equal to the number of queries). The j-th entry of the vector is 1 if query q_j accesses node s_i, and is 0 otherwise. Vectors that determine the contribution of a value to the queries are referred to as *coefficient* vectors (CVs). For example, in Figure 3, the initial directed edge of node s_2, which holds information about the locally generated reading, is labeled $(1, [110])$ to denote that the local sensor value 1 contributes to the queries q_1 and q_2, and does not contribute to the value of q_3. The result of a query q_j must be equal to the aggregate of all values of initial directed edges factored by their j-th coefficients, *i.e.* $Result(q_j) = aggr_{i=1}^{n}(u_i * CV_{u_i}[j])$, where n is the number of sensor nodes.

As the initial (value,CV) pairs are pushed towards the gateway, they can be partially processed at intermediate nodes. Let $InAnnot = [(v_1, CV_{v_1}), \ldots, (v_k, CV_{v_k})]$ be the

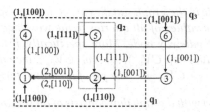

Fig. 3. NoOptimization: Node 2 linearly reduces the three input (value,CV) pairs into two output pairs

labels of the input edges and $OutAnnot = [(v_1', CV_{v_1'}), \ldots, (v_\ell', CV_{v_\ell'})]$ be the labels of the output edges of a sensor node. In any query plan, there should be no loss of information as data is routed through a node, *i.e.* the result of a query when evaluated based on the input edges must be equal to its result based on the output edges. Formally, each node must satisfy the *content preservation property*, *i.e.* for every query $j = 1, \ldots, m$, $aggr_{i=1}^k (v_i * CV_{v_i}[j]) = aggr_{i=1}^\ell (v_i' * CV_{v_i'}[j])$. This property is satisfied in Figure 3.

In a candidate plan, (i) each output (value,CV) pair of a node is computable as some function of the input pairs; and (ii) it should be possible to evaluate all query results based on the gateway's input pairs. The assumption in this paper is that a constant number of bits is dedicated to storing the semantics (CV - Coefficient Vector) of a value. For scalability, a node can use CVs of variable length to mark only queries affected by the values forwarded through the node. For simplicity, however, we consider a fixed CV length (equal to the number of queries m) for all nodes, and defer the study of compressing CVs to future work.

As queries are evaluated periodically over multiple rounds, the propagated values can potentially change at every round. Depending on whether we also allow the semantics of these values to change, we distinguish two different models of value propagation: static and dynamic. In the *static* model, the semantics remains unchanged at each edge, and it is propagated through the directed edge only once, as opposed to the corresponding value, which is propagated at every round. In the dynamic model, values must always be annotated with their semantics, to reflect changes due to network dynamics or variable sensor updates.

The assumption in this paper is a dynamic model in which a constant number of bits is dedicated to storing the semantics (CV - Coefficient Vector) of a value.

Content Preservation Principle: Let $InAnnot = [(v_1, CV_{v_1}), \ldots, (v_k, CV_{v_k})]$ be the labels of the input edges and $OutAnnot = [(v_1', CV_{v_1'}), \ldots, (v_\ell', CV_{v_\ell'})]$ be the labels of the output edges of a sensor node. In any query execution plan, there should be no loss of information as data is routed through a node. Informally, the result of a query when evaluated based on the input edges must be equal to its result based on the output edges. Formally, $\forall j = 1, \ldots, m$, $aggr_{i=1}^k (v_i * CV_{v_i}[j]) = aggr_{i=1}^\ell (v_i' * CV_{v_i'}[j])$. We call $aggr_{i=1}^k (v_i * CV_{v_i}[j])$ the *projection* of query q_j onto $[(v_1, CV_{v_1}), \ldots, (v_k, CV_{v_k})]$. The projection of a query onto the input edges of a node must be equal to its projection onto the output edges. This property is satisfied in the network of Figure 3.

Theorem 1. *If every node in the graph satisfies the content preservation property except for the gateway, then the values of all queries in the workload are given by the annotated input edges of the gateway node. More specifically, if the gateway has k input edges labeled with the pairs $(v_1, CV_{v_1}), \ldots, (v_k, CV_{v_k})$, then the value of a query q_j is $Result(q_j) = aggr_{i=1}^k (v_i * CV_{v_i}[j])$. The proof is omitted for space reasons.*

Optimization goal: *Start with a graph that consists of all sensor nodes and one directed dangling edge per node, carrying its source value. Minimize the number of directed edges that we need to add in the graph (excluding the initial dangling edges) such that the content preservation property is satisfied at each node.*

4   Algorithms

We now study the existing approach for processing aggregate queries, and propose two novel energy-efficient algorithms to improve its performance. All three algorithms consist of two phases: (i) a network configuration phase and (ii) a result propagation phase. The former phase is repeated every time the node connectivity graph changes, *e.g.* in case of link or node failures. The proposed heuristics are query-sensitive, and thus they also repeat the configuration phase every time the query workload changes. The role of the former phase is to set up routes to prepare the ground for the second phase, i.e. the forwarding of results to the gateway in regular rounds. The initial state of the graph in a given round is common for all algorithms: a node has an incoming edge annotated with an input pair (value,CV), as discussed in Section 3. The entries of the input CV denote which queries access that node.

4.1   The *NoOptimization* Algorithm

The existing state-of-the-art in optimizing multiple aggregate queries is the ECReduced algorithm proposed in [12]. It outperforms Tag [8] and Cougar [15] in the context of multiple queries, since these approaches were originally designed to process a single query, as shown in [12]. ECReduced is therefore a good basis for comparing the two proposed algorithms. In this paper, it is hereafter referred to as *NoOptimization*, to denote that it does not jointly optimize routing and processing taking into account the query workload. NoOptimization uses a predefined tree, and only optimizes the processing aspect of query execution.

Network Configuration Phase: Control messages are first flooded into the network, and every node selects as its *parent* the neighbor in the shortest path to the gateway node. If there are more than one candidate parents, the node selects its parent in one of the following ways: (i) randomly, (ii) the first node from which it received a query request, (iii) the node with which it consistently maintains better communication. In the experimental evaluation of Section 5, *NoOptimization* is implemented as in [12], *i.e.* breaking ties by random parent selection. Dynamic node or link failures are handled by a local flooding phase to repair affected tree routes, as in AODV [2].

Result Propagation Phase: The routes of query results are predefined in the network configuration phase, and the only decision that a node needs to make in this phase is how to convert its input (value,CV) pairs into output pairs. All output pairs, irrespective of their content, are forwarded to the node's *parent*. A naive application of the in-network aggregation technique to processing multiple queries would be to forward one partial aggregate value per query, and denote the query identifier in the coefficient vector. The NoOptimization algorithm uses a more elaborate technique to reduce the number of propagated (value,CV) pairs. In the case of algebraic aggregate functions, like *sum*, *count* or *avg*, a node running NoOptimization computes a basis of its input coefficient vectors and sends to its *parent* the basis vectors (and corresponding values) [12]. An example of the effect of linear reduction is shown in Figure 3, where node 2 receives three input (value,CV) pairs and reduces them to two output pairs. The linear reduction technique yields the optimal solution for these aggregates in terms of communication cost. The NoOptimization algorithm, which is used as a basis for comparison, is to our knowledge the most sophisticated existing approach to processing multiple algebraic aggregate queries.

In the simplest approach, every node sends a partial aggregate of each query for which it has data to its *parent*. If an input CV refers to q queries, it is split to q different CVs referring to one query each. Input CVs with one query are mapped to identical output CVs. Duplicate output CVs are eliminated, and the corresponding values are partially aggregated. The output (value,CV) pairs are sent to the *parent* node selected during the network configuration phase. This is a naive extension of the TAG approach for processing multiple queries.

4.2 The *SegmentToGateway (STG)* Algorithm

The first proposed heuristic algorithm exploits the fact that the intersecting query rectangles naturally divide the network into smaller segments. A *segment* S is a maximal set of nodes, s.t. $\forall s_i \in S, s_j \in S$, s_i and s_j are covered by the same set of queries and they are *internally connected*, *i.e.* there exists path from s_i to s_j consisting only of nodes in S. For example, the queries in Figure 5 form five segments $\{s_1, s_4\}$, $\{s_2\}$, $\{s_3, s_5, s_6\}$, $\{s_7\}$ and $\{s_8, s_9\}$. A segment S (or a node n in S) is represented by a bit vector that denotes which queries cover the nodes of S (*e.g.*, $SGVector(\{s_3, s_5, s_6\})$=[010]). STG performs aggregation of local sensor data by building a tree per segment, instead of building a tree per query, or a tree for all queries. The segment tree is rooted at the *SGLeader*, i.e. the node with the smallest hop count to the gateway. We refer to: (i) the number of hops from the SGLeader to the gateway as the *SGDistance* and (ii) the number of hops from a node to its SGLeader as the *distToSGLeader*. For instance, SGDistance(s_6)=2 and distToSGLeader(s_6)=1.

Network Configuration Phase: This is similar to the corresponding phase of the *NoOptimization* algorithm, except that in this case each node identifies not only a parent neighbor but also a SGParent (*i.e.*, a neighbor on a path to the SGLeader). Upon receiving a beacon message, a node updates the local list of neighbors and, if necessary, the *hopCount* value (as in NoOptimization). The next step depends on whether the beacon is sent from a node in the same or in a different segment. In the former case, the node compares the local knowledge about the *SGLeader* with that in the beacon. If the beacon knows of a *SGLeader* closer to the gateway (with smaller *SGDistance*), the local *SGDistance* value is updated and the sender node is selected to be the local

SGParent. In the latter case where a node receives a beacon from a node in a different segment, it realizes that it is on the border of the segment and thus it is eligible to become a *SGLeader*. It elects itself to be a *SGLeader* if its *hopCount* is smaller than the local *SGDistance*. The beacon message is updated accordingly and is rebroadcasted (Figure 4).

The cost of the network configuration phase of STG is similar to that of NoOptimization (or of TAG) (see Section 5). In addition, the insertion (or deletion) of queries has a local effect on segment formation, and does not require global network reconfiguration. Dynamic network failures are handled by adjusting the local repair mechanism used by NoOptimization to also update the segment-related state variables of nodes.

Result Propagation Phase: By the end of the network configuration phase, every node knows its parent and *SGParent*. In the result propagation phase, a node merges duplicate input CVs into the same output CV, aggregating values accordingly. An output (value,CV) pair is sent to the *SGParent* if and only if the CV is equal to the current node's *SGVector*. The remaining output (value,CV) pairs are forwarded to the *parent* node (after they have been linearly reduced in the case of algebraic aggregates). The gateway's neighbors send all their messages without exception directly to the gateway. Code for this phase is provided in the *send* command of Figure 4.

Discussion: STG identifies query commonalities (segments) and aggregates the values of all nodes within each segment separately following a mini-tree rooted at the *SGLeader*. The remaining values (whose CVs are not equal to the *SGVector*) are forwarded through the *parent* node (instead of the *SGParent*) and reach the gateway through the shortest path. By definition, STG performs better than NoOptimization.

4.3   The *SegmentToSegment (STS)* Algorithm

Although STG performs well in terms of merging readings of the same segment, it often fails to merge sub-aggregates of the same query that come from different segments. In the worst case, these sub-aggregates are propagated from the *SGLeader* nodes to the gateway through long disjoint paths. STS addresses the weakness of STG by sending messages towards neighbors that are likely to *reduce* them. STS manages to combine *segment-based* aggregation (introduced in STG), with merging of CVs from different segments, into a uniform mechanism.

Network Configuration Phase: The configuration phase of *STS* is similar to the corresponding phase of STG except that each node selects as a segment parent a node on the shortest (instead of on any) path to the SGLeader (Figure 4). In the flooding process, a node selects as its *SGParent* the node in the shortest path to the *SGLeader*, and stores the minimum distance to the *SGLeader* in the local variable *distToSGLeader*.

Result Propagation Phase: Initially, each node converts input to output (value,CV) pairs exactly as in NoOptimization and STG. In the latter algorithms, this processing step is followed by a well-defined routing step, namely NoOptimization forwards all output pairs to the *parent* node, whereas STG forwards them to either the *SGParent* or the *parent* node. It then interleaves two novel steps: 1) *neighbor-message matching*,

```
event TOS_MsgPtr RcvBeacon.rcv(TOSMsgPtr m)
{
  bool mustRebroadcastBeacon = FALSE;              else {// not equal vectors
  BeaconMsg * b = (BeaconMsg*)m → data;              if ((SGDistance > hopCount)
  addBeaconSenderToNeighbors(b);                     || (SGDistance == hopCount &&
  if (b → hopCount + 1 < hopCount) {                 b → source == parent &&
    mustRebroadcastBeacon = TRUE;                    b → source! = SGParent &&
    hopCount = b → hopCount + 1;                     closer(myLoc, leaderLoc))){
    parent = b → source;                               mustRebroadcastBeacon = TRUE;
  }                                                    SGParent = b → source;
  if (equalVectors(SG, b → SG)) {                      SGDistance = hopCount;
    if ((SGDistance > b → SGDistance)                  distToSGLeader = 0;
    || (SGDistance == b → SGDistance &&                leaderLoc = myLoc;
    b → distToSGLeader + 1 < distToSGLeader)      }}}
    || (SGDistance == b → SGDistance &&
    strictlyCloser(b → leaderLoc, leaderLoc)){
      mustRebroadcastBeacon = TRUE;
      SGParent = b → source;
      SGDistance = b → SGDistance;
      distToSGLeader = b → distToSGLeader + 1;
      leaderLoc = b → leaderLoc;
}}
```

Fig. 4. NesC code for the network configuration phase of STG (excl. lines in bold) and STS (incl. lines in bold)

which selects a suitable neighbor to forward each output pair, and 2) *message splitting*, which often splits the output pair before forwarding it.

Step 1: Neighbor-message matching. The idea behind the first feature is to forward output (value,CV) pairs towards nodes that are most likely to reduce them by merging them with their local or route-thru data. The first (value,CV) pair considered for matching is the one that contributes to most queries (with the greatest number of 1-bits in the CV). The process of matching it with the best neighbor node is detailed below:

Step 1.1: To ensure that messages are not forwarded away from the gateway, only neighbors closer to the gateway than the current node are considered, *i.e.* with lexicographically smaller (*hopCount,SGDistance,distToSGLeader,xCoord,yCoord*). For instance, node s_3 considers sending messages to s_2 (Figure 5). As an exception, a node also considers neighbors in the same segment that are not closer to the gateway, if (i) they are closer to their *SGLeader* and (ii) all queries that cover these nodes are also included in the message CV. For instance, s_3 also considers s_6 to forward its initial data $(1, [010])$ to, because *distToSGLeader*(s_6)<*distToSGLeader*(s_3) and the *SGVector*$(s_6) = [010]$ marks queries $\{q_2\}$ that are all marked in the message CV [010]. This exception cannot result in sending messages in cycles or away from the gateway, because the message is merged immediately with the receiving node's local data (input pairs of s_6 have equal CVs).

Step 1.2: Among neighbors selected in Step 1.1, consider only those that best match the message CV, *i.e.* which are covered by the maximum number of common queries with the message CV. If this number is 0 or the node is next to the gateway, send the message to its *parent*. Node s_3 has two candidate neighbors, s_2 and s_6, to send $(1,[010])$ (from Step 1.1). The *SGVectors* [011] and [010] of s_2 and s_6 both have one common query with the message CV ([010]). Among neighbors with equal number of common queries, select the one with the minimum number of queries (s_6).

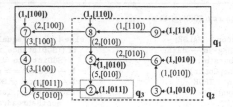

Fig. 5. Value-semantic pairs in the evaluation plan of the sum queries q_1, q_2 and q_3

Step 1.3: Among neighbors selected in Step 1.2, select the one with the lexicographically smaller (*SGDistance,distToSGLeader,xCoord,yCoord*). For instance, s_8 has two candidate neighbors s_5 and s_7 to send the output pair (2,[110]) to. Both have *SGDistance* equal to 2 and *distToSGLeader* equal to 0 (both nodes are segment leaders), so s_7 is selected because it has a smaller x coordinate.

Step 2: Message splitting. The rationale behind this step is that it is often beneficial to divide data into its components in order to give it greater potential for later merging. Most recent research efforts have focused on merging data to reduce their size. STS's novelty lies in offering further communication savings by means of data splitting. It is often beneficial to divide data into its components in order to give it greater potential for later merging. Let p be the pair considered for neighbor-message matching in the previous step. The pair p is split into two pairs p_1 and p_2, based on the *SGVector* of the selected neighbor. Assume that node s_8 chooses s_7 to forward $p = (2, [110])$ in Step 3. Notice that the CV of p has more queries (q_1 and q_2) than the SGVector of the selected neighbor ($SGVector(s_7) = [100]$ denotes that s_7 is covered only by q_1). In this case, p is split into two pairs, one contributing to the common queries $p_1 = (2, [100])$, and another contributing to the remaining queries $p_2 = (2, [010])$. Pair p_1 is sent to the selected neighbor and p_2 is re-inserted into the list of output pairs. During insertion, pairs with equal CVs are merged. If the list of (value,CV) pairs is not empty, steps 1 and 2 are repeated.

Discussion: Although STS is tailored specifically for optimizing spatial aggregate queries, two of its features - namely *neighbor-message matching* and *message splitting* - have broader applicability. For example, the idea of forwarding messages towards nodes that are most likely to reduce them is applicable in the context of optimizing GROUP-BY queries [10], where data is preferentially routed towards nodes that hold data belonging to the same group. By means of careful message routing, merging and splitting, STS ensures that all query subaggregates are merged together before they leave the query area, thus offering significant benefits wrt STG and NoOptimization.

The benefits of STS are more pronounced in the critical area around the gateway and increase with the number of nodes ensuring scalability (Section 5).

5 Experimental Evaluation

A thorough experimental evaluation was performed to compare the proposed heuristic algorithms with the existing *NoOptimization* approach using a home-grown simulator.

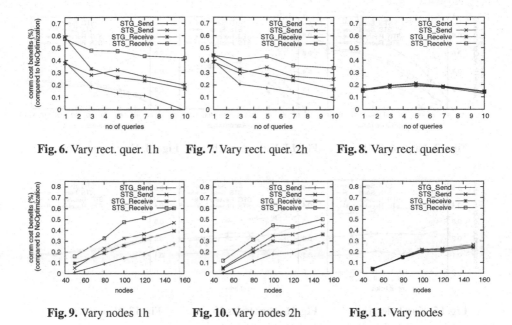

Fig. 6. Vary rect. quer. 1h   **Fig. 7.** Vary rect. quer. 2h   **Fig. 8.** Vary rect. queries

Fig. 9. Vary nodes 1h   **Fig. 10.** Vary nodes 2h   **Fig. 11.** Vary nodes

The experimental results below show the performance of the three algorithms varying: (i) the number of queries, (ii) the number of nodes, (iii) the radio communication range, and (iv) the number of holes (unpopulated areas in the network). The graphs below illustrate the communication benefits of STG and STS compared to NoOptimization. The benefit of STG is $(cost(NoOptimization) - cost(STG))/cost(NoOptimization)$ and the benefit of STS is defined similarly. It remains to define how the cost of an algorithm is calculated. In each graph two costs per algorithm are considered, the number of messages sent and the number of messages received during result propagation, thus resulting in four different measures of benefit (STG_Send, STS_Send, $STG\_Receive$ and $STS\_Receive$). Depending on which nodes are monitored, we provide three different types of graphs, those based on counts of messages sent (or received) (i) by nodes at most one hop away from the gateway (left), (ii) by nodes at most two hops away from the gateway (middle) and (iii) by all nodes in the network (right). The figure position and caption indicate whether global or local communication savings are considered.

The default simulation settings are as follows: We deploy 100 nodes uniformly at random in a 300m×300m network area. The radio communication range is set to 60m. The default query workload consists of five rectangular queries with randomly chosen dimensions ($x, y \in [30, 300]$). In our experiments below we vary the values of one parameter at a time, keeping the default values for the remaining parameters. Each point in a plot is drawn by averaging 40 repetitions in which we vary the query workload and network topologies within the scope of the experiment.

In the experiments below, the cost of the network configuration phase is very similar for the three algorithms, with NoOptimization sending 4%-10% less messages than STG and STS. This overhead is paid infrequently, and is counterbalanced by the benefits offered by STG and STS during the frequent result propagation phase.

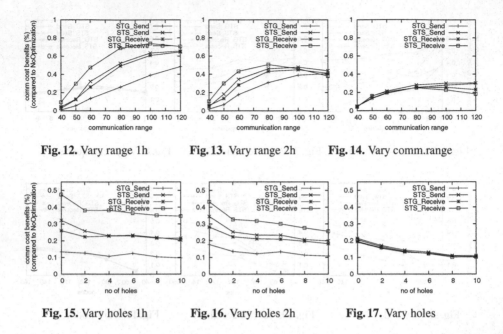

Fig. 12. Vary range 1h   **Fig. 13.** Vary range 2h   **Fig. 14.** Vary comm.range

Fig. 15. Vary holes 1h   **Fig. 16.** Vary holes 2h   **Fig. 17.** Vary holes

Vary number of queries: The first experiment illustrates the effect of the number of rectangular queries (sent together to the network for evaluation) on the communication benefits of STG and STS compared to NoOptimization. Figures 6, 7 and 8 concern traffic monitored within 1-hop, 2-hops, and max-hops (entire network) respectively. Notice that the two proposed algorithms perform similarly in the context of the entire network (Figure 8) obtaining a relative benefit of up to 20% compared to the *NoOptimization* algorithm. However, STS outperforms STG if we take into account only the traffic near the gateway (Figures 6 and 7). Notice in Figure 6 how STS saves up to 60% receive messages compared to *NoOptimization* when the number of queries is 1, and the gap between the benefits of STS and the benefits of STG increases as we increase the number of queries. The performance of STG for 10 queries falls considerably whereas STS continues to have a 42% advantage (for receive messages) and a 20% advantage (for send messages) over *NoOptimization* (Figure 6).

Vary number of nodes: Another experiment was done to measure the effect of the node cardinality in the performance of the proposed heuristic algorithms. Figures 9, 10 and 11 clearly show that as the number of nodes increases, and the network density increases, STG and STS demonstrate greater benefits compared to NoOptimization. Intuitively, when the number of nodes is very small (less than 60) the number of disjoing paths from a node to the gateway becomes small, leaving no flexibility for further reducing the communication cost. As the number of nodes increases, NoOptimization routes data through a large number of disjoint paths, whereas STG and STS manage to aggregate results earlier by selecting suitable common paths.

Vary communication range: The next step is to monitor the role of the radio communication range in the performance of the three algorithms (Figures 12, 13 and 14).

The increase in network connectivity (without increasing the number of nodes) initially increases the benefits of STS and STG compared to NoOptimization. Figure 12 shows that, for a communication range of 100m to 120m, nodes within one hop from the gateway receive up to 80% less messages with STS than with NoOptimization. STG outperforms NoOptimization, but it is inferior to STS.

Vary number of network holes: We also measured the ability of STG and STS to cope with network holes, *i.e.* areas completely void of sensors. Figures 15, 16 and 17 show that the number of holes (rectangles of dimension in the range [40, 80]) have a minor effect in the benefits of STS and STG over the NoOptimization algorithm. In the case of no holes, 48% less messages are received by the immediate 1-hop neighbors of the gateway (from the 2-hop nodes) in STS compared to NoOptimization, and this benefit decreases to 35% for 10 holes. The effect of holes is almost the same as the effect of decrease of nodes from 100 to 80 in Figure 9. Holes do not cause the proposed algorithms performance to deteriorate dramatically in unexpected ways.

6   Related Work

There has also been a plethora of work on energy-aware routing [3,13,16] but without considering the interplay of routing and query processing. The TinyDB [8,9] and Cougar [14,15] projects investigate tree-based routing and scheduling techniques for processing aggregate queries like *avg*, *count*, *sum*, *min* and *max* in sensor networks. The concept of semantic routing trees (SRTs) [9] is used to forward queries only to children that satisfy the query predicate. Zhao et al. [17] compute aggregate summaries over a reliable tree, utilizing a tree construction scheme based on high-quality links, similar to the one used in this work. More sophisticated aggregates are supported in [5], and the benefits of in-network aggregation are discussed in [1]. Directed diffusion [6] is a data-centric protocol that deals with continuous aggregate queries; the network is flooded with an interest for named data and the sources that contain the relevant data respond with the appropriate stream. Madden et al. consider the problem of managing multiple queries in [7], but without focusing on the routing aspect; they propose query plan data structures (Fjords) that handle both push-based and pull-based extraction of sensor data. Trigoni et al. [11,12] propose energy-efficient plans for optimizing multiple algebraic aggregate queries in a sensor network. The aforementioned efforts rely on tree-based aggregation and do not exploit the knowledge of the query workload to set up efficient routes for result propagation. The study of decentralized operator placement by Bonfils et al. is closer to our work since the idea is to place operators carefully in the network to minimize the communication cost. Their work considers optimizing a single query, and is more relevant to holistic aggregates, such as correlation or median, and materialized aggregates, such as storage points. Sharaf et al. propose a query-aware *tree* selection scheme, but for processing a different class of (GROUP-BY) queries [10]. We extend previous work on data aggregation in that we depart from the model of tree-based routing, and consider the interaction of processing and routing in reducing the volume of propagated data.

7   Conclusions and Future Work

This paper shows the interplay of routing and processing in evaluating aggregate queries in sensor networks, and proposes two novel algorithms that significantly outperform the existing approach. STG exploits the new concept of segment-based aggregation, and offers up to 60% energy savings compared to NoOptimization. STS, which avoids sending query sub-aggregates through disjoint paths, offers even higher savings (up to 80%). It consistently behaves better than STG, especially in the presence of many queries. The greatest savings of STG and STS are observed in the critical area around the gateway, which means that these savings directly reflect an increase in the network lifetime. In the future, we plan to study the effect of local route repairs on the cost of STS, as well as extensions of the algorithm to handle approximate aggregates. Another exciting direction is to explore multi-query optimization techniques for non-summary aggregates (*e.g. median*) and for queries without well-defined spatial coverage.

References

1. Krishnamachari, B.B., Estrin, D., Wicker, S.: Impact of data aggregation in wireless sensor networks. In: Int. Conf. on Distributed Computing Systems, pp. 575–578 (2002)
2. Broch, J., Maltz, D.A., Johnson, D.B., Hu, Y.-C., Jetcheva, J.: A performance comparison of multi-hop wireless ad hoc network routing protocols. In: Mobicom, pp. 85–97 (1998)
3. Chang, J.-H., Tassiulas, L.: Energy conserving routing in wireless ad-hoc networks. In: Infocom, vol. 1, pp. 22–31 (2000)
4. Gray, J., Chaudhuri, S., Bosworth, A., Layman, A., Reichart, D., Venkatrao, M., Pellow, F., Pirahesh, H.: Data cube: A relational aggregation operator generalizing group-by, cross-tab, and sub-totals. J. Data Mining and Knowledge Discovery 1(1), 29–53 (1997)
5. Hellerstein, J., Hong, W., Madden, S., Stanek, K.: Beyond average: towards sophisticated sensing with queries. In: IPSN, vol. 1, pp. 63–79 (2003)
6. Intanagonwiwat, C., Govindan, R., Estrin, D.: Directed diffusion: a scalable and robust communication paradigm for sensor networks. In: Mobicom, pp. 56–67 (2000)
7. Madden, S., Franklin, M.: Fjording the stream: an architecture for queries over streaming sensor data. In: ICDE, pp. 555–566 (2002)
8. Madden, S., Franklin, M., Hellerstein, J., Hong, W.: TAG: a tiny aggregation service for ad-hoc sensor networks. In: OSDI, vol. 1, pp. 131–146 (2002)
9. Madden, S., Franklin, M., Hellerstein, J., Hong, W.: The design of an acquisitional query processor for sensor networks. In: SIGMOD, pp. 491–502 (2003)
10. Sharaf, M., Beaver, J., Labrinidis, A., Chrysanthis, P.: Balancing energy efficiency and quality of aggregate data in sensor networks. The VLDB journal 13(4), 384–403 (2004)
11. Trigoni, N., Yao, Y., Demers, A., Gehrke, J., Rajaraman, R.: Hybrid push-pull query propagation for sensor networks. GI Jahrestagung 2, 370–374 (2004)
12. Trigoni, N., Yao, Y., Demers, A., Gehrke, J., Rajaraman, R.: Multi-query optimization for sensor networks. In: Prasanna, V.K., Iyengar, S., Spirakis, P.G., Welsh, M. (eds.) DCOSS 2005. LNCS, vol. 3560, pp. 307–321. Springer, Heidelberg (2005)
13. Woo, M., Singh, S., Raghavendra, C.S.: Power-aware routing in mobile ad hoc networks. In: Mobicom, pp. 181–190 (1998)

14. Yao, Y., Gehrke, J.: The Cougar approach to in-network query processing in sensor networks. SIGMOD Record 31(3), 9–18 (2002)
15. Yao, Y., Gehrke, J.: Query processing in sensor networks. In: CIDR, pp. 233–244 (2003)
16. Yu, C., Govindan, R., Estrin, D.: Geographical and energy aware routing: a recursive data dissemination protocol for wireless sensor networks. Technical Report UCLA/CSD-TR-01-0023, University of Southern California (2001)
17. Zhao, J., Govindan, R., Estrin, D.: Computing aggregates for monitoring wireless sensor networks. In: Int. Workshop on Sensor Network Protocols and Appl. (2003)

Exploiting Resource-Rich Actors for Bridging Network Partitions in Wireless Sensor and Actor Networks*

Ka. Selvaradjou, B. Goutham, and C. Siva Ram Murthy

Department of Computer Science and Engineering
Indian Institute of Technology Madras, India 600036
{selvaraj, goutham}@cse.iitm.ernet.in, murthy@iitm.ac.in

Abstract. Real-time and energy efficient Actor-Actor Coordination (AAC) is an important problem in Wireless Sensor and Actor Networks (WSANs). Actor nodes need to communicate with each other to perform joint actions on the environment. Unlike sensor nodes, actor nodes are resource-rich and their energy can be renewed. In WSANs, only a few number of actors will be deployed due to their cost and there is no guarantee that they form a connected network as the actor nodes frequently move. We address the problem of efficiently bridging the partitions in an actor network using resource-constrained sensor nodes. We propose a hybrid communication architecture in which actor nodes use dual-channel and directional antenna. We show by theoretical analysis and simulation results that exploiting resource-richness of actors and the use of directional antenna help enabling real-time actor-actor communication with minimum overhead in the energy-constrained sensor nodes. The results show that the use of narrow beam-width directional antenna at actor nodes reduces latency in AAC with minimum wastage of energy in sensor nodes for bridging the actor partitions.

1 Introduction

Developments in embedded systems coupled with wireless capabilities, enable newer class of ad hoc networking, known as Wireless Sensor Networks (WSNs). A sensor node consists of three subsystems, viz. sensing, computing, and communication. Such nodes are usually powered by a battery source and deployed in a large scale in a terrain under monitoring. Thus, the nodes form themselves, an ad hoc network, collect and forward environmental data towards a central sink. Typical applications of WSNs include habitat monitoring, battlefield surveillance, vehicle tracking, and health monitoring [1] [2].

In Wireless Sensor and Actor Networks (WSANs), a special class of nodes called Actors are deployed in addition to sensor nodes. These nodes are capable of acting on the environment. For example, an actor node may be capable of putting off fire by spraying water, activate heating elements if the observed temperature is below some threshold, etc. In addition, actor nodes may be mobile as in the case of robots or trucks. In WSANs, such actor nodes are also wireless enabled, so that they can either receive

---

* This work was supported by the Department of Science and Technology, New Delhi, India.

S. Rao et al. (Eds.): ICDCN 2008, LNCS 4904, pp. 416–427, 2008.

necessary commands from a central sink (semi-automated control) or they can directly receive events from sensor nodes and decide to take appropriate action(s) on the environment (fully-automated control) [3].

Sensor-to-Actor Coordination (SAC) and Actor-to-Actor Coordination (AAC) are two important issues in WSANs [4]. While the SAC deals with the issues of disseminating the events from sensor nodes to one or more number of actor nodes in an energy efficient and timely manner, the latter plays an important role when joint actions are required to bring the environment under control. Thus, AAC demands for real-time communication with high reliability. Moreover, as the number of deployed actor nodes is usually small and due to their frequent movement for performing actions, the topology of actor nodes becomes highly dynamic and results in partitions.

In this work, we propose a heterogeneous communication architecture and address the problem of healing the partitions in the actor network with the help of resource constrained sensor nodes. We also propose routing protocols that exploit resource-richness of actors in achieving real-time communications and in turn, maximize the sensor network lifetime. We carried out simulation studies and theoretical analysis to evaluate the performance of our scheme, both with and without using directional antenna at actor nodes.

The rest of the paper is organized as follows: In Section 2, we briefly outline the related work. Section 3, describes the problem in detail with our proposed hybrid architecture. In Section 4, we justify the need for directional antenna at sink nodes and an algorithm for actor discovery is explained. In Section 5, the performance gain of using directional antenna is analyzed and numerically evaluated for ideal settings. This is followed by Section 6, in which extensive simulation results are discussed. Finally, we conclude with summary of our contributions in Section 7 along with scope for future work.

2   Related Work

"Anycast" [5] considers the problem of multi-mobile sinks. The sensor nodes construct anycast trees in which the leaf nodes are the sinks. The sensor nodes route their data to any one of their leaf nodes. As the sink nodes are connected by out-band channel, the sink node which received the data packet from a sensor node, forwards the packet to the intended sink node in fewer hops, thereby reducing the latency. However, such an assumption of sink connectivity at all times, does not hold true always and hence we address the problem of bridging the actor partitions through resource-constrained sensor nodes. "Siphon" [6] considers the case of diverting the traffic generated by sensor nodes to the Physical Sink via a set of Virtual Sinks (static deployment) in case of congestion notification. Virtual Sinks are assumed to be resource-rich and have dual radio, viz. short-range (in-band, typically Mote radio) and far-range (out-band, typically IEEE 802.11). In case of network partition in the Virtual Sink backbone network, it is suggested that the intermediate sensors are used to bridge the gap. In bridging the network partition, the virtual sinks use their short-range radio, thus leading to increased end-to-end latency.

The use of directional antenna at sink node is proposed in [7] and [8] in order to extend the lifetime of the sensor nodes in relay zone. The key idea lies in effective scheduling of sensor nodes in relay zone such that nodes wake-up only during the period when sink node's directional beam focuses on them. However, these works do not address the problem of multiple sinks and network partitioning.

In our earlier work, We formulated the problem of optimal assignment of actor nodes in WSANs [9] as an optimization problem such that the energy required for the mobility of actors is minimized while maximizing the number of events visited. We proposed a suitable architecture and also distributed heuristics to obtain near optimal scheduling of actors. We have also studied different strategies of optimally placing the actors at the end of their scheduled events. However, this architecture relies on the presence of static agents at every zone in order to have undisturbed connectivity among them to take collaborative decisions.

In this work, we propose a heterogeneous architecture such that actors themselves act as sink nodes and they can collaboratively take decisions. In particular, we address the problem of healing the partitions in the actor network with the help of resource constrained sensor nodes.

3   Our Work

We address the problem of efficiently bridging the actor network partitions using resource-constrained intermediate sensor nodes. As explained in the following sections, the routing layer in our architecture, attempts to exploit the resource-richness of actors in order to minimize end-to-end latency in AAC while minimizing interference with sensor traffic using directional antenna at actor nodes.

3.1   System Model

We consider the model of WSAN in which N number of sensor nodes and M number of actors are placed randomly in a field which is to be monitored. The placement of nodes are such that sensor nodes are densely placed to meet the coverage requirements and they are static. But, the actor nodes are quite a few in number $(M \ll N)$ and they are mobile. While sensor nodes have single radio and use a single channel (as in motes), actor nodes are provided with dual radio and use two different channels (viz. *Sensor Channel* and *Actor Channel*).

Actors use the *Actor Channel* on a radio interface in order to have communications among neighbor actors thus forming a network of actors. They use *Sensor Channel* on a different radio interface, in order to have communication with their neighboring sensor nodes. Since the actor nodes are provided with dual interfaces, simultaneous communication, viz. actor-actor and actor-sensor communication is possible. In addition, actor nodes are equipped with *directional antenna* of n sectors. The need for and the use of such antennas are discussed in next section. Let the variables R_s, R_{ao}, and R_{ad} denote the transmission ranges of sensor node, actor node operating on omnidirectional antenna, and actor node operating on directional antenna, respectively. Then, the following relation holds among them: $R_s \ll R_{ao} \leq R_{ad}$ [10].

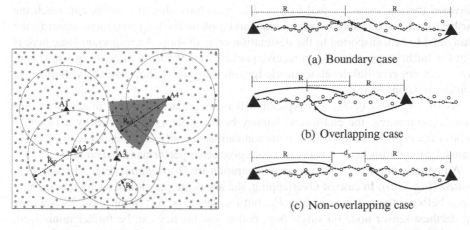

Fig. 1. WSAN Architecture

Fig. 2. Three cases of Actor separation

(a) Boundary case

(b) Overlapping case

(c) Non-overlapping case

3.2 Problem Description

Though the sensor nodes are static, the topology tends to be quasi static due to channel abnormalities and node deaths. But, the topology of actors in WSANs is highly dynamic due to frequent mobility of actor nodes to the places of events. Due to this and the fact that only a few number of actors are deployed in a given terrain of larger dimension, the connectivity among actors is not guaranteed most of the time. This results in partitions in the network of actors such that an actor from a partition can not directly communicate to another actor in a different partition using *actor channel*. For example, as shown in Figure 1, the actor node A4 is isolated from all other actors, while the remaining actors form a connected network. Under these circumstances, it may be necessary for A4 to exchange some vital information with one or more actors in the other partition. We address the problem of providing communication between partitions of actors through a set of intermediate sensor nodes.

The actor nodes flood their interest immediately after deployment or whenever they require, thus help forming routing paths originated from all the sensor nodes and destined to these sink nodes. It is to be noted that such interest propagation is initiated on the *sensor channel* with the transmission range adjusted such that R_{ao} is same as R_s. The *actor channel* is used only for data communication among actors. The topology is maintained by every actor by knowing at least one actor in its communication range.

An actor may get isolated from the rest of the actors due to mobility. In such a case, it makes an attempt to reach another actor through a set of intermediate sensor nodes. In doing so, it may flood a query on its *sensor channel* to find a sensor node which has a route to an actor whose node ID is different from that of this isolated actor. This is because, sensors near this isolated actor will have route towards this actor, but such an information will result in looping. Thus, only the sensor nodes which have route to an actor other than the one from where the query is originated, will reply back to this actor.

Three important cases wherein actors remain unconnected by their *actor channels* are depicted in Figures 2(a) to 2(c). If the actor positions are such that the distance between them is exactly equal to $2 \times R_a$ (Fig. 2(a)), then the actors can reach the farthest sensor node using *sensor channel* and push their data. From there onwards, the data need to be transported to the destination on multi-hop. An important issue here is that the farthest sensor node can receive packets from the actor node using single hop, but it can not give link level acknowledgment using single hop due to its short-range communication (R_s).

As the R_a (R_{ao} or R_{ad}) is typically 10 times greater than that of sensor node's transmission range, the end-to-end latency between actors is reduced by a factor of approximately 0.5. As actor-actor communication typically demands for real-time data transfers, exploiting actor resources would give better performance advantage.

An equally important cases of actor separation are *Overlapping* (Fig. 2(b)) and *Separated* (Fig. 2(c)). In case of Overlapping, the actors are positioned such that their distance between them is greater than R_a, but less than $2 \times R_a$. In this case, by reaching the farthest sensor node on single hop, end-to-end latency can be further minimized. If the actor positions are such that the distance between them is greater than $2 \times R_a$, then it leads to the Non-overlapping case. As can be seen from Figure 2(c), more the separation (d_s), then higher will be the end-to-end latency due to the involvement of several number of sensor nodes bridging the gap.

3.3   Challenges

The following are the important factors to be considered in designing efficient transport protocol between actors through a bridge of sensor nodes:

1. Heterogeneity of nodes: Actor nodes are resource-rich with respect to energy (renewable), communication and computation. Sensor nodes are limited by their available energy (non-renewable), shorter communication range, computation and memory capacity.
2. Asymmetrical link: While an actor can reach a sensor node with its maximum transmission range, the receiving sensor node can not acknowledge the actor directly, due to the differences between communication ranges ($R_{ad} \geq R_{ao} \gg R_s$). This necessitates careful design of MAC layer.
3. Collisions due to long-range communication: While the objective of exploiting actor's long-range communication is to minimize end-to-end latency in actor-actor communications, this happens at the cost of increased collisions at intermediate sensors. Hence, careful scheduling of sensor transmissions is required to keep the collisions minimum and thus saving scarce energy.

4   Need for Directional Antenna at Sink

As discussed earlier, the proposed WSAN architecture has heterogeneous nodes, viz. Actors and Sensors. The transmission range of actor nodes (R_a) is typically 10 times greater than that of sensor nodes. Thus, when an isolated actor needs to establish connection to another actor via a set of sensor nodes, it has the following two options:

1. It can establish a routing channel to another actor using intermediate sensors. While doing so, it can set its transmission range same as that of sensor node (R_s) and use *sensor channel*.
2. It can reach a sensor node having route to the destination actor, using its maximum transmit range (R_a) and from that sensor node onwards a multi-hop route towards the destination actor can be established.

The first option has a potential demerit of increased end-to-end latency between actor communications. This option would also decrease the network lifetime, as many intermediate sensor nodes are involved in carrying the actor traffic. The second option aims to exploit the actor node's powerful communication capability, thereby drastically minimizing the end-to-end latency. But, it has a potential demerit of collisions with all ongoing sensor communications in a circular area of radius R_a. This would happen only for a brief period during which transmission of control packet is taking place. Once the actor node knows a specific sensor node through which the destination actor has to be reached, then the actor traffic can be scheduled in such a way that the sensor nodes within R_a defer their transmissions, thereby saving their energy. As a consequence, end-to-end latency in sensor traffic will get badly affected.

In order to minimize number of collisions during actor route repair process and also to minimize the latency of sensor traffic, we propose to use directional antennas at actor nodes. Thus, whenever a *Route Repair* is initiated at an actor node, it would only affect ongoing transmissions within a sector rather than the entire circular area. Similarly, the use of directional antenna would only affect end-to-end latency of sensor traffic within a sector through which actor traffic is carried out.

Algorithm 1. Actor Discovery Algorithm

1:   Choose a sector arbitrarily
2:   Transmit *RREQ* packet at max. transmit power on *Sensor Channel*
3:   Wait for T_{resp} interval to receive *RREP* messages, if any
4:   **if** Timeout **then**
5:     choose the next sector in Clockwise Direction
6:   **end if**
7:   Repeat from step 2 till all sectors are explored
8:   **if** valid *RREP* messages are received **then**
9:     **if** $|RREP| > 1$ **then**
10:      Choose the node with highest hop count
11:     **else**
      Choose the node from where *RREP* arrived
12:     **end if**
13:   **end if**

4.1   Actor Discovery Process

As discussed in the previous sections, limited number of actor nodes in a terrain of larger dimension would result in partitioning of actor network. Thus, an isolated actor would need to communicate with a neighboring actor for performing joint actions.

When, an actor itself finds that it is isolated from the rest of the actor network, it can initiate a *Actor Discovery* process as outlined in Algorithm 1. As shown in Figures 2(b)-2(c), and in the Algorithm 1, the isolated actor broadcasts *Route Request (RREQ)* packet with its maximum transmit power, so that all the sensor nodes up to distance R_{ad} would listen to this control packet. If any sensor node has a route towards another actor, then it will send a *Route Reply (RREP)* message back to this actor. As the transmission range of a sensor is limited, such *RREP* messages would reach in a multi-hop fashion. In order to account for this multi-hop delay, the isolated actor should wait for T_{resp} duration to receive one or more *RREP* messages. This value will be typically set to slightly more than 10 times that of a packet transmission time, owing to the differences in communication ranges between actor and sensor nodes. If the isolated actor which initiated route repair process, is in receipt of one or more *RREP* messages, then it chooses a node to be its routing neighbor, whose *RREP* packet took higher number of hops. Ties are broken arbitrarily.

If no *RREP* messages arrive within T_{resp} interval, then it implies that none of the sensor nodes have route to any actor in the network. Then, the actor switches its directional antenna to the next sector and broadcasts the *RREQ* message. The actor scans through all the sectors after every T_{resp}, in case of no *RREP* messages received and finally gives up. Then, the application layer protocol can decide to move the actor node to a different place and try to find a closest actor for connectivity. It is assumed that the actors periodically beacon their presence and thus sensor nodes construct anycast tree with leaf nodes as actors.

5   Theoretical Analysis

Let N_{omni} and N_{θ} denote number of ongoing transmissions by sensor nodes within the communication range of actor when it uses omni-directional antenna and directional antenna, respectively. Then, the following equation governs the number of collisions as a function of directional angle, θ.

$$N_{\theta} \leq \frac{\theta}{360} \times N_{omni} \tag{1}$$

If the actor node initiates transmission of *RREQ* packet using its maximum transmission power, then all these ongoing transmissions will get collided. Thus, the sensor nodes need to retransmit the packets that did not reach destinations due to the occurrence of this collision. This extra retransmission would waste the scarce energy of node and also increases the latency in sensor traffic. Thus, a saving of collisions proportional to the ratio, $\frac{N_{omni}}{N_{\theta}}$ is possible when directional antennas are used at actor nodes. Also, the choice of directional angle, θ has direct impact on energy conservation by reducing the packet collisions. The numerical results in Figure 3 show the effect of θ on number of collisions.

Next, we see the gain in end-to-end latency between actors if long-range communication is preferred as shown in Figures 2(a) to 2(c). The one-way and end-to-end delay between separated actors can be given as

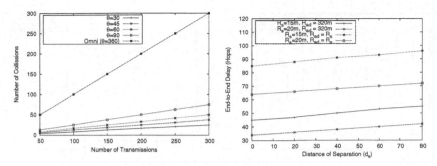

Fig. 3. Effect of angle, θ on collisions in sensor traffic

Fig. 4. End-to-End delay Vs d_s

$$Delay_{oneway} = 1 + \frac{d_s}{R_s} + \frac{R_{ad}}{R_s} \qquad (2)$$

$$End-to-End\ Latency = 2 \times Delay_{oneway} \qquad (3)$$

The value of 1 in the first term of equation 2 implies that communication between actor and farthest sensor is just one hop and d_s in second term denotes the distance of separation as depicted in Figure 2(c). The third term gives the number of hops a packet has to travel via sensor nodes to the destination actor. The effect of d_s on end-to-end delay is shown in Figure 4. The numerical results given in this plot compares the end-to-end latency (in hops) of long-range and short-range communications with values of R_s set to 15m and 20m. As can be seen from this figure, reduction in latency as high as 50% is possible when actors use long-range communication ($R_{ad} > R_s$) than when they use short-range ($R_{ad} = R_s$) communication between them.

Next, we establish from the fundamentals of antenna theory that the use of directional antenna indeed helps in further minimizing the end-to-end latency. The Friss formula [11] for transmission range is given by

$$P_r = P_t G_r G_t \left(\frac{\lambda}{4\pi}\right)^2 \left(\frac{1}{d^\alpha}\right) \qquad (4)$$

where G_r and G_t are the antenna gains of the receiver and the transmitter respectively, P_r and P_t are the corresponding signal powers, λ is the wavelength, d is the distance between receiver and transmitter and α (typically a value of 2 or 4 for free space and two-ray ground reflection propagation models, respectively) is the power loss exponent of the channel.

According to [12], the directional antenna gain (G_θ) of the main lobe is defined as

$$G_\theta = \left(\frac{360°}{\theta}\right) G_t \qquad (5)$$

where θ is a beam-width in azimuth for each beam pattern and G_θ is applied to the transmitter gain of the directional antenna with a beam-width θ.

Therefore, using equation 4 the communication range of omni-directional antenna, d_{omni} can be derived as,

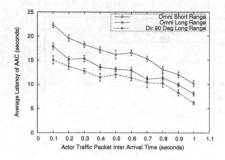

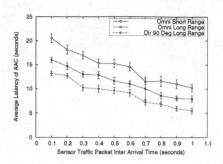

Fig. 5. Average latency in Actor Traffic vs. Varying Actor Traffic

Fig. 6. Average latency in Actor Traffic vs. Varying Sensor Traffic

$$d_{omni} = \left(\frac{P_t G_t G_r}{P_r} \left(\frac{\lambda}{4\pi} \right)^2 \right)^{\frac{1}{\alpha}} \tag{6}$$

Thus, when an actor is equipped with a directional antenna with beam-width of θ degrees, the communication range d_θ of the directional antenna can be derived from equations 4 and 5;

$$d_\theta = \left(\frac{360°}{\theta} \right)^{\frac{1}{\alpha}} d_{omni} \tag{7}$$

where d_{omni} is the communication range of omni-directional antenna.

Thus, for the case of $\alpha = 4$ (Two-Ray Ground Reflection Propagation Model) and $\theta = 90°$ (4 sectors), we have

$$d_\theta = \sqrt{2} \times d_{omni} \tag{8}$$

which shows that an extended communication range of about 40% is possible, if actor nodes use directional antennas. Let $R_{ao} = 300$m and $R_s = 30$m. Then from equation 8, the extended communication range of actor node due to the use of directional antenna is $R_{ad} = 420$m. Also, in ideal settings, single hop communication of the actor node is equivalent to 12 hops of sensor communications, thus saving of four hop delay in AAC.

6   Simulation Results

In the previous section, the performance advantage of using directional antenna is evaluated in the ideal settings. In order to verify the performance measures, we simulated a network with 250 sensor nodes and 5 actor nodes, randomly deployed in a terrain of dimension 450m × 450m. The figures 5 to 12 show the results of the simulation. The results are average of 10 simulation runs and the vertical bars in graphs indicate the confidence interval. The values shown conform to 95% confidence level.

In all the simulations, the values of R_s and R_{ao} are set to 15m and 150m, respectively. R_{ad} is set according to the equation 7. Only a subset of nodes generate data at regular intervals of time and they send them to the nearest actor. The actor nodes are deployed such that there exists at least one partition among the network of actors. A pair of

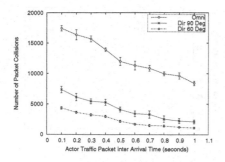

Fig. 7. Collisions vs. Varying Actor Traffic

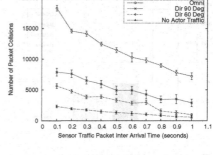

Fig. 8. Collisions Vs. Varying Sensor Traffic

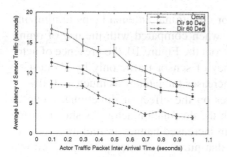

Fig. 9. Effect of Actor Traffic on Latency of Sensor Traffic

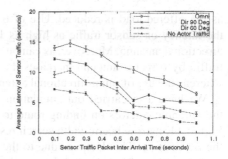

Fig. 10. Effect of Arrival Rate on Latency of Sensor Traffic

such actors which are out of communication range, attempt to communicate with each other with Packet Inter Arrival Times as shown in the figures. In figures 5 and 6, we compare the end-to-end latency of actor traffic by varying actor traffic and sensor traffic, respectively. From both the figures, we see the results of latency when actor nodes use short-range, long-range communication using omni-directional antenna and directional antenna with 4 sectors ($\theta = 90°$). It can be observed that the use of long-range omni-directional antenna helps minimizing the latency by about 30% when compared with that of short-range communication. Further reduction in latency of approximately 10% is due to the extended communication range of directional antenna.

Figures 7 and 8 show the results of collisions on sensor traffic, when actors use omni-directional antenna and directional antenna of 4 and 6 sectors. Though not much performance advantage is observed with respect to end-to-end latency of AAC, when directional antennas are used at actor nodes, but it is evident from Figures 7 and 8 that significant energy saving is possible if directional antennas are used with narrow beamwidth. The number of collisions are observed to be about 60% less at $\theta = 60°$ when compared with $\theta = 90°$.

Figures 9 and 10 show the effect of actor traffic on the latency of sensor traffic at various directional angles. The results are plotted by varying packet inter arrival rates of actor and sensor nodes, respectively. As shown in these figures, the latency decreases

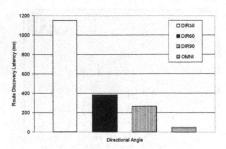

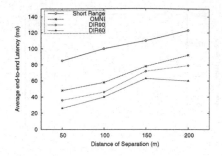

Fig. 11. Average Actor Discovery Delay

Fig. 12. Average latency of AAC traffic with respect to d_s

as the offered load is reduced. Use of 6 sector directional antenna helps minimizing the latency on sensor traffic as high as 100% when compared with the use of omnidirectional antenna. Moreover, as can be seen from the Figure 10, the presence of actor traffic by 6 sector antenna increases the latency of sensor traffic only by about 42% whereas the use of omni-directional antenna increases the latency as much as 100%.

We have also carried out simulation studies on the effect of directional angle of the antenna at actors on finding route to reach the destination actor. As shown in the Figure 11, narrow beam-width search results in increased latency in finding a route to the destination. This happens due to the fact that number of attempts is proportional to the number of sectors and T_{resp} is higher for narrow beam-width due to extended communication range (equation 7). Though rapid route discovery is observed with Omni-directional antenna, it happens at the cost of severe energy drain in the resource-constrained sensor nodes in actor's communication range, as shown in Figures 7 and 8.

In Figure 12, we show the results of average end-to-end latency of actor traffic by varying the distance between the end actors. In obtaining the simulation results, sensor traffic was totally suppressed. As shown, use of directional antenna at actor nodes reduces the latency to as low as 60% when compared with use of short-range communication. Similarly, the use of narrow beam-width directional antennas help further minimizing the latency due to their extended communication range.

Thus, it is evident from these results that the use of narrow beam-width directional antenna at actors helps minimizing the energy wastage in the sensor nodes and also minimizes the end-to-end latency of AAC due to its long-range communication capability.

7 Conclusions

We have presented in this work, a communication architecture for WSANs that use directional antenna at sink nodes. Using this architecture, we have proposed an energy efficient routing scheme that is designed to preserve connectivity among partitioned actor network using energy constrained sensor nodes. We have shown by theoretical analysis and simulation results that the use of directional antenna at actor nodes and exploiting the long-range communication capability of actors, sensor network lifetime can be maximized while enabling real-time communication among actors. We are currently investigating various strategies in choosing sectors so as to minimize the latency in finding the route to an isolated actor. We are also extending the work, to design an energy-efficient transport protocol for Actor-Actor Communication using this hybrid architecture.

References

1. Culler, D., Estrin, D., Srivastava, M.: Overview of Sensor Networks. IEEE Computer 37, 41–49 (2004)
2. Akyildiz, I.F., Su, W., Sankarasubramaniam, Y., Cayirci, E.: A Survey on Sensor Networks. IEEE Communications Magazine 40, 102–114 (2002)
3. Melodia, T., Pompili, D., Gungor, V.C., Akyildiz, I.F.: A Distributed Coordination Framework for Wireless Sensor and Actor Networks. In: Proceedings of the 6th ACM International Symposium on Mobile Ad Hoc Networking and Computing, pp. 99–110 (May 2005)
4. Akyildiz, I.F., Kasimoglu, I.H.: Wireless Sensor and Actor Networks: Research Challenges. Ad Hoc Networks 2(4), 351–367 (2004)
5. Hu, W., Jha, S., Bulusu, N.: A Communication Paradigm for Hybrid Sensor/Actuator Networks. In: Proceedings of the 15th IEEE International Symposium on Personal, Indoor and Mobile Radio Communications, pp. 47–59 (September 2004)
6. Wan, C.Y., Eisenman, S.B., Campbell, A.T., Crowcroft, J.: Siphon: Overload Traffic Management using Multi-Radio Virtual Sinks. In: Proceedings of the 3rd ACM Conference on Embedded Networked Sensor Systems, pp. 116–129 (November 2005)
7. Cho, J., Lee, J., Kwon, T., Choi, Y.: Directional Antenna at Sink (DAaS) to Prolong Network Lifetime in Wireless Sensor Networks. In: Proceedings of the 12th European Wireless Conference, pp. 1–5 (April 2006)
8. Mao, S., Hou, Y.T.: BeamStar: A New Low-cost Data Routing Protocol for Wireless Sensor Networks. In: Proceedings of IEEE GLOBECOM, vol. 5, pp. 2919–2924 (2004)
9. Selvaradjou, Ka., Siva Ram Murthy, C.: On Maximizing the Residual Energy of Actors in Wireless Sensor and Actor Networks. In: Proceedings of 8th International Conference on Distributed Computing and Networking, pp. 227–238 (2006)
10. Kumar, V., Arunan, T., Balakrishnan, N.: E-SPAN: Enhanced-SPAN with Directional Antenna. In: Proceedings of TENCON 2003, Conference on Convergent Technologies for Asia-Pacific Region, vol. 2, pp. 675–679 (2003)
11. Rappaport, T.S.: Wireless Communications: Principles and Practice. Prentice Hall, Englewood Cliffs (1996)
12. Kang, I., Poovendran, R., Richard, L.: Power Efficient Broadcast Routing in Ad Hoc Networks using Directional Antennas: Technology Dependence and Convergence Issues. In Technical Report UWEETR-2003-0015, Electrical Engineering Department, University of Washington, pp. 1–12 (2003)

A New Top-Down Hierarchical Multi-hop Routing Protocol for Wireless Sensor Networks

M.P. Singh[1,*] and M.M. Gore[2]

[1] Department of Computer Science and Engineering
National Institute of Technology Patna, India
writetomps@gmail.com
[2] Department of Computer Science and Engineering
Motilal Nehru National Institute of Technology, Allahabad, India
goremm@acm.org

Abstract. This paper proposes a new top-down hierarchical, multi-hop, routing protocol for the wireless sensor networks. The proposed solution is appropriate for random deployment and suitable for different sizes of target areas. This protocol forms clusters in which each cluster member is at one hop distance from the cluster head. This protocol ensures the participation of all the cluster heads in hierarchical topology formation. The proposed protocol is also capable of handling dynamic nature of the wireless sensor networks. The simulation results show the scalability of the proposed approach.

1 Introduction

Advancement in technologies has enabled the development of multi-functional tiny devices known as sensor nodes [1]. These nodes consist of sensing, data processing and communicating components. Network of sensor nodes is known as wireless sensor network (WSN). WSN is a specific kind of ad hoc network. WSN can be used in multiple applications in different spheres of life like monitoring applications, acoustic detection, seismic detection, military surveillance, inventory tracking etc.

The rest of the paper is organized as follows. Section 2 summarizes the related work. Section 3 describes the assumptions, notations, the algorithm, and provides comparison with PEGASIS [2] protocol. Section 4 presents implementation details and simulation results. Finally, section 5 concludes the paper.

2 Related Work

This section presents the related work on routing protocols for WSNs. These routing protocols shaped understanding of the problem.

---

* He is also a Ph.D. candidate at Motilal Nehru National Institute of Technology, Allahabad, India.

S. Rao et al. (Eds.): ICDCN 2008, LNCS 4904, pp. 428–433, 2008.

Low Energy Adaptive Clustering Hierarchy (LEACH) [3] is a hierarchical protocol. It uses single hop routing. This protocol assumes that all the nodes begin with equal energy capacity in each election round which is difficult to achieve. The above assumptions for the LEACH are not feasible for relatively larger target areas.

Threshold-sensitive Energy Efficient protocols (TEEN) [4], a hierarchical protocol, tries to minimize the communications by using two threshold values namely, hard and soft. TEEN protocol is not suitable for applications which require reporting of each event which occurs in the target area.

AdaPtive Threshold-sensitive Energy Efficient protocol (APTEEN) [5] is an extension to TEEN. APTEEN is a hybrid protocol. Transmission of sensed data is similar to TEEN except, if a node does not send data for a time period equal to the count time, it is forced to sense and retransmit the data.

Power-Efficient GAthering in Sensor Information Systems (PEGASIS) [2] forms a chain of sensor nodes in a greedy fashion. Sensed data moves from node to node, getting aggregated and eventually being sent to the end user. PEGASIS assumes that all sensor nodes send data to end user in one hop. It also assumes that all sensor nodes have same energy level and likely to die around the same time. For relatively larger network, chain formation will not be energy-efficient.

An extension to PEGASIS is Hierarchical-PEGASIS [6]. This is achieved by decreasing the delay occurred for packet transmission to base station. The chain based protocol with CDMA capable nodes, builds a tree of chains of nodes.

HEAR-SN: a new hierarchical energy-aware routing protocol for heterogeneous sensor networks [7]. Cluster-head nodes are superior in terms of computational power, communication range, and storage capacity over cluster-member nodes.

Two-Tier Data Dissemination (TTDD) [8] protocol provides a solution for multiple mobile sink problem. Sensor nodes are stationary and location-aware in TTDD.

The proposed protocol uses homogeneous sensor nodes. The proposed routing protocol falls into the category of hierarchical reactive network [4]. Cluster based hierarchical routing has advantages related to scalability and efficient communication. It minimizes the power consumption of sensor nodes by performing data aggregation, fusion, and multi-hop communication. This protocol is best suited for area monitoring applications such as environmental monitoring, military surveillance etc. In the next section proposed protocol is presented.

3   The Proposed Hierarchical Multi-hop Routing Protocol

This section describes the working of the proposed protocol that is a new top-down hierarchical multi-hop routing protocol for WSN. First, this section notes the assumptions about WSN and its components. Second, it provides the notations used. Third, this section presents the algorithm with explanation of each phase. Finally, a comparison for energy consumption with PEGASIS [2] is made.

Assumptions: Every sensor node has a unique ID. Broadcast messages sent by the cluster heads are received correctly within a finite time by all of its 1-hop neighbors. Network topology is static during the execution of algorithm. Packet broadcast by base station is correctly received by some of the cluster heads. The base station is static, and resourceful. All the sensor nodes in the sensor network have same capabilities in computation and have equal communication range.

Notations Used: *cid:* Cluster id. *holdback:* Holds randomly generated value which is used for cluster head making decision. *status:* Whether the node is cluster member or cluster head. *levelstatus:* Whether or not the cluster head is the part of hierarchical topology. *MN:* Member nodes of any cluster. *Connected Cluster Head (CCH):* Cluster head connected to partially or fully formed hierarchical topology.

The proposed protocol has been divided into six phases namely, *(1) Initialization phase, (2) Cluster setup phase, (3) Hierarchical topology setup phase, (4) Enquiry Phase, (5) Event detection and reporting to base station, and (6) Maintenance Phase.* These phases are presented in detail in Algorithm 1.1.

Algorithm 1.1 Proposed Hierarchical Multi-hop Routing Protocol
1   **Initialization phase:**
2   Each node initializes the following its own parameters
3   cluster id (cid) = null, *status* = null, *levelstatus* = false,
4   *holdback* value to some randomly generated number,
5   **Cluster setup phase**
6   after every t_c seconds each node decrements the *holdback* value by one
7   if (*holdback* == 0 && *status* == null)
8   set *status* = *cluster_head*, cid = node id,
9   Initialize the packet.type=*cluster_head_hello*, broadcast *cluster_head_hello*
10 On receiving the *cluster_head_hello* broadcast
11 if (*status* == null && *holdback* $\neq$ 0 && packet.type==*cluster_head_hello*)
12   cid = SendID, /*ID of node that has broadcast the *cluster_head_hello**/
13   set status = *cluster_member*,
14 **Hierarchical topology setup phase** /*Top-Down Approach*/
15 Base station initializes the following parameters
16 Packet type= *base_hello*, *levelstatus*=true, Level = 0
17 Now, base station initiates this phase by broadcasting the *base_hello* message
18 cluster head(s) on receiving first *base_hello* or *base_forward_hello* message
19 if((packet.type==*base_hello* || *base_forward_hello*) && status == *cluster_head* && *levelstatus*==false)
20   Set its own *levelstatus*=true,
21   Level = Level +1, Remembers its parent address,
22   Forward the *base_forward_hello* packet to form the next level
23 **Enquiry phase**
24 if (*levelstatus*=false && status == *cluster_head*)
25   the cluster heads send *scan_hello* packet to its members
26 on receiving *scan_hello*
27   Member nodes scan CCH by broadcasting the packet.type = *scan*,
28 on receiving *scan* packet
29 if(packet.type==*scan* && status==*cluster_head* && *levelstatus*==true)
30   cluster heads reply by sending the packet of type=*scan_reply*,
31 Member nodes receives the packet and decide to join the hierarchical topology

32 if(*packet.type*==*scan_reply* && *status*==*cluster_member* && *ReceiveID*==*NodeID*)∎

33   Call Function 1
34   Forward the packet.type==*scan_reply_forward* to its cluster head,
35 After receiving the *scan_reply_forward* packet
36   Call Function 1
37 **Function 1**
38   Enqueue the packets, Set its own *levelstatus*=true,
39   Level = Level +1, Maintain the list of parents,
40 **Event detection and reporting to base station**
41 if((status == *cluster_member*) && (*levelstatus* == true))
42   it sends *report* to its parents towards base station using hop-by-hop.
43 else
44   send *report* to its cluster head.
45   cluster head send the *report* to its parents hop by hop towards base station
46 **Maintenance phase**
47 Rerun the algorithm after t_r round time
48 **End of Algorithm 1.1**

Initialization phase: During this phase, each node initializes its own *cid* (Cluster id) to *null* value, randomly generated value into *holdack*, *status* to null, and *levelstatus* to false.

Cluster setup phase: This phase divides the WSN into clusters in which the MNs are at one hop distance from the cluster heads of respective clusters. This phase make sure that each active sensor nodes will be either cluster head or MN.

Hierarchical topology setup phase: Base station is at level 0. The base station starts this phase by broadcasting *base_hello* packet to find out the cluster heads for level 1. In turn, the cluster heads at level 1 broadcast the *base_forward_hello* packet to find out the cluster heads for level 2 and so on.

Enquiry phase: After the *hierarchical topology setup phase*, there may be some clusters / cluster heads which are not part of the hierarchical topology because these cluster heads are not directly reachable from any other cluster head. But member nodes of such clusters are connected to one or more CCHs. This phase make sure that all the left out cluster heads will be connected to hierarchical topology.

Event detection and reporting to base station: The member nodes of any cluster, which is part of hierarchical topology, send packets to its parents rather than to its cluster head. This saves the energy and reduces unnecessary delay in routing. This is also an energy efficient approach. Otherwise, the member nodes send the data to its cluster head and in turn to base station in hop by hop fashion.

Maintenance phase: In the last phase, the proposed protocol reruns the same algorithm after t_r round time. This adapts the change in population of sensor nodes. Worst case of the proposed protocol occurs when the same nodes become cluster heads in the next round, if all nodes get the same *holdback* values as in the previous round.

Comparison with PEGASIS: The proposed protocol uses the radio transmission model of [3].

Assumptions: each node has n neighbor nodes. Each neighbor is at d distance. Power consumption in computation is negligible in comparison with communication. Suppose, PEGASIS [2] forms a chain of m nodes. Hence maximum energy consumed to send a packet to base station

$$E_{pegasis-total} = (n+1)m * (k(E_{elec} + \epsilon_{amp} * d^2)) + (m * n + m - 1)k * E_{elec}. \quad (1)$$

The proposed protocol consumes maximum energy to transfer a packet to base station in using m clusters = m cluster heads transmit a packet + *(m-1)* cluster heads receive a packet.

$$E_{proposed-protocol} = 2 * m(k(E_{elec} + \epsilon_{amp} * d^2)) + (m * n + m - 1)k * E_{elec}. \quad (2)$$

Equations (1) and (2) show that the proposed protocol is approximately $(n+1)/2$ times energy efficient in comparison to PEGASIS [2].

4   Implementation Details and Simulation Results

The proposed protocol is implemented in NesC programming language with the underlying operating system TinyOS. Simulation is done by using TOSSIM simulator. Fig. 1(a) shows the relation between the component of the proposed protocol. *ClusterC* is the main component. It Contains the logic for initialization phase, cluster setup phase, hierarchical topology setup phase, enquiry phase, and maintenance phase. *EventDetetionC* component is responsible for monitoring the environment in which the sensor network is deployed, for occurrence of events of interest. *ReportC* component prepares the report of the occurred events and sends to the base station. For simulation purpose, the value of t_c is 700 milliseconds. After every 700 milliseconds *holdback* value of every node decreases by one. The graph in Fig. 1(b) shows the relationship between the number of sensor nodes and simulation time for the proposed protocol and cluster setup phase of the proposed protocol.

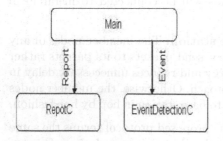
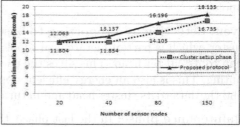

(a) Components of the proposed protocol

(b) Number of nodes Vs Simulation time

Fig. 1. Major Components and simulation result

5 Conclusion

A new top-down hierarchical, multi-hop, routing protocol for the wireless sensor networks has been presented. This protocol divides the WSN into non-overlapping clusters in which each cluster member is at one hop distance from the cluster head. In the proposed protocol, all the cluster heads participate in the hierarchical topology. The proposed protocol adapts the dynamic nature of wireless sensor network including changes in sensor node population and topology. The simulation results show that the proposed approach is scalable. Radio model equations of WSN show that the proposed protocol is approximately $(n+1)/2$ times energy efficient than PEGASIS [2].

The proposed protocol can be modified for hierarchical multi-hop secure routing protocol. Further, it can also be enhanced to support the mobility in wireless sensor networks.

References

1. Akyildiz, I.F., Su, W., Sankarasubramaniam, Y., Cayirci, E.: A survey on sensor network. IEEE Communication Magazine 40(8), 102–114 (2004)
2. Lindsey, S., Raghavendra, C.S.: PEGASIS: Power-efficient gathering in sensor information systems. In: Proceedings of IEEE Aerospace Conference, Big Sky, Montana, vol. 3, pp. 3–1125 – 3–1130 (2002)
3. Heinzelman, W.R., Chandrakasan, A., Balakrishnan, H.: Energy-efficient communication protocol for wireless micro sensor networks. In: IICSS 2000. Proceedings of the 33rd Hawaii International Conference on System Sciences, vol. 8, p. 8020. IEEE Computer Society, Washington, DC (2000)
4. Manjeshwar, A., Agrawal, D.P.: TEEN: A routing protocol for enhanced efficiency in wireless sensor networks. In: IPDPS 2001. Proceedings of the 15th International Parallel & Distributed Processing Symposium, pp. 2009–2015. IEEE Computer Society Press, Washington (2001)
5. Manjeshwar, A., Agrawal, D.P.: APTEEN: a hybrid protocol for efficient routing and comprehensive information retrieval in wireless sensor networks. In: Proceedings of the 2nd International Workshop on Parallel and Distributed Computing Issues in Wireless Networks and Mobile computing, pp. 195–202. IEEE Computer Society, Washington (2002)
6. Lindsey, S., Raghavendra, C., Sivalingam, K.: Data gathering in sensor network using the energy* delay metric. In: Proceedings of the IPDPS Workshop on Issue in wireless sensor network and mobile computing, San Francisco, CA, pp. 2001–2008 (2001)
7. Hempel, M., Hamid Sharif, P.R.: HEAR-SN: A new hierarchical energy-aware routing protocol for sensor networks. In: Proceedings of the 38th Hawaii International Conference on System Sciences (2005)
8. Ye, F., Luo, H., Cheng, J., Lu, S., Zhang, L.: A two-tier data dissemination model for large-scale wireless sensor networks. In: MobiCom 2002. Proceedings of the 8th annual international conference on Mobile computing and networking, pp. 148–159. ACM Press, New York (2002)

PROBESYNC: Platform Based Synchronization for Enhanced Life of Large Scale Wireless Sensor Networks

Virendra Mohan and R.C. Hansdah

Dept. of Computer Science & Automation, Indian Institute of Science,
Bangalore 560012, India
mohan.virender@gmail.com, hansdah@csa.iisc.ernet.in

Abstract. Optimization in energy consumption of the existing synchronization mechanisms can lead to substantial gains in terms of network life in Wireless Sensor Networks (WSNs). In this paper, we analyze ERBS and TPSN, two existing synchronization algorithms for WSNs which use widely different approach, and compare their performance in large scale WSNs each of which consists of different type of platform and has varying node density. We, then, propose a novel algorithm, PROBESYNC, which takes advantage of differences in power required to transmit and receive a message on ERBS and TPSN and leverages the shortcomings of each of these algorithms. This leads to considerable improvement in energy conservation and enhanced life of large scale WSNs.

1 Introduction

Large scale WSNs have attracted a great deal of attention due to their potential for applications in various areas such environmental monitoring, military surveillance, industrial applications, agriculture etc.[1]. The key constraint in the design of WSNs is the conservation of energy for each of the associated problems. According to [2], individual sensors can last only 100 to 120 h on a pair of AAA batteries in the active mode and it is usually difficult, if not impossible, to recharge or replace their batteries. Since a sensor network is usually expected to last several months to one year without recharging, minimizing energy consumption to extend the network lifetime, is an important design objective.

Time synchronization is an important requirement of most sensor networks since almost any form of sensor data fusion or coordinated actuation requires synchronized physical time for reasoning about events in the physical world. Providing synchronized time in WSNs poses challenges due to varying and contradictory requirements specification for precision, efficiency, lifetime, scope, availability for various applications. Time synchronization protocols in traditional networks are designed to achieve the highest possible accuracy. The higher the required accuracy, the higher is the resource requirements. In large scale WSNs, it may be useful to make a trade-off between accuracy and resource requirements.

An effort has been made in [3] to compare some of the state of art sensor network platforms based on a set of general platform metrics like radio physical

S. Rao et al. (Eds.): ICDCN 2008, LNCS 4904, pp. 434–439, 2008.

Table 1. Comparison of Salient Features of Mica2dot, Micaz and NMRC motes

Parameter	Mica2dot		Micaz	NMRC
	433MHz	916MHz		
Rx Current(mA)	8	10	19.7	18
Tx Current(mA), -5 db	25	27	17.4	10.5
Range(m)	300	150	75-100	10
R=Rx to Tx Power	.32	.37	1.13	1.71

properties and system core. However, it is difficult to compare different sensor network platforms for problematic metrics like power consumption and capacity due to the broad range of applications and architectures, each with their distinct characteristics. In [4], comparisons between sensor nodes, viz., Micaz, Mica2dot, NMRC and Intel motes have been made. The salient features Micaz, Mica2dot, and NMRC motes have been summarized in table 1.

A significant point to be noted in the table 1 is that while transmit current for Micaz motes is lower than its reception current, and it is other way round for Mica2dot motes, i.e., the two types of motes have different reception to transmission current ratio. It is this novel observation which forms the seed for our proposed algorithm PROBESYNC. In our proposed algorithm, we take advantage of the different power consumption characteristics of these platforms for reception and transmission of a message for overall savings in the clock synchronization algorithm for sensor networks.

The rest of the paper is organized as follows. In section 2, we present our algorithm, PROBESYNC, along with review and analysis of existing algorithms related to our sphere of work. The simulation experiments along with analysis of the results are presented in section 3. Finally, section 4 concludes the paper.

2   Our Synchronization Algorithm

Before we present our algorithm, PROBESYNC, we discuss and analyze RBS [7], ERBS [5] and TPSN [6], the protocols pertaining to our sphere of work. The two synchronization algorithms, RBS and its efficient version ERBS, are based on receiver-receiver synchronization approach and are more suited for a small network environment where receivers are less in number while TPSN uses sender-receiver synchronization approach for synchronization and is mainly suited for large networks.

2.1   RBS (Reference Broadcast Synchronization) and ERBS (Efficient RBS)

In Reference Broadcast Synchronization (RBS) [7] nodes send reference beacons to their neighbors, by making use of the broadcast possibility of the network.

Receivers use the arrival time of these beacons as points of reference for comparing their clocks. The simplest form of RBS is executed in three steps: (i) A node broadcasts a reference beacon. (ii) Each node that receives the beacon, records its arrival time according to the node's local clock. (iii) The nodes exchange their observations. Using this information, each node can compute its offset to any other node.

ERBS[5] is an improved version of RBS [7] in which only a percentage (called *p-ratio*) of the receiving sensor nodes exchange their observations. Authors of [5] have evaluated the performance of ERBS in terms of total number of messages at various p ratios and have claimed that the accuracy of ERBS when $p=.7$ is similar to that of the original RBS while there is considerable savings in the number of messages(43% of the original RBS).

2.2   Timing Sync Protocol for Sensor Network (TPSN)

The Timing-syncs Protocol for Sensor Networks (TPSN) [6] synchronizes time in a sensor network by first creating a hierarchical structure and then synchronizing nodes along this structure. When a hierarchical structure is established, pairwise synchronization is performed along the edges of the hierarchical structure in *synchronization phase* to calculate clock skew and propagation delay.

2.3   PROBESYNC

PROBESYNC is based on energy conservation in time synchronization based on number of messages exchanged . ERBS and TPSN described above report very high precisions, of the orders of few μ secs. However, an important point to note is that not only the number of messages used by the two methods is quite different for different number of receivers(children surrounding the node) but also ratio of number of received and transmitted messages is different in the two algorithms for different number of receivers. Below we analyze this message complexity of the two algorithms for n receivers.

For ERBS

$$No \, of \, Transmit \, Messages = pn$$

$$No \, of \, Reception \, Messages = n + \sum_{i=1}^{pn} i$$

$$= n + \frac{p^2 n^2}{2} + \frac{pn}{2}$$

$$Where \boxed{0 < p \le 1}$$

For TPSN

$$No \, of \, Transmit \, Messages = n + 1$$

$$No \, of \, Reception \, Messages = 2n$$

If R = Reception/Transmission power ratio for a platform, then in terms of number of equivalent transmission messages for energy consumption, we can say

For ERBS(p=.7)

$$
\begin{aligned}
Energy\ Consumption\ &= .7n + R(1.35n + .245n^2) \\
(Equivalent\ &Tx\ messages)
\end{aligned}
\tag{1}
$$

For TPSN

$$
\begin{aligned}
Energy\ Consumption\ &= (n+1) + R(2n) \\
(Equivalent\ &Tx\ messages)
\end{aligned}
\tag{2}
$$

R indicates the cost of receiving a message vis-a-vis transmitting the same message and it is different for different platform as can be seen from the table 1 and can be calculated based on the data sheet of various platforms. Depending upon R, there will be a critical number of n of receivers, for which one mechanism will be better than the other depending upon the platform. This critical number can be found by equating equation 1 and 2 with a given value of R for a platform thus enabling us to identify critical switch point for optimization of energy consumption. This forms the basis of PROBESYNC.

PROBESYNC follows a greedy strategy wherein in the initial phase, it carries out carries out level discovery(as in TPSN) to establish the hierarchical levels in the network based on the transmission range of the platform. In doing so, it also establishes the number of receivers(children) surrounding each node in WSN. In the second phase, depending upon the platform and therefore, R ratio supplied, it finds out critical number of receivers(children) for which the two algorithms (ERBS and TPSN) yield same energy consumption and follows a greedy synchronization strategy at each node to switch between two algorithm depending upon the number of receivers (children) ascertained in the level discovery phase. The pseudo code for the PROBESYNC is as given below.

PROBESYNC *(Input:Node_id each node, R ratio for the platform, P ratio for ERBS)* _____

find_levels_and_children;
receive_probesync
$$
= \frac{(.65R + .3) + \sqrt{(.65R + .3)^2 + 4(.245R)}}{2(.245R)};
$$
For each node
    if (*num_of_child* < *numreceiver_probesync*)
        // use ERBS to synchronize the children
        Broadcast *sync_request;*
        Designate p% of the children as *transmitters* ;
        For each child

        Note time of reception of *sync_request*;
        if (*transmitter*)
            Broadcast *obsn_packet* ;
            Receive *obsn_packet* from transmitters;
    else
            // use TPSN to synchronize the children
        Broadcast *sync_request*;
        For each child
            Note time of reception of *sync_request*;
            Send *ack* to parent after a random delay;

---

3   Performance Evaluation

Extensive simulations were carried out in Matlab 7.0 to compare the energy consumption and efficiency of the PROBESYNC with those of RBS, ERBS and TPSN in different WSNs with varying node density.

3.1   Simulation Experiments

Simulation experiments were carried out to ascertain the effectiveness of PROBESYNC in both high density as well as low density environment on different platforms. PROBE1 version of PROBESYNC finds critical number of receivers for which RBS and TPSN yield the same energy consumption for the given platform and uses a greedy strategy to switch between the two algorithms at each node based on this critical number while PROBE2 is the version described in section 2.3 and uses critical number of receivers to switch between the ERBS and TPSN. The two platforms selected for the simulation experiments are Mica2dot(433MHz) and Micaz as both exhibit totally different R ratio and their results could easily be used to draw the inferences for other platforms like NMRC which exhibits R ratio similar to Micaz and Mica2dot(916MHz) which exhibits R ratio similar to Mica2dot(433MHz) as seen from table 1. The experiments compared energy consumption in terms of number of equivalent transmission messages for the various algorithms for randomly deployed network of nodes ranging from 100 to 1500 Nodes in an area of **1000m x 1000m** and **500m x 500m**.

3.2   Simulation Results

The data obtained from simulation experiments was analyzed to compute the efficiency of both versions of PROBESYNC, i.e., PROBE1 over RBS and TPSN as well as PROBE2 over ERBS and TPSN on both types of sensors and in both, low as well as high, density configuration sets and the same is graphically shown in the figure 1.

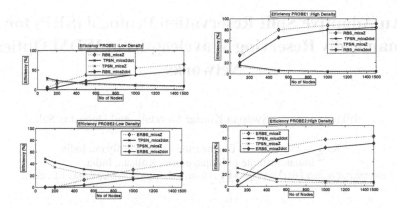

Fig. 1. Percentage Improvement in Performance of PROBE1 and PROBE2

4   Conclusions

PROBESYNC optimizes energy conservation in large scale networks by taking advantage of the difference in the energy requirements for transmission and reception of a message for a particular sensor network platform and recognizing varying density regions to fit in ERBS and TPSN to counter each others shortcomings without any additional overheads. While ERBS works efficiently in less denser areas, TPSN comes into play in more denser areas without any additional overhead, thereby enhancing the life of large scale WSNs. PROBESYNC apart from being scalable is also tunable through p ratio lending it an advantage to exploit the trade-off between the synchronization accuracy and energy conservation in applications with less stringent requirement for synchronization accuracy.

References

1. Akyildiz, I.F., Su, W., Sankara subramaniam, Y., Cayirci, E.: A survey on sensor networks. IEEE Communications Magazine (2002)
2. Power management and batteries: http://www.xbow.com/Support/appnotes.htm
3. Beutel, J.: Metrics for Sensor Network Platforms. In: Proceedings of REALWSN 2006, Uppsala Sweden (2006)
4. Bellis, S.J., Delaney, K., Flynn, B.O., Barton, J., Razeeb, K.M., Mathuna, C.O.: Development of Field Programmable Modular Wireless Sensor Network Nodes for Ambient Systems: Computer Communications (2005)
5. Lee, H., Yu, W., Kwon, Y.: Efficient RBS in Sensor Networks. In: ITNG 2006. Proceedings of the Third International Conference on Information Technology: New Generations, vol. 00, pp. 279–284 (2006)
6. Ganeriwal, S., Kumar, R., Srivastava, M.B.: Timing-Sync Protocol for Sensor Networks. In: Proceedings of the 1st International Conference on Embedded Networked Sensor Systems, Los Angeles, California, USA, pp. 138–149 (2003)
7. Elson, J., Girod, L., Estrin, D.: Fine-Grained Network Time Synchronization using Reference Broadcasts: Fifth Symposium on Operating Systems Design and Implementation (December 2002)

An Adaptive Split Reservation Protocol (SRP) for Dynamically Reserving Wavelengths in WDM Optical Networks

Malabika Sengupta[1], Swapan Kumar Mondal[1], and Debashis Saha[2]

[1] Kalyani Government Engineering College, Kalyani, India
[2] Indian Institute of Management, Kolkata, India
sengupta.malabika@gmail.com, ds.calcutta@gmail.com

Abstract. In WDM optical networks, prior to data transfer, lightpath establishment between source and destination nodes is usually carried out through a Wavelength Reservation Protocol (WRP), for which there are different approaches, such as Source Initiated Reservation Protocol (SIRP), Destination Initiated Reservation Protocol (DIRP) and Intermediate node Initiated Reservation Protocol (IIRP). At high load, due to scarcity of resources, a request is blocked primarily due to two important factors, namely 'outdated link information' (in case of DIRP) and 'over reservation' (in case of SIRP). To minimize the effect of both the factors (as attempted in IIRP), we propose to split a probe attempt into two concurrent (upstream and downstream) reservation attempts at some intermediate points (selected adaptively). This novel WRP, termed as Split Reservation Protocol (SRP) in the paper, is a potential competitor for IIRP. So we analyze SRP at length and compare it with IIRP for different network situations. The comparative results show that, for SRP, the blocking probability improves by even 90% in some cases, and the control overhead decreases by 29% sometimes. However, the average setup latency increases by 10% in most cases. So the proposed scheme appears quite promising especially for the applications (such as short messaging) where the blocking probability is the most important criteria.

1 Introduction

In Wavelength Division Multiplexing (WDM) [1] based optical networks, when a connection request arrives to a source, a proper route between the source and destination (called 'routing') is selected and an all optical path (commonly referred as a lightpath [2]-[3]) throughout the route is established. Though a complete lightpath establishment protocol is responsible for both routing and wavelength assignment, this work is restricted to wavelength assignment part only which can work with any standard routing. In this work, we consider fixed routing, based on the shortest path. Also, wavelength converters at intermediate nodes are not considered. Conventionally, lightpath establishment is handled in a centralized or distributed way and a signaling protocol is required to reserve resources along the selected route [1]-[5]. One major hurdle of the reservation protocols is updating of global information

S. Rao et al. (Eds.): ICDCN 2008, LNCS 4904, pp. 440–451, 2008.

about wavelength availability, which cannot be guaranteed at any particular place and time in a distributed system [2],[4],[5]. Basically, updating of information of availability of wavelengths at different links is done at regular intervals and due to propagation delay, the received information is outdated upon arrival. To cope up with this challenge, different protocols are suggested at various points of time [2],[7],[8],[10]-[13]. Intermediate node initiated reservation protocol (IIRP) [7] is one of them, which is supposed to perform better than its peers. However, there are some limitations of IIRP, for example, the problem of "over reservation" is not addressed completely, which can be further looked into. Intermediate nodes in IIRP are predefined and fixed and hence the protocol lacks in flexibility. Also, in absence of any such predefined nodes between source and destination, IIRP behaves simply like DIRP. We attempt to address these shortcomings in the proposed scheme, called split reservation protocol (SRP). SRP uses an adaptive reservation scheme, where reservations may be initiated at any one of some predefined nodes, which are decided dynamically using some system parameters. This modification improves the overall performance of the protocol considerably. The paper is organized as follows. In Section 2, relevant reservation protocols are discussed. The proposed protocol is discussed in Section 3. Theoretical analysis is presented in Section 4, whereas results and discussions are presented in Section 5. Finally, Section 6 concludes the paper. The following terms are used in this text: source, destination, PROB, RES, REL, ACK, NACK. Source and destination means source node and destination node. PROB, RES, REL, ACK and NACK are all control packets used in a designated route to probe and collect the availability of wavelengths, to reserve one or more wavelengths, to release one or more wavelengths, to acknowledge the acceptability of a connection request and to acknowledge the rejection of a connection request respectively.

2 Wavelength Reservation Protocols (WRPs)

WRPs may be primarily divided into three categories (Fig. 1), depending on the initiation of reservation from the source (S), destination (D), and intermediate (IN) node. Intermediate node initiation may be done statically or dynamically depending on the flexibility of the reservation process. In source initiated reservation protocol (SIRP) [1],[2], a RES is initiated from the source to reserve wavelength(s) in all hops

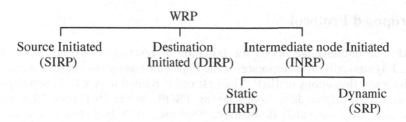

Fig. 1. Classification of protocols

along the selected route towards the destination. The scheme suffers from "over reservation" [6]-[8] as it starts reserving the wavelengths in forward path towards destination, much before the actual use of the same during transmission. In DIRP this problem is addressed and it is established that DIRP outperforms SIRP. In DIRP [1],[2], source sends a PROB, which proceeds towards the destination. If PROB reaches destination, the destination selects one wavelength from the available set of wavelengths and sends RES towards the source to reserve the selected wavelength throughout the route. If RES reaches the source successfully, the source initiates transmission. Though DIRP performs better than SIRP, it suffers from "outdated information" which is addressed in intermediate-node initiated reservation protocols (INRPs). The main idea in INRPs is to allow reservation (towards source) to be initiated by a set of intermediate nodes [7],[8]. These intermediate nodes may be predefined and fixed (e.g., IIRP) or dynamic (e.g., SRP as proposed in this work). The concept of IIRP is to allow the reservation to be initiated by a predefined set of intermediate nodes. These predefined intermediate nodes (special nodes) have adequate link-state information of the entire path. When a PROB proceeds forward and reaches the first special node, the node initiates a fast RES in the backward direction towards source. This RES tries to reserve a particular wavelength (say $\lambda 1$) upto source. The PROB then proceeds further until it reaches the next special node or the destination. In next special node, the node checks the availability of $\lambda 1$. If it is available, PROB proceeds forward. However, if $\lambda 1$ is not available, the node selects another wavelength (say $\lambda 2$) (if such is available) and initiates a new RES which reserves $\lambda 2$ towards source and releases $\lambda 1$. This is repeated until the PROB reaches the destination. The destination then initiates the normal RES to reserve either previously selected wavelength (if such is still available) or new wavelength from the set of available wavelengths (if any). Failure cases may arise due to non availability of wavelengths during PROB or during reservation. In such cases REL is used to release the reserved wavelengths (if any) by this request. IIRP suffers from extreme cases as reservation from an intermediate special node is initiated unconditionally. Say, for a particular request, if a special node exists next to the source in the route, it initiates backward reservation after traversing one hop only and suffers from over reservation which increases blocking probability (bp). Similarly, if the first special node exists just before last position in a particular route, it initiates the fast RES when only one hop is left and thus probability of getting any free wavelength is reduced due to outdated information. This problem is addressed in SRP.

3   Proposed Protocol

In SRP, the intermediate nodes for initiation of reservation are not static, rather selected dynamically. It incorporates some important features to improve the extreme situations and limitations of IIRP. The first one is related to types of control packets generated from intermediate nodes during PROB. While IIRP uses RES towards source and PROB towards destination, SRP uses RES both towards source and destination. The second one is related to selection of the position of splitting. While IIRP may initiate fast RES anywhere in the path unconditionally once the first special node is available, splitting in SRP takes place conditionally based on two parameters

(i) the path already traveled by PROB, (ii) the status of PROB result. Third important feature is related to the basic idea of retries. The characteristic of retries is embedded in IIRP as it generates RES from multiple special nodes (if required). But in case of SRP, from the splitting point, the RES towards destination reserves one or more wavelengths and RES towards source reserves one wavelength. If RES towards source is blocked, it may go for one or more retries. The scheme is discussed below.

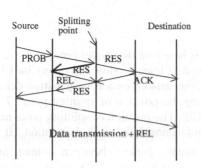

Fig. 2a. SRP for success with retry

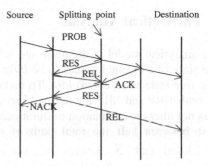

Fig. 2b. SRP for failure after retry

PROB is initiated by source (like IIRP), which moves towards the destination. If PROB result at any node (which contains the updated available set of wavelengths upto that node) does not fall below some predefined value (say c), and PROB reaches the destination, the request follows DIRP for the rest. However, on the way to destination, if (i) PROB result falls below c and (ii) the PROB has already traversed at least a pre-selected number of hops expressed as percentage (say x) of total number of hops on the designated route then splitting occurs and two separate RES are initiated from that node. A backward RES moves taking one wavelength (say λ_1 chosen randomly from the pool of available wavelengths) towards source and forward RES moves towards destination reserving predefined number of wavelengths (say m). This m includes the wavelength λ_1 and rest (m-1) wavelengths are chosen randomly from the available set of wavelengths so far (excluding λ_1). If forward RES reaches the node previous to destination and finds at least one wavelength available on the forward link (which is the last link of the route), an ACK is sent to the source by this node and reserves the last link. This ACK while passes through the splitting point, the node of splitting point retains the information of reserved wavelengths as confirmed pool which may be used in future during retries. If backward RES reaches source successfully and the ACK sent by forward RES is also received at source, source initiates transmission of data and also sends a REL to release all additional wavelengths (if any) reserved by forward RES from splitting point to destination. Also if any wavelength becomes unavailable during forward reservation, that particular wavelength is released using REL. If the forward RES is stuck at some node, a NACK is generated from that node which moves towards source releasing all the wavelengths reserved so far and the request is blocked. Now, if backward RES is stuck before it reaches the source, it comes back to the splitting point releasing the wavelength reserved so far. Then backward RES retries with another wavelength (if any) from the confirmed pool of available wavelengths or from the pool of expected available wavelengths (i.e., m which are attempted for reservation by forward RES) depending on whether the ACK from forward RES has reached the splitting point or not. It may be noted that maximum possible number of retries is one less than m. If reservation using retries becomes successful then transmission takes place as shown in Fig. 2a otherwise the request is blocked as shown in Fig. 2b. In this paper IIRP means static IIRP unless specified otherwise.

4 Theoretical Analysis

The analytical model of the proposed scheme is based on the model presented in [7]. The state of a channel is said to be *busy* during data transmission and otherwise (if it is in free state or reserved) *idle*. To make the comparisons easier, propagation delays for both IIRP and SRP are defined incorporating the position of splitting point. This does not alter the calculation of durations for IIRP. The position of splitting point may exist between half the total path of the route considered and destination. It is considered that S_R denotes the set of segments present between source and destination of route R. Also, it is considered that the kth segment includes the splitting point and segment $s_j(\in S_R)$ includes the link j (Fig. 3). The analysis consists of the following two sections.

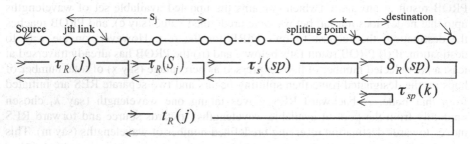

Fig. 3. Different time components of theoretical analysis

4.1 Wavelength Reservation Duration

The wavelength reservation duration $t_R^r(j)$ of jth link of route R is defined as the duration from the moment a channel on link j is reserved to the moment it becomes busy. Thus, the value of $t_R^r(j)$ can be expressed as,

for IIRP $t_R^r(j) = \tau_R(j) + \tau_R(s_j) + \tau_s^j(sp) + \delta_R(sp)$, $j = l_R^s$

$\qquad t_R^r(j) = \tau_R(j) + \tau_s^j(sp) + \delta_R(sp)$, $j \neq l_R^s$

for SRP, $t_R^r(j) = \tau_R(j) + \delta_R(sp)$,

where l_R^s is the last link of segment s_j and k is the number of segments present between source and splitting point. $\tau_R(j)$ is the round trip propagation delay between the source of R and the downstream node of link j, $\tau_R(s_j)$ is the round trip propagation delay between the downstream node of link j and the downstream node of last link of segment s_j. $\tau_s^j(sp)$ is the round trip propagation delay between downstream node of last link of segment s_j and the splitting point (sp).

$\delta_R(sp)$ is the round trip propagation delay between the splitting point and destination. From the above expressions it is clear that $t_R^r(j)$ for SRP is less than that of IIRP by at least $\tau_s^j(sp)$ and this will reduce the overall value of bp of SRP.

4.2 Vulnerable Period

We define vulnerable period $t_R^v(j)$ as the duration from the moment when the link state information is collected (during probe) and the moment when the reservation of wavelength is done on link j. Thus we can write the value of $t_R^v(j)$ as,

For IIRP, $t_R^v(j) = \tau_R(s_j)$

For SRP, $t_R^v(j) = \tau_R(s_j) + \tau_s^j(sp)$, when segment s_j varies between 1 and k-1

$\qquad = \tau_R(s_j) - \tau_{sp}(k)$, when s_j=k, for splitting before end node of the segment

$\qquad = \tau_R(s_j)$,   when s_j=k for splitting at the end node of the segment

$\qquad = 0$,   when s_j varies between k+1 and S_R

$\tau_{sp}(k)$ denotes the round trip propagation delay between splitting point and downstream node of the last link of kth segment. From the above expressions it can be found that $t_R^v(j)$ for SRP is better or at least equal to that of IIRP for $s_j \geq$ k. However for $s_j <$ k, $t_R^v(j)$ of SRP is more than that of IIRP by $\tau_s^j(sp)$.

4.3 Validation

As $\tau_s^j(sp)$ contributes in making the difference between IIRP and SRP to calculate $t_R^r(j)$ and $t_R^v(j)$, $\tau_s^j(sp)$ is analytically calculated for a particular route in the network and the same is compared with the simulated results. It is found that for a selected route R, and for the selected link j of segment sj (sj < k), simulated result of $\tau_s^j(sp)$ deviates by 7.05%.

5 Results and Discussions

It is reported that IIRP performs better or at least at par with DIRP at various situations. Hence, SRP is compared with IIRP only in this work. We assume the routing to be fixed shortest path. Connection requests in the net arrive following Poisson's distribution with mean rate of λ per second and connection holding times are exponentially distributed with an average holding time of $1/\mu$ second. λ is varied between 25 and 150 while μ is kept fixed at 25. The source and destination for each request are selected randomly with equal probability. One channel is used for exchange of control messages (i.e., out-band signaling is considered). The simulation model is event driven. It is assumed that no processing delay is involved at the nodes. There is no wavelength conversion device used in the network. Representative results for a fixed network using mesh topology with 40 nodes and 46 links are presented in this paper.

A key performance metric in lightpath establishment schemes is bp and hence bp is mainly considered to compare the performances. However as x and m decide the position of splitting which plays an important role to yield fairly optimized results, the behaviour of these two parameters are studied first for different situations and it is found that x has an optimum value of 0.5 which yields optimized results. A representative result in support of this is shown in Fig. 4. Fig. 4 shows variation of bp with m for different values of x for SRP keeping cr=70 and other parameters fixed. From the figure it is observed that x=0.5 gives best result. This is justified because if the splitting takes place near about 50 percent of the total path, then retry packets always travel a path between splitting point and some point between source and splitting point for retries (instead between destination and some point between source and destination), thereby reducing the average propagation delay. Hence in all subsequent results of SRP, x is considered as 0.5. Now the effect of m on bp for different values of cr and number of wavelengths (wls) is studied. It is observed from the results that for a given set of parameters, bp changes with m and becomes optimized for a particular value of m while other parameters remain fixed. This particular value of m is referred as m_{opt}. One such representative result is shown in Fig. 5. From the figure it can be seen that for wl=40, m_{opt} =3 and for wl=60, m_{opt} =5. However, as wl (a hardware dependent characteristic) remains fixed for a particular network, so depending on the values of cr, different values of m_{opt} can be used and that will yield best performance in respect of bp. But it may be noted that if m increases, the number of retries also increases (maximum number of retries may be = m-1) and hence the number of control packets also. This aspect restricts the use of very high values of m. So there should be a judicious choice of m ($<= m_{opt}$) if other parameters like control packet becomes equally important.

Now variation of bp with cr are shown in Fig. 6 for wl=40 and in Fig. 7 for wl=80. From these two figures the following can be observed: (i) As wl is increasing, bp in general is decreasing as more paths will be available. (ii) SRP is always better for any value of wl and cr, (iii) The betterment of SRP over IIRP has considerably increased

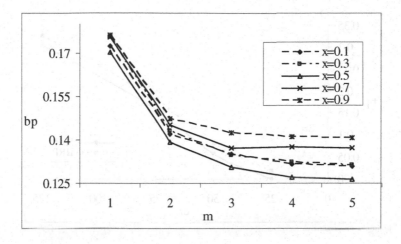

Fig. 4. Variation of bp with m for different values of x for cr=70

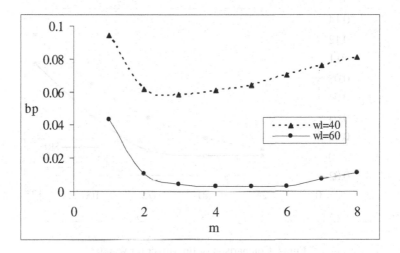

Fig. 5. bp vs m for different values of wl and for cr=50

with the increase of wl. Fig. 8 and Fig. 9 show average setup time versus cr for wl=40 and 80 respectively. It can be observed from Fig. 8 that setup time decreases with increase in cr and IIRP performs better. SRP improves rapidly and approaches towards the value of IIRP at higher values of cr. This happens because in case of SRP as cr increases the position of splitting tends towards the middle of the whole path which reduces the average path traveled and hence set up time. From Fig. 9, it can also be observed that setup time of SRP initially tends to increase and finally reaches to peak value and then decrease. This happens due to the fact that for a combination

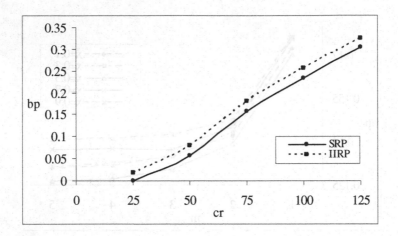

Fig. 6. Comparison of bp with cr for wl=40

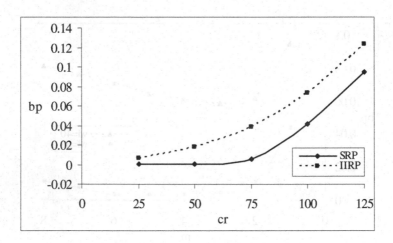

Fig. 7. Comparison of bp with cr for wl=80

of values of cr and wl, the number of retries for successful attempts reaches to a maximum value where setup time becomes maximum. Fig. 10 and Fig. 11 show the variation of average control packet with cr for wl=40 and 80. It is found that average control packet of IIRP is almost independent of cr as inter communication amongst the fast RES and normal RES is not used in this scheme. In case of SRP, average control packet remains considerably less at lower values of cr. This is because at lower values of cr, number of splitting is less. However it increases rapidly as more and more retries takes place with the increase of cr and thus the difference with that of IIRP reduces. At some value of cr it may even be more than IIRP in a given situation.

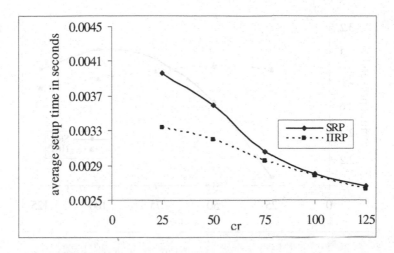

Fig. 8. Comparison of average setup time with cr for wl=40

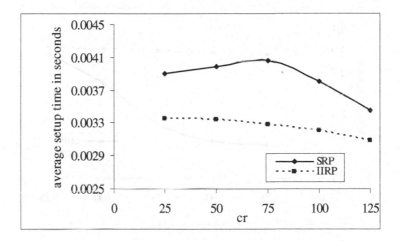

Fig. 9. Comparison of average setup time with cr for wl=80

In Fig. 10 average control packet of SRP becomes more than IIRP at cr=70. This crossover point is skewed towards higher values of cr (does not cross at all upto cr=125 for wl=80 as shown in Fig. 11). This happens because with the more available resources (higher values of wl), the need of retry is reduced for a given value of cr. So it is found that SRP is better than IIRP in terms of bp for all values of cr but at the cost of setup time. However set up time of SRP improves as cr increases and approaches towards the values of IIRP. Average control packets remain less for lower values of cr and becomes higher at higher values of cr. Considering all these aspects it can be justified that SRP may be the better choice with better bp at any situation and moderate control packets and setup time.

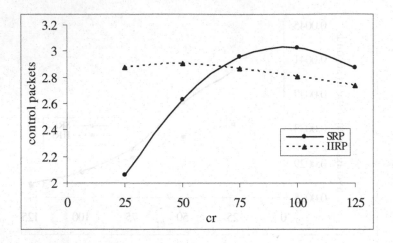

Fig. 10. Comparison of control packets with cr for wl=40

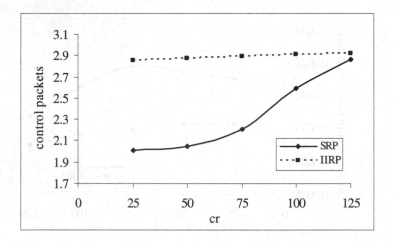

Fig. 11. Comparison of control packets with cr for wl =80

5 Conclusion

In WDM optical networks, prior to data transfer, lightpath establishment between source and destination is usually done through a wavelength reservation protocol. Different existing wavelength reservation protocols (DIRP and IIRP) are discussed in this paper. The analytical model is also outlined in reference of IIRP. In IIRP reservation is initiated at intermediate nodes without waiting for completion of probing up to destination. The proposed SRP, is basically dynamic in nature with the concept of conditional splitting and both way reservation. In SRP, PROB is split into two reservation packets to reserve wavelength(s) in both directions towards source and destination and splitting is done dynamically depending on some parameters of the network at that instant of time. If the availability of wavelength during probing falls below a certain level and the PROB travels a certain distance in the network, reservation is initiated from that intermediate node in both directions. This immediate reservation reduces the effect of outdated information and thus blocking becomes less compared to that of IIRP. Though the proposed SRP may require more average setup time but considering the betterment in blocking probability and average control packets used, the protocol can be considered as better performer.

References

[1] Zang, H., Jue, J.P., Mukherjee, B.: Review of routing and wavelength assignment approaches for wavelength-routed optical WDM networks. Optical networks 1(1), 47–60 (2000)

[2] Saha, D.: A Comparative study of distributed protocols for wavelength reservation in WDM optical networks. SPIE Opt. Netw. Mag. 3(1), 45–52 (2002)

[3] Zang, H., Jue, J.P., Sahashrabuddhe, L., Ramamurthy, R., Mukherjee, B.: Dynamic Lightpath Establishment in Wavelength-Routed WDM Networks. IEEE Communications Magazine, 100–108 (September 2001)

[4] Ozdaglar, A.E., Bertsekas, D.P.: Routing and Wavelength Assignment in Optical Networks. IEEE/ACM Trans. On Networking 11(2), 259–271 (2003)

[5] Feng, F., Zheng, X., Zhang, H., Guo, Y.: An efficient distributed control scheme for lightpath establishment in dynamic WDM networks. Photonic Netw. Commun. 7(1), 5–15 (2004)

[6] Jue, J.P., Xiao, G.: Analysis of blocking probability for connection management schemes in Optical Networks. In: Proc. IEEE GLOBECOM 2001, San Antonio, TX, November 2001, vol. 3, pp. 1546–1550 (2000)

[7] Lu, K., Jue, J.P., Xiao, G.: Intermediate-Node Initiated Reservation (IIR): A New Signaling Scheme for Wavelength-Routed Networks. IEEE Journal on Selected Areas in Communications 21(8), 1285–1294 (2003)

[8] Lu, K., Jue, J.P., Ozugur, T., Xiao, G., Chlamtac, I.: Intermediate-Node Initiated Reservation (IIR): A New Signaling Scheme for Wavelength-Routed Networks with Sparse Conversion. In: Proc. IEEE ICC 2003, An-chorage, AK (2003)

[9] Lu, K., Xiao, G., Chlamtac, I.: Blocking Analysis of Dynamic Lightpath Establishment in Wavelength-Routed Networks. In: Proc. IEEE ICC 2002, New York, vol. 5, pp. 2912–2916 (April 2002)

[10] Lin, W., Olff, R.S., Mumey, B.: A Markov-Based Reservation Algorithm for Wavelength Assignment in All-Optical Networks. IEEE Journal of Light wave Technologies 25(7), 1676–1683 (2007)

[11] Sengupta, M., Mondal, S.K., Saha, D.: Destination Initiated Multi-wavelength Reservation Protocol (DIMRP) in WDM Optical Networks: Finding the Optimal Selectivity for Wavelength Assignment. In: Chaudhuri, S., Das, S.R., Paul, H.S., Tirthapura, S. (eds.) ICDCN 2006. LNCS, vol. 4308, pp. 497–502. Springer, Heidelberg (2006)

Routing and Wavelength Assignment in All Optical Networks Based on Clique Partitioning

Tanmay De, Ajit Pal, and Indranil Sengupta

Department of Computer Science and Engineering,
Indian Institute of Technology, Kharagpur, West Bengal, India
{tanmayd, apal, isg}@cse.iitkgp.ernet.in

Abstract. Wavelength Division Multiplexing (WDM) offers the capability to handle the increasing demand of network traffic in a manner that takes the advantage of already deployed optical fibers. A lightpath is an all optical communication path between end-to-end over a same wavelength used on each intermediate link. Wavelengths are the main resources in WDM optical networks. The wavelength assignment problem has been solved by mapping it to a heuristic based clique partitioning problem under the wavelength continuity constraint. For routing, Dijkstra's shortest-path algorithm is used. Here, we propose two new polynomial time heuristics for wavelength assignment called CPWA1 and CPWA2, based on clique partitioning concepts for static traffic demand with the objective of minimizing the number of wavelengths. The performance of our proposed algorithms are analyzed through extensive simulations on different set of traffic demands under a wide range of network topologies. The results show that proposed mechanism requires less number of wavelengths per fiber for a given set of traffic demand as compared to an existing well known algorithms.

Keywords: WDM, RWA, clique partitioning, heuristics, lightpath.

1 Introduction

Wavelength Division Multiplexing (WDM) is becoming commonplace in the recent years, providing tremendous bandwidth of the optical fiber. The WDM technique divides the enormous bandwidth of an optical fiber into many non overlapping channels (wavelength), which can satisfy the demand of the high bandwidth applications in the next generation networks. The fundamental problem in WDM all-optical networks is routing and wavelength assignment (RWA) problem, which is NP-hard in general [1], [2]. In practice, RWA problem solved separately due to NP-hardness, that is, first solved the routing problem by determining the consecutive links between source and destination nodes and after that the wavelength assignment problem is solved by assigning wavelengths to each link. Lightpath is implemented by selecting a path of physical links between the source and destination nodes, and reserving a particular wavelength on each of these links for the path. A lightpath must use the same wavelength on all of its links if there is no wavelength converter

S. Rao et al. (Eds.): ICDCN 2008, LNCS 4904, pp. 452–463, 2008.
© Springer-Verlag Berlin Heidelberg 2008

at intermediate nodes, this is known as wavelength continuity constraint [1], [2]. The traffic assumptions generally fall into one of two categories: static or dynamic. In the static RWA model we assume that the demand is fixed and known, i.e. all the requests that are to be set up in the network are known beforehand. The objective is typically to accommodate the demand while minimizing the number of wavelengths used on all links. By contrast, in a stochastic/dynamic setting, we assume that requests between source-destination pairs arrive one by one at random, and objective in this case would be to minimize the call blocking probability.

In the routing aspect, there are three basic types of routing approaches: fixed routing, fixed- alternate routing, and adaptive routing. In fixed routing, there is only one fixed route (e.g. the shortest path) between a pair of source and destination nodes. In fixed-alternate routing, each node maintains a routing table that contains an ordered list of fixed routes to each destination node. In adaptive routing, routing is based on the current wavelength availability on each link. In particular, the optimal static lightpath establishment problem without wavelength converters was proven to be NP-complete in [3] by showing the equivalence of the problem to the graph-coloring problem. Relaxed linear programs have been used to get bounds on the desired objective function [4]. Due to computational complexity in obtaining an optimal solution, much of the previous work on RWA problem has focused on developing efficient heuristic methods.

In this paper, we have considered static RWA model and it treated as two separate problems, one routing and other wavelength assignment. For routing, Dijkstra's shortest-path algorithm is used. The wavelength assignment problem is formulated as clique partitioning problem and proposed two heuristics (based on algorithms in [5]) : Clique Partitioning Wavelength Assignment 1 (CPWA1) and other is Clique Partitioning Wavelength Assignment 2 (CPWA2) to partition and assign appropriate wavelengths to the given set of static connection requests. Both algorithms produce optimal or near optimal wavelength assignment in polynomial time.

The rest of the paper is organized as follows. In section 2, we give an overview of previous related work in this field. The routing and wavelength assignment problem modeled as clique partitioning problem is presented in section 3. Our proposed heuristics are present in section 4. The simulation results are reported and analyzed in section 5. Finally, the paper is concluded in section 6.

2 Related Work

A large number of heuristic algorithms have been developed in the literature to solve the RWA problem discussed here or its many variants. A review of various routing and wavelength assignment approaches is given in [1]. A new wavelength assignment scheme, called Distributed Relative Capacity Loss (DRCL), that works well in distributed controlled networks is also presented in [1]. Chlamtac et al. [3] used a greedy heuristic, called the Longest First Fixed Path (LFFP) algorithm to establish all lightpaths with minimum number of wavelengths. They used fixed shortest paths for all source-destination pairs. The shortest paths for a given connection requests are sorted in decreasing order and the longest request is assigned a wavelength first. One technique is to use LP-relaxation followed by rounding [6]. In this case, the integer constraints are relaxed to a non-integer problem which can be solved by linear programming method, and then a rounding algorithm is applied to obtain a new solution which obeys the integer constraints. A greedy approach taken in [7] is to create lightpaths between end nodes in order of decreasing traffic demands as long as the wavelength continuity and distinct wavelength constraints are satisfied. Raja Dutta et al. [8] presented a polynomial time algorithm that optimally assign a single wavelength to maximize one hop traffic in a tree topology. This algorithm used dynamic programming and also proposed a heuristic to use this optimal algorithm for general graph. The evolutionary algorithms in the design of general wide area mesh network that minimizes the network cost is studied in [9], and [10]. In [11], Baroni and Bayvel proposed an algorithm, called the minimum number of hops (MNH) algorithm, for minimizing the maximum load per link in arbitrarily connected networks. The work in [12] proposed two algorithms, called the Longest First Alternate Path (LFAP) and the Heaviest Path Load Deviation (HPLD) and shows these algorithms are better than algorithm MNH [11] and algorithm LFFP [3], to minimize the number of wavelengths used. In [14], J. Zhou and X. Yuan considered single fiber and multifiber systems and dynamic routing with three wavelength selection schemes, namely random-fit, first-fit and most-fit. A new ant-based algorithm for dynamic routing and wavelength assignment problem in WDM optical networks under the wavelength continuity constraint is presented in [15]. To best of our knowledge, clique partitioning based heuristic was first proposed for routing and wavelength assignment in [16]. In this paper, we have proposed two algorithms based on clique partitioning.

3   Network Model and Problem Formulation

The optical network can be modeled as a directed connected graph G(V,E) where V and E are the sets of nodes and bi-directional links (edges) of the network, respectively. Here each link e $\in$ E has a finite number of wavelengths. In the network a non-negative cost C(e) is assigned for every e $\in$ E. The cost of moving from one node i to another node j is assumed as infinity, if there is no link between i and j. A request is denoted as r(s : d), where s is the source node and d is the destination node.

The route for each connection request is determined based on the Dijkstra's shortest path algorithm, i.e., the shortest path is used to set up a connection from node s to node d, for all node pairs in the network. Now, we need to optimally assign wavelength to each of these connection requests. We can modeled as clique partitioning problem in routing and wavelength assignment. For this purpose, we determine the compatibility graph. The compatibility graph can be modeled as an undirected graph $G_C = (V_C, E_C)$, where V_C is the set of vertices (actually connection request) and $V_C = |R|$ i.e., total number of connection requests in the original network G. The set of edges is E_C and an edge (i, j) $\in$ E_C if routes of the two requests i and j do

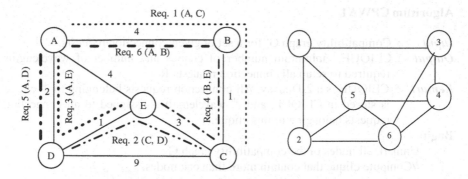

Fig. 1. Physical Topology and 6-connection requests with best route

Fig. 2. Compatibility Graph for connection requests in Fig. 1

not share a common link between them and i, j $\in$ V_C. Figure 1 shows the physical topology of a five node network and six different connection requests with best route. The compatibility graph shown in Fig. 2 corresponding to connection requests in Fig. 1.

In the compatibility graph, we can assign the same wavelength to all connection requests (nodes) those are connected with each other. For example, same wavelength can be assigned to three connection requests (nodes), if all these three nodes are connected with each other in the compatibility graph. So, we would like to partition the compatibility graph in such a way that it forms minimum number of complete graphs or cliques. Now, the same wavelength can be assigned to all the connection requests belonging to each clique. The total number of wavelengths required to establish the given set of connection requests R for the network is the minimum number of cliques in the compatibility graph. Therefore, the routing and wavelength assignment problem is mapped into a minimum clique partitioning problem. We know that the minimum clique partitioning problem is NP-complete. So, we have proposed heuristic based algorithms to find optimal or near optimal solutions.

4 Proposed Heuristics

In this section, we have proposed two heuristic based algorithms CPWA1 and CPWA2 (based on algorithms in [5]) for wavelength assignment (i.e., minimum number of cliques) that gives optimal or near optimal wavelength assignment in polynomial time.

4.1 Algorithms

In each iteration of algorithm CPWA1, consider a vertex x with minimum degree. Next, choose a vertex y which is neighbor of x and of minimum degree. If more than one y exist, then choose which has any common neighbor with x. Now combine x and y, call it x and delete edges from x and y that are not connected to their common neighbors in the compatibility graph. If the list of edges in the compatibility graph is empty then exit from algorithm, otherwise, repeat the said process.

Algorithm CPWA1

Input   : Compatibility graph G_c for a set of given connection requests.
Output : CLIQUE, minimum number of cliques and number of wavelengths required to setup all connection requests R.
Remark : CLIQUE is a 2-D array. All connection requests belonging to i^{th} clique is stored in CLIQUE$_i$ and i^{th} wavelength is assigned to all connection requests belonging to this clique.

Begin
    Unmark all nodes of the compatibility graph G_c.
    //Compute clique that contain more than one nodes.
    i = 1
    While (list of edges in compatibility graph G_c is nonempty)
        Pick a node x with minimum degree.
        If more than one x exist, consider x which has lowest index.
        Store x to CLIQUE$_i$
        Mark node x in G_c.
        While (x has any remaining neighbor)
            Pick a node y which is neighbor of x and with smallest degree.
            If more than one y exist, then consider y, which has any common neighbors with x. Otherwise, consider lowest index of y.
            Store y to CLIQUE$_i$
            Mark node y in G_c.
            Combine x & y and let it be x.
            Delete edges from x and y those are not connected to their common neighbors and accordingly update compatibility graph G_c
        End While
        i = i+1
    End While
    // Compute clique that contain single node.
    While (G_c has any unmarked node)
        Consider an unmarked node z and store it in CLIQUE$_i$
        Mark node z in G_c
        i = i+1
    End While
    NumberOfClique = NumberOfWavelengthNeed = i-1
    Return (CLIQUE, NumberOfWavelengthNeed)
End of Algorithm CPWA1.

Conceptually both algorithms, consider two vertices such that number of edges deleted can be minimized and the number of edges remains after they are merged is always maximum. Let, node x and node y are merged, then number of edges deleted,

$$E_d = e_x + e_y - c_{xy} - 1$$

where, E_d = number of edges deleted,

   e_x = number of edges of node x,

   e_y = number of edges of node y,

   c_{xy} = number of edges between common neighbors (of x & y) with node x

and y.

To minimize the number of edges deleted, we select x and y with minimum e_x & e_y and maximum c_{xy}. In algorithm CPWA1, consider nodes with minimum number of edges, i.e., with minimum e_x and e_y, Now we proposed algorithm CPWA2 for wavelength assignment that consider the node x with minimum number of edges and search for node y which has maximum number of nodes with x, i.e., we consider minimum e_x and maximum c_{xy} and others are similar concept of CPWA1.

Algorithm CPWA2

Input   : Compatibility graph G_c for a set of given connection requests.

Output   : CLIQUE, minimum number of cliques and number of wavelengths required to setup all connection requests R.

Remark : CLIQUE is a 2-D array. All connection requests belonging to i^{th} clique is stored in CLIQUE$_i$ and i^{th} wavelength is assigned to all connection requests belonging to this clique.

Begin

   Unmark all nodes of the compatibility graph G_c.

   //Compute clique that contain more than one nodes.

   i = 1

   While (list of edges in compatibility graph G_c is nonempty)

         Pick a node x with minimum degree.

         If more than one x exist, consider x which has lowest index.

         Store x to CLIQUE$_i$

         Mark node x in G_c.

         While (x has any remaining neighbor)

               Pick a node y which is neighbor of x and number of
               common neighbors with x is maximum.

               If more than one y exist, then consider y which has lowest
               index.

               Store y to CLIQUE$_i$

               Mark node y in G_c.

               Combine x & y and let it be x.

               Delete edges from x and y those are not connected to their
               common neighbors and accordingly update compatibility
               graph G_c

         End While

         i = i+1

   End While

   // Compute clique that contain single node.

   While (G_c has any unmarked node)

         Consider an unmarked node z and store it in CLIQUE$_i$

         Mark node z in G_c

                    i = i+1
            End While
            NumberOfClique = NumberOfWavelengthNeed = i-1
            Return (CLIQUE, NumberOfWavelengthNeed)
        End of Algorithm CPWA2.

4.2 Example

To explain how the proposed algorithm CPWA1 and algorithm CPWA2 work, let us consider a compatibility graph for 9 connection requests (numbered as 1 to 9) shown in Fig. 3. Both algorithms produce same set of cliques (also wavelength assignment to different connection requests) shown in Fig. 4(a). In algorithm CPWA2, first select node 2 as it is minimum degree and lowest index (since, minimum degree nodes are 2 and 8) i.e., $x = 2$ and put it to $CLIQUE_1$. The neighbors of node 2 are node 1, 6 and 9. Since, number of common neighbor of node 2 with node 1, 6 and 9 are 0, 1, and 1 respectively. So in first iteration of inner while loop node 6 is selected as y and put it to $CLIQUE_1$. Now combine x and y and assign it to x, i.e., $x = 2, 6$. Next statement is delete edges from x & y that are not connected to their common neighbor. So in this step edges (2, 1), (6, 3), (2, 6) and (6, 8) are deleted. Since, node 9 is common neighbor of node 2 and node 6, so node 9 is neighbor of x. Thus, inner while loop is satisfied for next iteration and node 9 is selected as y and insert it to $CLIQUE_1$. Set x as node 2, 6, and 9. Next delete edges (2, 9), (6, 9), (9, 7) and (9, 8) respectively. Now exit from inner while loop because there is no more neighbor of x (are node 2, 6, and 9) and we get first clique in $CLIQUE_1$. The element in $CLIQUE_1$ are   (2, 6, 9). Next iteration of outer while loop is started in a similar manner to find out the next clique. All the cliques returned by this algorithm (CPWA2) is shown in Fig. 4(a). Therefore, by this algorithm wavelengths 1, 2 and 3 are assigned to connection requests (2, 6, 9), (1, 3, 4, 5) and (7, 8) respectively. Fig. 4(b) shows the different cliques generated by algorithm CPWA2 for the compatibility graph (shown in Fig. 2). The CPWA1 algorithm generates the same set of cliques (shown in Fig. 4(a)) for the compatibility graph shown in Fig. 3.

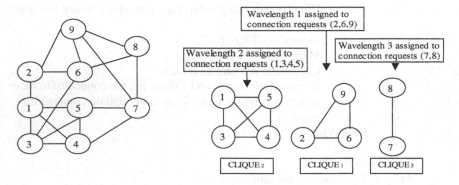

Fig. 3. Compatibility graph for 9 connection requests

Fig. 4(a). Different cliques result by algorithms CPWA1 and CPWA2 for the compatibility graph in Fig. 3

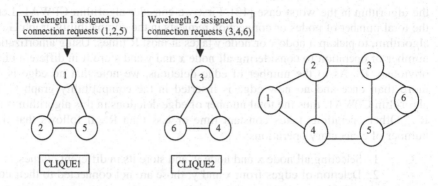

Fig. 4(b). Different cliques result by the algorithm CPWA2 for the compatibility graph in Fig. 2

Fig. 5. A small network of 6-nodes and 8-links

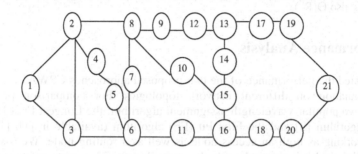

Fig. 6. ARPANET (21 nodes, 26 links)

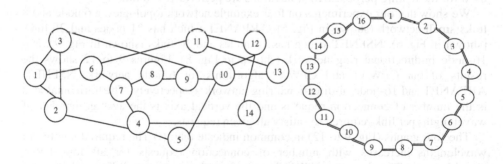

Fig. 7. NSFNET (14 nodes, 20 links)   **Fig. 8.** Bi-directional 16-node ring

4.3 Complexity

In amortized analysis, we average out the time taken by the operation throughout the execution of the algorithm and it guarantees the average cost of the operation and thus the algorithm in the worst case [13]. First we consider algorithm CPWA1. Let, R be the total number of nodes or connection requests in the compatibility graph G_c. In this algorithm, to pickup a node x or node y takes at most R times. Using amortization, the number of operation to considering all node x and y and store it in different cliques is obviously R^2. As to the number of edge deletions, we note that no edge is deleted more than once and no new edge is inserted in the compatibility graph G_c by the algorithm CPWA1, thus the total number of edge deletions in this algorithm is at most R^2. Other operations takes constant time or less than R^2. It follows that the total number of elementary operations:

1. Selecting all node x and node y, and store its in different cliques,
2. Deletion of edges from x and y, those are not connected to their common neighbor

altogether is $2R^2$. This implies that the time complexity of the algorithm CPWA1 is indeed $\Theta(R^2)$.

By similar amortized time analysis, we get the time complexity of the algorithm CPWA2 is also $\Theta(R^2)$.

5 Performance Analysis

We evaluated the performance of the two proposed approaches CPWA1 and CPWA2 using simulation on different network topologies. For comparison purpose we consider two popular wavelength assignment algorithm: the Longest First Fixed Path (LFFP) algorithm [3] and the First Fit (FF) algorithm (available in [1], [15]). Each node is working as both an access node as well as a routing node. We assume each physical link is bi-directional with the same length. The connection requests are randomly generated among all node pairs. The Dijkstra's shortest path algorithm is used for the routing purpose. All simulations are performed 100 times.

We show that our experiments on four example network topologies: a 6 node and 8 links small network (shown in Fig. 5), ARPANET which has 21 nodes and 26 links (shown in Fig. 6), NSFNET which has 14 nodes and 20 links (shown in Fig. 7), and 16-node bi-directional ring network (shown in Fig. 8). Figures 9 to 12 shows the results of our CPWA1 and CPWA2 algorithms for 6-node network, NSFNET, ARPANET and 16-node bi-directional ring network, respectively. The horizontal axis is the number of connection requests and the vertical axis is the average number of wavelengths per link required to satisfy all given requests.

The four graphs (Fig. 9 to 12) in common indicate that: (i) The required number of wavelengths increases with number of connection requests for all four RWA algorithms. (ii) The algorithm CPWA2 outperform the existing well known LFFP and FF algorithms. (iii) The performance of CPWA2 is better than CPWA1, one main reason may be the algorithm CPWA2 select node y (for clique) which is neighbor of node x and maximum common neighbor with x, is more effective than in the algorithm CPWA1, where y is neighbor of x and degree of node y is minimum. (iv) The algorithm CPWA1 perform much better than the existing algorithm FF and better performance than popular LFFP algorithm. (v) The performance of the LFFP is better than FF.

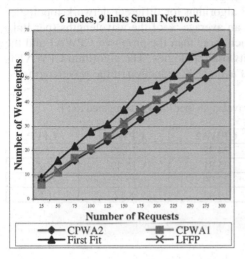

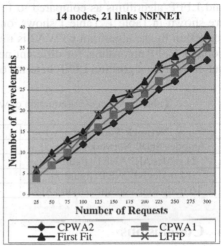

Fig. 9. Average number of wavelengths per link required versus number of requests for shown in Fig. 5

Fig. 10. Average number of wavelengths per link required versus number of requests for NSFNET

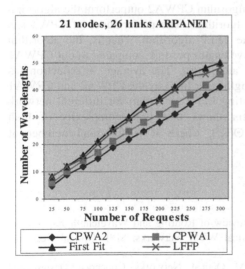

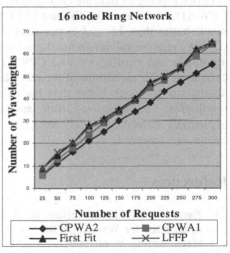

Fig. 11. Average number of wavelengths per link required versus number of requests for ARPANET

Fig. 12. Average number of wavelengths per link required versus number of requests for 16 node bi-directional ring network

Therefore, the performance of the CPWA2 is much better than proposed CPWA1 algorithm and the popular LFFP and FF algorithms, that is, the CPWA2 algorithm requires less number of wavelengths per link compared to CPWA1 algorithm and existing LFFP and FF algorithms.

The average % reduction of the wavelengths (per link) by the CPWA2, CPWA1 and LFFP algorithms as compared to FF algorithm for different network topologies are shown in Table 1. Table 1 shows, on an average % of the wavelengths (per link) reduction by the algorithm CPWA2 is much more than the proposed CPWA1 and the popular LFFP algorithms for different network topologies. The algorithm CPWA1 is better than the algorithm LFFP in terms of average % reduction of the wavelengths.

Table 1. Average % reduction of wavelength (per link) as compared to FF

Network Topology	CPWA2	CPWA1	LFFP
6 nodes Small Network (figure 5)	24.32	18.07	15.31
21 nodes ARPANET (figure 6)	25.81	16.49	3.28
14 nodes NFSNET (figure 7)	22.00	15.95	5.06
16 node Ring Network (figure 8)	19.40	8.12	1.61

6 Conclusions

In this paper, we have studied the problem of static routing and wavelength assignment in wavelength routed all optical networks and proposed two new efficient polynomial time heuristic algorithms CPWA1 and CPWA2 based on clique partitioning for wavelength assignment. Extensive simulation results for different network topologies indicate clearly that, algorithm CPWA2 outperform the algorithm CPWA1 and the existing FF and LFFP algorithms. The performance of CPWA1 is much better than FF and better than the LFFP algorithm. That is, the algorithm CPWA2 requires minimum number of wavelengths per link compared to our CPWA1 algorithm and existing FF and CPWA1 algorithms. The average % reduction (as compared to FF algorithm) of the wavelengths (per link) by the CPWA2 and CPWA1 algorithms are much better than the existing LFFP algorithm for different network topologies. The amortized time analysis shows that time complexity of both algorithms CPWA1 and CPWA2 are $\Theta(R^2)$, where R is the total number of connection requests.

References

1. Zang, H., Jue, J.P., Mukherjee, B.: A Review of Routing and Wavelength Assignment Approaches for Wavelength-Routed Optical WDM Networks. SPIE Optical Networks Magazine 1(1), 47–60 (2000)
2. Murthy, C.S.R., Gurusamy, M.: WDM Optical Networks Concepts, Design and Algorithms. Prentice-Hall of India Pvt. Limited, Englewood Cliffs (2002)
3. Chlamtac, I., Ganz, A., Karmi, G.: Lightpath Communications: An Approach to High Bandwidth Optical WAN's. IEEE Transactions on Communications. 40, 1171–1182 (1992)
4. Ramaswami, R., Sivarajan, K.N.: Routing and Wavelength Assignment in All-Optical Networks. IEEE/ACM Transactions on Networking 3, 489–499 (1995)
5. Kim, J.T., Shin, D.R.: New efficient Clique Partitioning Algorithms for Register-Transfer Synthesis of Data Paths. Journal of the Korean Physical Society 40(4), 754–758 (2002)

6. Banerjee, D., Mukherjee, B.: A Practical Approach for Routing and Wavelength Assignment in Large Wavelength-Routed Optical Networks. IEEE Journal on Selected Areas in Communications 14(5), 903–908 (1996)
7. Zhang, Z., Acampora, A.: A Heuristic Wavelength Assignment Algorithm For Multihop WDM Networks with Wavelength Routing And Wavelength Reuse. IEEE/ACM Transactions On Networking 3(3), 281–288 (1995)
8. Dutta, R., Mitra, B., Ghose, S., Sengupta, I.: An algorithm for Optimal Assignment of a Wavelength in a Tree Topology and Its Application in WDM Networks. IEEE Journal on Selected Areas in Communications 22(9), 1589–1600 (2004)
9. Banerjee, N., Sharan, S.: A Evolutionary Algorithm for Solving The Single Objective Static Routing Wavelength Assignment Problem in WDM Routing Network. In: ICISIP 2004. IEEE 2nd International Conference on Intelligent Sensing and Information Processing, pp. 13–18 (2004)
10. Saha, D., Purkayastha, M.D., Mukherjee, A.: An approach to Wide area WDM Optical Network Desig using Genetic Algorithm. Computer Communication 22(2), 156–172 (1999)
11. Baroni, S., Bayvel, P.: Wavelength Requirement in Arbitrarily Connected Wavelength-Routed Optical Networks. IEEE/OSA Journal of Lightwave Technology 15(2), 242–251 (1997)
12. Siregar, J.H., Takagi, H., Zhang, Y.: Efficient Routing and Wavelength Assignment in Wavelength-Routed Optical Networks. In: APNOMS 2003. 7th Asia-Pasific Network Operations and Management Symposium (2003)
13. Alsuwaiyel, M.H.: Algorithms Design Techniques and Analysis. World Scientific publishing Ltd., Singapore (2000)
14. Zhou, J., Yuan, X.: A Study of Dynamic Routing and Wavelength Assignment with Imprecise Network State Information. In: ICPPW. International Conference on Parallel Processing Workshops, pp. 1–5 (2002)
15. Ngo, S.H., Jiang, X., Horiguchi, S.: An ant-based approach for dynamic RWA in optical WDM networks. Journal of Photonic Network Communications 11, 39–48 (2006)
16. Pal, A., Patel, U.: Routing and Wavelength Assignment in Wavelength Division Multiplexing Networks. In: Sen, A., Das, N., Das, S.K., Sinha, B.P. (eds.) IWDC 2004. LNCS, vol. 3326, pp. 391–396. Springer, Heidelberg (2004)

Fault Detection and Localization Scheme for Multiple Failures in Optical Network

A. Pal[1], A. Paul[1], A. Mukherjee[2], M.K. Naskar[3], and M. Nasipuri[1]

[1] Dept. of CSE, Jadavpur University, Calcutta 700 032, India
amitangshupal@yahoo.co.in,
arghyadip.paul@yahoo.co.in,
nasipuri@vsnl.com
[2] Royal Institute of Technology, Stockholm, Sweden
and
IBM India Pvt Ltd, Calcutta 700091, India
amitava.mukherjee@in.ibm.com
[3] Dept. of ETCE, Jadavpur University, Calcutta 700 032, India
mrinalnaskar@yahoo.co.in

Abstract. This paper proposes fault detection and localization scheme to handle multiple failures in the optical network using wavelength-division multiplexing (WDM) technology. This proposed scheme is two-phased scheme containing (a) the detection of faults through monitoring devices raising alarms (fault detection) and (b) subsequently the localization of these faults (fault localization) by invoking an algorithm. The later phase will obtain a set of potential faulty nodes (links). We demonstrate the performance of the scheme on 14-node NSFNet and 28-node EuroNet. We compare our scheme with an existing algorithm [1] for locating faulty nodes (links). Our scheme outperforms the existing one.

Keywords: Fault Detection, Fault localization, WDM, Optical Network.

1 Introduction

High capacity optical networks are immensely used in industries due to its large transmission bandwidth and low cost. But these networks are also vulnerable to failures like malfunctions of optical devices, fiber cuts, soft failures i.e., the impairment due to subtle changes in signal power such as degrading signal to noise ratio (SNR), etc. One of the most important requirements to ensure high speed optical network survivable is to manage fault detection, localization and recovery. In this work we discuss only fault detection and localization and the block diagram of our proposed scheme is shown in Figure 1.

Fault diagnosis and localization is a challenging problem and hence it is an active field of research. Different approaches were used to solve the problem. Approximation algorithms were shown in [2]-[3] to reduce the number of monitoring elements. In [4] author showed that the optimal monitor placement (reduction) is an NP hard

S. Rao et al. (Eds.): ICDCN 2008, LNCS 4904, pp. 464–470, 2008

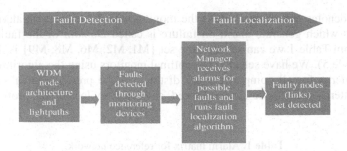

Fig. 1. Proposed fault detection and localization scheme

problem. Also in [1], [5] false and miss alarms are considered. In [5], authors showed that false alarms can be corrected in polynomial time but the correction of miss alarms is NP-hard.

We model the network by a directed graph $G = (V, E)$ where each node $v \in V$ of the graph represents an optical component, and the directed edge $(u, v) \in E$ represents a directed lightpath from u to v. We have taken 14-node NSFNet (shown in Fig 2) as our network model which is the backbone network for US. The Fig. 2 is self-explained.

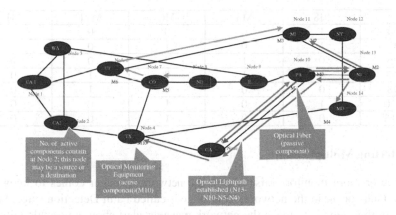

Fig. 2. Reference NSFNet

2 Proposed Scheme

2.1 Fault Monitoring: Monitors Placement with Dynamic Lightpaths

Monitors initially are placed to all possible number of locations so that the failures can be detected and located for all components distinctly. In Fig. 2, M1 – M11 i.e., 11 monitoring devices are placed to achieve maximum coverage. We propose a greedy algorithm which determines the optimal number of monitors in such a way that failures can be located for all components (i.e., for node(s) or link(s)) distinctly and no component remains unattended i.e., if a fault occurs in a component it must not remain undetected. The algorithm is described detail in [3]. In Table 1 (generated from

Fig 2), '1' denotes that if a node fails the monitor with '1' triggers an alarm. The set of monitors which generate alarm on failure is called *Domain* of the faulty component(s). From Table 1 we can say that the set {M1, M2, M6, M8, M9} is the domain of ND5 (node 5). We have selected the optimal monitors using the algorithm [3] until domain patterns for all components are distinct. In the pre-computing stage, these domain patterns (see Table 2) are stored and used to locate the probable faulty components.

Table 1. Alarm matrix for reference network

	M1	M2	M3	M4	M5	M6	M7	M8	M9	M10	M11
ND4	0	0	0	0	0	0	0	1	0	0	0
ND5	1	1	0	0	0	1	0	1	1	0	0
ND6	0	0	1	0	0	0	0	0	0	0	0
ND7	0	0	1	0	1	0	0	0	0	1	1
ND8	0	0	0	0	0	0	0	0	0	0	1
ND10	0	1	0	1	0	1	1	1	1	0	0
ND13	0	0	0	1	0	1	0	0	0	0	0

Table 2. Reduced Alarm matrix for reference network

	M8	M3	M6	M11	M1
ND4	1	0	0	0	0
ND5	1	0	1	0	1
ND6	0	1	0	0	0
ND7	0	1	0	1	0
ND8	0	0	0	1	0
ND10	1	0	1	0	0
ND13	0	0	1	0	0

2.2 Detecting Multiple Faults

When one or more monitors raise alarm, the network manager comes to know that probable faults occur in the network. This stage is called Fault Detection stage. So the function of this stage is to make the network manager alert about a possible failure in the network, so that he can run the fault localization algorithm (described later) to localize the faulty components.

2.3 Locating Multiple Faults

When there is any fault occurred in any component(s) some monitors which are in the domain of that component(s) will trigger alarms. But networks are frequently interrupted with corrupted alarms namely false and miss alarms. The fault localization algorithm (which also takes care for corrupted alarms) for multiple faults is described below. In this algorithm M is the set of all alarms, M_r is the set of all ringing alarms, M_s is the set of all silent alarms and C is the set of all components.

Algorithm for Locating Multiple faults
Set_of_multiple_fault(){
Initialize an empty set FC=$\varnothing$
Multiplefault(M_r)
for (i=1 to $|M_r|$){
    $D_r = M_r\backslash M_r(i)$ where $M_r(i) \in M_r$
    Multiplefault(D_r) }
for (i=1 to $|M_s|$){
    $B_r = M_r \cup M_s(i)$ for $M_s(i) \in M_s$
    Multiplefault(B_r) }
for (i=1 to $|M_r|$){
    $G_r = M_r\backslash M_r(i)$ for $M_r(i) \in M_r$
    for (k=1 to $|M_s|$){
        $H_r = G_r \cup M_s(k)$ for $M_s(k) \in M_s$
      Multiplefault (H_r) }}
Output set FC;}
Multiplefault(set M_r){
for (i=1 to $|C|$){
    search for a component $C_i \in C$ such that Domain ($C_i) \subseteq M_r$
    incorporate C_i to S
    FC=FC$\cup\{C_i\}$ }}

In our fault localization algorithm we have considered four cases i) No false alarm and no miss alarm ii) One false alarm and no miss alarm iii) No false alarm and one miss alarm iv) One false alarm and one miss alarm. We explain our algorithm using Table II. Let us consider at any time the *received alarm* (RAL) has been noticed {1 1 1 0 0} i.e., M3, M6, M8 have triggered alarms and M1, M11 remain silent. For case i) it is assumed that there are only correct alarms in the network. Now as Domain (ND4)$\subseteq M_r$, Domain (ND6)$\subseteq M_r$, Domain (ND10)$\subseteq M_r$, Domain(ND13)$\subseteq M_r$, {ND4, ND6, ND10, ND13} is included in faulty component (FC) (from Fault Localization algorithm). For case ii) we have made the all combination of received alarm pattern considering that there is one false alarm in the network. So, in the above mentioned received alarm pattern three more patterns are available. They are {(1 1 0 0 0), (1 0 1 0 0), (0 1 1 0 0)}. For case iii) where there is one miss alarm but no false alarm we have more combinations of received alarm pattern. They are {(1 1 1 1 0), (1 1 1 0 1)}. For case iv) where there are one false alarm and one miss alarm there are eight more possible combinations of received alarm pattern. They are {(0 1 1 1 0), (0 1 1 0 1), (1 0 1 1 0), (1 0 1 0 1), (1 1 0 1 0), (1 1 0 0 1)}.

3 Simulation Performance

We have implemented our scheme on 28 nodes EuroNet and the results are shown below. Fig. 3 shows that the cardinality of the set of possible faulty nodes in the case of single and double faults which is the output of fault localization algorithm. Fig. 4 and

Fig 5 show that the number of monitoring devices remains more or less same with the change of ligthpaths in three different situations namely a) during a single and double fault, b) after single and double fault and c) after addition of a new monitor (node) in the network.

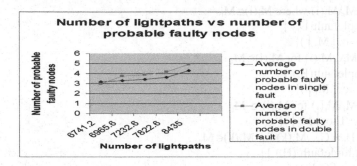

Fig. 3. Number of elements in faulty set vs. load

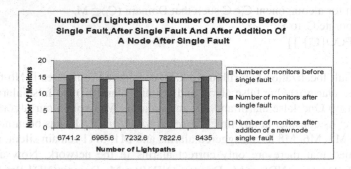

Fig. 4. Monitor number vs load before single fault, after single fault and after new node addition

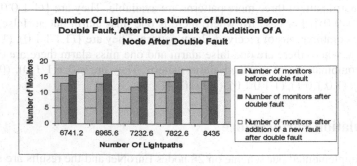

Fig. 5. Number of monitor vs load before double fault, after double fault and new node addition

4 Comparison Between Our Scheme and Algorithm Discussed in [1]

We have compared our scheme with the algorithm of [1] on the fault localization i.e., how the cardinality of the set of faulty nodes varies in both schemes (shown in Fig. 6 and Fig. 7). The cardinality set generated from [1] is higher in both cases. Therefore, our algorithm performs better in locating faults than existing one [1].

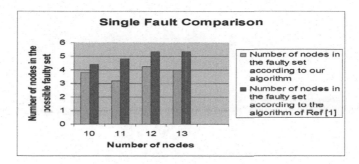

Fig. 6. Comparison of single fault

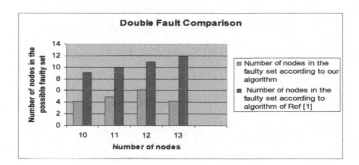

Fig. 7. Comparison of double faults

5 Conclusion

In this paper we have presented two-phased scheme containing (a) fault detection and (b) fault localization. We have shown the performance of our scheme on 28-node Eu-roNet and also compared fault localization scheme with an existing algorithm [1]. Clearly, it has been found that our algorithm outperforms the existing one.

References

[1] Mas, C., Thiran, P.: An Efficient Algorithm for Locating Soft and Hard Failures in WDM Networks. IEEE Journal of Selected Areas of Communications (October 2000)
[2] Stanic, Subramanium, Choi, H., Sahin, Choi, H-A.: On Monitoring Transparent Optical Networks. In: ICPPW. International Conference on Parallel Processing Workshops (2002)

[3] Pal, S., Nayek, P., Mukherjee, A.: Fault Localization Scheme for Multiple Failures in Optical Networks. In: Proceeding of SNCNW 2006, Lule, Sweden (2006)

[4] Rao, N.S.V.: Computational Complexity Issues in Operative Diagnosis of graph-based Systems. IEEE Transactions on Computers 42(4), 447–457 (1993)

[5] Nguyen, H., Thiran, P.: Failure Location in Transparent Optical Networks: The Asymmetry Between False and Missing Alarms. In: ITC 1919. Proceedings of The 19th International Teletraffic Congress, Beijing, China (August 2005)

A Heuristic Search for Routing and Wavelength Assignment in Distributed WDM Optical Networks with Limited Range Wavelength Conversion

Sahadeb Jana[1], Kajla Basu[2], and Subhabrata Chowdhury[2]

[1] Software Technology Parks of India, Electronics City, Hosur Road, Bangalore, India
[2] National Institute of Technology, M.G. Road, Durgapur, India
sahadeb_jana@rediffmail.com, kajla2007@rediffmail.com,
antuarka@yahoo.co.uk

Abstract. In today's broadband communication optical network is mostly used for backbone network establishment. In optical networks, it's the advent of wavelength division multiplexing, WDM, not only helps us to properly utilize available bandwidth of optical fiber but also helps us to manage the optical fiber medium in better way. Continuous lightpath would be treated as solution for lightpath establishment. And availability of the same wavelength throughout the whole path would be, only, cause of a lightpath establishment. It's the unavailability of the same wavelength throughout a path would cause lightpath not to be established and that would increase call blocking probability. Wavelength conversion in limited manner, one step wavelength conversion, is one solution to minimize call blocking probability. Here one wavelength assignment and one routing algorithm have been proposed which give us better results in terms of call blocking probability and processing time for wavelength assignment.

Keywords: WDM, One step conversion, Degree of conversion.

1 Introduction

If we see the trends in optical network technology, its clearly visible that the trend dynamic lightpath establishment or on demand lightpath establishment has become very popular in order to satisfy service providers' requests to respond quickly and economically to customer demands. For the efficient usage of network resources, the dynamic light- path establishment scheme should be able to maximize the number of connections that are established in the network [1]. However, there is always a possibility that the network resources are not sufficient to setup a lightpath when connection requests are issued, resulting in connection blocking. This blocking probability will increase if time taken to reserve wavelength in each link of a route path, returned by routing algorithm is high. Thus, wavelength assignment algorithm plays a pivotal role in dynamic light path establishment. In an optical network [3], it is usually not feasible to establish lightpaths on a single wavelength between every pair of nodes due to physical constraints on the number of wavelengths limited by the

S. Rao et al. (Eds.): ICDCN 2008, LNCS 4904, pp. 471–477, 2008.

ehium doped fiber amplifier bandwidth (35nm) [2], limited number and tunabilily of the optical receivers at each node and light wave dispersions that limit the physical length of the lightpath. A wavelength converter can transfer a signal on one wavelength to another wavelength at its output port (if there is no wavelength conflict). In all optical conversion, it is less costly to convert a wavelength to another wavelength not farther away [4]. In our study we have considered that all nodes in an optical network will have optical converter with one-step conversion capability. In other words, if incoming signals are with λ_i, the outgoing signal could be with either λ_{i-1} or λ_{i+1}. Here we should know why should we stress on less usage of conversion although available? The answer is too much conversion: a) causes signal loss and b) increases power consumption.

In recent studies [6]-[11], authors tried to solve the problems or it variants and have not considered the wavelength convertibility criteria. This motivates us to solve the assignment problem with assumption of limited convertibility at each node of the network.

The literatures [7], [12] have proposed different routing strategies and the best algorithm has been proposed in literature [7]. We have proposed one new routing algorithm, which performs better than the shortest path algorithm and the proposal in literature [8].

2 Network Model

The network consists of some nodes and connectivity by optical fiber. Each node of the network has switching and conversion capability to connect channels to form lightpaths. Conversion capability of each node is one step. The figure 1 depicts one node with one step wavelength convertibility. Here the term, one step wavelength conversion means - if λ_1, λ_2, λ_3 etc are the serially assigned wavelength of any link then λ_2 can be converted to either λ_1 or λ_3; λ_1 can only be converted to λ_2 and λ_3 only to λ_2 if available on the next link. The amount of switching and conversion capability at a node can be called as *wavelength degree* [5]. A node has *wavelength degree* (for some integer) if for each pair of incident links a channel in a link is attached to at most other channels in the other link. For this model, the limited conversion node shown in Fig 1 has wavelength degree two. Also note that a node with no or fixed conversion has wavelength degree one, while a node with full conversion has wavelength degree equal to total no of wavelength of each link. Here in presence of this one step conversion we have to find out a best path for any request so that the call blocking probability as well as number of conversion taken place in between nodes both can be reduced.

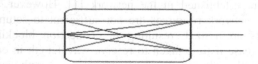

Fig. 1. One step conversion for wavelength degree 2

3 Mathematical Formulation

Let us assume that there are N nodes in a route path, P, returned by routing algorithm between any pair of nodes in an optical network. Each link in the network is having m wavelengths. For mathematical formulation let us consider the followings:

LP_k: k^{th} feasible lightpath in P, where k is positive integer
λ: Set of wavelength i.e $\lambda = \{\lambda_1, \lambda_2, \ldots \ldots, \lambda_m\}$
L: Set of links in the path i.e. $L = \{L_1, L_2, \ldots, L_{N-1}\}$
LS_i^j: Link status of ith link, $1 \leq i \leq N-1$ and $1 \leq j \leq m$
X_k: Assignment matrix where an element x_{ij}^k takes value 1 if wavelength λ_i is
    assigned to the lightpath, LP_k, on link, L_j, otherwise, 0 and $1 \leq i \leq m$, $1 \leq j \leq N-1$
λ^{UNU}: is a matrix where λ_{ij}^{UNU} takes value 1 if λ_i is free on the link L_j, otherwise 0, and
    $1 \leq i \leq m$, $1 \leq j \leq N-1$
Y_k: is the number of wavelength conversion in a lightpath, LP_k.
CH_i^j: j^{th} child generated by i^{th} parent, $1 \leq i \leq n-2$ and $1 \leq j \leq 2$ (m-2)
CON_{ij}^{kl}: Represents that to go from i^{th} link to j^{th} link k^{th} wavelength to be converted
    into l^{th} wavelength.
C_{ij}^k: Conversion cost from L_i to L_j calculated at node k.
SOL_COST: ΣC_{ij}^k, for $2 \leq k \leq N-1$

Objective of the problem:

$$Minimize \quad \Sigma C_{ij}^k, CBP \ and \ TC \tag{1}$$

Subject to:

$$\lambda_i = \lambda_{i+1} \ or \ \lambda_{i-1} \qquad if \ 1 < i < m \tag{2}$$

$$\lambda_i = \lambda_{i+1} \qquad if \ i = 1 \tag{3}$$

$$\lambda_i = \lambda_{i-1} \qquad if \ i = m \tag{4}$$

Here CBP is call blocking probability and TC is time consumption. The 2nd condition says that can be changed to either one step more or one step less if index of is greater than 1 and less than m. If its index is 1 then it can only be changed to one step more and in case of m it can be one step less.

4 Algorithm

Step 1: Branching at 2nd, 3rd, …..$(N-1)^{th}$ node is done in parallel as there are total N
    nodes on the routed path to find out CH_i^j.
Step 2: After branching, cost assigned to each and every child state. Left most
    children is the state itself and its cost is 0 and cost of all other is 1.
Step 3: For each child state of each parent intersection operation is done with the next
    link status value in parallel.

Step 4: Now cost of each intersection, $C_{ij}{}^k$, is calculated adding cost child state with cost of next link state, which is considered 0. This is calculated only if intersection value is not 0. If all the intersection values on a node are 0, request cannot be entertained. Here $CON_{ij}{}^{kl}$ is also calculated.

Step 5: At each node, pick up the least cost intersection and choose that as the best alternative for solution and calculate SOL_COST.

5 Routing Scheme

Routing algorithm may be based on shortest path routing (SPR) algorithm. But here a new approach for routing will be proposed which will be better than SPR.

This procedure will try to find a path keeping in mind two factors: length of path and wavelengths already used along the path. The total procedure is described below.

First of all we will find out a set of paths (P). The first path of that set will be shortest path; second one will be next shortest path; third one will be next to second one etc. P set is finite and depends upon user. Minimum value can be taken as 3.

Then we will calculate Wavelength Usage (WU) factor for each path. WU factor for each path is ratio of number of wavelengths presently in use and total number of wavelengths along that path.

WU factor = (No. of wavelengths presently in use) / (Total number of wavelengths along that path)

This says that if a path consists of two link each having three wavelengths and number of wavelengths in use along that path is three (i.e one link has used two wavelengths and another only one wavelength), WU factor for this example will be 3/ (2*3) = 0.5.

If WU factors for all the paths are calculated, we will calculate Deciding (D) factor for each path of the set. D factor is inverse of (L*WU factor), where L is length of the path.

D factor = 1/ (L*WU factor)

Once D factors are calculated, we will choose the path having maximum D factor as best path to be used for wavelength assignment.

Why does this scheme consider two different factors for path selection? Length of path factor is important because too much length increases probability of conversion. And the second factor is most important because too much wavelength usage on a path increases probability of not having suitable combination of wavelength even in presence of wavelength conversion.

Lastly, why did we take a finite set of paths? This has been considered in such a manner because too many paths in the set increases time consumption for selecting the best path.

6 Results

For testing the performance of the proposed algorithms, two different networks have been taken. The first one is a seven-node network with predefined connectivity as shown in the Figure 2. We will run our experiment on this network and it can be run on other any other network also.

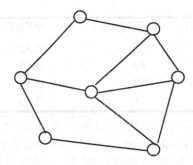

Fig. 2. A 7-node sample network

The results have been taken for different number of wavelength on each link and changing the total wavelength usage of the network. The percentage of wavelength usage means how much the network is loaded. Results on Table 1 show that the proposed concept, if applied, for wavelength assignment under one step wavelength conversion the call blocking probability can be improved to some significant amount. For simulation on this network total 28 calls were generated. From each source node 4 different calls were generated for four different destinations.

Legends which are used on the tables are as follows
Exp No.- Serial no of the experiments, WL - Wavelengths on each link, WLU - Wavelength Used, WTC - Call blocking probability without conversion, WOSC - Call blocking probability using SP routing with one step Conversion, NRA – Call blocking probability with new routing algorithm.

Table 1. Results show better performance of one step Conversion (WOSC) over without conversion (WTC)

Exp No.	WL	WLU(%)	WTC	WOSC
2	4	69	0.46	0.32
3	5	69	0.46	0.07
5	6	69	0.53	0.39
6	6	60	0.60	0.50

Results of the Table 2 show that applying the routing concept, on the same network varying number of wavelength and wavelength usage, we can improve the call blocking probability further to some noticeable amount. The routing algorithm, for simulation, takes three different paths for selecting the best one, according to the path selection formula already discussed, for any request.

Table 2. Results show better performance of new routing algorithm (NRA)

Exp No.	WL	WLU(%)	WOSC	NRA
2	4	75	0.32	0.28
4	5	64	0.14	0.03
5	5	84	0.39	0.35
6	6	76	0.50	0.35

Thus these two sets of result clearly say that the one step conversion wavelength assignment algorithm is a better concept and the routing algorithm proposed is also better one.

Now the time complexity and time consumption
The time complexity of the wavelength assignment algorithm proposed in literature [6] is $O(L*W)$. Where L is length of the path selected from the set of paths and it can be maximum $N(N-1)/2$, where N is the number of nodes of the network. Actually, in one-step conversion all the wavelengths except first and last one can be converted into two wavelengths and total number of calculation will be $2(W-2) = 2W-4$. Again, the first and last one can be converted to only one wavelength and the total computation will be $2W-4+2 = 2*W-2$. For intersection operation again we need $2*W-2$ computations. So total computations for the selected route are $L*2*(2*W-2)$ and complexity could be $O(L*W)$. For this algorithm the time complexity is $O(W)$. Because here for all the L-1 links computations will be going on in parallel and all the nodes can generate the output only with $2*(2*W-2)$ computations and this says that its complexity is $O(W)$.

7 Conclusion

Here one routing algorithm and one new approach for assigning wavelengths in presence of limited range wavelength conversion have been proposed. The routing algorithm has been proposed keeping two vital factors in mind: a) length of the path and b) wavelength usage over the path. And the wavelength assignment algorithm can be applied in distributed environment where each and every node has the computing capability to some extent. It has also been proved that this algorithm if applied in real networks can run consuming less time. The routing algorithm has been proposed and the results, applying this algorithm, show that this is a better proposition.

References

1. Mukherjee, B.: Optical Communication Networks. McGraw-Hill, New York (1997)
2. Lee, K.C., Li, V.O.K.: Routing of All-Optical Networks using wavelength Outside Erbium-Doped Fiber Amplifier Bandwidth. In: Proc. of IEEE/Infoocom 1994, Los Angles, CA (April 1994)
3. Ramswamy, R., Shivraja, K.: Optical Networks: A Practical Perspective, 2nd edn. Morgan Kaufmann Publishers, San Francisco
4. Venugopal, K.R, Achuth, A., SreenivasaKumar, P.: An Adaptive Algorithm lo Reduce Wavelength Conversion and Congestion in All-Optical Networks. In Technical Report. Departmat of Computer Science, UT Madras (December 1993)
5. Ramaswami, R., Segall, A.: Distributeed network control for optical networks. IEEE/ACM Trans. Networking 5, 936–943 (1997)
6. Mandal, S., Jana, S., Saha, D.: A Heuristic Search for Dynamic Lightpath Establishment in WDM Optical Networks with Limited Wavelength Conversion Capability. In: Proc. of ICCT 2003, Hydrabad, India, pp. 702–705 (April 2003)
7. Chu, X., Li, B.: Dynamic Routing and Wavelength Assignment in the Presence of Wavelength Conversion for All-Optical Networks. IEEE/ACM Transactions on Networking 13(3) (June 2005)
8. Hsu, C.-F., Liu, T.-L., Huang, N.-F.: On Adaptive Routing in Wavelength-Routed Networks. SPIE/Kluwer Optical Networks Magazine 3(1), 15–23 (2002)
9. Zang, H., Zue, J.P., Mukherje, B.: A Review of Routing and Wavelength Assignment Approaches for Wavelength-Routed Optical WDM Networks. Optical Networks Magazine, 47–60 (January 2000)
10. Kovacevic, M., Acampora, A.: Benefits of wavelength translation in all-optical clear-channel networks. IEEE Journal on Selected Areas in Communications 14, 868–880 (1996)
11. Chu, X.-W., Li, B., Chlamtac, I.: Wavelength converter placement for different RWA algorithms in wavelength-routed all-optical networks. IEEE Transactions on Communications 51, 607–616 (2003)
12. Harai, H., Murata, M., Miyahara, H.: Performance of Alternate Routing Methods in All-Optical Switching Networks. In: Proc. of IEEE INFOCOM 1997, pp. 516–524 (April 1997)

An Efficient Storage Mechanism to Distribute Disk Load in a VoD Server

D.N. Sujatha[1], K. Girish[1], K.R. Venugopal[1], and L.M. Patnaik[2]

[1] Department of Computer Science and Engineering
University Visvesvaraya College of Engineering Bangalore University
Bangalore-560001, India
suj_sat@yahoo.com
[2] Microprocessor Applications Laboratory, Indian Institute of Science
Bangalore-560012, India

Abstract. In this paper, a storage mechanism is devised to balance the load and to provide immediate service to the clients with a start-up delay of 2ms to 7 ms. The video storage is based on the probability of the clients requesting for the video. Videos with higher probability of being requested are stored and replicated to ensure guaranteed retrieval. Parity generation scheme is employed to provide reliability to non-popular videos. The system is also capable of handling disk failures transparently and thereby providing a reliable service to the clients.

Keywords: Fault Tolerance, Load Balancing, Start-up Delay, Video Server.

1 Introduction

Recent developments in storage mechanisms are making high performance Video-on-Demand (VoD) servers a reality. The video server stores heterogeneous information on array of high capacity storage servers and deliver them to the geographically distributed clients. The design constraint is to develop a large-scale cost-effective video server with a scalability to admit and service the client's requests simultaneously.

2 Previous Works

A comparison of different RAID levels is made to bring out Random Duplicate Assignment (RDA) [1]. In this strategy the video is striped and instead of being stored sequentially they are randomly allocated in different disks and each strip is mirrored to enable fault tolerance. The time required to access next block in the disk increase as the blocks are randomly allocated. A map between the blocks is to be maintained to handle this problem, which is an additional overhead. Golubchik et al. [2] discusses fundamental issues associated with providing fault tolerance in multi-disk VoD servers. In [3], [4] Replication of videos and placement of video blocks based on popularity is discussed.

S. Rao et al. (Eds.): ICDCN 2008, LNCS 4904, pp. 478–483, 2008.
© Springer-Verlag Berlin Heidelberg 2008

3   System Architecture

The overview of storage mechanism is shown in Fig. 1. The video is divided into blocks based on number of disks. Each block is stored in different disks sequentially so that only once a block of video stored on the disk. The first disk to store the video is rotated to ensure that the load is balanced among the disks. If the block requested is stored in a disk, which is serving another client, the request is queued. The requests in the request queue are serviced in round robin fashion. If the video is popular then, the video is stripped across the array of the disks and mirrored. The request is serviced by the mirrored storage, in case of increase load for the popular videos. The mirrored data is also accessed in case of disk failure containing the popular videos. If the video is non-popular video, it is stripped across the disks with the last disk in the set of disks to store the parity information. Performing XoR operation between all the blocks of data generates parity block. This helps to rebuild the video block in case of disk failure.

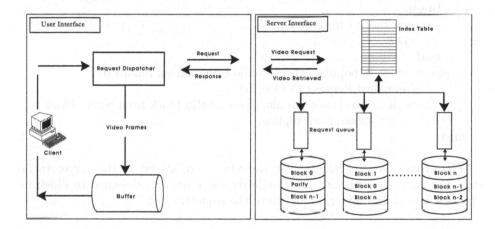

Fig. 1. Overview of the Storage Mechanism

4   Algorithm

A: Video_Storage (VideoId)
1. Determine the popularity of the video.
2. If (video is popular) *then* BlockSize = VideoSize / n
   else BlockSize = VideoSize / n-1
3. If(space available to store video at BlockSize on disk j)
   $While(VideoSize \geq 0)$
   begin
   $j = ((VideoId\%n) + i)\%n$
   $reduceVideoSizebyBlockSize.$
   $storeblockondisk$ j

        increment i by 1
end
4. $if (video is popular)$ *then mirror the blocks in mirror storage.*
            else $P_j = B_0 \oplus B_1$
  While $(i < n)$
  begin
         $p_j = p_j \oplus B_i$
         Store P_j in disk j
  end

B: Handle_Request (Video_id)
1. found = search index table for VideoId
2. While (found=EOF)
3. Retrieve video_info from index table.
  begin
     if (block not corrupted) and if (disk not loaded)
       begin
         stream block i from disk j
         j = j+1
       end
     else if (video is popular) then handle request from replica disk
       else Forward_Request (Video_Id)
         else if (video is not popular)then rebuild block from parity block
           else stream from replica.
  end

The storage routine shows how the videos are stored in the server to facilitate load balancing and the HandleRequest routine is designed to illustrate the behavior of the server on arrival of the request.

4.1   Illustrated Example

Consider the storage of 5 videos V_0, V_1, V_2, V_3, V_4 of file size 1500Mb, 1000Mb, 2000Mb, 800 Mb, and 3000 Mb respectively, where V_0, V_1, V_4 are popular videos and V_2, V_3 are non-popular videos. The disk-id of first block is disk-1, disk-2, disk-3, disk-4 and disk-5 with block size 300 Mb, 200 Mb, 800 Mb, 169 Mb and 600 Mb respectively. Considering 10 disks in the video server with 5 primary disks, the storage allocation for each video in their corresponding disks is given in Table 1. The request arrivals are indicated in Table. 2. The requests are served with each request being allocated bandwidth (Refer Table. 3). If the disk is busy serving different client it is moved to the request queue (Refer Table. 4). The request queue is checked for every 5 sec and if queue is not empty then, the clients are served in round robin fashion. It is assumed that the request queue capacity is 5. If the number of requests increases or the delay increases more than 10 ms then, the request is forwarded to other video server.

Table 1. Storage of Videos

Video-id	Block-size(Mb)	Disk-1	Disk-2	Disk-3	Disk-4	Disk-5
V_0	1500/5=300	B_0	B_1	B_2	B_3	B_4
V_1	1000/5=200	B_4	B_0	B_1	B_2	B_3
V_2	2000/4=500	B_3	P	B_0	B_1	B_2
V_3	800/5=160	B_2	B_3	P	B_0	B_1
V_4	3000/5=600	B_1	B_2	B_3	B_4	B_0

Table 2. Request Arrival

Request	Request-id	Arrival clock time(secs)
R_0	3	0
R_1	1	5
R_2	1	5
R_3	3	5
R_4	0	8
R_5	1	8
R_6	2	15
R_7	0	15
R_8	4	15
R_9	0	18

Table 3. Bandwidth Allocated to Requests

Time(ms)	Disk-1	Disk-2	Disk-3	Disk-4	Disk-5
T0=00	R_0(600Mb)	2Mbps			
T1=05	R_1(200Mb)	R_0(590Mb)	1Mbps	1Mbps	
T2=08	R_4(300Mb)	R_1(197Mb)	R_0(587Mb)	0.6Mbps	0.6Mbps
T3=10	R_4(298.2Mb)	R_0(200Mb)	R_3(160Mb)	0.6Mbps	0.6Mbps
T4=15	R_4(295.2Mb)	R_5(200Mb)	R_6(800Mb)	R_0(585.2Mb)	R_8(600Mb)
T5=18	R_4(294.2Mb)	R_5(200Mb)	R_6(499.4Mb)	R_0(584.6Mb)	R_8(599.4Mb)
T6=20	R_7(300Mb)	R_1(195.2Mb)	R_6(499Mb)	R_3(157Mb)	R_8(599.9Mb)

Table 4. Request Waiting in the Request Queue

Time(ms)	Disk-1	Disk-2	Disk-3	Disk-4	Disk-5
T0=00					
T1=05	R_2(200Mb)	R_3(160Mb)			
T2=08	R_2(200Mb)	R_3(160Mb)	R_5(200Mb)		
T3=10	R_2(200Mb)	R_3(585.2Mb)	R_1(195.2Mb)		
T4=15	R_7(300Mb)	R_1(195.2Mb)	R_3(157Mb)	R_2(197Mb)	
T5=18	R_7(300Mb)	R_7(197Mb)	R_0(584.2Mb)	R_9(300Mb)	R_2(199.7Mb)
T6=20	R_9(300Mb)	R_2(197Mb)	R_0(584.2Mb)	R_4(294.2Mb)	R_5(199Mb)

5   Simulation and Performance Analysis

Fig. 2, illustrates the start-up delay of the clients to begin downloading the video
after the request is made. The average delay increases with the increase of load, as

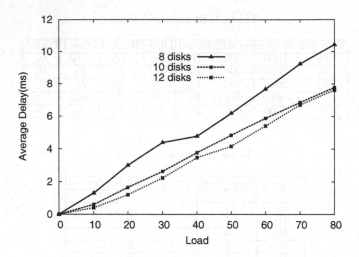

Fig. 2. Start-up Delay

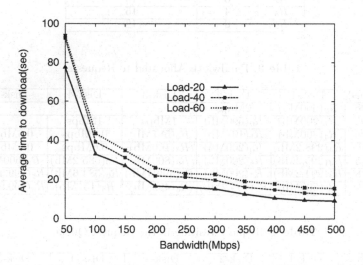

Fig. 3. Bandwidth Utilization for Varying Load

the clients are queued if the disk is busy serving other clients. The delay increases by 17% with the increase of load. The start up delay can be further decreased with increase in number of disks in the system which is evident from the graph. Fig. 2, also depicts the decrease in start up delay with increase in number of disks. Bandwidth utilization for varying load is ascertained in Fig. 3. The increase in bandwidth decreases time to download the entire video. Variations of load increase the time to download by 2% to 4%. Increase in bandwidth reduces the time to download by 75% reaching saturation at higher bandwidth rates.

6 Conclusions

An efficient storage mechanism has been proposed to balance the load in the video server. The system has a low delay of 2ms - 7ms for a varying load. The bandwidth is utilized efficiently and less time is required to download the videos. The feasibility of replication-on-demand is critically dependent on the replication bandwidth availability. We believe that the simplicity of their implementation and the flexibility they offer makes these policies especially attractive for implementation in scalable video servers. Our future work is to examine the possibility of providing fault tolerance along with balancing the load in a video server.

References

1. Choe, Y.R., Pai, V.S.: Achieving Reliable Parallel Performance in a VoD Storage Server Using Randomization and Replication. In: Intl. Parallel and Distributed Processing Symposium, pp. 1–10 (2007)
2. Golubchik, L., Muntz, R.R., Chou, C.-F., Berso, S.: Design of Fault-Tolerant Large-Scale VoD Servers: with Emphasis on High-Performance and Low-Cost. IEEE Trans on Parallel and Distributed Systems 12(4), 97–109 (2001)
3. Zhou, X., Xu, C.-Z.: Optimal Video Replication and Placement on a Cluster of Video-on-Demand Servers. In: Intl. Conference on Parallel Processing, pp. 547–555 (2002)
4. Huang, X.-M., Lin, C.-R., Chen, M.-S.: Design and Performance Study of Rate Staggering Storage for Scalable Video in a Disk-Array-Based Video Server. In: Intl. Workshop on Network and Operating Systems support for Digital Audio and Video, pp. 177–182 (2005)

Multi Level Pricing for Service Differentiation and Congestion Control in Communication Networks

Vineet Kulkarni, Sanjay Srivastava, and R.B. Lenin

Dhirubhai Ambani Institute of Information and Communication Technology,
Gandhinagar, 382007, India

Abstract. A desirable property of any system is that if a user is ready to pay for a specific level of service, the system should be able to meet his requirement. Currently, Internet does not provide a standard mechanism to price its resources. A multi level pricing scheme is proposed to reflect the hierarchical structure of the Internet, care being taken to ensure that it requires minimal changes to the Internet protocols. Data statistics are maintained as an aggregate, thus reducing the load on intermediate routers in the Internet. The proposed mechanism performs the dual functions of providing service differentiation according to budgets, and doing congestion control through feedback at time scale comparable to a round trip time. We investigate stability issues of the multi level pricing scheme. Simulation results for the different traffic scenarios show that the proposed pricing model increases the aggregate user utility function while adequately responding to congestion and providing service differentiation.

1 Introduction

The motivation for using pricing in communication networks is two-fold. Firstly, it provides a basis for signaling congestion. The price can indicate how desirable it is to begin a new transmission given the current state of the network. Secondly, pricing can be used to elicit how much the users value service relative to each other [1].

Price is an important parameter in determining the utilization of the network. One proposal is to choose representative applications for different classes, and determine the prices at equilibrium. These can be then be the default prices for the respective service classes [2]. Another idea is to use the TCP mechanism to determine prices for the end users [3]. The proposal is a modification to the existing TCP mechanism by using the ECN marks for pricing. On a slightly different note, in the case of slowly varying demand statistics time-of-day pricing suffices, and price changes at the scale of round trip times is not required [4].

Much of the work has focused on optimality of pricing schemes. There has been a proposal to move away from optimality and instead focus on the structural issues of the Internet, and design pricing schemes according to simplicity of

S. Rao et al. (Eds.): ICDCN 2008, LNCS 4904, pp. 484–489, 2008.

implementation and deployment [7]. A complete architecture for pricing in a DiffServ domain has been proposed [8], and it uses an underlying congestion control algorithm in the domain, on top of which the pricing only provides the required service differentiation.

Multi level pricing works at two different time scales. There is a first level scheme which adapts price at time scales comparable to round trip times and is similar in spirit to [5]. Its objective thus is to achieve congestion control. The second level scheme works at session time scales, and is similar to the hybrid schemes proposed in [6],[8]. The first and second level schemes are interconnected in that the feedback from the second level scheme is fed into the first level scheme.

While multi-level pricing is a combination of two separate mechanisms, it achieves much more than the individual schemes. It is compatible with the hierarchical structure of the Internet, and has been structured so as to require minimal changes to the current Internet. The question of increased load on intermediate routers has also been considered during the design of the scheme. Multi level pricing achieves the dual objectives of congestion control and service differentiation.

Details of formulation of the first level pricing scheme and its stability analysis can be found in Section 2. Second level pricing is necessary to identify misbehavior in the Internet. Details of the second level pricing scheme and its stability properties are discussed in Section 3. We have carried out simulation of multi-level pricing on ns-2. The simulation setup details as well as results can be found in Section 4.

2   First Level Pricing Scheme

In this model, a policing entity in the Internet regulates end users rates, and lets in traffic according to the residual capacity in the network. The policing entity, which is the ISP in case of the current Internet, does this regulation through a pricing scheme.

The pricing can be class-based or user-based. User based pricing can involve maintaining per user statistics and hence may be burdensome for the ISP. However, class based pricing needs information about the usage of specific classes of traffic only, and no per user state needs to be maintained. The treatment of users within a class cannot be differential though.

2.1   Formulation of the Pricing Scheme

Consider a network with a single bottleneck link of capacity C Mbps. Let there be n users accessing the network at a given instant. The instantaneous rate of user i at time instant t will be denoted by $x_i(t)$. Each user has a budget b_i, which indicates the maximum willingness to pay of that user. Let each user be the source of a CBR stream with the instantaneous rate.

According to our pricing scheme, the users will be charged based on their resource usage profile. There should also be a component in the price function that indicates congestion level on the link. This is required to bound the demand from the users to a maximum of up to the link capacity.

There are two components in the pricing scheme. The first is that of a service price. This is computed for user i based on the proportion of allocated resource used up by user i. Let this be denoted by p_i^s. It is given by the following formula

$$p_i^s(t) = \frac{x_i(t)}{\sum_i x_i(t)}. \tag{1}$$

The second component in the price function reflects the congestion state of the network. Congestion in networks is reflected through the queue buildup at intermediate routers. In the simple case of the traffic following Poisson arrivals with mean λ, and exponential service rate μ, the average queue length is given by $\frac{1}{\mu-\lambda}$. It is desirable that the pricing function tracks the congestion level as represented by the queue length in Eq. (2.1). Hence we choose the congestion price p_i^c as,

$$p_i^c(t) = \frac{1}{C - \sum_i x_i(t)}. \tag{2}$$

This can also be seen as the price depending on residual capacity in the network. For other traffic types represented by different arrival distributions, a pricing function can be determined along similar lines.

The price value for user i at time instant t is now given by,

$$p_i(t) = p_i^s(t) + p_i^c(t); \tag{3}$$

$$\Rightarrow p_i(t) = \frac{x_i(t)}{\sum_i x_i(t)} + \frac{1}{C - \sum_i x_i(t)}. \tag{4}$$

3   Second Level Pricing Scheme

The first level scheme works well at the ISP level in the Internet. But there is multiplexing of ISP traffic inside the core. Hence, resource overflow may happen at this point also. The ISP can regulate end users which it is servicing, but there should be some entity which signals the resources at the core to the ISP's. This is achieved through a two level pricing scheme, with a core entity performing the job of the second level of pricing.

In effect these are two markets, the retail market at the ISP and the wholesale market at the Core. The adaptation at the ISP-Core level happens at much larger time intervals than that of the User-ISP level.

Each ISP purchases some amount of resource from the Core. The core assigns different codepoints to ISP's to monitor their traffic for regulation. The usage statistics are maintained per ISP at the core, and not per class as in case of the ISP. Hence, the pricing is for a much higher aggregate of traffic here, than at the first level between the user and the ISP.

Let the amount of resource (bandwidth in the current case) purchased by a particular ISP, say ISP_j, is w_j. Let the contract between core and ISP be renegotiated at time interval of t seconds. The count of packets transmitted for a particular ISP are maintained at the core for each such interval. Let the count of packets for ISP_j be denoted by $pkts_j$. Let the average size of packets transmitted by ISP_j be $pktsize_j$. Thus, the actual bandwidth used by ISP_j during a given interval is,

$$\frac{pkts_j \times pktsize_j}{t}.$$

Overshoot O_j is thus determined as,

$$O_j = \left(\frac{pkts_j \times pktsize}{t} - w_j\right). \tag{5}$$

The price for ISP_j at the core p_{core}^j, when it overshoots the contract is thus determined as follows

$$p_{core}^j = p_{core}^j + \left(\frac{O_j}{w_j} \times p_{core}^j\right), \tag{6}$$

where O_j is determined by Eq. (5).

This price is fed into the price update equation at the ISP, Equation (4), giving

$$p_i(t) = \frac{x_i(t)}{\sum_i x_i(t)} + p_{core}^j \times \left(\frac{1}{C - \sum_i x_i(t)}\right). \tag{7}$$

3.1 Stability Analysis

According to the formulation in Equation (6), the value of p_{core}^j is proportional to $U(t) - w_j$, where $U(t)$ is the sum of all the user rates currently connected to ISP_j. Thus Equation (7) becomes,

$$p_i(t) = \frac{x_i(t)}{\sum_i x_i(t)} + \left(\frac{U(t) - w_j}{C - \sum_i x_i(t)}\right). \tag{8}$$

Again linearizing Equation (8) about the equilibrium point (U_o, x_o^i) we get,

$$\delta x_i = \left(\frac{-b_i}{U_o p_o^2}\right)\delta x_i + \left(\frac{-b_i}{p_o^2}\right)\left(\frac{(C - w_j)}{R_o^2} - \frac{x_i^o}{U_o^2}\right)\delta U; \tag{9}$$

$$\delta p_i = \left(\frac{1}{U_o}\right)\delta x_i + \left(\frac{-x_i^o}{U_o^2} + \frac{C - w_j}{R_o^2}\right)\delta U. \tag{10}$$

The Eigenvalues are,

$$\left(\frac{-b_i}{U_o p_o^2}\right), \left(\frac{-x_i^o}{U_o^2} + \frac{(C - w_j)}{R_o^2}\right) \tag{11}$$

The first eigenvalue is always negative. For the second eigenvalue to be negative the following condition needs to be satisfied,

$$x_i^o > \frac{U_o^2}{R_o^2}(C - w_j). \tag{12}$$

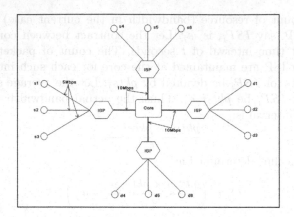

Fig. 1. Topology used for simulation of two level pricing

4   Results

Simulations have been done on the *ns-2* simulator [9]. The ISP and core counterparts have been implemented as agents. ISP and core agents make use of this underlying model for contract establishment, marking of packets, and policing.

The topology used for the simulation of two level pricing is as shown in Fig. 1.
The scenario depicted in Fig. 2 is a case when the demand at the ISP exceeds its allocated capacity. The ISP provides price feedback to the users at 0.01 second intervals, while the Core provides feedback to the ISP at 5 second intervals. The ISP keeps track of which users overshooted their contract. If the users are permitted to go beyond the capacity reserved for the ISP, then congestion can

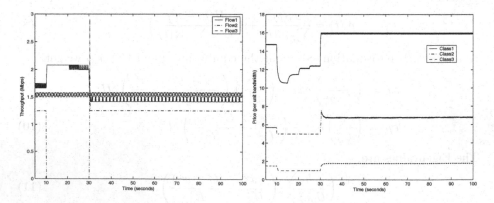

Fig. 2. End users misbehaviour results in the ISP violating its contract with the Core

Fig. 3. The core levies charge on the ISP depending on the magnitude of overshoot, and eventually the end users are forced to cut back on the rate and obey the contract of the ISP

set in. The core, identifies the misbehavior and communicates it back to the ISP. The rates at equilibrium are in the ratio of their budgets.

The proposed two level pricing identifies and penalizes misbehaving users through communicating with the ISP's. The Core maintains statistics about the achieved rates for each of the ISP's, and at regular intervals compares this with the contracted rates. Overshoot, if any, is penalized through a price component which is communicated to the ISP by the core. The ISP in turn conveys this information to the end users. Since no user's budget is infinite, the regulation happens eventually.

5   Conclusion

This paper has proposed a mechanism for providing effective service differentiation based on budgets of users, and also perform congestion control functions. A mathematical proof for the local asymptotic stability of the pricing mechanism is provided. The pricing function is also validated through simulation results. To reduce the amount of information to be maintained, the pricing algorithm has been split across two levels. Data is thus maintained in an aggregated manner at the individual levels, and the lower level has the capability to split up the aggregated data communicated from the upper level into its constituents. The proposed scheme can be scaled to higher degree of hierarchy. The scheme has been designed so as to require minimal changes to the current Internet, and can be implemented incrementally.

References

1. Cocchi, R., Shenker, S., Estrin, D., Zhiang, L.: Pricing in computer networks:Motivation, formulation and example. IEEE/ACM Transactions on Networking 6, 614–627 (1993)
2. Ganesh, A., Laevaens, K., Steinberg, R.: Congestion pricing and user adaptation. In: INFOCOM, pp. 959–965 (2001)
3. Gibbens, R.J., Kelly, F.P.: Resource pricing and evolution of congestion control. Automatica, 35–99 (1999)
4. Paschalidis, I.Ch., Tsitsiklis, J.N.: Congestion dependent pricing of network services. IEEE/ACM Transactions on Networking, 171–184 (2000)
5. O'Donnell, A.J., Sethu, H.: Congestion control, differentiated services and efficient capacity management through a novel pricing strategy. Computer Communications, 1457–1469 (2003)
6. Wang, X., Schulzrinne, H.: Performance study of congestion price based adaptive service. In: NOSSDAV. Proceedings of International Workshop on Network Operating System Support for Digital Audio and Video, pp. 1–10 (2000)
7. Shenker, S., Clark, D., Estrin, D., Herzog, S.: Pricing in computer networks:Reshaping the research agenda. ACM Computer Communications Review, 19–43 (1996)
8. Yuksel, M., Kalyanaraman, S.: Distributed dynamic capacity contracting: A congestion pricing framework for diffserv. In: Almeroth, K.C., Hasan, M. (eds.) MMNS 2002. LNCS, vol. 2496, p. 198. Springer, Heidelberg (2002)
9. Fall, K., Varadhan, K.: The ns manual (2003)

Revenue-Driven Bandwidth Management for End-to-End Connectivity over IP Networks

K. Ravindran, M. Rabby, and X. Liu

City College of CUNY and Graduate Center,
Department of Computer Science,
Convent Avenue at 138th Street,
New York, NY 10031, USA
ravi@cs.ccny.cuny.edu, mfrabby@yahoo.com, xliu@gc.cuny.edu

Abstract. The paper describes a policy-based model for cost-effective 'data connectivity' provisioning between session-level end-points. Data flows with closely-similar QoS needs are aggregated over an end-to-end logical path. The available infrastructure bandwidth is apportioned between various paths that carry (aggregated) data flows with distinct QoS levels. Flow aggregation over a path allows reaping the statistical multiplexing gains in bandwidth. Whereas, a path-level bandwidth allocation allows meeting the QoS needs of data flows sharing this path. The SP installs policy functions at the end-points that can make the connectivity provisioning cost-optimal in different operating regions of the system.

1 Introduction

To offer data-level connectivity as a service, end-to-end paths may be set up between data aggregation points — say, between New York and London. Individual clients may then exchange high volume information over these data paths for sports, business, and entertainment applications.

In commercial settings, the service provider (SP) may lease the bandwidth from infrastructure networks (say, telecom companies such as AT&T) to provide a session-level 'data connectivity' between end-points. In public Internet however, the raw bandwidth between end-points is available free of cost but the availability of bandwidth is itself not guaranteed. From the SP's standpoint, the internet bandwidth is of use only if it can be packaged into a usable commodity, i.e., a bandwidth that can be measured and made available to the end-users with some guarantee of stability and predictability over meaningful time-scales. This packaging of bandwidth into a usable form incurs a cost to the SP. Thus, revenue incentives become a part of bandwidth management strategies when providing transport connectivity as a service to the users.

The SP is faced with two conflicting goals: reducing the bandwidth costs incurred for data transfers (to maximize the SP's revenues) and allocating enough bandwidth to meet the QoS needs of application sessions (to satisfy the end-user's utility). Our end-point admission control function aggregates a large number of data flows with closely-similar QoS needs over a single logical connection.

S. Rao et al. (Eds.): ICDCN 2008, LNCS 4904, pp. 490–495, 2008.

The resource management function then suitably apportions the available infrastructure bandwidth between the various connections that carry (aggregated) data flows with distinct QoS levels. In contrast with the flow aggregation model employed in [1], our model employs a session-level object, namely, 'data connection', to effectively manage the data flows.

The SP may use *policy* functions that prescribe how distinct the flow specs of data over various paths are and what cost the per-flow bandwidth apportionment over a data path incurs. Our architecture allows installing a repertoire of policy functions at end-points and selecting the appropriate ones to make the connectivity provisioning cost-optimal. The paper describes the end-point mechanisms to realize architecture, and evaluates it using simulation studies.

2   Bandwidth-Provisioned Connectivity

In our model, the links that provide the physical connectivity between end-points constitute the 'infrastructure', and the available capacities in a path chosen to connect peer entities constitute the 'resource'.

2.1   A Management View of Connectivity

The management control is exercised on two types of session-level objects: 'data flow' and 'data connection'. A 'data flow' is a sequence of packets transported from the source to the receiver with a certain end-to-end QoS. A 'data connection' is set up over the transport path between the source and receiver end-points, with a prescribed amount of bandwidth allocation to carry a group of data flows with a closely-similar QoS characteristics. See Figure 1. A 'data connection' is the object granularity for bandwidth allocation purposes, whereas a 'data flow' is the object granularity for end-to-end admission control.

Suppose a flow parameter r captures, at a macro-level, the bandwidth usage. Typically, r is a tuple: $[p, A, \Delta, \mathcal{D}]$, where p is the peak rate, A is the average rate, Δ is the loss tolerance, and $\mathcal{D}$ is the allowed delay[1]. An estimation of the bandwidth needs may be represented as a mapping function:

$$\mathcal{F} \ : \ r \in \mathcal{Q} \ \rightarrow \ b \in (0, \mathcal{W}),$$

where $\mathcal{Q}$ and $\mathcal{W}$ represent the flow parameter space and network capacity respectively. $\mathcal{F}$ depicts a policy to determine the level of bandwidth allocation needed to carry the flow r. We say that a flow r has a stronger QoS need than a flow r' (i.e., $r \succ r'$) if $\mathcal{F}(r) > \mathcal{F}(r')|_{\forall \mathcal{F}}$. Likewise[2], a policy $\mathcal{F}$ is more aggressive than a policy $\mathcal{F}'$ if $\mathcal{F}(r) < \mathcal{F}'(r)|_{\forall r}$.

---

[1] The $[p, A, \Delta, \mathcal{D}]$ tuples may be viewed as prescribing distinct 'virtual link classes' (see [2]). The admission controller then maps an application-generated data flow to one of these 'virtual links'.

[2] [3] gives guidelines to prescribe the '$\succ$' relation over $\mathcal{Q}$.

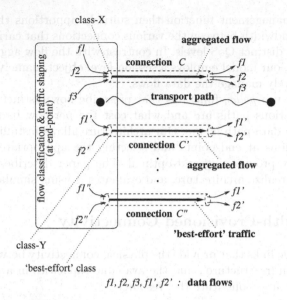

Fig. 1. 'data connection' versus 'data flows'

2.2   Cost Reduction by Bandwidth Sharing

Given a bandwidth allocation $b_r = \mathcal{F}(r)$ for a data flow r, the total bandwidth usage incurred by a 'data connection' C can be transcribed into a cost $\Theta(\sum_{\forall r} b_r)$ for transporting multiple data flows $\{r\}$ over C. The function $\Theta(\cdots)$ maps a bandwidth usage onto a cost — which may include the infrastructure-level tariffs incurred for bandwidth and any fixed cost of maintaining the connection.

With flow aggregation, $b(r) = \frac{\mathcal{R}_{bw}(n)}{n}$, where $\mathcal{R}_{bw}$ is the total bandwidth allocated and n is the number of flows of type r sharing this bandwidth. The SP reduces $b(r)$ by multiplexing r with other data flows to reap statistical bandwidth gains, whereby the QoS needs of r can be met with a lower $b(r)$.

The SP's goal is to reduce the overall cost of data connectivity by exploiting the statistical multiplexing gains that accrue when bandwidth is shared between multiple data flows. This revenue-oriented incentive forms the basis for a dynamic control of connectivity mechanisms. The latter are anchored on our architectural notion of 'data connection'.

3   End-System Control and Management

The control mechanisms are built around: i) 'packet scheduling' over data connections weighted by their bandwidth allocations, and ii) connection-level packet delay checks against the tolerance parameter $\mathcal{D}$. Both (i) and (ii) do not require any per-flow state tracking at the infrastructure level.

3.1 Effective Bandwidth with Policy-Based Control

Figure 2 illustrates how a policy function $\mathcal{F}$ may capture these gains, so that it can be plugged in by the SP at appropriate control points. The study is based on subjecting the packet flows generated from the video traffic traces of a *JurassicPark* movie segment to our policy-based bandwidth allocations. Three policies are employed: A, B and C — as indicated in the tables. Policy C incurs the least amount of bandwidth allocation, policy B incurs the most, and policy B is in-between. The tables are pre-computed based on a traffic analysis of the traces, namely estimating the burstiness and average rate parameters from the packet size distributions.

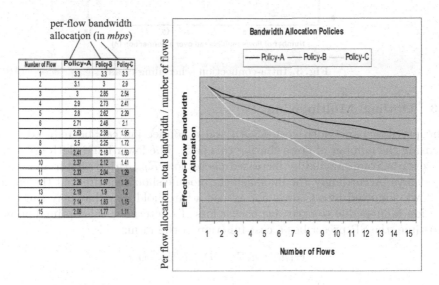

per-flow bandwidth allocation (in *mbps*)

Number of Flow	Policy-A	Policy-B	Policy-C
1	3.3	3.3	3.3
2	3.1	3	2.9
3	3	2.85	2.54
4	2.9	2.73	2.41
5	2.8	2.62	2.29
6	2.71	2.48	2.1
7	2.63	2.38	1.95
8	2.5	2.25	1.72
9	2.41	2.18	1.53
10	2.37	2.12	1.41
11	2.33	2.04	1.29
12	2.26	1.97	1.24
13	2.19	1.9	1.2
14	2.14	1.83	1.15
15	2.06	1.77	1.11

Per flow allocation = total bandwidth / number of flows

policy C is more aggressive than policy B;
policy B is more aggressive than policy A

Fig. 2. Bandwidth allocation policies for shared connections

3.2 Impact on End-User QoS

The multiplexing of data flows over a connection C can degrade the QoS due to excessive levels of path sharing and sustained higher rates in many of the data flows. It has been shown [4] that the queuing delay of packets monotonically increases with the number of flows n that feed packets into the queue. This condition is captured by the relation $\mathcal{R}_{loss}(n) > \mathcal{R}_{loss}(n')$ for $n > n'$.

Figure 3 corroborates this delay behavior based on our simulation studies of policy functions A, B and C — c.f. Figure 2. Policy C incurs longer packet delays than policy B, and the latter incurs longer delays than policy A. Thus, beyond a certain level of sharing (say, for $n > n''$), the end-to-end delay of packets may increase to a level where the client-prescribed loss tolerance limits are not met.

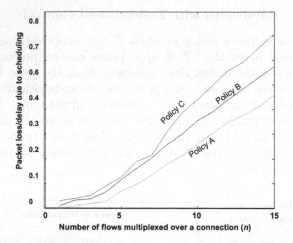

Fig. 3. Intra-connection scheduling costs

3.3 Optimal Multiplexing

The per-flow bandwidth cost $\mathcal{R}_{bw}(n)$ on a connection can be reduced by increasing the number of flows sharing this path. The lower bandwidth usage may however be counteracted by increased packet loss $\mathcal{R}_{loss}(n)$ arising from scheduling delays. Accordingly, the management module should ensure that the number of flows admitted into C does not exceed a threshold n_{opt} that may cause connection failures due to excessive packet loss. To determine this optimal point at run-time, the SP prescribes a cost function of the form:

$$\Theta(n) = a.\mathcal{R}_{bw}(n) + b.\mathcal{R}_{loss}(n)$$

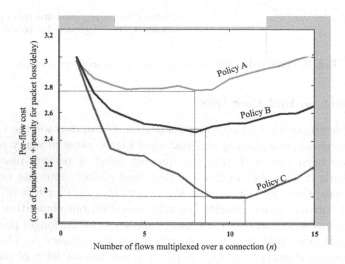

Fig. 4. Cost optimality behavior observed in our simulation study

for use by the SP, where a and b are normalization constants. There is a unique global optimal point n_{opt} for each allocation policy.

Figure 4 shows this cost optimality behavior in our experimental study using video traffic traces under policies A, B and C. An aggressive policy has a higher n_{opt}, yielding a lower cost minimum — such as the policy-B over policy-A.

The SP may determine the grouping of data flows by estimating the service-level costs using the $\Theta(n)$ relation. The decision as to when a re-grouping of data flows into distinct connections is necessary may be based on a policy that interprets the cost changes with respect to n.

4   Conclusion

The paper described a new model of session-level connectivity provisioning for use by QoS-sensitive networked applications. The connectivity provider (SP) employs policy functions to map the application-prescribed flow specs onto the bandwidth needs of connections that carry the data flows. The strategy is to reduce the per-flow cost incurred by multiplexing many closely-similar data flows on a single connection. The multiplexing brings in two benefits to the SP. First, it reduces the per-flow bandwidth allocation due to the gains accrued from a statistical sharing of connection bandwidth. Second, it amortizes the connection-level overhead across many flows. The level of cost reduction, and hence the revenue accrual, can be controlled by the SP using policy functions that take into account the burstiness and loss/delay tolerance of data flows.

Our studies indicate that the model can be employed in large network settings (such as IP networks), while dealing with the scalability issues arising therein.

References

1. Breslau, L., Knightly, E.W., Shenker, S., Stoica, I., Zhang, H.: End-point Admission Control: Architectural Issues and Performance. In: Proc. ACM SIGCOMM 2000, Stockholm (2000)
2. Floyd, S., Jacobson, V.: Link-sharing and Resource Management Models for Packet Networks. IEEE/ACM Trans. on Networking 4(3) (August 1995)
3. Wroclawski, J.: Specification of the Controlled-load Network Element Service. In Internet RFC 2211 (1997)
4. Guerin, R., Orda, A.: QoS Routing in Networks with Inaccurate Information: Theory and Algorithms. IEEE/ACM Trans. on Networking 3(7) (June 1999)

Modeling and Predicting Point-to-Point Communication Delay of Circuit Switching in the Mesh-Connected Networks

F. Safaei[1,3], A. Khonsari[1,2], M. Fathy[3], and M. Ould-Khaoua[4]

[1] IPM School of Computer Science, Tehran, Iran
[2] Dept. of ECE, Univ. of Tehran, Tehran, Iran
[3] Dept. of Computer Eng., Iran Univ. of Science and Technology, Tehran, Iran
[4] Dept. of Computing Science, Univ. of Glasgow, UK
{safaei, ak}@ipm.ir,{f_safaei, mahfathy}@iust.ac.ir,
mohamed@dcs.gla.ac.uk

Abstract. Several analytical performance models for Circuit Switching (CS) in
k-ary n-cubes have been reported in the literature. However, to the best of our
knowledge, the performance properties of CS have not been investigated in the
mesh networks. To address this shortcoming, this paper proposes the first
analytical modeling approach to predict the mean message latency in 2-D mesh
interconnect networks using CS augmented with virtual channels. Analytical
approximations of the model are confirmed by comparing with those obtained
through simulation experiments.

1 Introduction

Recently there has been a renewed interest for Circuit Switching (CS) in the
communication systems and Internet [1]. Although several analytical performance
models for CS in k-ary n-cubes have been reported in the literature [2, 3], there has been
hardly any attempt to assess the performance properties of CS in mesh networks
augmented with virtual channels. In an effort to fill this gap, this paper proposes the first
analytical model for 2-D $k \times k$ mesh networks employing CS with virtual channels.

The structure of the paper is organized as follows. Our model assumptions are
illustrated in Section 2. Moreover, the performance modeling approach is presented in
this section. Section 3 compares the massage latencies predicted by analytical model
with those obtained through simulation experiments. Finally, Section 4 summarizes
our findings and concludes the paper.

2 The Analytical Model

2.1 Assumptions

The proposed model is based on the following assumptions that are widely used in the
literature [2-6].

S. Rao et al. (Eds.): ICDCN 2008, LNCS 4904, pp. 496–502, 2008.
© Springer-Verlag Berlin Heidelberg 2008

1. Each node generates messages independently, which follows a Poisson process with a mean rate of λ_{node} messages per cycle.
2. The arrival process at a given communication network is approximated by an independent Poisson process.
3. The destination of each message would be any node in the network with uniform distribution.
4. Message length is fixed at M flits, each of which requires one cycle to cross from one node to the next.
5. V (≥ 1) virtual channels are used per physical channel. When there is more than one virtual channel available that bring a message closer to its destination, one is chosen at random.

2.2 Derivation of the Model

The analytical model computes the mean message latency using the following steps. First, the mean time to establish a path is calculated. Second, the mean network latency, i.e., the time for a message to cross the network from source to destination, is determined. Then, the mean waiting time seen by a message at the source before entering the network is derived using M/G/1 queuing system [6]. Finally the mean message latency is obtained by including the effects of virtual channel multiplexing.

Let us first calculate the average message arrival rate on a given channel $<a, b>$ where a and b are two adjacent nodes. In general, if there are n dimensions numbered 0 to $n-1$ and there are Δ_i hops from a to b in the ith dimension, then the total number of minimal routes from a to b is calculated by

$$\left\| \aleph \right\|_{<a,b>}^{n} = \prod_{i=0}^{n-1} \left(\frac{\sum_{j=i}^{n-1} \Delta_j}{\Delta_i} \right) = \left(\sum_{i=0}^{n-1} \Delta_i \right) ! / \prod_{i=0}^{n-1} \Delta_i ! \qquad (1)$$

For every source-destination pair of nodes, s and d, for which channel $<a, b>$ may be used, the probability that channel $<a, b>$ is traversed can be expressed as

$$P_{(s,d),<a,b>} = \left(\left\| \aleph \right\|_{<s,a>}^{2} \times \left\| \aleph \right\|_{<b,d>}^{2} \right) / \left\| \aleph \right\|_{<s,d>}^{2} \qquad (2)$$

With uniform traffic pattern, messages generated at a node have an equal probability of being destined to any other node. Hence, the rate of messages produced at a specific node and destined to another node is equal to the ratio of the message generation rate, λ_{node}, to the number of nodes in the network except itself. Therefore, the rate of messages generated at a specific node, s, and destined to another node, d, that traverse the channel $<a, b>$ along its path is given by

$$\lambda_{(s,d),<a,b>} = \left(\lambda_{node} / (N-1) \right) P_{(s,d),<a,b>}, \text{ where } N = k^2 \qquad (3)$$

The rate of messages traversing a specific channel can be calculated as the aggregate of Equation (3) over all source-destination pairs that have at least one path between each other that traverses channel $<a, b>$. This parameter is denoted by

$$\lambda_{<a,b>} = \sum_{(s,d) \in G_{<a,b>}} \lambda_{(s,d),<a,b>} = \left(\lambda_{node} / (N-1) \right) \sum_{(s,d) \in G_{<a,b>}} P_{(s,d),<a,b>} \qquad (4)$$

where $G_{<a, b>}$ is the set of all pairs of source and destination nodes that have at least one path between each other that traverses channel $<a, b>$. Let $S=(S_x, S_y)$ be the source node and $d =(d_x, d_y)$ denote the destination node. We define the set $H=\{h_x, h_y\}$, where h_x and h_y indicate the number of hops that the message makes along X and Y dimensions, respectively. We get

$$h_x = \|s_x - d_x\| \quad , \quad h_y = \|s_y - d_y\| \tag{5}$$

where $\|x - y\|$ indicates the distance between a source node x and a destination node y. Moreover, the total number of hops made by the message between source and destination node is given by

$$\|H\| = h_x + h_y \tag{6}$$

We define $\bar{S}_{(s,d)}$ as the network latency seen by a message crossing from source node s to destination node d. This parameter consists of two parts: One is the delay due to actual message transmission time, $\|H\| + M$, and another term accounts for the average set-up time, $\bar{C}_{(s,d)}$, needed to reserve a dedicated path. Thus, $\bar{S}_{(s,d)}$ is determined by

$$\bar{S}_{(s,d)} = \|H\| + M + \bar{C}_{(s,d)} \tag{7}$$

where M and $\|H\|$ denote the message length and mean message distance (given by Equation (6)), respectively. In order to compute the quantity of $\bar{C}_{(s,d)}$, we employ a Markov chain (details of the model can be found in [2]) to model the header actions to cross the network. Let $\bar{C}_{(s,d),i}$ be the expected time for a header to reach the final state starting from state i. When the header advances to the next node, the residual expected duration becomes $\bar{C}_{(s,d),i+1}$. On the other hand, when the header backtracks to the source node, the residual expected duration is $\bar{C}_{(s,d),0}$. Given that the header requires one cycle to move from one node to the next, the expected time $\bar{C}_{(s,d),i}$ satisfies the following recurrence relation

$$\bar{C}_{(s,d),i} = \begin{cases} (1 - P^b_{(s,d),i})(\bar{C}_{(s,d),i+1} + 1) + P^b_{(s,d),i}(\bar{C}_{(s,d),0} + i) & 0 \le i \le \|H\| - 1 \\ 0 & i = \|H\| \end{cases} \tag{8}$$

Once the header reaches its destination, an acknowledgment flit is transmitted back to the source via the reserved path. Thus, the mean time to set-up a path for the $\|H\|$-hop message can be written as

$$\bar{C}_{(s,d),H} = \bar{C}_{(s,d),0} + \|H\| \tag{9}$$

where the term $\|H\|$ accounts for the number of cycles that are required to send the acknowledgement flit back to the source. Averaging over the $(N - 1)$ possible destination nodes in the network gives the mean time to set-up a path, $\bar{C}_{(s,d)}$, from source node s and destination node d as

$$\overline{C}_{(s,d)} = \left(1/(N-1)\right)\sum_{d \in G-\{s\}} \overline{C}_{(s,d),H} \tag{10}$$

The probability of blocking depends on the number of output channels, and thus on the virtual channels that a message can use at its next hop. A message is blocked at its ith hop, if all the virtual channels that can be chosen for its next hop, are occupied. Let T_i be the set of possible ways that i hops can be distributed over two dimensions such that the number of hops made in dimensions X and Y be at most h_x and h_y. T_i can be expressed as

$$T_i = \{(i_x, i_y) : i_x + i_y = i \; ; i_x \leq h_x, \; i_y \leq h_y, i_x, \; i_y \geq 0\} \tag{11}$$

The probability that a message has entirely crossed dimension X on its ith hop is given by

$$P_{(s,d),i}^X = \left(\|T_i\|_{i_x = h_x} / \|T_i\|\right) \cdot P_{(s,d),i,V}^X \tag{12}$$

where $P_{(s,d),i,V}^X$ is the probability that all virtual channels used by a message over all the possible paths from s to d in dimension X are busy; this probability is denoted by

$$P_{(s,d),i,V}^X = \left(\sum_{j=1}^{\|T_i\|_{i_x = h_x}} \cdot P_{<a_j,b_j>,V}\right) / \|T_i\|_{i_x = h_x} \tag{13}$$

On the equation above, $P_{<a_j,b_j>,V}$ is the probability that V virtual channels at a specific physical channel in path j, $<a_j, b_j>$, are busy. This probability is obtained later from Equation (21). Similarly, the probability that a message has entirely crossed dimension Y on its ith hop is given by

$$P_{(s,d),i}^Y = \left(\|T_i\|_{i_y = h_y} / \|T_i\|\right) \cdot P_{(s,d),i,V}^Y, \qquad P_{(s,d),i,V}^Y = \left(\sum_{j=1}^{\|T_i\|_{i_y = h_y}} P_{<a_j,b_j>,V}\right) / \|T_i\|_{i_y = h_y} \tag{14}$$

On the other hand, the probability that a message has not entirely passed dimension X on its ith hop can be expressed as

$$P_{(s,d),i}^{\overline{XY}} = \left(\|T_i\|_{i_x < h_x, i_y < h_y} / \|T_i\|\right) \cdot P_{(s,d),i,V}^{\overline{XY}}, \text{ where } P_{(s,d),i,V}^{\overline{XY}} = \left(\sum_{j=1}^{\|T_i\|_{i_x < h_x, i_y < h_y}} P_{<a_j,b_j>,V}\right) / \|T_i\|_{i_x < h_x, i_y < h_y} \tag{15}$$

Finally, the blocking probability, $P_{(s,d),i}^b$, is calculated as the aggregate of the blocking probabilities at the ith hop. Therefore, the $P_{(s,d),i}^b$ can be obtained as

$$P_{(s,d),i}^b = P_{(s,d),i}^X + P_{(s,d),i}^Y + P_{(s,d),i}^{\overline{XY}} \tag{16}$$

When the header does not experience any blocking during the path set-up stage, a minimum duration to establish a path is $2\|H\|$ cycles. So, the minimum average network latency seen by the message can be written as

$$\overline{S}_{\min,(s,d)} = M + 3\|H\|, \quad \overline{S}_{\min} = \left(1/(N-1)\right)\sum_{d \in G-\{s\}} \overline{S}_{\min,(s,d)} \tag{17}$$

For a given node s in the network, the average latency seen by a message originated at that node to enter the network, $\bar{S}_s$, is equal to the average of all $S_{(s,\,d)}$ resulting in

$$\bar{S}_s = \left(1/(N-1)\right) \sum_{d \in G-\{s\}} \bar{S}_{(s,d)} \tag{18}$$

Since a message can enter the network through any of the V virtual channels, the average traffic rate on each injection virtual channel is λ_{node}/V. Using adaptive routing under the uniform traffic pattern results in the mean service time seen by messages at all source nodes being the same, and equal to the average network latency, i.e., $\bar{S}_s$. As a result, modeling the local queue in the source node as an M/G/1 queue, with the average arrival rate of λ_{node}/V and service time $\bar{S}_s$ with an approximated variance $(\bar{S}_s - \bar{S}_{min})$ [5] yields the average waiting time, $\bar{W}_s$, seen by a message at the source node s as

$$\bar{W}_s = \left(1/N\right) \sum_{d \in G-\{s\}} \left((\lambda_{node}/V)\bar{S}_s^2 \left(1 + (\bar{S}_s - \bar{S}_{min})^2 / \bar{S}_s^2\right) / \left(2\left(1 - (\lambda_{node}/V)\bar{S}_s\right)\right)\right) \tag{19}$$

Equation (19) gives the network latency seen by a message to cross from the source node s to the destination node d. By averaging over all the N possible nodes in the network, the mean network latency is approximated as

$$\bar{S} = \left(1/N\right) \sum_{s \in G} \bar{S}_s \tag{20}$$

The probability $P_{<a,b>,v}$ that v ($0 \le v \le V$) virtual channels at a given physical channel $<a, b>$ are busy can be determined using a Markovian model [2, 4]. In the steady state, the model yields the following probabilities

$$Q_{<a,b>,v} = \begin{cases} 1 & v=0 \\ Q_{<a,b>,v-1}\lambda_{<a,b>}\bar{S} & 0<v<V \\ Q_{<a,b>,v-1}\lambda_{<a,b>}/(1/\bar{S} - \lambda_{<a,b>}) & v=V \end{cases}, \quad P_{<a,b>,v} = \begin{cases} (\sum_{v=0}^{V} Q_{<a,b>,v})^{-1} & v=0 \\ P_{<a,b>,v-1}\lambda_{<a,b>}\bar{S} & 0<v<V \\ P_{<a,b>,v-1}\lambda_{<a,b>}/(1/\bar{S} - \lambda_{<a,b>}) & v=V \end{cases} \tag{21}$$

When multiple virtual channels are used per physical channel in dimension X or Y, they share the bandwidth in a time-multiplexed manner. The average degree of virtual channel multiplexing that takes place at a specific channel $<a, b>$, can be estimated as

$$\bar{V}_{<a,b>} = \sum_{v=1}^{V} v^2 \cdot P_{<a,b>,v} \Big/ \sum_{v=1}^{V} v \cdot P_{<a,b>,v} \tag{22}$$

Let $V_{max,\,(s,\,d),\,j}$ be the maximum $\bar{V}_{<a,b>}$ of channels traversed by the path j, between source s and destination d. $V_{max,\,(s,\,d),\,j}$ can be calculated as

$$\bar{V}_{max,(s,d),j} = \left(1/\|H\|\right) \sum_{i=1}^{\|H\|} \bar{V}_{<a_i,b_i>,j} \tag{23}$$

where j is a specific path between s and d, and $\|H\|$ is the distance (in terms of the number of hops made by the message) between the source and destination nodes. The parameter $\overline{V}_{<a_i,b_i>,j}$ is the average multiplexing degree of channel $<a_i,b_i>$, which is the channel traversed by the ith hop of path j. Let there be L different paths of minimal length from s to d. We then calculate the average degree of virtual channel multiplexing from source s to destination d along path j ($1 \leq j \leq L$) as

$$\overline{V}_{(s,d)} = (1/L) \sum_{j=1}^{L} \overline{V}_{max,(s,d),j} \qquad (24)$$

Averaging over all possible source-destination pairs, results in the overall virtual channels multiplexing degree as follows

$$\overline{V} = (1/N(N-1)) \sum_{s \in G} \sum_{d \in G-\{s\}} \overline{V}_{(s,d)} \qquad (25)$$

Scaling the mean network latency and waiting time at the injection channel by the factor $\overline{V}$ to model the effects of virtual channel multiplexing yields the mean message latency as [4]

$$Mean\ message\ latency = (\overline{S} + \overline{W}_s)\overline{V} \qquad (26)$$

Examining the equations of the analytical model reveals that it is very difficult to give closed-form solutions to the various variables of the model. Therefore, these equations are solved iteratively [6].

3 Model Validation

In order to validate the proposed model, the analytical model was simulated. The results of simulation and analysis for the 8×8 (N =64) and 16×16 (N =256) networks with message length M =32 and 64 flits, and V =1, 6 virtual channels per physical channel are depicted in Fig. 1. The figure demonstrates that the analytical model predicts the mean message latency with a good degree of accuracy in all regions. However, some discrepancies around the saturation point are apparent. This is a result of the approximations made when constructing the analytical model. This approximation greatly simplifies the model by avoiding the computation of the exact distribution of the message service time at a given channel.

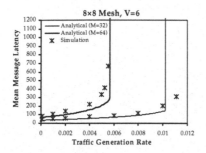
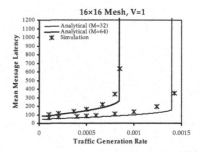

Fig. 1. The mean message latency predicted by the model vs. simulation results for the 8×8 and 16×16 mesh networks with CS under Poisson traffic, V=1, 6 virtual channels per physical channel, and message lengths M =32, 64 flits

4 Conclusions

This paper has described the first analytical model to capture the mean message latency in circuit-switched 2-D mesh networks when fully adaptive routing and virtual channels flow control are used. The proposed model is general and can easily be extended to other topologies. Results from simulation experiments have revealed that the model predicts latency with a good degree of accuracy. Another interesting line of research for future work may be the extent of the modeling approach described here to consider the behavior of CS with other traffic patterns, e.g. hotspot traffic, and in the vicinity of failures in mesh networks.

References

1. Molinero-Fernandez, P., McKeown, N.: The Performance of Circuit Switching in the Internet. Journal of Optical Networking 2, 82–96 (2003)
2. Ould-Khaoua, M., Min, G.: Circuit switching: an analysis for k-ary n-cubes with virtual channels. IEE Proc.-Comput. Digit. Tech. 148(6), 215–219 (2001)
3. Sharma, V., Varvarigos, E.A.: Circuit switching with input queuing: an analysis for the d-dimensional wraparound mesh and the hypercube. IEEE TC 8(4), 349–366 (1997)
4. Ould-Khaoua, M.: A Performance Model of Duato's Adaptive Routing Algorithm in k-ary n-cubes. IEEE TC 48(12), 1–8 (1999)
5. Draper, J.T., Ghosh, J.: A Comprehensive Analytical Model for Wormhole Routing in Multicomputer Systems. JPDC 32(2), 202–214 (1994)
6. Kleinrock, L.: Queuing Systems, vol. 1. John Wiley & Sons, New York (1975)

Maximizing Aggregate Saturation Throughput in IEEE 802.11 Wireless LAN with Service Differentiation

A.V. Babu* and Lillykutty Jacob

Department of Electronics and Communication Engineering,
National Institute of Technology, Calicut - 673601, India
Tel: 91-495-2286706
babu@nitc.ac.in

Abstract. In this paper, we determine class specific optimal minimum contention window (CW_{min}) values that simultaneously maximizes aggregate saturation throughput and provides proportional throughput differentiation meeting deterministic target throughput ratios among multiple priority classes in IEEE 802.11 wireless LAN (WLAN). We show that, with the current default CW_{min} setting, IEEE 802.11e Enhanced Distributed Channel Access (EDCA) cannot provide satisfactory throughput differentiation among multiple priority classes. Compared to EDCA, the proportional throughput differentiation can provide consistent and adjustable differentiation among different service classes. With these optimal CW_{min} values, the aggregate throughput remains maximum and insensitive to the number of active nodes in the network, thus improving the scalability of the protocol.

Keywords: IEEE 802.11e EDCA, performance analysis, proportional throughput differentiation, quality of service, saturation throughput.

1 Introduction

IEEE 802.11 has become one of the most successful MAC protocols for wireless infrastructure and ad hoc LANs. The IEEE 802.11 standard [1] provides two access methods: (i) the Distributed Coordination Function (DCF), also known as the basic access method; (ii) the Point Coordination Function (PCF), an access method similar to a polling system, which uses a point coordinator to arbitrate the access right among nodes. DCF is based on carrier sense multiple access with collision avoidance (CSMA/CA) and supports only best effort service. Due to significant demand for Quality of Service (QoS) sensitive multimedia applications, the 802.11 Task Group E has recently ratified final proposals and specifications for the QoS aware MAC protocol with service differentiation mechanism (named 802.11e) [2]. The 802.11e MAC protocol employs a channel access function called Hybrid Coordination Function (HCF) that includes a contention based Enhanced Distributed Channel Access (EDCA) and a contention-free HCF Controlled Channel Access (HCCA). The EDCA mode of operation of 802.11e is an extension of the DCF with the goal to

---

* Corresponding author.

S. Rao et al. (Eds.): ICDCN 2008, LNCS 4904, pp. 503–514, 2008.
© Springer-Verlag Berlin Heidelberg 2008

provide priorities and traffic differentiation in the wireless access. Each traffic flow is classified into an appropriate Access Category (AC). Four AC's are defined, each one has associated MAC transmission queue. The behavior of an AC depends on a number of MAC layer parameters: initial Contention Window size (CW_{min}), maximum Contention Window size (CW_{max}), Arbitration Inter Frame Space (AIFS) and Transmission Opportunity limit (TXOP_limit). If one AC has a smaller AIFS or CW_{min}, that class's traffic has a better chance to access the medium earlier [2].

EDCA support CW_{min} based tuning to achieve differentiation among multi-priority classes. It has been proved that relative service differentiation can be achieved by varying CW_{min} alone [8]. It is well known that the aggregate throughput under DCF significantly degrades as the number of competing nodes increases [3]. Thus a distributed channel access mechanism such as DCF does not scale with the number of contenders. EDCA, which is a DCF based protocol also exhibit the scalability problem. In the case of EDCA, the throughput achieved by nodes of low priority class significantly degrades as the number of higher priority class nodes increases [9]. Further, under EDCA, selection of default CW_{min} values for service differentiation does not maximize aggregate throughput. In this paper, we determine the class specific optimal CW_{min} values to maximize aggregate throughput and provide proportional throughput differentiation among multiple priority classes. Through analysis and simulation, we demonstrate that proportional throughput differentiation and aggregate throughput maximization can be simultaneously achieved through appropriate assignments of per class optimal CW_{min}. Further, with the selection of optimal CW_{min} values, the maximum aggregate throughput of the WLAN approaches a constant value for large number of active nodes.

Rest of the paper is organized as follows: Section 2 gives a brief account of related work. In Section 3, we derive the expression for class specific optimal CW_{min}. Section 4 presents the results, both analytical and simulation. The paper is concluded in Section 5.

2 Related Work

Several papers have appeared in the literature on the performance analysis of IEEE 802.11 DCF [4, 5]. Several schemes have been proposed in the literature to enhance DCF and achieve service differentiation [6] - [9]. There have been several studies on evaluating the performance of EDCA in the context of IEEE 802.11e using analytical models or by simulation [9] - [13]. Most of the papers, mentioned above, analyze the effect of variation of CW_{min} on service differentiation, while the analytical model for EDCA discussed in [10] consider the effect of varying both CW_{min} and AIFS on service differentiation. Most of the existing literatures on EDCA consider relative service differentiation, where higher priority classes have better performance than lower priority classes based on differentiation of EDCA parameters. The issue of adjusting the degree of service differentiation so as to achieve a deterministic target differentiation ratio is not addressed.

Several papers have been proposed in the literature to improve the performance of DCF and EDCA [14]-[20]. In [14], authors propose a fair medium access control (PMAC) protocol to maximize wireless channel utilization subject to weighted fairness among multiple data traffic flows. In [15], authors address the issue of finding the optimal configuration of 802.11e EDCA with respect to the weighted max–min fairness criterion. Authors of [17] conduct simulation study of a method for proportional QoS control between low and high priority classes in 802.11eWLAN. In [18], authors propose Spacing Based Channel Occupancy Regulation (SCORE) MAC protocol to provide proportional service differentiation in WLAN. In [19], authors propose a class based p-persistent analytical model for EDCA and present a constraint optimization problem to maximize the system throughput while satisfying the QoS requirements. Work in [20] address the issue of finding the class specific optimal CW_{min} values that yield the maximum aggregate throughput while maintaining throughput differentiation between classes. It may be noted that in [19] and [20], closed-form analytical expressions for the optimal MAC parameters are not solved explicitly. In this paper, differently from the above, we consider a proportional throughput differentiation model of [16] in which the throughput ratio of different service classes is proportional to the ratio of their differentiation parameters.

3 Proportional Throughput Differentiation and Maximum Aggregate Throughput

For maximizing aggregate system throughput simultaneously with providing proportional throughput differentiation, we consider tuning CW_{min} values of multiple priority classes, assuming all other MAC parameters including the frame size to be same for all the classes. In this section, first we consider the throughput differentiation under EDCA employing tuning of CW_{min} [7, 8]. We, then present an analytical model to determine the class specific optimal CW_{min} values to meet the desired objectives. We also derive expression for optimal value of maximum aggregate throughput.

3.1 Saturation Throughput Ratio between Two Priority Classes in EDCA

We assume saturation condition (i.e., each node has always frames to send). N different types of traffic flows are considered with n_i flows for class-i traffic ($i = 1$, $2,..,N$). It is assumed that each node carries only one traffic flow. The effects of bit errors due to noise are ignored. Consequently, packets are lost only due to collisions. Also the effect of hidden terminals is not considered. For class-i traffic, contention window size in the j–th retry/retransmission be $W_{i,j}$. Assume that, at each transmission attempt for a class-i traffic flow, regardless of the number of retransmissions suffered, each frame collides with constant and independent probability p_i, where p_i is the conditional collision probability seen by a class-i frame at the time of its being transmitted on the channel. The probability that a node senses the channel to be idle p_{idle} is:

$$p_{idle} = \prod_{i=1}^{N}(1-\tau_i)^{n_i} \tag{1}$$

where τ_i is the probability that a node with class-i traffic transmits during a time slot, and can be expressed as [9]:

$$\tau_i = \frac{(1-2p_i)(1-(p_i)^{L_i+1})}{W_{i,0}(1-(2P_i)^{m+1})(1-p_i)+(1-2p_i)(1-p_i^{L_i+1})+W_{i,0}(1-2p_i)(2p_i)^m p_i(1-(p_i)^{L_i-m})} \tag{2}$$

where L_i represents the retry limit for class i traffic and m represents the maximum back off stage. The collision probability for class i traffic is:

$$p_i = 1-(1-\tau_i)^{n_i-1}\prod_{\substack{r=1 \\ r\neq i}}^{N}(1-\tau_r)^{n_r} \tag{3}$$

Let S_i be the normalized saturation throughput for class-i traffic, which is defined as the fraction of time the channel is used to successfully transmit the payload bits corresponding to class i traffic and is calculated as follows.

$$S_i = \frac{p_{tr,i}p_{s,i}E[L]}{E[\sigma]} \tag{4}$$

Here $E[\sigma] = (1-p_{tr})\sigma + p_{tr}p_s T_s + p_{tr}(1-p_s)T_c$, where p_{tr} is the probability that there is at least one transmission in a given time slot, p_s is the probability that this transmission is successful, and $p_{s,i}$ is the probability that successful transmission occurs for class i traffic. These probabilities are calculated as follows:

$$p_{tr} = 1-\prod_{i=1}^{N}(1-\tau_i)^{n_i}; p_{s,i} = \frac{n_i\tau_i(1-\tau_i)^{n_i-1}\prod_{h=1,h\neq i}^{N}(1-\tau_h)^{n_h}}{p_{tr,i}}; p_s = \frac{1}{p_{tr}}\sum_{i=1}^{N}n_i p_{s,i} \tag{5}$$

In (4), $E[L]$ denotes the average frame size corresponding to class i (assumed to be equal for all i). σ, T_s and T_c, respectively, represent the duration of an empty time slot, the average time channel is sensed busy because of successful transmission, and the average time the channel is sensed busy because of a transmission failure due to collision. Let the per node saturation throughput ratio between class i and class 1 be D_i. As in [8], the following approximate expression can be obtained:

$$D_i = \frac{S_i/n_i}{S_1/n_1} \approx \frac{\tau_i(1-\tau_1)}{\tau_1(1-\tau_i)} \tag{6}$$

3.2 Proportional Throughput Differentiation

We apply the proportional service differentiation model of [16], which was introduced for DiffServ architecture in IP networks to provide quantitative service differentiation, for a WLAN with N number of classes. Let s_i be the per station throughput of class i traffic. The proportional differentiation model for WLAN is defined as follows: $s_i/s_j = \phi_i/\phi_j$ for all i,j, where ϕ_i is the differentiation weight for class i. Assuming that class-1 stations have the highest priority, we define the differentiation ratio for class i stations, D_i as follows: $D_i = s_i/s_1 = \phi_i/\phi_1$ with $D_1 = 1$ and $0 < D_i < 1; i = 2,...,N$. It may be noted that D_i here represents a quantitative measure for proportional throughput differentiation among different traffic classes. Analytical expressions for class specific optimal CW_{min} to achieve the desired proportional throughput differentiation and maximum aggregate throughput are determined in the following subsection.

3.3   Evaluation of Class Specific Optimal CW_{min} Values

Let S be the aggregate system throughput. The throughput maximization problem with proportional differentiation is formulated as follows.

$$\text{Max } S = \sum_{i=1}^{N} S_i \text{ such that } s_i / s_1 = D_i \; ; \; i = 2,3,...,N \tag{7}$$

Proposition 1. The optimal frame transmission probabilities τ_i^* ; $i = 2,...,N$ corresponding to (7) are given as follows:

$$\tau_i^* = \frac{D_i \sqrt{2/(bT_c')}}{1 + D_i \sqrt{2/(bT_c')}} \; ; \; i = 1,2,...,N \tag{8}$$

where $D_1 = 1$ and $0 < D_j < 1$; $j = 2,...,N$; $b = \sum_{j=1}^{N}\sum_{\substack{k=1 \\ j \neq k}}^{N} n_j n_k D_j D_k + \sum_{j=1}^{N} \frac{n_j(n_j-1)D_j^2}{2}$

and $T_c' = T_c / \sigma$ is the collision duration expressed as number of idle slot time, σ.

Proof: Combining (4), (5) and (6) and on simplifying, we get

$$S = \sum_{i=1}^{N} S_i = \sum_{i=1}^{N} \frac{K_2 n_i D_i (\tau_1 /(1-\tau_1))}{(1/p_{idle}) - K_1 + (\delta/T_c)\sum_{i=1}^{N} n_i D_i (\tau_1 / 1-\tau_1)} \tag{9}$$

where $K_1 = 1 - \sigma/T_c$, $K_2 = E[L]/T_c$ and $\delta = T_s - T_c$. Similarly, combining (1) and (6), we have

$$P_{idle} = \prod_{i=1}^{N}(1-\tau_i)^{n_i} = \prod_{i=1}^{N}(\frac{1}{1+(\tau_1 / 1-\tau_1)D_i})^{n_i} = \frac{1}{\prod_{i=1}^{N}(1+(\tau_1 / 1-\tau_1)D_i)^{n_i}} \tag{10}$$

Expanding $[1 + D_i(\tau_1 / 1-\tau_1)]^{n_i}$ using binomial series and neglecting higher order terms, the following expression can be obtained for $(1/p_{idle})$:

$$\frac{1}{P_{idle}} \approx 1 + (\sum_{i=1}^{N} n_i D_i)(\frac{\tau_1}{1-\tau_1}) + \frac{1}{2}[\sum_{j=1}^{N}\sum_{\substack{k=1 \\ j \neq k}}^{N} n_j n_k D_j D_k + \sum_{j=1}^{N} \frac{n_j(n_j-1)D_j^2}{2}](\frac{\tau_1}{1-\tau_1})^2 \tag{11}$$

We define $a = \sum_{i=1}^{N} n_i D_i$ and $b = \sum_{j=1}^{N} \sum_{\substack{k=1 \\ j \neq k}}^{N} n_j n_k D_j D_k + \sum_{j=1}^{N} \frac{n_j(n_j - 1)D_j^2}{2}$.

Substituting (11) in (9), and replacing with a and b, the corresponding terms,

$$S = \frac{K_2 a(\tau_1/1 - \tau_1)}{1 - K_1 + a(\tau_1/1 - \tau_1) + (b/2)(\tau_1/1 - \tau_1)^2 + a(\tau_1/1 - \tau_1)(\delta/T_c)} \quad (12)$$

The value of τ_1 corresponding to maximum throughput is obtained by solving $\frac{dS}{d\tau_1} = 0$. Thus

$$\tau_1^* = \frac{\sqrt{2/(bT_c')}}{1 + \sqrt{2/(bT_c')}} \quad (13)$$

Combining (13) with (6), we obtain

$$\tau_j^* = \frac{D_j \sqrt{2/(bT_c')}}{1 + D_j \sqrt{2/(bT_c')}}; \quad j = 2,..., N \quad (14)$$

∎

Using (1), (3) and (11), the optimal collision probabilities p_i^* can be deduced as follows:

$$p_i^* \approx 1 - \frac{1}{(1 - \tau_i^*)(1 + a(\tau_1^*/1 - \tau_1^*) + \frac{b}{2}(\tau_1^*/1 - \tau_1^*)^2)}; \quad i = 1,2,..., N \quad (15)$$

Using (2) and (15), the class specific optimal CW_{min} values to achieve the desired objectives are obtained.

$$W_{i,0}^* = \frac{(1 - 2p_i^*)(1 - (p_i^*)^{L_i+1})((2/\tau_i^*) - 1)}{(1 - (2P_i^*)^{m+1})(1 - p_i^*) + (1 - 2p_i^*)(2p_i^*)^m p_i^*(1 - (p_i^*)^{L_i - m})}; i = 1,2,3,..., N \quad (16)$$

The optimal values are numerically computed as follows. Given D_i; $i = 1,2,3,....,N$, and 802.11b parameters, the optimal frame transmission probabilities τ_i^*; $i = 1,2,3,....,N$ are computed using (8). Then the corresponding collision probabilities p_i^* are computed using (15). The class specific optimal CW_{min} values are then determined using (16).

Proposition 2. As the number of active stations increases unboundedly, the maximum aggregate throughput of the WLAN approaches a constant value and is given by:

$$S^* \approx \frac{E[L]}{\sigma\beta + T_s + T_c[\beta(e^{1/\beta} - 1) - 1]} \quad (17)$$

Proof: Let p_{idle}^* be idle slot probability corresponding to the optimal transmission attempt probabilities τ_i^* ; $i = 2,...,N$. From (12), we get the following expression for the maximum aggregate system throughput S^*.

$$S^* = \frac{E[L]a(\tau_1^*/1-\tau_1^*)}{\sigma + a(\tau_1^*/1-\tau_1^*)T_s + [(1/p_{idle}^*)-1-a(\tau_1^*/1-\tau_1^*)]T_c} \tag{18}$$

From (13), we have $\tau_1^*/1-\tau_1^* = \sqrt{2/(bT_c')}$. Let $\beta = \sqrt{T_c'/2}$ and note that $a^2 \approx b$. Then $a(\tau_1^*/1-\tau_1^*) \approx 1/\beta$. Further, from (10), we have $1/p_{idle}^* = \prod_{i=1}^{N}[(1+(\tau_1^*/1-\tau_1^*)D_i]^{n_i}$. For very large n, $[1+(\tau_1^*/1-\tau_1^*)D_i]^{n_i} \approx [1+(\tau_1^*/1-\tau_1^*)]^{n_i D_i}$. Hence

$$\frac{1}{p_{idle}^*} \approx [1+(\tau_1^*/1-\tau_1^*)]^{\sum_{i=1}^{N}n_i D_i} = [1+(\tau_1^*/1-\tau_1^*)]^a \approx [1+(1/a\beta)]^a = e^{1/\beta} \tag{19}$$

Substituting (19) in (18), we get the result.   ∎

Hence we conclude that, in a WLAN with very large number of active stations, the optimal values of aggregate saturation throughput, is insensitive to the number of active stations as well as the number of priority classes in the network.

4 Performance Evaluation

In this section, we present the numerical results obtained from the analytical model of the previous section. We also present simulation results to validate the analytical model. The simulation model was developed using NS-2 [21] based on IEEE 802.11e draft and IEEE 802.11b standard [3]. In our simulation set up, all nodes in the network were within range of each other (no hidden terminal problem) and there was no mobility in the system. An ad hoc topology was used and stations were arranged at random positions in a rectangular grid with dimensions $500m \times 500m$. The interface queues at each station used a drop-tail policy and the queue length was set at 50 packets in order to approximate an infinite buffer. We assumed in each station a single application. This corresponds to having only one MAC layer queue and one access category (AC) for each station. Because we consider all nodes under saturation, CBR type of traffic was considered. The traffic rate at each active node was selected to be larger than the raw physical transmission rate of the network so as to keep the nodes in saturation. Each simulation was run for 100 seconds of simulation time. All the reported results were averaged over three to five independent simulation runs. To obtain the numerical results, we have implemented the analytical model developed in Section 3 in MATLAB.

First we consider a WLAN with two traffic classes: class-1 stations have high priority ($D_1 = 1$) and for class-2 stations, the target throughput differentiation ratio is $D_2 = 0.5$. Stations of both classes are configured with same AIFS values; n_1 and n_2 respectively represents the number of nodes belonging to class 1 and class 2; and $n_1 = n_2 = n$. For EDCA with prioritized CW_{min} control, we select $W_{1,0} = 16$ and $W_{2,0} = 32$. The optimal CW_{min} values for class-1 and class-2 stations are tabulated in Table 2.

Table 1. Optimal $W_{1,0}{}^*$ and $W_{2,0}{}^*$

Number of nodes	$W_{1,0}{}^*$	$W_{2,0}{}^*$
$n_1 = n_2 = 1$	31	62
$n_1 = n_2 = 2$	77	154
$n_1 = n_2 = 5$	213	425
$n_1 = 2$ & $n_2 = 1$	61	121
$n_1 = 5$ & $n_2 = 1$	151	300
$n_1 = 1$ & $n_2 = 2$	48	96
$n_1 = 1$ & $n_2 = 5$	95	190

Next, we use these optimal values of CW_{min} to investigate further results. We measure the achieved aggregate throughput and throughput ratio between the two traffic classes for various values of n. Under proportional throughput differentiation, the differentiation ratio remains insensitive to the number of nodes n. We observe that the aggregate throughputs obtained with optimal CW_{min} values are much greater than those achieved for EDCA. Table 2 shows the throughput achieved by each class as well as the aggregate throughput for different values of n. With $n_1 = n_2 = 5$, the proposed method achieves about 19% increase in aggregate throughput over EDCA while for $n_1 = n_2 = 10$, the total throughput is greater than EDCA by 35%. Fig. 1 shows the variation of aggregate saturation throughput against n. The maximum aggregate throughput is almost insensitive to the number of stations, while under EDCA, the throughput reduces significantly as the network size increases. The throughput degradation in EDCA is mainly due to the increased frame collision probability as a result of more contending nodes in the network. The selection of proposed optimal CW_{min} values reduces probability of collision, still maintaining very high throughput and proportional differentiation. Figure 2 shows the probability of collision for the two traffic classes against n for EDCA as well as the optimal CW_{min} method. It may be noted that the probability of collision in the former case (EDCA) increases drastically as the network size grow, while for the latter case, the collision probability is almost a constant for large n. For $n = 5$, compared to EDCA, the collision probability reduces by about 70% and for $n = 10$, it reduces by 82%. Figure 3 shows the variation of aggregate throughput against CW_{min} of class-1 stations, $W_{1,0}$, while

$W_{2,0}$ is selected to achieve target proportional differentiation among the classes. These results establish the claim that the proposed optimal CW_{min} value of class-1 stations $W_{1,0}^{*}$ indeed maximizes the aggregate throughput.

Table 2. Throughput achieved by nodes in a wireless LAN with two classes of traffic

Differentiation Criterion		Throughput (s_i) Mbps		Throughput Ratio	Total network throughput (Mbps)
		Class 1 Analysis/ simulation	Class 2 Analysis/ simulation	s_2 / s_1 Analysis/ simulation	Analysis/ simulation
EDCA $W_{1,0} = 16$ & $W_{2,0} = 32$	$n=1$	0.603/ 0.605	0.27/ 0.252	0.446/ 0.417	0.873/ 0.857
	$n=5$	0.4977/ 0.51	0.23/ 0.214	0.462/ 0.42	0.727/ 0.724
	$n=10$	0.439/ 0.445	0.2087/0.184	0.482/ 0.445	0.6477/ 0.629
Proportional Differentiation	$n=1$	0.587/ 0.58	0.293/ 0.287	0.5/ 0.495	0.88/ 0.867
	$n=5$	0.577/ 0.569	0.288/ 0.29	0.5/ 0.5	0.865/ 0.861
	$n=10$	0.576/ 0.569	0.284/ 0.28	0.494/ 0.49	0.86/ 0.85

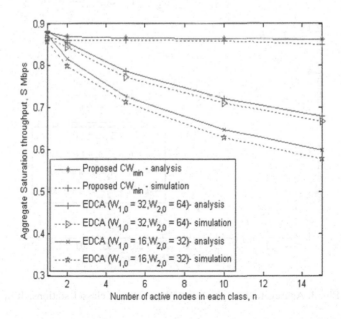

Fig. 1. Aggregate saturation throughput vs number of nodes in each class

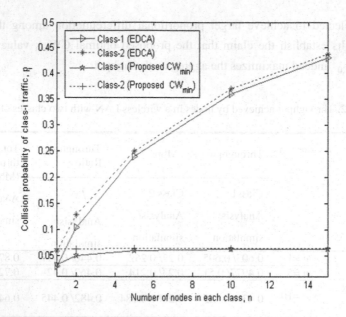

Fig. 2. Collision probability vs number of nodes in each class

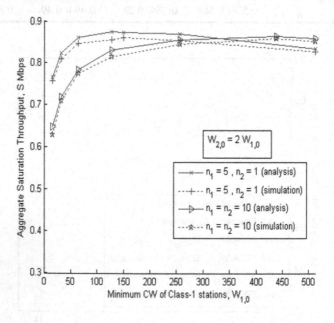

Fig. 3. Aggregate throughput vs CW$_{min}$ value of class-1 stations, $W_{1,0}$

5 Conclusions

In this paper we determined the maximum aggregate throughput of a wireless LAN with multiple priority classes. We computed class specific optimal CW_{min} values for multiple priority classes to achieve maximum aggregate throughput and proportional throughput differentiation simultaneously. We also obtained approximate closed-form expressions for maximum aggregate throughput, optimal collision probability and optimal idle slot probability, assuming large number of active nodes. We have shown that, with the current differentiation parameter setting, EDCA cannot provide satisfactory throughput differentiation between multiple priority classes. Compared to EDCA, the proportional throughput differentiation can provide consistent, adjustable proportional differentiation among different service classes. Further more we demonstrated that, with optimal CW_{min} values, the maximum aggregate throughput remains insensitive to number of nodes in the network while in EDCA, the aggregate throughput reduces drastically as the network size increases. Extensive simulations were conducted to corroborate the analytical findings.

Acknowledgement

The work reported in this paper was supported in part by Ministry of Human Resources and Development (MHRD), Government of India.

References

1. IEEE 802.11 WG Part II: Wireless LAN Medium Access Control (MAC) and Physical (PHY) layer specifications (1999)
2. IEEE 802.11 WG, Part 11: Wireless LAN MAC and PHY specifications: MAC Quality of Service Enhancements (November 2005)
3. IEEE 802.11b WG, Part II: Wireless LAN MAC and PHY Specifications: High-speed physical layer extension in the 2.4 GHz band (September 1999)
4. Bianchi, G.: Performance analysis of the IEEE 802.11 Distributed Co-ordination Function. IEEE Journal on Selected Areas in Communication 18(3), 535–547 (2000)
5. Tay, Y.C., Chua, K.C.: A Capacity Analysis for the IEEE 802.11MAC Protocol. Wireless Networks 7, 159–171 (2001)
6. Aad, I., Castelluccia: Differentiation Mechanism for IEEE 802.11. In: Proceedings of IEEE INFOCOM, Alaska (2001)
7. Li, B., Battiti, R.: Performance Analysis of an Enhanced IEEE 802.11 DCF Supporting Service Differentiation. In: Proceedings of IEEE QFIS, Stockholm (2003)
8. He, J., Zheng, L., Yang, Z., Chou, C.T.: Performance Analysis and Service Differentiation in IEEE 802.11 wireless LAN. In: Proceedings of IEEE LCN, Bonn (2003)
9. Xiao, Y.: Performance Analysis of Priority Schemes for IEEE 802.11 and IEEE 802.11e Wireless LANs. IEEE Transactions on Wireless Communications 4(4) (July 2005)
10. Robinson, J.W., Randhawa, T.S.: Saturation Throughput Analysis of IEEE 802.11e Enhanced Distributed Coordination Function. IEEE JSAC 22(5) (2004)

11. Mangold, S., Choi, S., May, P., Kein, O., Hiertz, G., Stibor, L.: IEEE 802.11e Wireless LAN for Quality of Service. In: Proceedings of European Wireless Conference, Florence (February 2002)
12. Ni, Q., Romdhani, L., Turletti, T.: A Survey of QoS Enhancements for IEEE 802.11 Wireless LAN. Wireless Communications and Mobile Computing 4(5), 547–566 (2004)
13. Lindgren, A., Almquist, A., Schelen, O.: Quality of Service Schemes for IEEE 802.11 Wireless LANs - An Evaluation. MONET 8(3), 223–235 (2003)
14. Qiao, D., Shin, K.: Achieving Efficient Channel Utilization and Weighted Fairness for Data Communications in IEEE 802.11 wireless LAN Under the DCF. In: Proceedings of the Tenth International Workshop on Quality of Service, Miami (2002)
15. Banchs, A., Vollero, L.: Throughput analysis and optimal configuration of 802.11e EDCA. Computer Networks 50(11), 1749–1768 (2006)
16. Dovrolis, C., Ramanathan, P.: A Case for Relative Differentiated Services and the Proportional Differentiation Model. IEEE Network 13(5), 26–34 (1999)
17. Tanigawa1, Y., Kim, J.-O., Tode, H., Murakami, K.: Proportional Control and Deterministic Protection of QoS in IEEE 802.11e Wireless LAN. In: Proceedings of IWCMC, Canada (2006)
18. Xue, Q., Gong, W., Ganz, A.: Proportional Service Differentiation in Wirless LANs Using Spacing-based Channel Occupancy Regulation. MONET 11, 229–240 (2006)
19. Zhaoy, J., Zhang, Q., Guo, Z., Zhu, W.: Throughput and QoS Optimization in IEEE 802.11 wireless LAN. In: IEEE conference on 3Gwireless2002 & WAS2002, USA (2002)
20. Yoon, J., Yun, S., Kim, H., Bahk, S.: Maximizing Differentiated Throughput in IEEE 802.11eWireless LANs. In: Proceedings of LCN, Florida (2006)
21. The ns-2 Simulator, http://www.isi.edu/nsnam/ns/

Overloading Cellular DS-CDMA: A Bandwidth-Efficient Scheme for Capacity Enhancement

Preetam Kumar[1], M. Ramesh[2], and Saswat Chakrabarti[1]

[1] G.S. Sanayal School of Telecommunications
[2] Dept. of Electronics and Electrical Communication Engineering
Indian Institute of Technology, Kharagpur
preetam@gssst.iitkgp.ernet.in, ramu_mudumba@yahoo.co.in,
saswat@ece.iitkgp.ernet.in

Abstract. Overloading is a technique to accommodate more number of users than the spreading factor N. This is an efficient way to increase the number of users in a fixed bandwidth, which is of practical interest to mobile system operators. In this paper we have reviewed the different overloading schemes proposed in the literature for the DS-CDMA systems. The performance of an Orthogonal/Orthogonal (O/O) overloading scheme, using two sets of orthogonal codes (O/s-O) has been evaluated. Iterative multistage detector (IMSD) is used to reduce the multiple access interference between the users of two sets. The BER performance of IMSD is evaluated with hard and soft decisions functions using Monte-Carlo simulations. It is found that, this scheme provides 19% and 11% channel overloading for synchronous DS-CDMA system in an AWGN channel, with a SNR degradation of less than 0.5 dB at a BER of 10^{-5} compared to single user bound for N=16 and 64 respectively.

1 Introduction

In a conventional direct sequence code division multiple access (DS-CDMA) communication, each user is assigned a unique spreading code or signature. The performance of CDMA system is dependent on the correlation properties of spreading codes, which determines the multiple access interference (MAI) power. The number of users supported in a DS-CDMA cellular system is typically less than spreading factor (N), and the cells are underloaded. To make a better use of radio spectrum, it is of considerable interest to assign more sequences than the spreading factor, i.e., to overload the channel. Hence the cellular system becomes overloaded, when the number of supported users exceeds the spreading factor. Infact this type of channel overloading is provisioned in the 3G standard [1].

The concept of overloading a DS-CDMA cell using orthogonal codes is illustrated in Fig.1. Let us consider two sets of spreading codes, set1: N mutually orthogonal codes of length N and set 2: another set of mutually orthogonal codes. Let there be a demand for more than N code channels and let the first N users be given N unique spreading codes of length N form set 1. The cell gets overloaded if additional M users are assigned spreading codes from a new set of codes, i.e., form set 2.

S. Rao et al. (Eds.): ICDCN 2008, LNCS 4904, pp. 515–527, 2008.

In a single set, if all codes are synchronized, orthogonal signatures are optimal due to complete elimination of multiple access interference (MAI).Synchronism between signatures can be maintained in the downlink of cellular systems with relative ease and hence, orthogonal signatures (Walsh functions) are used in the downlink of IS-95 and UMTS mobile radio standards. Even in the uplink of UMTS, usage of orthogonal signatures has been advocated to realize multi-code channelization to increase the overall data rate. Also in the uplink, some systems that combine multicarrier modulation with CDMA can maintain orthogonality by inclusion of an appropriate cyclic prefix, and single-tap equalization [2].

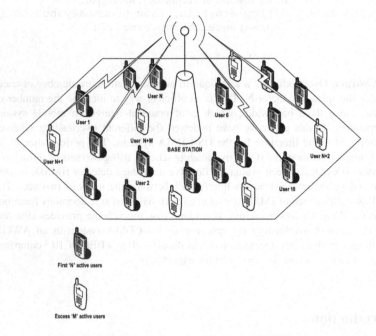

Fig. 1. Overloading concept in a single cell CDMA system

The Capacity or the number of active users (K) in a conventional synchronous orthogonal CDMA environment is limited by the spreading factor, which is W.T, where W is the transmission bandwidth and T is the duration of the symbol. When K exceeds N, the system is overloaded and signatures are no longer orthogonal. This leads to MAI between the two sets.

In an overloaded system, a conventional matched filter receiver is not optimal due to high level of MAI. Multiuser detection (MUD) is required in order to obtain a satisfactory performance of the users in any overloaded system. Linear MUD's, such as the decorrelator, the minimum mean-squared error detector or linear decision directed interference cancellation are devised to detect users in an underloaded system. The Maximum Likelihood (ML) detection is not an option because of its complexity that is exponential in the number of users. The nonlinear MUDs such as multistage parallel interference cancellation (PIC) and successive interference cancellation (SIC) [3], have good complexity-performance trade-off as compared to other MUD's. Hence these MUDs are suitable for overloaded systems. Thus, the problem of overloading DS-CDMA systems may be stated as follows: How to increase the number of spreading codes, or the number of users K, without increasing the dimension N, while keeping minimum MAI to ensure low complexity of the receiver.

In the next section, we give a detailed overview of five different overloading schemes that have been proposed in the literature. In Section-3, the system model of Orthogonal/Orthogonal (O/O) is presented. In section-4 Iterative multistage detection for the proposed scheme is explained. The Monte-Carlo simulation results of Orthogonal/scrambled-Orthogonal (O/s-O) overloading scheme are presented in Section-5. Finally, section-6 summarizes the results and concludes the paper.

2 Overloading Schemes for CDMA Systems: A Review

Let us consider an overloaded system with spreading factor N and the number of active users K (>N). We assume perfect power control and synchronous users. The received vector $\mathbf{y}$ over an AWGN channel after demodulation and chip sampling is given in each symbol interval by

$$\mathbf{y} = \mathbf{Sa} + \mathbf{n} = \sum_{i=1}^{K} a_i \mathbf{s}_i + \mathbf{n} \qquad (2.1)$$

where $\mathbf{a}$ contains the BPSK modulated data symbols of K users and $\mathbf{S}$ is the signature matrix of dimensions $K \times N$ with unit norm sequences. All sequences are assumed to have equal energy. The Gaussian noise is represented by the real valued vector $\mathbf{n}$ and consists of independent Gaussian noise samples with variance $\sigma^2 = N_0/(2E_b)$, where $N_0/2$ is the variance of the noise and E_b is the bit energy. In Fig. 2, the classification of overloading schemes based on signature sequence selection is shown. First we will discuss two schemes using single set of signature sequence and then three schemes based on multiple sets. These schemes are briefly explained below:

(1) The signature sequence can be chosen randomly, i.e. random spreading. In each symbol interval, each signature is chosen independently and completely at random out of the set $\{1/\sqrt{N}, -1/\sqrt{N}\}^N$. This is an evident choice for the signatures, as orthogonality between the users is impossible if K > N. Moreover, for high channel loads (K/N $\rightarrow \infty$) or for very high signal-to-noise ratios, random spreading incurs almost no loss in spectral efficiency as compared to optimal signature sets [4].

(2) One can look for signatures that are "as orthogonal as possible". A popular measure in oversaturated channels for this is to look for unit-norm signatures that minimize the Total Squared Correlation (TSC) among the signatures. A lower bound to the TSC of any set of K unit-norm signatures of length N (Welch-Bound) is given by

$$TSC = \sum_{i=1}^{K} \sum_{j=1}^{K} (s_i^T \cdot s_j)^2 \geq TSC_{min} = K^2/N \qquad (2.2)$$

For K<N, this bound cannot be achieved and the best code can be orthogonal sequences. For $K \geq N$, this lower bound TSC_{min} can be achieved by so-called Welch-Bound Equality (WBE) [5] sequences, satisfying

$$\mathbf{S}.\mathbf{S}^T = \frac{K}{N}\mathbf{I}_N \qquad (2.3)$$

Where $\mathbf{I}_N$ is the identity matrix of order N. Signatures sets satisfying (2.3) can be considered 'as orthogonal as possible' since TSC is minimized.

These WBE sequences can be generated by means of an iterative procedure [6], but are not binary-valued in general. WBE sequences have some very interesting properties: they maximize the sum capacity among all possible signature sets, and maximize at the same time the network capacity. However, WBE sequences have the important drawback that they are not scalable: if the number of users in the system changes dynamically, these sequences have to be recomputed for every change in K.

(3) A third approach is to design a scalable signature set that is especially suited to be detected by means of a particular multiuser detector. Examples are the tree-structured channel overloading [7] and excess signaling [8], where the signatures are designed so that they can be detected easily by means of a Maximum Likelihood (ML) detector. Both overloading schemes allow for a restricted number of excess users (K-N) only, and do not have binary spreading sequences. In order to allow for a high number of excess users with binary spreading sequences and suboptimal Multiuser Detectors (MUD's), schemes have been introduced such as the OCDMA/OCDMA (O/O) in [9], PN/OCDMA (PN/O) in [10]. In these schemes, the users are divided into two groups: the first N users are the 'set 1 users', while the M (=K-N) excess users are the 'set 2 users'. Expression (2.1) can now be modified as:

$$\mathbf{y} = \mathbf{S}_1\mathbf{a} + \mathbf{S}_2\mathbf{b} + \mathbf{n} = \sum_{i=1}^{N} a_i \mathbf{s}_i^1 + \sum_{j=1}^{M} b_j \mathbf{s}_j^2 + \mathbf{n} \qquad (2.4)$$

where $\mathbf{a}$ and $\mathbf{b}$ contain the data symbols of se1-users and set2-users respectively. In O/O scheme, the first N users (set-1 users) are assigned orthogonal sequences, while the excess users (set-2 users) are assigned other orthogonal sequences (O/O), while in PN/O set2-users are assigned random sequences (PN/O). The signature matrix $\mathbf{S}_1 = [\mathbf{s}_1^1......\mathbf{s}_N^1]$ of the set1-users is the orthogonal Walsh-Hadamard matrix $\mathbf{W}_N$ of order N in both the schemes. In PN/O, the signature of the set-2 users is chosen independently and completely at random in every symbol interval out of $\{1/\sqrt{N}, -1/\sqrt{N}\}^N$. In this way, the set 1 users suffer from less interference in O/O scheme as compared to random spreading (PN), while the set 2 users suffer from less (O/O) or the same amount of interference (PN/O) as compared to random spreading with the same values of K and N. Because of the special structure of these signatures, both O/O and PN/O can be detected easily by means of iterative multistage interference cancellation [11] schemes, where in every stage, the set 1 users are detected first, followed by a detection of the set 2 users. Also, we can combine two different orthogonal multiple access schemes like TDMA/OCDMA [12]. Recently, we have proposed a new overloading scheme [13], where set1 users are assigned synchronous orthogonal sequences, while set2 users are asynchronous with PN sequences to improve the overloading performance.

(4) Another kind of overloaded OCDMA is presented in [14], where signals are divided into groups that are orthogonal to each other. A similar idea is exploited in [15], where the N-dimensional global signal space is divided into a number of L-dimensional orthogonal subspaces. Each L-dimensional subspace is assigned to L+s users. This method of arranging oversaturation is referred as group orthogonal CDMA (GO-CDMA). Each subspace is allocated to L+s users, which results in oversaturation efficiency equal to (1+s/L).

(5) In the cdma2000 system, binary suboptimal Quasi-Orthogonal Sequences (QOS) [16] are used in the downlink instead of the WBE sequences. For N<K<2N, a binary QOS signature set is obtained for any spreading factor N that is a power of 2, by assigning the Walsh-Hadamard sequences $\mathbf{WH}_N^{(i)}$ (i = 1, ..., N) of order N to the first N users (set 1 users), while the (K−N) excess users (set 2 users) are assigned the same Walsh-Hadamard sequence, but overlaid by a common (quasi-) bent sequences. These sequences have balanced crosscorrelation between users of the two sets. Although they have a lower user capacity than systems with WBE sequences, they are much more appealing from a practical point of view.

From an information-theoretical point of view, WBE sequences are the best choice, since they maximize the sum capacity. The O/O signature set is almost as good as these WBE-sequences with respect to the sum capacity [17], while random spreading can remain substantially inferior to both WBE sequences and O/O, if the load is not too high [4]. It has been shown in [18], that O/O outperforms random, WBE sequences and PN/O schemes using multistage SIC as MUD when the spreading length $N \geq 64$.

3   System Model for O/O Overloading Scheme for DS-CDMA

In the sequel we will consider the DS-CDMA system with processing gain N and the number of users K (=M+N). We assume that the channel is a nondispersive additive white Gaussian noise (AWGN) channel and that the different user signals are in perfect time synchronism. The signal $s_{u,k_u}(t)$ is the signature waveform of the k-th user in set-u, where $u \in \{1,2\}$, $k_1 \in \{1,2,3.......N\}$ for set-1 and $k_2 \in \{1,2,3.......M\}$ for set-2 users ($M \leq N$). Here N is number of users in set-1 and M number of users in set-2. The signature waveform may be expressed as:

$$s_{u,k_u}(t) = \sum_{j=1}^{N} s^j_{u,k_u} p_c(t - jT_c)$$ (3.1)

where $s^j_{u,k_u} \in \{-1,1\}$, T_c is chip duration and $p_c(t)$ is the rectangular pulse shape of the chip wave form with unit energy. We assume that all set-1 users are operational and hence N=Maximum number of users in set-1 (=Spreading factor). Let us denote $\mathbf{S}_1$ and $\mathbf{S}_2$ as the signature matrices of the set-1 and set-2 users respectively, which are generated from two different orthogonal sequence sets. The dimensions of signature matrix $\mathbf{S}_1$ is $N \times N$ and dimensions of $\mathbf{S}_2$ is $N \times M$. All users signatures are normalized such that $\left\| s_{u,k_u}(t) \right\| = 1$, i.e. unit norm signatures.

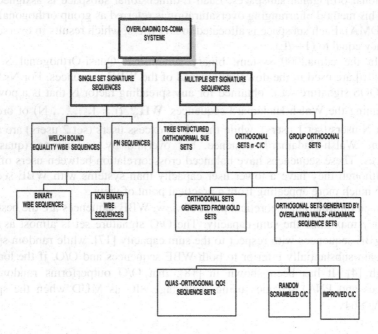

Fig. 2. Classification of overloading schemes based on the selection of signature sequence

Let us denote $\mathbf{b}_1$ and $\mathbf{b}_2$ as the data matrices of the set-1 and set-2 users respectively. The signal $b_{u,k}(t)$ is the data waveform of the k-th users in set-u, and is given as

$$b_{u,k_u}(t) = \sum_{l=-\infty}^{\infty} b^l_{u,k_u} P_{T_b}(t - lT_b) \qquad (3.2)$$

where, data sequences $b^l_{u,k_u} \in \{-1,1\}$ are i.i.d. and equiprobable random variables. In (3.2), T_b is bit duration, N=spreading factor and $P_{T_b}(t)$ is the rectangular pulse shape of the information data bits.

Matrices A1 and A2 are diagonal matrices of received signal amplitudes of both groups of users and are expressed as:

$$\mathbf{A}_1 = diag[A_{1,1}\cos(\phi_{1,1}),...,A_{1,N}\cos(\phi_{1,N})]$$
$$\mathbf{A}_2 = diag[A_{2,1}\cos(\phi_{2,1}),..,A_{2,M}\cos(\phi_{2,M})] \qquad (3.3)$$

Equation (3.3) models the channel attenuation and phases of the carriers of set-1 and set-2. In (3.3) A_{u,k_u} is the complex channel attenuation for the k-th user of the set-u. For AWGN channel $A_{u,k_u} = 1$ and for Rayleigh fading channel model, fading amplitudes are generated according to $A_{u,k_u} = A_{u,k_u}^{(I)} + jA_{u,k_u}^{(Q)}$, where $A_{u,k_u}^{(I)}$ and $A_{u,k_u}^{(Q)}$ are independent zero mean real Gaussian distributed random variables with variance $\sigma_{A_{u,k_u}^{(I)}}^2 = \sigma_{A_{u,k_u}^{(Q)}}^2 = \frac{1}{2}$. The phase term ϕ_{u,k_u} is the carrier phase of the k-th user of the set-u.

The discrete-time matrix model of the received BPSK modulated CDMA signal after demodulating and chip-matched filtering is given as:

$$\mathbf{r} = \mathbf{r}_1 + \mathbf{r}_2$$
$$= \mathbf{S}_1\mathbf{A}_1\mathbf{b}_1 + \mathbf{S}_2\mathbf{A}_2\mathbf{b}_2 + \mathbf{n} \tag{3.4}$$

where

$$\mathbf{r}_1 = \mathbf{S}_1\mathbf{A}_1\mathbf{b}_1 \tag{3.5}$$
$$\mathbf{r}_2 = \mathbf{S}_2\mathbf{A}_2\mathbf{b}_2 . \tag{3.6}$$

The vector $\mathbf{n}$ is the sampled AWGN noise with zero mean, and variance equal to σ^2. An effective multistage iterative interference cancellation receiver is discussed in the next section, which reduces the high level of interference due to overloading.

An important type of O/O scheme has been first discussed in [9], which is termed as scrambled-O/O (s-O/O) scheme. In this scheme set-1 users are assigned Walsh-Hadamard codes scrambled with set specific random scrambling sequence. Once the number of users exceeds 'N', excess users are assigned the same Walsh- Hadamard codes of set 1 but with different random scrambling sequence. The scrambling sequences are considered to change randomly from symbol to symbol in both sets. In this paper, we have shown the overloading performance of an O/O scheme, where scrambling sequence are used for the set 2 users WH codes only. This scheme is termed as O/s-O. The scrambling sequence for the set 2 is found by computer search such that the binary scrambling sequence provide equal crosscorrelation values ($\pm 1/\sqrt{N}$) between set 1 and set 2 spreading sequences. This balanced crosscorrelation property between two sets ensures same BER performance for all users in each set.

4 Iterative Multistage Detection

The amount of overloading depends upon the spreading sequence design and the ability of MUD to remove the high level of interference caused due to extra users. An efficient multiuser detection scheme can be used to improve the BER performance and overload the system for a given BER requirement. We will explain the iterative multistage interference cancellation receiver, which removes interference iteratively between the two sets.

In conventional matched filter receiver, the received demodulated and chip sampled signal (3.4) is despreaded and we obtain soft outputs of the transmitted bits embedded in multiple access interference (MAI) and AWGN noise. In conventional matched filter detection, these outputs are fed to the decision device to make the hard decision of the transmitted information bits. In this work, iterative multistage detection (IMSD) technique is used to remove the MAI between two sets users. The basic principle of this receiver is to iteratively remove the estimated interference from each set due to users of other set in multiple stages such that near single user performance is achieved. The interference power from set2-user (assuming that the useful signal power is normalized) is 1/N, and therefore the total interference power that affects set1-users is M/N. As long as M remains small compared to N, preliminary decisions can be made on the symbols transmitted by set1-users with some good reliability. But each of the set2-users gets an interference power of N (1/N) =1 from set1-users. Clearly the bit error (BER) performance will be poor for this set of users if detection is made prior to interference cancellation. As set1-users are detected with some good reliability, we can estimate the interference created from this set on set2-users. This estimated interference is removed from set2-uers before making the decision. Now in second iteration, interference from set2-users on set-1 are estimated form the first iteration outputs of set-1 and a more reliable set1 bits are obtained. This process continues till we get a near single user performance.

To explain the operation the following notations are used: $\hat{\mathbf{b}}_1^i$ and $\hat{\mathbf{b}}_2^i$ are decisions about set-1 & set-2 user data bits at i^{th} iteration respectively, $\mathbf{y}_1^i$ and $\mathbf{y}_2^i$ are set 1 and set 2 matched filters output at i^{th} iteration. At each iterative stage of the IMSD detector, the decision on the information bits are made according to the following expressions,

$$\hat{\mathbf{b}}_1^i = \phi\left(\mathbf{S}_1^T(\mathbf{r} - \delta_{2,i}.\mathbf{I}_2^{(i-1)})\right) \tag{4.1}$$

$$\hat{\mathbf{b}}_2^i = \phi\left(\mathbf{S}_2^T(\mathbf{r} - \delta_{1,i}.\mathbf{I}_1^i)\right) \tag{4.2}$$

where,

$$\mathbf{I}_1^i = \mathbf{S}_1\mathbf{A}_1\hat{\mathbf{b}}_1^i ; \tag{4.3}$$

$$\mathbf{I}_2^i = \mathbf{S}_2\mathbf{A}_2\hat{\mathbf{b}}_2^i \tag{4.4}$$

are estimated Multiple Access Interference (MAI) of set 1 on set 2 and set 2 on set 1 respectively. $\delta_{1,i}$ and $\delta_{2,i}$ ($0 \leq \delta \leq 1$) are the partial cancellation factor (pcf) which decides the amount of estimated interference cancellation for set 2 and set 1 respectively in the ith iteration. Generally as the iterations increases these pcf values approaches unity. The value of pcf is selected to minimize the BER. In this paper $\delta_{1,i}$ is set to unity as the set-1 data estimates are reliable as compared to set 2 (M < N).

In equations (4.1) and (4.2), $\phi(x)$ is the nonlinear decision function. According to the decision function $\phi(x)$, IMSD can be classified as Hard Decision Interference Cancellation (HDIC) or Soft Decision Interference Cancellation (SDIC). For HDIC, the decision function is defined as

$$\phi(x) = sgn(x) = \begin{cases} -1 & x < 0 \\ 1 & x > 0 \end{cases} \tag{4.5}$$

For SDIC except for the last iteration, where we take hard decision, in other iterations several nonlinear decision functions can be used. In some of the proposed schemes iteration dependent decision functions (ISDIC) are used. Computational complexity of SDIC is the limiting factor for its practical implementations. We have used piecewise linear approximation of hyperbolic tangent and is defined as:

$$\phi(x) = \begin{cases} x/\theta & |x| < \theta \\ sgn(x) & |x| \geq \theta \end{cases} \tag{4.4}$$

where θ is selected to minimize the average BER.

5 Simulation Results

In this section we show the overloading performance of Orthogonal/scrambled-Orthogonal (O/s-O) overloading scheme for DS-CDMA system. The Monte-Carlo simulation has been carried out in MAT-Lab to evaluate the BER performance of O/s-O overloading schemes in an AWGN channel. We have considered equal power and equal phase (assumed zero) synchronous users in both the sets. In the situation when users are synchronous and with equal phase, maximum level of MAI power results between the sets. The BER performance of hard decision interference cancellation (HDIC) and soft decision interference cancellation (SDIC) has been investigated. The amount of overloading is obtained for an average BER with a maximum SNR degradation of less than 0.5 dB compared to single user bound. We present the amount of overloading as the ratio of the total number of users K (=M+N) and the spreading length N, i.e., (M+N)/N % for a given BER and SNR degradation. The value of the parameter θ is 0.7 for SDIC and it is fixed for all iterations.

The overloading performance of HDIC technique for N=16 and 64 is shown in Fig. 3 and Fig. 4 respectively. For 6% overloading, the SNR degradation is less than 0.5 dB as compared to single user performance, for both spreading factors. But as we increase the overloading to 11%, the SNR degradation is more than 1 dB. Hence the amount of overloading for HDIC scheme is less even we increase the value of N from 16 to 64, as observed from Fig. 4.

To increase the amount of overloading SDIC scheme is used. As can be observed from Fig. 5, 19% overloading is possible with less than 0.5 dB degradation for a BER of 10^{-5} when the value of spreading length N is 16. This is considerably higher than

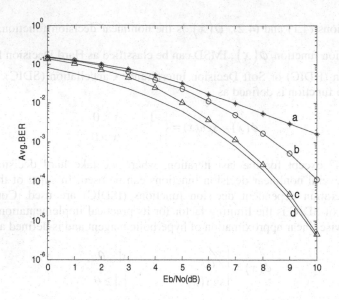

Fig. 3. BER performance comparison with Hard decision Interference cancellation (HDIC) with N=16 for overloading a) 19%; b) 11%; c) 6%; d) Single user performance

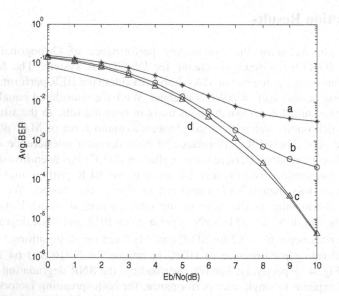

Fig. 4. BER performance comparison with Hard decision Interference cancellation (HDIC) with N=64 for the overloading a) 19%; b) 11%; c) 6%; d) Single user performance

the corresponding HDIC scheme. In Fig. 6, the BER performance of SDIC scheme for N=64 is shown at different values of overloading. It is interesting to observe that the amount of overloading is reduced to 11% for a BER of 10^{-5}.

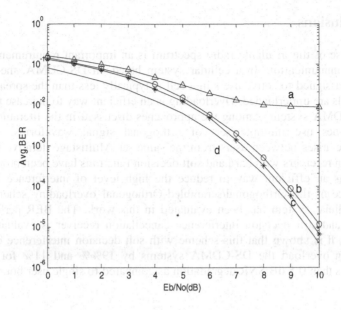

Fig. 5. BER performance comparison with Soft decision Interference cancellation (SDIC) with N=16 for overloading a) 30%; b) 19%; c) 11%; d) Single user performance

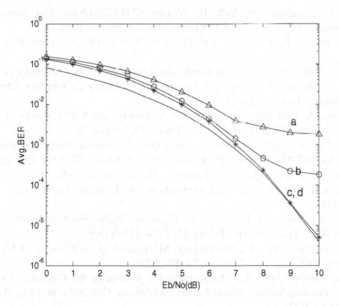

Fig. 6. BER performance comparison with Soft decision Interference cancellation (SDIC) with N=64 for overloading a) 30%; b) 19%; c) 11%; d) Single user performance

6 Conclusions

Efficient use of the available radio spectrum is an important requirement for future wireless communication. In a cellular system based on DS-CDMA, the number of sequences assigned to active users in a cell is typically less than the spreading factor, and the cells are underloaded. Overloading is an efficient way to increase the capacity of a DS-CDMA system. Among the approaches discussed in the literature, the most efficient ones use multiple sets of orthogonal signal waveforms, so that no interference arises between users from the same set. Multistage iterative interference cancellation receivers with hard and soft decision functions have been proposed in the literature as an efficient way to reduce the high level of interference level. The performance of the Orthogonal/scrambled-Orthogonal overloading scheme for DS-CDMA cellular system has been evaluated in this work. The BER performance of both hard and soft decision interference cancellation receiver is evaluated through simulation. It is shown that this scheme with soft decision interference cancellation (SDIC) can overload the DS-CDMA systems by 19%% and 11% for N=16 and 64 with less than 0.5 dB SNR degradation as compared to single user bound at a BER of 10^{-5}.

References

1. Adachi, F., Sawahashi, M., Suda, H.: Wideband DS-CDMA for Next- Generation Mobile Communication Systems. IEEE Commun. Mag. 36, 56–59 (1998)
2. Hara, S., Prasad, R.: Overview of multicarrier CDMA. IEEE Commun. Mag. 35, 126–133 (1997)
3. Verdu, S.: Multi - user Detection. Cambridge University Press, Cambridge (1998)
4. Verdu, S., Shamai, S.: Spectral Efficiency of CDMA with Random Spreading. IEEE Trans. Inform. Theory. 55, 622–640 (1999)
5. Viswanath, P., Anantharam, V.: Optimal Sequences and Sum Capacity of Synchronous CDMA Systems. IEEE Trans. Inform. Theory. 45, 1984–1991 (1999)
6. Ulukus, S., Yates, R.D.: Iterative Construction of Optimum Signature Sequence Sets in Synchronous CDMA Systems. IEEE Trans. Inform. Theory 47, 1989–1998 (2001)
7. Learned, R.E., Willisky, A.S., Boroson, D.M.: Low complexity joint detection for oversaturated multiple access communications. IEEE Trans. Signal Processing 45, 113–122 (1997)
8. Ross, J.A.F., Taylor, D.P.: Multiuser Signaling in the Symbol- Synchronous AWGN Channel. IEEE Trans. Inform. Theory 41, 1174–1178 (1995)
9. Sari, H., Vanhaverbeke, F., Moeneclaey, M.: Extending the Capacity of Multiple Access Channels. IEEE Commun. Mag. 38, 74–82 (2000)
10. Sari, H., Vanhaverbeke, F., Moeneclaey, M.: Increasing the Capacity of CDMA using Hybrid Spreading Sequences and Iterative Multistage Detection. In: Proc. IEEE VTC, pp. 1160–1164 (1999)
11. Vanhaverbeke, F., Moeneclaey, M., Sari, H.: DS/CDMA with Two Sets of Orthogonal Sequences and Iterative - Detection. IEEE Commun. Lett. 4, 289–291 (2000)
12. Sari, H., Vanhaverbeke, F., Moeneclaey, M.: Multiple access using two sets of orthogonal signal waveforms. IEEE Commun. Lett. 4, 4–6 (2000)

13. Kumar, P., Chakrabarti, S.: A New Overloading Scheme for DS- CDMA System. In: National Conference on Communication, IIT Kanpur, pp. 285–288 (2007)
14. Djonin, D., Bhargava, V.K.: New results on low complexity detectors for oversaturated CDMA systems. In: Proceedings of Globecom 2001, pp. 846–850 (2001)
15. Paavola, J., Ipatov, V.: Oversaturating Synchronous CDMA Systems on the Signature Per User Basis. In: Proc. 5th European Personal Mobile Communications Conf., pp. 427–430 (2003)
16. Yang, K., Kim, Y.K., Kumar, P.V.: Quasi-orthogonal Sequences for Code-division Multiple-Access Systems. IEEE Trans. Inform. Theory. 46, 982–993 (2000)
17. Vanhaverbeke, F., Moeneclaey, M.: Binary signature sets for increased user capacity on the downlink of a CDMA systems. IEEE Trans. on Wireless Communication 05, 1795–1804 (2006)
18. Vanhaverbeke, F., Moeneclaey, M.: Performance Evaluation of Three Different Types of Channel overloading. In: IEEE PIMRC, pp. 569–572 (2003)

Enhancing DHCP for Address Autoconfiguration in Multi-hop WLANs

Raffaele Bruno, Marco Conti, and Antonio Pinizzotto

Institute for Informatics and Telematics (IIT)
Via G. Moruzzi, 1 - 56124 Pisa, Italy
{r.bruno,m.conti,a.pinizzotto}@iit.cnr.it

Abstract. To extend the coverage area of conventional WLANs and to provide better mobility support, multi-hop WLANs are emerging as a viable and cost-effective solution. A possible way to construct such a multi-hop WLAN system is to employ an ad hoc routing protocol to discover and maintain the multi-hop paths between the clients and the access points. A prerequisite of proper routing is that all the nodes have a unique network-layer identifier. However, traditional autoconfiguration protocols commonly used in infrastructure-based WLANs, such as DHCP, are not directly applicable in this context due to multi-hop relaying between hosts. In this paper we propose an enhancement of DHCP to enable dynamic address allocation of mobile nodes in multi-hop WLAN systems, without changing the legacy implementation of the DHCP servers. We have implemented a prototype of our solution, and we have measured the maximum delay needed to configure an IP address under various topology configurations and network loads. Our experimental results indicate that the proposed mechanism is quite fast in lightly loaded networks, while the contention between data traffic and control messages may significantly increase the configuration delay.

1 Introduction

In recent years, IEEE 802.11 wireless LAN (WLAN) systems have been widely established on campuses, in public places and in indoor environments to provide convenient data transmission between mobile devices and the Internet. A typical WLAN consists of two different entities: access points (APs), which are connected to the backbone infrastructure, and clients (or stations), which are associated with an AP that is reachable through one-hop wireless transmissions. However, due to radio signal attenuation the coverage area of WLAN systems is limited. To extend WLAN coverage and to provide better mobility support two approaches are traditionally followed in real practice. On the one hand, it would be possible to increase the transmission power of an access point in order to reach farther nodes. However, the main shortcoming of this solution is to induce poor channel reuse and to increase the number of users that access the network through the same access point. This results in the increase of the contention level within each cell, which generally degrades the per-user throughput performance. In addition, the extent of this technique is limited by the fact that the IEEE 802.11 technology operates in the unlicensed frequency spectrum (i.e. ISM band) and most governments restrict the maximum transmission power level. On the other hand, we may opt for deploying

S. Rao et al. (Eds.): ICDCN 2008, LNCS 4904, pp. 528–539, 2008.

more access points at a closer spacing so as to increase the network capacity. However, a number of reasons, including increasing possibility of co-channel interference between nearby access points, availability of a limited number of orthogonal non-interfering frequency channels, as well as cost and management overheads, limit the effectiveness of this approach.

To overcome the limitations of the above-discussed approaches, recently several authors have advocated the idea of enabling multi-hop communications inside WLAN systems so that clients can have also multi-hop paths to reach the AP via other clients that act as relays [1, 2, 3, 4]. Figure 1 shows an illustrative example of such network organization. According to this view, the APs have to implement specific gateway functionalities to interconnect the ad hoc components (basically a MANET network) to the wired local infrastructure and the Internet [5]. A possible way to build such a multi-hop WLAN system is to employ routing protocols that have been designed to construct multi-hop paths among the nodes of an ad hoc network. In general, both proactive (e.g., OLSR [6]) and reactive (e.g., AODV [7]) ad hoc routing protocols can be used to discover and maintain the appropriate multi-hop routes between the clients and the APs. However, using a network-layer based solution (i.e., an ad hoc routing protocol) to construct this multi-hop WLAN system brings also a number of fundamental design challenges. In particular, a prerequisite for proper routing is that all nodes are configured with a unique network-layer (e.g., IP) address. Since pre-configuration is impractical in such networks, an address autoconfiguration protocol is crucial to allow dynamic assignment of nodes' network addresses. However, the autoconfiguration protocols commonly used in conventional infrastructure-based WLANs to configure unique addresses, such as the Dynamic Host Configuration Protocol (DHCP) [8] or the Zeroconf protocol [9] are not applicable in this context due to multi-hop relaying between clients.

In this paper we propose an enhancement of DHCP to enable dynamic IPv4 address allocation of mobile nodes in multi-hop WLAN systems. Important features of the proposed solution are the following: i) it is a fully distributed scheme that does not require changes of the legacy DHCP server implementation, but all the modifications are restricted to the clients; ii) it is designed to efficiently cope with node mobility, and iii) the mobile clients do not need any *a priori* information on the identity or location of the DHCP servers. In principle, it may be argued that any address autoconfiguration protocol already designed to work in ad hoc networks might be also employed to assign a unique identifier to mobile clients in a multi-hop WLAN system. However, on the one hand these schemes assume *stand-alone* ad hoc networks not connected to any external network (e.g. [10]). In this case, the autoconfiguration protocol assigns an address valid only within that particular ad hoc network. Our proposed solution is not restricted to configure only local addresses but it is specifically designed to assign *globally* routable IP addresses. On the other hand, in case of an ad hoc network connected to the Internet, ad hoc nodes may use the Internet gateway for network prefix allocation (e.g. [11]). This design choice makes the autoconfiguration protocol simpler but introduces additional issues such as how each gateway provides a topologically correct routing prefix. To avoid this complication our proposed scheme does not require any network prefix pre-allocation for the wireless nodes. In other words, we permit that all the nodes in

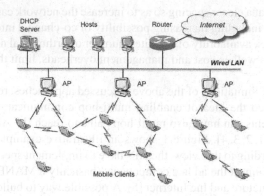

Fig. 1. Illustrative example of a multi-hop WLAN system

the multi-hop WLAN system, both ad hoc nodes and static ones, have an IP address with the same network identifier. As shown in [4] this architectural design allows transparent support for node mobility and reduced overheads. We have prototyped the main components of our scheme in a realistic test-bed using the OLSR protocol [6] as ad hoc routing protocol. In this test-bed, we have conducted several experiments to evaluate the efficiency of our solution in terms of the maximum delay that is needed to configure an IP address. The shown experimental results indicate that: *i*) in lightly loaded networks the total configuration delay is quite small and stable, even when the client is several hops far from the DHCP server, and *ii*) heavily loaded data traffic may interfere with DHCP control messages causing a significant increase of the time needed to complete the address allocation.

The remaining of this paper is organized as follows. The basic idea of the proposed solution is presented in Section 2, while the protocol details are described in Section 3. Section 4 presents the experimental evaluation. Section 5 concludes the paper and discusses future work.

2 Design Principles

The main goal of our autoconfiguration scheme, named *AH-DHCP*, is to assign a globally routable IPv4 address to the mobile nodes of a multi-hop WLAN using, in a transparent way, the DHCP-based mechanisms already implemented in the wired part of the network. This means that a wireless node establishing a multi-hop path through other wireless nodes to reach the closest access point, must be able to perform a standard DHCP request when interacting with the available DHCP servers. On the other hand, from the point of view of the DHCP servers, requests generated from wired or wireless nodes must be undistinguishable. This implies that our solution can rely on legacy DHCP servers, without requiring any change of the standard server implementation.

To enable a new joining node to deliver its address request to the available wired DHCP servers, we exploit the standard DHCP relay functionalities. More precisely, a DHCP Relay Agent is a device capable of intercepting DHCP_DISCOVER and

DHCP_REQUEST packets from clients. Then, the DHCP relay rebroadcasts the request to other networks, or send the client's request to DHCP servers the relay has been configured to contact. The DHCP server then responds back to the relay agent that, in turn, forward the servers' replies directly to the clientÕs hardware address. In our solution, a mobile node not yet associated with the multi-hop WLAN executes a preliminary message handshake to discover reachable and already configured wireless nodes. Then, the unconfigured node elects one of the discovered neighbours as DHCP relay agent, which will forward all the client's DHCP messages to the known DHCP server. Note that the DHCP standard does not define any specific mechanism to discover the available DHCP relay agents, but client-originated DHCP packets are implicitly forwarded by the DHCP relay agents located on the same physical network segment of the client. This behaviour is acceptable in wired networks because they are controlled environments, and both the location and number of DHCP relay agents is carefully planned. Specifically, DHCP relay agents are usually enabled only on routers' interfaces interconnecting different subnets. On the contrary, in a multi-hop WLAN each wireless node is a potential DHCP relay agent. Therefore, if multiple DHCP relay agents are used simultaneously to pass client's messages to DHCP servers, the DHCP servers may be overloaded by the concurrent requests. Moreover, multiple copies of the same DHCP messages will travel in the multi-hop WLANs increasing the control traffic overheads.

There is another shortcoming in the original design of DHCP that prevents its efficient use in multi-hop WLAN systems. Specifically, DHCP standard assumes that nodes are static during a client-server transaction and that message losses are infrequent. For these reasons, DHCP clients adopts a simple retransmission strategies that relies on timeouts to detect messages losses [8]. However, a multi-hop WLAN is a dynamic environment where nodes are free to move almost arbitrarily. Thus, the selected DHCP relay and the unconfigured node may move out of their respective transmission ranges and become unreachable before the address assignment is completed. This may lead to unacceptable delays in the address allocation. On the contrary, our scheme incorporates a mechanism to allow a timely detection of DHCP relay's movements in order to ensure a prompt selection of a new valid DHCP relay. Note that after the completion of the allocation procedures, each wireless node has to periodically interact with the DHCP server to renew its address. Some authors [10, 12] observed that it might be difficult to guarantee a continuous access to DHCP servers since ad hoc networks can become partitioned due to node mobility. However, in the considered network scenarios this limitation does not appear problematic because the multi-hop WLAN system we envision will be mostly used as a flexible and cost-effective extension of the fixed networking infrastructure in enterprise buildings or campus facilities. In these contexts, users are semi-static or nomadic and are interested in having a continuous access to Internet and its centralized services.

3   AH-DHCP Description

We assume that the access points in the network implement the gateway functionalities described in [4]. This means that the access points can provide Internet and Intranet connectivity through multi-hop wireless paths to wireless nodes implementing a proactive ad hoc routing algorithm. Note that our scheme does not need a specific initialization procedure, because the first nodes to join the multi-hop WLAN are the access points themselves, which may interact with the DHCP servers using their wired interfaces. Thus, in the following we describe the AH-DHCP operations when a new wireless node (other that the access point) wants to join the multi-hop WLAN system. Figure 2 summarizes the state machine of the AH-DHCP client, and it will be used as the reference flow diagram during the protocol description.

DHCP Relay Discovery. Let node C be a new wireless node that wants to acquire a network address. It boots up its AH-DHCP client module and it starts to broadcast special messages, named RELAY_DISCOVERYs. Other wireless nodes that are already part of the multi-hop WLAN and that are in radio visibility of node C responds with a RELAY_ACK message that expresses the willingness of that node to act as DHCP relay agent for node C. Note that these replay messages are unicast packets sent to node C's hardware address. In addition, each RELAY_ACK message conveys the distance, in terms of hops, between the relay and its closest gateway. Node C allocates a fixed time, say T_O, to collect the neighbors' responses. After this timer expiration, node C selects the relay that is at the minimum hop-distance to an access point as forwarder of its DHCP messages. To this end, node C sends an unicast DHCP_DISCOVERY message to the selected relay, say R. Note that conventional DHCP clients transmit broadcast DHCP_DISCOVERY messages because they are not aware of the available DHCP relays. On the contrary, an AH-DHCP client scans its radio coverage area to discover available DHCP relays in order to activate only one of them, which will act as unique initiator of the address allocation process. This avoids sending multiple copies of the same allocation request to the DHCP servers.

To increase the probability of receiving at least a response from one of the neighbor wireless nodes, node C periodically broadcasts new RELAY_DISCOVERY messages with period T_R. However, to avoid synchronization with other AH-DHCP clients in radio visibility of node C and transmitting RELAY_DISCOVERY messages, the generation of control traffic should be randomized. To this end, we add a variable jitter for the transmission of RELAY_DISCOVERY messages. More precisely, if t_k is the time instant at which node C should transmit the k-th RELAY_DISCOVERY message, the real transmission is scheduled at time $t'_k = t_k + jitter$, where $jitter$ is a random value selected in the interval $[-MAX_j, MAX_j]$. In our prototype implementation we selected $MAX_j = 0.1 \cdot T_R$. Note that this randomization strategy is similar to the one adopted in the OLSR specification [6] to avoid synchronization of control messages. Similarly, it is possible to have collisions between the RELAY_ACK replays, because node C may have a large number of neighbor wireless nodes with DHCP relaying capabilities. Again, we adopt as collision avoidance strategy the randomization of RELAY_ACK transmissions. However, since the collision probability may be higher for reply messages than for relay discovery messages, for the former type of packets we selected a maximum jitter value equal to 50% of T_R. Finally, it would be possible that after the T_O expiration, node C did not receive any response. In this case, node C initializes the T_O timer and keeps transmitting RELAY_DISCOVERY messages.

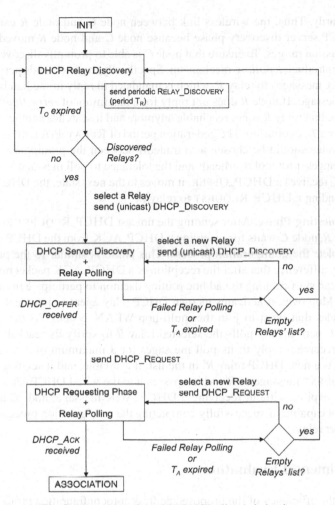

Fig. 2. Flow chart of the AH-DHCP client's behavior

DHCP Server Discovery. After sending the unicast DHCP_DISCOVERY to the selected DCHP relay R, node C waits for receiving a DHCP_OFFER from the DHCP sever, which the relay agent forwards the message to. However, it can occur that between node R and the access point there are persistent communication problems (e.g., poor quality wireless links or an overloaded channel) that may introduce unacceptable delays in the configuration procedure. To control the maximum delay introduced by the DHCP server discovery phase, node C initializes another timer, say T_A. If the reception of a DHCP_OFFER does not occur before the T_A expiration, node C checks the list of DHCP relays discovered during the last DHCP relay discovery phase. If this list is not empty, then node C selects a new DHCP relay R' and it sends a unicast DHCP_DISCOVERY to node R' to activate a new configuration procedure. On the contrary, if node R is the only discovered relays, node C starts a new DHCP relay discovery phase to find additional neighbor nodes. In our envisaged scenario, nodes are free to move arbitrarily. Thus, the wireless link between node C and node R can break during the DHCP server discovery phase because node C and node R moved away from their transmission ranges. To ensure that node C is able to promptly discover a topology change, we introduce a *polling* mechanism. Specifically, node C sends periodic unicast RELAY_POLL messages to relay R, which is mandated to reply immediately with a RELAY_ACK message. If node R does not reply for a maximum of *retry_limit* times, node C can assume that relay R is not reachable anymore and it searches another valid DHCP relay, as after a T_A expiration. The generation period of RELAY_POLL messages and the *retry_limit* value should be chosen as a tradeoff between the promptness in detecting topology changes, protocol overheads and the tolerance to poll message losses. Finally, when node C receives a DHCP_OFFER, it moves to the next state, the DHCP requesting phase, by sending a DHCP_REQUEST to relay R.

DHCP Requesting Phase. After sending the unicast DHCP_REQUEST to the selected DCHP relay R, node C waits for receiving a DHCP_ACK from the DHCP sever, which would complete the configuration process. This phase is similar to the previous one, with the only difference that after the reception of a DHCP_ACK packet node C is configured and can start running the ad hoc routing daemon to participate in the multi-hop forwarding. Moreover, it activates its own DHCP relay agent to intercept the requests of future nodes that want to join the multi-hop WLAN system. As described previously, node C periodically polls the selected relay R to verify its reachability. If node C does not receive a reply to its poll messages for a maximum of *retry_limit* times, node C selects a new DHCP relay R' in the list, if available, and it sends a new unicast DHCP_REQUEST message to R', which passes it to the wired DHCP server. Finally, if the T_A timer expires without receiving a DHCP_ACK message, node C assumes that relay R is not capable of successfully completing the configuration process and it tries to use another relay.

4   Experimental Evaluation

To evaluate the efficiency of the proposed address autoconfiguration protocol, we have deployed a small-scale test-bed with one access point and five nodes operating in static configurations. We did not use a commercial access point, but a computer instrumented as an access point and implementing the required functionalities to manage multi-hop paths with the clients. We have adopted as reference implementation the DHCP server, client and relay agent public source code provided by the Internet Systems Consortium (ISC), which is one of the most popular DHCP implementations for POSIX-compliant operating systems [13]. Then, we made the necessary modifications to the DHCP client and relay agent software modules to implement the mechanisms described in Section 2. Our prototype does not implement the polling mechanisms, and the following experimental evaluation consider only static relay agents. Regarding the system hardware configuration, our test-bed consists of six laptops running Linux 2.6.12 OS kernel. To provide Internet connectivity to the configured mobile nodes we adopted the multi-hop WLAN architecture described in [4], which is based on OLSR ad hoc routing protocol [6]. All nodes were located in the same room, and the *IP-tables* feature of Linux was used to emulate the multi-hop topologies. To generate the background UDP traffic

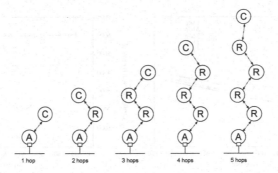

Fig. 3. Network layouts used for the experiments described in Section 4.1

we used the *iperf* tool [14]. If not otherwise stated, the UDP payload size is fixed and set to 1448 bytes.

It is worth point out that we conducted the performance tests in an area of CNR building covered by other wireless networks, which introduced uncontrollable radio interference. However, we believe that the randomness due to the external interference is well representing the characteristics of real radio environments and it is useful to attain more realistic results. To measure steady-state performance we have replicated each test fifty times. The following graphs report both the averages and the 95% confidence intervals. Note that the confidence intervals are often very tight (≤ 1 percent), and are not appreciable from the plots.

4.1 IP Address Configuration

First of all, we carried out a set of experiments to evaluate the IP address configuration delay, say D_{conf}, which is defined as the interval from the time the new joining node boots up its AH-DHCP client and the time it receives the DHCP_ACK message with the committed IP configuration parameters. Several factors can affect this delay, such as the duration of the 4-message exchange adopted by the DHCP protocol and the processing delays on the DHCP servers [15]. However, in a multi-hop WLAN system also the distance of the DHCP server from the mobile node plays a crucial role in determining the configuration delay. For instance, the configuration requests delivered by the new joining node may have to traverse multiple wireless hops before reaching the closest access point, which acts as gateway between the ad hoc domain and the wired infrastructure. To estimate this component of the total D_{conf} delay we performed several tests in the network scenarios illustrated in Figure 3. More precisely, we considered a single client C that is n wireless hops far from the access point A. Thus, at least $n-1$ relays are needed to establish this n-hop path between C and A. Obviously, each wireless hop adds its own medium access delay, processing delay and queuing delay. Regarding the DHCP server, we used the legacy server deployed on the LAN, which the access point is attached to.

Figure 4(a) shows the IP address assignment delay for different n values. The shown delays have been measured without background traffic, i.e., when OLSR routing messages and AH-DHCP messages are the only packets transmitted over the wireless

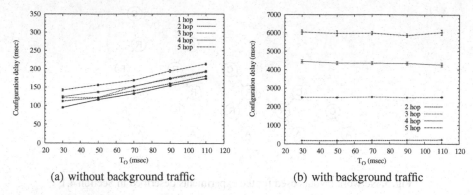

(a) without background traffic   (b) with background traffic

Fig. 4. IP address assignment delay

links. Beside the length of the route between C and A, the other system parameter we varied during the tests was the observation period (T_O) duration. Specifically, we configured $T_O = m \cdot T_R + \Delta$, where T_R is the repeat period of RELAY_DISCOVERY messages and Δ is a guard time. In all experiments, the T_R value was fixed to 20 msec and $\Delta = T_R/2$. The m value is an integer varying in the range $[1,5]$. From the shown experimental results, we observe that the D_{conf} value increases almost linearly with T_O and that it is slightly dependent on the n value. To explain this behaviour it is useful to introduce two additional variables. The first one, say D_{disc}, expresses the time between the first RELAY_DISCOVERY message sent by the AH-DHCP client running on the new joining node and the DHCP relay activation (through the unicast DHCP_DISCOVERY message sent by the AH-DHCP client to the selected relay). The second one, say D_{assign}, expresses the time between the DHCP relay activation and the reception of the DHCP_ACK message concluding the IP address assignment. It is intuitive to write that $D_{conf} = D_{disc} + D_{assign}$. Without background traffic, the network contention induced by control traffic (i.e., OLSR and DHCP messages) is negligible and the transmission buffers are empty most of the time. Consequently, packet losses are rare events and they are mainly due to the radio disturbance caused by external interfering radio sources. In these conditions, new joining node was always capable of discovering the neighbor relay node within one T_O interval. This implies that $D_{disc} \approx T_O$ and $D_{conf} \approx D_{assign}+T_O$. In addition, by inspecting the traces we observed that the D_{assign} value does not depend on the T_O parameter but only on the path length between C and A. Since the network load is negligible, the D_{assign} contribution to the total configuration delay is quite limited and it ranges from 60 mses, in case of a client directly connected to the access point, to 100 msec, in case of a 5-hop chain of relay agents.

The protocol behaviour changes radically with background traffic, as shown in Figure 4(b). The background traffic consists of $n-1$ UDP flows. Specifically, each relay R is a CBR (Constant Bit Rate) source sending UDP packets to a server in the wired LAN, which the access point A is attached to. The per-flow UDP load was set in such a way to saturate the wireless channel. From the experimental results we notice that the total configuration delay varies from 200 ms, in case of a single relay node between client C and access point A, up to 6 seconds, in case of four relay nodes between the C and A. To explain the observed values we should clarify the impact of data traffic on

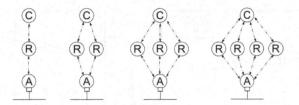

Fig. 5. Network layouts used for the experiments described in Section 4.2

DHCP control traffic. Specifically, client's DHCP messages are encapsulated into UDP packets that are sent as broadcast frames, which are particularly vulnerable to collisions because they are not acknowledged. For these reasons, loss probability for DHCP packets is much higher that for data frames. The first effect of these losses is that the D_{disc} increases, because a single T_O interval is not generally sufficient for discovering the neighbor DHCP relay. From the experimental results we found out that the D_{disc} delay, with background traffic, ranges from 65 msec (for $T_O = 30$ msec) to 110 msec (for $T_O = 110$ msec). In addition, the D_{assign} delay is significantly higher than the D_{disc} delay due to the high queuing delay observed in overloaded networks. Finally, DHCP messages forwarded by DHCP relays may get lost due to various factors (e.g., retry limits at MAC layer, buffer overflows, radio interference). DHCP protocol relies on timeouts to detect messages losses and introduces randomized delays before retransmissions. Thus, DHCP message losses may significantly increase configuration delay in challenged environments. Our measurements indicate that, in the considered overloaded networks, each additional wireless hop adds about one second to the total configuration delay.

4.2 Relay Discovery

In the previous section, we considered network scenarios where the new joining node has a single neighbor DHCP relay agent. However, in general the client C may be in radio visibility with a greater number of configured nodes. Hence, it is important for the client to discover all the possible relays in order to select the best one (e.g., the relay at a shortest distance from the access point). To evaluate the efficiency of the discovery phase we have carried out several tests in the network scenarios illustrated in Figure 5. More precisely we considered a single client (C) that is in radio visibility with n different relays. All these potential DHCP relays are in radio visibility with the same access point A. Thus the client C is two hops far from the access point A. In the experiments we varied the T_R parameter, i.e., the repetition frequency of RELAY_DISCOVERY messages. Note that in these tests the T_O period was unbounded and we forced the client to execute a continuous DHCP relay discovery procedure. Figure 6(a) shows the minimum observation period needed to discover all the available relays in a network without background traffic. From the experimental results we observe that in the case of a single relay, the discovery phase is very short and the first RELAY_DISCOVERY message sent by node C is sufficient to trigger the RELAY_ACK reply. On the contrary, with more than one relay it is possible that RELAY_ACK messages sent by relay nodes get lost due collisions. This leads to an increase of the time required to discover all the relays.

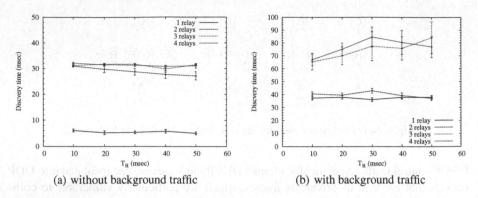

(a) without background traffic   (b) with background traffic

Fig. 6. Duration of relay discovery phase

Note that the smaller the T_R interval and the higher the probability of collision because RELAY_DISCOVERY packets are sent more frequently.

Figure 6(b) shows the results obtained when the same experiment is replicated in overloaded networks. The background data traffic consists of n CBR (Constant Bit Rate) UDP flows established with a server in the wired LAN, one for each relay R. The per-flow UDP load was set in such a way to saturate the wireless channel. The first observation we may derive from the experimental results is that there is an increase in the minimum time needed to discover all the available relays. This was expected, since data traffic increases the contention level on the channel, inducing an higher number of collisions that negatively affect the delivery rate of broadcast frames (such as RE-LAY_DISCOVERY messages). The second observation concerns the increased variability of the measured delays and the more evident dependency on the T_R value. This can be explained by noting that the longer the T_R interval, and the longer the time between consecutive RELAY_DISCOVERY messages. Hence, the time needed to recover a message loss increases. However, we may observe that the DHCP relay discovery phase is quite fast even with background traffic.

5   Conclusions

In this paper we have described AH-DHCP, an address autoconfiguration protocol for multi-hop WLAN systems. The main goal of our work was to show the applicability of DHCP, originally designed to provide configuration parameters to hosts in a fixed network, also when traditional WLANs integrate ad hoc networking technologies to discover and maintain multi-hop wireless path within the network. The basic idea is to take advantage of DHCP relay capabilities available in already configured nodes. To this end, we have proposed an enhancement of DHCP to enable a new joining node to dynamically choose a reachable wireless node as the DHCP relay that transparently passes all the client-originated messages to the DHCP servers located in the wired part of the network. Experiments conducted with a prototype implementation of AH-DHCP have shown that the proposed solution has low latency in lightly loaded networks, while the contention between data traffic and control messages increases the address configuration delay. Especially when the mobile node is far from the DHCP server, this increase may be remarkable. However, the causes of these delays may be rooted to the inefficiencies of multi-hop ad hoc networking rather than to the AH-DHCP overheads. For future work, we intend to investigate mechanisms to reduce the impact of multi-hop forwarding on address assignment, e.g. by introducing a hierarchy of DHCP relay agents. Another key research issue is the extension of our solution to IPv6.

References

1. Lee, S., Banerjee, S., Bhattacharjee, B.: The Case for a Multi-hop Wireless Local Area Network. In: Proc. of IEEE INFOCOM 2004, Hong Kong, China, vol. 2, pp. 894–905 (2004)
2. Karrer, R., Sabharwal, A., Knightly, E.: Enabling Large-Scale Wireless Broadband: The Case for TAPs. ACM SIGMOBILE Comp. Comm. Review 34, 27–34 (2004)
3. Narayanan, S., Liu, P., Panwar, S.: On the Advantages of Multi-hop Extensions to the IEEE 802.11 Infrastructure Mode. In: Proc. of IEEE WCNC 2005, New Orleans, LA, USA, vol. 1, pp. 132–138 (2005)
4. Ancillotti, E., Bruno, R., Conti, M., Gregori, E., Pinizzotto, A.: A Layer-2 Framework for Interconnecting Ad Hoc Networks to Fixed Internet: Test-bed Implementation and Experimental Evaluation. The Computer Journal (2007), doi:10.1093/comjnl/bxm013
5. Sun, Y., Belding-Royer, E., Perkins, C.: Internet Connectivity for Ad hoc Mobile Networks. International Journal of Wireless Information Networks 9(2), 75–88 (2002) (Special issue on Mobile Ad hoc Networks: Standards, Research, Application)
6. Clausen, T., Jaquet, P.: Optimized Link State Routing Protocol (OLSR). RFC 3626 (2003)
7. Perkins, C., Belding-Royer, E., Das, S.: Ad hoc On-Demand Distance Vector (AODV) Routing. RFC 3561 (2003)
8. Droms, R.: Dynamic Host Configuration Protocol. RFC 2131 (1997)
9. Cheshire, S., Aboba, B., Guttman, E.: Dynamic Configuration of IPv4 Link-Local Addresses. RFC 3927 (2005)
10. Nesargi, S., Prakash, R.: MANETconf: Configuration of Hosts in a Mobile Ad Hoc Network. In: Proc. of IEEE INFOCOM 2002, New York, NY, USA, vol. 2, pp. 1059–1068 (2002)
11. Wakikawa, R., Malinen, J., Perkins, E., Nilsson, A., Tuominen, A.: Global connectivity for IPv6 Mobile Ad Hoc Networks. Internet Draft (2002)
12. Weniger, K., Zitterbart, M.: Address Autoconfiguration on Mobile Ad Hoc Networks: Current Approaches and Future Directions. IEEE Network 18, 6–11 (2004)
13. Internet Systems Consortium: ISC DHCP Version 3.0.5 (2006)
14. NLANR/DAST: Iperf Version 2.0.2 (2005)
15. Park, A., Kim, P., Lee, M., Kim, Y.: Fast Address Configuration for WLAN. In: Liew, K.-M., Shen, H., See, S., Cai, W. (eds.) PDCAT 2004. LNCS, vol. 3320, pp. 396–400. Springer, Heidelberg (2004)

Channel Assignment in Multimedia Cellular Networks

Goutam K. Audhya[1] and Bhabani P. Sinha[2]

[1] BSNL, Calcutta - 700 001, India
gkaudhya@gmail.com
[2] ACM Unit, Indian Statistical Institute, Kolkata - 700 108, India

Abstract. This paper deals with multimedia channel assignment in a hexagonal cellular network with two-band buffering. After deriving a lower bound on the minimum bandwidth for real-life situations, we present an algorithm for assigning channels using Genetic Algorithm (GA). We also propose an elegant technique for *re-use* of the channels, using only eighteen distinct frequency bands on a nine-node subgraph of the network, and then extend it for assignment of the complete network. The proposed algorithm converges very rapidly with required bandwidth close to the derived lower bound.

1 Introduction

The Channel Assignment Problem (CAP) for a mobile cellular network is the task of assigning frequency channels to the calls satisfying some frequency separation constraints with a view to avoiding channel interference and using as small bandwidth as possible [5]. A lower bound on bandwidth requirement for assigning multimedia channels to a hexagonal cellular network has been derived in [6], considering only two types of multimedia signals, say type A and type B, with a single demand of each type at each node of the network. In this paper, we use the same system model as used in [6] and first estimate the lower bounds on the required bandwidth for assigning channels in some real-life situations. We next present an algorithm for solving the multimedia channel assignment problem, using genetic algorithm (GA), under the condition of 2-band buffering and with only two types of multimedia signals where each cell has a single demand for each type of signal. We then select a subset of only nine nodes of the network and propose a clever technique of re-using the frequency channels so that by repeatedly using only eighteen bands (two bands for each node for assigning both the types of multimedia signals), the required assignment for the whole network can be completed. For this purpose, we first find the required frequency separation constraints among the channels to be assigned to the different nodes of the network, and then use our proposed GA-based algorithm for assigning the multimedia channels for the complete network. Experiments show that the proposed assignment algorithm converges very rapidly and assigns channels with a bandwidth close to the derived lower bound.

S. Rao et al. (Eds.): ICDCN 2008, LNCS 4904, pp. 540–545, 2008.
© Springer-Verlag Berlin Heidelberg 2008

2   Notations

We denote the bandwidths required for type A and type B signals as BW_A and BW_B, respectively. W.l.o.g, we assume that $BW_A \geq BW_B$. The required frequency separations for avoiding interference in a 2-band buffering system between two calls in the same cell, in two cells distance 1 apart and in two cells distance 2 apart are denoted by 1) s_0, s_1 and s_2, respectively for the two type A calls, 2) s'_0, s'_1 and s'_2, respectively for the two calls, one of type A and the other of type B, and 3) s''_0, s''_1 and s''_2, respectively for the two type B calls. Because $BW_A \geq BW_B$, we assume that $s_0 \geq s'_0 \geq s''_0, s_1 \geq s'_1 \geq s''_1$ and $s_2 \geq s'_2 \geq s''_2$. We further assume that $s_0 \geq s_1 \geq s_2, s'_0 \geq s'_1 \geq s'_2$ and $s''_0 \geq s''_1 \geq s''_2$.

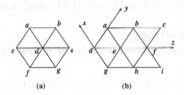

Fig. 1. Hexagonal Cellular network: a) A 7-node subgraph, b) A 9-node subgraph

3   Lower Bound on Bandwidth

Considering the seven-node subgraph of Fig. 1 (a), for different relative values of the parameters $s_0, s_1, s_2, s'_0, s'_1, s'_2, s''_0, s''_1, s''_2$, we first state the result from [6].

Result: *To assign one band for type A signal and one band for type B signal to each of the nodes in a hexagonal cellular network, the required minimum bandwidth is given by the following expressions:*

i) $\min[s'_0 + s'_1 + 4s_2 + 2s'_2 + 5s''_2, \ s_1 + 2s'_1 + 3s_2 + 2s'_2 + 5s''_2, \ s_1 + s'_1 + s''_1 + 4s_2 + s'_2 + 5s''_2, s_1 + s'_1 + 4s_2 + 2s'_2 + 5s''_2]$, *for* $s_2 + s''_2 \leq 2s'_2$, *and ii)* $\min[s'_0 + s'_1 + 10s'_2 + s''_2, s_1 + s'_1 + s''_1 + 9s'_2 + s''_2, \ s_1 + s'_1 + 10s'_2 + s''_2]$, *for* $s_2 + s''_2 \geq 2s'_2$.

3.1   Approximations in Practical Situations

Assuming that the frequency response curves for the bands assigned to type A and type B signals are typically of trapezoidal shape with $BW_A \geq BW_B$, it has been shown in [6] that $s_1 - s'_1 = s_2 - s'_2 = s'_1 - s''_1 = s'_2 - s''_2$. Hence, $s''_2 + s_2 = 2s'_2$. Thus, the result in [6] now reduces to the following under such real-life constraints:

Theorem 1. *To assign one band for type A signal and one band for type B signal to each of the nodes in a hexagonal cellular network, the required minimum bandwidth is* $\min[s'_0 + s'_1 + 4s_2 + 2s'_2 + 5s''_2, \ s_1 + 2s'_1 + 3s_2 + 2s'_2 + 5s''_2, \ s_1 + s'_1 + s''_1 + 4s_2 + s'_2 + 5s''_2, s_1 + s'_1 + 4s_2 + 2s'_2 + 5s''_2]$.

4   Genetic Algorithm for Multimedia Channel Assignment

We now use the elitist model of genetic algorithm (EGA) for solving the multimedia channel assignment problem. First, we form a Channel Assignment Problem (CAP) graph similar to that in [1], in which a node represents a call generated from a cell, and two nodes v_i and v_j are connected by an edge with weight c_{ij}, where $c_{ij} (> 0)$ is the minimum separation between the channels assigned to the corresponding calls. Let $C = c_{ij}$ be the frequency separation matrix for the CAP graph consisting of n nodes. Let M be the population size which is an even integer. Let cp be the crossover probability, for which we take a high value, say 0.95, in our algorithm. We start with a mutation probability of $q = 0.5$ and then vary it with the number of iterations similar to that used in [5].

We now describe the fitness function $Fit(S)$, used in our algorithm, as follows:

function Fit(S) // S is a string.//
        $t[0] \leftarrow 0$; *// t [i] is the frequency assigned to the i-th node $node_i$ of S //*
        for $i = 1$ to $n - 1$ do
                Set t[i] to smallest integer without violating the frequency separation
                requirements specified by the matrix C with all the previously
                assigned values $t[0], t[1], ..., t[i - 1]$.
        return max $t[0], t[1], ..., t[n - 1]$.

4.1   Algorithm GA

Step 1: Set the iteration number $t \leftarrow 0$; Set $cp \leftarrow 0.95$; Set $M \leftarrow 20$.

   Step 2: *(initial population)* For $i = 0$ to $M - 1$, generate a random order of the nodes in the CAP graph and consider it as a string S_i; set $q_t \leftarrow \{S_0, S_1, ..., S_{M-1}\}$ as the initial population.

   Step 3: Compute $Fit(S_i)$ for each string $S_i (0 \le i \le M - 1)$ of q_t. Find the best string S_{best1} (i.e., the string with the least fitness value) and the worst string S_{worst1} (i.e., the string with the highest fitness value) of q_t. If S_{best1} or S_{worst1} is not unique, choose one arbitrarily.

   Step 4: *(Selection or reproduction)* a) Calculate the probability p_i of selection of $S_i (i = 0, 1, ..., M - 1)$ as $p_i = \frac{\frac{1}{Fit(S_i)}}{\sum_{i=0}^{M-1} \frac{1}{Fit(S_i)}}$

   b) Calculate the cumulative probability q_i for $S_i (i = 0, 1, ..., M - 1)$ as $q_i = \sum_{j=0}^{i} p_i$.

   c) Generate a random number r_j from $[0, 1]$ for j = 0,1,...,M - 1. Now, if $r_j \le q_0$, select S_0; otherwise select $S_i (1 \le i \le M - 1)$, if $q_{i-1} < r_j \le q_i)$.

   Note: $p_0 = q_0$ and $p_i = q_i - q_{i-1}$ for $1 \le i \le M - 1$.

   Step 5: *(Crossover)* Form $M/2$ pairs of pairing the i-th and $(M/2 + i)$-th string from $q_{mat}(1 = 0, 1, ..., (M/2 - 1))$. For each pair of strings, generate a random number R from $[0, 1]$. If $(R \le cp)$then generate two random numbers from $\{0, n - 1\}$ to define a matching section. Use this matching section to effect a cross through position-by-position exchange operation (to produce two offsprings for the next generation).

Step 6: *(Mutation)* Set $q \leftarrow m$ probability(t). For each string S_i of q_{tempi} $(0 \leq i \leq M - 1)$, and for each node $node_j (0 \leq i \leq M - 1)$ of string S_i, generate a random number from $[0, 1]$, say m. If $(m \leq q)$ then exchange $node_j$ of S_i with any other randomly selected node $node_k$ of $S_i, (0 \leq k \leq n - 1, k \neq j)$.

Step 7: Calculate $Fit(S_i)$ for each string $S_i (0 \leq i \leq M - 1)$ of q_{temp2}. Find the best string S_{best2} and the worst string S_{worst2} of q_{temp2}. If S_{best2} or S_{worst2} is not unique, choose one arbitrarily.

Step 8: *(elitism)* Compare S_{best1} of q_t and S_{best2} of q_{temp2}. If $Fit(S_{best2}) > Fit(S_{best1})$, then replace S_{worst2} with S_{best1}. Rename q_{temp2} as q_t.

Step 9: $t \leftarrow t + 1$. If $t < T$ then go to stpe 3; otherwise stop.

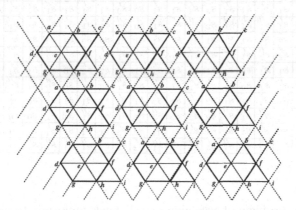

Fig. 2. Frequency assignment of the whole network using eighteen bands

5   Assignment Technique with Reuse of Channels

The algorithm developed above can now be applied to any CAP graph. However, in case of a hexagonal cellular network, we propose an elegant technique for reusing the channels in a very effective way. For this, we first consider a 9-node subgraph with nodes a, b, c, d, e, f, g, h and i, as shown in Fig. 1(b), where each node represents a cell. We refer to it as a 9-node *block*. We assign only eighteen bands to this 9-node *block*, i.e., one band for type A and one band for type B calls to each of the nine nodes, satisfying all the frequency separation constraints within the *block*, as well as, with the neighboring *blocks*. We then repeat this 9-node *block* along with the assigned eighteen bands, over the entire cellular network to complete the whole assignment.

Let $\phi_A(\alpha)$ be the band assigned to a type A call and $\phi_B(\alpha)$ to a type B call, at node α, where $\alpha \in \{a, b, c, d, e, f, g, h, i\}$. We consider three directions x, y and z on the cellular graph as shown in Fig. 1(b). In x direction, there are three different sequences of node alignments identified by their repetitive nature as type $x_1 : a, b, c, a, b, c, \cdots$; type $x_2 : d, e, f, d, e, f, \cdots$; and type $x_3 : g, h, i, g, h, i, \cdots$. However, in cases of y and z directions, each has only one type of node sequence, identified by their repetitive natures as type $y : a, h, f, c, g, e, b, i, d, \cdots$, and type $z : d, c, i, f, b, h, e, a, g, \cdots$, respectively.

Table 1. Frequency Separation matrix for 9-node block

Nodes	a_A	a_B	b_A	b_B	c_A	c_B	d_A	d_B	e_A	e_B	f_A	f_B	g_A	g_B	h_A	h_B	i_A	i_B
a_A	s_0	s_0'	s_1	s_1'	s_1	s_1'	s_1	s_1'	s_1	s_1'	s_2	s_2'	s_1	s_1'	s_1	s_1'	s_2	s_2'
a_B	s_0'	s_0''	s_1'	s_1''	s_1'	s_1''	s_1'	s_1''	s_1'	s_1''	s_2'	s_2''	s_1'	s_1''	s_1'	s_1''	s_2'	s_2''
b_A	s_1	s_1'	s_0	s_0'	s_1	s_1'	s_2	s_2'	s_1	s_1'	s_1	s_1'	s_2	s_2'	s_1	s_1'	s_1	s_1'
b_B	s_1'	s_1''	s_0'	s_0''	s_1'	s_1''	s_2'	s_2''	s_1'	s_1''	s_1'	s_1''	s_2'	s_2''	s_1'	s_1''	s_1'	s_1''
c_A	s_1	s_1'	s_1	s_1'	s_0	s_0'	s_1	s_1'	s_2	s_2'	s_1	s_1'	s_1	s_1'	s_2	s_2'	s_1	s_1'
c_B	s_1'	s_1''	s_1'	s_1''	s_0'	s_0''	s_1'	s_1''	s_2'	s_2''	s_1'	s_1''	s_1'	s_1''	s_2'	s_2''	s_1'	s_1''
d_A	s_1	s_1'	s_2	s_2'	s_1	s_1'	s_0	s_0'	s_1	s_1'	s_1	s_1'	s_1	s_1'	s_2	s_2'	s_1	s_1'
d_B	s_1'	s_1''	s_2'	s_2''	s_1'	s_1''	s_0'	s_0''	s_1'	s_1''	s_1'	s_1''	s_1'	s_1''	s_2'	s_2''	s_1'	s_1''
e_A	s_1	s_1'	s_1	s_1'	s_2	s_2'	s_1	s_1'	s_0	s_0'	s_1	s_1'	s_1	s_1'	s_1	s_1'	s_2	s_2'
e_B	s_1'	s_1''	s_1'	s_1''	s_2'	s_2''	s_1'	s_1''	s_0'	s_0''	s_1'	s_1''	s_1'	s_1''	s_1'	s_1''	s_2'	s_2''
f_A	s_2	s_2'	s_1	s_1'	s_1	s_1'	s_1	s_1'	s_1	s_1'	s_0	s_0'	s_2	s_2'	s_1	s_1'	s_1	s_1'
f_B	s_2'	s_2''	s_1'	s_1''	s_1'	s_1''	s_1'	s_1''	s_1'	s_1''	s_0'	s_0''	s_2'	s_2''	s_1'	s_1''	s_1'	s_1''
g_A	s_1	s_1'	s_2	s_2'	s_1	s_1'	s_1	s_1'	s_1	s_1'	s_2	s_2'	s_0	s_0'	s_1	s_1'	s_1	s_1'
g_B	s_1'	s_1''	s_2'	s_2''	s_1'	s_1''	s_1'	s_1''	s_1'	s_1''	s_2'	s_2''	s_0'	s_0''	s_1'	s_1''	s_1'	s_1''
h_A	s_1	s_1'	s_1	s_1'	s_2	s_2'	s_2	s_2'	s_1	s_1'	s_1	s_1'	s_1	s_1'	s_0	s_0'	s_1	s_1'
h_B	s_1'	s_1''	s_1'	s_1''	s_2'	s_2''	s_2'	s_2''	s_1'	s_1''	s_1'	s_1''	s_1'	s_1''	s_0'	s_0''	s_1'	s_1''
i_A	s_2	s_2'	s_1	s_1'	s_1	s_1'	s_1	s_1'	s_2	s_2'	s_1	s_1'	s_1	s_1'	s_1	s_1'	s_0	s_0'
i_B	s_2'	s_2''	s_1'	s_1''	s_1'	s_1''	s_1'	s_1''	s_2'	s_2''	s_1'	s_1''	s_1'	s_1''	s_1'	s_1''	s_0'	s_0''

For the given problem of assigning two channels uniformly to each node of the 9-node subgraph, we have to construct a CAP graph with eighteen nodes, and the corresponding the frequency separation matrix with the above strategy of re-using the channels is shown in Table 1. Note that the frequency separations shown in Table 1 takes care of the adjacency of other neighboring nodes (outside the 9-node subgraph) in the network.

We next apply the *AlgorithmGA* over the 9-node *block* of Fig. 1(b), for assigning bands to one type A and one type B calls at each of the nine nodes for minimum bandwidth, satisfying all the frequency separation requirements of Table 1. Note that from the equality $s_1 - s_1' = s_2 - s_2' = s_1' - s_1'' = s_2' - s_2''$ and Fig. 2, there can be five different conditions C_1, C_2, C_3, C_4 and C_5 as listed below:

1) $C_1 : 2s_2'' < s_1'', 2s_2 < s_1$ and $s_2 + s_2' < s_1''$, 2) $C_2 : 2s_2'' < s_1'', 2s_2 < s_1$ and $s_2 + s_2' \geq s_1''$, 3) $C_3 : 2s_2'' < s_1'', 2s_2 \geq s_1$ and $s_2'' + s_2' < s_1''$, 4) $C_4 : 2s_2'' < s_1'', 2s_2 \geq s_1$ and $s_2'' + s_2' \geq s_1''$, and 5) $C_5 : 2s_2'' \geq s_1''$.

The GA-based assignment algorithm with the above technique of channel re-use has been run on the entire hexagonal cellular network under all these five different conditions. The resulting bandwidth requirements under different conditions are stated in the following theorem.

Theorem 2. *The bandwidth BW required by our proposed assignment technique under different conditions is given as follows:*

for C_1, $BW = 2s_1 + 4s_1' + 2s_1'' + s_2'$;   for C_2, $BW = s_1 + 5s_1' + 2s_1'' + s_2$;
for C_3, $BW = 2s_1' + s_1'' + 6s_2 + 3s_2'$;   for C_4, $BW = s_1 + 4s_1' + 3s_2 + 4s_2'$; and
for C_5, $BW = 5s_2 + 6s_2' + 6s_2''$.

Proof: The proof follows from the details of channels assigned to each of the 9-nodes of the network under the above constraints for each of these five conditions. All these details are, however, omitted due to brevity.

6 Conclusion

We have first derived a lower bound on the bandwidth for multimedia channel assignment in cellular netywork for real-life situations. We have next presented an algorithm for multimedia channel assignment based on genetic algorithm (GA). Exploiting the hexagonal symmetry of the cellular network, we have then proposed an elegant technique of reusing the frequency channels. Use of this idea causes a rapid convergence of our allocation algorithm with a resulting bandwidth close to the lower bound. Future work includes improving the lower bound on bandwidth for a feasible assignment of the whole network.

References

1. Sen, A., Roxborough, T., Sinha, B.P.: On an optimal algorithm for channel assignment in cellular network. In: Proc. Int. Conf. Comm., Canada, pp. 1147–1151 (1999)
2. Goldberg, D.E.: Genetic Algorithm: Search, Optimization and Machine Learning. Addison Wesley Publishing Company, Inc., Reading (1989)
3. Chakraborty, G.: An efficient heuristic algorithm for channel assignment problem in cellular radio networks. IEEE Trans. Veh. Tech. 50(6), 1528–1539 (2001)
4. Ghosh, S.C., Sinha, B.P., Das, N.: An efficient channel assignment technique for hexagonal cellular networks. In: Proc. 6th Int. Symp. Par. Arch. Alg. and Networks, Philippines, pp. 361–366 (May 2002)
5. Ghosh, S.C., Sinha, B.P., Das, N.: Channel assignment using genetic algorithm based on geometric symmetry. IEEE Trans. Veh. Tech. 52(4), 860–875 (2003)
6. Audhya, G.K., Sinha, B.P.: Lower Bound on Bandwidth for Channel Assignment in Multimedia Cellular Network with 2-Band Buffering. In: Proc. Int. Conf. Comput.: Theory and Applications, Kolkata, India, pp. 59–65 (March 2007)

On Routing with Guaranteed Delivery in Three-Dimensional Ad Hoc Wireless Networks

Stephane Durocher[1,*], David Kirkpatrick[2], and Lata Narayanan[3]

[1] School of Computer Science, McGill University, Montréal, Canada
durocher@cs.mcgill.ca
[2] Department of Computer Science, University of British Columbia, Vancouver, Canada
kirk@cs.ubc.ca
[3] Department of Computer Science, Concordia University, Montréal, Canada
lata@cse.concordia.ca

Abstract. We study routing algorithms for three-dimensional ad hoc networks that guarantee delivery and are k-local, *i.e.*, each intermediate node v's routing decision only depends on knowledge of the labels of the source and destination nodes, of the subgraph induced by nodes within distance k of v, and of the neighbour of v from which the message was received. We model a three-dimensional ad hoc network by a unit ball graph, where nodes are points in $\mathbb{R}^3$, and nodes u and v are joined by an edge if and only if the distance between u and v is at most one.

The question of whether there is a simple local routing algorithm that guarantees delivery in unit ball graphs has been open for some time. In this paper, we answer this question in the negative: we show that for any fixed k, there can be no k-local routing algorithm that guarantees delivery on all unit ball graphs. This result is in contrast with the two-dimensional case, where 1-local routing algorithms that guarantee delivery are known. Specifically, we show that guaranteed delivery is possible if the nodes of the unit ball graph are contained in a slab of thickness $1/\sqrt{2}$. However, there is no k-local routing algorithm that guarantees delivery for the class of unit ball graphs contained in thicker slabs, *i.e.*, slabs of thickness $1/\sqrt{2} + \epsilon$ for some $\epsilon > 0$. The algorithm for routing in thin slabs derives from a transformation of unit ball graphs contained in thin slabs into quasi unit disc graphs, which yields a 2-local routing algorithm. We also show several results that further elaborate on the relationship between these two classes of graphs.

1   Introduction

Mobile ad hoc networks (MANETs) have been the subject of intensive study over the last decade. Communication between different nodes in a MANET is achieved by means of a multi-hop routing protocol, which dictates how a packet from a source node should be forwarded along the edges of the network to a given

---

* Research for this work was supported by NSERC.

S. Rao et al. (Eds.): ICDCN 2008, LNCS 4904, pp. 546–557, 2008.

destination node. Many routing algorithms for MANETs model the network as a two-dimensional geometric graph [12,19,20,25]. This captures a large number of possible application scenarios for ad hoc networks, where nodes might be vehicles moving through city streets or some other terrain. However, there is increasing interest in applications where ad hoc and sensor networks may be deployed in three-dimensional space, such as in an ocean, the atmosphere, or in a building [5,13]. For example, underwater networks that perform ocean column monitoring would require nodes to be placed at different depths in the water, creating a three-dimensional network [4]. In this paper, we study the problem of routing in three-dimensional ad hoc networks, and the extent to which they differ from two-dimensional ad hoc networks from the perspective of routing protocols. In brief, our results show that the two settings are indeed quite different.

Two-dimensional ad hoc networks are usually modelled as *unit disc graphs* (UDG). Every node in a UDG can be mapped to a point on the plane, in such a way that any two nodes at distance at most one are connected by an edge. In other words, a node v is connected to every node u occurring within the disc of radius one centred at v. The unit disc centred at a point represents the transmission range of the corresponding host. In reality however, the transmission range of a wireless node is affected by many unpredictable factors, and is unlikely to be a perfect disc. In [6], the notion of a *quasi unit disc graph* (QUDG) was introduced to address the issue of unstable transmission ranges. Roughly, a d-QUDG is a geometric graph in which any two nodes at distance at most d are always connected, nodes at distance greater than one cannot be connected, and nodes at distance between d and one may or may not be connected.

The ad hoc nature of the networks under consideration, and the mobility of the nodes implies that the topology of the network is arbitrary, and moreover, it changes over time. In the absence of any information about the location of nodes, routing protocols are obliged to flood control packets through the network in order to obtain information about the topology of the network [24]. However, in many cases, it is reasonable to assume that nodes do have access to information about not only their own locations, but also the location of their immediate neighbours, and correspondent nodes, via GPS and location servers. There is a large body of work on routing protocols that utilize position information in order to achieve efficiency in routing (see the surveys [12,25]). Most of these are heuristics, and there may be graph instances on which the routing algorithm fails to deliver the packet. In *greedy routing*, for example, a node transmits the packet to its neighbour that minimizes the Euclidean distance to the destination [21]. In *compass routing*, the next node is chosen to the neighbour that minimizes the angle between itself, the current node, and the destination node [16]. In both these algorithms, the packet can get stuck in a loop, resulting in a routing failure. The only class of algorithms that is guaranteed to deliver the packet is based on *face routing*, in which a planar subgraph of the unit disc graph is extracted locally, and then routing proceeds by traversing the faces of this planar graph that intersect the line segment between the source and destination [16]. Face routing can be combined with greedy routing [9,15], and can be limited in space [17] to achieve faster delivery times. Face routing can also be simulated on d-QUDGs where $d \geq 1/\sqrt{2}$, as shown in [6,18].

A *unit ball graph* (UBG) is the natural generalization of a UDG to three dimensions, where nodes correspond to points in $\mathbb{R}^3$. A node v is accordingly connected to every node within the unit-radius ball centred at v. Similarly, the quasi unit disc graph model can be extended to a *quasi unit ball graph* model. All the algorithms that have been proposed so far for routing in UBGs are based on heuristics [1,2,3,11,14]. As yet, there is no known algorithm for routing that guarantees delivery in such networks. In this paper, we address the question of what kind of UBGs admit a routing algorithm that guarantees delivery.

The answer to this question depends on the kind of information that is available to a routing algorithm in deciding where next to forward a packet. At one end of the spectrum are algorithms that have complete information about the entire graph, and that can store routing tables that contain next-hop information along shortest paths for every possible destination. At the other end are the so-called online and *memoryless* algorithms [8], where a node makes its forwarding decision based only on the labels[1] of itself, the destination node, and its neighbours. Bose et al. show that there is no deterministic memoryless algorithm that is guaranteed to succeed even if the graphs are limited to convex subdivisions [7].

Routing algorithms with complete information are entirely unsuitable for the application domain of mobile ad hoc networks, with their changing topologies, autonomous nodes, and low-bandwidth wireless links. On the other hand, memoryless algorithms are far too restrictive. For example, in practice, when a node receives a message, it knows which of its neighbours sent it. Yet, it is precisely the lack of this information that makes it impossible for a memoryless algorithm to route on all convex subdivisions; the only information outside the memoryless model available to face routing, which does succeed on all convex subdivisions, is knowledge of the previous node. Similarly, it would be reasonable to allow a node knowledge of the topology of its k-hop neighbourhood for small and fixed values of k. We say an algorithm is k-*local* if a node has access to the topology of its k-hop neighbourhood, as well as the previous node on the path, in making its forwarding decision. There has been increased recent interest in distributed algorithms that are sensitive to locality; see for example the book by Peleg [23]. Routing algorithms with information about $O(1)$ other nodes in the graph are related to k-local algorithms and have been studied in [16,17]. In this paper, we restrict ourselves to routing algorithms that are k-local. While our algorithm for a restricted class of unit ball graphs is 2-local, the impossibility results apply to k-local algorithms for any fixed k.

Our Results

In essence, we show that routing in three-dimensions is harder than routing in two dimensions. As far as routing is concerned, it is possible to "lift off" the

---

[1] In a geometric graph, a node is labelled by its coordinates.

plane to a certain extent, but not beyond. We consider unit ball graphs where nodes are contained in a slab of fixed thickness. We show that if the thickness of a slab is less than $1/\sqrt{2}$ times the transmission radius of nodes, then there is a 2-local algorithm that guarantees delivery in the graph. Conversely, for unit ball graphs in thicker slabs, we show that if a k-local routing algorithm were to exist, then a k-local algorithm for routing would also exist for an arbitrary graph, which we show is impossible.

The algorithm for UBGs contained in thin slabs derives from the fact that such a UBG can be transformed via projection into a d-QUDG with $d \geq 1/\sqrt{2}$, for which a 2-local algorithm with guaranteed delivery was outlined in [18]. We explore the relationship between UBGs and QUDGs further in Section 4. We show that neither the class of all UBGs nor the class of d-QUDGs is contained in the other, for fixed values of d. In particular, for every $d < \sqrt{3}/2$, we exhibit a d-QUDG that cannot be embedded as a UBG. While it is straightforward to see that any graph can be embedded as a d-QUDG for small enough d, we show that for any fixed d, there are UBGs that cannot be embedded as a d-QUDG. Finally, our negative results on routing in UBGs contained in slabs of large enough thickness imply the non-existence of a k-local algorithm for d-QUDGs with $d < 1/\sqrt{2}$. This shows that the results of Barrière et al. [6] and Kuhn et al. [18] on routing in QUDGs are tight.

2   Definitions

Given a labelled, connected, undirected graph, $G = (V, E)$, and two vertices, s and t in V, the problem of routing is to send a packet from s to t using the edges in G. To this end, an algorithm for routing is implemented in a distributed manner at every node in the graph, in such a way that when the packet arrives at a particular node u, the routing algorithm implemented at u must deterministically choose a unique neighbour of u to which the packet should be forwarded. An algorithm halts once the message is forwarded to the destination vertex t. In this case, we say the algorithm *delivers* the message. We say routing algorithm $\mathcal{A}$ *succeeds* for a class of graphs $\mathcal{G}$ if, for all $G \in \mathcal{G}$, $\mathcal{A}$ delivers a message from any origin s to any destination t in G. Otherwise, we say A is *defeated* by some $G \in \mathcal{G}$.

Let the k-*neighbourhood* of a vertex v, denoted $G_k(v)$, be the subgraph of G induced by vertices within graph distance k from v (including the corresponding vertex labels). The vertex labelling scheme should be independent of the graph; in particular, the labelling should not encode additional information about the topology of the graph or the neighbourhood of a vertex. For example, in a geometric graph, each vertex is labelled by its coordinates.

Let Σ denote the set of possible vertex labels for a given class of graphs and let $\mathscr{P}(A)$ denote the power set of set A. Given a fixed k, we say a routing algorithm is k-*local* if it can be defined by a *routing function* $f : \Sigma^4 \times \mathscr{P}(\Sigma^2) \to \Sigma$ with the following interpretation: $f(s, t, v, u, G_k(u))$ specifies the neighbour to which node u should forward the packet, provided (a) the packet was received from its neighbour v, (b) the source and destination of the packet are s and t respectively, and (c) $G_k(u)$ is the k-neighbourhood of u.

A k-local algorithm must therefore make the forwarding decision at a node u based only on the source and destination nodes, its k-neighbourhood, and the previous node on the path. It has no additional information about the route. In particular, no memory or state information may be stored in the message other than s, t, and v, nor may the state of a vertex be modified after forwarding a message.

Given a set of points P in $\mathbb{R}^2$, the *unit disc graph* induced by P, denoted $UDG(P)$, is an embedded graph whose vertices correspond to P and for which edge (u, v) exists if and only if $\|u - v\| \leq 1$. Given a set of points P in $\mathbb{R}^3$, the *unit ball graph* induced by P, denoted $UBG(P)$, is defined analogously.

Given $d \in [0, 1]$, graph $G = (V, E)$ can be realized as a *d-quasi unit disc graph*, denoted d-QUDG, if there exists an embedding of G, $f : V \to \mathbb{R}^2$, such that for all $u, v \in V$,

1. $\|f(u) - f(v)\| \leq d \Rightarrow (u, v) \in E$, and
2. $\|f(u) - f(v)\| > 1 \Rightarrow (u, v) \notin E$.

If $\|f(u) - f(v)\| \in (d, 1]$, then no conclusion may be drawn about the membership of edge (u, v) in E: both $(u, v) \in E$ and $(u, v) \notin E$ are possible. Observe that a 1-QUDG is a UDG and any graph is a 0-QUDG. See Barrière et al. [6] and Kuhn et al. [18] for a discussion of quasi unit disc graphs.

Given a fixed d, let $\mathcal{UDG}$, $\mathcal{UBG}$, and d-$\mathcal{UBG}$ denote the classes of graphs that can be realized as a UDG, a UBG, or a d-QUDG, respectively.

Finally, if P_1 and P_2 denote parallel planes in $\mathbb{R}^3$, we refer to the closed region between P_1 and P_2 as a *slab* and to the minimum distance between P_1 and P_2 as its *thickness*.

3   Routing in Unit Ball Graphs

In this section we present our main results on routing in unit ball graphs in Theorems 1 and 2. Together, these two results characterize the class of UBGs for which a k-local routing algorithm is possible. Our first observation, stated formally in the following lemma, is that any UBG contained in a slab of thickness $\lambda < 1$ can be transformed into a QUDG by projecting the points in the UBG to a plane parallel to the slab.

Lemma 1. *Choose any $\lambda \leq 1$ and let P denote a set of points in $\mathbb{R}^3$ contained in a slab of thickness λ. Let $f : \mathbb{R}^3 \to \mathbb{R}^2$ denote the projection onto a plane parallel to the slab. Let $G = (V, E)$ denote the embedded graph such that $V = \{f(v) \mid v \in P\}$ and $E = \{(f(u), f(v)) \mid \|u - v\| \leq 1, u, v \in P\}$ (V and E may be multisets). G is a $(\sqrt{1 - \lambda^2})$-QUDG.*

Proof. Choose any two points $u, v \in P$. If $\|f(u) - f(v)\| > 1$ then $\|u - v\| > 1$ and $(f(u), f(v)) \notin E$. Similarly, if $\|f(u) - f(v)\| \leq \sqrt{1 - \lambda^2}$ then $\|u - v\| \leq 1$ and $(f(u), f(v)) \in E$. Therefore, the projected graph G is a $(\sqrt{1 - \lambda^2})$-quasi unit disc graph. $\qquad\square$

Kuhn et al. [18] propose a 2-local routing algorithm for d-quasi unit disc graphs that succeeds for any $d \geq 1/\sqrt{2}$. The following theorem is an immediate consequence of Lemma 1.

Theorem 1. *For every finite set of points P in $\mathbb{R}^3$ contained within a slab of thickness $1/\sqrt{2}$, there exists a 2-local routing algorithm that succeeds for $UBG(P)$.*

Proof. By Lemma 1, the projection of $UBG(P)$ onto a plane parallel to the slab is a $1/\sqrt{2}$-QUDG, G. Since $UBG(P)$ and G are isomorphic, the k-neighbourhood of a vertex v in $UBG(P)$ determines the k-neighbourhood of the corresponding vertex in G. Therefore, a 2-local routing algorithm in $UBG(P)$ can be achieved by projecting the 2-neighbourhood of the current vertex v and simulating a 2-local routing algorithm such as the one in [18] on the corresponding QUDG. □

Note that Theorem 1 requires knowledge of a normal to the plane since, in general, this cannot be determined from the 2-neighbourhood of a vertex.

In the remainder of this section, we show that the result in Theorem 1 is tight: there is no k-local routing that can guarantee delivery on all UBGs contained in slabs thicker than $1/\sqrt{2}$. To prove this, we first show that any such algorithm would imply the existence of a 1-local routing algorithm for arbitrary graphs (Lemma 2). Next we show the impossibility of a 1-local routing algorithm for arbitrary labelled graphs (Lemma 3).

Lemma 2. *If there exists some $\epsilon > 0$, some $k \geq 1$, and a k-local routing algorithm that succeeds for $UBG(P)$, for every finite set of points P in $\mathbb{R}^3$ contained within a slab of thickness $1/\sqrt{2} + \epsilon$, then there exists a 1-local routing algorithm that succeeds for any connected, labelled graph G.*

Proof. Suppose for some $\epsilon > 0$, there exists a k-local algorithm $\mathcal{A}$ that succeeds in routing on every UBG contained in a slab of thickness at most $1/\sqrt{2} + \epsilon$. For any arbitrary graph G, we show how to construct a UBG G' such that routing on G can be accomplished by simulating $\mathcal{A}$ on G'. Let $G = (V, E)$ be an arbitrary connected labelled graph. Let $n = |V|$. Without loss of generality, assume the vertices are labelled $0, \ldots, n-1$; that is, $V = \{0, \ldots, n-1\}$. The proof holds regardless of whether the set of vertex labels is a contiguous subset of the integers.

We define a transformation from G to a set of points $P(G)$ in $\mathbb{R}^3$. Let $\epsilon' = \min\{\epsilon, \sqrt{3} - 1/2\}$. For each vertex $v \in V$, create two sets $C_v = \{(2vk, y \pm 1/2, 0) \mid y \in \{2k \cdot \min(N(v)) - (k-1), \ldots, 2k \cdot \max(N(v)) + (k-1)\}\}$ and $R_v = \{(x \pm 1/2, 2vk, 1/\sqrt{2} + \epsilon') \mid x \in \{2k \cdot \min(N(v)) - (k-1), \ldots, 2k \cdot \max(N(v)) + (k-1)\}\}$, where $N(v)$ denotes the set of labels of neighbours of v and v itself. That is, C_v is a column of points in the xy-plane starting at $(2vk, 2k \min(N(v)) - k + 1/2, 0)$ and R_v is a row of points in the xy-plane starting at $(2vk, 2k \min(N(v)) - k + 1/2, 2vk, 1/\sqrt{2} + \epsilon')$. For each edge $(u, v) \in E$, add a point $p_{u,v} = (2uk, 2vk, (1/\sqrt{2} + \epsilon')/2)$. Finally, for each $v \in V$, add the point $p_{v,v} = (2vk, 2vk, (1/\sqrt{2} + \epsilon')/2)$. The graph $UBG(P(G))$ is defined in the usual way; every pair of points within distance one of each other is connected by an edge. Figure 1 shows a graph G and the corresponding graph $UBG(P(G))$ for $k = 1$.

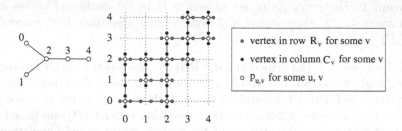

Fig. 1. A graph G and the corresponding graph $UBG(P(G))$ for $k = 1$

For each $v \in V$, the set C_v (similarly, R_v) is a sequence of points, each at distance one from the previous point, and therefore, C_v (R_v) corresponds to a path in $UBG(P(G))$. For any $u \neq v$, columns C_u and C_v are at distance at least two apart and rows R_u and R_v are at distance at least two apart. If edge $(u, v) \notin E$, where $u \neq v$, then the distance between any point $i \in C_u$ and any point $j \in R_v$ is greater than one; therefore, i and j are not adjacent in $UBG(P(G))$. Since $\epsilon' \leq \sqrt{3} - 1/\sqrt{2}$, if edge $(u, v) \in E$, then the distance between some point $i \in R_u$ and $p_{u,v}$ is at most one and the distance between some point $j \in C_v$ and $p_{u,v}$ is at most one; therefore, i and $p_{i,j}$ are adjacent in $UBG(P(G))$, as are j and $p_{i,j}$. See Figure 2.

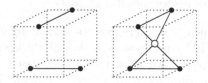

Fig. 2. The region $[2ik \pm 1/2] \times [2jk \pm 1/2] \times [0, 1/\sqrt{2} + \epsilon']$ in $UBG(P(G))$ if i and j are not adjacent in G and the same region if i and j are adjacent in G

It is straightforward to see that $UBG(P(G))$ is contained within a slab of thickness $1/\sqrt{2} + \epsilon' \leq 1/\sqrt{2} + \epsilon$ and therefore algorithm $\mathcal{A}$ should succeed on it. We claim that a straightforward simulation of $\mathcal{A}$ in $UBG(P(G))$ constitutes a 1-local routing algorithm for G. That is, upon reaching a vertex $v \in V$, it suffices to simulate $\mathcal{A}$ on the subgraph of $UBG(P(G))$ that corresponds to vertex v and its 1-neighbourhood in G. The simulation begins at point $p_{v,v}$ with the goal of reaching the destination vertex $p_{t,t}$. When the simulation moves to a point outside $C_v \cup R_v \cup \{p_{v,v}\}$ in $UBG(P(G))$, it must reach a point $p_{v,u}$ or $p_{u,v}$ for some $u \neq v$. This corresponds to forwarding the message to vertex u, which must be a neighbour of v in G. The computation of the k-local subgraph of

$UBG(P(G))$ around any vertex in $C_v \cup R_v \cup \{p_{v,v}\}$, and hence the simulation, can be performed completely locally for any vertex v, given the the 1-neighbourhood of v in G. Furthermore, knowledge of the number of vertices in G is not required to simulate the local neighbourhood of v in $UBG(P(G))$. Since the simulation results in a 1-local routing algorithm guaranteed to succeed on an arbitrary graph G, the lemma follows.   □

We proceed to show the non-existence of a 1-local routing algorithm for an arbitrary labelled graph G.

Lemma 3. *For any 1-local routing algorithm $\mathcal{A}$, there exists a labelled graph for which $\mathcal{A}$ is defeated.*

Proof. A 1-local routing function f must be defined for all valid combinations of input. In particular, $f(s, t, v_i, u, \{(u, v_1), \dots, (u, v_k)\})$ must be defined for all $i \in \{1, \dots, k\}$, where s denotes the origin, t denotes the destination, v_i denotes the last vertex visited, u denotes the current vertex, and $\{v_1, \dots, v_k\}$ denotes the set of neighbours of u. Let $f'_u(v_i) = f(s, t, v_i, u, \{(u, v_1), \dots, (u, v_k)\})$ for a given s, t, u, and its set of neighbours. We refer to f'_u as a *local routing function*.

Function $f'_u : \{v_1, \dots, v_k\} \to \{v_1, \dots, v_k\}$ is one of k^k possible functions. Function f'_u must be bijective. Assume otherwise. Without loss of generality, say $f'_u(v_i) \neq v_1$ for all $i \in \{1, \dots, k\}$. Function f'_u is defeated by a tree with t in the subtree of u rooted at v_1 and s in any other subtree of u. Furthermore, if $k > 1$ then f'_u must be a derangement. Assume instead that $f'_u(v_i) = v_i$ for some $i \in \{1, \dots, k\}$. Function f'_u is defeated by a tree with s in the subtree of u rooted at v_i and t in any other subtree of u. Therefore, it suffices to consider local routing functions f'_u that are derangements.

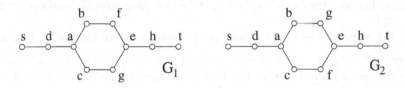

Fig. 3. Any routing algorithm is defeated by G_1 or G_2 if all local routing functions are derangements

A set of cardinality two has a unique derangement. Therefore, f'_u is uniquely defined when u has degree two. A set of cardinality three has two possible derangements. Therefore, f'_u is one of two functions when u has degree two. Observe that f'_u is also uniquely defined when u has degree one.

Let G_1 and G_2 denote the graphs illustrated in Figure 3. Graphs G_1 are G_2 are automorphic upon permuting vertices f and g. As discussed, the local routing function is uniquely defined for all vertices of degree two or less. There are two vertices of degree three: a and e. Let $f'_a(v) = f(s, t, v, a, \{(a, b), (a, c), (a, d)\})$ and $f'_e(v) = f(s, t, v, e, \{(e, f), (e, g), (e, h)\})$ denote the local routing functions

Table 1. The four combinations of derangements for local routing functions f'_a and f'_e

routing function 1				routing function 2				routing function 3				routing function 4			
u	$f'_a(u)$	u	$f'_e(u)$	u	$f'_a(u)$	u	$f'_e(u)$	u	$f'_a(u)$	u	$f'_e(u)$	u	$f'_a(u)$	u	$f'_e(u)$
b	c	f	g	b	d	f	g	b	c	f	h	b	d	f	h
c	d	g	h	c	b	g	h	c	d	g	f	c	b	g	f
d	b	h	f	d	c	h	f	d	b	h	g	d	c	h	g

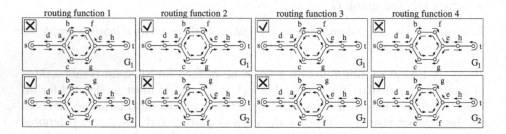

Fig. 4. Four routing functions are possible for graphs G_1 and G_2 such that each local routing function is a derangement. Each routing function is defeated by G_1 or G_2 when delivering a message from s to t. A defeat is denoted by X.

for vertices a and e, respectively. Each of f'_a and f'_e may be defined by one of two derangements, resulting in four possible routing functions for graphs G_1 and G_2, given in Table 1. As shown in Figure 4, each of the four routing functions is defeated by either G_1 or G_2. □

Remark: It is straightforward to show the non-existence of a k-local routing algorithm for any fixed k by replacing the edges in graphs G_1 and G_2 by paths of length k.

The following theorem is an immediate consequence of Lemmas 2 and 3.

Theorem 2. *For every $\epsilon > 0$, every $k \geq 1$, and every k-local routing algorithm $\mathcal{A}$, there exists a finite set of points P in $\mathbb{R}^3$ contained within a slab of thickness $1/\sqrt{2} + \epsilon$ such that $\mathcal{A}$ is defeated by $UBG(P)$.*

Theorem 2 and Lemma 1 also give the following corollary:

Corollary 1. *For every $\epsilon \in (0, 1/\sqrt{2}]$, every $k \geq 1$, and every k-local routing algorithm $\mathcal{A}$, there exists a $(1/\sqrt{2} - \epsilon)$-QUDG, G, such that $\mathcal{A}$ is defeated by G.*

In [6] and [18], algorithms for routing in d-QUDGs for $d \geq 1/\sqrt{2}$ are given. Corollary 1 implies that these results are tight: it is impossible to extend the range of d for which the class of d-QUDGs would admit a k-local algorithm.

4   Unit Ball Graphs and Quasi Unit Disc Graphs

In Section 3 we showed that any UBG contained within a slab of thickness $\lambda \leq 1$ is isomorphic to some $(\sqrt{1 - \lambda^2})$-QUDG. In this section we present additional observations on unit ball graphs and their relationship to quasi unit disc graphs and more general graphs. We show the following general result which follows from Lemmas 4 and 5.

Theorem 3. *(1) Given any fixed d, $UBG \not\subseteq d\text{-}QUDG$. (2) Given any fixed $d' < \sqrt{3}/2$, $d'\text{-}QUDG \not\subseteq UBG$.*

We first show that the class UBG is not contained within the class $d\text{-}QUBG$ for any fixed d:

Lemma 4. *For every d, there exists a finite set of points P in $\mathbb{R}^3$ such that $UBG(P)$ is not isomorphic to any $d\text{-}QUDG$.*

The proof of Lemma 4 was omitted due to space limitations. If d is not fixed, then any graph can be realized as a $d\text{-}QUDG$ for some d:

Proposition 1. *For every finite labelled graph G, there exists a d and a $d\text{-}QUDG$, G' such that G is isomorphic to G'.*

Proof. Choose any graph G. Embed all vertices of G at distinct points contained within a disc of radius $1/2$ in the plane. Add the edges of G. Choose $d > 0$ such that d is less than the minimum distance between any two points. The resulting graph is a $d\text{-}QUDG$ since all edges have lengths in the range $[d, 1]$.   □

By Lemma 1, any UBG contained in a slab of thickness $\lambda < 1$ is isomorphic to some quasi unit disc graph. The converse is not true; as we show in Lemma 5, there exist quasi unit disc graphs that are not isomorphic to any UBG.

Lemma 5. *$K_{3,3}$ is forbidden as an induced subgraph of a UBG but can be realized as a $(\sqrt{3}/2 - \epsilon)\text{-}QUDG$ for any $\epsilon > 0$.*

The proof of Lemma 5 was omitted due to space limitations. It follows that $d\text{-}QUDG \subseteq UBG$ when $d = 1$ but $d\text{-}QUDG \not\subseteq UBG$ when $d \le \sqrt{3}/2$. It remains open to determine for which range of values of $d \in (\sqrt{3}/2, 1)$ the predicate $d\text{-}QUDG \subseteq UBG$ remains true.

The definition of a d-quasi unit disc graph has a natural generalization to three dimensions as a d-*quasi unit ball graph*, denoted $d\text{-}QUBG$. We note the following straightforward relationship between $d\text{-}QUBG$ and $d\text{-}QUDG$:

Proposition 2. *For every $d \le 1$, every $\lambda < d$, and every $d\text{-}QUBG$, G, contained in a slab of thickness λ, there exists a $(\sqrt{d^2 - \lambda^2})\text{-}QUDG$ G' such that G is isomorphic to G'.*

Proof. The proof is analogous to the proof of Lemma 1.   □

Proposition 2 and the 2-local routing algorithm of Kuhn et al. [18] give:

Corollary 2. *There exists a 2-local routing algorithm that succeeds for any $d\text{-}QUBG$, G, such that $d \ge \sqrt{\lambda^2 + 1/2}$ and G is contained in a slab of thickness λ.*

5   Discussion

We have shown the impossibility of routing algorithms that guarantee delivery in three-dimensional ad hoc networks, modelled by unit ball graphs, when nodes are constrained to have information only about their k-hop neighborhood. This result is in direct contrast to the two-dimensional case, where a 1-local algorithm such as face routing guarantees delivery on all unit disc graphs.

The results from the planar case do "lift off" the plane to a limited extent. We showed that unit ball graphs for which the nodes are contained in a slab of thickness $1/\sqrt{2}$ admit a 2-local routing algorithm that guarantees delivery. On the other hand, we also showed that for any fixed k, there is no k-local routing algorithm that is guaranteed to succeed on all unit ball graphs, even if the nodes are contained in a slab of thickness of $1/\sqrt{2} + \epsilon$ for arbitrarily small $\epsilon > 0$. An interesting question would be to characterize precisely the class of unit ball graphs in thicker slabs that do have routing algorithms. Since distributed algorithms for routing in unit ball graphs remain an urgent necessity, the question of the kind of information with which a routing algorithm might be augmented, in order to circumvent the negative results in this paper would be useful to answer.

In this paper, we have begun an exploration of the relationship between unit ball graphs, quasi unit disc graphs, and quasi unit ball graphs. Many questions remain open. For example: does there exist a $\delta > 0$ such that any $(1 - \delta)$-QUDG is isomorphic to some UBG? If so, what is the supremum of all such δ? By Lemma 5, $\delta < 1 - \sqrt{3}/2$. Several graph problems that are NP-complete are efficiently approximable (*e.g.,* maximum independent set, graph coloring, and minimum dominating set [22]) or tractable (*e.g.,* max-clique [10]) on unit disc graphs. A similar investigation of which graph problems are tractable or approximable on unit ball graphs and the other classes of graphs studied here might be a fruitful avenue of research.

Acknowledgements

The authors would like to thank Prosenjit Bose for providing helpful answers to our questions regarding hardness results for memoryless routing algorithms as well as Stephen Wismath, Ethan Kim, and John Iacono for discussing ideas which resulted in a preliminary algorithm for routing in unit ball graphs at the 2007 Bellairs Workshop on Computational Geometry.

References

1. Abdallah, A., Fevens, T., Opatrny, J.: Hybrid position-based 3-D routing algorithms with partial flooding. In: IEEE CCECE (2006)
2. Abdallah, A., Fevens, T., Opatrny, J.: Randomized 3-D position-based routing algorithms for ad-hoc networks. In: Mobiquitous (2006)
3. Abdallah, A., Fevens, T., Opatrny, J.: Power-aware 3D position-based routing. In: IEEE ICC (to appear, 2007)

4. Akyildiz, I.F., Pompili, D., Melodia, T.: Underwater acoustic sensor networks: Research challenges. Ad Hoc Net. (2005)
5. Alam, S.M.N., Haas, Z.J.: Coverage and connectivity in three-dimensional networks. In: ACM MobiCom, pp. 346–357 (2006)
6. Barrière, L., Fraigniaud, P., Narayanan, L., Opatrny, J.: Robust position-based routing in wireless ad-hoc networks with unstable transmission ranges. Wireless Comm. & Mob. Comp. 3/2, 141–153 (2003)
7. Bose, P., Brodnik, A., Carlsson, S., Demaine, E.D., Fleischer, R., López-Ortiz, A., Morin, P., Munro, I.: Online routing in convex subdivisions. Int. J. Comp. Geom. App. 12, 283–295 (2002)
8. Bose, P., Morin, P.: Online routing in triangulations. In: Aggarwal, A.K., Pandu Rangan, C. (eds.) ISAAC 1999. LNCS, vol. 1741, pp. 113–122. Springer, Heidelberg (1999)
9. Bose, P., Morin, P., Stojmenovic, I., Urrutia, J.: Routing with guaranteed delivery in ad hoc wireless networks. Wireless Net. 7, 609–616 (2001)
10. Clark, B., Colbourn, C., Johnson, D.: Unit disk graphs. Disc. Math. 86, 165–177 (1990)
11. Fevens, T., Kao, G., Opatrny, J.: 3-D localized position-based routing with nearly certain delivery in mobile ad hoc networks. In: ISWPC (2007)
12. Giordano, S., Stojmenovic, I.: Position based routing algorithms for ad hoc networks: A taxonomy. In: Cheng, X., Huang, X., Du, D.Z. (eds.) Ad Hoc Wireless Networking, pp. 103–136. Kluwer, Dordrecht (2003)
13. Heidemann, J., Ye, W., Wills, J., Syed, A., Li, Y.: Research challenges and applications for underwater sensor networking. In: IEEE WCNC (2006)
14. Kamali, S., Opatrny, J.: Posant: A position based ant colony routing algorithm for mobile ad-hoc networks. In: ICWCM, vol. 3 (2007)
15. Karp, B., Kung, H.: GPSR: Greedy perimeter stateless routing for wireless networks. In: ACM MobiCom, vol. 6, pp. 243–254 (2000)
16. Kranakis, E., Singh, H., Urrutia, J.: Compass routing on geometric networks. In: CCCG, vol. 11, pp. 51–54 (1999)
17. Kuhn, F., Wattenhofer, R., Zollinger, A.: Asymptotically optimal geometric mobile ad-hoc routing. In: DIALM, vol. 6, pp. 24–33 (2002)
18. Kuhn, F., Wattenhofer, R., Zollinger, A.: Ad-hoc networks beyond unit disk graphs. In: ACM DIALM-POMC (2003)
19. Li, X.Y.: Applications of computational geomety in wireless ad hoc networks. In: Cheng, X., Huang, X., Du, D.Z. (eds.) Ad Hoc Wireless Networking, Kluwer, Dordrecht (2003)
20. Li, X.Y., Wang, Y.: Wireless sensor networks and computational geometry. In: M.I., et al. (eds.) Handbook of Sensor Networks, CRC Press, USA (2003)
21. Lin, X., Stojmenović, I.: GEDIR: Loop-free location based routing in wireless networks. In: PDCS, pp. 1025–1028 (1999)
22. Marathe, M.V., Breu, H., Hunt III, H., Ravi, S.S., Rosenkrantz, D.J.: Simple heuristics for unit disk graphs. Networks 25, 59–68 (1995)
23. Peleg, D.: Distributed computing: A locality-sensitive approach. In: SIAM (2000)
24. Perkins, C.: Ad Hoc Networking. Addison-Wesley Professional, Reading (2001)
25. Stojmenovic, I.: Position based routing in ad hoc networks. IEEE Comm. 40, 128–134 (2002)

Energy-Efficient Dominating Tree Construction in Wireless Ad Hoc and Sensor Networks[*]

Ruiyun Yu[1], Xingwei Wang[2], Yonghe Liu[3], and Sajal K. Das[3]

[1] Computing Center, Northeastern University, China
yury@cc.neu.edu.cn
[2] College of Information Science and Engineering, Northeastern University, China
wangxw@mail.neu.edu.cn
[3] Department of Computer Science and Engineering, The University of Texas
at Arlington, USA
yonghe@uta.edu, das@cse.uta.edu

Abstract. Motivated by reducing communication overhead and prolonging network lifetime in wireless ad hoc and sensor networks, we propose an energy-efficient dominating tree construction ($EEDTC$) algorithm to construct a dominating tree that can serve as a communication backbone in wireless infrastructures. The algorithm has a theoretical approximation factor of at most 9, and has $O(n)$ message complexity and $O(n)$ time complexity. Due to the low message complexity, $EEDTC$ performs well on energy consumption. The energy-aware ranking technique introduced can also balance energy consumption in the network, and hence reduce the probability of network failures caused by energy depletion of backbone nodes.

1 Introduction

Wireless ad hoc and sensor networks have drawn lots of attention in recent years. Unlike other traditional networks, they are decentralized and have no physical backbone infrastructure. Broadcasting feature is a nature of wireless networks and can cause high communication overhead.

To reduce communication overhead, many researchers proposed to use a connected dominating set (CDS) as a virtual backbone for hierarchical routing in wireless ad hoc and sensor networks [1][2][3][4][5][6][7][8][9][10].

But constructing and maintaining a CDS will impose other control overhead onto overall communication, so a CDS-construction algorithm should be efficient enough. On one hand, the size of a CDS should be as small as possible, so that overhead will be minimized when an application is executed on the CDS. On the other hand, the algorithm also should have good performance on time complexity and message complexity, and try its best to reduce control overhead.

[*] This work is supported by the National High-Tech Research and Development Plan of China under Grant No. 2006AA01Z214, the National Natural Science Foundation of China under Grant No. 60673159, and the Program for New Century Excellent Talents in Universities.

S. Rao et al. (Eds.): ICDCN 2008, LNCS 4904, pp. 558–569, 2008.

Among existing literature, the algorithms proposed in [1], [4] and [5] are tree-based schemes. A dominating tree seems more appropriate in many application scenarios, such as data dissemination, data fusion, routing, and so on. While constructing a dominating tree always introduces high algorithm complexity.

To construct a dominating tree with lower algorithm complexity, we propose an energy-efficient dominating tree construction (*EEDTC*) algorithm, that is a quite different approach from those in [1], [4] and [5]. The differences lie in execution processes, as well as in the amount of nodes involved.

EEDTC consists of two phases: *Marking Phase* and *Connecting Phase*. The *Marking Phase* constructs a maximal independent set (*MIS*), and meanwhile forms a forest consisting of trees rooted at several initiators. In the *Connecting Phase*, the forest is connected to a dominating tree by connecting some adjacent trees.

Compared with other tree-based algorithms [1][4][5], *EEDTC* simplifies the execution process by combining *MIS* construction and forest formation together which are separated in other schemes. Moreover, only a small proportion of nodes get involved to connect the forest in *EEDTC*, while every node is involved up to n times in other schemes. Therefore *EEDTC* gains better algorithm complexity.

EEDTC has an approximation factor of at most 9, $O(n)$ message complexity and $O(n)$ time complexity. To the best of our knowledge, *EEDTC* outperforms all existing tree-based *CDS*-construction schemes on message complexity.

Simulations show that *EEDTC* performs well on energy consumption, energy balance, and message complexity.

The rest of this paper is organized as follows. We survey some of related schemes in Section 2, and introduce our contribution in Section 3. Some preliminaries and assumptions are presented in Section 4. In Section 5, we propose the *EEDTC* algorithm. Then we analyze the performance of *EEDTC* by theoretical analysis in Section 6 and by simulations in Section 7. Section 8 concludes this paper.

2   Related Work

In this section, we briefly survey several schemes of constructing connected dominating sets in wireless ad-hoc and sensor networks.

Wu and Li [2] first find a connected dominating set (*CDS*) of a connected graph G in the *Marking Process*. The algorithm then removes all redundant nodes from the initial *CDS* in the *Reducing Process*.

Stojmenovic et al. [3] improve the algorithm proposed in [2] by replacing larger-id priority with highest-degree priority to remove redundant nodes in the *Reducing Process*.

Literature [6] and [7] take energy issue into consideration. Instead of the id-based removal approach exploited in [2], Wu et al. [6] consider two extended rules for selective removal. In [7], Kim et al. propose an algorithm similar to the one in [11], but Kim et al. consider residual energy of each node.

The algorithms in [8], [9] and [10] are based on the multipoint relays (*MPR*) approach proposed in [12]. Adjih et al. [8] propose a source-independent *MPR* that constructs a *CDS* based on the original *MPR* algorithm. Wu et al. [9] extend the source-independent *MPR* by providing several extensions. Liang et al. proposed a gateway multipoint relays (*GMPR*) scheme in [10].

The algorithms proposed in [1], [4] and [5] are tree-based.

Sivakumar et al. [1] first construct a dominating set *S*. Then it connects *S* to a connected dominating set by using the minimum spanning tree (*MST*) algorithm proposed in [13].

The algorithm proposed by Wan et al. [4] consists of two phases which construct a maximal independent set (*MIS*) and a dominating tree, respectively. The algorithm runs on the basis of a spanning tree constructed by the distributed leader-election algorithm in [14].

Min et al. [5] also first construct a spanning tree using the same approach as in [4] prior to the *MIS* formation. Then it interconnects nodes in the *MIS* to a spanning tree using the distributed algorithm proposed in [14].

3 Our Contribution

The *EEDTC* algorithm we propose is different from those in [1], [4] and [5] on execution processes.

The algorithm in [1] first constructs a dominating set which is then connected by the *MST* algorithm in [13]. The algorithms in [4] and [5] all construct a tree using the algorithm in [14] before the *CDS* construction.

The tree construction approaches in [13] and [14] all have high message complexity, because every node is involved up to n times to collect information for combination decision. Either all nodes report to the root [14], or the root broadcasts a query and gets response over the tree [13].

EEDTC first constructs a *MIS*, and meanwhile a forest consisting of some multi-hop trees is formed with a little extra overhead. Then it connects the forest using the shortest paths between some pairs of adjacent trees.

EEDTC combines *MIS* construction and forest formation together, and only a small proportion of nodes are involved to connect the forest, therefore it use less messages than in other schemes.

The algorithm in [1] has $O(n|C| + m + nlogn)$ message complexity, and the algorithms in [4] and [5] both have $O(nlogn)$ message complexity, while the message complexity of *EEDTC* is $O(n)$.

Lower message complexity definitely leads to lower energy consumption. Moreover, *EEDTC* also has good performance on energy balance. So *EEDTC* is energy-efficient, and can greatly prolong the lifetime of wireless networks.

4 Preliminaries and Assumptions

We assume that the transmission ranges of all nodes in the network are equal. Without losing generality, we model the network as a unit disk graph $G(V, E)$ [15], where V denotes the vertex (node) set and E denotes the edge set.

A subset S of V is a dominating set if each node u in V is either in S or is adjacent to a certain node v in S. A subset C of V is a connected dominating set (CDS) if C is a dominating set and C also induces a connected subgraph of G. Naturally, the nodes in C can communicate with each other without using nodes in $(V - C)$, and every node in G can be accessed by a certain node in C within one-hop distance.

A subset R of V in a graph G is an independent set if, for any pair of vertices in R, there is no edge between them. A subset M of V is a maximal independent set (MIS) if no more vertices can be added into it to generate a larger independent set. From the definition, it is easy to know that a maximal independent set (MIS) is also a dominating set.

We assume that nodes in the network are uniquely indexed and can gauge its residual energy. Furthermore, through message exchanges, a node is aware of its neighbor nodes, including their IDs and residual energy.

We also assume that nodes are static or can be viewed as static during a reasonable period of time.

Since the connected dominating set (CDS) we construct in $EEDTC$ is also a dominating tree, we will use these two phrases interchangeably in the remainder of this paper.

5   The Energy-Efficient Dominating Tree Construction ($EEDTC$) Algorithm

Our algorithm towards the construction of a dominating tree is named $EEDTC$ (the energy-efficient dominating tree construction). It consists of two phases: *Marking Phase* and *Connecting Phase*. The *Marking Phase* constructs a MIS (as discussed in the previous section, a maximal independent set (MIS) is also a dominating set), and a forest composed of trees rooted at several initiators is generated at the same time, then the *Connecting Phase* connects the forest to a single spanning tree, in which a subset of nodes form a dominating tree.

5.1   Marking Phase

The goal of this phase is to construct a MIS. Meanwhile, the MIS will be connected to a forest by some intermediate nodes.

We first introduce an energy-aware ranking technique. A node has a higher *rank* if it has more residual energy, and node IDs are used to break a tie when nodes have equal energy.

During the *Marking Phase*, each node is initially a candidate, and subsequently becomes a dominator, a connector or a dominatee. All dominators form a MIS, connectors are intermediate nodes responsible for connecting the MIS to a forest, and other nodes are dominatees.

At the beginning, a candidate with the highest rank compared with all its neighbors turns into a dominator, then broadcasts a DOMINATOR message. It also becomes the root of a tree, and the tree is marked by the ID of this node.

Upon receiving a DOMINATOR message, a candidate changes to a dominatee, and selects the sender as its parent. Subsequently, it broadcasts a DOMINATEE message.

Upon receiving a DOMINATEE message, a candidate changes to a dominator if there are no candidates with a higher rank than itself in its vicinity. Then it selects the neighbor closest to the root (with fewest hops to the root) while with higher rank as its parent (When selecting a parent, the node first considers its connector neighbors if there exist such neighbors). Then the new dominator sends a REQUESTPARENT message to its parent, and broadcasts a DOMINATOR message.

Upon receiving a REQUESTPARENT message, if the node is a dominatee, it changes to a connector and broadcasts a CONNECTORNOTIFY message notifying the change.

The *Marking Phase* terminates when there are no candidates left in the network.

Fig. 1 depicts an example with twenty-one nodes. After the *Marking Phase*, a forest with four trees is constructed (see 1(b)). The *MIS* is comprised of five dominators (nodes with *rank* 15, 17, 19, 20 and 3) and a connector (the node with *rank* 13).

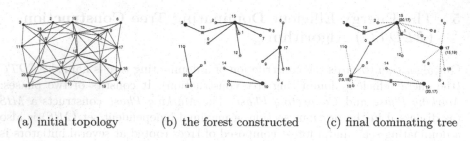

(a) initial topology   (b) the forest constructed   (c) final dominating tree

Fig. 1. The dominating tree construction

5.2   Connecting Phase

In this phase, we will connect the forest constructed in the *Marking Phase* to a single spanning tree.

The tree construction approaches in [13] (exploited in [1]) and [14] (used by [4] and [5]) all have high message complexity, because, in each combination round, all nodes in related trees are involved to collect information for next combination decision, and some nodes will be involved n times in an extreme instance (for example, a chain structure).

To minimize amount of messages used in this phase, we now propose a novel approach to connect the forest to a spanning tree. By this approach, the forest will be connected only through communication along the shortest paths between pairs of adjacent trees, and nodes not in these paths will not be involved in the execution.

For ease of explanation, we use an *edge node* to denote a node in a tree that has more than one neighbor in other trees.

The *Connecting Phase* runs as follows.

At the beginning, each edge node sends a FEEDBACK message to the root of the tree it belongs to along its tree branch.

Upon receiving a FEEDBACK message, a non-root node just forwards the message.

After receiving FEEDBACK messages from all edge nodes in the tree, a root node gets information of adjacent trees, and knows the shortest paths to all adjacent trees. In the paths, only edge nodes might be dominatees, and the other nodes are either dominators or connectors.

Then, all trees in the forest will gradually be merged into the tree with the largest ID, and eventually there is only one tree left that spans the network. The dominatees in the shortest paths that connect the forest will become connectors.

We define a *merging rule* here. If a tree has at least one adjacent tree, and has the smallest ID compared with all its adjacent trees, it will be merged into the adjacent tree with the highest ID.

If a tree satisfies the *merging rule*, it first sends a MERGE message to the root of the tree it is about to be merged into, and changes its ID to the ID of that tree. Then it sends a MERGENOTIFY message to the roots of any other adjacent trees notifying the ID change.

Both a MERGE message and a MERGENOTIFY message are sent along the shortest paths between pairs of adjacent trees.

Each sender or forwarder of a MERGE message select its next-hop node in the path as its new parent. Upon receiving a MERGE message, a node changes to a connector if it is a dominatee.

When receiving a MERGE message or a MERGENOTIFY message, a root node starts another merging round if it satisfies the merging rule.

The *Connecting Phase* terminates when there are no root nodes satisfying the merging rule, and there is just one tree left that spans the network. All dominators form a maximal independent set(*MIS*), and all connectors are responsible for connecting the *MIS* to a dominating tree.

Fig. 1(c) shows the dominating tree we finally get. The dominators (marked with solid dots) and the connectors (marked with solid squares) form the dominating tree.

6   Features of *EEDTC*

EEDTC constructs a maximal independent set(*MIS*) in the *Marking Phase*. The size relation between any *MIS* and any optimal connected dominating set(*CDS*) in a unit disk graph G is shown in *Lemma 1* which has been proved in [4].

Lemma 1. *The size of any maximal independent set (MIS) of a graph* G *is at most 4opt + 1, where opt is the size of any optimal connected dominating set* (CDS) *of a graph* G.

Lemma 2. *Algorithm EEDTC has an approximation factor of at most 9.*

Proof. The *Marking Phase* generates a *MIS M*, and a forest. We assume the number of trees in the forest is k. Let M_i be the set of dominators in tree i, so $M = \sum_{i=1}^{k} M_i$

In the *Marking Phase*, each non-root dominator selects a connector as its parent if there is a connector neighbor. Otherwise it selects a dominatee as its parent and the selected dominatee becomes a connector. In an extreme situation, every non-root dominator selects a distinct connector as its parent, and the number of connectors in tree i is $|M_i|-1$. So the number of connectors introduced in the *Marking Phase* is at most

$$\sum_{i=1}^{k}(|M_i| - 1) = \sum_{i=1}^{k} |M_i| - k = |M| - k \qquad (1)$$

In the *Connecting Phase*, since there are k trees in the forest, we will use $k - 1$ paths to connect them together. Each path introduces no more than two dominatees which become connectors in the *Connecting Phase*. So the number of connectors added into *CDS* in this phase is at most $2(k - 1)$.

Hence the number of connectors in *CDS* is no more than

$$|M| - k + 2(k - 1) = |M| + k - 2 \qquad (2)$$

And the size of *CDS* is at most

$$|M| + (|M| + k - 2) \leqslant 2(4opt + 1) + k - 2 = 8opt + k \qquad (3)$$

For k is the number of trees in the forest F and is equal to the number of higher *rank* initiators, it couldn't be larger than the size of any optimal connected dominating set (*CDS*), i.e. k is less than or equal to *opt*.

So the approximation factor of *EEDTC* is at most 9*opt*.

Lemma 3. *Algorithm EEDTC has message complexity of $O(n)$ and time complexity of $O(n)$.*

Proof. Before the execution of *EEDTC*, every node should know all its neighbors' id and residual energy. This can be achieved from broadcasting a HELLO message by each node in the *Neighbor Discovery Phase*, and the execution time is constant. The amount of massages sent is exact one per node in this phase, so this phase is bounded by $O(1)$ time and $O(n)$ messages.

In the *Marking Phase*, every node sends either a DOMINATOR message or a DOMINATEE message. A non-root dominator also sends a REQUESTPARENT message, and a dominatee sends a CONNECTORNOTIFY message when it changes its state from *dominatee* to *connector*. These also use linear execution time. The message complexity introduced in this phase is $O(n)$, and the time complexity is $O(logn)$.

In the *Connecting Phase*, every *edge node* in a certain tree sends a FEED-BACK message to its *root node* along its branch, and only nodes in the shortest paths between adjacent trees are involved while the forest are connected, therefore the amount of messages introduced is comparable with that in the *Marking*

Phase. The *Connecting Phase* also takes linear time. So the *Connecting Phase* also takes $O(n)$ message complexity and $O(n)$ time complexity.

Altogether, *EEDTC* has $O(n)$ message complexity and $O(n)$ time complexity.

Instead of involving all nodes to connect a forest in [1], [4] and [5], we just use a small proportion of nodes which are in the shortest paths between pairs of adjacent trees. Hence *EEDTC* gains better message complexity, and consume less energy than other schemes. Due to the energy-aware techniques, *EEDTC* also performs well on energy balance. These together earn a prolonged lifetime for wireless networks, which is verified by the simulations in Section 7.

7   Simulation

In this section, we evaluate energy consumption, *CDS* size, approximation factor, and message complexity of *EEDTC* through simulations. For performance comparison, We also simulate the tree-based algorithm proposed by Wan et al. [4] (marked with *WAN*).

The simulations run in the discrete event simulator OMNeT++ (version 3.3) [16]. The Mobility Framework (version 2.0) model [17] is used to support simulations of wireless networks within OMNeT++.

We assume that all nodes remain stationary throughout the simulation, and wireless nodes are randomly deployed in a $600 \times 600m^2$ playground. The communication range is set to 150m.

7.1   Energy Consumption and Lifetime

According to the model proposed in [18], power consumption for sending is set to 1 unit per packet (we assume all packets in our simulations are of the same size), and power consumption for receiving is set to 0.5 unit per packet. We neglect power consumption in idle phases and computation processes. The initial energy of each node is assigned a random value between 2950 and 3000 unit.

We compare *EEDTC* algorithm with *WAN*, and also evaluate the *EEDTC* with no energy awareness in which an id-priority ranking is exploited and the energy issue is neglected.

We randomly deploy 40, 60, and 80 nodes in the playground, and simulate three schemes for 10 rounds respectively. We don't change the topology in each deployment after it is generated in the first round.

First, we simulate plain dominating tree construction processes, in which we only construct a dominating tree in each round. As shown in Fig. 2, compared with *WAN*, *EEDTC* is much more efficient on energy consumption. The average amount of energy consumed in *EEDTC* is only about one-fourth of that in *WAN*.

The dominators and the connectors are always responsible for forming a virtual backbone of wireless networks, and consume more energy in a communication process than other nodes. To evaluate this feature, we build a set of simulations where a simple data query application is executed 10 times after the dominating tree construction in each round.

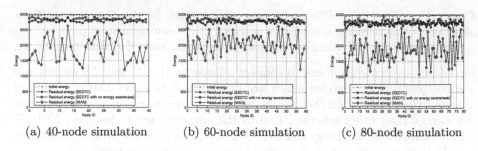

(a) 40-node simulation   (b) 60-node simulation   (c) 80-node simulation

Fig. 2. Energy Consumption of Plain Dominating Tree Construction

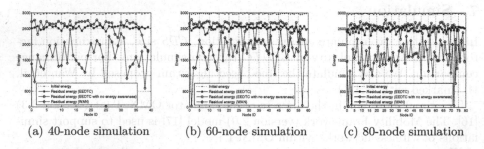

(a) 40-node simulation   (b) 60-node simulation   (c) 80-node simulation

Fig. 3. Energy Consumption with Query Applications

As illustrated in Fig. 3, energy of some nodes in *WAN* and in the *EEDTC* with no energy awareness is consumed rapidly. Due to the energy-priority ranking, *EEDTC* performs well on energy balance in every deployment. This remarkably prolongs lifetime of wireless networks.

7.2   The Size of CDS

To observe the size of *CDS*, we run simulations with 30, 40 ,50, 60, 70, 80, 90 and 100 nodes respectively, and each case is measured by 20 different topologies which are generated randomly.

Fig. 4(a) shows the number of dominators, connectors and *CDS* nodes (the union of dominators and connectors) in 8 cases. The number of dominators in *EEDTC* is almost the same as in *WAN*, but the number of connectors is less than that of *WAN*, which leads to less *CDS* nodes. This owes to the connector selection technique used in *EEDTC*.

However, the size of *CDS* varies a little when wireless nodes are evenly deployed in a fixed size playground and communicate at a fixed communication radius. So when the network becomes dense, the ratio of *CDS* nodes to simulation nodes drops remarkably (see Fig. 4(b)).

7.3   Approximation Factor

The simulation setup in this part is the same as in section 7.2.

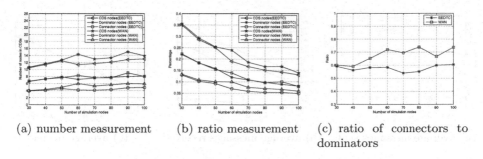

(a) number measurement   (b) ratio measurement   (c) ratio of connectors to dominators

Fig. 4. CDS size measurement

Lemma 1 indicates that the size of any maximal independent set (*MIS*) is at most $4opt+1$, and we also proved in *Lemma 2* that *EEDTC* has an approximation of at most 9. According to Fig. 4(c), the number of the connectors is about 55 to 60 percent of that of the dominators in *EEDTC*. So the approximation factor of *EEDTC* approaches to about

$$4opt + 1 + 0.6(4opt + 1) \approx 6.5opt \tag{4}$$

The ratio of connector number to dominator number in *WAN* ranges from 0.6 to 0.75, so the approximation factor of *WAN* is about

$$4opt + 1 + 0.75(4opt + 1) \approx 7opt \tag{5}$$

From simulation results, the approximation factor of *EEDTC* is slightly better than that of *WAN*.

7.4 Message Complexity

The simulation setup in this part is the same as in section 7.2.

Fig. 5 illustrates the average messages sent and received in the simulations.

According to the aforementioned discussions, in *EEDTC*, the number of messages sent in the *Neighbor Discovery Phase* is exact one per node, and the *Marking Phase* introduces no more than two messages per node. Number of messages received in those two phases is decided by the average degree (see Fig. 5(c), the denser the network is, the higher the average degree is). When the average degree goes up, the number of messages received increases accordingly.

In the *Connecting Phase*, each message is unicasted along the branch its sender belongs to or the shortest path between pairs of adjacent trees. Only a small proportion of nodes are involved in this phase. Although some nodes may send or receive more than one message, there are not many messages transmitted in this phase.

As depicted in Fig 5(a), number of messages sent in *EEDTC* is about 4.5, and number of messages sent is directly proportional to the average degree (see Fig. 5(b) and Fig. 5(c)).

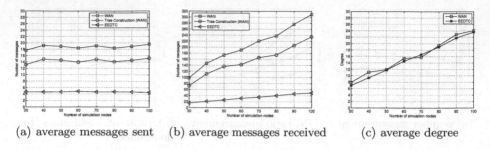

(a) average messages sent   (b) average messages received   (c) average degree

Fig. 5. Messages measurement and average degree

WAN constructs a spanning tree using the distributed leader-election algorithm [14] which has $O(nlogn)$ message complexity. As shown in Fig. 5, it sends about 15 messages per node, and receives about 70 to 240 messages when the simulation nodes ranges from 30 to 100. The number of overall messages sent and received in *WAN* subsequently increases.

These verify *Lemma 3* that *EEDTC* has $O(n)$ message complexity, while *WAN* has $O(nlogn)$ message complexity. Compared with *WAN*, *EEDTC* has much better message complexity, which leads to a better performance on energy consumption in *EEDTC* (see section 7.1).

8   Conclusion

In this paper, we propose an energy-efficient dominating tree construction (*EEDTC*) algorithm to construct a connected dominating set (*CDS*), and the final *CDS* we get is a dominating tree. *EEDTC* has a good approximation factor, as well as low message complexity and time complexity. Compared with Wan's algorithm, *EEDTC* performs well on message complexity and energy consumption, and can greatly prolong the lifetime of wireless networks.

References

1. Sivakumar, R., Das, B., Bharghavan, V.: Spine routing in ad hoc networks. Cluster Computing 1, 237–248 (1998)
2. Wu, J., Li, H.: On calculating connected dominating set for efficient routing in ad hoc wireless networks. In: DIALM 1999. Proceedings of the 3rd international workshop on Discrete algorithms and methods for mobile computing and communications, Seattle, USA, pp. 7–14 (November 1999)
3. Stojmenovic, I., Seddigh, M., Zunic, J.: Dominating sets and neighbor elimination-based broadcasting algorithms in wireless networks. IEEE Transactions on Parallel and Distributed Systems 13, 14–25 (2002)
4. Wan, P.-J., Alzoubi, K., Frieder, O.: Distributed construction of connected dominating set in wireless ad hoc networks. In: INFOCOM 2002. Proceedings of the Twenty-First Annual Joint Conference of the IEEE Computer and Communications Societies, New York, USA, pp. 1597–1604 (June 2002)

5. Min, M., Wang, F., Du, D.-Z., Pardalos, P.: A reliable virtual backbone scheme in mobile ad-hoc networks. In: MASS 2004. IEEE International Conference on Mobile Ad-hoc and Sensor Systems, Fort Lauderdale, USA, pp. 60–69 (October 2004)

6. Wu, J., Gao, M., Stojmenovic, I.: On calculating power-aware connected dominating sets for efficient routing in ad hoc wireless networks. In: IPPN 2001. International Conference on Parallel Processing, Valencia, Spain, pp. 346–354 (September 2001)

7. Kim, B., Yang, J., Zhou, D., Sun, M.-T.: Energy-aware connected dominating set construction in mobile ad hoc networks. In: ICCCN 2005. 14th International Conference on Computer Communications and Networks, San Diego, USA, pp. 229–234 (October 2005)

8. Adjih, C., Jacquet, P., Viennot, L.: Computing connected dominated sets with multipoint relays. Ad Hoc and Sensor Networks 1, 27–39 (2005)

9. Wu, J., Lou, W., Dai, F.: Extended multipoint relays to determine connected dominating sets in manets. IEEE Transactions on Computers 55, 334–347 (2006)

10. Liang, O., Sekercioglu, Y.A., Mani, N.: Enhanced gateway multipoint relays for constructing a small connected dominating set in wireless ad hoc networks. In: ICCS 2006. 10th IEEE International Conference on Communication systems, Singapore, pp. 1–5 (October 2006)

11. Zhou, D., Sun, M.-T., Lai, T.-H.: A timer-based protocol for connected dominating set construction in ieee 802.11 multihop mobile ad hoc networks. In: SAINT 2005. The 2005 Symposium on Applications and the Internet, Trento, Italy, pp. 2–8 (January 2005)

12. Qayyum, A., Viennot, L., Laouiti, A.: Multipoint relaying for flooding broadcast messages in mobile wireless networks. In: HICSS 2002. The 35th Annual International Conference on System Sciences, Hawaii, pp. 3866–3875 (January 2002)

13. Awerbuch, B.: Optimal distributed algorithms for minimum weight spanning tree, counting, leader election and related problems. In: STOC 1987. Proceedings of the 19th Annual ACM Symposium on Theory of Computing, New York, USA, pp. 230–240 (May 1987)

14. Cidon, I., Mokryn, O.: Propagation and leader election in a multihop broadcast environment. In: DISC 1998. 12th International Symposium on DIStributed Computing, Andros, Greece, pp. 104–119 (September 1998)

15. Clark, B.N., Colbourn, C.J., Johnson, D.S.: Unit disk graphs. Discrete Mathematics 86, 165–177 (1990)

16. Omnet++ discrete event simulator (2007), http://www.omnetpp.org

17. Mobility framework model for omnet++ (2007), http://mobility-fw.sourceforge.net

18. Kubisch, M., Karl, H., Wolisz, A., Zhong, L., Rabaey, J.: Distributed algorithms for transmission power control in wireless sensor networks. In: WCNC 2003. Wireless Communications and Networking Conference, IEEE, New Orleans, USA, pp. 558–563 (March 2003)

A Location-Aided Content Searching Mechanism for Large Mobile Ad Hoc Network Using Geographic Clusters

Parama Bhaumik[1] and Somprokash Bandyopadhyay[2]

[1] Dept. of Information Technology, Jadavpur University,
Kolkata, India
parama@it.jusl.ac.in
[2] MIS group, Indian Institute of Management, Calcutta, India
somprokash@iimcal.ac.in

Abstract. An interesting and useful application in ad hoc wireless mobile community is searching and locating information in a distributed and decentralized manner. Locating and collecting information in a highly dynamic network while minimizing the consumption of scarce resources such as bandwidth and energy is the main challenge in this domain. In this paper we present a radically new location aided content searching mechanism that can determine the location and the content as well of the information searched that incurs minimum overhead. Here we have used a stable geographically clustered network that enables us to distribute the search message in a location-aided manner. In disastrous scenarios the access of emergency information, services or resources is considered to be of special interest to the user groups. Mobile terminals are there to gather information from sensors and other sources. The location-Aided content searching mechanism discussed here is concerned with efficiently delivering this information together with the geographical location of the information to the person in the field on need basis. The mobility tolerant clusters structures are used to lower the proactive traffic while minimizing the query cost. We present results from detailed simulations that demonstrate the efficiency of our mechanism and discuss the scalability of this model to larger networks.

1 Introduction

Ad hoc networks are multihop wireless networks consisting of 1000s or more radio equipped nodes that may be as simple as autonomous (mobile or stationary) sensors or PDAs, laptops carried by peoples. These types of networks are useful in any emergency or disastrous scenario where temporary network connectivity is needed, such as in disaster relief or in the battlefields.

In this paper we have used Geographical clusters for locating information which were specially designed to support and manage highly dynamic mobile nodes.

For the same we have introduced a content search mechanism that can be easily deployed for searching information in a resource poor infrastructure less decentralized

S. Rao et al. (Eds.): ICDCN 2008, LNCS 4904, pp. 570–580, 2007.
© Springer-Verlag Berlin Heidelberg 2007

network where the communication overhead due to searching matters a lot. In general a content-based network is a novel communication infrastructure in which the flow of message through the network is driven by the content of the message, rather than by explicit addresses assigned by sender. In a content-based network, receivers declare their interests to the network by means of filters, while senders simply inject messages into the network. The network is responsible for delivering any and all messages to each receiver matching the filter declared by that receiver. The content – search mechanism that we have introduced in this paper is distinct from existing content based search models in that we are not allowing the senders to inject information in the network and as such there is no need of centralized servers to publish the contents. Here the users are to declare the information needed in the form of search messages, and the message itself using the location aided routing mechanism reaches the appropriate senders. Now delivering the information to the intended searchers while minimizing the message overhead and reducing battery consumption is a challenge made harder because of node mobility. In location aided search mechanism information is delivered back to the users using same path discovered by location aided routing and in this case route failures during data transfer due to mobility can be managed incurring little overhead.

In order to explain the location-aided content searching mechanism model better, let us focus on an obvious application area. Imagine the effect of a severe Gas leak in Bhopal, India. It is likely that the effected area will contain a variety of threats to disaster relief personnel such as gas leaks, intense fires, toxic leaks, riots etc. Disaster relief personnel sent into these areas will need to be kept appraised of the location and types of existing threats to ensure their safety. They will also need to be kept informed of deployment of other relief personnel, equipments and resources (such as food, emergency medicine etc) made available in the affected area. Thus a person in the emergency field is typically most interested in obtaining information that will provide him with a complete picture of his surroundings.

In the above scenario, all this emergency information can be collected by autonomous sensors dropped into the affected area and can be further forwarded to the intended users together with the location information. For example in emergency like Gas leak case think of a person who wants to know about the maximum intensity of the poisonous gas and the exact location of the affected area. He can generate this query from any node in the field. It is the task of the searching protocol to discover the maximum intensity zone in the network and deliver the information back to the person. *Thus the location-Aided content searching mechanism we discuss here is concerned with efficiently delivering the information together with the geographical location of the information content (from sensors and other sources) to the person in the field on an as need basis.*

1.1 Over View of the Search Mechanism

It is very natural that when disasters like fire breakouts, rise in water level, Gas Leaks, explosions etc happens people will be more concerned for obtaining information not only about the situation but also about the exact location of affected area. The knowledge Sensors and other nodes can sense the situation and can generate information about the intensity and location of threats. In Location-Aided Content search mechanism, all this information can be searched and send to those nodes that need it on emergency basis. However, the search takes place in a manner that minimizes the network traffic overhead. The problem arises as the information flows through a multihop wireless mobile set of nodes; it becomes difficult to maintain the route from the source to the destination. When there are multiple senders the receiver have no way of knowing which sender's location information is nearest and modify the search accordingly as they themselves are moving. In the remainder of this section we discuss the challenges in conducting the content searching in a mobile scenario incurring minimum overhead.

Our mechanism assumes that all devices in the network know their own location (using GPS Receivers). Since this protocol is meant to operate in an ad hoc network, it is important to summarize some of the properties of the environment as they relate to the content location service.

- First, we cannot assume a static topology. Nodes may join and leave the network at any time and node mobility is an accepted occurrence. To handle this situation we will be using mobility tolerant stable cluster structures to partition the network [1] and will describe the clustering mechanism used in section 3.
- Second, since the cost of making sure that every one knows every thing is prohibitive, to locate a specific content, a device is not allowed to be aware of all the contents available in the network. In this context our proposed mechanism takes the help of cluster heads, which timely collects the information from other nodes when needed and sends them only to the source node. So nodes that attempts to locate content need only to contact the cluster heads within the definite locations of cluster boundaries discussed in section 4.
- The proposed mechanism must be scalable, fault-tolerant, adaptable and accurate. We attempt to work in an environment where communication cost is high and we want our queries can be made relatively cheap while allowing for lower overhead. We can show the possibility of lowering the overhead cost in a scalable network in the performance and evaluation section.

1.2   Overview of the Paper

In section 2, we describe other content based searching mechanism used for ad hoc networks and describe how our mechanism differs from them. Section 3 describes the clustering protocol used in detail and section 4 describes our model in detail. We present results of simulations in section 5. The work reported in this paper is on going and we conclude with our current research focus in section 6.

2   Related Works

Recently several authors have begun developing a variety of algorithms to solve the problem of resource location in ad hoc networks. Some of the first approaches to appear followed the centralized client-server architecture. Some examples of such approaches are presented in [4,5]. What all these models have in common is the reliance upon a centralized storage that would handle queries by users. This assumption violates the requirements of ad hoc networks where all node should be considered equal and no one should be given extra responsibility when compared to peers.

Decentralized approaches [6,7] remove the reliance upon a central directory server but do not take link cost into account when computing routes. This makes them impractical for use in ad hoc networks. Some protocols have been proposed specifically for such resource poor environments [8] but these still rely heavily on the use of broadcast making them too expensive to operate.

A novel approach to disseminating service information is described in [7,8]. The authors propose the use of location information for routing, but the protocol requires all nodes to periodically send advertisements along geometric trajectories, which again congest the network with overhead traffic.

It is easy to see that the Location-Aided content searching mechanism proposed in this paper is very different from any of the above models. This is because here the searches are performed in parallel within the geographical cluster boundaries. As the location of the information changes, there is no problem in finding them within the mobility tolerant clusters. This feature of our mechanism makes it unique as well as extremely powerful in disastrous scenarios where the goal is to maximize message efficiency while ensuring minimum overhead.

3   The Framework Used with Geographical Cluster Structures

The clustering approach proposed in this paper is based on positional concepts (individual node position), which is available via reliable position locating system (i.e. GPS). A good clustering scheme will tend to preserve its structure when a few nodes are moving and the topology is slowly changing. Otherwise, high processing and communication overheads will be paid to reconstruct the cluster.

The objective of the algorithm is to form a set of geographically stable clusters, which do not, changes their structures with the member mobility. We propose to define a geographic boundary for each cluster with the information of the GPS of the nodes lying at the boundary. Generally the existence of a cluster in a mobile scenario depends on the existence of its member node and so it keeps changing. In this framework once the clusters have been defined by their boundaries they remain absolutely fixed over the whole network area and only the mobile nodes move over these geostationary clusters. Thus there is no need to run the clustering algorithm frequently for managing the mobile nodes and to keep the cluster member information updated. In this stable network framework the initial clustering algorithm is required only when the member list of a cluster head is empty, or when a node enters a region and no periodic messages are received from any of its neighbor. So the clustering algorithm is triggered with a long interval.

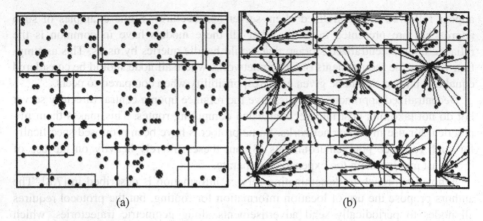

(a)	(b)

Fig. 1. a) The cluster Structures with their Geographical boundaries. b) The cluster Heads and their member node mappings.

3.1 GPS Bounded Cluster Structure Algorithm

To obtain the initial set of clusters in an ad hoc environment, we referred a leader election algorithm - Max-Min D –Cluster Formation algorithm proposed by Alan D. Almis, Ravi Prakash, Vuong Duong and T. Huynh [2]. There are several advantages for using Max-Min D–Cluster Formation algorithm over other existing clustering algorithms like the nodes can asynchronously run the heuristics so no need for synchronized clocks, we can customize the number of clusters as a function of d.

In our GPS based clustering algorithm [1] we have used the initial leader election part of the Max-Min D–Cluster algorithm in the first phase. In the second phase the elected leader or the cluster head will be able to recognize its boundary by getting the GPS information from all of its member nodes and will announce this boundary location values within d hop. Thus all the member nodes get alarmed about the current cluster boundary and will utilize this value while going out of this cluster.

The GPS based clustering algorithm will partition the network into a number of geographically overlapping clusters. These cluster boundaries are static, and are not required to be redefined with the mobility of the boundary nodes. This boundary value will be once notified to all the members of a cluster and will remain fixed until the region becomes completely empty. In that case the cluster-head will recall the initial clustering algorithm to remain connected and the cluster boundary does not exists any more. This particular technique of defining the clusters with fixed boundaries has following advantages.

1. The cluster structure becomes robust in the face of topological changes caused by node motion, node failure and node insertion /removal.
2. Conventional beacon-based cluster management algorithms require the entire network to reconfigure continuously, while in GPS based cluster management protocol the impact of node mobility has been localized within the cluster and its immediate neighboring clusters.

3. The ability of surrogating cluster headship from a mobile cluster head to any of its neighbor.
4. Independent and autonomous cluster control and maintenance by the mobile members only.
5. No performance degradation of the network due to cluster management protocol.

Here in this framework to make the network knowledgeable we will use the flooding mechanism to inform all the cluster heads about all other clusters formed in the network. Thus after the initial clusters were formed using our GPS Bounded Cluster structuring mechanism each CH will start flooding its boundary value within the network. In this case we cannot avoid flooding because the formed cluster structures are not known to the network. Though the network over head is reasonably high but as the cluster boundaries are stable so this one kind of static information needs to be percolated only once in the network.

3.2 Cluster Management Protocol with Mobile Cluster Heads

For periodic beacon based cluster maintenance protocols if a cluster member is moving out of the transmission range of the CH, the member node searches for the new head by detecting the new CH beacon signal. There is no other intelligent way to track the mobility of a member node. Here we have proposed a cluster maintenance protocol using GPS technology, which is able to maintain a stable cluster structure even in presence of high mobility incurring little overhead. In this protocol any node including the cluster head automatically gets alarmed while crossing the geographical boundary of a cluster using the program, which continuously compares the current GPS value of the node with that of the boundary values. Thus it is quite easy for a departing node to make a timely arrangement for rebinding with a new CH and unbind with the old one. This work uses a novel optimistic cluster head-surrogating scheme for achieving efficiency in mobile cluster management process. In this scheme a cluster-head is also free to leave its cluster after delegating the leadership to any member-node of its current cluster. This member-node will now act as a surrogate cluster-head of the cluster. The process actually duplicates a copy of headship program and related member information list to the selected surrogate-head.

4 Location-Aided Content Searching

Based on the above discussion we can now apply the searching mechanism on a geographically clustered network. The proposed mechanism treats all the member nodes in the network as equal and only selected cluster heads are allowed to take more responsibility than others. Once the clusters are formed with definite boundaries the boundary location information is flooded through out the network and all the cluster heads keep the record of all other cluster boundaries in the network. As these cluster boundary information are absolutely stable there is no need to send the clustering update message periodically. The nodes inside the clusters may change their position, but using the surrogating scheme of cluster headship there is always one node to take the responsibility of head and as such the cluster structures remains absolutely stable. This significantly decreases the amount of proactive traffic, as the cluster boundary information is flooded only once in the network though the network can be highly dynamic in nature. To make sure that all nodes within a cluster are informed timely about the accurate position of the cluster heads which can also change position, the cluster heads are allowed to periodically broadcast their node ID and location value (GPS) amongst it's d hop neighbors. But in the said framework the cluster head change notification traffic is restricted to the cluster boundary only. The basic mechanism follows from the scheme described in section 3.2.

In this geographically clustered network a node can easily locate any content in the network by sending a query messages first to the cluster head. The cluster head on behalf of a node sends the query to all other cluster heads. In a dense network, the messages are guaranteed to reach all the clusters through greedy geographical packet forwarding technique (forward the packet to the neighbor closest to the destination). A node where content is found informs its own cluster head about the information. The CHs are now responsible for delivering the information to the source clusterhead from where query generates. In this way it keeps the cost low while finding the closest path to the destination node in the vast majority of situations. Finding the closest path is an important benefit as it generally means fewer hops between the source and the destination [1,3] which in turn, translates into lower connection cost.

4.1 Detail Description of the Content Discovery Mechanism

To illustrate how this strategy works suppose a source node (shown in Fig 2) generates a search message in the network. As the node knows the location of its cluster head it forwards the message to the head. The clusterhead then searches the content among its own member by announcing the message within d hop cluster boundary. In this case the CH simply uses restricted broadcast method to flood the message within the cluster boundary only. If the searched message is found within the local cluster then there is no need to forward the search message further and the cluster head sends the current position (GPS) and the Node ID of the resultant node. But if the content cannot be found within the cluster the search message is sent towards all the cluster locations. A cluster head can easily forward the packet to all these predefined directions as it carries these cluster boundary information from the initial stage of the clustering of network.

The content searching process is exemplified in Fig 2. The next hop in the message forwarding is selected using the same regular geographic routing [8] with each node forwarding the packet to its neighbor closest to the destination (Here destination is the GPS value of the Cluster Boundaries described). The message on reaching the cluster boundaries is forwarded to the corresponding cluster heads by the gateway nodes (nodes lying at the boundaries). In this way all the cluster heads (if reachable) get the search message request packet. Each CH then advertises (restricted broadcast) this message within d hop of its boundary, which finds the result of the search at the destined node in a cluster. Once the result is discovered at a particular node, it immediately replies with a response message to its CH. The clusterhead is here responsible to contact the source CH from where the search request arrived. The source node may receive more than one response message corresponding to the same query. In such case it selects the response identifying the destination closest to its geographical location. Now a definite geographical route is possible to establish from source node to

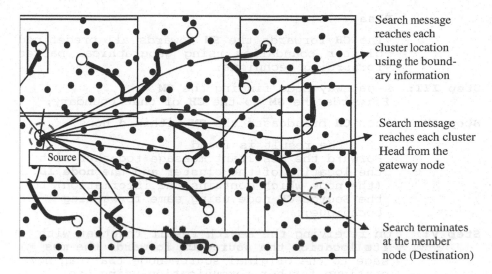

Fig. 2. Location-Aided content searching using Geographical cluster boundaries

destination node for seamless data communication, which remains valid as long as the destination remains within the current cluster. During the course of information flow from the destination to the source using our cluster management protocol [1] we can timely register the moment a node crosses the cluster boundary and calls for de-registration. Here the CH can timely inform the source about the unavailability of the node. The source then again sets a fresh search message. This way by timely inform-ing the source node about the unavailability of the information resource we can reduce the frequency of packet drops and can significantly reduce the searching over-head due to mobility.

Note that the idea behind choosing Location-Aided content searching comes as a result of the following observations:

1. In a large mobile network all cluster heads are easily reachable using stable geo-graphical cluster boundaries.
2. The end-to-end delay during data transmission and probability of packet failures may decrease due informing the source about the absence of the destination node in the early stage.
3. In a large dense network, the use of large cluster structures can significantly re-duce searching overhead, as much lesser number of search messages will be gen-erated to reach those clusters.

4.2 Algorithm for Location-Aided Content Searching

Step I: The Source node sends Search Message **(SM)** to
              its cluster head **(CH)**;

Step II: If the **SM** is found in the local Cluster
              The **CH** sends the GPS of the discovered node to
              the source node and route is established from
              source to destination;

Else

The **CH** forwards the **SM** towards all predefined cluster boundaries using geographical packet forwarding technique;

Step III: A gateway node finding the **SM**
Forwards the **SM** to the **CH** of that boundary;

Step IV: Each **CH** broadcasts the **SM** within **d** hops;

If   the result is found
Forward the Resultant message together with the location of the cluster and the **node ID** (the node which contains the information) to the Source **CH** node using same forwarding technique;

Step V: On receiving the search result together with its location the source **CH** forwards the message to the original source node that can now continue further communication using geographical routing.

5   Simulation Results

In this section we evaluate the performance of our protocol in a simulated environment. A java simulation program was developed to simulate a variety of network conditions. To study the effects of mobility a moderate density network of 100 nodes was evaluated with varying node speeds. Several measures were considered when evaluating the search mechanism. In this case we have only evaluated the on demand overhead traffic generated during the message searching.

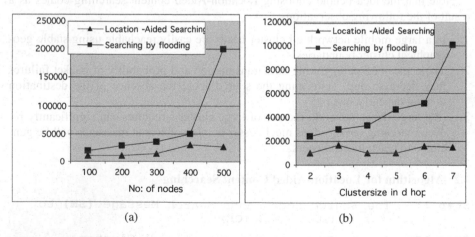

(a)   (b)

Fig. 3. a) Searching overhead with varying node density. b) Searching overhead with varying Cluster size in d hops.

5.1 Effects of Network Density

This section studies the effects of node density on the performance of Location-aided content searching as measured by the factors specified in the discussion. To simulate a low to high-density network we have placed 100 to 500 nodes on an area of 1000 by 1000 meters. As seen in Figure 3a, in case of content searching by simple flooding the amount of search message in the network grows exponentially with the increase in the node density. This is because with the addition of nodes in the network a huge number of search messages were generated. On the other hand a lowering curve for location aided searching shows that with the increase of network density the number of search messages produced in the network remains almost unaffected. As in this case the search messages are forwarded towards the cluster boundaries using the same geographic routing [1,3] and there is no scope of generation of redundant packets in the network. The above-mentioned figures clearly demonstrate the scalability of the mechanism.

5.2 Effects of Cluster Size

Here we have allowed our d (the input which determines the cluster size) to vary from 2 to 7 i.e. from 2 hops cluster size to large 7 hops clusters. We can find from figure 3b. that the searching overhead involved with flooding does not vary with the cluster size as simple broadcast protocol does not utilizes any advantage of clustering in the network. Here maximum overhead has been used for tracking the mobile nodes. But the overhead curve shown in figure [3b] for location aided content searching has a general trend to get lowered. Because in this case with increase in d the larger clusters have formed in the network forcing the total number of clusters formed in the network to be less. Due to the above reason the number of search messages required to forward for the cluster boundaries have also become reduced which shows that with the use of large clusters for larger networks the searching over head can be significantly reduced using our mechanism.

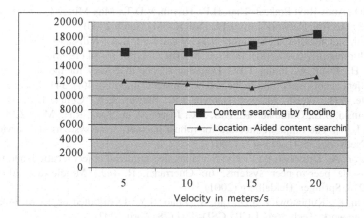

Fig. 4. Searching overhead incurred with varying node velocity

5.3   Effects of Mobility

To get the effects of mobility during the simulation runs we have considered mobile nodes whose speed varies from 5 m/sec to 20 m/sec. Fig. 4 shows that at high mobility, the overhead required to search content in the network is much lower than the broadcast based content searching. This is an expected behavior from the network as in this network the mobility of the nodes are managed timely using the cluster boundary information.

6   Conclusions

The high level contribution of this paper is in proposing a location aided search technique in a mobility-managed framework. Discovering any resource in mobile ad hoc networks while minimizing the searching overhead and reducing network maintenance cost is a challenge made harder because of node mobility. In this context we have developed a radically new mechanism to search information in mobile ad hoc networks using fixed geographical cluster boundaries. Proposed Location-Aided content searching mechanism aims to support geographical position based searching. It achieves its goal with the introduction of stable cluster structures and proposes low overhead methods for discovering resourceful nodes. A special scheme of mobility management and cluster maintenance solves the problem of constant location updating of the nodes.   We have presented simulation results, which show that with the use of large clusters for larger networks the searching overhead can be significantly reduced using our mechanism.

References

[1] Bhaumik, P., Bandhopadhyay, S.: A Mobility Tolerant Cluster Management Protocol with Dynamic Surrogate Cluster-heads for A Large Ad Hoc Network. In: Chaudhuri, S., Das, S.R., Paul, H.S., Tirthapura, S. (eds.) ICDCN 2006. LNCS, vol. 4308, Springer, Heidelberg (2006)

[2] Alan, D., Amis Ravi Prakash Thai, H.P., Huynh, V.D.T.: Max-Min D-Cluster Formation in Wireless Ad Hoc Networks. In: IEEE INFOCOM (March 2000)

[3] Basagni, S., Chlamtac, I., Syrotiuk, V.R., Woodward, B.A.: A distance routing effect algorithm for mobility (DREAM). In: Proc. MOBICOM, pp. 76–84 (1998)

[4] Chen, H., Joshi, A., Finin, T.W.: Dynamic service discovery for mobile computing: intelegellent agents meet jinni in the aether. Cluster Computing 4(4), 343–354 (2001)

[5] Gribble, S.D., Welsh, M., von Behren, J.R., Brewer, E.A., Culler, D.E., Borisov, N., Czerwinski, S.E., Gummadi, R., Hill, J.R., Joseph, A.D., Katz, R.H., Mao, Z.M., Ross, S., Zhao, B.W.: The ninja architecture for robust internet- scale systems and services. Computer Networks 35(4), 473–497 (2001)

[6] Rowstron, A., Druschel, P.: Pastry: Scalable, decentralized object location, and routing for large scale peer-to-peer systems. In: Guerraoui, R. (ed.) Middleware 2001. LNCS, vol. 2218, Springer, Heidelberg (2001)

[7] Hildrum, K., Kubiatowicz, J.D., rao, S., Zhao, B.Y.: Distributed object location in a dynamic network, Tech. Rep. UCB? CSD-02-1178 (April 2002)

[8] Doval, D., O'Mahony, D.: Nom: Resource location and discovery for ad hoc mobile networks. In: Med-hoc-Net 2002, Sardegna, Italy (September 2002)

A Centralized Algorithm for Topology Management in Mobile Ad-Hoc Networks through Multiple Coordinators

Abhishek Bhattacharyya, Anand Seetharam, and M.K. Naskar

Advanced Digital and Embedded Systems Laboratory
Department of Electronics and Telecommunications Engineering
Jadavpur University
abhishek.bhattacharyya@gmail.com,
anandsthrm@yahoo.co.in, mrinalnaskar@yahoo.co.in

Abstract. The topology of a MANET is maintained enduring transmission failures by suitably selecting multiple coordinators among the nodes constituting the MANET. The basic philosophy behind the algorithm is to isolate four coordinators based on positional data. Once elected, they are entrusted with the responsibility to emit signals of different frequencies while the other nodes individually decide the logic they need to follow in order to maintain the topology, thereby eliminating the need for routing. The algorithm is going to be formulated in such a way, that the entire network is going to move in one direction while each node can move freely. As far as our knowledge goes, we are the first ones to conceive the concept of multiple coordinators. The simulation results prove the efficacy of the scheme in topology maintenance.

1 Introduction

Ad-hoc networks are an emerging domain in wireless communications for mobile hosts (nodes) where there is no fixed infrastructure such as base stations or mobile switching centers.[1,2] Mobile nodes that are within each other's radio range communicate directly via wireless links, while those that are far apart rely on other nodes to relay messages as routers. Node mobility in an ad hoc network causes frequent changes of the network topology. Thus routing is necessary to find the path between source and destination and to forward the packets appropriately [3].Mobile ad-hoc networks are extensively used to retain connectivity of nodes in inhospitable terrains, disaster relief etc. where preconceived infrastructure is absent and sudden data acquisition is necessary [3-5].

Random node movement makes routing an essential requirement for MANET. Due to frequent node movement it may so happen that when the source node wants to transmit packets, the destination node may be out of range of the source node. Further, transmission losses occurring due to different natural phenomena may be another cause of frequent network disruption. Hence, the current focus of many researchers is to find out an efficient topology management algorithm, which ensures node connectivity without much delay and unnecessary overhead.

S. Rao et al. (Eds.): ICDCN 2008, LNCS 4904, pp. 581–586, 2008.

The two widely accepted approaches for topology management are centralized and distributed algorithms [5]. However in the centralized algorithms considered so far, there being only one coordinator, the workload on the coordinator is immense. Moreover as far as our knowledge goes, all of them assume multiple transmission ranges, which is not possible in many practical situations. The distributed approaches on the other hand suffer form the drawback that it is very difficult to maintain complete connectivity among the nodes.

The paper is organized as follows: in the following section we formally state the topology management problem. Section three contains the primary assumptions. The next section is the coordinator election procedure. Section five deals with the movement algorithm. We finally conclude with simulation results and a comparative study with previous algorithms in section seven.

2 Topology Management Problem

Given a physical topology of a mobile ad-hoc network the problem is to control the movements of the individual nodes so as to maintain a stable neighborhood topology. In a system of n nodes (n_0, n_1....n_{n-1}) constituting a MANET, two nodes n_i and n_j are said to be neighboring if and only if they can communicate without the need of routing. Now if we assume that the transmission range of each node be R_{max} and D_{ij} denotes the relative distance between the nodes then the network neighborhood topology will be maintained provided $\exists$ at least one j such that

$$D_{ij} \leq R_{max} \; \forall \; i,j = 0,1,2....n-1$$

3 Primary Assumptions

1. The network moves in only one direction, here the x-direction while the nodes can move in any direction they please. 2. Initially all the nodes can communicate with one another. 3. Each node knows its initial position through a GPS set.

4 Coordinator Election Algorithm

Among the set of all x-coordinates $\{x_1, x_2..., x_i..., x_n\}$ and the set of all y-coordinates $\{y_1, y_2, ..., y_i, ... ,y_n\}$ received by a node, the minimum and maximum x-coordinate and the minimum and maximum y-coordinate are selected, denoted by x_{min}, x_{max}, y_{min}, y_{max} respectively. Now let p_{min} and p_{max} respectively denote

$$p_{min} = \min \{x_{min}, y_{min}\}, \; p_{max} = \max \{x_{max}, y_{max}\} \tag{1}$$

Let '4a' denote the distance between (p_{max}, p_{max}) and (p_{min}, p_{min}).

$$4a = \sqrt{2} * (p_{max} - p_{min}) \tag{2}$$

Considering a square with coordinates P (p_{max}, p_{max}), Q (p_{max}, p_{min}), R (p_{min}, p_{min}), S (p_{min}, p_{max}), the diagonals PR and QS are divided into four equal parts as shown in Figure 1 and the points of division are obtained as D,O,B and A,O,C with

$A = ((p_{max}+3p_{min})/4, (3p_{max}+p_{min})/4), B = ((p_{max}+3p_{min})/4, (p_{max}+3p_{min})/4)$
$C = ((3p_{max}+p_{min})/4, (p_{max}+3p_{min})/4) D = ((3p_{max}+p_{min})/4, (3p_{max}+p_{min})/4)$

Now, following the initial coordinator movement procedure stated in section 4.1, 4 nodes occupy positions A, B, C, D and declare themselves as coordinators C_1, C_2, C_3 and C_4 respectively and emit messages in this regard. The coordinators now emit signals continuously of frequencies f_1, f_2, f_3 and f_4 respectively and of range $R_{max} = a = (p_{max}-p_{min})/(2\sqrt{2})$. Thus all nodes initially lie within the square PQRS as is evident from Figure1.

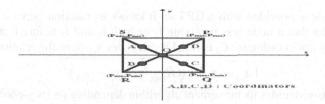

Fig. 1. Election of Coordinator

4.1 Initial Coordinator Movement Procedure

At first each node calculates its distance from A, B, C and D and sends it to all the other (n-1) nodes in the network. A node now checks if its distance from A is less than the other (n-1) nodes. If the answer is positive then it moves to the point A by moving along the x direction for a time T_x and then along the y direction for a time T_y with $T_x = |x_i - x_A| / V_{imaxx}$ and $T_y = |y_i - y_A| / V_{imaxy}$. Thus the total time required for the node to move to A is $T_A = T_x + T_y$. However if the answer obtained is negative a similar procedure is repeated for points B, C and D.

5 Movement Algorithm

The nodes now forward their maximum velocities along the x-direction V_{imaxx} to the coordinators. Let $V_x = min \{V_{imaxx}\}$. The coordinators now decide to move with a velocity $V_c < V_x$ and inform it to all other nodes.

Since all the nodes are initially in the region PQRS as referred to Figure 1, it receives either of f_1, f_2, f_3 or f_4. During movement only when it does not receive any frequency, it realizes it has moved just out of range. Since the algorithm is instantaneous the instant a node fails to receive f_1, f_2, f_3 or f_4, it is at the edge of the circles with C_1, C_2, C_3 or C_4 as centers.

5.1 Failure of a Node to Receive f_1 or f_2

As soon as a node fails to receive f_1 or f_2, it realizes that it has moved out through arcs 12 or 23 as in Figure 2. It then decides to shoot to regain a stable position in the topology.

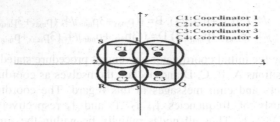

Fig. 2. Movement of nodes on failing to receive f_1 or f_2

Since a node is provided with a GPS set it knows its position (x_i, y_i) at that instant. Let us consider that a node was receiving f_1 or both f_1 and f_2 before it moved out of range. Since y_{c1} of coordinator C_1 is fixed it calculates x_{c1} from the relation

$$|x_{c1} - x_i| = \sqrt{R_{max}^2 - (y_i - y_{c1})^2}.$$

The node now decides its movement algorithm depending on its y-coordinate.

If $|y_i - y_{c1}| \leq R_{max} / \sqrt{2}$ then it is on the arc 1' 2 as shown in Figure 3. It then shoots along the direction of movement with a velocity V_{imaxx} for a time $t_{shoot} = |x_{c1} - x_i|/(V_{imaxx} - V_c)$.

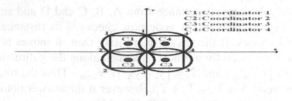

Fig. 3. Movement of nodes on failing to receive f_1 or f_2 depending on y –coordinates

However, if for a node $|y_i - y_{c1}| > R_{max} / \sqrt{2}$ it lies on the arc 1' 1 as depicted in figure 3. It then moves forward with a velocity $V = V_c\hat{i} - V_{imaxy}\hat{j}$ for a time $t_1 = (R_{max} - (R_{max}/\sqrt{2}))/V_{imaxy}$ .After moving for t_1, it shoots forward for a time t_{shoot1} with V_{imaxx} as stated earlier. The movement algorithm is similar if a node fails to receive f_2.

Lemma 1. The maximum value for t_{shoot} for a particular node is $R_{max}/(V_{imaxx} - V_c)$.

5.2 Failure of a Node to Receive f_3 Or f_4

As soon as a node fails to receive f_3 or f_4, it realizes that it has moved out through arcs 14 or 43 as in Figure 3. It then decides to stop to regain a stable position in the topology. Let us consider that a node was receiving f_3 or both f_3 and f_4 before it moved out of range. Since y_{c3} of coordinator C_3 is fixed it calculates x_{c3} from the relation

$$|x_{c3} - x_i| = \sqrt{R_{max}^2 - (y_i - y_{c3})^2}.$$

If $| y_i - y_{c3} | \le R_{max} / \sqrt{2}$ it stops for a time $t_{stop}=|x_{c3}-x_i|/V_c$. If however $| y_i - y_{c3} | > R_{max} / \sqrt{2}$ it initially moves with a velocity $V=V_c\hat{\imath}-V_{imaxy}\hat{\jmath}$ for a time t_1 as calculated in section 5.1 and then it stops for a time t_{stop}. The movement procedure is identical if a node fails to receive f_4.

Lemma 2. The maximum value of t_{stop} for all nodes is R_{max}/V_c.

5.3 Transmission Losses

The movement algorithm ensures that even if there is a loss of a single frequency for an extended time period none of the nodes diverge out.

Suppose that a node, which was previously receiving f_1 or f_2 suddenly fails to receive any frequency. Following the movement algorithm stated in section 5.1 it checks for its y-coordinate. If $| y_i - y_{cj} | \le R_{max} / \sqrt{2}$ where j=1 or 2 depending on f_1 or f_2, this node is in the shaded region 1 as shown in the Figure 4. The node now shoots in the positive x-direction for a time t_{shoot}. The maximum shooting period is $R_{max}/(V_{imaxx}-V_c)$ vide Lemma 1. Thus the maximum distance that the node covers relative to the coordinators during this period is R_{max}. Hence even if the node initially was in the unstable positions X or Y as shown in Figure 4 or at any other position at the rim of the circles with centers C_1 or C_2, at the end of shooting it is either going to receive f_3 or f_4. Thus even after t_{shoot} if a node does not receive any frequency it realizes transmission loss and moves with a velocity V_c in the positive x-direction until it receives a frequency again. Again if $| y_i - y_{cj} | > R_{max} / \sqrt{2}$ where j=1 or 2 then the node is in the shaded region 1' as shown in figure. If it suddenly fails to receive any frequency then it moves with a velocity $V = V_c\hat{\imath}-V_{imaxy}\hat{\jmath}$ or $V=V_c\hat{\imath} + V_{imaxy}\hat{\jmath}$ for a time t_1 according as whether it received f_1 or f_2 previously vide section 5.1. This brings it back within the square PQRS. Now it shoots forward in the positive x-direction for a time t_{shoot} whence by previous arguments we conclude that after a time t_1+t_{shoot} the node must receive a frequency. If it does not, it realizes transmission loss and moves with velocity V_c until it receives a frequency again.

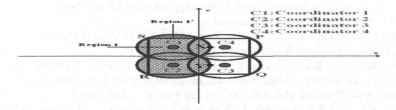

Fig. 4. Transmission Loss of f_1 or f_2: Region Division

A similar argument can be put forth for nodes which previously received f_3 or f_4. In this case the nodes converge after a period a period t_1+t_{stop}.

6 Simulation Results

Extensive simulations in several synthetically designed situations establish that none of the nodes ever diverge out from the topology. A sample illustration is provided in Figure 5.

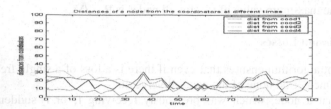

Fig. 5. Distance of a node from the coordinators at various times. Initial position of node (-7,17). V_{imaxx}=11 units. V_{imaxy}=10 units. Coordinator positions (-8,8), (-8,-8), (8,-8) and (8,8). R_{max} = 11.5 units. V_c = 5 units.

7 Conclusion

As proposed earlier, we have been able to develop a novel algorithm in which the nodes of the network always maintain the topology. In addition as compared to single coordinator systems proposed in [3-5] multidirectional node movement becomes feasible. Moreover, the system never becomes static as a whole and hence no time is wasted in maintaining the network topology thereby ensuring greater efficiency. Apart from this no node ever diverges out of communication range. Elongated transmission time loss periods can also be endured. Number of messages transmitted and received being reduced the workload on the coordinator is decreased. Apart from these advantages the requirement of three communication ranges is also eliminated.

References

1. National Institute of Standards and Technology, Mobile Ad Hoc Networks (MANETs), http://w3.antd.nist.gov/wahn_mahn.shtml
2. IEEE 802.11. "Wireless LAN Medium Access Control (MAC) and Physical Layer (PHY) specification", Standard, IEEE, New York (November 1997)
3. Gupta, S.S., Ray, S.S., Samanta, S., Naskar, M.K.: An Efficient Topology Management Algorithm for Mobile Ad-Hoc Networks. In: EPMDS 2006. International Conference on Electronic and Photonic Materials, Devices and Systems - 2006 (2006)
4. Gupta, S.S., Ray, S.S., Samanta, S., Naskar, M.K.: A Stochastic Algorithm for Managing Network Configuration of a Mobile Ad-Hoc Network. In: AMOC 2007. 5th Asian International Conference on Mobile Computing - 2007 (2007)
5. Basu, S.S, Choudhury, A.: Self adaptive topology management for mobile ad-hoc networks. IE(I) Journal-ET 84 (July 2003)

Author Index

Agarwal, Arun   176
Ahmed, Maruf   257
Ananthanarayana, V.S.   251
Attiya, Hagit   112
Audhya, Goutam K.   540

Babu, A.V.   503
Balasooriya, Janaka   39
Balasubramanian, Bharath   124
Bandyopadhyay, Somprokash   570
Baruah, Sanjay   215
Baskaran, R.   393
Basu, Kajla   471
Bezawada, Bruhadeshwar   387
Bhattacharyya, Abhishek   581
Bhattacharyya, Dhruba Kumar   239
Bhaumik, Parama   570
Biswas, Debmalya   363
Boulinier, Christian   191
Bruno, Raffaele   528

Cameron, Kirk   263
Chakrabarti, Anirban   227
Chakrabarti, Saswat   515
Chatterjee, Punyasha   332
Choi, Kyu Young   345
Chowdhury, Morshed   310
Chowdhury, Sharif M.H.   257
Chowdhury, Subhabrata   471
Christou, Ioannis   350
Conti, Marco   528

Das, Abhijit   298
Das, Nabanita   332
Das, Rosy   239
Das, Sajal K.   558
Das, Shantanu   292
De, Tanmay   452
Dey, Sandip   170
Dimitriou, Tassos   350
Dolev, Danny   54
Domaszewicz, Jaroslaw   322
Doss, Robin   310
Durocher, Stephane   546

Effantin, Brice   209

Farahabady, M. Hoseiny   280
Fathy, M.   496
Fisher, Nathan   215

Garg, Vijay K.   124
Girish, K.   478
Goddard, W.   182
Gore, M.M.   428
Goutham, B.   416
Guitton, Alexandre   401
Gupta, Arobinda   203

Haddar, M.A.   286
Hansdah, R.C.   434
Hasan, Masud   257
Hedetniemi, S.T.   182
Hillel, Eshcar   112
Huang, Hongtao   158
Huang, Song   263

Jacob, Lillykutty   503
Jacobs, D.P.   182
Jana, Prasanta K.   274
Jana, Sahadeb   471
Jmaiel, M.   286
Joshi, Jaimini   39

Kacem, A. Hadj   286
Kannan, A.   393
Karame, Ghassan   350
Karmakar, Sushanta   203
Kheddouci, Hamamache   209
Khonsari, A.   496
Kim, Yong Ho   345
Kirkpatrick, David   546
Kothapalli, Kishore   387
Koziuk, Michal   322
Kulkarni, Vineet   484
Kumar, Preetam   515

Lee, Dong Hoon   345
Lenin, R.B.   484
Levert, Mathieu   191

Li, Dong   263
Li, Gang   310
Lim, Jongin   345
Liu, X.   490
Liu, Yonghe   558
Locher, Thomas   25
Lu, Mingming   13
Lucas, Keny T.   274

Mak, Vicky   310
Mallick, Dheeresh K.   274
Meraji, Sina   375
Métivier, Y.   286
Mizrahi, Tal   73
Mohan, Virendra   434
Mondal, Swapan Kumar   440
Mosbah, M.   286
Moses, Yoram   73
Mostefaoui, Achour   99
Mukherjee, A.   464
Mukherjee, Partha   339
Murthy, C. Siva Ram   416

Nalla, Pradeep Kumar   176
Narayanan, Lata   546
Nasipuri, M.   464
Naskar, M.K.   464, 581
Navathe, Shamkant   39

Ogale, Vinit   124
Ould-Khaoua, M.   496

Pal, A.   464
Pal, Ajit   452
Pal, Sankar K.   1
Pandu Rangan, C.   86, 304
Patnaik, L.M.   478
Paul, A.   464
Pedone, Fernando   147
Petit, Franck   191
Pike, Scott M.   135
Pinizzotto, Antonio   528
Prasad, Sushil K.   39

Rabby, M.   490
Rajeswari, L. Prema   393
Ramesh, M.   515

Ravindran, K.   490
Raynal, Michel   99
Rezazad, Mostafa   280
Roy, Bimal Kumar   298

Safaei, F.   496
Saha, Debashis   440
Sarbazi-Azad, Hamid   280, 375
Sarmah, Sauravjyoti   239
Sastry, Srikanth   135
Schiper, Nicolas   147
Schneider, Fred B.   54
Seetharam, Anand   581
Selvaradjou, Ka.   416
Sen, Sandip   339
Sengupta, Indranil   452
Sengupta, Malabika   440
Sengupta, Shubhashis   227
Shankar, Bhavani   304
Shareef, Amjed   86
Singh, M.P.   428
Sinha, Bhabani P.   540
Skordylis, Antonios   401
Song, Yantao   135
Song, Yee Jiun   54
Srimani, Pradip K.   182
Srinathan, Kannan   304
Srivastava, Sanjay   484
Sujatha, D.N.   478
Sun, Huang   209

Thilagam, P. Santhi   251
Travers, Corentin   99
Trigoni, Niki   401

van Renesse, Robbert   54
Venugopal, K.R.   478
Vidyasankar, Krishnamurthy   363
von Rickenbach, Pascal   25

Wang, Xingwei   558
Wankar, Rajeev   176
Wattenhofer, Roger   25
Wu, Jie   13

Yu, Ruiyun   558
Yu, Shui   310

Lecture Notes in Computer Science

Sublibrary 1: Theoretical Computer Science and General Issues

For information about Vols. 1– 4545
please contact your bookseller or Springer

Vol. 4904: S. Rao, M. Chatterjee, P. Jayanti, C.S.R. Murthy, S.K. Saha (Eds.), Distributed Computing and Networking. XVIII, 588 pages. 2008.

Vol. 4878: E. Tovar, P. Tsigas, H. Fouchal (Eds.), Principles of Distributed Systems. XIII, 457 pages. 2007.

Vol. 4873: S. Aluru, M. Parashar, R. Badrinath, V.K. Prasanna (Eds.), High Performance Computing – HiPC 2007. XXIV, 663 pages. 2007.

Vol. 4863: A. Bonato, F.R.K. Chung (Eds.), Algorithms and Models for the Web-Graph. X, 217 pages. 2007.

Vol. 4860: G. Eleftherakis, P. Kefalas, G. Păun, G. Rozenberg, A. Salomaa (Eds.), Membrane Computing. IX, 453 pages. 2007.

Vol. 4855: V. Arvind, S. Prasad (Eds.), FSTTCS 2007: Foundations of Software Technology and Theoretical Computer Science. XIV, 558 pages. 2007.

Vol. 4851: S. Boztaş, H.-F.(F.) Lu (Eds.), Applied Algebra, Algebraic Algorithms and Error-Correcting Codes. XII, 368 pages. 2007.

Vol. 4847: M. Xu, Y. Zhan, J. Cao, Y. Liu (Eds.), Advanced Parallel Processing Technologies. XIX, 767 pages. 2007.

Vol. 4846: I. Cervesato (Ed.), Advances in Computer Science – ASIAN 2007. XI, 313 pages. 2007.

Vol. 4838: T. Masuzawa, S. Tixeuil (Eds.), Stabilization, Safety, and Security of Distributed Systems. XIII, 409 pages. 2007.

Vol. 4835: T. Tokuyama (Ed.), Algorithms and Computation. XVII, 929 pages. 2007.

Vol. 4783: J. Holub, J. Žďárek (Eds.), Implementation and Application of Automata. XIII, 324 pages. 2007.

Vol. 4782: R. Perrott, B.M. Chapman, J. Subhlok, R.F. de Mello, L.T. Yang (Eds.), High Performance Computing and Communications. XIX, 823 pages. 2007.

Vol. 4771: T. Bartz-Beielstein, M.J. Blesa Aguilera, C. Blum, B. Naujoks, A. Roli, G. Rudolph, M. Sampels (Eds.), Hybrid Metaheuristics. X, 202 pages. 2007.

Vol. 4770: V.G. Ganzha, E.W. Mayr, E.V. Vorozhtsov (Eds.), Computer Algebra in Scientific Computing. XIII, 460 pages. 2007.

Vol. 4769: A. Brandstädt, D. Kratsch, H. Müller (Eds.), Graph-Theoretic Concepts in Computer Science. XIII, 341 pages. 2007.

Vol. 4763: J.-F. Raskin, P.S. Thiagarajan (Eds.), Formal Modeling and Analysis of Timed Systems. X, 369 pages. 2007.

Vol. 4746: A. Bondavalli, F. Brasileiro, S. Rajsbaum (Eds.), Dependable Computing. XV, 239 pages. 2007.

Vol. 4743: P. Thulasiraman, X. He, T.L. Xu, M.K. Denko, R.K. Thulasiram, L.T. Yang (Eds.), Frontiers of High Performance Computing and Networking ISPA 2007 Workshops. XXIX, 536 pages. 2007.

Vol. 4742: I. Stojmenovic, R.K. Thulasiram, L.T. Yang, W. Jia, M. Guo, R.F. de Mello (Eds.), Parallel and Distributed Processing and Applications. XX, 995 pages. 2007.

Vol. 4739: R. Moreno Díaz, F. Pichler, A. Quesada Arencibia (Eds.), Computer Aided Systems Theory – EUROCAST 2007. XIX, 1233 pages. 2007.

Vol. 4736: S. Winter, M. Duckham, L. Kulik, B. Kuipers (Eds.), Spatial Information Theory. XV, 455 pages. 2007.

Vol. 4732: K. Schneider, J. Brandt (Eds.), Theorem Proving in Higher Order Logics. IX, 401 pages. 2007.

Vol. 4731: A. Pelc (Ed.), Distributed Computing. XVI, 510 pages. 2007.

Vol. 4728: S. Bozapalidis, G. Rahonis (Eds.), Algebraic Informatics. VIII, 291 pages. 2007.

Vol. 4726: N. Ziviani, R. Baeza-Yates (Eds.), String Processing and Information Retrieval. XII, 311 pages. 2007.

Vol. 4719: R. Backhouse, J. Gibbons, R. Hinze, J. Jeuring (Eds.), Datatype-Generic Programming. XI, 369 pages. 2007.

Vol. 4711: C.B. Jones, Z. Liu, J. Woodcock (Eds.), Theoretical Aspects of Computing – ICTAC 2007. XI, 483 pages. 2007.

Vol. 4710: C.W. George, Z. Liu, J. Woodcock (Eds.), Domain Modeling and the Duration Calculus. XI, 237 pages. 2007.

Vol. 4708: L. Kučera, A. Kučera (Eds.), Mathematical Foundations of Computer Science 2007. XVIII, 764 pages. 2007.

Vol. 4707: O. Gervasi, M.L. Gavrilova (Eds.), Computational Science and Its Applications – ICCSA 2007, Part III. XXIV, 1205 pages. 2007.

Vol. 4706: O. Gervasi, M.L. Gavrilova (Eds.), Computational Science and Its Applications – ICCSA 2007, Part II. XXIII, 1129 pages. 2007.

Vol. 4705: O. Gervasi, M.L. Gavrilova (Eds.), Computational Science and Its Applications – ICCSA 2007, Part I. XLIV, 1169 pages. 2007.

Vol. 4703: L. Caires, V.T. Vasconcelos (Eds.), CONCUR 2007 – Concurrency Theory. XIII, 507 pages. 2007.

Vol. 4700: C.B. Jones, Z. Liu, J. Woodcock (Eds.), Formal Methods and Hybrid Real-Time Systems. XVI, 539 pages. 2007.

Vol. 4699: B. Kågström, E. Elmroth, J. Dongarra, J. Waśniewski (Eds.), Applied Parallel Computing. XXIX, 1192 pages. 2007.

Vol. 4698: L. Arge, M. Hoffmann, E. Welzl (Eds.), Algorithms – ESA 2007. XV, 769 pages. 2007.

Vol. 4697: L. Choi, Y. Paek, S. Cho (Eds.), Advances in Computer Systems Architecture. XIII, 400 pages. 2007.

Vol. 4688: K. Li, M. Fei, G.W. Irwin, S. Ma (Eds.), Bio-Inspired Computational Intelligence and Applications. XIX, 805 pages. 2007.

Vol. 4684: L. Kang, Y. Liu, S. Zeng (Eds.), Evolvable Systems: From Biology to Hardware. XIV, 446 pages. 2007.

Vol. 4683: L. Kang, Y. Liu, S. Zeng (Eds.), Advances in Computation and Intelligence. XVII, 663 pages. 2007.

Vol. 4681: D.-S. Huang, L. Heutte, M. Loog (Eds.), Advanced Intelligent Computing Theories and Applications. XXVI, 1379 pages. 2007.

Vol. 4672: K. Li, C. Jesshope, H. Jin, J.-L. Gaudiot (Eds.), Network and Parallel Computing. XVIII, 558 pages. 2007.

Vol. 4671: V.E. Malyshkin (Ed.), Parallel Computing Technologies. XIV, 635 pages. 2007.

Vol. 4669: J.M. de Sá, L.A. Alexandre, W. Duch, D. Mandic (Eds.), Artificial Neural Networks – ICANN 2007, Part II. XXXI, 990 pages. 2007.

Vol. 4668: J.M. de Sá, L.A. Alexandre, W. Duch, D. Mandic (Eds.), Artificial Neural Networks – ICANN 2007, Part I. XXXI, 978 pages. 2007.

Vol. 4666: M.E. Davies, C.J. James, S.A. Abdallah, M.D. Plumbley (Eds.), Independent Component Analysis and Blind Signal Separation. XIX, 847 pages. 2007.

Vol. 4665: J. Hromkovič, R. Královič, M. Nunkesser, P. Widmayer (Eds.), Stochastic Algorithms: Foundations and Applications. X, 167 pages. 2007.

Vol. 4664: J. Durand-Lose, M. Margenstern (Eds.), Machines, Computations, and Universality. X, 325 pages. 2007.

Vol. 4661: U. Montanari, D. Sannella, R. Bruni (Eds.), Trustworthy Global Computing. X, 339 pages. 2007.

Vol. 4649: V. Diekert, M.V. Volkov, A. Voronkov (Eds.), Computer Science – Theory and Applications. XIII, 420 pages. 2007.

Vol. 4647: R. Martin, M.A. Sabin, J.R. Winkler (Eds.), Mathematics of Surfaces XII. IX, 509 pages. 2007.

Vol. 4646: J. Duparc, T.A. Henzinger (Eds.), Computer Science Logic. XIV, 600 pages. 2007.

Vol. 4644: N. Azémard, L. Svensson (Eds.), Integrated Circuit and System Design. XIV, 583 pages. 2007.

Vol. 4641: A.-M. Kermarrec, L. Bougé, T. Priol (Eds.), Euro-Par 2007 Parallel Processing. XXVII, 974 pages. 2007.

Vol. 4639: E. Csuhaj-Varjú, Z. Ésik (Eds.), Fundamentals of Computation Theory. XIV, 508 pages. 2007.

Vol. 4638: T. Stützle, M. Birattari, H. H. Hoos (Eds.), Engineering Stochastic Local Search Algorithms. X, 223 pages. 2007.

Vol. 4630: H.J. van den Herik, P. Ciancarini, H.H.L.M.(J.) Donkers (Eds.), Computers and Games. XII, 283 pages. 2007.

Vol. 4628: L.N. de Castro, F.J. Von Zuben, H. Knidel (Eds.), Artificial Immune Systems. XII, 438 pages. 2007.

Vol. 4627: M. Charikar, K. Jansen, O. Reingold, J.D.P. Rolim (Eds.), Approximation, Randomization, and Combinatorial Optimization. XII, 626 pages. 2007.

Vol. 4624: T. Mossakowski, U. Montanari, M. Haveraaen (Eds.), Algebra and Coalgebra in Computer Science. XI, 463 pages. 2007.

Vol. 4623: M. Collard (Ed.), Ontologies-Based Databases and Information Systems. X, 153 pages. 2007.

Vol. 4621: D. Wagner, R. Wattenhofer (Eds.), Algorithms for Sensor and Ad Hoc Networks. XIII, 415 pages. 2007.

Vol. 4619: F. Dehne, J.-R. Sack, N. Zeh (Eds.), Algorithms and Data Structures. XVI, 662 pages. 2007.

Vol. 4618: S.G. Akl, C.S. Calude, M.J. Dinneen, G. Rozenberg, H.T. Wareham (Eds.), Unconventional Computation. X, 243 pages. 2007.

Vol. 4616: A.W.M. Dress, Y. Xu, B. Zhu (Eds.), Combinatorial Optimization and Applications. XI, 390 pages. 2007.

Vol. 4614: B. Chen, M. Paterson, G. Zhang (Eds.), Combinatorics, Algorithms, Probabilistic and Experimental Methodologies. XII, 530 pages. 2007.

Vol. 4613: F.P. Preparata, Q. Fang (Eds.), Frontiers in Algorithmics. XI, 348 pages. 2007.

Vol. 4600: H. Comon-Lundh, C. Kirchner, H. Kirchner (Eds.), Rewriting, Computation and Proof. XVI, 273 pages. 2007.

Vol. 4599: S. Vassiliadis, M. Bereković, T.D. Hämäläinen (Eds.), Embedded Computer Systems: Architectures, Modeling, and Simulation. XVIII, 466 pages. 2007.

Vol. 4598: G. Lin (Ed.), Computing and Combinatorics. XII, 570 pages. 2007.

Vol. 4596: L. Arge, C. Cachin, T. Jurdziński, A. Tarlecki (Eds.), Automata, Languages and Programming. XVII, 953 pages. 2007.

Vol. 4595: D. Bošnački, S. Edelkamp (Eds.), Model Checking Software. X, 285 pages. 2007.

Vol. 4590: W. Damm, H. Hermanns (Eds.), Computer Aided Verification. XV, 562 pages. 2007.

Vol. 4588: T. Harju, J. Karhumäki, A. Lepistö (Eds.), Developments in Language Theory. XI, 423 pages. 2007.

Vol. 4583: S.R. Della Rocca (Ed.), Typed Lambda Calculi and Applications. X, 397 pages. 2007.

Vol. 4580: B. Ma, K. Zhang (Eds.), Combinatorial Pattern Matching. XII, 366 pages. 2007.

Vol. 4576: D. Leivant, R. de Queiroz (Eds.), Logic, Language, Information and Computation. X, 363 pages. 2007.

Vol. 4547: C. Carlet, B. Sunar (Eds.), Arithmetic of Finite Fields. XI, 355 pages. 2007.

Vol. 4546: J. Kleijn, A. Yakovlev (Eds.), Petri Nets and Other Models of Concurrency – ICATPN 2007. XI, 515 pages. 2007.